Lidia Hidalgo

Computers and Information Processing

with Business Applications

The O'Leary/Williams Supplement Package

Instructor's Guide by Marvin Clark

Study Guide by James Adair

Transparency Masters

Test Bank by Carole Colaneri

Instructor's Resource Box containing all of the above

Lab Manual: Introduction to WordStar and Lotus 1-2-3 on the IBM PC by T.J. O'Leary

Computerized Testing Service for mainframe and minicomputers

TestGen for microcomputers

For more information on the above titles, please call 800-227-1936
or (in California) 800-982-6140

Computers and Information Processing

with Business Applications

T.J. O'Leary / Brian K. Williams
Arizona State University

The Benjamin/Cummings Publishing Company, Inc.
Menlo Park, California › Reading, Massachusetts › Don Mills, Ontario › Wokingham, U.K. › Amsterdam › Sydney › Singapore › Tokyo › Mexico City › Bogota › Santiago › San Juan

Sponsoring Editor: Susan Nelle
Developmental Editor: Pat Burner
Production Manager: Laura Argento
Production Coordinator: Pat Franklin Waldo
Designer: Al Burkhardt
Photo Research: Roberta Spieckerman Associates
Illustrations: George Omura
Copy Editor: Alice Spears
Composition: Graphic Typesetting Service, Los Angeles
Color Separations: Color Response, Inc.

Credits appear at the end of this book. Company names used in parts of the text are fictitious and for educational purposes; any resemblance to actual company names is purely coincidental.

Library of Congress Cataloging in Publication Data
O'Leary, T. J. (Timothy J.)
Computers and information processing: with business applications.

Includes index.
1. Business—Data Processing. 2. Office practice—Automation. I. Williams, Brian K., 1938–
II. Title.
HF5548.2.044 1985 658'.054 84-28339
ISBN 0-8053-6920-1
DEFGHIJ–DO–8987

The Benjamin/Cummings Publishing Company, Inc.
2727 Sand Hill Road
Menlo Park, California 94025

To my wife, Linda Perley Coats O'Leary, and my son, Daniel Albert O'Leary

—T. J. O'L.

To my mother, Gertrude Smoyer Williams

—B. K. W.

Brief Contents

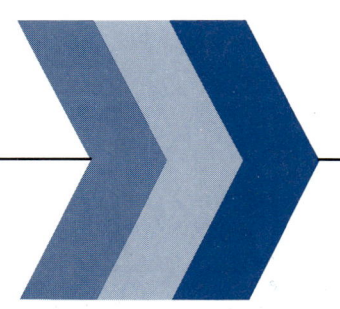

Detailed Contents

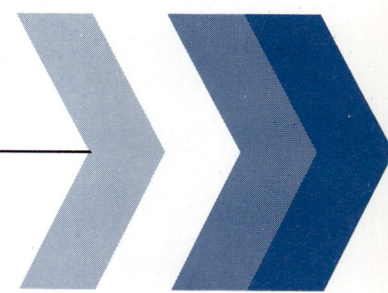

Part 2

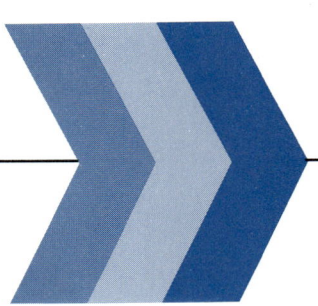

The Uses of Software 87

Part 3

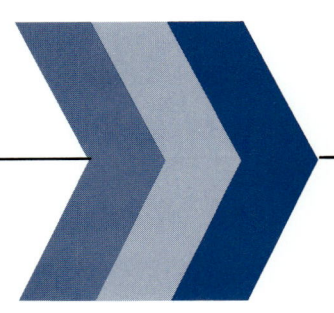

The Uses of Hardware 201

CHAPTER 7

Input and Output: Problems In, Solutions Out 203

CHAPTER 10

Networks and Data Communications: Bringing Us Together 343

Part 4

CHAPTER 11

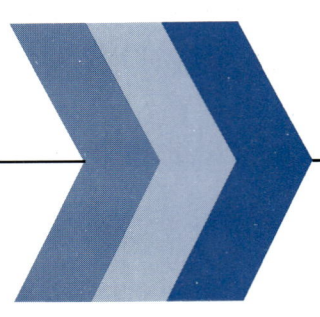

CHAPTER 12

CHAPTER 13

CHAPTER 14

Part 5

The Rewards and Risks of the Information Age 513

APPENDIX

Corporate Reports

Color Reports on the Computer as a Tool

The "Corporate Reports"—five special color layouts interspersed throughout the book—depict the uses of the computer as a tool in various kinds of enterprises. Like the annual reports that companies publish for their shareholders, the Corporate Reports present recent breakthroughs in ways of doing business. Our Corporate Reports offer future managers an inside look at some new, computer-oriented business environments in which they may pursue careers.

Corporate Report 1

(follows page 62)

Computers in Business: New Tools, New Careers

The Information Revolution launched by the computer is having a profound effect on business. Here we see the making of a silicon chip; the effects of office automation; the computer revolution in banking; the changes in communications brought about by networks and satellites; the uses of computers in the energy and transportation industries; computerized factories, including industrial robotics; and—harbinger of the future—personal robots.

Corporate Report 2

(follows page 158)

The Software Industry: Inside Look at a Software Development Firm

One of the most successful computer software companies around, with sales in the millions, ASK was founded in 1973 from a second-hand desk in Sandra Kurtzig's apartment bedroom. In this Corporate Report we look at the software packages that ASK develops to boost productivity of manufacturing operations; the company's network service; and their user education and support operation.

Corporate Report 3
(follows page 254)

The Health Industry: Inside Look at a Modern Hospital

What happens behind the scenes in a modern hospital? This report follows the hypothetical course of a patient admitted with a sports injury. Today's health administrators must deal with an array of computer-based technology if they are in a high-tech hospital like the one we examine in this Corporate Report. Computer involvement extends from admissions, patient records, and financial data, to laboratory technology, pharmacies, development of prostheses, patient education, implants, and brain scans, among other activities.

Corporate Report 4
(follows page 350)

The Information Industry: Inside Look at a Computer Magazine Publisher

Publisher of magazines for IBM and Apple computers and a member of the world's largest publisher of computer-related information, PC World Communications also makes extensive use of microcomputers. Here we examine the use of these tools in putting out *Macworld*, the magazine for users of Apple's Macintosh computer.

Corporate Report 5
(follows page 510)

Computers for Decision Making: The Tasks of Business

The four principal departments of business are Marketing, Accounting and Finance, Production, and Research and Development. Each of these departments uses computer-based information systems for management decision making. Computers are also used to carry out the tasks of the department, as depicted here.

To the Instructor: Why Use This Book?

We have become used to surprises, but perhaps the real surprises are yet to come.

We have become used to startling developments in such separate industries as telephone, overnight delivery, information processing, microcomputers, data base, telecommunications, and office automation. But perhaps the most significant new development is that all these industries have begun to fuse into one—the Information Industry, the product of the 30-year revolution in electronics we have all been living through.

To anyone contemplating or engaged in a career in business—or in management of any sort, public sector as well as private—ignoring this monumental change is to concede the advantage before the game has even begun. For the name of the game is not so much courage or luck or even superior position or intelligence. To managers in the rest of the twentieth century, the name of the game is handling information.

The Promise of This Book: The Student Business Tool

Computers and Information Processing with Business Applications is designed as a textbook for an introductory college course in business information processing. No academic prerequisites in business, mathematics, computer science, or programming languages are necessary. We introduce terminology as needed throughout the text.

A question many students ask is: How much does one *really* have to know about computers in order to pursue a business career? Our answer is: Only as much as is useful. This book is intended for people who plan to go into business—or management or administration in some form—and who therefore will become *users* of the computer. Our aim is to introduce students to the business tool they will be using in the workplace in the rest of this century.

Accordingly, the book has the following features:

1. The book takes a "user-oriented," business applications approach. It is possible to learn a great many technical things about computers and information processing. A future manager, however, does not *need* to know all of them. Thus, we present only the technical material that people planning careers in accounting, finance, marketing, or the like need to know to do their jobs. Those planning technical careers in computers and information processing will want to go on to further work in the field after reading this text.

2. Office automation and applications software are described early in the book—indeed, software precedes hardware. "The Promise of Office Automation" appears as Chapter 2, showing students how word processing, electronic filing, electronic mail, and the like are rapidly revolutionizing white-collar work. "Personal Software You Can Use"—which shows the workings of popular commercial software packages for word processing, electronic spreadsheets, filing, and business graphics—appears as Chapter 4, giving students an early look at software uses in the business environment. Other aspects of software—structured programming and programming languages—are also described before the main discussion of hardware, so that students can be better prepared for hands-on manipulation of computers as early in the course as possible.

3. The book has a strong systems orientation. We believe business students should not study hardware and software in a vacuum but rather within the framework of a total business information *system*. Accordingly, quite early in the book, in Chapter 3, we present an overview of how business systems and computer systems work together. We return to this treatment in detail in Part 4 when we describe systems analysis and design, operations information systems (OIS), management information systems (MIS), data base management systems (DBMS), and decision support systems (DSS).

4. The computer is treated as a tool. The computer has been subjected to endless mystification by many data processing professionals. This book presents the computer for what it is—a valuable part of the manager's tool kit. On the one hand, we show it as a tool for personal professional activities—for file management, spreadsheets, word processing, and graphics. On the other hand, we show it as a tool for managing corporate information through business information systems.

5. The microcomputer is given a starring role. Because the microcomputer has revolutionized the workplace, it is essential that it have the emphasis it deserves, and we try to accomplish this in this book. However, we have been careful not to diminish the importance of larger computers. We do not believe that microcomputers will replace mainframes but rather will be integrated with these and other computers; in this way, microcomputers will significantly change the role of and the control of computer resources within the organization. We also believe that microcomputers offer managers a tool for greater productivity in their business activities.

6. The book offers many cases and applications. Because we want managers to learn how best to develop and use computer-based information, we offer three kinds of case examples covering a variety of industries:

- **Case studies beginning each chapter.** Drawn from highly readable reports in publications ranging from *Computerworld* to the *Wall Street Journal,* from *Personal Computing* to the *Harvard Business Review,* these boxed-off "curtain-raiser" case studies, which appear on the second page of each chapter, generally present actual uses of the technology and processes to be discussed. Students thus become engaged in each chapter with a sense of the real-world problems and opportunities associated with the material they are about to read.
- **Ongoing "You Are There" cases covering several chapters.** With these in-text cases, we give the student a "hands-on" feeling of participation as the right-hand assistant to a manager or chief executive in four industries: health, films, banking, and clothing. The student thus becomes closely identified with business problem-solving processes.
- **Realistic case problems concluding each chapter.** How do you present business problems for people without business experience? How do you make case problems meaningful and not silly or superficial? We have tried to present case problems that students will *want* to read—because they provide added information of value and alert them to challenges and opportunities they may actually face. Thus, the case problems introduce topics such as computerized recruitment services, managing cash flow, determining billable time for professionals, "just-in-time" systems, and other subjects we hope students will be reluctant to pass up.

7. We have tried to make the material interesting and meaningful. All of us are dazzled every day by television programs, magazines, and advertising with lively writing and flashy graphics. These are the seductive messages with which education must compete. We believe that, without trivializing the material at hand, we can enhance the educational process by avoiding dullness. Thus, we have tried to write with liveliness and style, using many journalistic devices to hold reader interest. We have also tried to pay attention to the importance of graphics, offering vivid, well-conceived illustrations and eye-catching color "Corporate Reports"—sections of photographs and art designed much like shareholder annual reports—to depict the uses of the computer as a tool in business environments. And throughout the text and in boxed-off material we have provided historical perspectives, biographical profiles, commentary, how-to tips, and other material that sheds light on the immediacy and pervasiveness of computers in business.

8. We have included extensive pedagogy to make this text an excellent student learning tool. A **Preview** at the beginning of each chapter outlines the topics to be covered in the chapter. The material at the end of each chapter includes a **Summary** that students will find especially useful when reviewing for tests; a list of **Key Terms,** including the page in the chapter where each term is first introduced; **Review Questions** for student self-testing; and **Case Problems** that require students to apply the concepts they have learned in the chapter. Additionally, a **Glossary/ Index** appears at the back of the book.

Finally, we should mention that this book expresses a viewpoint or vision. Facts by themselves are not enough; they are given coherence when expressed with a philosophical viewpoint. Students want to know how to be prepared to deal with computers in business; however, we believe that technology is changing the ways of doing business so rapidly that one cannot possibly be prepared for everything. But one can be prepared with an *attitude*—the attitude that one must be able to cope with all kinds of changes. One must be ready to deal both with old technology and with very new, with a great deal of business information and with very little, with commonplace ways of doing business and with cutting-edge surprises. This is a viewpoint you will find expressed repeatedly throughout this book.

Organization: Options for Using This Book

Computers and Information Systems with Business Applications is divided into five parts.

Part 1, The New Tool for Business Enterprise, introduces the computer as a business tool from a macro point of view. After this introduction, we describe the exciting advances in office automation. In the all-important third chapter, we explain how business systems work, how computer systems work, and then how the two worlds of computers and business are fused together as computer-based business information systems. Chapter 3 gives the student sufficient background so that the instructor may then customize the rest of the book to his or her course requirements. For instance, if the reading in this text must be foreshortened in order to accommodate other course readings or laboratory work, it is possible to omit Part 3, "The Uses of Hardware," and/or Part 5, "The Rewards and Risks of the Information Age." Instructors will find that their students have derived enough material about hardware in Chapter 3 to permit them to understand any of the remaining parts should they want to adjust the organization of their reading.

Part 2, The Uses of Software, starts with material most useful to business students: how to use some prominent commercial software packages in word processing, spreadsheets, data bases (files), and business graphics. We believe that it is important to have students using computers in a computer lab as early as possible in the course in order to begin to quench their thirst for hands-on experience and to stimulate their interest in using the computer as a business tool. Consequently, we have deliberately organized the book so that practical matters of software precede the issues of hardware—although any instructor who feels that hardware (Part 3) should be taught before software will find the text organization flexible enough to permit this.

Part 2 also covers programming. Although we think it is important that students learn at least some programming logic and problem solving, it is our belief that the ordinary business user of computers in the rest of this century will not be using today's programming languages such as BASIC so much as integrated business software packages and fourth-generation languages. Nevertheless, we believe that structured programming concepts are important—both because of their general applicability to logical thinking and because managers must be able to communicate their needs to programmers—and so we have included a chapter on application programming and a chapter on programming languages.

Part 3, The Uses of Hardware, covers input and output devices, CPU and operating systems, external storage and file organization, and data communication systems. As we mentioned above, this part can be introduced whenever the instructor desires—or covered in part or skipped altogether. We have written Part 3 from the point of view of the professional of the 1990s who will be *using* computers, not designing and installing them, yet who needs to be on speaking terms about hardware to communicate his or her wants to people with more technical backgrounds.

Part 4, Business Information Systems, covers systems analysis and design, operations information systems, management information systems, data base management systems, and decision support systems—the crucial business-related disciplines a future manager needs to know. We have illustrated the conceptual information with case studies in order to give students a feel for the problems of the business world and some of the solutions that computers can provide.

Part 5, The Rewards and Risks of the Information Age, addresses some top concerns about the use of computers in our time. Chapter 15 describes the evolution of information systems, the importance of information resource management, and the possible course of business information systems in the future. Chapter 16 covers privacy, security, and ethics—important and necessary concerns for all of us. The last chapter describes some of the risks in computer technology, including the problems of automation and employment. It also presents some ideas on the impact of the technology of the future.

The **Appendix** offers a course in BASIC programming.

Supplements Available

Because teaching a large introductory course can be a rigorous activity, we believe a solid package of supplementary materials is almost as important as a solid textbook. Accordingly, our publisher has produced a supplementary package that provides a complete system of instruction. The supplements are packaged in a handsome box that is easy to store on a bookshelf. The supplements are sensitive to the needs not only of full-time instructors but also of part-time instructors and teaching assistants. The supplements include the following:

1. Instructor's Guide. Written by Professor Marvin Clark of the College of Business, Boise State University, the instructor's guide offers many practical suggestions for using the textbook. For each chapter in the text, the guide features

- Learning objectives
- Chapter overview
- Key terms from the chapter
- Lecture outline
- Answers to review questions and case problems

The guide also includes program solutions to programs in the BASIC appendix.

2. Study Guide. Written by Professor James Adair of the Department of Computer Information Systems, Bentley College, the study guide is available for students interested in further study of the book's contents. For each chapter in the text, the study guide includes

- What to look for in the chapter
- Key terms
- Self-tests, including terms to be defined; short-answer, multiple-choice, true/false, and matching questions; comparisons between terms; and application problems.

The study guide also has five review tests, one for the end of each of the five parts of the text. Answers to all self-tests are included in the back of the study guide.

3. Test Bank. Developed by Professor Carole Colaneri of the Department of Computer Science, Mid-Florida Technical College, the test bank includes more than 1800 questions in the following formats:

- True/false
- Multiple choice
- Matching
- Sentence completion

For qualified adopters, two types of computerized testing services are available—one designed for mainframes and most minicomputers, the other (TestGen) designed for IBM PC and Apple II microcomputers. Further information is available from the publisher.

4. Transparency Masters. A number of illustrations from the text are also available as transparency masters. All such transparency masters are drawn with thick lines and large type for the most readable projection.

5. Laboratory Manual. Written by Professor T. J. O'Leary of the School of Business, Arizona State University, this lab manual is an introduction to WordStar and Lotus 1-2-3 for the IBM PC. The manual, which is designed to acquaint students with two of the most popular commercial software packages available, presents explanations of how to use the packages with hands-on exercises. A template data disk is available for instructors adopting the lab manual.

To the Student: What's in This Book for You?

You are probably a member of a generation that is not afraid of technology. Television has been around as long as you have. You probably use the phone more often than you write letters. An automatic teller machine is a convenience, not an irritation. Personal computers may be unfamiliar, but they are not threats, only curiosities.

But whether you are of this generation that has grown up with three decades of the revolution in electronics or of an older one, you are probably aware that the knowledge of technology will only become *more* essential to future careers. That indeed is the concern we are addressing in this book: We expect that computers will be the ordinary tools of the future and that business people will be required to use them as a matter of course. Our aim is to help you succeed with these tools.

To assist you, we have employed a number of devices:

1. We have tried to make the material both entertaining and meaningful. Business and computers are not dull—far from it. Thus, we have tried to convey the fast pace of the Information Revolution that you are living in, the rewards and risks of business, the spirit of enterprise and entrepreneurship. What helps some managers succeed? What makes some companies outlast others? How does technology help you compete? Such questions suggest stories worth telling, for they are questions that will no doubt be of vital concern to you beyond the classroom.

2. We have included extensive, varied examples and applications. Because the book should above all be practical, we have tried to show in great detail how the Information Revolution is permeating business, as follows:

- **Case studies at the beginning of each chapter:** These descriptions of computers and information processing in action are intended to give you a real-world taste of the concepts to come.
- **Case examples within chapters:** How does it feel to be using computer technology and concepts in business? We put you in a "hands-

on" situation as the valued assistant of a top executive in four business enterprises: a health services company, a film production company, an international bank, and a stylish clothing manufacturer.

- **Case problems at the end of each chapter:** These are case problems we hope you will not want to miss, for they are not just repetitions of chapter material but additional valuable information, not so much problems as opportunities.
- **Boxes:** These include how-to tips, explanations, historical perspectives, flashbacks, further examples, and other interesting topics that flesh out the text discussion.
- **"Corporate Reports":** These special color layouts that appear throughout the book show how the computer as a tool is used in various kinds of enterprises. They also give you a sense of what a career is like in some of the more forward-looking companies.

3. We have provided many learning aids. The following are designed to help you get a grasp on the material. The **Preview** at the beginning of each chapter does just that—preview the important headings in the chapter, to help orient you to the main topics being covered. A **Summary** appears at the end of each chapter, which we hope you will find especially helpful when reviewing for tests. The summary also includes important words in boldface (darker) type, the same boldfaced terms that appear throughout the text. The list of **Key Terms** repeats these terms, and indicates the page in the chapter where each term is first mentioned. The **Review Questions** at the end of each chapter consist of questions designed for self-testing before examinations. The **Case Problems** at the end of the chapter, as mentioned, pose situations that invite you to apply the concepts learned in the chapter. Finally, a **Glossary/Index** appears in the back of the book to provide a concise definition of each key term and to refer you to the appropriate discussion within the text.

How you feel about this book is important to us. Any comments, favorable or unfavorable, will be welcomed and will be read carefully. Write to us in care of our publisher, The Benjamin/Cummings Publishing Company, 2727 Sand Hill Road, Menlo Park, CA 94025.

T. J. O'Leary
Brian K. Williams

Acknowledgments

There are only two names on the front of this book, but there are many others who have contributed to it and made us even prouder to have our names on it.

Chief among them are the many hardware and software companies and users of their products who have been so generous with the photographs that you see throughout the book. They are listed on pages 669–673. In particular, we must single out the following for special thanks because of their generosity in permitting Roberta Spieckerman and her photographers access to their premises and employees: ASK Computer Systems, Inc.; El Camino Hospital; PC World Communications and Macintosh magazine. We are indebted to Allison Hartman of ASK, Karen Fischer of El Camino Hospital, and Bruce Charonnat and Janet McCandless of Macworld for their kindness in making these special arrangements.

We must also express our appreciation to the publishers, authors, and artists who gave us permission to reprint from previously published materials; they are listed on pages 666–668.

Several instructors took part in discussion groups about the manuscript or reviewed the material in whole or in part. We are delighted to have had their participation and owe them all many thanks. Their names are listed at the end of the front matter.

Many friends and publishing professionals helped in the writing, design, graphics, and production stages of this book, and we are extremely grateful for their efforts. They include the Derman brothers, Randy Dunagan, Rhonda Harris, Peter Menzel, Brenn Lea Pearson, Stacey C. Sawyer, Louise Sessions, Marcia Shenk, Steve Sorensen, Alice Spears, and Peeter Vilms. In particular, Chris Kozakis helped us tremendously with his ideas, programming experience, editorial reviews, and consultations. Tom Coury gave us invaluable support by organizing and developing the BASIC appendix. Roberta Spieckerman made an enormous contribution with her ideas for and creation of the color sections of this book, along with her many other ideas for text photos; there is no question that she and her staff are top-notch in photo research. George Omura should be singled out for the quality and creativity of the line art; we feel we were lucky to have him. Al Burkhardt, one of the best book designers we have ever worked with, deserves applause for his dignified yet exciting design, including the different layouts for the color sections. Pat Franklin Waldo, the production coordinator, is absolutely in a class by herself, performing broken-field running while remaining the epitome of calmness and good humor; there are not many others who can do what she can do, and we are very fortunate in having had her services.

At Benjamin/Cummings, we are grateful to Laura Argento for her production management of a project under difficult conditions and to Allan Wylde, Jim Behnke, Sally Elliott, and Jane Gillen for their publishing support. We have been lucky to have had the assistance of the very fine mind of senior developmental editor Pat Burner, whose writing, organization, and ideas appear incognito throughout this book; there is no doubt that she was a strong, constructive force. Finally, we must extend our greatest tribute to Susan Nelle, our sponsoring editor. This book is in great part an expression of her vision, a vision she has held to steadfastly throughout; without her, this text would not exist.

There are those close to us who gave up what we have yet to pay back—time—so that we might work on this book. Linda, Danny, Kirk, Sylvia, and Stacey: We remember what we missed and are grateful for your patience.

T. J. O'Leary
Brian K. Williams

Reviewers and Participants in Market Research

James Adair
Bentley College

Herbert Bomzer
Central Michigan University

Lloyd Brooks
Memphis State University

Marvin Clark
Boise State University

Eli Cohen
California State University, Sacramento

Carole Colaneri
Mid-Florida Technical College

Chris Edwards
Carnegie-Mellon University

Richard Fleming
Northlake College

James Kasum
University of Wisconsin—Milwaukee

David Kay
University of California, Los Angeles

Richard Kearns
East Carolina University

Michael Kelly
City College of San Francisco

James Kho
California State University, Sacramento

Ken Lebeiko
California State University, Hayward

John Lehene
San Jose State University

Helen Ligon
Baylor University

Robert Lind
University of New Orleans

Alan Lord
Ohio State University

C.G. Mallonee
Essex Community College

Anne McClanahan
Ohio University

Robert C. Meier
West Washington University

Leon Pearce
Drake University

Norman Pendegraft
University of Idaho

Sheila Pickett
San Jose State University

Herbert Rebhun
University of Houston

Steven Schmidt
Butte College

Thomas Schriber
University of Michigan

Anne Steele
University of North Carolina

E. Burton Swanson
University of California, Los Angeles

Neil Swanson
Arizona State University

Steve Teglovic
University of Northern Colorado

Julie Tinsley
Indiana Central University

Robert van Spyk
California State University, Hayward

David Whitney
San Francisco State University

Prologue: The Business of Change

Shepherd's Mill is still. Built in the 1730s in Shepherdstown, West Virginia, as one of many rural water mills that converted grain into flour, Shepherd's Mill is now a silent monument to the industrial age that once formed the whole order of our society.

In the century and a half of its existence, the mill was modified several times in response to advances in milling and water power technology. In the late 1700s, a conveyor system was introduced that automated the movement of grain through the various stages. In the 1890s, grindstones were replaced by chilled iron rollers, which milled a finer, better flour. The new technique required greater power than before: other millers went to steam power or water turbines, but the owner of Shepherd's Mill installed the 40-foot-diameter waterwheel shown here. At the same time, he added the wood-frame third floor to the original stone structure.

Today, however, Shepherd's Mill is still, a relic of an economic and technological order long gone by. Though a monument, it has lessons for the present, for it shows how business institutions must adapt to technological change. The mill changed much during its long life. For us living in the Computer Age, however, the changes we will witness in our institutions will be far more dramatic and certainly far more rapid. Indeed, for the rest of our lives, we will need to make it our business to understand the business of change.[1]

Part 1

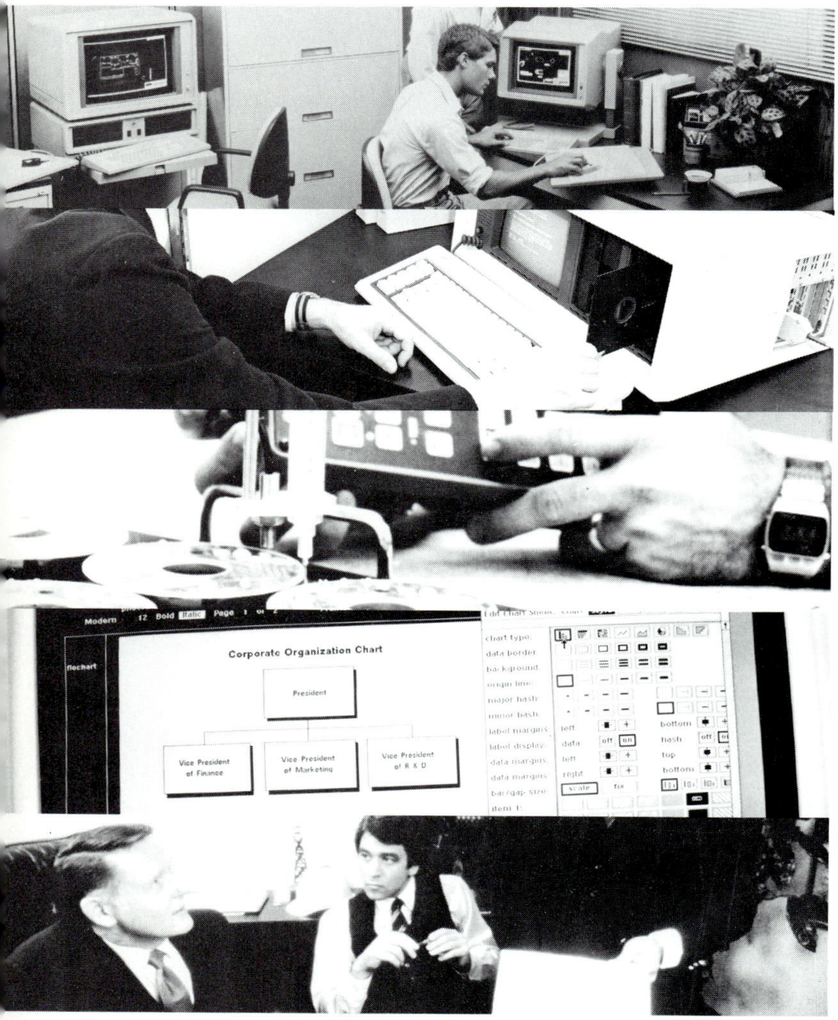
Corporate Organization Chart
President
Vice President of Finance
Vice President of Marketing
Vice President of R & D

The New Tool for Business Enterprise

The old ways are changing, and changing fast. Once upon a time, the pace of business enterprise was measured in weeks and days and hours—by the speed of clipper ships or transcontinental trains or the Western Union wire. Today it is measured in hours and minutes and seconds—by the speed of the Concorde jetliner or the Telex message or the COMSAT satellite signal. Once, back in 1874, Philo Remington began marketing a curious printing machine, known as a "typewriter," which began the retirement of the quill pen. Today the workplace is being revolutionized by word processing and other office technology, changing the nature of white-collar work more rapidly than at any time in the past 100 years. Once, less than a decade and a half ago, the Wall Street stock exchanges almost collapsed under the pressure of trading 11 million shares a day. Today they are capable of trading more than 237 million shares a day.

The midwife of these changes is, of course, the computer. The chief characteristic of the computer is that by its speed and its ability to handle enormous amounts of data *it greatly extends our human capabilities.* The result has been the Information Revolution, a revolution in the production, dissemination, and handling of all the information that business people need to know to bring goods and services to market. The key to controlling this revolution, however, is not to be fearful of the computer but to learn to use it, to become familiar with it as an everyday business tool.

Let us now begin to examine this tool—first presenting some background in computers, then seeing how the computer is automating office work, then showing how computer systems and business systems are fused into business information systems.

CHAPTER 1

The Computer Solution

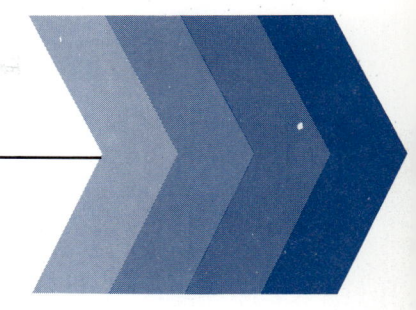

The Information Revolution and New Realities

PREVIEW

The Information Revolution—how shall we sing its song?

The uses to which computers can be put are varied and profound, and the high hopes that business people have—that computers will enhance productivity, reduce drudgery, speed responses to the marketplace—are mainly justified. And the changes still to come promise to be on the grand scale. The box on the next page, for example, is a paean to the computer revolution about to affect the Securities and Exchange Commission, regulator of the nation's stock exchanges. Such changes, it is hoped, will drastically curtail mountains of paper and speed up the delivery of information to those who need it. Indeed, we will find many occasions throughout this book on which to sing the praises of computers.

Computer Dreams, Computer Nightmares

When you become involved with computers in business, however, there is another song you *do not* want to sing—a dirge. Computers have fostered and will probably continue to foster unrealistic expectations about what they can do. Let us show what we mean.

When the U.S. Supreme Court ruled in 1977 that lawyers could run advertisements for themselves—just like restaurants, banks, and most other businesses—two Oakland, California, lawyers thought they saw a way to take this opportunity, combine it with a novel business strategy and computers, and mass-market legal services to become the "McDonald's of law firms."

How well did the plan work?

First, the advertising: "THERE ARE TIMES YOU NEED A LAWYER, AND TIMES YOU DON'T. YANELLO & FLIPPEN HELPS YOU DECIDE," ran

CASE STUDY: NEW ERA FOR INVESTORS

The Computer Revolution for the Securities and Exchange Commission

The S.E.C.—the Securities and Exchange Commission—was established a few years after the stock market crash of 1929 in which so many people suffered economic disaster. It is designed to protect investors by requiring full disclosure of relevant financial information from companies wishing to sell new stock or bond issues to the public.

ITTF
ITT
ITTC
SPECIAL
DAILY
MATURITIES
DATE
ITTF
ITT
ITTC

WASHINGTON, April 1—The Federal Express and Purolator Courier trucks lined up two deep in front of the Securities and Exchange Commission on Friday, and every few minutes another rounded the corner of Fifth Street at the base of Capitol Hill. By noon a makeshift receiving center in the lower lobby was a blizzard of paper.

The S.E.C. hopes that this frenzy, marking the quarterly deadlines for companies to turn in their required reports, will be eliminated by late next year. The line of overnight express service mail trucks and some six million pages of documents a year will be replaced by a neat stream of electrons.

Companies will file quarterly, annual and other reports with the S.E.C. electronically, computer to computer. And instead of waiting weeks, sometimes months, for copies of these documents, brokers and investors will be able to call the information up on the screens of their personal computers the same afternoon.

The system will revolutionize the quantity and timeliness of the most valuable corporate information that publicly held companies are forced to disclose. It will also radically improve the quality of research: With the press of a few buttons, investors in living rooms across the United States will be able to peruse the auditor's report of a company's latest results. .

Under the S.E.C. system, called Edgar, for Electronic Data Gathering and Retrieval, a company filing its report would transmit it directly to the S.E.C. much the way that many now send material electronically to financial printers.

The S.E.C. would transfer the material to a large computer, connected by high-speed telephone lines to a popular switching system like Tymshare or GTE's Telenet system.

Investors seeking information for their portfolios would dial a local telephone number for the switching system, and enter a code to identify themselves for billing purposes.

Then they would identify the name of the company they wanted to learn about. On the screen, a menu would appear, listing the company's filings or asking whether some specific information was sought, such as the company's latest quarterly earnings report, or a specific proxy statement. With the press of a button, the information would appear on the screen.

—David E. Sanger, *The New York Times,* April 4, 1984

one of their ads. They blanketed TV, radio, billboards, newspapers, and mass transit with a $250,000-a-year advertising campaign.

Second, the business strategy: Law has typically been a tradition-bound field, but Yanello & Flippen thought they saw a way to reach clients who had had little contact with lawyers before. Initial consultation fees would be only $20. Other fees would be 20–30% less than those of competing lawyers. They would go after bread-and-butter cases: divorces, wills, contracts, and the like. Clients would pay with credit cards or in installments.

Third, the computer: The computer was as essential to success as any of the other parts, for it would allow Yanello & Flippen to speed up paperwork (the law utilizes a great deal of repetitious material, such as standard "boilerplate" clauses in contracts), decrease the use of high-priced lawyers, and keep track of billings.

The novel strategy appeared to pay off. In the next four years, Yanello & Flippen Law Offices grew to 20 attorneys in eight Oakland and San Francisco Bay area offices, attracted 16,000 clients, and gathered annual revenues of more than $1 million.

A year later, however, cofounder Ralph Yanello had declared himself personally bankrupt; his partner, Thomas Flippen, had left the business; and the firm itself was down to five attorneys operating on the brink of insolvency.

What went wrong? Part of the answer, according to a *San Francisco Chronicle* article, was that the advertising worked so well that the staff of lawyers, most of them young and inexperienced, was quickly overwhelmed with 100 cases each. Probably equally important, however, were the high expectations for, and misuses of, the computer.

Says the *Chronicle* story:

> The computer system that was supposed to be the firm's ally turned out to be a nemesis. The office went through four different [computers] in as many years. Bills were fouled up, and clients were not billed for as long as a year, attorneys said. Hundreds of thousands of dollars were never collected.
>
> The billing snafu drained endless hours, diverting the firm from creating the legal programming that was supposed to reduce the high cost of legal services.
>
> After the first computer arrived late, with accounting software that Yanello found inadequate, he plunged into developing his own programs, although he had no formal computer training and was advised against it.
>
> Yanello never stopped believing in computers, as if the machines embodied all the rationality that the firm lacked. . . .[1]

On October 11, 1983, Yanello & Flippen filed a multimillion-dollar lawsuit accusing a local vendor, Mini Systems, of failing to provide them with a time-and-billing system, word processing package, and adequate programming and training services, which were deemed "crucial" to their survival.

Winners and Losers: Who Will Gain by the Information Revolution?

There are many "war stories" about computers in business, and you will no doubt hear more. We have introduced our book with the sad case of Yanello & Flippen, however, because we feel it is important to go about the study of computers pragmatically. If business people are to make sound judgments, of course, they must realize that computers and their information are only as good as the people who design them, program them, and—most importantly, for readers of this book—use them.

As we stated in the introduction to this part of the book, the computer is a *business tool*. There are two facts about tools: First, tools change. The spade becomes plow becomes tractor. The pen becomes typewriter becomes word processor. While the tools that evolve may make our lives easier, as the tools change, we must change with them.

Second, tools can do both harm and good. That familiar tool the car causes around 50,000 deaths a year in the United States, but the car-as-ambulance saves more lives (probably over 30,000 in one month in New York City alone). The computer unquestionably puts some people out of work, but it also brings a good many benefits.

Who will be the winners and losers in the Information Revolution? Let us consider the losers first—since, needless to say, none of us wants to be counted among them.

The Losers

Hardly a job now exists that will not be affected by computer technology. Some, however, will be affected adversely. Blue-collar manufacturing jobs—the numbing but often well-paying jobs that exist for unskilled workers in auto plants and the like—are particularly vulnerable to industrial robots, such as the computer-controlled welders and paint-sprayers now found in automobile plants. Many tedious but easily learned white-collar jobs—such as those involving filing, sorting, and the typing of lists—are also disappearing. Jobs that consist largely of dispensing information over a telephone—the ones currently occupied by stockbrokers, airline reservations personnel, and the like—are other endangered species. People serving business travel, such as airline pilots, will find themselves reduced in numbers as business people come to depend more on computerized communications than on travel. Clearly, with 30 million people already unemployed throughout the Western

Steel-collar worker. Many blue-collar workers fear the prospect of computer-related automation, such as the robot welders used in new-car assembly plants.

industrialized world, the loss of such jobs to computers is certain to become an urgent social issue.

But the computer will do more than displace jobs. It will also, some observers point out, narrow some jobs, make others more complicated, compartmentalize still others, and generally strain previous work styles. Librarians, travel agents, and employment personnel, to name a few occupations, will no doubt find extraordinary changes in their lives. So will business managers. Yet one Harris Poll survey for *Business Week* found that 55% of business managers reported they had taken no formal computer training—even though 91% felt it would increase their productivity.[2] Such managers may not exactly be losers—yet. But it would be interesting to see if they emerge among the winners.

The Winners

The biggest winners will probably be those enterprising "surfers," as they have been called, who, anticipating the wave of technological change, ride the crest of that wave to success. These are the risk-takers and innovators represented, for instance, by the Silicon Valley overnight millionaires behind such names as Hewlett-Packard or Intel or Apple Computer.

But there are a great many other people who are not innovators who clearly will emerge as winners also. Robots may displace some blue-collar workers in industry, but they also are able to rescue others from doing some jobs that humans should not have to do—for instance, working with radioactive materials, handling molten steel, or doing welding in dangerous situations. Computers may remove low-level white-collar clerical jobs, but they also remove a great deal of tedium. Word processing, for example, eliminates the repetitious typing of revised drafts, and computerized filing systems can do away with laborious alphabetizing by hand. Computers may remove the human presence in many business transactions, such as that of the bank teller or the airline reservations clerk, but they also make those transactions faster. Computerized telecommunications not only allows banking or ticket-buying to be done via telephone and home computer, it also benefits some single parents, disabled people, and others who need to be able to work at home and communicate with co-workers.

Another class of winners consists of those whose careers are directly tied to the computer's existence—people with job titles like computer programmer, systems analyst, and data base manager. Often having such a job is like riding a tiger, however, because of the rapidity with which the industry changes.

But, of course, the winners we are most concerned about in this book are business people. Some of the ways in which business people will or do benefit are as follows:

- Electronic message systems, both text and voice, allow managers to transmit memos and reports to several people at the same time and reach people more easily in different time zones.
- Large data banks, both within and outside the organization, enable managers to put together studies of businesses, markets, and so on, in hours instead of weeks.
- Desktop computers give executives the ability to do "what-if" calculations, using electronic spreadsheets, and to turn numbers into colorful charts and graphs that make information easier to grasp.
- Computerized systems allow executives to maintain electronic calendars and to schedule meetings with many people with much more ease.
- Television linkups enable managers in dispersed geographical locations to hold "face-to-face" conferences, thus saving travel time and expense.

In short, new electronic business information systems can improve job satisfaction, raise productivity, and eliminate much of the drudgery and wasted time that has long plagued many business professionals.

Nowhere are the benefits to executives more apparent than in that newest of white-collar tools, the microcomputer.

The Marvelous Microcomputer: The Business Productivity Tool

Every profession and every trade has its specialized tools, from the hammer of a carpenter to the stethoscope of a physician. Even desk-bound white-collar workers have tools, such as telephones, calculators, dictaphones, and photocopiers. Recently, however, the microcomputer has emerged as an essential instrument for business people.

If you have not already put your fingers on the keyboard of a microcomputer, there is virtually no doubt that you will. Indeed, much of the

Appleseed. The seed of the microcomputer revolution in offices occurred when special software was developed for the Apple II microcomputer, shown here. The Apple II was first available in 1977 but was mainly thought of as a game or hobbyists' machine. The most important business software developed was VisiCalc, first shipped in 1979, an "electronic spreadsheet" that allowed managers to manipulate projected costs more easily. A great many other programs are now available, including those that allow an Apple user to send and receive messages over telephone lines.

rest of this book is predicated on the assumption that you *should* learn to use this machine—that is, it is a necessary skill not just to survive in business but to prevail.

As we shall see in Chapter 3, there are four different sizes of computers (supercomputers, mainframes, minicomputers, and microcomputers), but it is the microcomputer that is currently having the most dramatic effect—that is, in fact, redefining the roles of other computers—and thus has a crucial role in the future of anyone going into business. Also known as *personal computers* and *desktop computers,* **microcomputers** are the smallest and least expensive, costing generally between $100 and $10,000 and being small enough to put on a table top or even hold in your hand. Price and size are what have made the microcomputer one of the most exciting developments of modern times, for they have made computing power available to many more people than it was possible before.

The dramatic advances in microcomputers are due to the technological advances in the microprocessor. Some people confuse the terms *microprocessor* and *microcomputer,* but the two are not the same. A **microprocessor**—microscopic processor—is the actual part of the computer responsible for processing information. Microprocessors put the computing power once possible only with room-sized computers into a chip the size of a dime (see box).

Because microcomputers are becoming so important in our lives, let us look at how they can be used in homes, schools, and businesses.

HISTORY OF THE INFORMATION AGE

The Challenge of the Chip

Nothing can be fully understood without context, and history is context. The story of the Information Age is told in installments throughout this book, but if you prefer this history all at once, the installments may be read in one sitting. To set the scene for the present, however, let us begin with the recent past.

The principal driving force of the Information Revolution is a device no thicker than your thumbnail and half its size—the microchip or integrated circuit. Ordinary consumers probably first became aware of the impact of these chips during the 1970s when pocket calculators began to appear. More dramatic are the chips now found in home or personal computers, which consume less than one watt of power yet have the computational ability of a 1946-era room-size computer requiring 140,000 watts of power, enough electricity to run a small power station. Today, machines ranging from cardiac pacemakers to communications satellites are familiar applications of microchip technology. And, of course, so are the new business machines of interest to us:

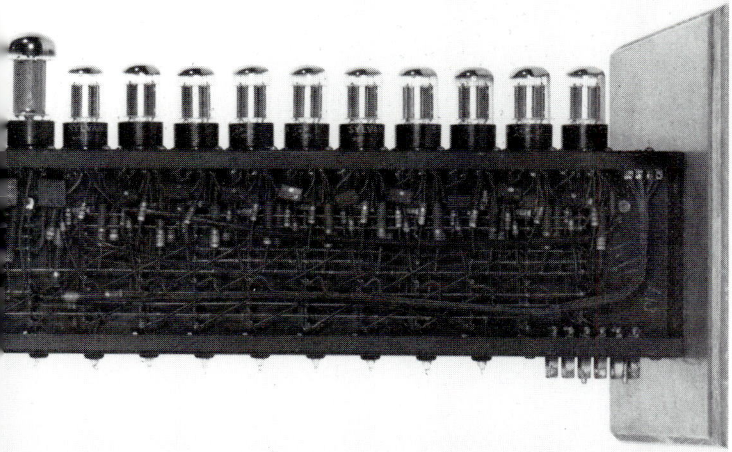

Three generations of technology. Vacuum tubes *(top left)* gave way to transistors and then to integrated circuits or chips *(bottom right)*. The relative sizes of the three forms of technology are shown at top right.

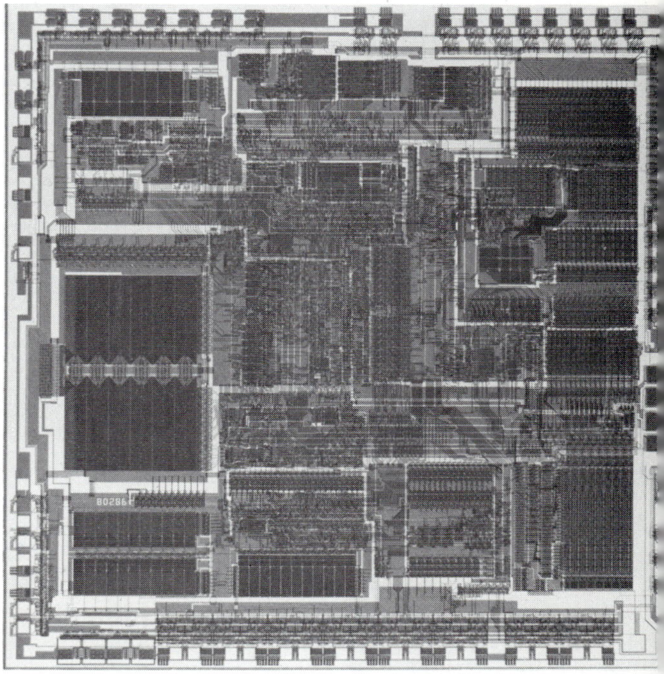

word processors, automated teller machines, telecommunications equipment, and so on.

The Vacuum Tube

The power of the computer is intimately linked to the size of the electronic device within it that controls the flow of electric current. The earliest device was the **vacuum tube,** an electronic tube about the size of a light bulb. In one of the earliest computers, the 1946 ENIAC, 18,000 vacuum tubes were required—and all had to operate simultaneously. One critic objected that because "the average life of a vacuum tube is 3000 hours, a tube failure would occur every 15 minutes. Since it would average more than 15 minutes to find the bad tube, no useful work could ever be done." Nevertheless, the ENIAC was able to complete ten months' worth of calculations in one day.

The Transistor

In 1959, the vacuum tube was succeeded by the **transistor,** a type of electrical circuitry several times smaller than the vacuum tube. Invented by three Bell Laboratories scientists—John Bardeen, Walter Brattain, and William Shockley, who later shared a Nobel prize for their efforts—transistors also had other advantages in that they needed no warm-up time, consumed less energy, and were faster and more reliable.

The Integrated Circuit

Beginning in 1965, the transistor began to be replaced by the **integrated circuit,** which was much smaller. Indeed, an integrated circuit less than one-eighth inch square now may contain hundreds of components and replace an entire circuit board of transistors. This further miniaturization set the stage for "democratizing" computers. No longer were they the exclusive property of business, university, and government organizations. The real revolution was about to begin: computers for everybody.

Integrated circuits are made with one of the earth's most abundant materials, a nonmetallic substance called **silicon,** found in common beach sand and in practically all rocks and clay. The element has given rise to the name "Silicon Valley" for California's Santa Clara County, an hour's drive south of San Francisco and originally the principal site of the electronics industry making what came to be known as the **silicon chip,** another name for integrated circuit. Silicon is used because it is a **semiconductor**—that is, a crystalline substance that will conduct electric current when it is "doped" with chemical impurities. A cylinder of silicon is sliced into wafers, each about 3 inches in diameter, and each wafer is etched repeatedly with patterns of electrical circuitry, then divided into several hundred small chips. A chip 1 centimeter square is so powerful it can hold 10,000 words—the length of a daily newspaper. Integrated circuits have proved to be extremely reliable, because semiconductor firms give them rigid work/not work tests. Mass production has also made them inexpensive to manufacture, and their compactness has made them inexpensive to operate because of reduced travel time for the electricity and hence low power use.

The Microprocessor

In 1969, an Intel Corporation design team headed by Ted Hoff developed the microprocessor. In this event, the integrated circuits evolved from specialized chips designed for either computer memory or logic into general-purpose processors-on-a-chip, or **microprocessors.** It is these devices that are found in the variety of products we see today, from microwave ovens to personal computers.

What about the future? Futurists speculate about entire wafers being used for superpowerful chips, about an office-on-a-chip, about biochips. We will describe these fascinating possibilities later.

Next history installment: **The Beginning: Babbage, Lady Byron, and the Brass and Pewter Computer,** p. 67.

Microcomputers in the Classroom and the Living Room

Perhaps you have encountered personal computers earlier in your education. Apple, Commodore, and Tandy–Radio Shack in particular have been active in marketing to schools. The number of programs being written for educational uses is dramatically increasing, ranging from vocabulary development to preparation for college entrance exams.

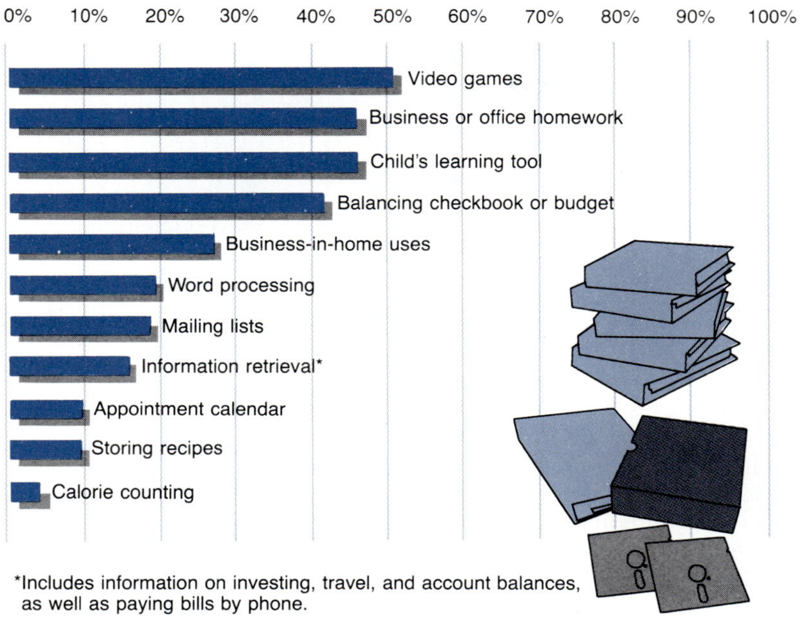
0%
10%
20%
30%
40%
50%
60%
70%
80%
90%
100%
Video games
Business or office homework
Child's learning tool
Balancing checkbook or budget
Business-in-home uses
Word processing
Mailing lists
Information retrieval*
Appointment calendar
Storing recipes
Calorie counting

*Includes information on investing, travel, and account balances, as well as paying bills by phone.

Figure 1-1 Uses of home computers. Percentage of home-computer users who said they use their computer for a particular task. Owners were able to give multiple responses.

Or perhaps you were first introduced to the microcomputer as a home computer. The extremely volatile market for home computers has been dominated by such names as Apple, Tandy–Radio Shack, Commodore, Atari, and IBM. In one survey (see Figure 1-1), it was found that most people use their personal computers for video games—available games range from Swamp War to (literally!) Kitchen Sink—but the second most common use was for business or office homework, tying with use as a child's learning tool. One of the more interesting services available to home-computer owners are so-called "information utilities," such as CompuServe or The Source, which give users access via telephone lines to data banks—massive stores of data—and news and financial services. People also are able to do home banking and buy and sell stocks through their home computers.

Some people also use home computers to handle personal money matters: checkbook balancing, tax preparation, stock portfolio evaluation, and so on. In addition, they are finding their computers useful as word processors to handle report writing and correspondence, as devices for keeping records, and as organizers of personal calendars and schedules.

Will the home computer ever become as commonplace as the TV set or stereo? It depends on which futurist you want to listen to. Some believe that nearly half the households in the United States will have a personal computer by the end of this decade.

Microcomputers in Business

The reaction to the appearance of microcomputers in business has been fascinating. Some executives have simply ignored their presence, either being afraid of them or feeling it is demeaning to lay hands on a keyboard. One writer described the situation this way:

> Executives feel that sitting at a computer terminal ill-suits the executive image. Secretaries type; managers feel foolish and unprofessional when they do. . . .
>
> Still another unexpressed fear stems from the widespread notion that computer systems are temperamental gadgets. Managers are afraid that a missed keystroke will result in a nasty headquarters memo that reads in effect: "Who was the jerk who blew up the system?"
>
> Senior vice president Harvey Poppel of Booz Allen points out that a computer's ability to give instantaneous notice of mistakes further intimidates many managers. "In a corporate environment, people sugarcoat the ways they tell you you're wrong," Mr. Poppel says. "The computer just comes out and says you're wrong with blinding speed. It is an immediate rebuke."[3]

Others view micros simply as toys or as status symbols in the office power struggles, boasting about the number-crunching abilities of their computers the way car enthusiasts brag about horsepower.

Most forward-looking business people, however, have found the machine a definite asset. Indeed, the cry "Computer liberation!" might describe the way many businesses have received it. Small businesses—businesses with fewer than 100 employees—can use microcomputers to free themselves from outside services for their computing needs or from expending much of their efforts on acquiring larger computers and hiring staffs to use them. Large businesses have also been liberated from being tied exclusively to large computers. In fact, the appearance of microcomputers has enhanced the efficiency of the large ones: the micro can be used to communicate with larger computers as if it were a **terminal**—a device with a keyboard and video screen (and possibly a printer) which is used to input data and output information. Yet the micro can also operate by itself, removing the workload from the larger computer. In addition, microcomputers have brought computing power from the guarded mysteries of the data processing department right to users' desks.

Microcomputers have many uses in business, among them:

- **To enhance productivity:** A manager's job is to plan and schedule the people and material resources available to get a task done. Microcomputers can aid in this task. Employees at Bank of America, for example, use micros to obtain corporate data from the bank's large computer. The data is then used by individual users on their desktop computers for financial analysis.
- **For communications:** A microcomputer can communicate with a larger computer and enhance the larger one's efficiency. A billion-dollar Canadian chemical company, C-I-L, uses microcomputers to transfer small amounts of data from one large computer to another—a job that previously had been done by physically transporting reels of magnetic tape. More dramatically, microcomputers have opened up a new people-to-people form of communications through telephone networks.
- **For automating offices:** Just as factories have long been automated, now offices are becoming so, and microcomputers are having a big impact, whether for communicating between executives, for word processing, or for storing information to reduce paperwork.

The New Frontier of the Information Revolution

"Can there really be anything new under the sun?" asks organizational psychologist Evan Peelle. "It may seem somewhat paradoxical, but at the close of the 20th century there still appears to be an ever-growing number of uncharted areas to explore. The enigma of our modern world is that the more we advance, the more of the unknown we discover."[4]

Because the human mind has a unique curiosity and drive to grow, says Peelle, we continue to create new frontiers to challenge ourselves and new ideas for meeting those challenges—the latest frontier being high technology.

Information technology—computers, telecommunications, data banks, graphics equipment, and the like—will change everything about the way we do business. It will change the products and services we provide, speeding up production and distribution. It will change the markets, erasing geographic and other boundaries. It will change production economics, so that in some cases it will be just as cheap to make products singly as to make them in quantity. And it will change the relationships between people in business—suppliers and buyers, producers and customers, employers and employed. To readers of this book, there is only one question:

Will you be ready for these changes?

SUMMARY

- The computer is a business *tool*, which means it is only as good as the people who design, program, and use it. There are two facts about tools. First, tools change; to utilize tools effectively, we must change with them. Second, tools can do both harm and good; the computer will put some people out of work while bringing benefits to others.
- The computer is changing the nature of work. Some jobs are affected adversely: jobs are being displaced by computers, while others are made more complicated, more narrow, or more compartmentalized. Blue-collar jobs such as unskilled workers in auto plants and white-collar jobs such as filing, giving information over a telephone, and serving business travel are particularly vulnerable.
- Some jobs are enhanced and made more productive by the computer, and the computer will continue to create new jobs and business opportunities. People who will benefit will be those who are technological innovators, blue-collar workers delivered from doing dangerous work, white-collar workers doing tedious work, and those who gain by doing business via telephone and home computer such as single parents and disabled people.
- Business people will benefit by having electronic message systems with which to transmit memos and reports, large data banks—massive stores of information—with which to put together studies in rapid time, desktop computers to help do "what-if" calculations of different possible numerical outcomes and turn numbers into colorful graphs, electronic calendars for scheduling meetings, and television linkups for having long-distance conferences without business travel.
- There are four sizes of computers, but the smallest and least expensive, the microcomputer, is one that readers of this book are apt to be familiar with. The **microcomputer** is also known as a personal or desktop computer.
- The microcomputer owes its existence to the **microprocessor**—microscopic processor—which is the part of the computer responsible for processing information. The history of the microprocessor is described at the end of this summary.
- Among the personal uses of microcomputers, it has been found that most people use their home computers principally for video games. The second most common use, business and office homework, ties with the use of computers as a child's learning tool. The home computer is also used for personal finances, for word processing, and for access to "information utilities," which give viewers access via telephone lines to data banks and news and financial services.

- Some executives have ignored or been intimidated by microcomputers and others view them as toys or status symbols. However, people in small business find that the microcomputer frees them from outside services for computing needs or from having to expend efforts on acquiring large computers and staffs to use them. People in large business find microcomputers can be used to communicate with larger computers; that is, the microcomputer is either used as a **terminal**—a device with keyboard and videoscreen used to input and output information—or used as a computer by itself, removing the workload from larger computers.
- Among the uses of microcomputers in business are (1) to enhance productivity, such as helping to plan and schedule people and material resources to get a task done; (2) for communications, such as to communicate with a larger computer or with other microcomputer users; and (3) for automating offices, such as for communicating between executives, for word processing, or for storing information to reduce paperwork.
- The microcomputer came about because of the microprocessor. Early computers, such as the 1946 ENIAC, used **vacuum tubes,** electronic tubes about the size of light bulbs that controlled the flow of electric current; vacuum tubes failed quite frequently. In 1959, the vacuum tube was succeeded by the **transistor,** a smaller type of electrical circuitry that needed no warm-up time, consumed less energy, and was faster and more reliable than the vacuum tube.
- In 1965, the transistor began to be replaced by the **integrated circuit,** which was less than one-eighth of an inch square and could replace an entire circuit board of transistors. Integrated circuits are made of **silicon,** a nonmetallic substance found in sand, which is a **semiconductor**—it will conduct electric current when doped with chemical impurities. Integrated circuits are known as **silicon chips.** They are extremely reliable, compact, and inexpensive to operate because of reduced travel time for electricity and thus low power use.
- In 1969, integrated circuits evolved from specialized chips designed for either computer memory or logic into general-purpose processors-on-a-chip or **microprocessors.** These are devices found in many appliances today, including microcomputers.

KEY TERMS

Integrated circuit, p. 16
Microcomputer, p. 14
Microprocessor, p. 14
Semiconductor, p. 16
Silicon, p. 16
Terminal, p. 18
Transistor, p. 16
Vacuum tube, p. 15

REVIEW QUESTIONS

1. What went wrong with Yanello & Flippen's strategy for success?
2. What effects, both good and bad, will the computer have on the nature of work in the near future?
3. Name various personal, business, and educational uses for the microcomputer.
4. Describe the benefits of the microcomputer to business.
5. Describe the history of electronic devices from vacuum tube to microprocessor.

CASE PROBLEMS

Case 1-1: Survival of the Paper Clip

Suppose you have some money to invest, and you are considering buying stock in companies involved in supplying offices. You have been reading about offices using less paper because of the switch to electronic equipment. You then read in the *Los Angeles Times*[5] (itself made of paper, of course!) that despite predictions of paperless electronic offices, technology is generating more paper than ever: electronic data storage makes more information available on paper for those who need it or think they need it; photocopiers make it easier to generate multiple copies; fear of power blackouts makes office workers generate backup copies of printouts. Thus, there seems to be more paper being produced. On the other hand, American offices have only begun to phase in the electronic gear that could reduce traditional ways of using paper.

Your assignment: The survival of the paper clip depends on the survival of paper. Do you think you should put your money into ClipCo, a paper-clip manufacturing company, for a long-term investment? Why or why not?

Case 1-2: The Future of Microcomputers

One of the ironies that you may face in your business career is that there is a need for simplicity in gadgetry, but the microprocessor has given manufacturers many more options. As the *New York Times* (March 8, 1984) reported, "Appliances are beeping, blinking, flashing messages and signaling when doors are ajar, [wash] cycles over and motors burned out. And the pace of the revolution [in electronics] will probably pick up. Manufacturers are already tinkering with appliances that listen and speak." Yet the people who use these devices probably want ease of use. As the director of marketing services for the Whirlpool Corporation told the *Times*, "The family is changing. . . . More than half of all women are working. Men and children are operating appliances. Plus we've got an aging population. Overall that means a need for ease of operation. We're not there yet. Appliances are probably too complex for lots of people."[6]

Your assignment: Let us say you go to work for a microcomputer company, Americomputer. Knowing what you know about the complexity of appliances and the problems with consumers, what recommendations for the future would you make to Americomputer about the design and marketing of microcomputers?

CHAPTER 2

The Promise of Office Automation

The Electronic White-Collar Future

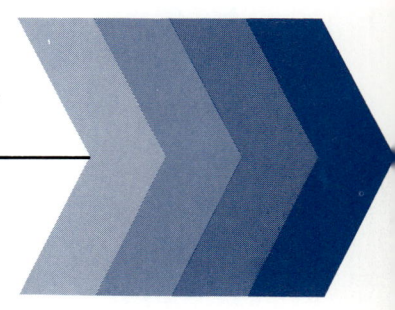

How do you stay a winner in an era of constant technological change?

Some people seem to know how to do it—and we hope that this book will help you learn to be one of them. Other people lag behind. Listen in, for instance, to the frustrating phone call salesman Fred Coldcall is making to his home office from a roadside pay phone, as described in the box on the following page. Clearly, Fred is not a winner. The fault is not entirely his, however. He is working for a company that is using old technology—technology that may not even seem old because we are all so used to it.

PREVIEW

Staying Ahead in an Era of Technological Change

How do some companies stay winners in an era of constant technological change? Like certain people, certain companies seem to know how to do it—computer makers IBM and Hewlett-Packard, for example, or pharmaceutical house Eli Lilly, or Dow Chemical. They may not be successful every time, but they continually do well enough to put themselves in the forefront of technological change in their industries. What is their secret?

Richard N. Foster, who is director in the New York office of McKinsey & Co. and who heads the consulting firm's work on technology management, has taken a look at this question:

> Everyone knows the sad tales of companies that seemingly did everything right, yet lost competitive leadership as a result of technological change. Du Pont was beaten by Celanese when bias-ply tire cords changed from nylon to polyester. B. F. Goodrich was beaten by Michelin when the radial overtook the bias-ply tire. NCR wrote off $139 million in

CASE STUDY: WAITING FOR THE OFFICE OF THE FUTURE

The Office of the Present: The Frustrations of Fred

"Darn it, Mary, I was within 20 minutes of Quick Industries this morning."

"Well, Mr. Coldcall, I tried to reach you at the field office. It's lucky that you just phoned in. Anyway, a Mr. Buysome at Quick Industries said that if you still want to bid on their contract, you've got to see him tomorrow at the latest and your proposal has to be in by Friday."

"Which proposal? We've talked about three different jobs."

"He said it was the one with the new specs."

"Oh, no! Peter in sales engineering has those at the district office along with the pricing sheets. Please transfer me to Peter. I'll get back to you."

"Sorry, he's on his line; it's busy."

"I guess I'll have to hold, but I'm in a phone booth."

Some minutes later: "Pete? Fred. Listen. I need the Quick specs and pricing. Can you get them to the field office by noon tomorrow? I'll make a special trip to pick them up."

"Those old things! I suppose I can find them somewhere, but we've changed some of the components and the pricing, so I'll have to update them. I'll try to get them to you by the end of the day."

"Pete, you've got to do better than that."

"Sorry, Fred. I'm already working on three other rush proposals, and I'm expediting two other jobs through some bottlenecks in the factory."

"Pete, for Fred's sake, do your darnedest! Now please transfer me back to Mary."

"Mary, two things: arrange the delivery with Peter. Then call Joan at the field office. Tell her we're going to have to work late tomorrow night after I come back from my meeting with Buysome. Tell her also to pull the Quick files and proposal boilerplates. She's the only one there who knows where everything is, how to work the word processor, and the high quality copier, and. . . ."

"Oh, Fred, Joan just called me from O'Hare [Airport]. Remember, she's off to Acapulco? Fred . . . Fred . . . are you there?"

—Harvey L. Poppel,
"Who Needs the Office of the Future?"
Harvard Business Review,
November–December 1982

Poor Fred is dead—or is he? In the office of the future, or automated office, he could probably pull off a quick sale with Quick Industries. *To see how, turn to the box on p. 46 at the end of this chapter.*

electromechanical inventory, and the equipment to make it, when solid-state point-of-sale terminals entered the market. . . .

These companies lost even though they were low-cost producers. They lost even though they were close to their customers. They lost even though they were market-share leaders. They lost because they failed to make an effective transition from old to new technology.[1]

Moving from old to new technology—that, in a nutshell, is the requirement facing all of us. How can it be done?

Foster believes strong companies owe their relative success to a recognition of "five realities of technically based economic competition":

- **Recognize that all products and processes have performance limits.** This means that "the closer one comes to these limits, the more expensive it becomes to squeeze out the next generation of performance improvements," says Foster. Industry leaders thus do research to understand the limits of each technology. This was what Bell Laboratories did, for example, in recognizing that the size of vacuum tubes could never be significantly reduced. It therefore formed the team that developed the transistor, which, as we saw in Chapter 1, was a keystone of the miniaturization process that is part of the Computer Revolution.

- **Take all competition seriously.** This means not assuming the strongest competitors will be the ones with the largest resources. Boeing Aircraft was nearly bankrupt when it introduced the commercial jet plane against larger, more financially secure airplane makers such as Lockheed.
- **Attack to win—or even play in—the game.** This means investing in promising new technology in an aggressive way and not investing in old products. Most companies are reluctant to do this, feeling they have to recover their prior investment in the old technology and believing consumers will continue to buy the old product even if it is less economical. This is rarely the case, as Lever found when it was beaten by Procter & Gamble's introduction of the first synthetic detergent.
- **Begin the attack early.** "The substitution of one product or process for another," says Foster, "proceeds at a slow pace and then explodes—rarely in a predictable fashion. One cannot wait for the explosion to occur to react. There is simply not enough time." B. F. Goodrich, he points out, lost 60% of its market share to Michelin in four years when the radial overtook the bias-ply tire. Moreover, economic measures of performance are not sufficient for an early warning. The market may be changing too fast.
- **There should be close ties between the CEO—the chief executive officer—and the chief technical officer.** Without this, there will not be the leadership to translate business needs into technical programs or technological possibilities into business strategies. "In the U.S. today," says Foster, "only one CEO in five considers his top technical officer a part of the inner circle."

The preceding survival advice is directed toward the processes and products that a company produces. But it also largely applies to the *business skills* that we as individuals must learn in order to stay current and stay ahead in an era of technological change. It is our contention in this book that to survive in the new Information Age one must learn to use new tools. These tools have been grouped under the heading of the *automated office,* sometimes called the "office of the future." Before we look at these tools, however, let us look at the office of the present.

Nine to Five: What Is an Office?

No matter what line of work you are in—butcher, baker, candlestick maker, or computer consultant—there is usually some place you call an office. Even people who do not do much indoor work, such as farmers and construction workers, have an office: a place in which to pay bills, order supplies, send invoices, plan the work, and so on. Indeed, an **office** may be defined as a place where people generate, store, retrieve, and communicate the information necessary for the conduct of a business. In the last decade, there has been mushrooming growth in office work, so that now about half of the nation's work force is employed in handling information.[2]

Misimpressions of the Office

A man from Mars might have some interesting impressions or misimpressions about what an office and the business world are like, based on their portrayal in advertising and the media. Television business people, for example, are often depicted as venal and corrupt; like J. R. Ewing in *Dallas,* they spend most of their time cutting ethically questionable deals. Print advertising shows executives in corner offices with lofty views and uncluttered desks. Movies like *Nine to Five* show a white-collar chain gang of office workers enslaved to arbitrary bosses and balky photocopying machines. Perhaps, viewing the culture at large, the Martian visitor might get the most common impression of all—that working in an office is *boring,* that it consists of handling an endless stream of pieces of paper and telephone calls, making office work the indoor equivalent of hoeing weeds.

Of course all of these impressions apply to certain cases, but with the amount of misinformation projected about what an office is, small wonder that many students might not want to spend their lives working in one. The experience of the office, however, is as varied as people. While we cannot possibly describe all the different circumstances of office work, what is important for our purposes is this: offices are organized around the flow of business information, and the ways of handling that information are changing.

The Activities of the Office

Whether you are in an old-fashioned office or a new one, there are seven office activities concerned with handling business information:

- Creating it
- Storing it
- Retrieving it
- Organizing it
- Summarizing it
- Communicating it
- Using it to make decisions

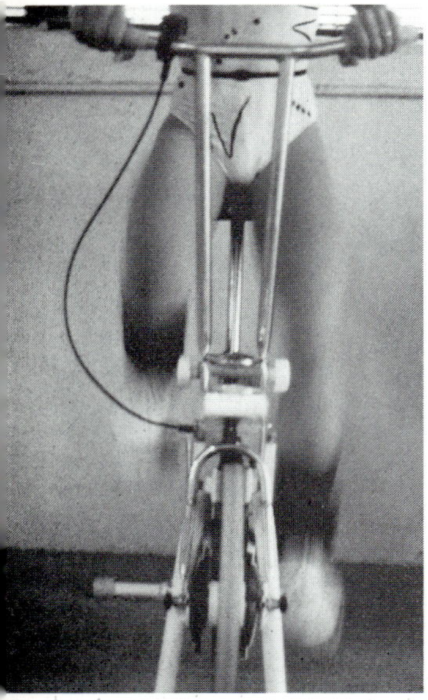

Some businesses might not seem to require much in the way of these seven activities. A health club or exercise studio, for example, might seem to consist principally of Nautilus equipment and changing rooms. Let us suppose, however, that your uncle is an executive with a nationwide corporation, Health Inc., that owns a number of health-related businesses, and let us suppose that you have gone to work part-time in the office of one of the corporation's chain of exercise studios, named Exercise! Unlimited. Here is how the information-handling activities apply.

You receive information generally in number, symbol, or text form—for instance, the names, addresses, ages, sex, and monthly dues of people who have signed up for membership in the studio. This information is used to *create* a document, such as a membership record card for each member. As new members join and new membership record cards are created, you *store* them in a manila folder (labeled NEW MEMBERS) in a drawer in a filing cabinet next to your desk. At the end of every month, you *retrieve* the folder and *organize* the membership record cards in alphabetical order by members' last names. The cards of the new members are then merged with the record cards of the old members. Periodically you *summarize* the information on the members—the age range, sex, and types of exercise activities most are interested in, for instance—and *communicate* that summary to your supervisor, who forwards it on to her boss. That information is used by executives of Exercise! Unlimited to plan their promotion for reaching new prospective members.

Figure 2-1 shows how this flow of information might look. Perhaps you and the manager are the only two employees in the office (there are exercise instructors in the studio). But the purposes and tasks are the same whether an office has one person in it or hundreds—and whether it is a traditional or an automated office.

The Changing Office Worker

Let us take a snapshot of the traditional office hierarchy—and be prepared to modify the picture because it describes an organizational structure that was developed precisely because there *was* no way to automate most office activities until now. In a large corporation there have traditionally been three categories of office workers:

- Clerical and secretarial
- Technical and professional
- Executive manager

Clerical and secretarial jobs have tended to deal with predictable, standardized tasks that make up the first three of the seven office activities described above—that is, the *creation, storing,* and *retrieving* of documents. Such jobs tend to be very text oriented: filing, typing letters,

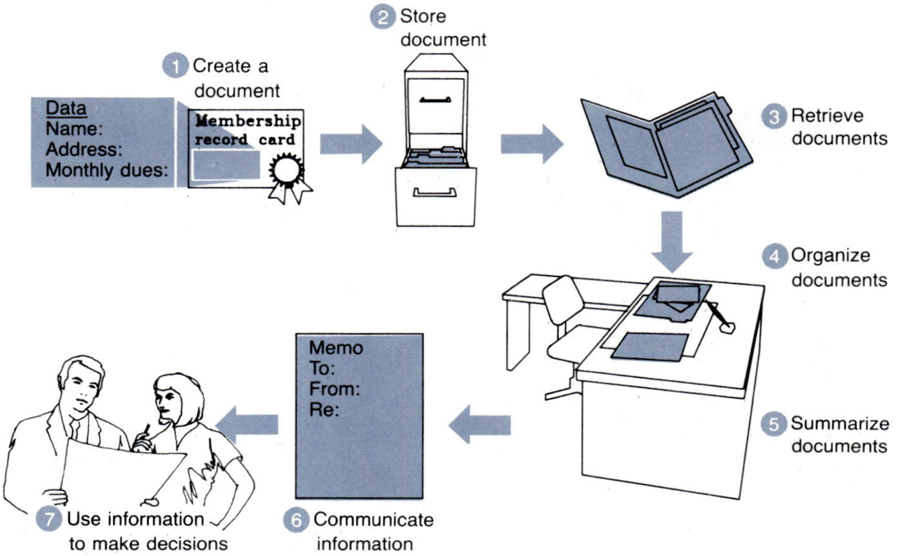
1 Create a document
Data
Name:
Address:
Monthly dues:
Membership record card
2 Store document
3 Retrieve documents
4 Organize documents
5 Summarize documents
Memo
To:
From:
Re:
6 Communicate information
7 Use information to make decisions

Figure 2-1 **Info flow.** How information flows in a standard office. This shows how information about new members in a health club is handled.

sorting mail, transcribing dictation, and performing similar low-level paperwork activities. Although there are still executives around today who started out working in the mailroom and other jobs at this level, this stepping-stone is almost certain to disappear, since the tasks these jobs comprise are the most easily automated.

Today most upwardly mobile white-collar workers with college degrees begin at the second level, in the *technical and professional* category. This group includes what many readers of this book may well become: managers, accountants, marketing specialists, financial analysts, lawyers, computer information systems people. Responsibilities in these jobs vary—financial analysts work with corporate data, lawyers search cases for legal precedents, and so on—but by and large they work with both text and data and they cover all seven of the office activities mentioned previously.

Executive managers have the most varied responsibilities of all and in general are more concerned with decision making.Top managers are less likely to *create* data and reports—except, perhaps, for their superiors, boards of directors, or the stockholders—but they are concerned with taking in a lot of information from inside and outside the company, *organizing* it, *summarizing* it, *communicating* it, and *making decisions* about it. Thus, they need text and data, but they are more concerned with decisions and communications than are personnel in the other two groups. For example, the board of directors of Health Inc. might ask the chief executive officer to explore opportunities for expanding the Exercise! Unlimited chain of exercise studios into eastern Canada. The CEO would get external information about the population in the target areas and compare it with internal information about the studio chain's present members, organize it, summarize it into a report, and communicate the report to the board, which would make decisions about expansion.

Now we know what the functions and traditional jobs of an office are. Let us see how they will begin to change.

The Automated Office: Speeding Up the Future

Office automation—which you often see designated by its abbreviation, **OA**—may be both briefly and broadly defined.

Briefly defined, **office automation** is the *convergence of a number of data processing and communication technologies designed to increase the efficiency of creating, storing, retrieving, organizing, and communicating business information.* You will note that this frees up executives for dealing with the two remaining office information-handling activities—summarizing information and making decisions about it.

Broadly defined, office automation is as follows:

- **It is a system for enhancing office productivity.** It is a system of data processing and communication technologies that allow not only clerks and secretaries, but also, more importantly, technical and professional people and executive managers to work more efficiently and productively.
- **It is electronic.** It uses electronic **data processing,** which is concerned with the logical operations of numbers and symbols, and electronic **text processing,** which is concerned with the creation and reproduction of letters, reports, memos, and so on. It also uses electronic communication systems and electronic filing systems.
- **It links people and information.** The automated office connects people in an office—or in several offices—electronically with each other and with other data and information.

The promise of office automation is fascinating, and we will describe the details shortly. Before we do, however, let us consider the all-important question: *Why* is it needed?

The Need for OA

As we mentioned, over half the U.S. work force consists of white-collar workers—people in office jobs, from chairman or -woman to file clerk—and the percentage is increasing every year. Yet office workers have not increased their productivity as fast as people in blue-collar or laboring occupations have. The reason is plain: a great deal more money has been invested in machinery to support farm and factory workers than in equipment to support office workers. The capital investment for each type of worker and the increased productivity over the past decade are as follows:

- Factory worker—$50,000 investment, productivity up 183%
- Farm worker—$35,000 investment, productivity up 90%
- Office worker—only *$3000* investment, productivity up only *3%*

At the same time, operating costs for offices have doubled in the last ten years, with labor costs—that is, salaries and wages—accounting for most of the increase. Indeed, of the $1.3 trillion paid for wages, salaries, and benefits in the United States, nearly two-thirds goes to office workers. *Total* office costs are approaching a trillion dollars a year and are increasing at a rate of 16% a year.

It is clear that automation of the office represents the most promising way of controlling costs and increasing productivity, as automation of the factory did in years past. Why, then, has it not been done sooner?

Office Automation Now

Typewriters, telephones, and photocopying machines significantly improve our office productivity over that of our forebears two or three generations ago, but this equipment does not constitute the kind of radical form of white-collar automation that we are contemplating here.

There are several good reasons why the changes are developing now:

- The cost of electronic equipment has been falling at a dramatic rate—30% per year—owing to the technological advances in communications and computers.
- Microcomputers have demonstrated that a relatively small investment can yield large returns and can assist technical, professional, and executive management as well as clerks and secretaries.
- Manufacturers are investing heavily in the development of sophisticated integrated office systems. **Integrated** equipment is able to coordinate or accomplish a number of different tasks. A microcomputer, for instance, can process data, do word processing, or communicate with other computers. In an integrated office system, all of the pieces of equipment are compatible with each other so they can work together. This may sound simple, but it has not been the case so far.

By 1990, according to industry sources, companies in the United States could save $300 billion by installing office automation.You can be sure business people are not going to overlook possible savings of this magnitude.

Much of what is already an outdated phrase—the "office of the future"—is now here, the tools an executive must now learn to use. In the following five sections, we will describe what the tools of the automated office look like and what they mean to you:

- Word processors
- Electronic files
- Electronic mail
- Electronic conferencing
- Workstations

Word Processors: The New-Age Typewriters

The term "word processor" might seem to suggest that there is some logical way by which a computer sorts unprocessed words into processed words, but, of course, it does nothing of the kind. A **word processor** is an electronic typewriter with a keyboard linked to a video screen and computer (see Figure 2-2). You do not type immediately onto a piece of paper, however. Rather, the words appear on the video screen and are temporarily stored (either within the computer or on an outside storage device). When you are ready, you can then electronically send these words from the computer to a printer—a typewriterlike device—for printing out on paper.

Unlike the standard office electric typewriter, the word processor can do several marvelous things. Writing becomes more like working with soft clay than like working with hammer and chisel and marble. No more erasing, inserting, or cutting and pasting by hand. With word processing, you can rearrange words and sentences and do deletions and insertions with the punch of a button. As one novelist said about his word processor, "Once I learned it could do the two essential things a writer really needs—insert and delete—I knew I'd finally moved from the Stone Age to the Space Age."[3]

Word processors can be either **dedicated word processors,** machines that do nothing but word processing, or microcomputers that can perform word processing as one of their many capabilities. From the writer's standpoint, the advantage of dedicated machines is that they have more **function keys**—special keys for specific writing, editing, and typing tasks, such as "Delete," "Insert," "Move forward," and so on. Micro-

codex

Figure 2-2 A word processor. This word processor consists of a unit with a video screen, an internal computer, built-in disk drives, and a detached keyboard. Not shown is the printer. Word processors are revolutionizing executive work habits.

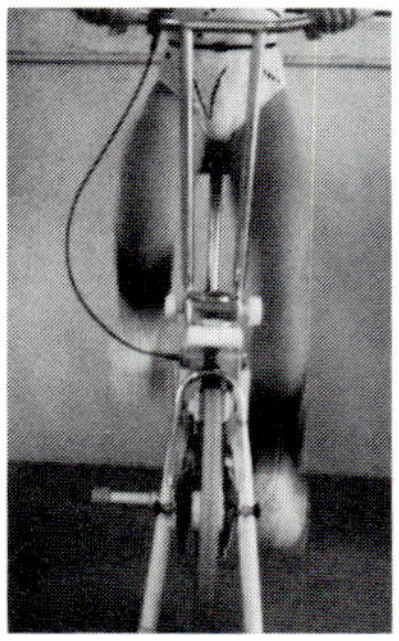

computers have fewer if any word processing function keys because their keys are used for a variety of tasks.

Word processing is the first step in office automation and usually is considered the cornerstone. This you may begin to appreciate when your uncle announces that the parent company, Health Inc., has decided to join the electronic revolution and to install an OA system throughout the corporation. For Exercise! Unlimited this is manifested in the delivery of a microcomputer with a printer to the studio manager's office.

After a few hours spent at the keyboard, you can see why typewriters are no match for word processors—why word processing can boost productivity over typewriters by 50% to as high as 400%.[4] When you write to studio clients politely reminding them that their membership fees are past due, you no longer have to send a "Dear Sir or Madam" form letter or type the same letter over and over again with a new name and address at the top. Rather, you can type the text of a letter once and then change the name and address with just a few keystrokes; the printer will print out a different, typewritten letter each time. The studio manager particularly appreciates the machine because she is a terrible typist, and she can easily correct her typing mistakes electronically instead of using erasers and whiting-out correction fluid.

We will give a more detailed example of how word processing works in Chapter 4.

Electronic Filing: Replacing the Manila Folder

What does a worker produce? Factory workers can look at the parts or products sitting on the skids at the end of the assembly line. Office workers can look at—paper.

Clerks and secretaries spend 90% of their time handling paperwork, and the results are there for all to see in the four-drawer filing cabinets found in most offices. To fill only a couple of those drawers costs as much as a new car—$9600. At these prices, it makes sense to look for other solutions. For legal documents, insurance forms, patient records, railroad shipping documents, and other high-volume records and documents, the solution is electronic filing.

Electronic filing may be defined as technically enhanced storage and retrieval of data or information. There are several kinds of electronic media, the most popular being:

- **Magnetic disks and tapes:** As we will see in the next chapter, a great deal of computerized information is stored on phonograph-record-like magnetic disks or reels or cassettes of magnetic tape.
- **Microfilm and microfiche:** These consist of computer-generated documents in which the information is significantly reduced in size photographically yet can be called up to full size for later use, as shown in Figure 2-3. As you no doubt know from the library, **microfilm** consists of a roll of film on which the images of documents are stored in reduced size. **Microfiche** consists of 4-by-6-inch sheets of film. Information from a computer can be converted directly onto microfilm or microfiche to produce what is known as **computer output on microfilm,** abbreviated **COM.**

These electronic media allow easy access from one computer to another. For example, files may be stored on a large computer and then "downloaded" to a small computer, such as a desktop computer.

A central notion to electronic filing—and to a great deal of this book—is that of data base. A **data base** consists of several files, most likely stored on magnetic disk, which are *cross-referenced.* That is, each file is like a single file folder in a file cabinet which you can find by looking it up in different indexes—alphabetically by last name, by social security number, by birth date, and so on.

Data bases may be internal or external. An *internal data base* might be Ford Motor Company's list of dealers, which might be stored in the main computer room at company headquarters. An *external data base* might be a large public data source called an "information utility" or a

Figure 2-3 Microfiche and electronic filing. *Top right:* This 4-by-6-inch sheet of microfiche has approximately 250 frames, or the equivalent of 250 paper pages. *Bottom left:* A microfiche camera. This machine takes only one second to film a document image, such as a page from the computer forms printer. *Bottom right:* A computer output on microfilm (COM) system. Such systems can accept stored data or data received directly from a computer. The data is converted directly to images on sheets of microfiche, like that the man is holding. Thus, the data never needs to be printed out on paper.

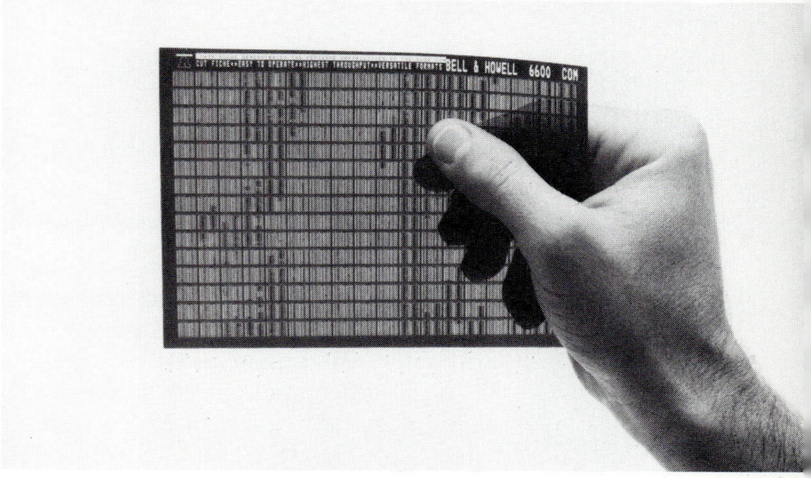
BELL & HOWELL 6600 COM

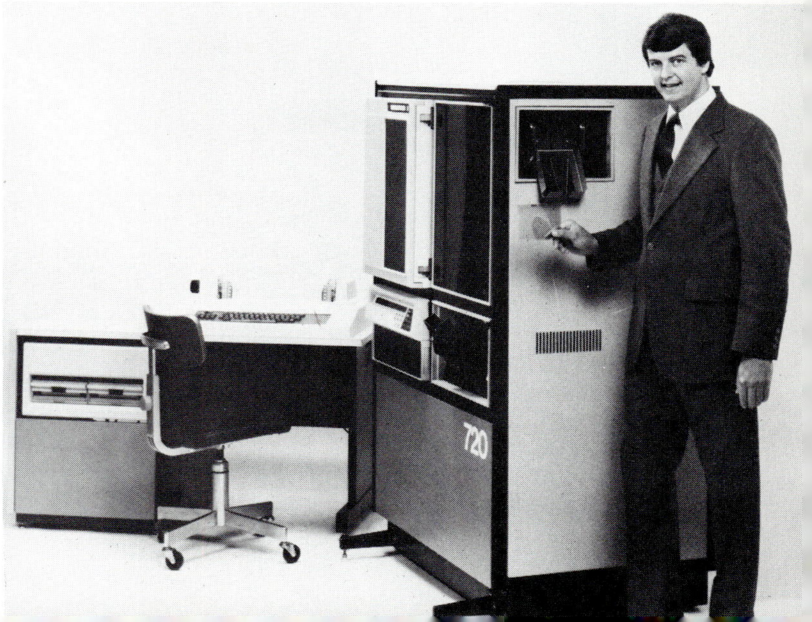
720

specialized data bank, either of which make entire encyclopedias' worth of information available via telephone lines to a subscriber's desktop computer.

Such sophisticated electronic filing may not seem particularly useful in your two-person office at Exercise! Unlimited. You find, however, that having information about studio members on a small magnetic disk that works with your microcomputer is actually quite helpful. Alphabetizing of names is done automatically, address changes are easily updated on the files (no crossing out with ink), and it is easy to have the computer give you birthday reminders so that you can send customers a birthday card.

As we mentioned, however, an important concept of office information is that technology is *linked together.* The studio manager finds that by hooking up your microcomputer by telephone line to the Health Inc. headquarters, she is able to connect to corporation files, avail herself of new health and marketing knowledge in various data bases, and so on.

Electronic Mail: End of Telephone Tag and Mailroom Drag

Next to word processing, electronic mail—sometimes referred to as **electronic mail/message system (EMMS)**—is the most widely used of the new tools. **Electronic mail** consists of using electronic means to send, store, and deliver messages that you would otherwise deliver orally by phone or send by mail (either inside or outside the office).

What, you may think, could improve on the telephone for speed in delivering messages? Actually, studies have shown that, for business telephone calls, 70% of the time when a person calls, the other person is not available to take the call. This game, called "telephone tag," is one that we have all played: you call someone, who is not in, and you leave a message for that person to call you back. He or she calls back, and you are not in—and so on.

As for mail, we all know how long it can take to get a document from one far-flung state to another—usually not possible on the same day—but quite often business people find the same lag even within an in-house mail system. This slowness has been dubbed "mailroom drag." Quite often the drag is so long that it takes a company two days to transmit its mail from one floor to another floor in the same building.

To appreciate what effect this tag and drag have, consider that the principal activity of middle- and upper-level managers is *transferring information*—either by person-to-person contact or by written documents. Consider also that *half* the conversations executives have are composed of one-way information transfers—that is, no discussions are needed. Clearly, the information could be communicated by written documents—except for the delay of mailroom drag. The alternative is the telephone—except for the delays of telephone tag. Electronic mail, then, is ideal for the one-way communication of information. And, of course, one of its greatest attractions is that it gives the option of providing a permanent copy of the message.

Information in electronic mail is communicated in three ways:

- In the **facsimile method,** copies (facsimiles) of documents are transmitted electronically from one location to another via telephone lines or by satellite signal; this is often the case with wire-service photos seen in the daily newspaper.
- In **computer message switching,** the caller sends a message to another person's personal computer terminal, where it is displayed on the screen. If the intended receiver is unavailable, the message is electronically stored in the terminal until the receiver can pick it up. A variation is the **electronic mailbox,** in which the message is stored in a centralized computer "post office," which users must check periodically.
- Perhaps the most exciting breakthrough in electronic mail is the **voice store and forward (VSF) system,** in which the sender's voice message is electronically stored, then retrieved and reconstructed by the person receiving the message. The technique relies on speech recognition equipment that analyzes and classifies speech patterns and translates them into electronic impulses that can be accepted by the computer.

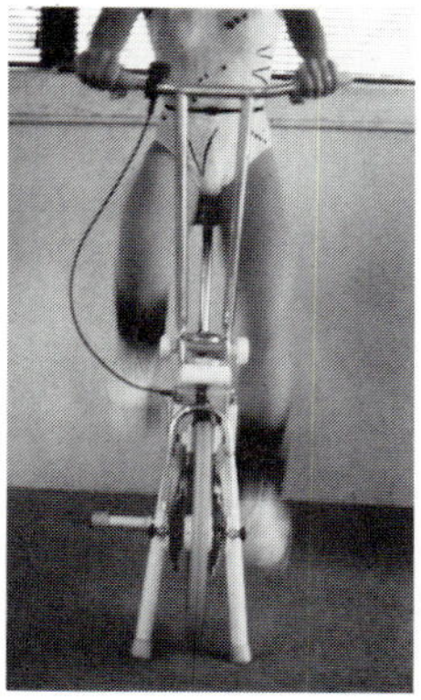

The Exercise! Unlimited studio you work at already has a telephone answering machine. Why, you wonder, do you need electronic mail? Actually, in an exercise studio run by two people you certainly do not. But when you visit your uncle in his office in the Public Relations Department at Health Inc. headquarters in St. Louis, you begin to see the benefits. Your uncle does not deal just with short memos from other executives. He also deals with long documents relating to health legislation, which are sent to him by the corporation's lobbyist and government-watcher in Washington, D.C. He must keep abreast of new health administrative rulings out of the Department of Health and Human Resources and of the health bureaucracies in all 50 state capitals. He also has people around the country watching local newspapers for articles that affect Health Inc.'s business. While much of this information could be sent by overnight package-delivery, your uncle needs to have it quickly enough to formulate a corporate response. And nearly all of it is too long to be left as a message on an answering machine.

Electronic Conferencing: Easing the Stress of Business Travel

A business trip to Rio de Janeiro at Mardi Gras time may be exciting and romantic, but most business travel is not. As Louis Hagopian, chairman of the New York–based advertising agency NW Ayer, says:

> There's much more fatigue and stress than there is personal pleasure in business travel.
>
> It isn't fun. It's a chore business people accept, like late hours at the office, conventions and breakfast meetings, where the needs of the job take precedence over personal time that most of us would rather spend at home. . . .
>
> The man or woman who flies on business isn't the corporate freeloader. Business fliers are among the most productive people in the shop. . . .
>
> One recent survey found that more than 90% of business travelers spend most of their time working while they are in the air. The majority of our business-flying hours are before or after the 9-to-5 office hours. . . .[5]

Business travel is big business. Indeed, 90% of all air travel is still done for business purposes, despite the fact that travel costs have doubled in the last three years. But are such business trips really efficient? Some observers think that 40% of all fly-in business conferences could be held by telephone.[6]

Even if there were no change in meetings that required air travel, there would still be an enormous number of other meetings held every day to serve purposes that might be better handled in other ways. Your uncle tells you that of the 20 million business meetings held every business day, 80% last only half an hour or less, over a third are for information exchange only, and 60% could be handled by voice communication alone.[7]

With these statistics in mind, you can see that there is a clear case for some sort of use of electronic technology to link people for conferencing. EMMS is the technology that allows such electronic conferencing or the communication of several people through an electronic medium. Such conferencing takes two forms:

- Computer conferencing
- Teleconferencing

Computer Conferencing: Meeting by Typing

The direct result of electronic mail technology, **computer conferencing** allows people to confer with each other without their having to be present at the same location or at the same time. At your uncle's office at Health Inc., you see how this works. In a typical "meeting" (if that is the word), he dials up a computer conferencing service and couples his telephone handset to his desktop computer terminal (see Figure 2-4). He

codex

Figure 2-4 Telecommunications. *Left:* An acoustic coupler, which accepts a telephone handset, allows computer data to be transmitted over telephone lines. *Right:* A modem, or data communications module, which connects computer and telephone, allows the operator to still use the telephone handset.

and all other conference participants have access to the same computer file or information, and all of them can ask questions and give answers to each other by typing on their respective keyboards.

Before the conference you wonder why the same thing could not be handled by a conference *telephone* call—that is, with the various participants being linked together through the company headquarters telephone switchboard. However, a look at the conferees and the importance of the meeting topic show you why. Important new legislation is being developed in Congress regulating the health care industry, which will substantially affect Health Inc.'s profit picture. The corporation hopes to get its recommendations incorporated into the legislation, but time is of the essence and the materials to be reviewed are fairly long. Not only your uncle, but also lawyers, financial analysts, and the chief executive officer must be consulted. All have different demands on their time and, moreover, are working in different time zones around the country.

The result is an all-day meeting in which participants are called away from and then return to their desks, where they catch up on the status of the discussion by looking at the screens of their desktop computers. At the end of the day, there is not only a transcript representing everyone's point of view, but the whole conference is stored in a computer file, which can easily be called up later.

The advantage of computer conferencing, of course, is convenience. Participants can interact with each other without following a strict schedule format and without having to travel. In addition, several conferees can "talk"—that is, type messages on their keyboards—at about the same time from many different geographical areas.

The disadvantages are that such conferences tend to be very structured and therefore somewhat rigid. Moreover, communication is restricted because of the lack of face-to-face contact, and spontaneity and mutual creativity are inhibited. And, of course, the speed of communication is determined by how well the participants can type. This is an example of how the automated office may require different skills from those required in the traditional office.

Teleconferencing: Meeting by Voice

Teleconferencing allows several people at different locations to communicate electronically. Unlike computer conferencing, participants can talk and listen rather than type and read. However, all must be present at the same time.

There are three main forms of teleconferencing:

- **Audio conferences** consist of several parties connected simultaneously by telephone—a fairly common event at present.
- **Audiographic conferences** are the same as audio conferences except that in addition graphics (illustrations) are transmitted, using facsimile devices.
- **Audiovisual conferences** are those in which participants sit in specially equipped rooms in different geographical locations, looking at and conversing with each other via projection screens on the walls (see Figure 2-5). Not only do audiovisual conferences permit people to talk to each other face to face, they may also exchange documents, which are transmitted by space satellite. In other words, audiovisual conferences are the next best thing to being there. (Maybe even better, if you can skip a plane trip you would rather not make.)

There are many advantages to teleconferencing. Not only does it improve job satisfaction, quality of work life, and productivity by sparing executives the hardships of airline food and cramped seats, it also makes meetings themselves better. Because of the expense and rigid

Figure 2-5 Audiovisual conferencing. *Left:* AT&T Information Systems' Picturephone Meeting Service allows meeting participants in specially equipped rooms to talk while viewing each other on television screens. *Right:* AT&T also offers a portable modular system, with monitor, camera, and audio system in one console, so that any office can be turned into a site for video teleconferencing.

time schedule of the conference, participants are more likely to be on time for meetings. Meetings may also be shorter, better structured, more task-oriented—in theory, more productive—than typical conferences. Finally, teleconferencing provides a way for people in dispersed locations to react quickly to emergency situations.

Despite the expense, more and more large businesses are using audiovisual conferencing, especially for sales, new product introduction, coordination, problem solving, and executive board meetings. Exxon Corporation, for instance, has used teleconferencing to connect specialists in oil-drilling disasters with workers on site trying to control a wellhead emergency.

Workstations: The Electronic Desk

What, would you guess, are the most popular business tools? Answer: the pen and the pencil, used by professional, technical, and managerial people for two-thirds of their activities.

Figure 2-6 An executive workstation. This microcomputer system produced by Burroughs can be used to connect with other workstations or a larger computer.

Clearly, although this group of people accounts for most of office salary costs, they have been relatively untouched by office automation. Indeed, a recent survey found that professionals use computers less than 1% of their time. Workstations are designed to increase the productivity of this group, although they can be used by others as well.

The **workstation**—also called the **executive workstation**—is constructed around a microcomputer or terminal, either of which is linked to a larger computer or processing unit in another room or at another site. The large computer controls communication and allows access to data banks. Figure 2-6 shows an example of a workstation.

What can you do with this new version of an executive desk? A great many things, as follows:

- **Intraoffice message transmittal:** Sending and receiving intraoffice messages by electronic mail is probably the most frequent use for an executive workstation.
- **Meeting scheduling:** This is a much more useful benefit than it might seem. Setting up a meeting between 16 busy executives may require several hours of secretaries phoning each other, whereas with the electronic gear in a workstation it can take two seconds. Each executive has a personally controlled electronic calendar programmed into his or her workstation; when a meeting is required, all the calendars are scanned for a mutually convenient open date and time, and all participants are notified by electronic mail.
- **Word processing, electronic filing, data processing:** These tasks are particularly easy to do with a workstation containing a microcomputer, which can not only communicate with the main computer, but also process text and data independently.

It has been estimated that the 1 million workstations in use in 1983 will grow to 10 million by 1993. This development may not hold particular significance for clerical-secretarial personnel or executive managers, but it promises to revolutionize the work habits and increase the flexibility of many professional and technical people. Financial analysts will have direct access to financial data, such as the Dow-Jones Industrial Averages; accountants will be able to call on the corporation's accounting data in many forms; and marketing specialists will have access to current sales information and market trend analysis.

Some Barriers in the OA Steeplechase

None of the office technology just described is in the future—only the application of it. It is possible *today* for executives to communicate across the ocean as easily as across a room, to send memos instantaneously to employees over 10,000 miles away, to use electronic systems to set up meetings without unduly disturbing busy executives, and to extract vital data from electronic files during an executive board meeting. Why, then, do we not see more companies using office technology—*today?*

We have already looked at some of the human issues, including the reluctance of people to confront new technology, and business issues, including the enormous investments required. Still to be overcome are some technological issues, as follows.

CASE STUDY: OA RELIEF FOR FRED

When Fred's Office of the Future Becomes Present

A great deal of the equipment described in this chapter—and more that we will describe later—can be helpful not only to business people indoors but also to those on the outside. Here, for instance, is how new technology would keep Fred from losing those sales opportunities:

A sales professional like Fred Coldcall would be equipped with an easy-to-use, portable intelligent display terminal enabling him to access information and contact people in a variety of timesaving ways. First, Fred would scan publicly available data bases to select his prospect lists. Next, a "traveling salesman" algorithm [command] could be used to display a minimum-time travel path among prospects and existing customers. Fred and his office-based assistant, Mary, would use an electronic mail system operating through Fred's terminal to stay in close touch as she scheduled Fred's appointments to match the minimum-travel path. Naturally, the system would reconfigure the path should any appointments be unavailable or canceled. Mary would use her desk-based communicating word processor to send and receive such messages.

Next, Fred would use his terminal while visiting Quick Industries to access the Quick file, as well as the latest specifications and pricing information. Thus he could elicit Mr. Buysome's reaction to the main points of his proposal on the spot and adjust accordingly instead of wasting substantial time and effort preparing a formal proposal. In simpler situations, such as selling personal home insurance, the sales professional could display and print a complete proposal in front of the prospect.

In addition to a portable data terminal, Fred would have a portable telephone that he could use "hands-free" in his automobile and thus convert idle auto travel time to productive time. Not only would this unit enable Fred to place and receive telephone calls while he was on the move but it would also connect him with a central voice message computer. Since this type of system can send and receive messages to and from any telephone, it would enable Fred to communicate with customers and the internal support people who did not have access to a data terminal.

Without having to leave his car, Fred could check the status of an order, coordinate invoice reconciliation efforts, arrange proposal preparations or sales engineering assistance, and even change his appointment schedule at any hour of the day.

Video technology would also help Fred. Full sound and motion product demonstrations on a videodisc would be accessed, along with standard pricing and availability, through an inexpensive videodisc player attachment to Fred's . . . data terminal. Depending on the type of product, he could view this material with prospects or use it solely to prepare himself. Fred could also keep current with new product and marketing plans by attending videoconferences available periodically at a nearby motel.

—Harvey L. Poppel,
"Who Needs the Office of the Future?"
Harvard Business Review,
November–December 1982

The Problem of Equipment Incompatibility

One reason business has been slow to fully adopt OA technology is that a great deal of equipment is incompatible. In many cases, even types of OA equipment manufactured by the same firm will not work with each other—that is, they are **incompatible**. The word processors, for instance, will not communicate with the electronic message systems. Multiply this problem by the number of different manufacturers making office equipment, from Apple Computer to Zenith/Heath, and you see why compatibility is such a problem.

The Need for Integration: Networking

Integration is the promised land of office automation. The real payoff in OA comes from not just automating the various office tasks but *linking* them—that is, **integrating** them—so that information can flow freely in many forms. As we will see in later chapters, the key to this concept is networking. A **network** is a computer system that uses data communications equipment to connect two or more computers and their resources.

Here, also, lack of standardization has been a real problem. However, progress is under way—Xerox Corporation, for example, has devised a system (Xerox System 8000) capable of connecting several workstations together, using not only Xerox equipment but other manufacturers' equipment as well.

Because about 85% of all information exchanges occur in a relatively small geographic area between two or more persons, local networking appears to have especially high potential. **Local area network systems (LANSs)** use special cabling to allow users to link office automation equipment from different manufacturers, for the purpose of sharing resources or for electronic message transfer systems. An alternative, **private branch exchange (PBX),** uses existing telephone lines to transmit data and voice—thereby offering larger geographic range at lower cost, although the quality of transmission is lower and information is not as secure.

Onward

The development of technology, it has been observed, advances rapidly and usually well ahead of the willingness of a large portion of the population to adapt readily and comfortably to it. In this chapter, we have tried to provide a glimpse of the developing technology to which we will need to adapt. In the next chapter, we will begin to take a look at the systems underlying much of the technology and how they apply to business.

SUMMARY

- For companies to compete successfully in an era of technological change, they must move from old to new technology by (1) recognizing that all products and processes have performance limits, (2) taking all competition seriously, (3) attacking to win (or just play in) the game, (4) beginning the attack early, and (5) keeping close ties between the chief executive officer (CEO) and the chief technical officer. In addition, individuals must learn to use new tools and keep business skills current.
- An **office** is where people generate, store, retrieve, and communicate the information necessary to conduct a business. Currently, about half of the nation's work force is employed in handling information. Offices vary greatly, and the ways of handling business information are changing; however, the same basic seven office activities apply to handling business information: (1) creating it, (2) storing it, (3) retrieving it, (4) organizing it, (5) summarizing it, (6) communicating it, and (7) using it to make decisions. Different businesses emphasize different activities.
- Traditionally, large corporations comprise three categories of office workers: (1) clerical and secretarial, (2) technical and professional, and (3) executive manager. However, automation is changing these categories.
- Clerical and secretarial jobs have tended to deal with predictable and standardized tasks concerning creating, storing, and retrieving business information. These jobs are very text-oriented and are the most easily automated.
- Technical and professional jobs, the starting level for most upwardly mobile white-collar workers with college degrees, include responsibilities in middle management and in varying professions (finance, law, computer systems). People in this category work with both text and data and are involved in all seven office activities.
- Executive managers have the most varied responsibilities and are more concerned with decisions and communications than the first two categories of office worker. Executive managers are less likely to create data but are more concerned with organizing, summarizing, communicating, and using it to make decisions. Office automation frees up executives for more summarizing and decision making.
- **Office automation** is the convergence of a number of data processing and communication technologies designed to increase the efficiency of conducting the seven office activities. (1) It is a system for enhancing office productivity. (2) It is electronic. (3) It links people and information.
- Office automation is needed to help white-collar workers increase their productivity as fast as blue-collar workers have done to help control mushrooming office operating costs.

- Several new developments have made white-collar automation possible: (1) Technological advances in communications and computers have dramatically cut the cost of electronic equipment. (2) Through the use of microcomputers, a relatively small investment can yield large returns. (3) Sophisticated integrated office systems are available to coordinate or accomplish a number of different tasks.
- The tools of the automated office are (1) **word processors,** (2) **electronic files,** (3) **electronic mail,** (4) **electronic conferencing,** and (5) **workstations.**
- A word processor is an electronic typewriter with a keyboard linked to a video screen and a computer; the typed words appear on the screen and are stored for later printing out. Word processing allows the user to rearrange words and sentences, delete, and insert, by punching a button. **Dedicated word processors** do only word processing and have many **function keys,** specialized keys for deleting, inserting, and the like; microcomputers, which have a limited number of function keys, can perform word processing among many other things. Word processing (covered in more detail in Chapter 4) is the first step in office automation and can significantly boost productivity over that possible with typewriters.
- Electronic filing is the technically enhanced storage and retrieval of data or information. It cuts the time needed for handling paperwork, eliminates the need for filing cabinets, and enables office-information systems to link electronically with other systems. Electronic filing makes use of two kinds of electronic media: (1) magnetic disks and tapes, and (2) **microfilm** and **microfiche**—computer-generated documents (**computer output on microfilm,** or **COM**) photographically reduced in size for later use (microfilm is a roll of film, whereas microfiche are 4-by-6-inch sheets of film). These media allow easy access from one computer to another, permitting, for instance, files stored on a large computer to be "downloaded" to a smaller one.
- A central notion to electronic filing is that of data base. A **data base** consists of several files that are cross-referenced so that an item of information can be found by looking it up in several indexes. Data bases may be internal—within a company—or external, which means they can be large public data sources called information utilities or they can be specialized data banks; both make information available over the telephone to subscribers with microcomputers.
- Electronic mail (**electronic mail/message system,** or **EMMS**), ideal for fast one-way communication of information and quick response, uses electronic means to send, store, and deliver messages in three ways: (1) by the **facsimile method,** which transmits documents electronically via telephone or satellite; (2) by **computer message switching,** in which the message is sent to be displayed on or stored in a computer (the **electronic mailbox**); and (3) by the **voice store and forward (VSF) system,** in which the message sender's voice is stored and later retrieved.

- Electronic conferencing uses EMMS to eliminate the need for costly and inefficient business travel and meetings by linking people in two ways: (1) Through **computer conferencing**, which uses a computer conferencing service to couple telephone handsets to desktop computer terminals. All participants have access to the same computer file and can communicate—without all having to be present at the same time—by typing on their keyboards. The conference is stored in a computer file. Computer conferencing is convenient but also has some disadvantages, such as lack of spontaneity. (2) Through **teleconferencing**, which allows meeting by voice when all participants are present. **Audio conferences** use telephones to link the parties; **audiographic conferences** use facsimile devices to transmit graphics in addition to using telephones to transmit voices; **audiovisual conferences** use specially equipped rooms with projection screens to allow people in different geographical locations to meet and exchange documents. Teleconferencing allows meetings to be shorter, better structured, more responsive, more task-oriented, and more productive than typical conferences.
- The workstation, or **executive workstation**, is a "desk" constructed around a microcomputer or a terminal linked to a larger computer or remote processing unit. Workstations are designed to increase the productivity of professional office workers, although they can also be used by other workers. They (1) allow intraoffice messages to be sent electronically, (2) help schedule meetings and maintain calendars, and (3) do word processing, electronic filing, and data processing. The workstation promises to revolutionize work habits and increase the flexibility of many professional and technical people.
- Not all of the office automation technology available today is commonly used because of people's reluctance to confront new technology and because of various business issues, such as required investments, equipment **incompatibility**—different machines not able to work together—need for integration, and lack of standardization.
- Networking is the key to **integration**—that is, linking office tasks. A **network** is a computer system that uses data communications equipment to connect two or more computers and their resources. **Local area network systems (LANs)** use special cabling to allow users to link office automation equipment from different manufacturers. **Private branch exchanges (PBXs)** use existing telephone lines to transmit data and voices.

KEY TERMS

Audio conference, p. 42
Audiographic conference, p. 42
Audiovisual conference, p. 42
Computer conferencing, p. 40
Computer message switching, p. 39
Computer output on microfilm (COM), p. 36
Data base, p. 37
Data processing, p. 32
Dedicated word processor, p. 34
Electronic filing, p. 36
Electronic mail, p. 38
Electronic mailbox, p. 39
Electronic mail/message system (EMMS), p. 38
Executive workstation, p. 44
Facsimile method, p. 39
Function keys, p. 34
Incompatibility, p. 47
Integration, p. 33
Local area network system (LANS), p. 47
Microfiche, p. 36
Microfilm, p. 36
Network, p. 47
Office, p. 29
Office automation (OA), p. 32
Private branch exchange (PBX), p. 47
Teleconferencing, p. 42
Text processing, p. 32
Voice store and forward system (VSF), p. 39
Word processor, p. 34
Workstation, p. 44

REVIEW QUESTIONS

1. What are the five ways companies can move from old to new technology and successfully compete? Why are these strategies important to the individual as well as to the company?
2. Why are white-collar office workers less productive than blue-collar workers?
3. Name the seven office activities concerned with handling business information.
4. Describe one of the tools of the automated office.
5. What is the principal activity of upper-level managers? How does EMMS facilitate this activity?
6. Contrast computer conferencing with audio conferences.
7. What are the advantages of electronic conferencing over business travel? What are the disadvantages?

CASE PROBLEMS

Case 2-1: Popularity Contest: Dvorak versus QWERTY

In moving from typewriter to word processor, perhaps the time has come to get rid of old QWERTY. What is QWERTY, you query? They are the top left letter keys on any ordinary typewriter keyboard—and have been ever since Christopher Sholes designed the modern typewriter in 1867. The reason for laying out the letters in that particular way is that Sholes was afraid that fast typists would jam the works on his primitive machine. Thus, he deliberately removed the most useful keys from the middle row—the home row—to slow down the typists' flying fingers. Even after the technology improved, the arrangement of keys persisted, particularly after the touch-typing system became popular.

In 1930, August Dvorak, of the University of Washington, invented his own keyboard. All vowels and punctuation marks were placed on the left side. The most common consonants were placed on the right. The arrangement allowed 70% of the keys to be hit in the home row, whereas QWERTY typists use the home row less than a third of the time. Tests have shown Dvorak to be the more efficient system. Speeds can be improved by 5 to 25%, with roughly half the number of errors.

Of course, QWERTY lingers on, because—with 30 million keyboards in the United States alone—no one has wanted to be retrained. In 1983, however, the American National Standards Institute (ANSI) officially adopted Dvorak as an alternative to QWERTY. This is important news because ANSI is the body that sets so many industrial standards for American products.[8]

Your assignment: Let us say you are in charge of long-range planning for an organization that does not do a great deal of word processing but wants to have executives communicate with each other by terminals. More than half the executives do not know how to type, so in-house training will be required. Which kind of keyboards would you order, QWERTY or Dvorak, and why? In weighing your decision, consider that there have been cases in which entire countries have changed important standards overnight (Sweden switched from driving on the left-hand side of the road to driving on the right; Great Britain switched to a decimal system for its currency). Do you think this could be accomplished with Dvorak?

Case 2-2: Tractors of the Future

Looking at electronic office technologies today, says a work and technology specialist at Massachusetts Institute of Technology, is like having an opportunity over a century ago to say, "What do we want to do about the [factory] assembly line?" That is, there is an opportunity now to address issues of the effects of technology while their installation and use is in an early stage. As a *New York Times* (March 28, 1984) article pointed out, there have been few examples to show that people have thought through the impact of new technologies such as the automobile, the tractor, the elevator, or the superhighway, even though they had profound effects on workers and on how the nation operates and functions.[9]

Your assignment: What do you think OA will mean for shifting office work from cities to rural or suburban areas or even out of the country? What will OA do for the "social office"—make work more lonely and tedious or bring people together more? Already some computers can understand simple voice commands; how would all the technologies discussed thus far be changed if voice technology is expanded so that less keyboarding is required?

CHAPTER 3

Overview of Business Systems and Computer Systems

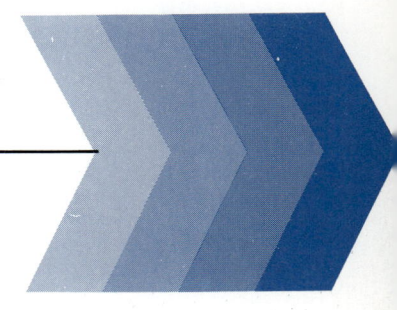

How the Two Can Work Together

How often do we operate by principles of rationality when making decisions?

If you got to a theater and discovered you had lost the $10 ticket to the play, would you simply buy another ticket? Probably not, says one researcher—yet if you had not bought your ticket yet and found you had lost a $10 *bill*, you would probably still go ahead and spend another $10 for a ticket. If you developed tennis elbow shortly after paying a membership fee at a tennis club, would you continue playing tennis? Probably—because most people are willing to accept a negative outcome if it is considered as a "cost" rather than as a "loss." If you buy a one-in-a-million lottery ticket, do you think you will have a chance of winning? Probably you will assume you will either not win at all or you will grossly overestimate the likelihood that you *will* win—because most people are simply unable to deal with very improbable events such as this.[1]

Clearly, psychological factors greatly influence people's decisions. Yet it is crucial that we bring some sort of rationality to decision making—in a word, impose some sort of a *system*. Business managers are not the only ones concerned with bringing a systems approach to solving individual problems. So also are public administrators, as the case study on the next page makes clear.

Some Systematic Definitions

In this chapter we will see how business as a system works. We will also see how a computer system works. We will then put the two together to see how business is enhanced with computer-based information systems.

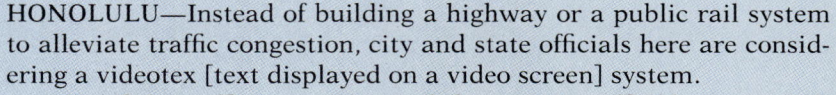

CASE STUDY: PROPOSED NEW SYSTEM

Trafficking in Computers

HONOLULU—Instead of building a highway or a public rail system to alleviate traffic congestion, city and state officials here are considering a videotex [text displayed on a video screen] system.

Honolulu traffic is so congested that . . . city officials are considering rationing automobile travel and implementing road pricing, which would charge people for using certain roads, to alleviate congestion.

But "there is a limit to what rerouting and traffic control can accomplish," said Carl Takamura, an aide to Hawaii's governor. . . . "What Honolulu needs is a revolutionary method to ease congestion."

One method, proposed by Aegis Systems Corp. in Tigard, Ore., is the purchase of a personal computer for every Honolulu home, business and office, along with the development of Autoride, an on-line transportation application. "Autoride will be a 24-hour, on-line system matching riders and drivers, arranging special transportation for elderly or handicapped people and possessing security features," explained Malcolm McLeod, a Department of Transportation economist. . . .

Autoride would match riders to taxis or private automobiles traveling to nearby areas. . . .

In the proposed system, riders enter pickup points, destinations, and times when rides are needed [into a special microprocessor-containing credit card]. Drivers enter routes, destinations, times of departures, and vehicle registrations [onto their cards]. Drivers may be either professional taxi drivers or residents.

A mainframe [large computer] would check driver registration to ensure that the driver has no criminal record and that the car is insured, then match riders to drivers. "The key is providing door-to-door service," [Aegis president Robert] Benke said.

Drivers and riders will not exchange money. "The system would be cashless," Benke noted. "At the end of the month, riders would be billed and drivers would be paid."

—Paul Korzenlowski
Computerworld,
January 23, 1984

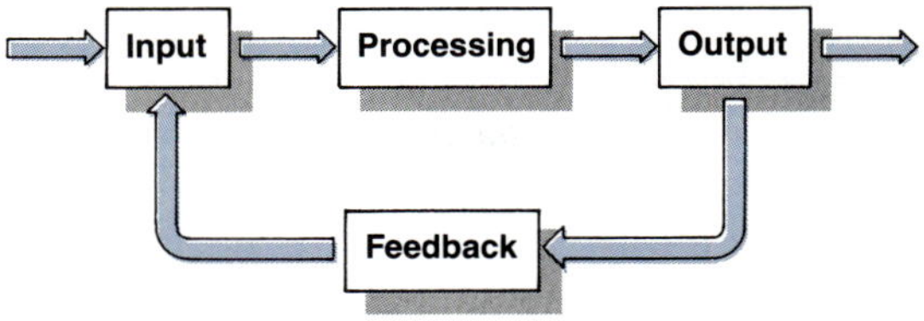
Input
Processing
Output
Feedback

Figure 3-1 The basis of a system. This chart, called an IPO chart (IPO stands for input, processing, and output), shows the four parts of a system as it will be understood in this book.

"System" is a common but loosely used word. Is a freeway system the same as a nervous system? Is a grading system the same as a betting system? (Some might say so.) Let us give some definitions: A **system** is a *collection of interrelated parts that work together for a common purpose.* For our purposes, we will consider a system with four parts:

- **Inputs:** things that enter the system from the environment.
- The **processor:** the part that operates on the inputs to transform them into something.
- **Outputs:** the products of the processing.
- **Feedback:** communication back to the system, either from the environment or from within the system itself.

These four parts are shown in Figure 3-1, which is called an **IPO chart.** IPO stands for input, processing, and output.

We can see how these parts can be used to describe a number of systems—the circulatory system of the human body, the electrical power system of New York City, some of the ecosystems of nature—but let us apply them to business and computers.

What a Business System Is

What is the purpose of a business firm? Beyond simple survival, there are two purposes—to make goods and services and to make a profit. To achieve these purposes, of course, requires a certain amount of effort—the funds of investors, the labors of employees, and so on. As Figure 3-2 shows, the purposes and activities of a business can be described as a system with the same four parts mentioned in Figure 3-1:

- **Input** is the investment in materials, money, employees, and facilities.
- **Processing** is the activity of converting the input—the investment and materials—into a finished product or service and selling it.

- **Output** consists of the goods and services that are produced and the profit or perhaps, unfortunately, the loss.
- **Feedback** consists of market forecasts and status reports about the products and profitability, which may suggest that there should be more investment if profits are up and less investment if profits are down.

The Four Subsystems of Business

The overview of the business shown in Figure 3-2 is a *macro* or overall view of a business system. But there is also a *micro* view, a closer examination of the business that shows the system can be broken down into smaller parts or **subsystems.** The important subsystems of a business—and the ones that you will see referred to throughout this book—are its four *functional* areas, namely:

- **Marketing:** the area concerned with sales forecasting, advertising, pricing, selling, and logistics (the movement of goods to market).
- **Accounting and finance:** the area concerned with generating and investing capital (money) and with accounting operations.

Figure 3-2 Macro view of firm.

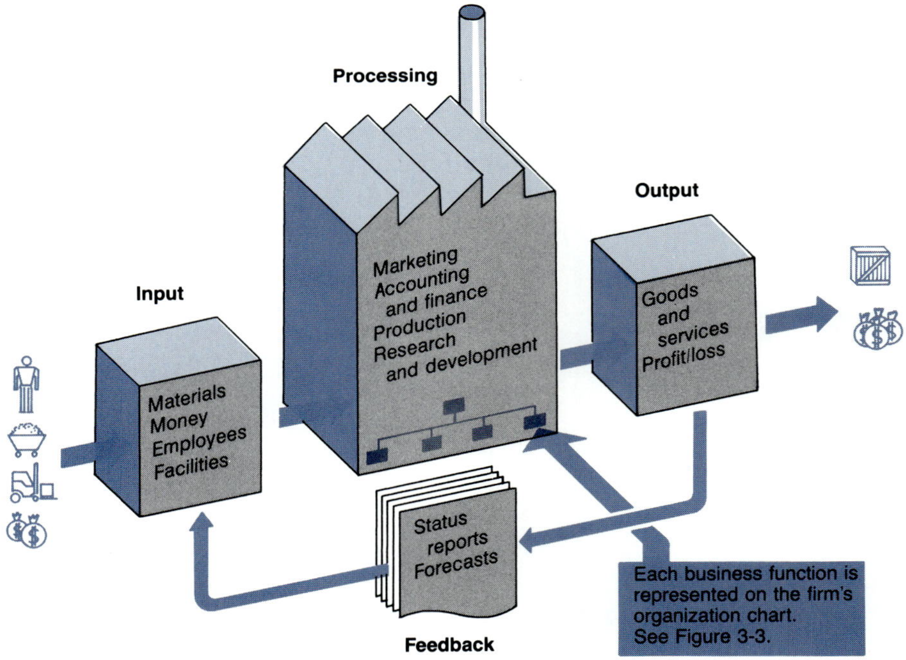
Processing
Input
Materials
Money
Employees
Facilities
Marketing
Accounting
and finance
Production
Research
and development
Output
Goods
and
services
Profit/loss
Status
reports
Forecasts
Feedback
Each business function is represented on the firm's organization chart.
See Figure 3-3.

- **Production:** the area concerned with purchasing raw materials, inventory control (**inventory** consists of physical goods on hand), and production scheduling.
- **Research and development:** the area concerned with developing new products and improving existing products.

The four functional subsystems of a business are frequently reflected in the firm's **organization chart**—a drawing depicting the formal lines of authority within an organization—an example of which appears in Figure 3-3. The role of managers, of course, is to coordinate these subsystems for the common goal of producing company products and profits.

Note that there are three levels of management within each functional area: *top, middle,* and *lower* or *supervisory.*

The Responsibilities of Managers

Picture yourself, then, as the chief executive officer (CEO) of a company, standing in your office looking at your company's organization chart, which shows you at the top. Now let us, in essence, take that chart down off the wall, lay it flat, and spread it out around you, changing it into a wheel—see the lower half of Figure 3-3. You, the CEO, are sitting at the hub of the wheel, surrounded by your four departments. This wheel is important because it shows how the four functions must be coordinated for a company to achieve its purposes.

For this coordination to happen, managers must perform their primary activity—decision making. The decision making must occur in five areas:

- Planning
- Organizing
- Controlling
- Communicating
- Staffing

These five areas, considered the classic tasks of management, are as follows:

Planning. Planning, of course, is what you do to try to get yourself or your organization from your present position to an even better position. **Planning** requires that you set objectives and develop strategies and policies for achieving them. Whatever you do in planning lays the foundation for the other four management tasks.

Organizing. To achieve company goals, you must organize all parts of the company in a coordinated and integrated effort. **Organizing** is the act of making orderly arrangements and structures to best use company resources.

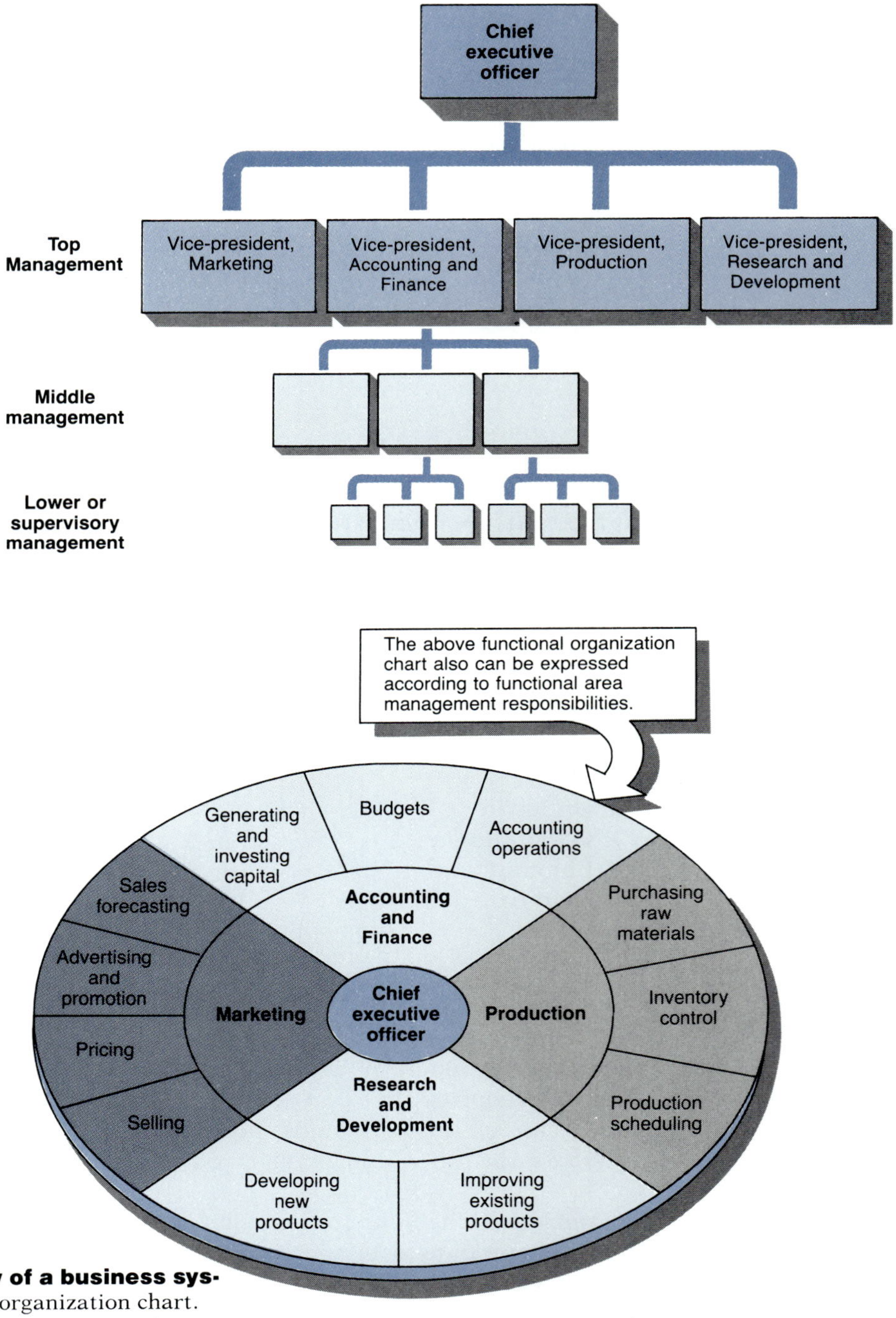
Chief executive officer
Top Management
Vice-president, Marketing
Vice-president, Accounting and Finance
Vice-president, Production
Vice-president, Research and Development
Middle management
Lower or supervisory management
The above functional organization chart also can be expressed according to functional area management responsibilities.
Generating and investing capital
Budgets
Accounting operations
Accounting and Finance
Sales forecasting
Advertising and promotion
Pricing
Selling
Marketing
Chief executive officer
Production
Purchasing raw materials
Inventory control
Production scheduling
Research and Development
Developing new products
Improving existing products

Figure 3-3 One view of a business system. *Top:* Functional organization chart. *Bottom:* Functional area management responsibilities.

Controlling. There you are, planned and organized, but how do you accomplish the results? By **controlling,** the process by which you establish standards of performance, measure employee results, correct mistakes, and minimize deviations from the objectives. The key to control is *feedback*. Feedback enables you as a manager to head off problems before they get too severe.

Communicating. **Communicating** is sharing information between people, whether face to face or over the phone, via memo or by closed-circuit television. Communicating may be more important than any of the other four tasks: after all, if you cannot explain what you are planning and organizing for, how can you expect to accomplish results? Once again, of course, feedback is important.

Staffing. **Staffing** has to do with people, of course—selecting them, training them, developing them.

With all this, we see that a business organization is a complex enterprise. It consists of four functional areas, with three levels of managers performing five management tasks—all of which must be coordinated for the success of the enterprise.

How can computers assist in this effort? Before we answer that question, let us consider what a computer system is.

What a Computer System Is

A computer needs four components to operate—hardware, software, data, and people.

- **Hardware** consists of the machines in the system—the keyboard, the video screen, the computer itself, and so on.
- **Software** consists of the programs available to run the system. A **program** is a set of step-by-step instructions directing the computer to perform specific tasks.
- **Data** consists of the raw facts that have not yet been processed into information. When raw facts have been turned into *useful* facts, they are called **information**.
- **People** need no definition, of course, but it is people that make the other three components work. Whatever one's fears about the takeover of a machine society, the machines cannot run by themselves.

Input, Processing, and Output

As Figure 3-4 shows, a computer system closely resembles the system we showed in the IPO chart in Figure 3-1. That is, a computer system consists of:

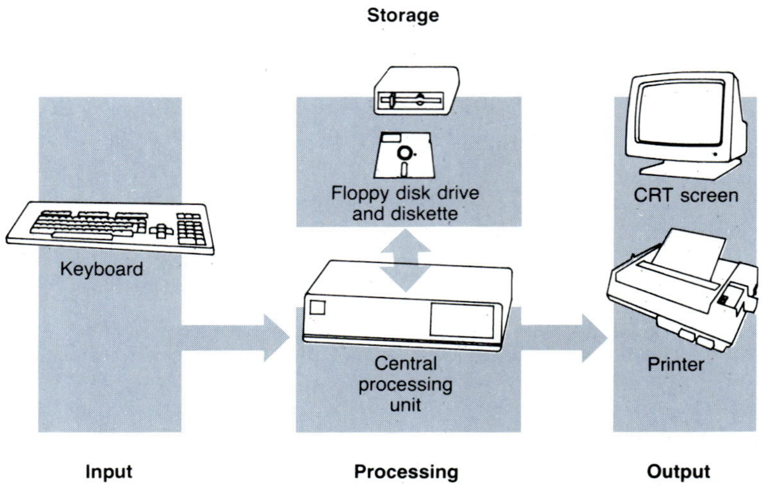
Storage
Floppy disk drive and diskette
CRT screen
Keyboard
Central processing unit
Printer
Input
Processing
Output

Figure 3-4 A computer system. All computer systems follow essentially the same arrangement: input, processing (including storage), and output. Shown here is the arrangement for a microcomputer system such as one might have at home.

- Input
- Processing (including storage)
- Output

Figure 3-4 shows the arrangement for a microcomputer system, but the principle is the same for larger systems. The hardware responsible for this process works as follows:

- **Input units** take data (such as dates, hours worked, pay rates) in machine-readable form and send it to the processing unit.
- The **processor** is the central processing unit, a machine with electronic circuitry that converts input data into information. It executes the computer instructions called for by a program. The processor contains **primary storage,** which holds the data and instructions while they are being worked on by the processor. **Secondary storage** consists of devices *outside* the processor that can store additional data. This storage *supplements* the primary storage in the processor.
- **Output units** make the processed data, now called information, available for use in the form of printed reports, columns of figures, pie charts or bar graphs, and so on.

Text continues on p. 63

Corporate Report 1

Computers in Business: New Tools, New Careers

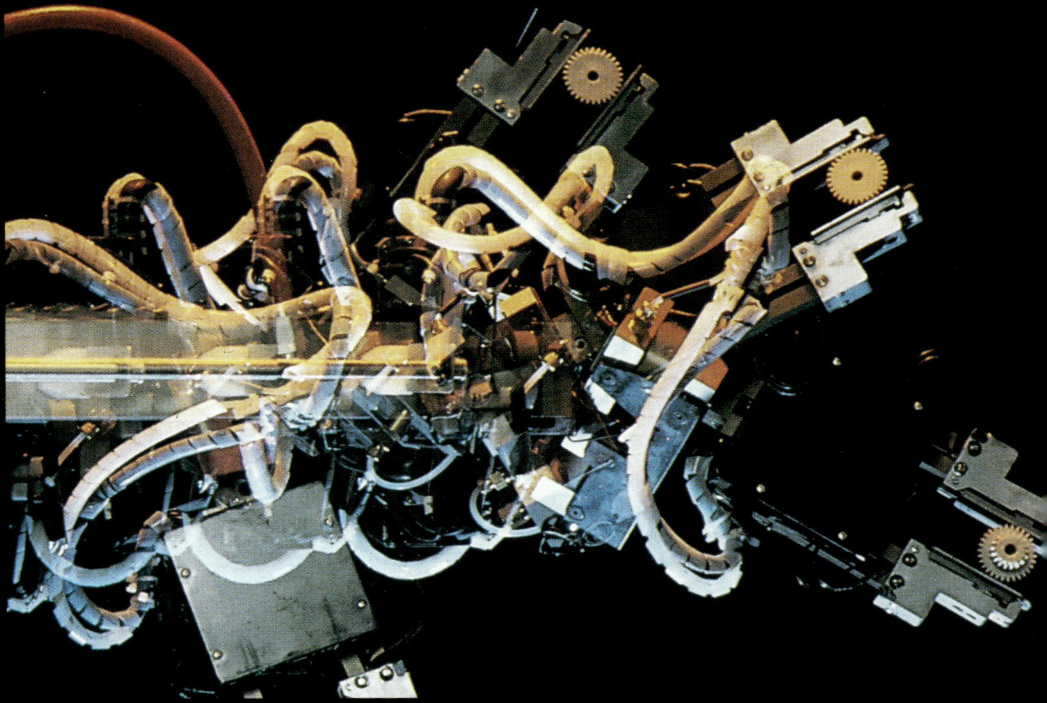

1

2

Rapid changes: they are symbolized by the movements of a factory robot in a multiple-exposure photograph *(photo 1)* and by the compactness of a portable computer *(photo 2)* that is more powerful than the two-ton, room-size computers of two decades ago. Computers are becoming the ordinary tools of the workplace, and they promise to have a profound effect on future careers. In these pages—and in other color Corporate Reports in this book—we show how these tools are being used.

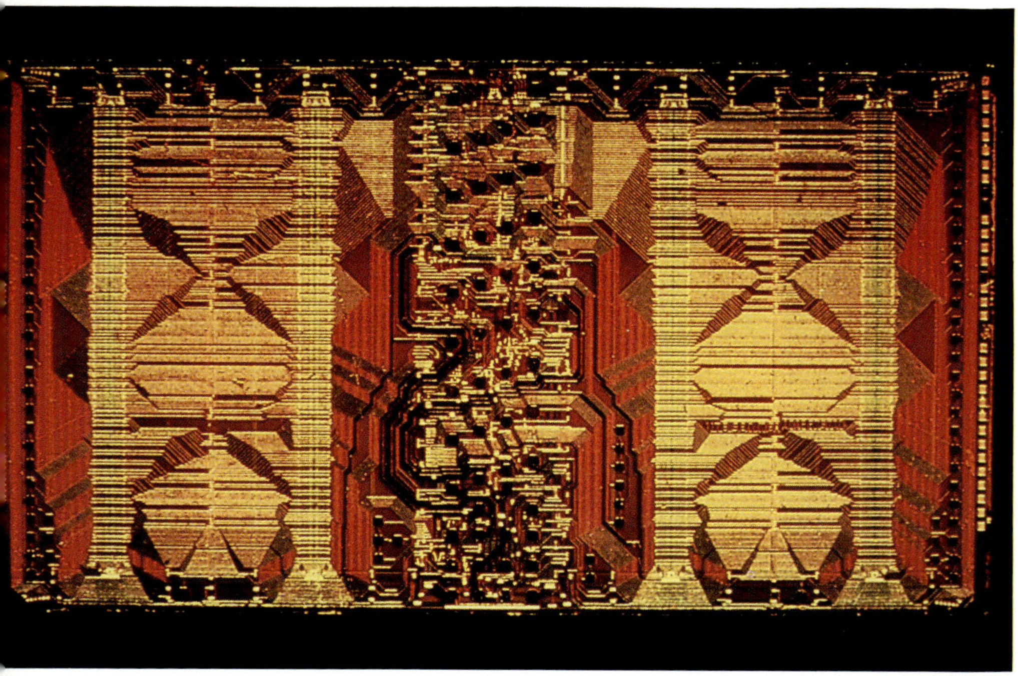

3

The Underlying Electronics

The power for the Information Revolution begins with the silicon chip, a wonder of miniaturization that is smaller than your fingernail—one experimental IBM memory chip *(photo 3)* is only three-eighths of an inch long but can store 280,000 characters of information. The circuits on such chips are first drawn on a wall-sized scale, then photographically reduced to microscopic size and developed in clusters on 3- or 4-inch "wafers" of silicon, such as those being held here *(photo 4)*. The wafers are baked in an oxygen furnace *(photo 5)* then cut apart into separate chips by an automated die-cutting machine *(photo 6)*. Chips are later mounted along with other electronic components on circuit boards *(photo 7)*.

Advances in circuit technology have

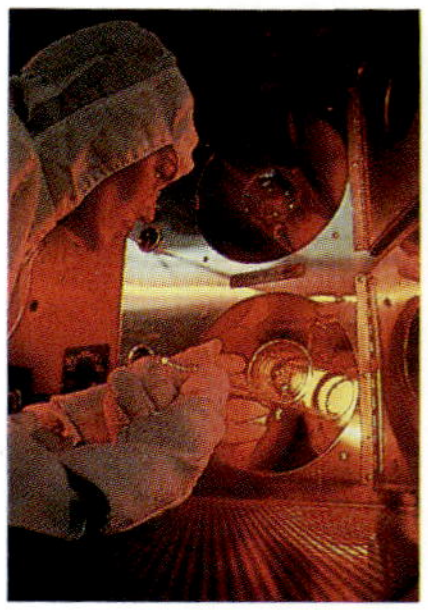

5

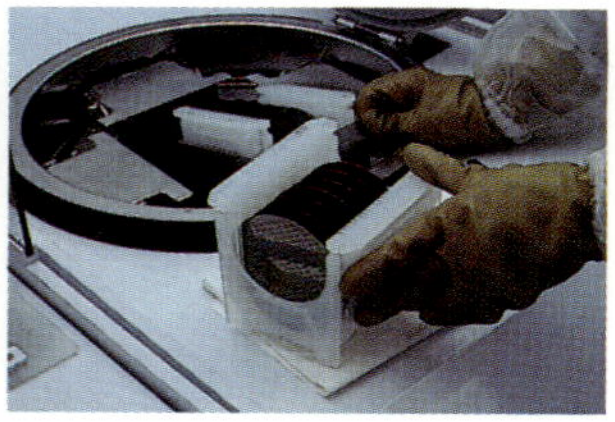

4

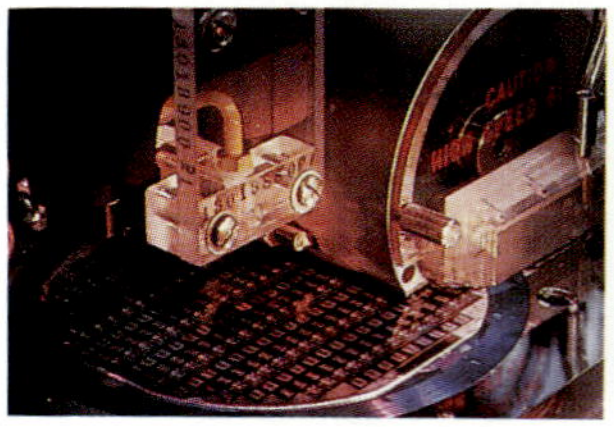

6

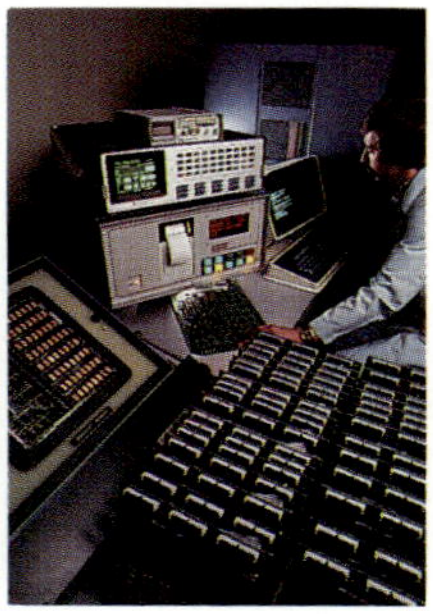

7

affected the kind of computer products available and the kinds of communications required, as the first chart below indicates. In the 1960s, the development of discrete and small-scale integrated (SSI) circuits allowed large, centralized mainframe computers to come into use. In the 1970s, medium- and large-scale integrated (MSI and LSI) circuits led to the development of minicomputers, which gave companies the ability to adopt distributed data processing—distribution of computer power outward from a central computer. In the 1980s, very large-scale integrated (VLSI) circuits allow microprocessors to be placed into all kinds of equipment: microcomputers, workstations, and various kinds of communication devices. This permits new forms of networking and distributed sharing of resources. The arrival of the microprocessor has boosted microcomputer sales *(chart)*. In 1984, worldwide personal computer shipments surpassed those of minicomputers; by 1987 they will be even with mainframe shipments. From 1977 to 1987, the worldwide installed base of personal computers will have grown from 200,000 to over 80 million.

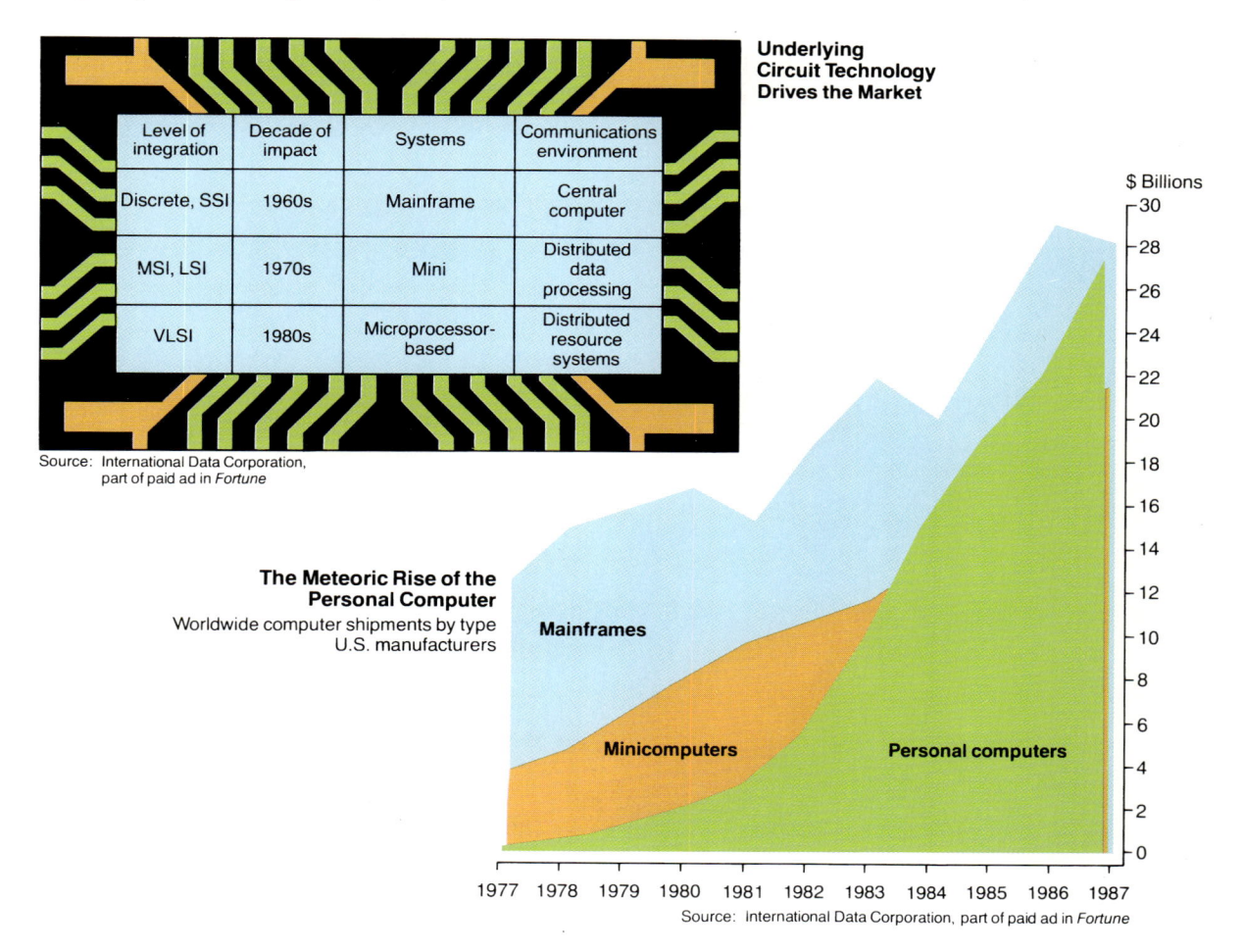

Underlying Circuit Technology Drives the Market

Level of integration	Decade of impact	Systems	Communications environment
Discrete, SSI	1960s	Mainframe	Central computer
MSI, LSI	1970s	Mini	Distributed data processing
VLSI	1980s	Microprocessor-based	Distributed resource systems

Source: International Data Corporation, part of paid ad in *Fortune*

The Meteoric Rise of the Personal Computer

Worldwide computer shipments by type
U.S. manufacturers

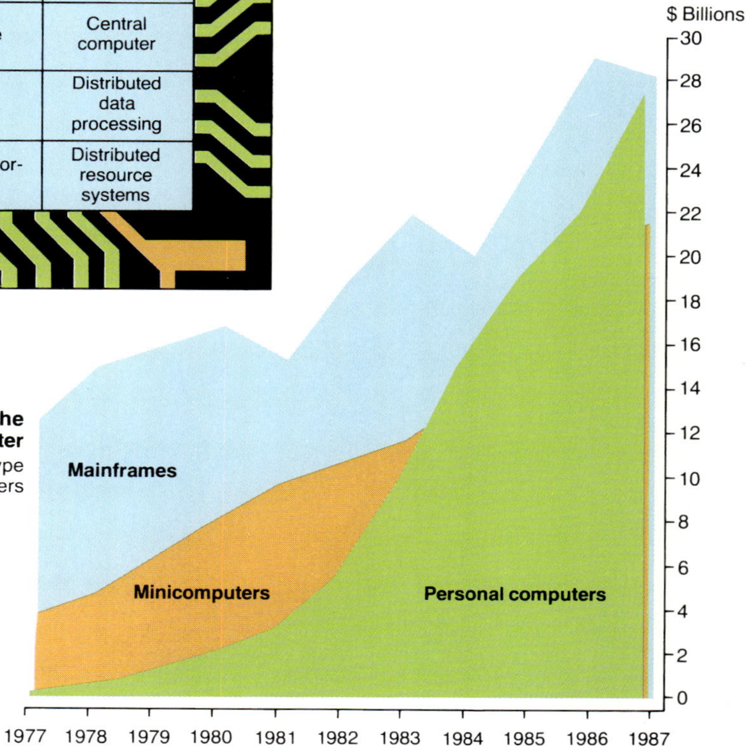

$ Billions
30
28
26
24
22
20
18
16
14
12
10
8
6
4
2
0
Mainframes
Minicomputers
Personal computers
1977
1978
1979
1980
1981
1982
1983
1984
1985
1986
1987

Source: International Data Corporation, part of paid ad in *Fortune*

The Automated Office

Most of the work force in the United States is made up of office workers, from mail clerks to top executives. Office workers are concerned with seven ways of handling business information or data—creating, storing, retrieving, organizing, summarizing, communicating, and making decisions about it.

Today the declining cost of integrated circuits has produced a revolution in the handling of these tasks. Called office automation, this revolution consists of the convergence of a number of data processing and communication technologies which has made a great many devices available to office workers: personal computers, word processors/electronic typewriters, electronic mail, voice/data workstations, facsimile devices, low-cost printers, and local area networks (LANs). These devices of the automated office have put today's managers and their staffs on a steep learning curve as they try to master business graphics and other software—shown below *(photo 8)* being taught to customers at IBM's Information Networks education center.

The automated office gives managers information such as sales forecasts in graphically and hence easier-to-grasp form *(photo 9)*. It also provides the tools of word processing—and not just for clerical workers, as shown here *(photo 10)*; executives

CHART REPORTS
"BEHIND EVERY GREAT CHART, THERE'S A GREAT REPORT"

8

also use word processing to produce and revise work. In addition, managers may use computers as filing systems to organize data into usable form and to draw information from remote sources such as data banks and data bases, using telecommunications systems *(photo 11)*.

The result of all this activity has been that in the United States digital office devices were being installed in offices at about the same rate as business phones in 1983 *(chart)*. By 1988, however, electronic keyboards will be going in four times as fast and be almost as numerous as business phones—and will surpass the number of white-collar workers.

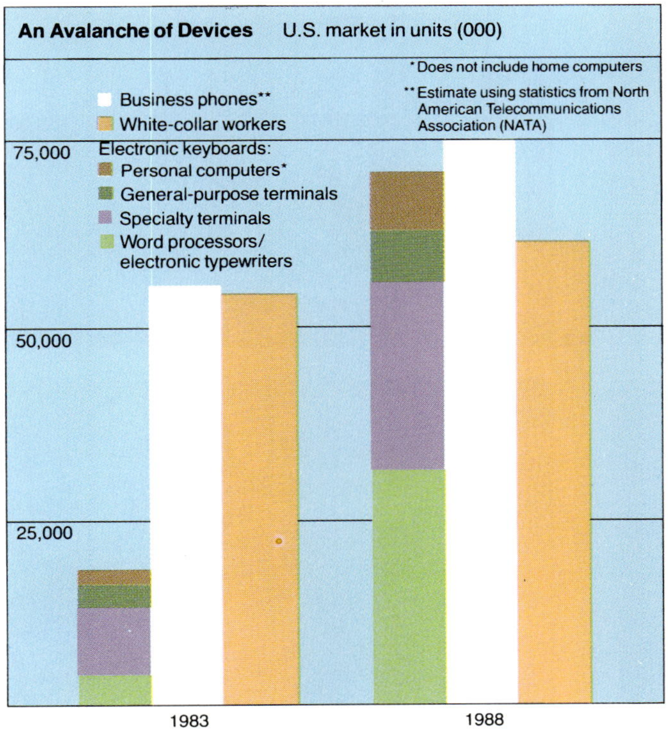

An Avalanche of Devices
U.S. market in units (000)
*Does not include home computers
**Estimate using statistics from North American Telecommunications Association (NATA)
Business phones**
White-collar workers
Electronic keyboards:
Personal computers*
General-purpose terminals
Specialty terminals
Word processors/ electronic typewriters
75,000
50,000
25,000
1983
1988

Source: International Data Corporation, part of paid ad in *Fortune*

9

10

11

12

Banking

We associate money with the stuff that is locked in the vault at night. But in modern banking, money is an electronic signal on a videoscreen—whether viewed by the teller behind the counter or a customer at an outside automatic teller machine *(photos 13 and 14)*. This technology also permits a per-

13

CROCKER BANK
Crocker Automated Teller
Crocker Automated Teller

14

15

son with a microcomputer linked to a telephone to subscribe to a home-banking service, which allows customers to transfer funds, check balances, and pay certain bills from the comfort of their homes. Although these are the more recent innovations, banking has used computer technology for years to process checks, as this woman *(photo 15)* is doing with a magnetic ink character reader (MICR) device, which "reads" the futuristic numbers printed on checks.

Anyone contemplating a career in banking or finance will find knowledge of personal computers a necessity. Loan officers, for instance, use electronic spreadsheets—which enable managers to make "what-if" projections using different numbers—to analyze customer needs and determine different payment schedules. They may also use business graphics, as shown on this page, which may be of two types. Analytical graphics are usually for a firm's internal use and are to help people analyze data and see trends by enabling them to visualize information. Presentation graphics, as shown here, are in color and are useful when making a presentation to the boss, clients, or investors.

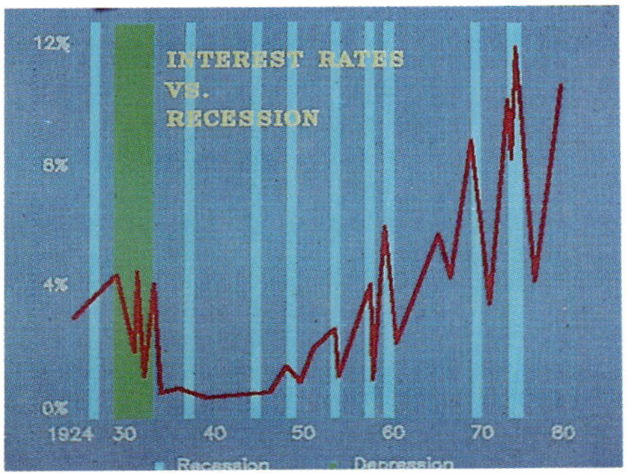
INTEREST RATES
VS.
RECESSION
12%
8%
4%
0%
1924
30
40
50
60
70
80

16

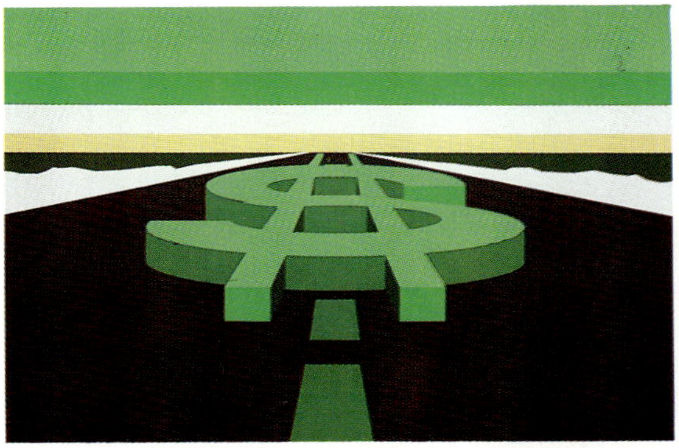

17

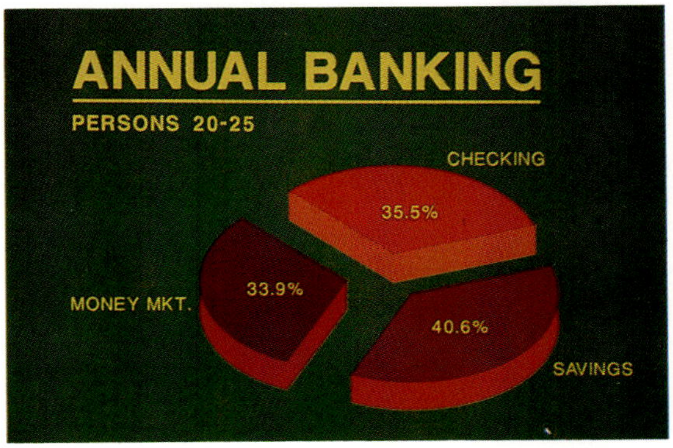
ANNUAL BANKING
PERSONS 20-25
CHECKING
35.5%
MONEY MKT.
33.9%
40.6%
SAVINGS

18

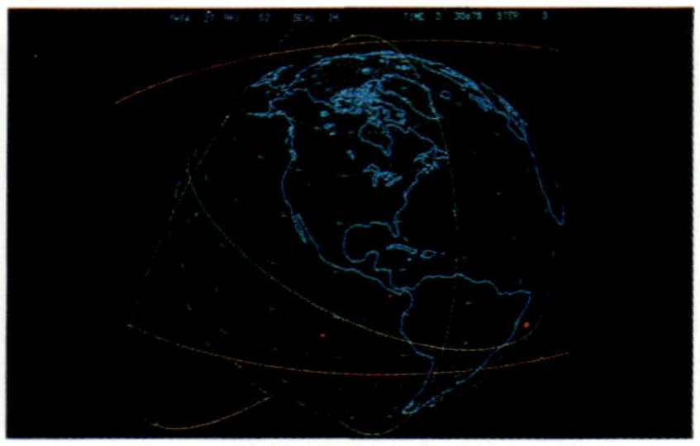

20

19 21

Communications

One of the most exciting career fields—and one of the most to benefit from high technology—communications has come to be symbolized by the orbital satellite, which accepts message signals from one point on the earth and beams to a receiving dish on another point. There are a great many communications satellites in orbit and more are being boosted into orbit every year. The three-dimensional computer graphics system shown here *(photo 20)* helps keep track of satellites at different altitudes.

Satellite companies—such as RCA, Western Union, and American Telephone & Telegraph—began by sending voice and TV signals, and, of course, much of TV traffic is still routed this way. Indeed, the television industry is highly computerized, from the control room to making graphics for the weather forecast *(photo 21)*.

Of particular interest to us, satellites are now being used extensively in computer-to-computer communication. High-speed data circuits are what make possible such communications as electronic mail, in which one transmits messages typed on a computer keyboard; voice mail, in voice-store-and-forward message systems; local area networks (LANs), which tie together local computer systems; private branch exchanges (PBXs), which the telephone system has used for years, integrated with LANs; and voice recognition systems, whereby there is machine recognition of the spoken voice. As the chart *(opposite)* indicates, the technology for these aspects of the automated office is evolving rapidly.

22

23

"We are witnessing a shift of tidal proportions in the way we handle information, in the way we move it from place to place," says Robert Hall, president of Satellite Business Systems. "And satellites are superb information handlers." Satellites, in fact, can "talk" 160 times faster than is practical over land lines. Indeed, two-thirds of the transatlantic telephone calls are carried by satellite rather than undersea cable. As the two photos at left illustrate, satellite communications requires sophisticated technology: the control center for Satellite Business Systems *(photo 22)*; the control center for Westinghouse Electric Corporation *(photo 23)*.

Source: Gartner Group, Inc., part of ad in *The New York Times*

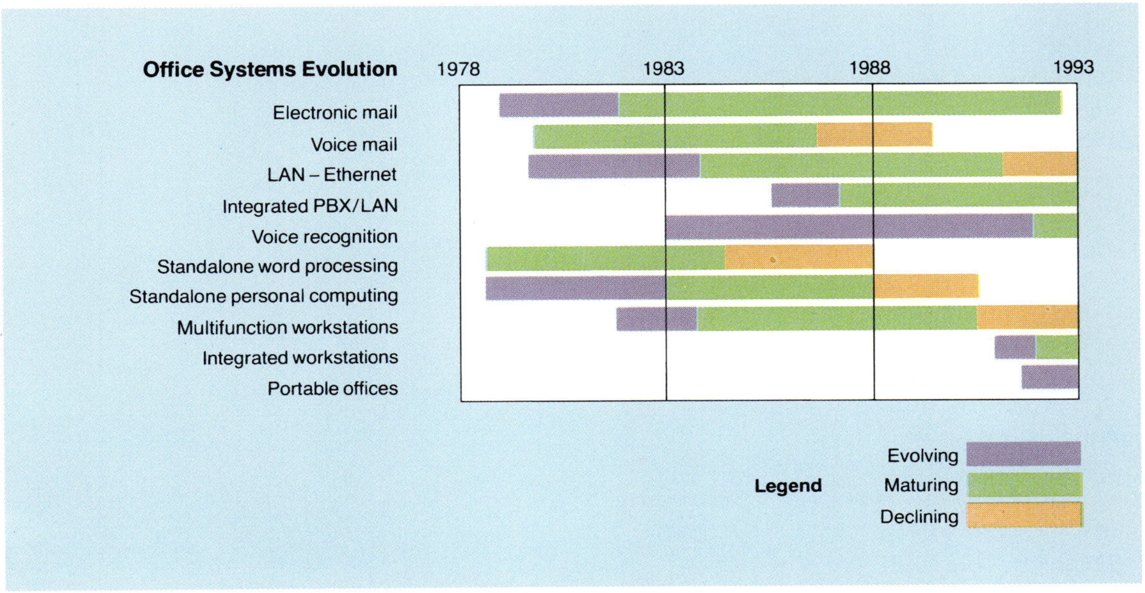
Office Systems Evolution
1978
1983
1988
1993
Electronic mail
Voice mail
LAN – Ethernet
Integrated PBX/LAN
Voice recognition
Standalone word processing
Standalone personal computing
Multifunction workstations
Integrated workstations
Portable offices
Legend
Evolving
Maturing
Declining

24

25

26

27

Energy Industries

Energy is big business in North America, and computers are a big part of that business. As the photos on these pages show, computers are used to locate and develop new sources of energy—oil, natural gas, coal, geothermal, uranium, and solar—and do it more productively.

Located in Southern California, Solar One *(photo 24)* is the world's largest solar electricity-generating station. It uses electricity-producing solar collectors, which catch the sun's rays, shown here reflecting off a 300-foot central receiving tower. The positions of the computer-directed collectors are adjusted in the control room *(photo 25)* for maximum exposure to solar rays.

Computers also make customer service more efficient. At the Southern California Edison Company, customer service representatives use computers and data bases to call up customer billing records *(photo 26)*. In 1983, 800 such representatives responded to about 4 million telephone calls.

Meter readers at the utility read an average of 380 electricity meters a day, and the data is computer-processed for customer billing. In the future, however, it is likely that utilities will monitor energy use with the help of computers at a central facility rather than use meter readers.

The energy backbone of industrial countries is, of course, oil, and computer technology is used to help regulate the control valves in oil refineries *(photo 28)*. Computers and computer-aided design programs are even used to design refineries *(photo 30)*.

28

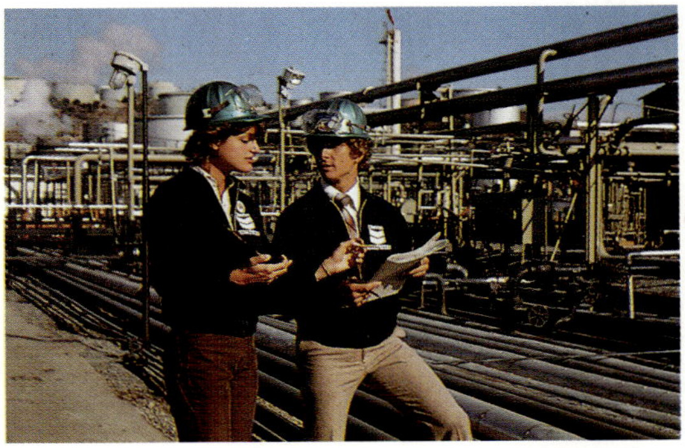
29

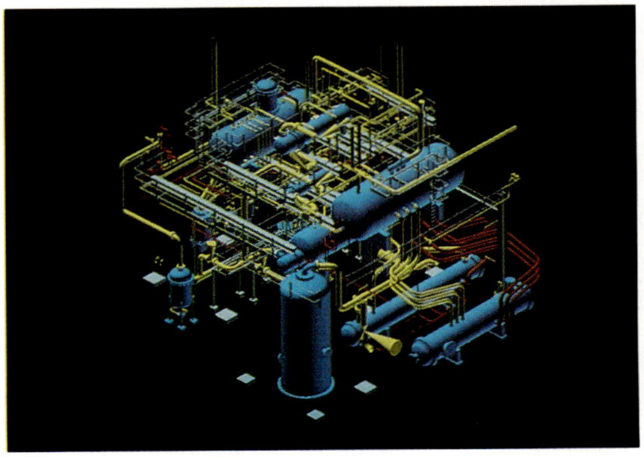
30

31

35

Transportation

32

33

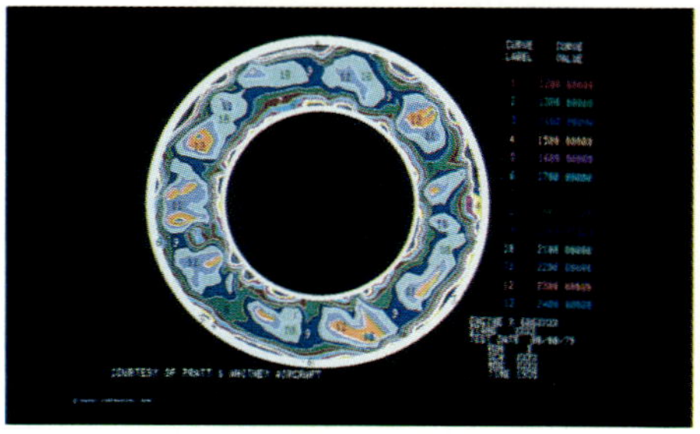

34

A night flight into Chicago looks quite dramatic—the more so when captured with a photographer's fish-eye lens *(photo 31)*. There may be fewer business people experiencing this, however, if teleconferencing—meetings arranged through computer networks or using television cameras—begins to replace business travel. In addition, telecommuting—working at home, using a computer and telecommunications—may replace motor vehicles as a way of getting to the office.

Whatever the prospects for the transportation industry, computers are already being used extensively to simulate solutions to problems. Aeronautical engineers use

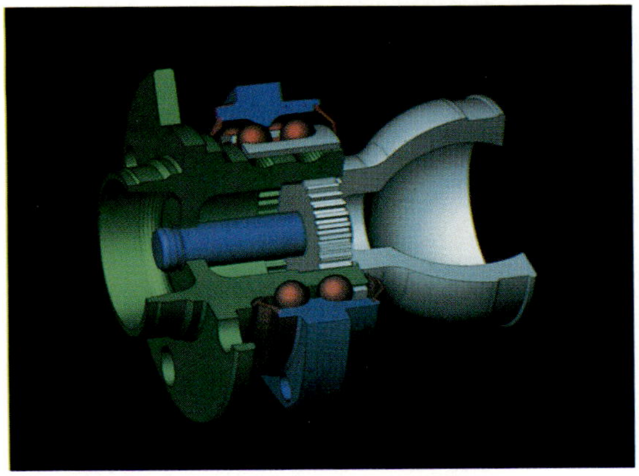

36

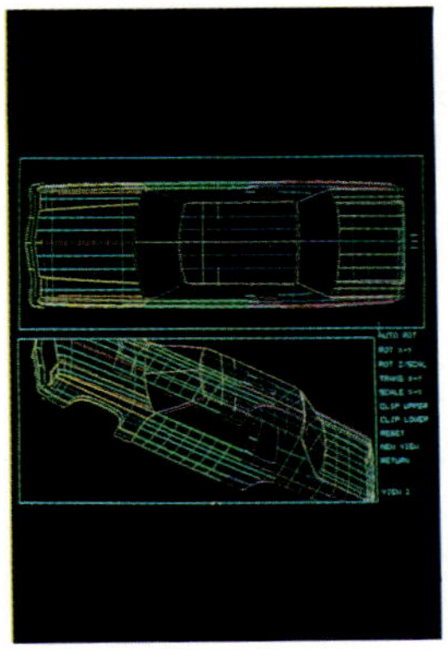

37

computer-assisted engineering (CAE) systems to transform specifications into three-dimensional models on a CRT screen *(photo 32)*: the model may be turned, enlarged, reduced, and otherwise manipulated. Light pens are used to test simulations of fuel-indicating systems *(photo 33)*. Computerized imaging systems can simulate aircraft engine stresses *(photo 34)*. Even pilot training is simulated; this instrument panel *(photo 35)* includes computerized radar simulation.

Trucks and cars also benefit from computerized design. CAD/CAM—which stands for computer-assisted design and computer-assisted manufacturing—is used to create graphic models of automobile bodies and parts *(photos 36 and 37)*. Computerized equipment is also used to verify each part dimension against its blueprint specification *(photo 38)* and to sculpt clay models to exact dimensions *(photo 39)*.

38

39

41

42

40

Manufacturing

Those considering careers in industrial engineering, production management, or other jobs related to manufacturing should consider the factory of the future—which is already in the present. Located in a striking building in Erie, Pennsylvania *(photo 41)*, this completely computerized factory is part of General Electric's locomotive manufacturing division. From the second-floor balcony *(photo 42)*, supervisors have a view of the entire system, one of the first so-called flexible manufacturing systems

43

(FSMs) in the United States. Unlike conventional factories, which follow a fixed pattern of steps, FMSs can be reprogrammed for different production requirements—new parts, design changes, or differing quantities of product. This flexibility significantly alters the economics of manufacturing.

Designed to make frames for traction motors, the Erie factory has nine huge milling machines *(photo 43)*, which eat into gigantic blocks of metal on steel pallets. A plant based on conventional manufacturing processes would have required 240 workers, but the GE plant requires only 15 workers on the day shift, four on the evening shift, and none but a night watchman at night, although the factory runs three shifts.

Flexibility is the key word in future manufacturing, and this is clearly evident in industrial robots, which, unlike most machines on an assembly line, can be programmed and reprogrammed for a variety of tasks *(photo 44)*. As labor costs rise and technology costs decline, robots will become more attractive. Although we are used to thinking of robots as people-like, it is clear from these photos that the large, industrial robots, at least, have little resemblance to humans. Indeed, they can do some things better than humans. Once its movements are calibrated exactly, as this technician is doing here *(photo 45)*, an industrial robot can do a number of repetitious chores—including the most detailed, mind-numbing, and dangerous, such as arc welding *(photo 46)*.

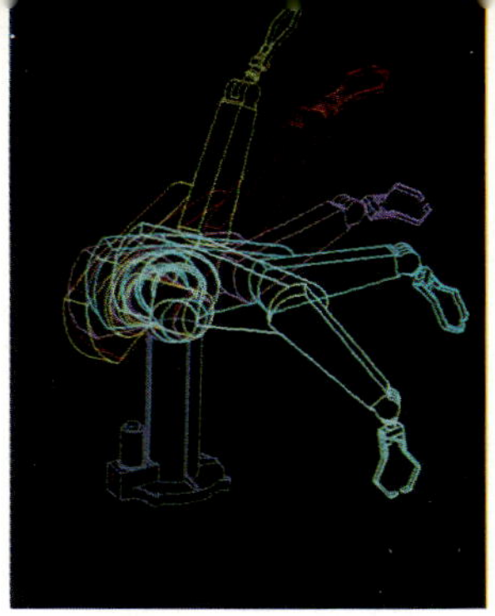
44

45

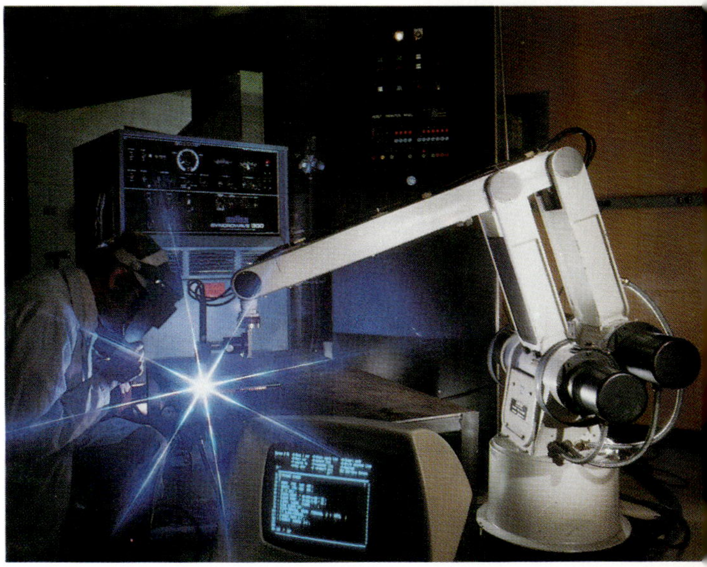
46

INTERNATIONAL SPACE
HALL OF FAME

47

Personal Robots

So far, personal robots—like RB5X here at the International Space Hall of Fame in Alamagordo, New Mexico—are mainly just cute toys. They have yet to show people they are practical—even at the level of washing dishes or walking the dog. Some observers, however, think that personal robots are about at the point that personal computers were a few years ago, mainly of interest to hobbyists. Today, of course, the microcomputer is one of a manager's most valuable business tools. Might the same thing yet happen with a descendant of RB5X?

48

Let us now get into the all-important discussion of how a computer system works. This discussion is principally about hardware, for we will begin to describe software in the next several chapters. In order to understand how software is supposed to work, however, you need to understand the arrangement of hardware in a computer system.

Input: Taking It All In

As Figure 3-5 shows, there are several different kinds of input devices and input **media**—the materials such as tape on which data are recorded. The following devices represent some of the most common ways of inputting—putting in—data to the computer system for processing.

Keyboard. Probably the most common input device, a **keyboard** is a typewriterlike keyboard of letters, numbers, and special characters; it may also have special keys peculiar to computer or word processing usage. The keyboard usually appears along with a video screen called a **CRT screen**—CRT stands for **cathode-ray tube**—and together they are called a **terminal.** Sometimes, however, the keyboard is marketed separately, as with those intended for home computer use which are supposed to be attached to a television set.

Magnetic Tape. Magnetic tape looks like audio cassette tape, but it comes on a reel.

Magnetic Disk. A magnetic disk is a round platter with a magnetized surface that stores data as electronic impulses. There are two kinds of magnetic disks—hard and flexible.

- **Hard disks:** A **hard disk** is made of rigid metal and coated with ferrous oxide, and it looks something like a long-playing stereo record. Hard disks usually come in stacks known as **disk packs,** with space between the disks. Both top and bottom surfaces are used for recording data (except for the surfaces on the very top and bottom of the stack). Hard disks require hard **disk drives** (see Figure 3-5)—mechanical machines with a spindle in the middle on which a disk pack can be mounted and which is rotated at very fast speeds—to record or input data. The disk drive translates the data on the disk into electronic impulses, which are sent to the part of the computer called the central processing unit.
- **Flexible disks:** A **flexible disk**—also known as a **diskette** or **floppy disk**—is made of oxide-coated flexible plastic and looks something like a 45 rpm phonograph record. Used with microcomputers, the flexible disk requires a floppy disk drive (shown in Figures 3-4 and 3-5) to translate data on the disk into electronic impulses.

We will describe this array of input devices in more detail in Chapter 7.

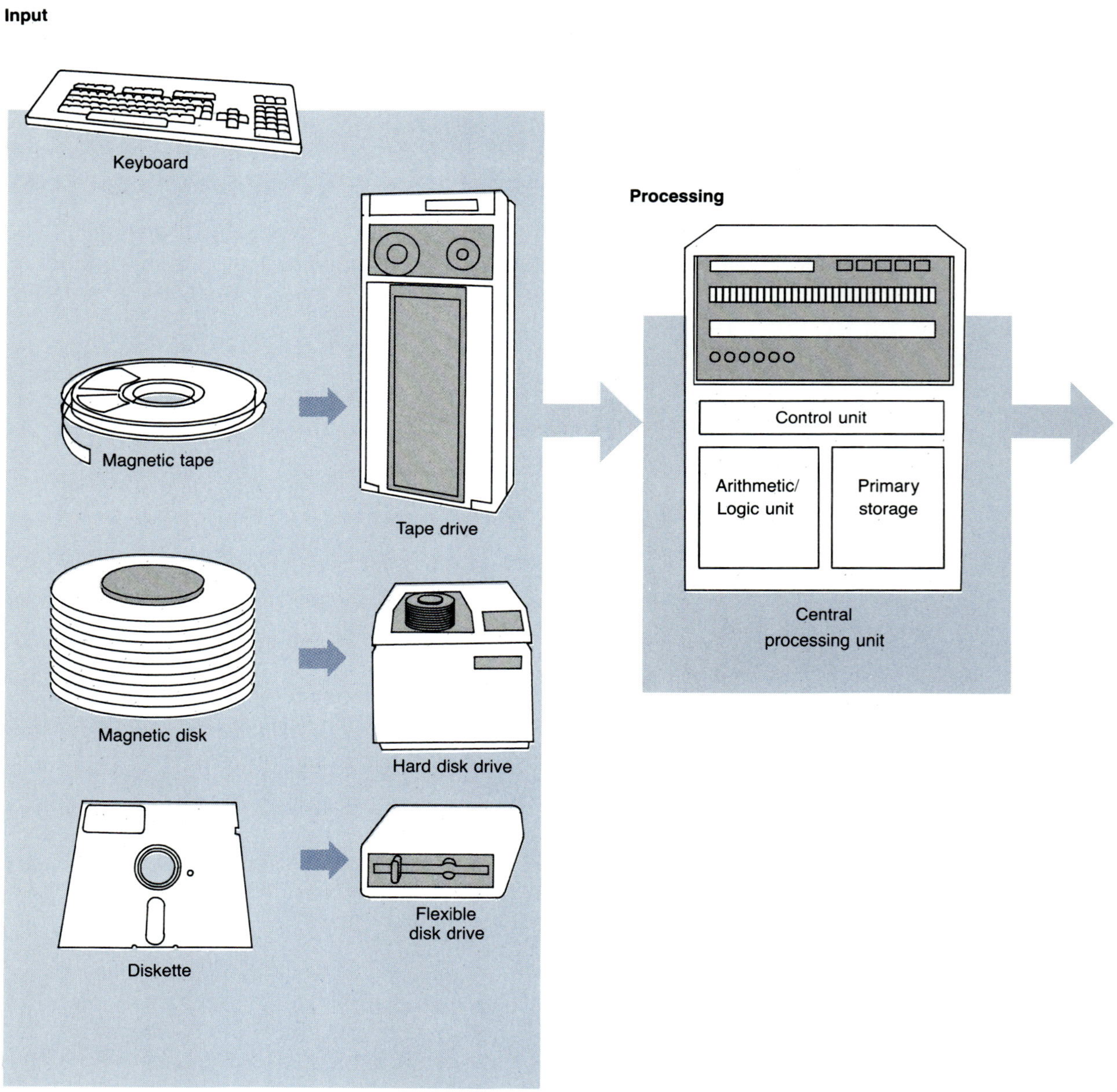
Input
Keyboard
Magnetic tape
Tape drive
Magnetic disk
Hard disk drive
Diskette
Flexible disk drive
Processing
Control unit
Arithmetic/ Logic unit
Primary storage
Central processing unit

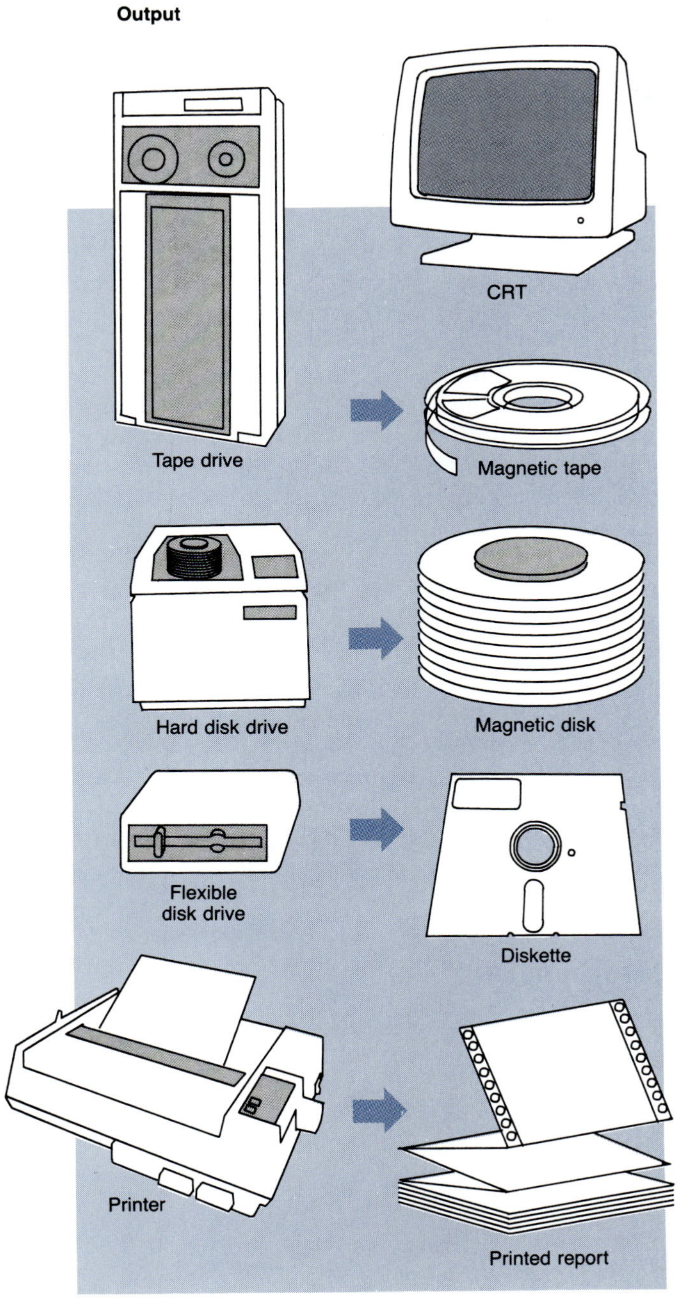
Output
CRT
Tape drive
Magnetic tape
Hard disk drive
Magnetic disk
Flexible
disk drive
Diskette
Printer
Printed report

Figure 3-5 Input, processing, and output of a computer system. Not all computer systems are capable of using all these forms of input or of producing all these forms of output.

Processing and Storage: Brains and Backup

The processor itself—the **central processing unit,** or **CPU,** which is often called the computer's "brain"—consists of three parts. As Figure 3-5 shows, these are:

- The control unit
- The arithmetic/logic unit
- Primary storage

The Control Unit. The **control unit** contains circuitry that directs the entire computer system to carry out or execute the program instructions; that is, it coordinates the other parts of the computer.

The Arithmetic/Logic Unit. The **arithmetic/logic unit** contains the electronic circuitry that controls all arithmetic operations and logical operations. **Arithmetic operations** are the four standard math operations: addition, subtraction, multiplication, and division. **Logical operations** consist of the three basic comparison operations: equal to (=), less than (<), and greater than (>).

Primary Storage. **Primary storage** is referred to by a variety of names: **main memory, main storage, internal storage,** and simply **memory.** The main memory is the part of the computer that holds data and instructions for processing—at least temporarily, until you turn the computer off or someone else wants to use it for his or her programs. The capacity or size of primary storage is often expressed by the letter **K** for **kilobyte,** which represents 1024 bytes. A **byte** represents one character (letter, number, symbol) of data. You may hear a salesperson in a computer store say that a computer has "128 K" of memory, which translates into 128 times 1024 bytes, or 131,072 characters of memory.

Secondary Storage. **Secondary storage** (also called **auxiliary storage**) is found physically *outside* the processor. Secondary storage can take many forms, but three of the most common are:

- Magnetic tape
- Hard disk
- Flexible disk

Both the processor and secondary storage are explained in more detail in Chapters 8 and 9, respectively.

Output: The Uses of Computing

As Figure 3-5 shows, many input media and devices can be used for output:

- Magnetic tape
- Hard disk
- Flexible disk

HISTORY OF THE INFORMATION AGE

The Beginning: Babbage, Lady Byron, and the Brass and Pewter Computer

The abacus—beads strung on wires—has been used in the Orient for 5000 years to do calculations, and a French mathematician named Blaise Pascal developed a cigar-box-sized mechanical adding machine in 1642. However, the computer itself—the basis for office automation and the Information Revolution—was conceived in Victorian England over 160 years ago.

The tale of Charles Babbage, called "the father of the computer," is one of genius, obsession, and disappointment. Born in England in 1791, Babbage was a man of inherited wealth who became a well-known mathematician and inventor. As a young man, he conceived the notion that logarithmic tables, which at that time were laboriously computed by hand, might be calculated more accurately by machinery. In 1822, he assembled the basic scheme for a machine that would calculate the successive differences in polynomial equations and presented the idea as a paper to the Royal Astronomical Society, which awarded the paper its gold medal. Encouraged by this success, Babbage then undertook the building of a demonstration model of what he called a **difference engine** *(see illustration)*, using a grant from the English government.

A model of the difference engine.

Charles Babbage.

In a workshop on the Babbage estate, craftsmen began manufacturing rods, ratchets, wheels, and gears, which were then assembled into a giant machine. However, it was soon discovered that the smallest irregularities were enough to throw the tons of brass and pewter parts into fits of grinding and shaking, bringing the steam-driven machine to a halt. The state of the art of Victo-

The analytical engine. This model was built by Babbage's son.

rian technology failed to support Babbage's vision. As the machine became increasingly expensive, the government withdrew its financial support.

Undaunted, Babbage conceived of another mechanical marvel called the **analytical engine** *(illustration)*, which he hoped could do not just one kind of calculation but a variety of tasks. The analytical engine was the first machine to possess the five key concepts of modern computers: (1) an input device; (2) a processor, or number calculator; (2) a control unit to direct the task to be performed and the sequence of calculations; (4) a storage place or memory, to hold information waiting to be processed; and (5) an output device.

The government considered this project hopeless also, but Babbage attracted support from an unexpected quarter, the poet Lord Byron's daughter, the beautiful Augusta Ada Byron, who later became the Countess of Lovelace. If Babbage was the "father of the computer," Lady Lovelace was the "first programmer." A woman not only of leisure but also of intellectual accomplishments, including that of mathematician, Lady Lovelace was 27 when she came to Babbage's work and over the next ten years she helped develop the instructions for doing computations on the analytical engine. Her notes, "Observations on Mr. Babbage's Analytical Engine," contain thoughts not only on the machine but also on the nature of mechanical intelligence. ("The Analytical Engine has no pretensions whatever to originate anything. It can do whatever we know how to order it to perform. It can follow analysis; but it has no power of anticipating any analytical relations or truths." In other words, a computer by itself cannot be considered creative.)

Augusta Ada Byron.

Lady Lovelace died of cancer at age 36. Babbage continued to persevere on his machines, without completing either one. Ironically, late in life he saw another engineer complete a simpler model of the difference engine. He died in 1871 at age 80, suffering the disappointment of having an idea ahead of its time, an idea that the technology of his era could not fulfill.

Next history installment: **Hollerith and the Punched-Card Revolution**, p. 208.

And let us add two other common ones:

- The CRT
- The printer

The device that gets the most use, perhaps, is the CRT; however, the printer is a close second. **Printers** are machines that produce printed documents under the control of the program in the computer. Printers can be **impact printers,** which form images as typewriters do, striking characters against a ribbon and forming an image on paper. Or they can be **nonimpact printers,** which form images using specially coated papers that respond to electrostatic impulses. Some printers print a character at a time, others a line at a time.

We shall have more to say about output devices in Chapter 7.

Those Marvelous Machines: Monsters, Mainframes, Minis, and Micros

Computers have been classified into four categories, from large to small (although some people classify the first two in one category):

- Supercomputers—sometimes called "monsters"
- Mainframes
- Minicomputers
- Microcomputers

Examples of each of the categories are shown in Figure 3-6.

Supercomputers. Referred to as "monsters" or maxicomputers, **supercomputers** are the fastest and most powerful computers. One, the Cray-1, is available for between $6 million and $17 million. The Cray-2 is supposed to be 12 times as powerful as the Cray-1. Supercomputers being built by the Japanese are reputedly 1000 times more powerful than those presently found in the U.S. It is unlikely that you will encounter a supercomputer, since the machines are principally used for worldwide weather forecasting, weapons research, and very special applications requiring an enormous number of calculations in a very short period of time.

Mainframes. Before the other sizes of computers were built, all data processing was done on mainframes, and thousands are in use today in large and medium-sized companies as well as hospitals, universities, and government agencies. A **mainframe** is the largest, fastest, and most expensive category of general-use computers. The cost of a mainframe and supporting equipment and services can range from $250,000 to $10 million or more, and primary storage is capable of holding several million characters of information and able to process around 5 million instructions per second. Because of their size and speed, mainframes usually must be placed on special raised floors that allow wiring and cooling systems.

Supercomputer. A Cray X-MP.

Microcomputer. Introduced in 1981, the IBM Personal Computer has become very popular with business users.

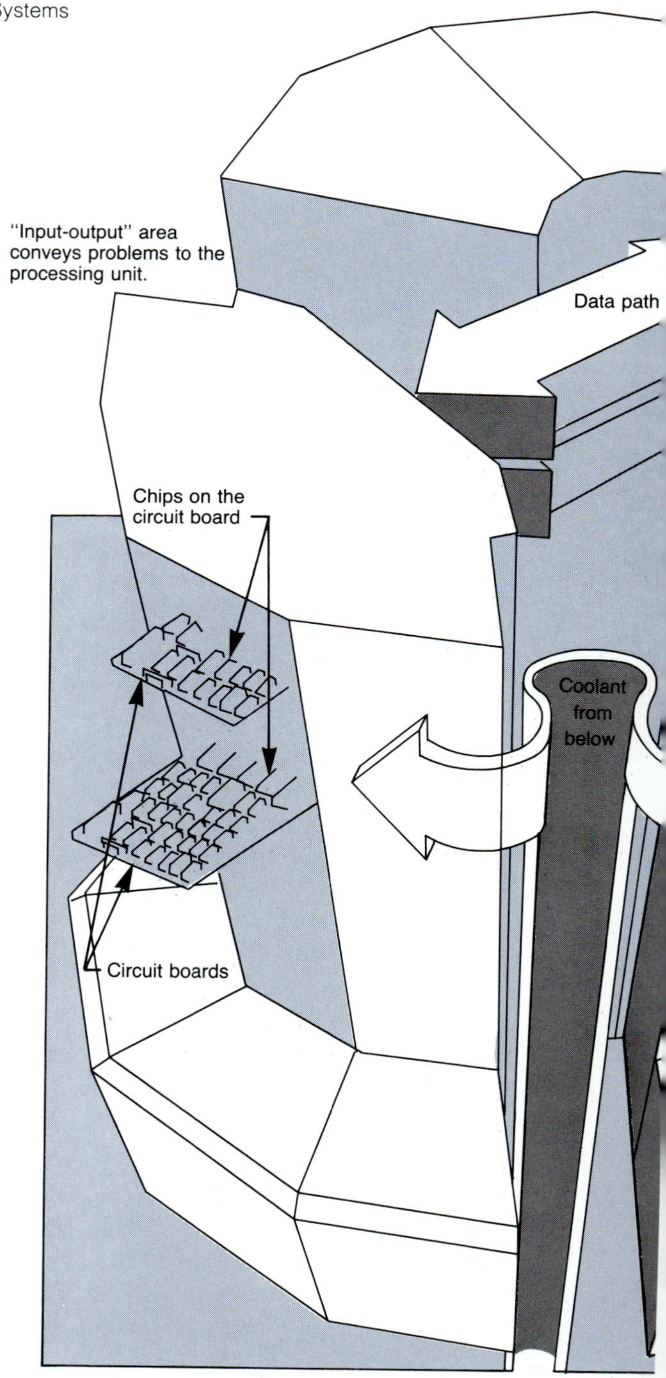
"Input-output" area conveys problems to the processing unit.
Data path
Chips on the circuit board
Coolant from below
Circuit boards

Figure 3-6 Computer world. The four types of computers are shown on these pages. *Center:* The Cray-1 supercomputer operates in terms of 100 million operations per second; a microcomputer only thousands.

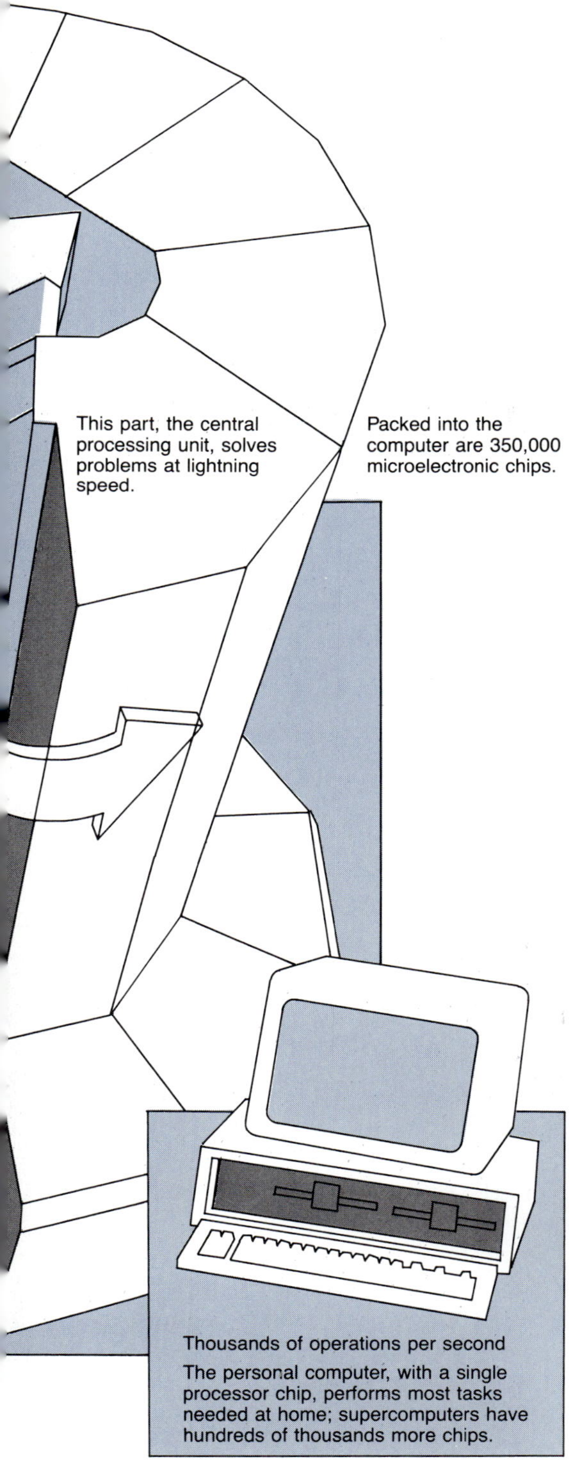
This part, the central processing unit, solves problems at lightning speed.
Packed into the computer are 350,000 microelectronic chips.
Thousands of operations per second
The personal computer, with a single processor chip, performs most tasks needed at home; supercomputers have hundreds of thousands more chips.

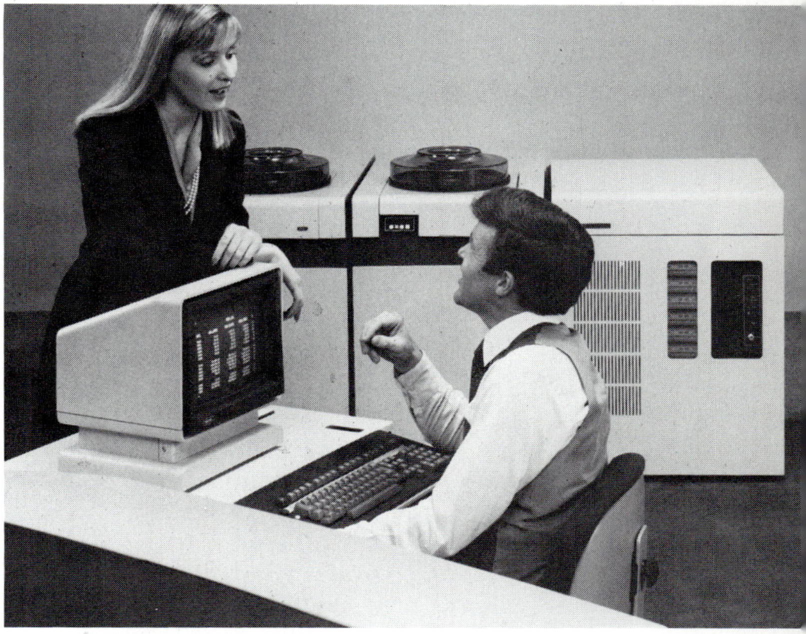

Minicomputer. This Wang model has many small business uses.

Mainframe computers. These are used in the design and development of new commercial aircraft.

Mainframes are useful not only because they can store an enormous amount of data—all the information on students in a university, for example, or all the policy holders for a large nationwide insurance company—but also because they can support several terminals. Some hospital systems, for instance, have over 200 terminals, which are used to enter medical records into the computer as well as for other tasks.

Minicomputers. The **minicomputer** resembles the mainframe but is of medium size and speed and costs considerably less—$10,000 to about $250,000. Developed in the late 1960s for special purposes, minicomputers were adopted as general-purpose machines by small businesses in much the same way that large businesses have used mainframes. Business people like them because they can support several terminals and can handle most accounting functions efficiently. Some minicomputers do not require special wiring and air conditioning or an extensive support staff.

Prior to the 1970s, most organizations put their computer facilities and all related activities in one location. In other words, there was **centralized data processing.** However, in the seventies the trend was toward **decentralized** or **distributed data processing.** As business needs and computer applications increased and central computer departments became overloaded, users began to supplement their large, central mainframe computers with a number of minicomputers located in branch offices and regional quarters. In the distributed data processing system, however, the minicomputers located at the remote sites are connected to the mainframe—known in this usage as the **host** computer—by communications lines such as telephone lines.

Microcomputers. We have already covered microcomputers in Chapter 1. As mentioned, **microcomputers** are desktop or personal computers costing between $100 and $10,000.

With the arrival of micros, small businesses have been freed from having to rely on three traditional sources for their computer needs: (1) **service bureaus,** outside companies that sell standard computer capabilities or services, such as pickup-and-deliver payroll services; (2) **time-sharing services,** outside companies that sell computer time to several clients, linked by telephone lines from the time-sharing computer to the clients' terminals; and (3) **purchase** of a large computer (usually a minicomputer), with supporting staff. Small businesses can use microcomputers for such general applications as payroll, yet still use them for special purposes, such as terminals to connect with time-sharing services via telephone lines.

Computer Choices

The microcomputer, as we saw in Chapter 1, is having a significant effect on business today. The mainframe has been around longer and will probably continue to be the mainstay of computing power for large business. However, its use will no doubt be changed by its relationship to the micro, which can be used by itself for many purposes, but which also can be used to gain access to the mainframe when necessary.

The appearance of microcomputers in mainframe organizations has created some interesting problems, however. Some data processing department directors worry that chaos will result if individual managers are allowed to order any kind of micros; so they have attempted to prohibit the purchase of micros altogether—a futile gesture, since microcomputers are so inexpensive that some managers have purchased them out of their own pockets. Other data processing directors have simply ignored the appearance of companywide micros—also a mistake, since too many different makes of microcomputers may be incompatible with the company mainframe and may be difficult to maintain. Probably the best approach is that taken by firms such as Mobil Oil, which has introduced a pilot project encouraging the purchase of microcomputers but giving support and direction to employee acquisitions and providing a training program.

This concludes our overview of how a business system operates and how a computer system operates. Let us now try to put the two systems together as a computer-based information system.

The Computer-Based Information System

As we saw in Figure 3-3, the flow of information within the organization can be quite complex. Information flows across the functional areas. Sales forecasts by the marketing area, for instance, are essential to production schedules for the production department if people in that group are to know what kinds of priorities to assign. The flow of information must also work vertically within a functional area. For example, middle managers need status reports from supervisory personnel beneath them in order to coordinate their work.

The study of how information flows and the creation of better systems of information flow is called **systems analysis and design.** Information can exist in file cabinets, but computer-based information systems can enhance the flow of information.

Information flows in several ways:

- Information follows the IPO model as was shown in Figure 3-2. It comes into the organization as *input* in the form of employees, materials, facilities, and money. It is *processed and stored* in the four functional areas of marketing, accounting and finance, production, and research and development. It is *output* as goods and services and as profit or loss.

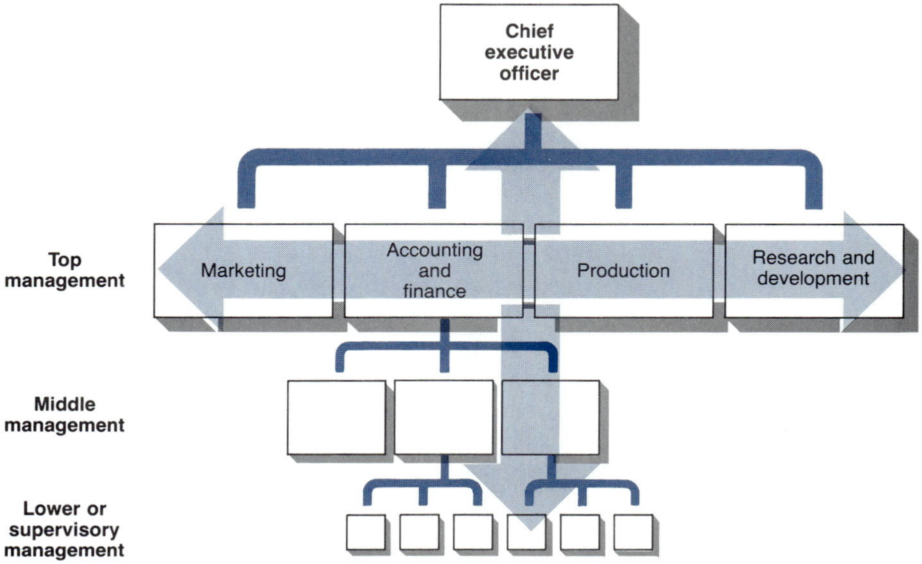
Chief executive officer
Top management
Marketing
Accounting and finance
Production
Research and development
Middle management
Lower or supervisory management

Figure 3-7 Four functional areas with three levels of management. Information flows up and down the ranks of managers as well as between the functional areas.

- Within each of the four functional areas—marketing, accounting and finance, production, and research and development—information flows up and down through three levels of managements: top, middle, and lower. This is shown in Figure 3-7.
- The managers within these three levels and four areas do the things managers are paid to do—namely, make decisions about planning, organizing, controlling, communicating, and staffing.

Now let us introduce a new concept: Within each of the three levels of management there is—or should be—some sort of **centralized business information system,** shared by managers in the four functional areas, as shown in Figure 3-8. The information for this system may be stored in a collection of filing cabinets, but what we are talking about is a computerized information system. If you are a manager, what this means is that you most likely have a CRT terminal on your desk, so that you can make inputs to the information system and draw outputs from it in order to help you make your decisions.

There are three levels or subsystems of information systems. These correspond to one of the three levels of management:

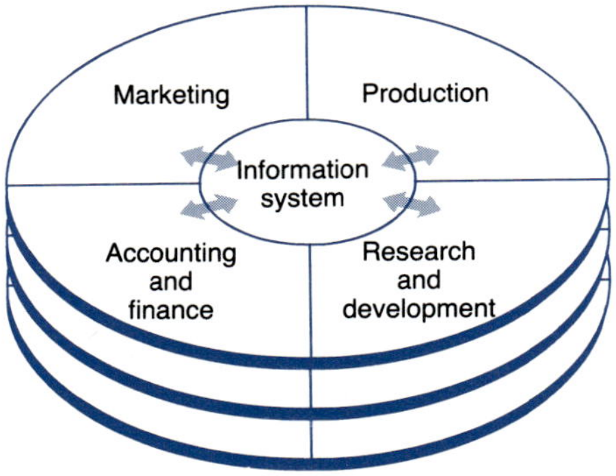
Marketing
Production
Information system
Accounting and finance
Research and development

Figure 3-8 The centralized business information system. Such an information system exists for each of the three levels of management—top, middle, and lower.

- For lower-level or supervisory management: Operations information systems (OISs)
- For middle management: management information systems (MISs)
- For top management: decision support systems (DSSs)

Some overlaps occur, but each system is intended for a particular level of manager, as Figure 3-9 shows. Moreover, each type of information system is truly different from the other, as we shall see.

The three systems are described below.

Operations Information Systems

An **operations information system (OIS)**—also known as a **transaction processing system** or an **electronic data processing system**—is defined as a computer-based means of capturing transactions so that they can be reproduced when necessary. A **transaction** is an event that is to be recorded—for example, an employee hiring or termination, the sale of a product, the receipt of materials for inventory, records of client complaints, and so on.

The outputs of a transaction processing system are:

- Documents needed to do business—invoices, shipping orders, paychecks, mailing lists, and the like.
- Listings of transactions that have occurred, for confirmation or reference—such as a listing of all past due customer accounts.
- Electronic records for a corporate data base for later use in making decisions about a variety of applications.

An operations information system is the first information system that a company develops. As mentioned, it is usually oriented toward assisting the lower-level or supervisory manager. It is concerned with the actual operation of the company, with the performance of standard operations and procedures, particularly accounting operations.

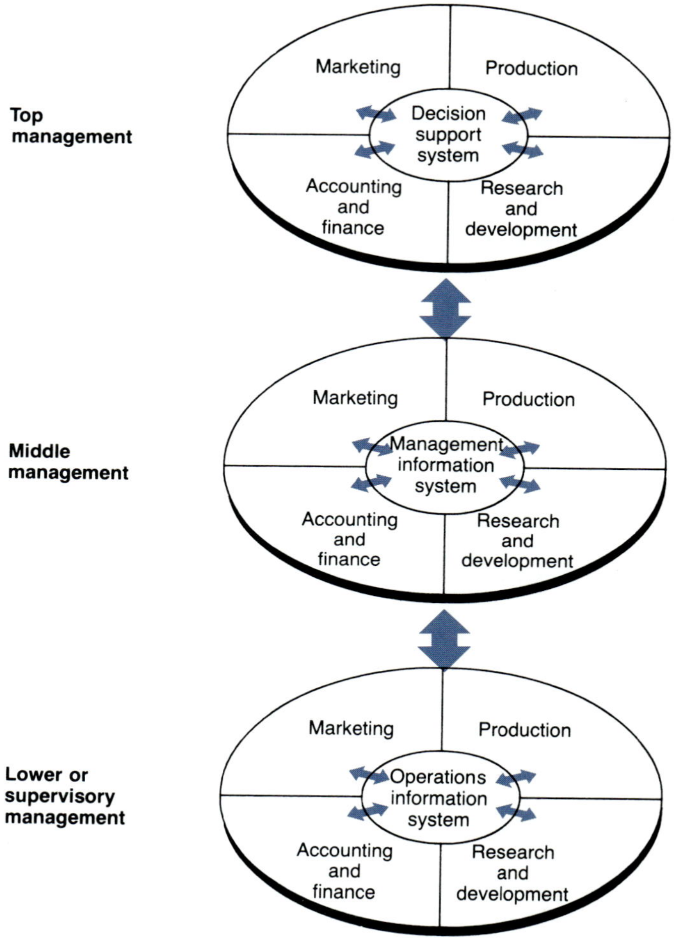
Top management
Marketing
Production
Decision support system
Accounting and finance
Research and development
Middle management
Marketing
Production
Management information system
Accounting and finance
Research and development
Lower or supervisory management
Marketing
Production
Operations information system
Accounting and finance
Research and development

Figure 3-9 The three business information systems.

Management Information Systems

Operations information systems first became popular during the 1950s. In the sixties, managers became aware of another use for the information systems concept. Not only could low-level managers avail themselves of computer-produced information to help with day-to-day problems, middle-level managers also could use the same information in summarized form as standardized reports to help them make decisions.

Management information systems (MISs) are concerned with creating standard reports that summarize transaction processing data. Typically developed by companies as the next step after they have developed operations information systems, MISs are characterized by the following features:

- Their information is aimed at middle managers.
- The information is intended to generate reports.
- Reports are predetermined and inflexible.

Decision Support Systems

MIS reports were found to be appropriate for middle managers, but not flexible enough to support many decision-making tasks, particularly those of top-level managers, who required information in less structured form. In the 1970s, interest began to shift to providing better information assistance to top-level managers. The result has been **decision support systems (DSSs).**

Unlike MIS, which tends to produce standard, predetermined reports, DSS is designed to have greater flexibility and be capable of helping managers analyze unstructured kinds of problems. Whereas OIS is oriented toward lower-level managers and MIS toward middle-level managers, DSS is oriented toward top-level managers. (For the record, we should mention that some people consider DSS part of MIS.)

Some characteristics of DSS are as follows:

- Information is oriented toward top managers and executive decision makers.
- DSSs are **interactive**—that is, they are initiated and controlled by the user.
- The systems emphasize flexibility, adaptability, and quick response.

The recent growth in software that is easy to use has greatly facilitated the use of DSS by top-level managers.

Forward Spin

"Forward spin" is not a term encountered often, but it is one of those business jargon phrases that means something—an idea, product, or information—that is not useful yet but will be soon. Perhaps "forward spin" characterizes the information you have learned in this chapter—not yet useful but soon to be.

Useful very soon, in fact: In the next chapter we will begin to put the computer to use in a serious way as a tool for business enterprise.

SUMMARY

- In business management, as well as public administration, some sort of rationality—a system —must be imposed on the process of decision making.
- **A system** is a collection of interrelated parts that work together for a common purpose. Business systems may be enhanced by computer-based information systems.
- A system, for our purposes, has four parts: (1) **inputs**—things that enter the system from the environment; (2) **processor**—the part that operates on the inputs to transform them into something; (3) **outputs**—the products of the processing; (4) **feedback**—communication back to the system. An **IPO chart** (input, processing, output) shows how these parts are related.
- Businesses have two purposes: to make goods and services and to make a profit. These purposes are served by activities that correspond to the four parts of a system: (1) *Input* is the investment in employees, materials, facilities, and money. (2) *Processing* converts the input into a finished product or service and sells it. (3) *Output* is the goods and services produced plus the profit or loss. (4) *Feedback* consists of market forecasts and status reports.
- The four parts of the system constitute the *macro* view. The *micro* view reveals smaller parts, or subsystems. The important subsystems of a business are its four functional areas: (1) **accounting and finance**—concerned with generating and investing capital and with accounting operations; (2) **marketing**—concerned with sales forecasting, advertising, pricing, selling, and logistics; (3) **production**—concerned with purchasing raw materials, inventory control, and production scheduling; (4) **research and development**—concerned with improving products and developing new ones.
- The four functional subsystems of a business are frequently reflected in an **organization chart**—a drawing depicting the formal lines of authority within an organization.
- The three levels of management within each functional area are (1) top, (2) middle, and (3) lower, or supervisory.
- The role of managers is to coordinate the subsystems to produce company products and profits. Decision making is the primary activity of managers, and it occurs in five areas: (1) planning, (2) organizing, (3) controlling, (4) communication, and (5) staffing.
- **Planning** attempts to get the organization from its present position to a better one; it requires setting objectives and developing strategies and policies for achieving them. Planning lays the foundation for the other four management tasks.
- **Organizing** coordinates and integrates all the parts and efforts of the com-

pany; it is the act of making orderly arrangements and structures to best use company resources.

- **Controlling** establishes standards of performance, measures employee results, corrects mistakes, and minimizes deviations from the objectives. The key to control is feedback, which enables managers to head off problems before they become severe.
- **Communicating** is sharing information between people by any means. Communicating may be more important than any of the other four management tasks.
- **Staffing** involves selecting people and training and developing them for their jobs.
- The four parts of a computer system are (1) **hardware**—the machines in the system, such as the keyboard, the video screen, and so on, (2) **software**—the **programs** (step-by-step instructions that direct the computer to perform specific tasks) that run the system, (3) **data**—the raw facts that have not yet been processed into information (raw facts turned into useful facts are called **information**), and (4) people, to make the system work.
- A computer system resembles the IPO chart in that it also involves input, processing, and output. The hardware components of this system are (1) **input units,** which take data in machine-readable form and send it to the (2) **processor,** the central processing unit, a machine with electronic circuitry that converts input data into information and then sends it to (3) **output units,** which make the information available for use.
- Processors contain **primary storage,** which holds data and instructions while they are being worked on by the processor, and **secondary storage,** which consists of devices outside the processor that can store additional data. This storage supplements the primary storage.
- Some of the common input devices and input **media** are the keyboard, magnetic tape, and magnetic disks, both hard disk and flexible disk.
- The **keyboard,** probably the most common input device, is a typewriterlike keyboard of letters, numbers, special characters, and usually some specialized keys. The keyboard usually is connected to a **cathode-ray-tube** (CRT) **screen** (a video screen), and together they are called a **terminal.**
- **Magnetic tape** looks like audio cassette tape, but it comes on a reel.
- **Magnetic disk** is a round platter with a magnetized surface. It may be hard or flexible.
- **Hard disk** is made of rigid metal and coated with ferrous oxide. Hard disks generally come in stacks called **disk packs,** with space between the disks. **Hard disk drives**—machines with a spindle in the middle on which a disk pack can be mounted and rotated at very high speed—are required to record or input data to the central processing unit.

- **Flexible disks,** which are also known as **diskettes** or **floppy disks,** are made of oxide-coated plastic and are used with microcomputers. They require a **floppy disk drive** to translate data on the disk into electronic impulses, which are sent to the central processing unit.
- The processor—the **central processing unit,** or **CPU,** often called the computer's "brain"—has three parts: (1) the control unit, (2) the arithmetic/logic unit, and (3) primary storage.
- The **control unit** contains circuitry that directs the entire computer system to carry out, or execute, the program instructions.
- The **arithmetic/logic unit** contains the electronic circuitry that controls all **arithmetic operations** (addition, subtraction, multiplication, division) and **logical operations** (the three basic comparison operations: equal to, less than, and greater than).
- Primary storage is referred to by a variety of names: **main memory, main storage, internal storage,** and simply **memory.** The main memory holds data and instructions for processing. Its capacity is often expressed by the letter **K** for **kilobyte,** which represents 1024 bytes. A **byte** represents one character of data.
- Secondary storage, or **auxiliary storage,** is outside the processor. The three most common forms of secondary storage are (1) magnetic tape, (2) hard disk, and (3) flexible disk.
- For output, one can use magnetic tape, hard disks, flexible disks, CRT screens, and printers. **Printers** produce printed documents under the control of the computer program. Printers can be **impact printers,** which form images as typewriters do, or they can be **nonimpact printers,** which form images using specially coated papers that respond to electrostatic impulses. Some printers print a character at a time, others a line at a time.
- There are four categories of computers, in order from large to small: (1) supercomputers, (2) mainframes, (3) minicomputers, and (4) microcomputers.
- **Supercomputers,** also called monsters or maxicomputers, are the fastest and most powerful computers. They are principally used for worldwide weather forecasting, weapons research, and other very special applications requiring an enormous number of calculations in a short time.
- **Mainframes,** built before the other computers, are the largest, fastest, and most expensive general-purpose computers. Primary storage can hold around several million characters of information and process around 5 million instructions per second. Mainframes are useful because they can store an enormous amount of data and because they have numerous terminals.
- **Minicomputers** resemble mainframes but are of medium size and speed and cost less. Minicomputers were developed in the late 1960s for special pur-

poses but were later adopted as general-purpose machines by small businesses. They can support several terminals and handle most accounting functions.

- **Microcomputers** are desktop or personal computers. Micros have freed small businesses from relying, for their computer needs, on: (1) **service bureaus**—outside companies that sell standard computer services; (2) **time-sharing services**—outside companies that sell computer time to clients linked by telephone; and (3) purchasing large computers with supporting staffs.
- Before the 1970s, most organizations put their computer facilities and related activities in one location for **centralized data processing.** In the 1970s, the trend was toward **decentralized** or **distributed data processing:** users began to supplement their large, central mainframe computers with a number of minicomputers located in branch offices or other data processing areas. The minicomputers link up to the mainframe, or the **host** computer, by communications lines such as telephone lines.
- Although the mainframe continues to be the mainstay of computing power for large businesses, the microcomputer is having a significant effect on business and is presenting various problems that require well-planned purchasing and training programs to solve.
- The study of how information flows and the creation of better systems of information flow is called **systems analysis and design.** Information flows in several ways: (1) It follows the IPO model in that it comes into the organization as *input* in the form of employees, materials, facilities, and money; it is *processed and stored* in the four functional areas—marketing, accounting and finance, production, and research and development; it is *output* as goods and services and as profit or loss. (2) Within each of the four functional areas, it flows up and down through three levels of managements—top, middle, and lower. (3) People within the three management levels and four functional areas make decisions about planning, organizing, controlling, communicating, and staffing.
- Each of the three management levels should have a centralized business information system, shared by managers in the four functional areas.Three levels of information systems correspond to the three levels of management: (1) for lower-level or supervisory management, operations information systems (OISs); (2) for middle management, management information systems (MISs); (3) for top management, decision support systems (DSSs).
- **Operations information systems (OISs)**—also known as **transaction processing systems** or **electronic data processing systems** and which became popular during the 1950s—are computer-based means of capturing **transactions** (events to be recorded) to be reproduced when necessary. The outputs of a transaction processing system are (1) documents needed to do business, (2)

listings of transactions that have occurred, and (3) electronic records for a corporate data base for later decision making.

- An operations information system is the first information system that a company develops. It concerns the actual operation of the company—standard operations and procedures, particularly accounting operations.
- **Management information systems (MISs),** which were developed during the 1960s, create standard reports that summarize transaction processing data. They are typically developed after operations information systems and have the following characteristics: (1)Their information is aimed at middle managers. (2) The information is intended to generate reports. (3) Reports are predetermined and inflexible.
- **Decision support systems (DSSs)** were developed in the 1970s to assist top-level managers. These systems have greater flexibility and can help analyze unstructured kinds of problems. Some DSS characteristics are as follows: (1) Information is oriented toward top managers and executive decision makers. (2) They are **interactive** (initiated and controlled by the user). (3) They emphasize flexibility, adaptability, and quick response. (4) They accommodate the personal decision-making styles of individual managers.

KEY TERMS

Accounting and finance, p. 58
Arithmetic/logic unit, p. 66
Arithmetic operations, p. 66
Auxiliary storage, p. 66
Byte, p. 66
Cathode-ray-tube (CRT) screen, p. 63
Central processing unit (CPU), p. 66
Centralized data processing, p. 72
Communicating, p. 61
Controlling, p. 61
Control unit, p. 66
CRT terminal, p. 63
Data, p. 61
Decentralized data processing, p. 72
Decision support system (DSS), p. 77
Disk drives, p. 63
Diskettes, p. 63
Disk packs, p. 63
Distributed data processing, p. 72
Electronic data processing system, p. 75
Feedback, p. 57
Flexible disk, p. 63
Floppy disk drive, p. 63
Floppy disk, p. 63
Hard disk, p. 63
Hardware, p. 61
Host, p. 72
Impact printer, p. 69
Information, p. 61
Inputs, p. 57
Input unit, p. 62
Interactive, p. 77
Internal storage, p. 66
Inventory, p. 59
IPO chart, p. 57
Keyboard, p. 63
Kilobyte, p. 66
Logical operations, p. 66
Magnetic disk, p. 63
Magnetic tape, p. 63
Mainframes, pp. 69, 72
Main memory, p. 66
Main storage, p. 66
Management information system (MIS), p. 76
Marketing, p. 58
Media, p. 63
Memory, p. 66
Microcomputer, p. 72
Minicomputer, p. 72

Nonimpact printer, p. 69
Operations information system (OIS), p. 75
Organization chart, p. 59
Organizing, p. 59
Outputs, p. 57
Output unit, p. 62
Planning, p. 59
Primary storage, p. 62, 66
Printer, p. 69
Processor, p. 57, 62
Production, p. 59
Program, p. 61
Research and development, p. 59
Secondary storage, pp. 62, 66
Service bureau, p. 72
Software, p. 61
Staffing, p. 61
Supercomputer, p. 69
System, p. 57
Systems analysis and design, p. 73
Time-sharing service, p. 72
Transaction, p. 75
Transaction processing system, p. 75

REVIEW QUESTIONS

1. Define *system*. Describe the parts of a system. How can a business be described as a system?
2. What are the four subsystems of business?
3. Name the five areas of decision making that are the concern of managers.
4. Discuss the four components that a computer needs to operate.
5. What are the four categories of computers? Compare them.
6. Describe the flow of information within a computer-based information system. What are the three kinds of computer-based information systems and to which levels of management do they correspond?

CASE PROBLEMS

Case 3-1: AirLetter and the Irrational Marketplace

The importance of having ways to systematize business decisions is suggested by the following example of Jim Hanifin, a Boulder, Colorado, businessman who in 1981 began studying the U.S. Postal Service's sorting procedures and came up with a plan for his own overnight airmail delivery service. This was reported in *Inc.* (November 1983).

Calling the service AirLetter, Hanifin struck a partnership deal with Western Airlines, Inc. and hired a designer to make up some stamps commemorating Western's early years of flight. Customers would buy the stamp for $1, slap it on an envelope already bearing a normal 20¢ stamp, and give the envelope to AirLetter. Hanifin's people would then sort the letters and airfreight them via

Western or the most direct route to their destinations, where they would be deposited with the local post office. Second-day delivery was guaranteed—for $1.20.

The idea seemed like a surefire winner. The price, after all, was about $10 to $20 below Federal Express's next day delivery service, and roughly four times cheaper than the Post Office's Express Mail, AirLetter's nearest competitor. In February 1982, Western AirLetter was officially launched with service from Denver to 26 major U.S. population centers. Hanifin sat back and waited for the money to start rolling in.

And waited.

For some reason, the service did not take off, despite an extended local advertising campaign. Finally, a Los Angeles research firm was brought in to find out what was going wrong. Nobody was quite prepared for the answer: The AirLetter had priced itself out of the bottom of the market. Quite simply, consumers thought the $1.20 price was too good to be true. They were, in fact, *10 times* as likely to try the service at $4.25.

Since then, Western AirLetter has raised its prices and begun offering next-day delivery for $6.50. . . .[2]

Your assignment: If you had been running Western AirLetter, do you think an information system could have helped? Which of the departments—Marketing, Accounting and Finance, Production, or Research and Development—might have had need of an information system?

Case 3-2: Careers in the Information Industry

As the preceding three chapters make clear, business enterprise is undergoing a great deal of transition. This is sure to be reflected in the jobs of the future. Writing in *The Futurist* magazine, Washington, D.C. psychologist S. Norman Feingold points out, for example, that 28% of the work force in the United States was in manufacturing in 1980, but in the year 2000 it will probably be only 11% and in the year 2030 only 3%. Today, he says, 55% of the workers in the U.S. are in information industries, and by the end of the century it will probably be 80%. Some of the emerging career areas in the information industry are: operation of information systems—abstractors, indexers, biographic searchers, information brokers; management of information systems—supervisors of facilities that organize knowledge of a specific subject area; design of information systems—programmers who write or modify programs to solve information problems; research and teaching—computational linguists, information scientists, teachers of information science; and consulting or selling of information. "Information is a limitless resource," says Feingold. "Unlike finite industrial resources such as oil, ore, and iron, there is an inexhaustible supply of knowledge, concepts, and ideas as people gain further education."

Your assignment: Based on your reading in the last three chapters, what possible emerging career areas in the information industry or business information processing can you determine that might be of interest to you? Your opinion may be guided by what Feingold has called the following characteristics of an emerging career. An emerging career is one that:

- Has become increasingly visible as a separate career area in recent years.
- Has developed from pre-existing career areas, such as medical care and personal or business services.
- Has become possible because of advances in technology or actual physical changes in our environment. . . .
- Shows growth in numbers of people employed or attending emerging education and training programs.
- Requires skills and training.
- Does not appear and then disappear in a short period of time.[3]

Part 2

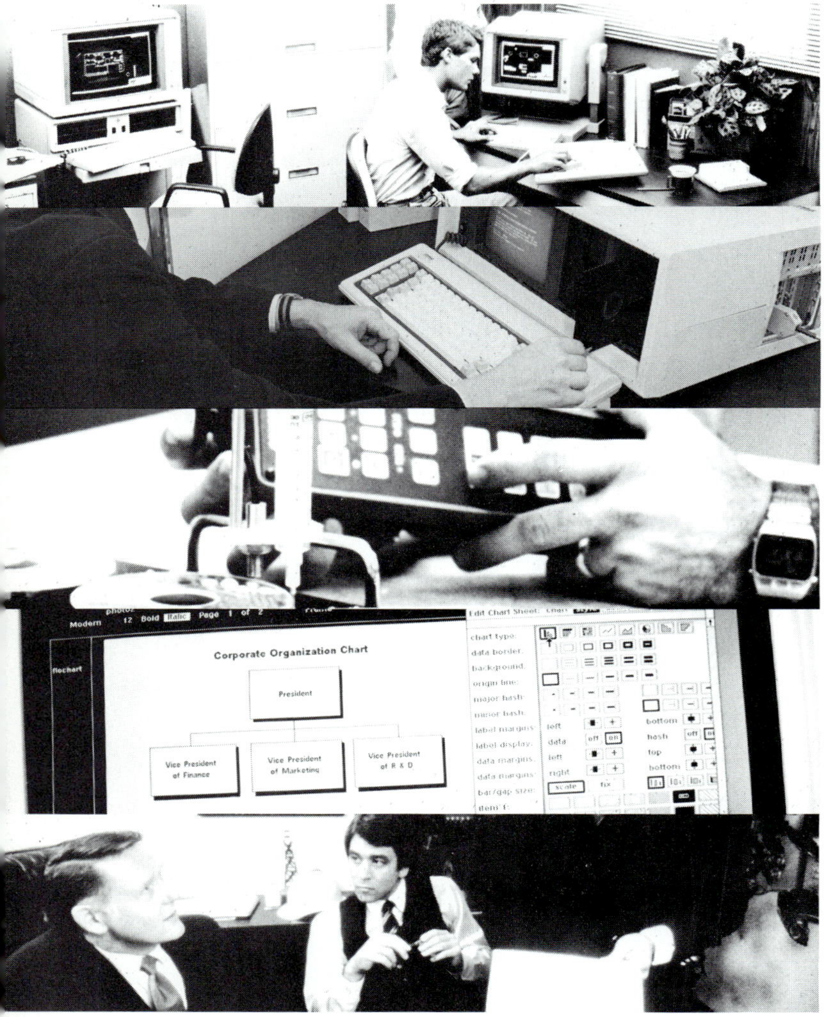
Modern
12 Bold Italic Page 1 of 2
Corporate Organization Chart
President
Vice President of Finance
Vice President of Marketing
Vice President of R & D
Edit Chart Sheet
chart type
data border
background
origin line
major hash
minor hash
label margins
label display
data margins
bar/gap size
left
data
off
on
right
bottom
hash
top
scale
fix

The Uses of Software

Where are you now? Where do you want to be? How do you want to get there? These are the questions business people continually ask.

As we stated earlier, the business of business is dealing with change—and when dealing with computerized information systems, software is the principal means of handling the problems of change. Want to put out a report in a hurry, get comments on it from several departments, and rewrite it in time to get it out on the noon plane tomorrow? Word processing can cut the time by hours or even days. Want to figure out different possibilities for pricing a product, opening a new store, or hiring new staff? You can easily project different alternatives using so-called electronic spreadsheets, as we shall describe. We are rapidly reaching the era of the "easy computer," with software that makes computing truly, in that overused term of the computer industry, "user-friendly."

It is in your interest to get up and running on computers as soon as possible. In the next three chapters, we show you how, beginning first with ready-made software of particular interest to business users, then describing application programming and the programming languages you need to be able to talk about for a career in business.

CHAPTER 4

Personal Software You Can Use

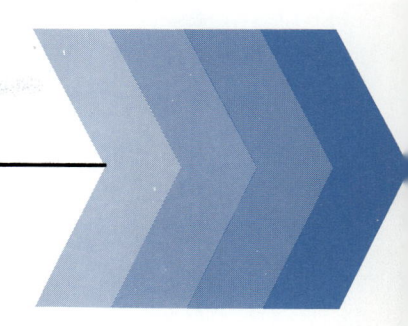

Word Processing, Spreadsheets, File Management, Graphics, and Integrated Packages

P R E V I E W

Ultimately, perhaps, there is no completely escaping boredom. A certain amount of tedium is simply built in to the process of being alive. No doubt this partly explains why people take risks in mountain climbing and sky-diving. It—and the quest for profits—also partly explains why the business entrepreneurial spirit is alive and well: people not only seek fortune and fame, they seek adventure, stimulation, and relief from boredom.

But what is more boring than doing work over or doing work that is not useful because of management inefficiencies? Computers may not necessarily make work more interesting—although in many cases they can indeed do that. However, as the case study on the next page makes clear, computers and software can take a lot of the waste and inefficiency—and thus some of the boredom—out of work.

The Software Explosion

Computers have been around for over 30 years, becoming more powerful on the one hand and smaller and more accessible on the other. Yet for most of their history, computers have remained the province of a priesthood of specialists in corporate data processing departments. Why is it that only recently have we begun to see computers on general managers' desks? The answer is software. The software that makes computers genuinely useful and accessible to nearly everyone has been a fairly recent development.

CASE STUDY: THE BUSINESS OF CHARITY

Making the Most of the Money You Raise

While most of this book is concerned with for-profit organizations, it is interesting to note that many charities and volunteer organizations need to run on sound business principles also.

Even when the donations stop flowing so freely, *someone* has to come up with the financial means to keep the charitable organizations and the political campaigns going. Cutting costs and developing new and innovative ways to seek donations are obvious solutions, but they require a sharp degree of organization.

For an increasing number of people, that organization lies in the form of an affordable personal computer paired with data-base management software. One of the most popular of these combinations is the Apple II computer with PFS:File and PFS:Report software from Software Publishing Corporation of Mountain View, Calif. "Since last April, when we first got our Apple and the PFS software, we've saved around $2000 a month," says Sarah Ball, bookkeeper at the Christian Child Health Foundation in Houston, Texas. "We used to have all our records prepared by an outside computer firm—and believe me, we were paying an arm and a leg for their services."

In an effort to cut those costs, Ball's organization made the decision to buy a computer and bring the record keeping in-house. According to Ball, it was the right move. "We rely almost totally on PFS:File and PFS:Report to keep up with all our activities," she explains, "and it does a better job than any of us could do alone." PFS:File works like an electronic index-card filing system, allowing individual users to design custom forms to meet specific needs; no predefined forms are used. PFS:Report allows the individual to retrieve the information and generate reports comparing a number of variables.

Ball currently uses her Apple/PFS system to maintain records on about 50 adoption cases, 95 foster care families, and a substantial number of children involved in the Foundation's counseling program. She also uses the system to list the organization's board members and staff. "We're a church-affiliated foundation, and we count heavily on financial support from individuals and groups," Ball explains. "PFS helps us keep track of all contributors, so when we need to write a note of thanks or ask for further support, we sit down at the computer, and have the information we need in a matter of minutes."

Having had no previous computer experience, Ball was somewhat anxious about incorporating the new system into the organization's daily activities. "I'm naturally intimidated by machines, so I really had to get my nerve up the first time I sat down with the Apple and PFS software," Ball says. "But after a couple of hours, I felt completely comfortable. I was amazed at how easy it was to operate."

—*Personal Computing*,
November 1983

But what a development! There has been a veritable explosion in software use. As one magazine writer puts it, "The hottest disks these days aren't those in jukeboxes." They are the business software diskettes for microcomputers.

Some computer trade magazines keep a list of business software blockbusters, sort of like the top 40 hits in the record industry. The best sellers are intended for general business applications: word processing, filing and manipulating data, financial modeling, and accounting. Among them are WordStar and VisiCalc, which have each sold half a million copies since their introduction in 1979; SuperCalc, with sales of 250,000; PFS:File, with 130,000; and dBASE II, with 120,000.[1] A list of the top ten hits in business software is shown in Figure 4-1.

Software is developed by three different sources:

- **Internal programmers,** people employed by companies to do such tasks as developing payroll programs. The demand for experienced programmers is high and is expected to continue.
- **Software consultants,** also known as third-party suppliers—freelancers or employees of consulting firms who can bring a corporate client certain types of expertise or offer temporary personnel who can bring solutions to the client's programming problems (and who do not cost the client in fringe benefits).
- **Packaged software manufacturers,** who develop programs in accounting, payroll, inventory management, and the like, that are not tailored to the requirements of any particular client but are available "off the shelf" for anyone to use. Examples of such developers—often called "publishers"—of software for microcomputers are MicroPro, publisher of WordStar, and Lotus Development, publisher of Lotus 1-2-3.

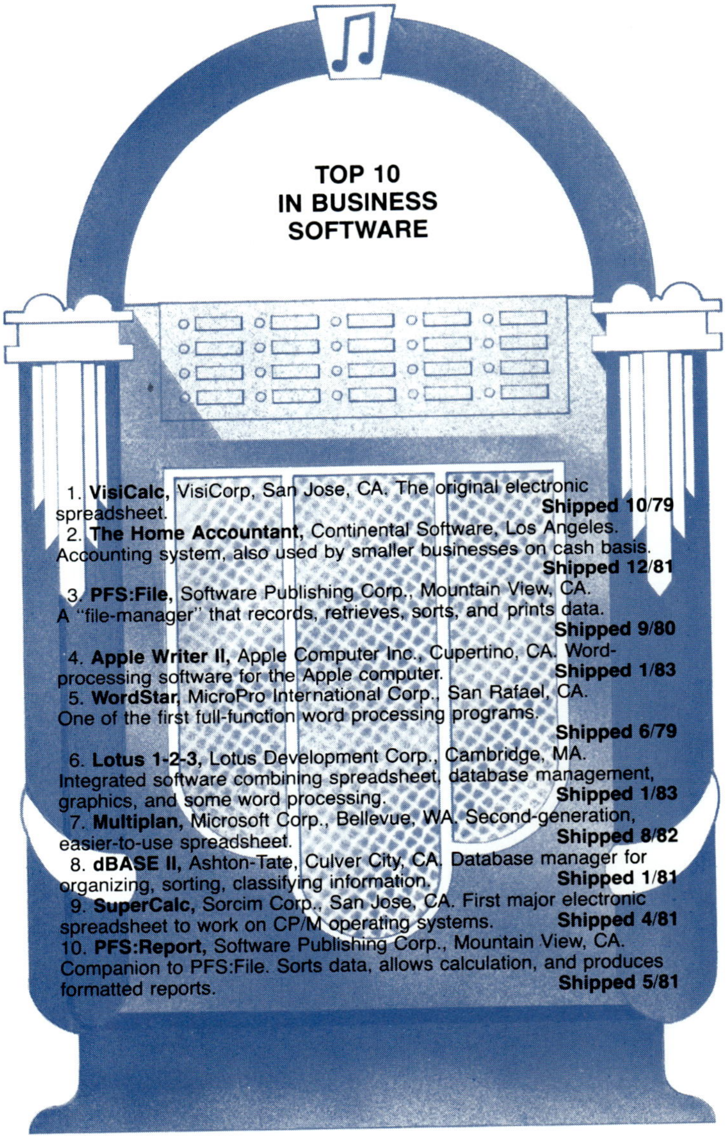
TOP 10
IN BUSINESS
SOFTWARE
1. **VisiCalc,** VisiCorp, San Jose, CA. The original electronic spreadsheet. **Shipped 10/79**
2. **The Home Accountant,** Continental Software, Los Angeles. Accounting system, also used by smaller businesses on cash basis. **Shipped 12/81**
3. **PFS:File,** Software Publishing Corp., Mountain View, CA. A "file-manager" that records, retrieves, sorts, and prints data. **Shipped 9/80**
4. **Apple Writer II,** Apple Computer Inc., Cupertino, CA. Word-processing software for the Apple computer. **Shipped 1/83**
5. **WordStar,** MicroPro International Corp., San Rafael, CA. One of the first full-function word processing programs. **Shipped 6/79**
6. **Lotus 1-2-3,** Lotus Development Corp., Cambridge, MA. Integrated software combining spreadsheet, database management, graphics, and some word processing. **Shipped 1/83**
7. **Multiplan,** Microsoft Corp., Bellevue, WA. Second-generation, easier-to-use spreadsheet. **Shipped 8/82**
8. **dBASE II,** Ashton-Tate, Culver City, CA. Database manager for organizing, sorting, classifying information. **Shipped 1/81**
9. **SuperCalc,** Sorcim Corp., San Jose, CA. First major electronic spreadsheet to work on CP/M operating systems. **Shipped 4/81**
10. **PFS:Report,** Software Publishing Corp., Mountain View, CA. Companion to PFS:File. Sorts data, allows calculation, and produces formatted reports. **Shipped 5/81**

Figure 4-1 Top 10 in business software. Whereas home computer-game best-seller lists tend to vary from month to month, this Top 10 list of business software sales compiled by *Inc.* magazine tends to feature the same golden oldies. This list is based on data for the first six months of 1983. It is drawn from information provided by Al Tommervik, publisher of Softalk Publishing Inc. (*Softalk* magazine and *Softalk for the IBM Personal Computer*); Egil Juliussen, chairman of Future Computing Inc.; Bob Leff, president of Softsel Computer Products Inc. (the country's largest distributor of software for personal computers); and Bill Slapin, publisher of *Computer Merchandising* magazine.

The software packages are the ones making up the best-seller lists mentioned above. Their advantage over internally developed and third-party–developed software is that they are generally widely tested and are mass produced, thus being relatively inexpensive. However, their flexibility is limited and modifications can be costly if not impossible.

For the general manager, however, packaged software is not merely the wave of the future; indeed, the wave has already washed well up on the beach, as the above sales figures show. The software market for microcomputers is expected to boom fourfold from 1984 to 1987, when total sales are predicted to exceed $10 billion. Clearly, this means that we will all be seeing packaged software used increasingly in a variety of businesses. This means that it will be more important for you to learn how to use packaged software than to learn to do programming.

Let us, then, take a look at those software packages you will probably find useful in your college and professional careers to create documents, analyze data, and file information. You may also find some of these useful for your personal needs on a home computer. We will examine four software packages that appear on the best-seller "jukebox" shown in Figure 4-1, namely:

- Word processing, using *WordStar*
- Financial spreadsheets, using *VisiCalc*
- File management, using *PFS:File*
- Graphics, using *Lotus 1-2-3*

Word Processing: The Electric Pencil and Eraser

Without a word processor, you cannot imagine that you need one. With one, you cannot imagine doing without it.

As we saw in Chapter 2, a **word processor** includes the following basic components: a computer, a keyboard, a CRT screen, a printer, and a word processing program. Some word processors also have a **mouse,** a device that you can roll on a table top to move a cursor on the CRT screen. A word processor can be a machine that does nothing else (a dedicated word processor) or it can be a computer (typically a microcomputer) that can do word processing in addition to other tasks.

The word processing software is designed to allow the creation, editing, formatting, storing, and printing of text. There are numerous commercial word processing systems in which computer hardware and software are bundled together as a unit; the most well known of these are the IBM Displaywriter, the Wang Wangwriter, and the DEC Decmate. For personal computers or microcomputers, word processing soft-

The Mouse that Rolled

In using a computer, it helps to know how to type, since most *data*—the words in your report or numbers in your spreadsheet, for example—are entered through the keys on a keyboard. In our examples in the text we have also been showing you how to enter certain *commands* through the keyboard. However, with the right kind of computer, a great many commands can be entered using a marvelous device called a mouse.

We are not talking about biotechnology here. The mouse is not a rodent but a small, movable, hand-held device that can be rolled on a table or desk top and in turn will manipulate a graphic pointer on the CRT screen. The pointer can be used to activate commands such as "Delete" or "Save" without one's having to use the keyboard. The mouse can also be used to pick out certain objects and information and go directly to the place on the screen where you wish to insert a word or other data.

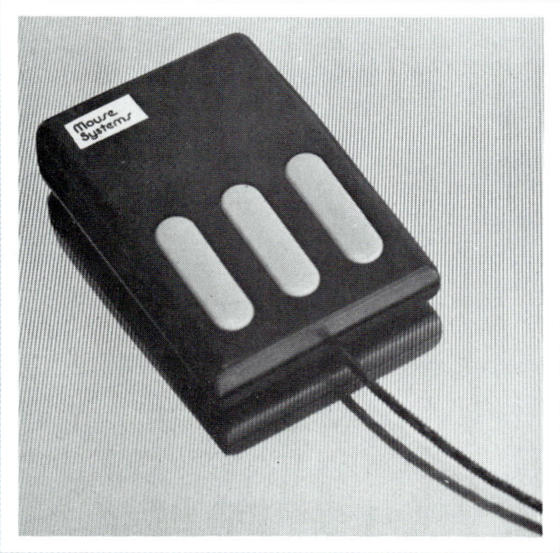
Mouse Systems

Why do people call it a mouse? When it was first invented in the 1960s, it had three protruding control buttons that looked like mouse ears and a connecting cable to the computer that looked like a mouse tail. Now, with Apple's Macintosh personal computer, for example, the mouse has one button.

What is the benefit of a mouse? Daniel Farber, writing about the mouse on the Macintosh, describes it this way:

> Using a mouse draws on an innate human skill: pointing. It's as natural as throwing a ball, but more importantly, it increases your productivity and frees you from the constraints of the keyboard. Because the mouse minimizes use of the keyboard, you can concentrate on what's happening on the screen, and you won't have to memorize or look up all sorts of keyboard command codes to do your work. For tasks that don't require extensive typing, a mouse in the hand is an efficient device.
>
> —Daniel Farber, "A Mouse in the Hand," *Macworld*, February 1984

ware packages are sold separately, usually recorded on a floppy disk; some of the best known of these are WordStar, Apple Writer II, MultiMate, Magic Wand, EasyWriter, PFS:Write, Peachtext, VisiWord, Microsoft Word, Electric Pencil, Scripsit, The Bank Street Writer, ScreenWriter II, Word Handler II, and Leading Edge Word Processing. Let us give an example of how word processing works, using a program often used for business purposes, WordStar.

Writing with Word Processing: Getting a Job in the Film Industry

BUSTER KEAT
THE GENER
LAS FAIRBANK

Let us pretend you are about to finish school and are seeking that first career job. This is no summer job search. You are going to take some risks and try to find the job you want. Indeed, you are going to try to find a job in one of the most competitive, highly paid industries there is—the movie industry.

This is not going to be a job in front of the camera, however. You are looking for something on the business side. You have read that over 75% of the feature films made in the industry today never turn a profit, so that it is crucial to keep track of costs and expenses on individual pictures. Maybe, you think, with your business background, the industry could use your help. You decide to compose a job-inquiry letter to the head of a film production company, using your WordStar word processing program on your microcomputer (see Figure 4-2).

You load WordStar into your machine by inserting the WordStar diskette into one of the two disk drives *(drive A)* and a blank diskette into the other *(drive B)*. You turn on the computer—an Apple IIe, let us say.

Figure 4-2 An Apple IIe microcomputer. This popular personal computer is often used for tasks such as word processing. (To run WordStar, however, it requires a special circuit board.) Note that there are two disk drives and a printer, in addition to the keyboard and video screen.

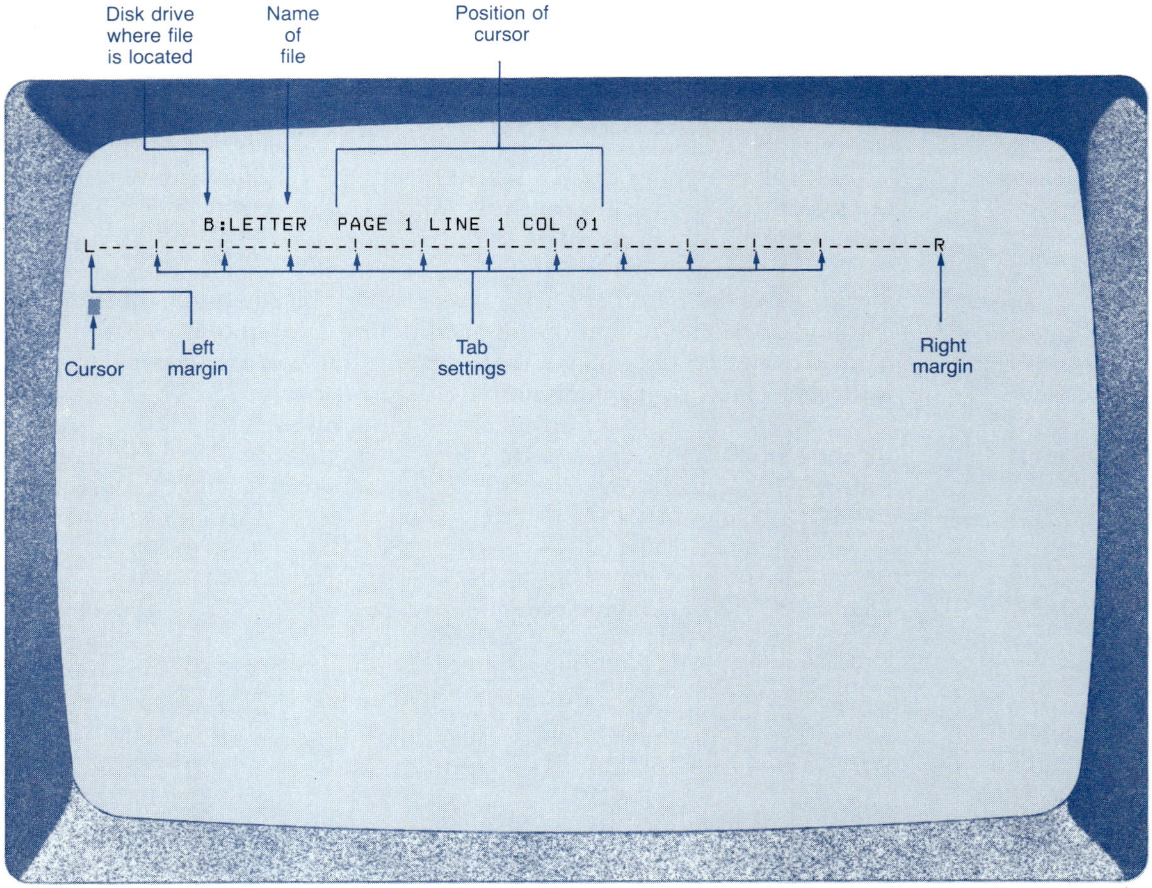
Disk drive where file is located
Name of file
Position of cursor
B:LETTER PAGE 1 LINE 1 COL 01
Cursor
Left margin
Tab settings
Right margin

Figure 4-3 WordStar format. These notations appear at the top of the screen: L stands for left margin, R for right margin. The exclamation points (!) in between represent tab settings, for use in constructing tables. (WordStar also has a menu or list of word processing commands on the screen, which is not shown here.)

Even before you start typing, WordStar automatically sets the margins and tabs, as shown in Figure 4-3. Notice at the far left side of the illustration the **cursor,** a rectangular mark that acts as a pointer and indicates the location of the next character to be typed. Using a combination of keys on the keyboard, the cursor can be moved anywhere on the screen. At the top of the screen appear certain notations: a letter (A or B) indicating which disk drive holds the file or diskette on which you are writing your letter, the name of your file, and the page, line, and column in the letter or manuscript where the cursor currently appears.

A **file,** incidentally, is anything you store as a unit, like a file in a filing cabinet. In WordStar, you create or get into a file with two keystrokes.

Let us now begin the process of writing the letter.

Creating Text. You can create a rough draft of your letter by simply typing it on the keyboard, watching the text appear on the screen. You will no doubt find that typing in WordStar is faster than it is on a typewriter, since you need not hit a carriage return key; any word that crosses the right-hand margin is automatically moved to the left on the next line down—a feature called **automatic carriage return** or **word wrap.** You will also find that you need not be concerned about making a few typing errors, as we will explain. Your first draft of the letter is shown in double-spaced form in Figure 4-4.

Editing and Formatting Text. Word processing is not magic, but it almost feels that way when it comes to correcting typographical errors. Notice, for instance, in the first line the error "discruss"; the word is easily changed to "discuss" by repositioning the cursor close by the "r" and pressing the DELETE key to remove it. Whole words and phrases can also be removed; the words "part-time" can be deleted from the first line with little effort.

Inserting material is also easily accomplished. You decide an introductory touch of humility is in order, and so you add the phrase "taking the liberty of" to the first sentence, without having to retype the entire letter. Some word processing programs, including WordStar, have an **overtyping** feature, whereby you can simply type over what you have just written. The inserting and deleting functions are probably the most useful features of a word processor.

Moving words, phrases, and other material within the text is performed so easily as to have no comparison with the same task on a regular typewriter. You decide, for instance, that the next-to-last paragraph makes a better conclusion to the letter, and in ten seconds this is done. This rearrangement feature is known as a **cut and paste** or **block move** feature and is probably the second-most-used feature of a word processor.

Perhaps you have a tendency to transpose letters as you type, as in the case of "yuo" for "you." In this case, you can use the **search and replace** function, in which the program asks you what words you want to search for and replace, you indicate the error and replacement, and then the push of a few buttons lets the machine go through the entire document and make the change.

All these editing changes are shown in the right-hand portion of Figure 4-4.

It is also easy to change the format or appearance of the text, as

Mr. R. J. Elliott
President
Starfire Film Production Company
1 Sam Goldwyn Boulevard
Century City, California 90067

8060 East Lewis Avenue
West Milford, New Jersey 07480

March 2, 1986

Dear Mr. Elliott:

I am writing to you to discruss the possibility of part-time employment in your office in a business position. I believe you will find my background in marketing, communications, and administration has provided me with exceptional skills for assisting yuo in making day-to-day management decisions.

As the enclosed resume shows, I have a particularly strong accounting background, which yuo may find useful in helping yuo meet the requirements of government tax and payroll reporting, in keeping good accounting records, and in identifying all the real costs of films produced by your firm.

If my qualifications seem of interest to you, I would welcome the opportunity to come to your offices for an interview.

Because of my previous jobs in sales, I believe I would also be able to communicate well with film crews, cast, film laboratories, distributors, and others with whom yuo must deal on financial matters.

Sincerely yours,

[Your name]

Enclosure

8060 East Lewis Avenue
West Milford, New Jersey 07480

March 2, 1986

Mr. R. J. Elliott
President
Starfire Film Production Company
1 Sam Goldwyn Boulevard
Century City, California 90067

Dear Mr. Elliott:

I am taking the liberty of writing to you to discuss the possibility of employment in your company in a business position. I believe you will find my background in marketing, communications, and administration has provided me with exceptional skills for assisting you in making day-to-day management decisions.

As the enclosed resume shows, I have a particularly strong accounting background, which you may find useful in helping your company meet the requirements of government tax and payroll reporting, in keeping good accounting records, and in identifying all the real costs of films produced by your firm.

Because of my previous jobs in sales, I would also be able to communicate well with film crews, cast, film laboratories, distributors, and others with whom you must deal on financial matters.

If my qualifications seem of interest to you, I would welcome the opportunity to come to your office for an interview.

Sincerely,

[Your name]

Enclosure

Figure 4-4 Writing a letter on a word processor. *Opposite page:* This is how the first draft of a letter might look using a WordStar word processing program. *Above:* This is the final draft, after editing and reformatting.

shown in the right half of Figure 4-4. **Text formatting** is concerned with the look of your letter. It includes underlining, margin setting, line centering, and **justification**—evening up the ends of the lines like the type in this book (as opposed to the "ragged right" look of typed manuscripts). You decide that for your final draft you will single-space rather than double-space the letter. You also want to remove the indented paragraphs. These changes are accomplished with just a few keystrokes. Finally, you decide to change the width of the page margins from 1 inch to $1\frac{1}{2}$ inches, using right and left margin-set commands.

Storing and Printing Text. A few simple keystrokes, and *voila!*—you have saved or stored your letter on a diskette for later use (including applying for other jobs, revising only the address and salutation). You then print out your letter on paper on the printer—again by just pressing a couple of keys. If you decide the printed letter still does not seem right, you can simply throw it away, call up the letter onto the screen from the diskette, re-edit it, and print it out again. Perhaps you can begin to see how word processing can make you a *better* writer: the inclination you might feel working at a typewriter to let small flaws go by because you cannot bear the thought of retyping an entire page is not such an issue here because the flaws are so easily and quickly corrected.

What to Look for in Word Processing Programs

As mentioned, there are numerous word processing programs and the costs vary dramatically. Some of the desirable features are as follows:

- **Screen oriented.** Whenever you enter or edit text, you can see the changes directly on the screen.
- **Live screen.** Corrections can be made to the text immediately as you see it on the screen. You do not have to shift the word processor into a special editing mode.
- **80-column screen.** Some word processors allow only 40 characters (columns) to be displayed on a line on the screen, which will not resemble what the page looks like when printed out. If you want to see how the page will look while you are typing it, a screen allowing 80 characters is necessary.
- **Menus and Help options.** A **menu** is a list of commands that you can type in through the keyboard to make editing, formatting, and other changes. Commands may be few on a simple word processing program such as those intended for children (The Bank Street Writer), but complex on a program like WordStar, in which case a menu that appears on the screen is useful. A **Help option** is also useful when you do not know what to do next on the system.
- **Backup capability.** Some word processing systems have a "failsafe" capability, so that in case you erase part of a file by mistake there is a backup file you can use.

- **Form letter generator or "mail-merge."** This feature allows you to merge files, such as names and addresses from mailing lists along with a letter, so that you can produce letters that appear to be individually typed.
- **Spelling checker.** Some word processing programs can be linked to a proofreading program consisting of a dictionary of correctly spelled words (SpellStar, which works with WordStar, consists of 20,000 words).
- **Memory-based versus disk-based.** Some word processing systems will only be able to type documents that are shorter than a certain length because most of the program is in the computer memory. Others hold most of the program as well as the document you are typing on disk. The first method is faster, because all the information is in the computer's memory, but disk-based systems allow storage of longer documents.

Some word processing programs offer a feature that consists of a split screen, called **windowing,** which allows you to look at one file while you are working on another. As we will see, windowing has become a principal feature of integrated packages—software that combines word processing along with other capabilities such as financial modeling and graphics. We shall discuss integrated packages at the end of this chapter.

Financial Spreadsheets: Nimble Number Manipulation

What is a **spreadsheet?** Traditionally, it was simply a blank sheet of paper divided into rows and columns which accountants and financial analysts used to produce a wide range of reports, from income and balance sheets to cash budget plans. The tyranny of the spreadsheet has been described by one writer thus:

> In the old days . . . a financial spreadsheet was manufactured out of actual paper and ink. It often measured two feet across and was unlikely to remain long on top of a desk without having coffee spilled on it. Against its typically dull-green Eye-Ease background were crosshatched some 7,500 spaces into which accountants, bookkeepers, treasurers, and business planners squeezed their numbers, tiny oblong by tiny oblong, pencil by resharpened pencil. It was white-collar sweatshop work; a manager performing a five-year projection involving even a handful of products could count on many weekends in the office and wastebaskets full of jettisoned calculations.[2]

All that began to change in October 1979, when a program known as VisiCalc, an electronic spreadsheet, was shipped to customers. *(See box.)* Since then, there have emerged perhaps five dozen such electronic financial programs.

FLASHBACK

The Invention of VisiCalc

VisiCalc is probably the most widely imitated software in business, with an estimated 60 clones (nicknamed "VisiClones" and "CalcAlikes"), according to its maker's chairman, Dan Fylstra, 32, of VisiCorp in San Jose, California. Fylstra and a friend, with an initial investment of $500, founded VisiCorp in 1978 under the name of Personal Software as a project for a marketing course while graduate students at the Harvard Business School. VisiCorp's first and main product is VisiCalc, the electronic spreadsheet for personal computers.

Fylstra did not invent VisiCalc. The idea for the spreadsheet occurred to another student, Daniel Bricklin, now 31, while staring at columns of numbers on a blackboard during classes at the Harvard Business School. In those days, when a figure in one column of such a spreadsheet was changed, all the rest had to be recomputed and changed by hand. "Just one mistake on my calculator," Bricklin recalled for *Time* magazine, "and I would end up moaning, 'My God, I got the whole series of numbers wrong!' "

Dan Fylstra of VisiCorp.

Daniel Bricklin of Software Arts.

During the winter of 1978 he and another student, Robert Frankston, now 33, both M.I.T. graduates, worked long hours developing their VisiCalc (visible calculator) spreadsheet.

However, when the pair attempted to market the new software, it received a lukewarm reception. It was then that Fylstra entered the picture and began an energetic marketing campaign, eventually turning it into the most popular small business program. Personal Software moved to California's Silicon Valley in 1979. The change in the company name to VisiCorp has been accompanied by the introduction of other Visiproducts, such as VisiSchedule and VisiPlot. Of particular interest is Visi On, an integrated program that shares commands and information easily and uses a "mouse," a tabletop movable device that allows users to communicate more easily than through a keyboard.

In 1983, however, VisiCorp's fortunes started to slip. VisiCalc sales withered as easier-to-use products such as Lotus 1-2-3 began to appear. VisiCorp was paying royalties for VisiCalc to

Software Arts, which had been formed by Bricklin, but the relationship between the companies soured, and the two became engaged in a deep legal battle. While Software Arts began marketing a new version of VisiCalc, in August 1984 VisiCorp announced it sold most of the rights to Visi On—perhaps because it needed to raise cash.

Perhaps particularly interesting is that VisiCalc alone is credited with selling thousands of microcomputers for business uses. Indeed, it has been observed that the electronic spreadsheet marked the first legitimate business application of what until then had been a machine for hobbyists and game players. Because VisiCalc was originally programmed to operate on an Apple II computer, this one piece of software alone had an enormous impact on altering the Apple image from a game computer to a business computer. VisiCalc has since been followed by SuperCalc, which owed its popularity to the fact that it could run on several more machines besides the Apple, and Multiplan and Lotus 1-2-3, both of which are "second generation" and much easier to use.

The reason for the popularity of electronic spreadsheets is their simplicity, flexibility, and, most important, their "what-if" capability. The "what-if" part can be demonstrated if, for example, you are thinking about buying a new car and are wondering whether you can afford the monthly payments. With an electronic spreadsheet you can vary the number of possibilities—the total price of the car (what if it is $15,000? what if $10,000?), the size of the down payment ($2000? or $3000?), the number of months over which to pay off the loan covering the balance (36 months? or 48?), and the interest rate on the loan (13%? 14%?). By holding three of these factors constant and varying the fourth (the down payment, say), you can figure out the different possible monthly payments you could make.

This is the kind of financial analysis that goes on all the time in business, not only by accountants, but by others as well. Spreadsheets are used for sales projections, expense reports, income statement and balance sheet preparation, and nearly any other numerical problem that used to be attacked with pencil and paper.

Let us demonstrate in detail how a spreadsheet works, using VisiCalc, the oldest and probably best-known of these programs.

"What If . . . ?": Calculating the Affordable Apartment

You got the job, and you are moving out to southern California to work for Starfire!

Based on this offer, you decide to see what you can afford in the way of an apartment. You also decide to continue your schooling, probably at night, and so you need to allow for tuition and other school expenses. Thus, you need to figure out your projected income versus your projected

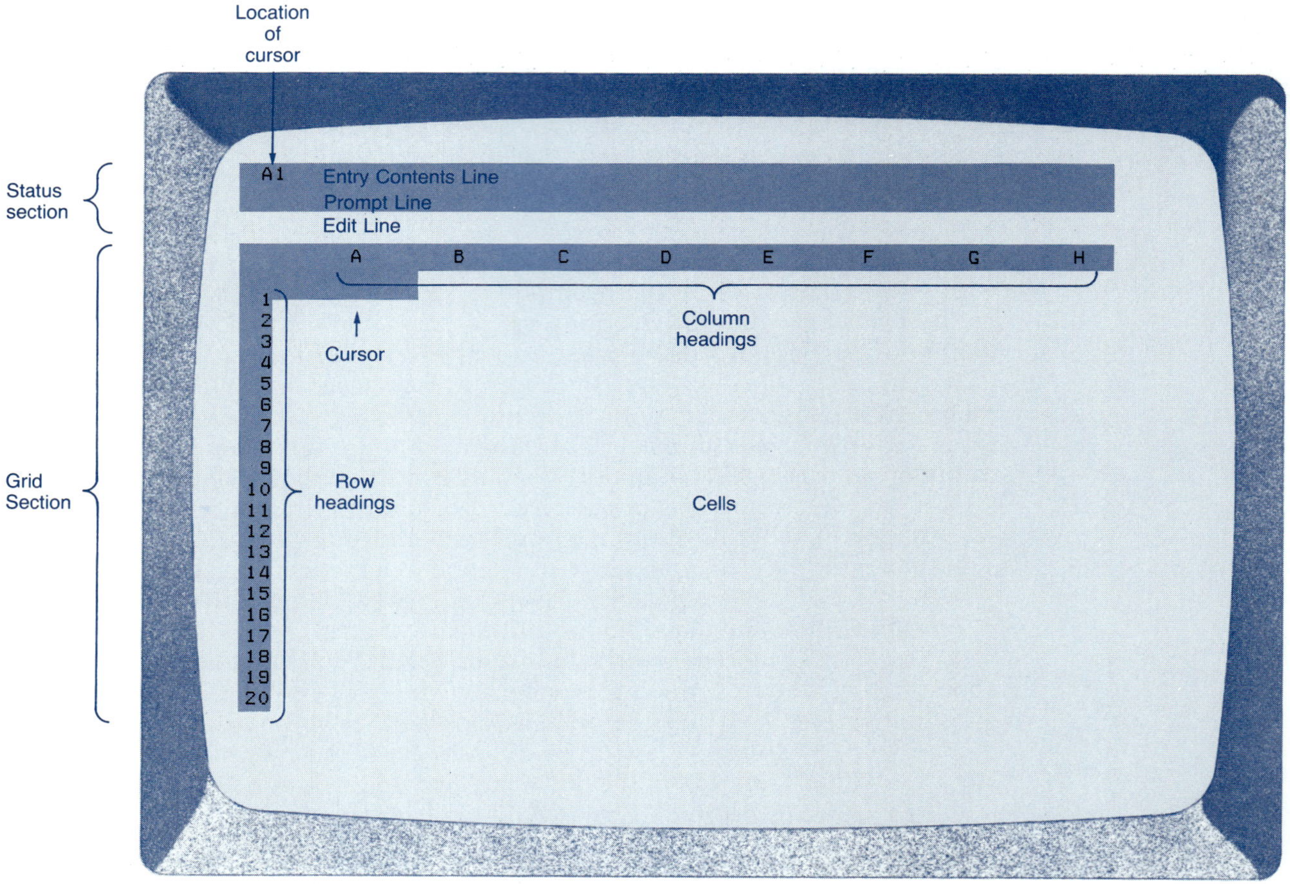
Location of cursor
Status section
Grid Section
A1
Entry Contents Line
Prompt Line
Edit Line
A
B
C
D
E
F
G
H
1
2
3
4
5
6
7
8
9
10
11
12
13
14
15
16
17
18
19
20
Cursor
Column headings
Row headings
Cells

Figure 4-5 A spreadsheet screen. *Left:* Screen format for VisiCalc spreadsheet before any data has been entered. *Right:* Example of how an electronic spreadsheet can be expanded to several screens, thus giving the user more rows and columns, even if not all of them can be viewed at one time.

expenses. What better instrument to use than a spreadsheet such as VisiCalc?

Screen Format. Notice, in the left half of Figure 4-5, how VisiCalc looks on your video screen. It consists of a status section and a grid section. The *status section* consists of the top three lines: the entry contents line (displays information about the format of the cell and what the cell contains), the prompt line (describes the options in a sequence of commands), and the edit line (displays each character as it is typed). The

Figure 4-5 (continued).

grid section consists of the *column* headings across the top (A, B, and so on), the *row* headings down the left side (1, 2, 3, and so on), and the *cells* in the middle. The cells are invisible here (unlike the little rectangles on a paper spreadsheet), but each is capable of holding nine spaces or digits, as shown in Figure 4-5 by the location of the cursor in the upper left corner. Each cell can be designated by its coordinate of column letter and row number; here the cursor is in column A row 1, or cell A1.

Actually, the VisiCalc screen shown in the left half of Figure 4-5 is just a small part of the entire spreadsheet available to you. As the right part of Figure 4-5 shows, the spreadsheet can be expanded from 21 rows and 8 columns to 254 rows and 63 columns. (The Lotus 1-2-3 electronic spreadsheet, which its manufacturer claims is the largest, is made up of 2048 rows by 256 columns—equivalent to 524,288 cells. With this you

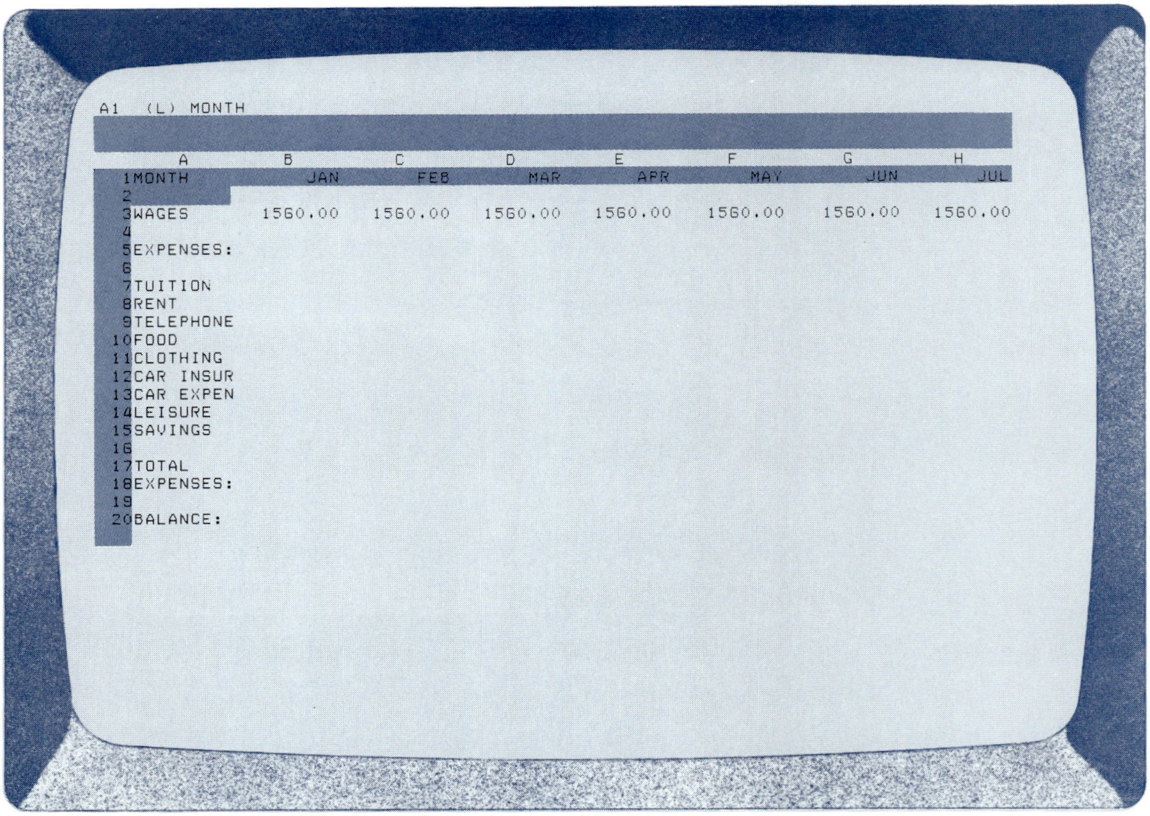
A1 (L) MONTH
A B C D E F G H
1MONTH JAN FEB MAR APR MAY JUN JUL
2
3WAGES 1560.00 1560.00 1560.00 1560.00 1560.00 1560.00 1560.00
4
5EXPENSES:
6
7TUITION
8RENT
9TELEPHONE
10FOOD
11CLOTHING
12CAR INSUR
13CAR EXPEN
14LEISURE
15SAVINGS
16
17TOTAL
18EXPENSES:
19
20BALANCE:

Figure 4-6 Spreadsheet screen with labels and values. The labels consist of months at the head of the columns and the wages, types of expenses, and totals to the right of the rows. The values are numbers entered on the spreadsheet—in this case, the values for wages.

should be able to express all the possible monthly car payments of all the different new-car models in the world.)

Labels and Values. Column and row headings are known as *labels.* Labels must begin with a letter or word (not a number). In your case, you want to project your income and expenses over a seven-month period. Thus, as Figure 4-6 shows, you type months for labels as column headings and types of expenses and income for row headings. To enter labels (or any other information) on the spreadsheet, you use the keyboard to move the cursor to the appropriate place and type in whatever you need to type. Correcting information is done the same way; it is like erasing and rewriting with pencil and eraser on paper.

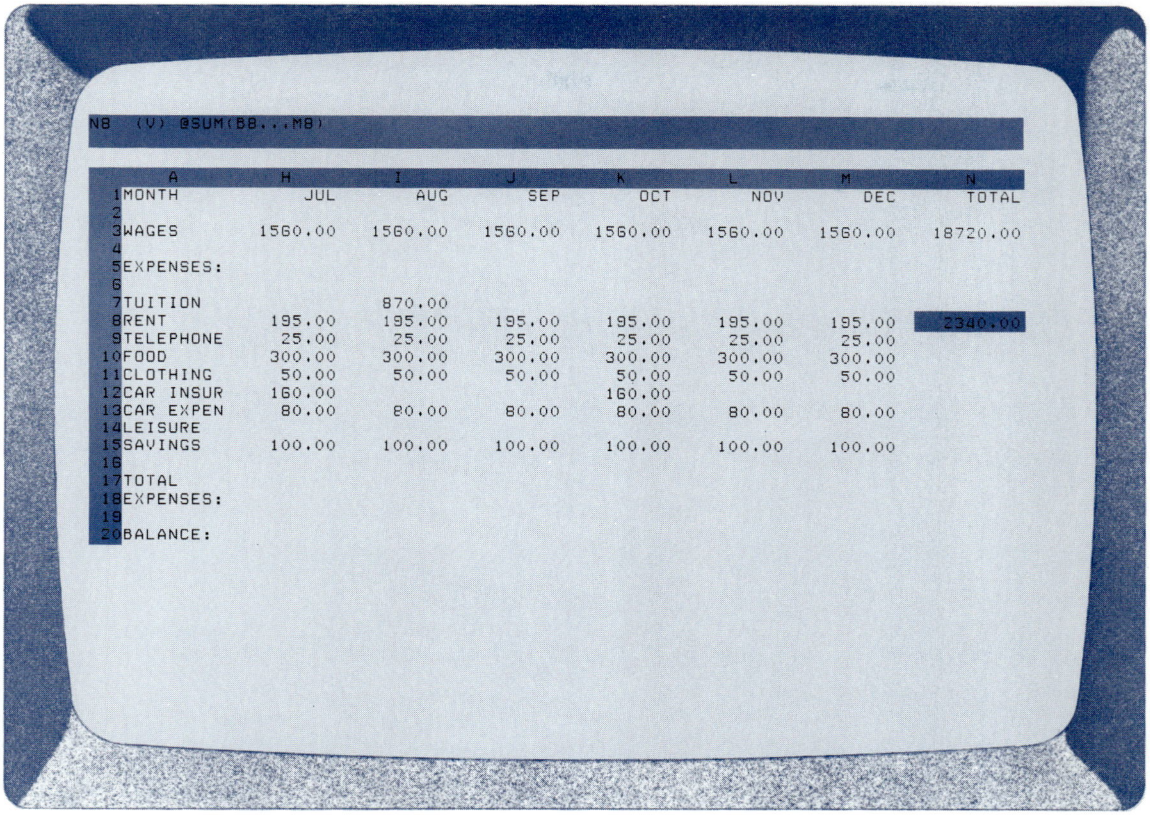

N8 (V) @SUM(B8...M8)

	A	H	I	J	K	L	M	N
1	MONTH	JUL	AUG	SEP	OCT	NOV	DEC	TOTAL
2								
3	WAGES	1560.00	1560.00	1560.00	1560.00	1560.00	1560.00	18720.00
4								
5	EXPENSES:							
6								
7	TUITION		870.00					
8	RENT	195.00	195.00	195.00	195.00	195.00	195.00	2340.00
9	TELEPHONE	25.00	25.00	25.00	25.00	25.00	25.00	
10	FOOD	300.00	300.00	300.00	300.00	300.00	300.00	
11	CLOTHING	50.00	50.00	50.00	50.00	50.00	50.00	
12	CAR INSUR	160.00			160.00			
13	CAR EXPEN	80.00	80.00	80.00	80.00	80.00	80.00	
14	LEISURE							
15	SAVINGS	100.00	100.00	100.00	100.00	100.00	100.00	
16								
17	TOTAL							
18	EXPENSES:							
19								
20	BALANCE:							

Figure 4-7 Calculating formulas. The formula is given on the top line; the result is indicated at the far right, column N, row 8.

A *value* is a number contained in a cell. As Figure 4-6 shows, row 3, Wages, expresses the values for what you will earn in the months of January through December. (Although at this point the screen you are viewing does not extend past July, the values from August through December are still there.) You also insert values for your expenses; Figure 4-7 shows the expenses for the last six months of the year.

Formulas. Now you can begin to run some computations. Looking at row 8, Rent, we see that you have budgeted \$195 a month for rent each month for a twelve-month period. To calculate what the total will be for the entire year—as shown in cell N8 in Figure 4-7—we use the formula expressed on the top line: N8 (V) @SUM(B8 . . . M8). This translates as: "In cell N8 give us the sum of all the values, (V), in cells B8 through M8." The result, indicated by the cursor in cell N8, is \$2340. The totals of other expenses are computed in a similar manner.

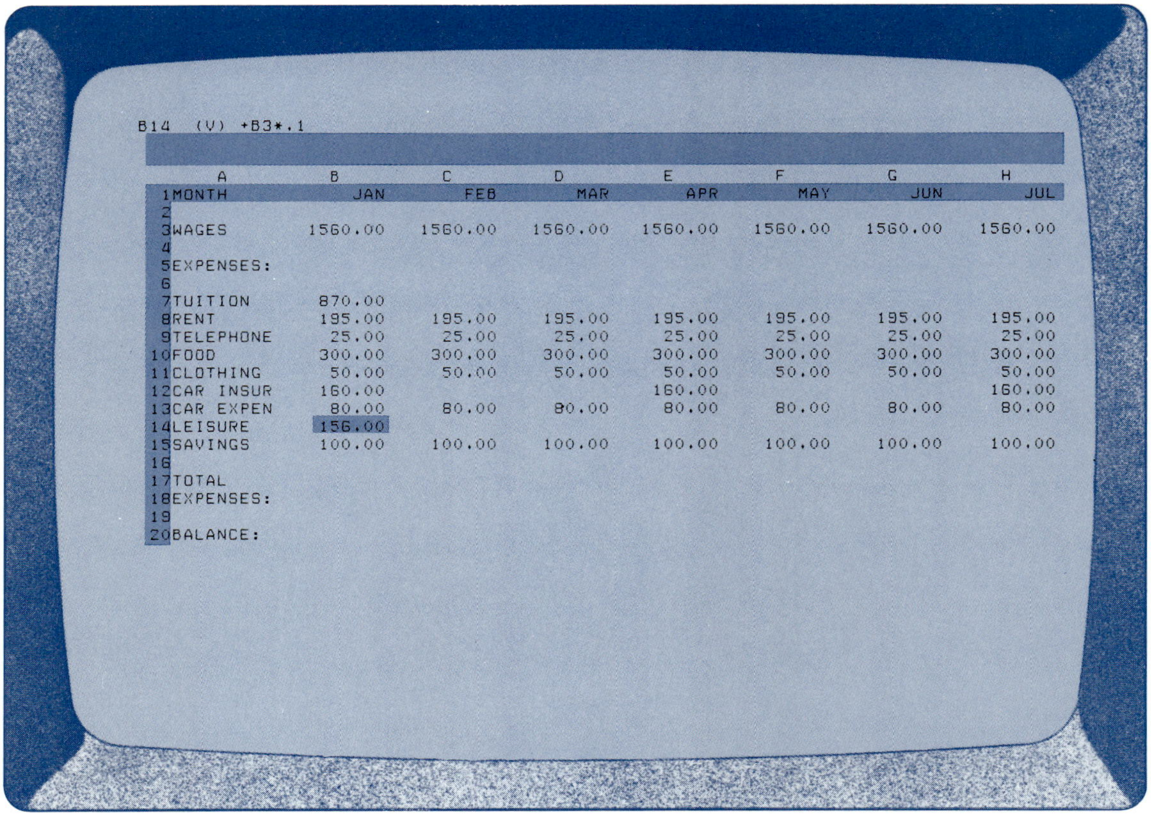
B14 (V) +B3*.1
A B C D E F G H
1MONTH JAN FEB MAR APR MAY JUN JUL
2
3WAGES 1560.00 1560.00 1560.00 1560.00 1560.00 1560.00 1560.00
4
5EXPENSES:
6
7TUITION 870.00
8RENT 195.00 195.00 195.00 195.00 195.00 195.00 195.00
9TELEPHONE 25.00 25.00 25.00 25.00 25.00 25.00 25.00
10FOOD 300.00 300.00 300.00 300.00 300.00 300.00 300.00
11CLOTHING 50.00 50.00 50.00 50.00 50.00 50.00 50.00
12CAR INSUR 160.00 160.00 160.00
13CAR EXPEN 80.00 80.00 80.00 80.00 80.00 80.00 80.00
14LEISURE 156.00
15SAVINGS 100.00 100.00 100.00 100.00 100.00 100.00 100.00
16
17TOTAL
18EXPENSES:
19
20BALANCE:

Figure 4-8 Calculating another formula.
This shows the formula for computing leisure-time expenses in January.

Another formula: Let us say you have arbitrarily decided to budget 10% of each month's wages for leisure-time expenses. (You want to go see a few of those films whose business aspects you will be handling for Starfire.) You place the cursor in cell B14, as shown in Figure 4-8, and type the formula expressed above on the entry contents line: B14 (V) +B3*.1. This translates as: "In cell B14 give us the value, (V), which is the total of the value in cell B3 multiplied by 10%." (The sign "*" means "multiplied by." The number ".1" is the same as ".10" or 10%; the zero has been omitted.) So $156.00 is the amount that you have allowed yourself to spend on leisure-time activities in January. The leisure budgets for the other 11 months are calculated by the same formula.

Of course, you are also interested in how you are going to come out

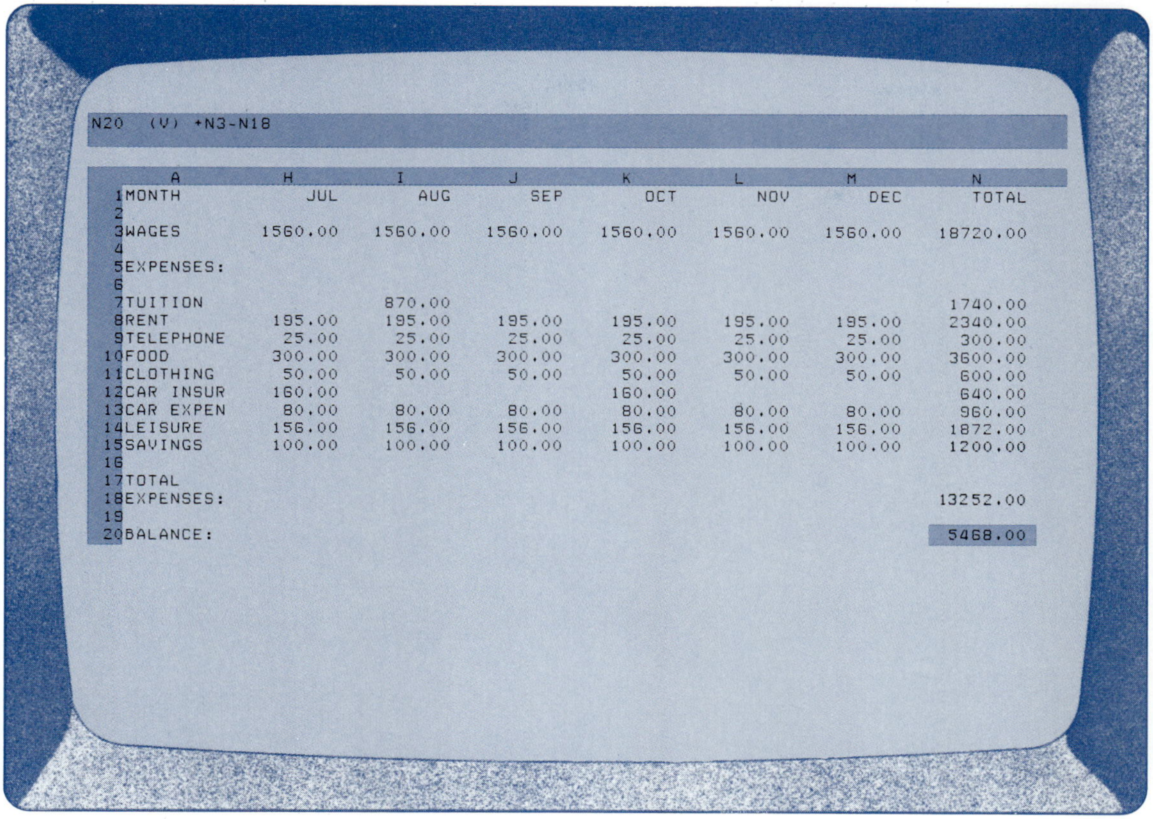
N20 (V) +N3-N18
A H I J K L M N
1MONTH JUL AUG SEP OCT NOV DEC TOTAL
2
3WAGES 1560.00 1560.00 1560.00 1560.00 1560.00 1560.00 18720.00
4
5EXPENSES:
6
7TUITION 870.00 1740.00
8RENT 195.00 195.00 195.00 195.00 195.00 195.00 2340.00
9TELEPHONE 25.00 25.00 25.00 25.00 25.00 25.00 300.00
10FOOD 300.00 300.00 300.00 300.00 300.00 300.00 3600.00
11CLOTHING 50.00 50.00 50.00 50.00 50.00 50.00 600.00
12CAR INSUR 160.00 160.00 640.00
13CAR EXPEN 80.00 80.00 80.00 80.00 80.00 80.00 960.00
14LEISURE 156.00 156.00 156.00 156.00 156.00 156.00 1872.00
15SAVINGS 100.00 100.00 100.00 100.00 100.00 100.00 1200.00
16
17TOTAL
18EXPENSES: 13252.00
19
20BALANCE: 5468.00

Figure 4-9 **Ahead or behind?** This screen shows that you will come out ahead at the end of the year in income over expenses.

at the end of the year, whether you are ahead or behind financially. You can do this by calculating your balance, as shown in Figure 4-9, which means subtracting your total expenses from your total wages. The formula for this, given on the entry contents line, is N20 (V) +N3−N18, which means: "For the value in cell N20, calculate the value of N3 (which is total wages) minus the value of N18 (which is total expenses)." You are pleased to see, of course, that you are coming out ahead, with $5468.00 at the end of the year—a nice cushion in case things fall through at Starfire.

Split Screens. Once we have inserted all of the monthly wages and expenses, our interest naturally tends to focus on the yearly totals. It

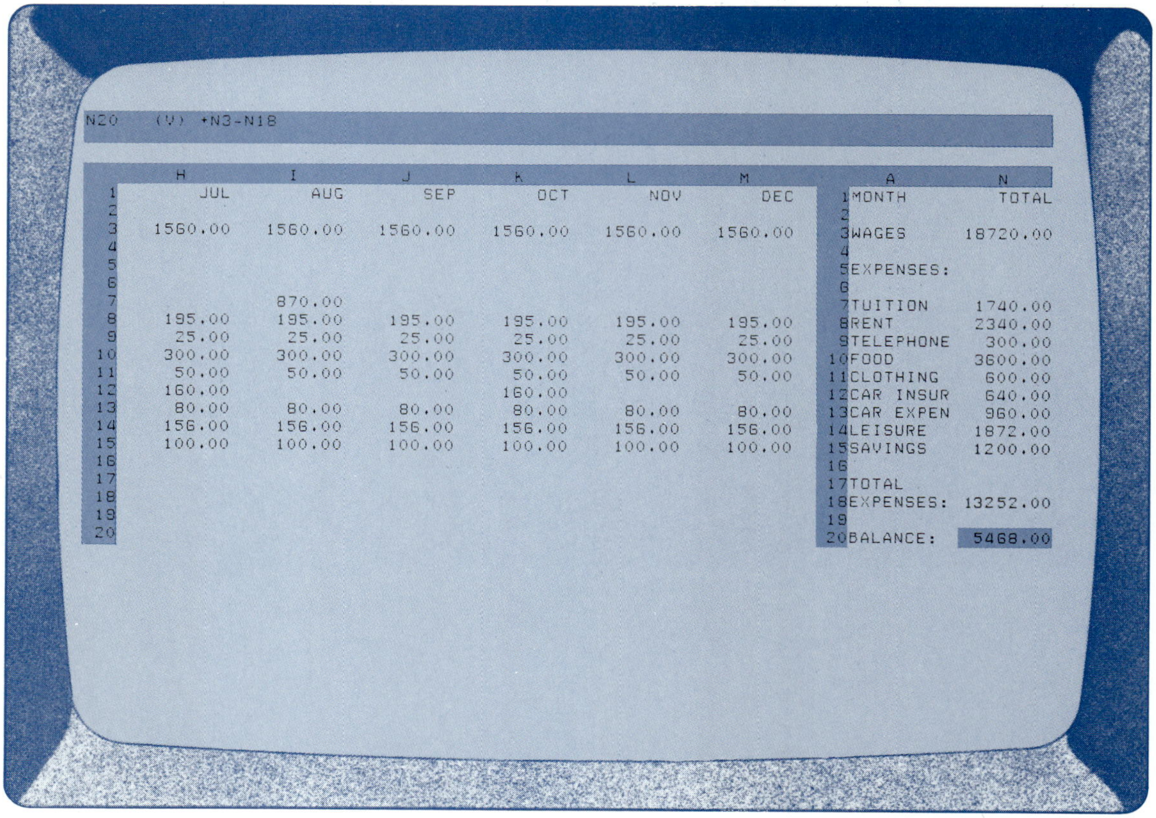

N20 (V) +N3-N18

	H	I	J	K	L	M	A	N
1	JUL	AUG	SEP	OCT	NOV	DEC	MONTH	TOTAL
2								
3	1560.00	1560.00	1560.00	1560.00	1560.00	1560.00	WAGES	18720.00
4								
5							EXPENSES:	
6								
7		870.00					TUITION	1740.00
8	195.00	195.00	195.00	195.00	195.00	195.00	RENT	2340.00
9	25.00	25.00	25.00	25.00	25.00	25.00	TELEPHONE	300.00
10	300.00	300.00	300.00	300.00	300.00	300.00	FOOD	3600.00
11	50.00	50.00	50.00	50.00	50.00	50.00	CLOTHING	600.00
12	160.00			160.00			CAR INSUR	640.00
13	80.00	80.00	80.00	80.00	80.00	80.00	CAR EXPEN	960.00
14	156.00	156.00	156.00	156.00	156.00	156.00	LEISURE	1872.00
15	100.00	100.00	100.00	100.00	100.00	100.00	SAVINGS	1200.00
16								
17							TOTAL	
18							EXPENSES:	13252.00
19								
20							BALANCE:	5468.00

Figure 4-10 **Split screen.** Column A, containing the row labels, has been positioned next to column N, the totals column, for ease in identifying final results.

would be more convenient and easier to read if the row labels (column A) were right next to the row totals (column N). To see both the first column and the last column at the same time you need to split the screen. This is shown in Figure 4-10, where both columns A and N appear together at the right.

"What-If" Analysis. Now let us try the feature that has made VisiCalc the best-seller that it is—the ability to change figures to see what will happen.

After talking to your friend John, who once lived in Los Angeles, you

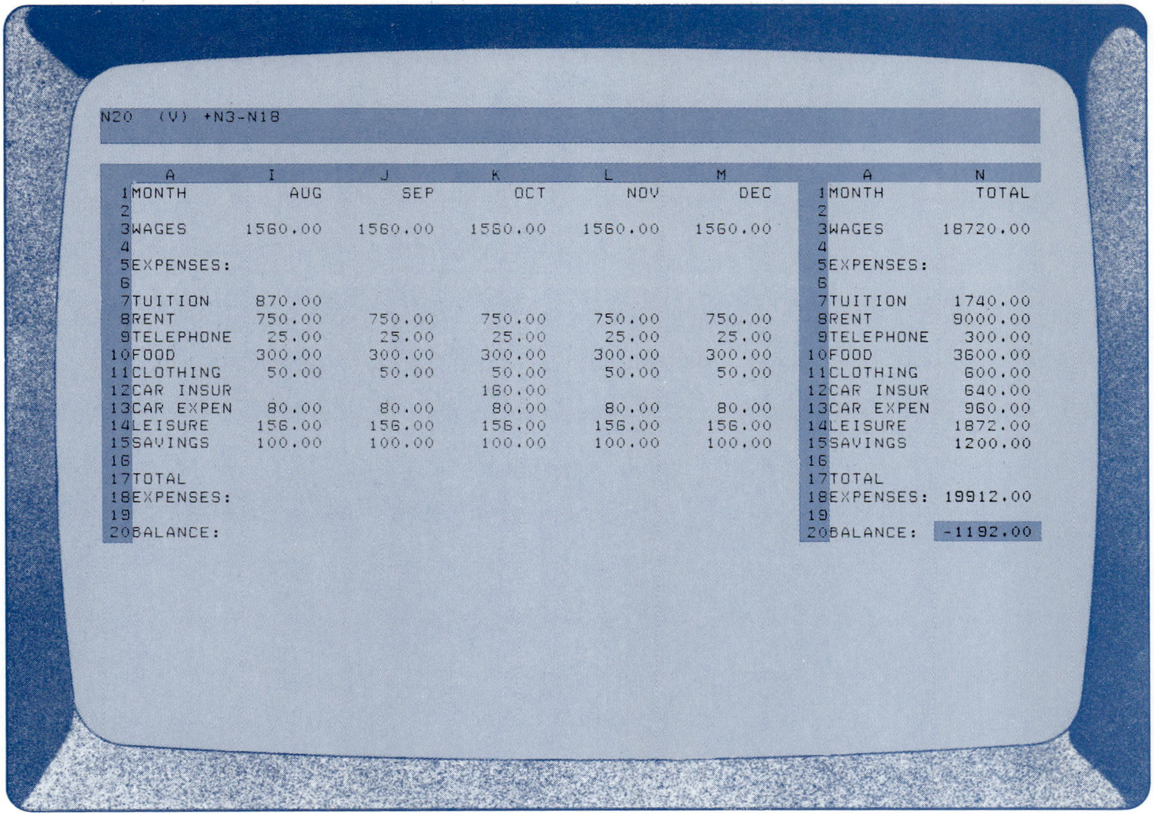

N20 (V) +N3-N18

	A	I	J	K	L	M		A	N
1	MONTH	AUG	SEP	OCT	NOV	DEC	1	MONTH	TOTAL
2							2		
3	WAGES	1560.00	1560.00	1560.00	1560.00	1560.00	3	WAGES	18720.00
4							4		
5	EXPENSES:						5	EXPENSES:	
6							6		
7	TUITION	870.00					7	TUITION	1740.00
8	RENT	750.00	750.00	750.00	750.00	750.00	8	RENT	9000.00
9	TELEPHONE	25.00	25.00	25.00	25.00	25.00	9	TELEPHONE	300.00
10	FOOD	300.00	300.00	300.00	300.00	300.00	10	FOOD	3600.00
11	CLOTHING	50.00	50.00	50.00	50.00	50.00	11	CLOTHING	600.00
12	CAR INSUR			160.00			12	CAR INSUR	640.00
13	CAR EXPEN	80.00	80.00	80.00	80.00	80.00	13	CAR EXPEN	960.00
14	LEISURE	156.00	156.00	156.00	156.00	156.00	14	LEISURE	1872.00
15	SAVINGS	100.00	100.00	100.00	100.00	100.00	15	SAVINGS	1200.00
16							16		
17	TOTAL						17	TOTAL	
18	EXPENSES:						18	EXPENSES:	19912.00
19							19		
20	BALANCE:						20	BALANCE:	-1192.00

Figure 4-11 **"What if. . .?"** What if the rent were higher? A rent of \$750 a month (row 8) yields a deficit for the year. (Figure continued, p. 112.)

are convinced that your original estimate of \$195 per month for rent is much too low. You want to revise your estimate to \$750 per month. Now, you ask, "Can I afford it?"

Look at the first part of Figure 4-11 (page 111). You have changed all the values on row 8, Rent, to \$750 each month. VisiCalc recalculates your entire financial picture almost immediately. Unfortunately, as cell N20 shows, this kind of rent is too much: it puts you in the hole \$1192.00 for the year. It looks like you will not be able to live that well. You try a monthly rent of \$500 instead. As the second part of Figure 4-11 (page 112) shows, this works out better: you come out with \$1808.00 left over for the year.

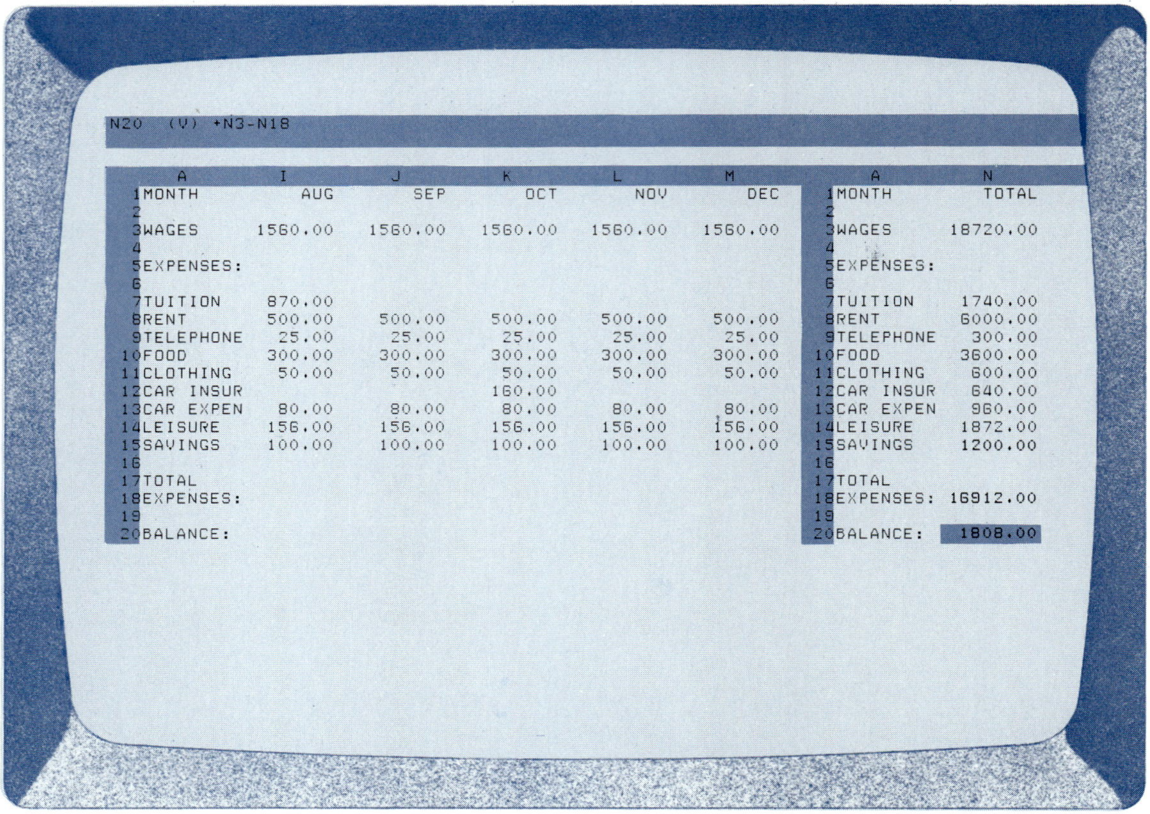

N20 (V) +N3-N18

	A	I	J	K	L	M
1	MONTH	AUG	SEP	OCT	NOV	DEC
2						
3	WAGES	1560.00	1560.00	1560.00	1560.00	1560.00
4						
5	EXPENSES:					
6						
7	TUITION	870.00				
8	RENT	500.00	500.00	500.00	500.00	500.00
9	TELEPHONE	25.00	25.00	25.00	25.00	25.00
10	FOOD	300.00	300.00	300.00	300.00	300.00
11	CLOTHING	50.00	50.00	50.00	50.00	50.00
12	CAR INSUR			160.00		
13	CAR EXPEN	80.00	80.00	80.00	80.00	80.00
14	LEISURE	156.00	156.00	156.00	156.00	156.00
15	SAVINGS	100.00	100.00	100.00	100.00	100.00
16						
17	TOTAL					
18	EXPENSES:					
19						
20	BALANCE:					

	A	N
1	MONTH	TOTAL
2		
3	WAGES	18720.00
4		
5	EXPENSES:	
6		
7	TUITION	1740.00
8	RENT	6000.00
9	TELEPHONE	300.00
10	FOOD	3600.00
11	CLOTHING	600.00
12	CAR INSUR	640.00
13	CAR EXPEN	960.00
14	LEISURE	1872.00
15	SAVINGS	1200.00
16		
17	TOTAL	
18	EXPENSES:	16912.00
19		
20	BALANCE:	1808.00

Figure 4-11 (continued). A rent of $500 a month still allows a surplus overall for the year.

Adding and Deleting Rows and Columns. A surprise—your parents have decided that, now that you have a job, it is time for you to pick up the car loan payments that they have been paying for until now. VisiCalc allows you to add this new expense to the budget, inserting additional rows and (if necessary) columns, using just three keystrokes. Deleting rows and columns is also easily accomplished.

What to Look for in Spreadsheets

As mentioned, there are numerous spreadsheet programs and they differ greatly in cost and performance. Some guidelines as to what to look for are as follows:

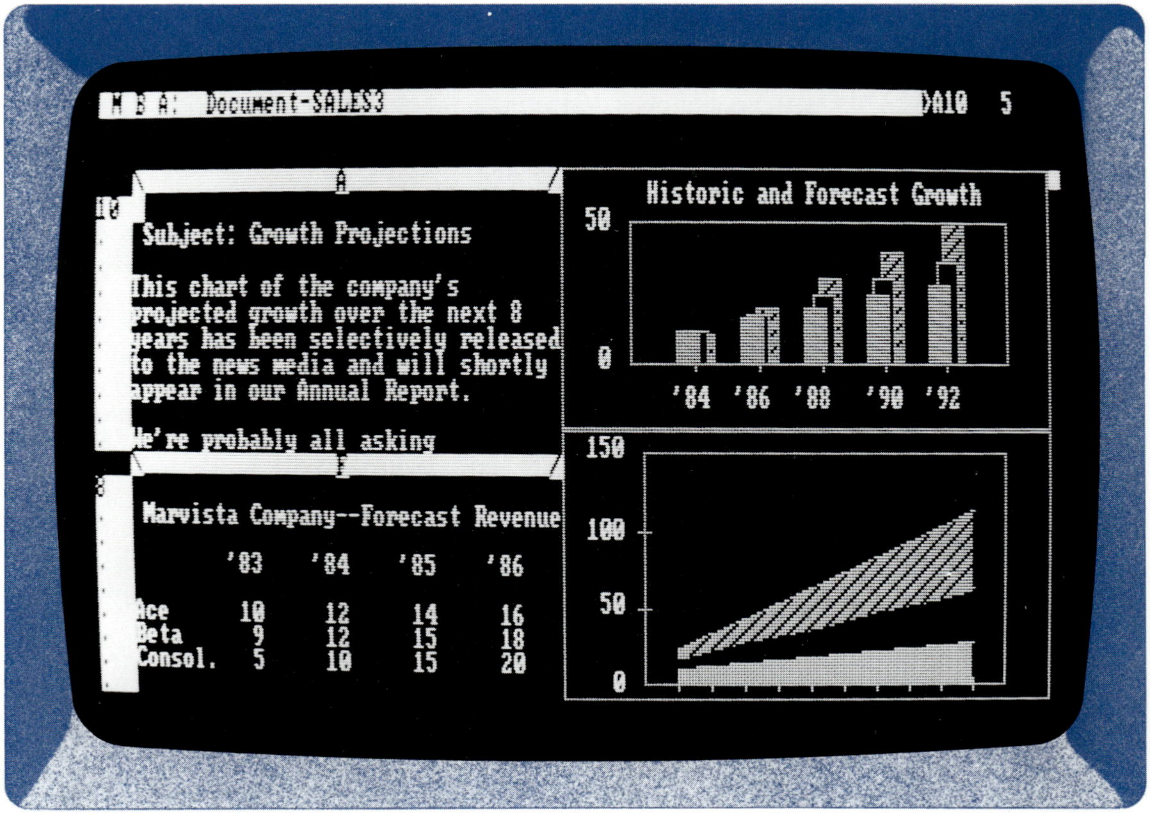
Document-SALES3
A10 5
Subject: Growth Projections
This chart of the company's
projected growth over the next 8
years has been selectively released
to the news media and will shortly
appear in our Annual Report.
We're probably all asking
Marvista Company--Forecast Revenue
'83 '84 '85 '86
Ace 10 12 14 16
Beta 9 12 15 18
Consol. 5 10 15 20
Historic and Forecast Growth
50
0
'84 '86 '88 '90 '92
150
100
50
0

Figure 4-12 We do windows. Some software, such as the Context MBA, allows "windows," or sectors from different programs, to be visible at the same time.

- **Screen format:** The spreadsheet must allow clear presentation and insertion of labels for rows and columns and must allow information appearing on the screen to be edited easily.
- **Size of spreadsheet:** As mentioned, some spreadsheets are larger than others. However, some spreadsheets cannot be used all at once because of the limitations of the computer's memory. Some have more cells, but, on the other hand, some have cells that can hold more characters. (Context MBA holds 502 characters in each cell, as opposed to 240 for Lotus 1-2-3.)
- **Multiple windows:** Some spreadsheets allow for multiple windows. The MBA spreadsheet, for example, can show graphs in three win-

dows with values changing as data is changed in a table in the fourth window. Figure 4-12 shows windows.

- **Calculation flexibility:** A spreadsheet should be able to work for both an engineer and a financial analyst or other specialist. That is, the equations used to define cell relationships should include not only the basic arithmetic operations but also any specialized formulas.
- **File access:** The spreadsheet should be able to interact with files from other programs. Often you may wish to display an entire spreadsheet in a report, but this is best accomplished if the spreadsheet and word processing files can be combined.
- **Good documentation: Documentation** is computer industry jargon for instruction manuals. The bane of the industry is that, in the past, documentation has been badly written or otherwise inadequate. Although spreadsheets are easy to use, clear and complete documentation helps. Valuable parts of the documentation are tutorials, sample problems, discussion of various applications, and reference sections.

File Management and Data Base Management

We have considered two of the most common business activities—creating documents (word processing) and analyzing and summarizing data (spreadsheets). Now let us consider the third: filing information.

Individuals seem to be able to get along for years with their important records—birth certificates, tax records, and so on—simply thrown in a box in the back of a closet, although, of course, it is somewhat time-consuming to dig the records up when they are needed. Businesses, however, cannot operate this way. Imagine, after all, the number of irate customers, employees, suppliers, and tax collectors if such things as customer accounts, payroll records, supplier invoices, and past income tax statements were left in disarray. The success of a business is quite often linked to its having orderly and accessible files, as we saw in the case of the Yanello & Flippen law firm in Chapter 1.

File folders might help you organize that material in your closet, but manual filing systems are often inefficient for business files because they occupy too much space, are difficult to organize, and are not always easily accessible (a file may be located in the marketing department, for instance, but the sales and engineering departments may need it also). Instead, files are often computerized. Programs designed to assist in this filing task are called **data base managers** or **data base management sys-**

tems, which you will often see expressed in management literature and software ads as the common abbreviation **DBMS.**

A data base has become a key concept in business and will become even more so in the years ahead. A **data base** is defined as a collection of information. More specifically, it is a collection of *integrated* data that can be used for a variety of applications.

It has been said that a data base management system is to text what an electronic spreadsheet is to numbers. With some types of computerized filing systems, you can put in whatever information you need to file and update—say, all customer orders with amounts and dates—and later pull it out in different ways. Some filing software allows you just to feed in data however you see fit, then retrieve it and combine it for display on the screen and printing out according to how you want it. For instance, you could make a list of all apartment possibilities in southern California (based on a reading of the for-rent ads in several editions of the *Los Angeles Times* in your college library). For each apartment you could include zip code, how long ago the ad ran, and whether the landlord requires up-front payment of security deposits and first and last months' rent (Figure 4-13). You could then rank the apartments according to how inexpensive the initial outlay would be (Figure 4-14), their closeness to your job (based on zip code), or how recently the ad ran. You could also pull out all apartments based on one key variable, such as all apartments in Sherman Oaks.

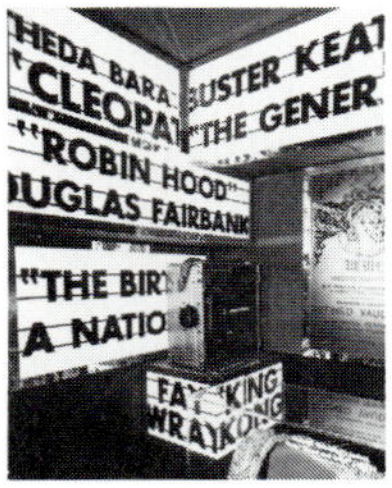
HEDA BARA
CLEOPAT
USTER KEAT
THE GENER
"ROBIN HOOD"
UGLAS FAIRBANK
"THE BIR
A NATIO

A sales representative could find another use for such an electronic filing system, putting all customer orders in with amounts and dates and then, right before the next trip to New Orleans, say, getting a printout that listed all customers in that city who had made purchases within the last year, spent more than $1000 in a single order, and ranked by total orders. This way he or she could organize the New Orleans trip according to which customers were worth spending the most time seeing.

Computer Graphics: Picture This!

What is the most effective way to communicate information and ideas for decision making? Graphics, says one 1981 study (see Figure 4-15, pages 118–119). According to a survey by the Wharton Applied Research Center at the University of Pennsylvania, we retain only 10% of information we hear but 50% of information presented with visual aids.

Maybe you already sense this intuitively just because you know what it is like to live in the television age. But imagine being a manager grappling with a computer printout of numbers late at night, trying to make sense out of them, and you can probably understand why business

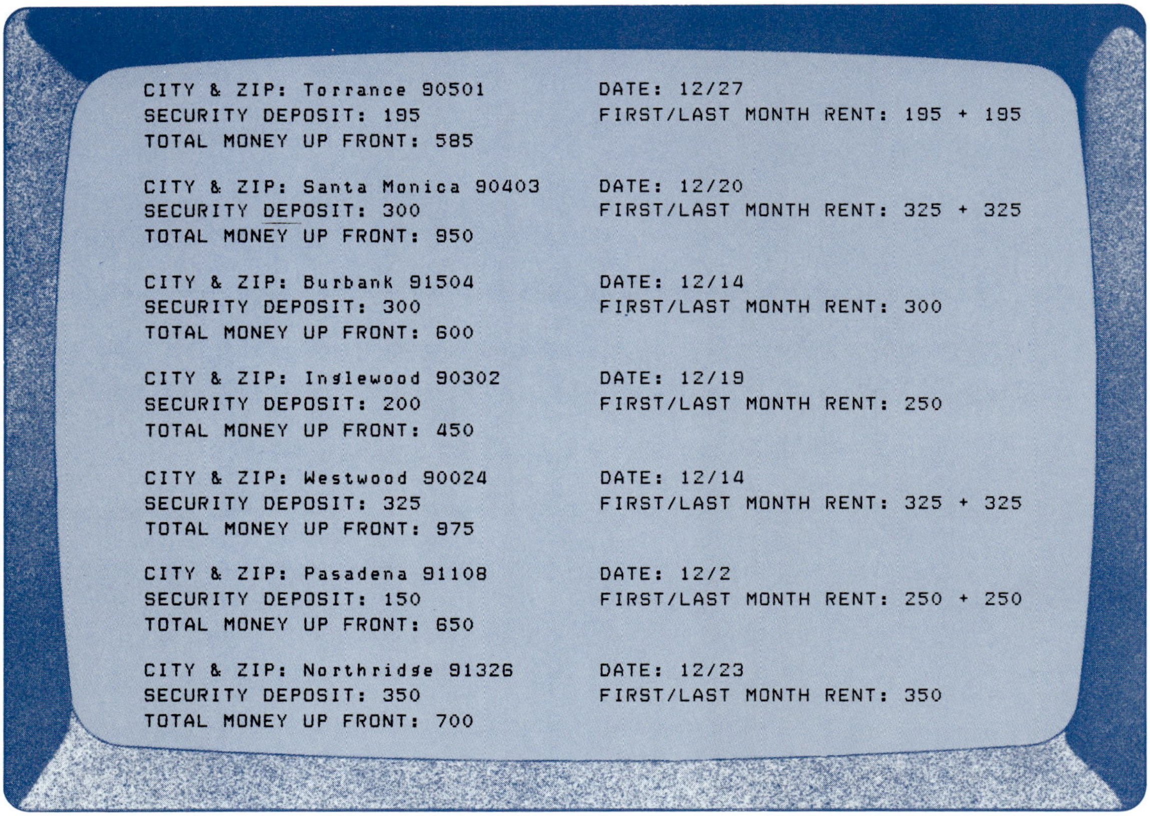
CITY & ZIP: Torrance 90501
DATE: 12/27
SECURITY DEPOSIT: 195
FIRST/LAST MONTH RENT: 195 + 195
TOTAL MONEY UP FRONT: 585
CITY & ZIP: Santa Monica 90403
DATE: 12/20
SECURITY DEPOSIT: 300
FIRST/LAST MONTH RENT: 325 + 325
TOTAL MONEY UP FRONT: 950
CITY & ZIP: Burbank 91504
DATE: 12/14
SECURITY DEPOSIT: 300
FIRST/LAST MONTH RENT: 300
TOTAL MONEY UP FRONT: 600
CITY & ZIP: Inglewood 90302
DATE: 12/19
SECURITY DEPOSIT: 200
FIRST/LAST MONTH RENT: 250
TOTAL MONEY UP FRONT: 450
CITY & ZIP: Westwood 90024
DATE: 12/14
SECURITY DEPOSIT: 325
FIRST/LAST MONTH RENT: 325 + 325
TOTAL MONEY UP FRONT: 975
CITY & ZIP: Pasadena 91108
DATE: 12/2
SECURITY DEPOSIT: 150
FIRST/LAST MONTH RENT: 250 + 250
TOTAL MONEY UP FRONT: 650
CITY & ZIP: Northridge 91326
DATE: 12/23
SECURITY DEPOSIT: 350
FIRST/LAST MONTH RENT: 350
TOTAL MONEY UP FRONT: 700

Figure 4-13 Data input for a filing system. This screen shows several southern California apartments listed according to city and zip code, date apartment appeared in the for-rent ads, security deposit required, first and last months' rent, and total amount of money required up front. These data were entered using PFS:File, a popular filing software package.

Figure 4-14 Data resorted. *Top:* Using PFS:Report, we now show the data from Figure 4-13 organized as a table. *Bottom:* This screen shows the apartments reordered according to those which require the least money up front. They could also be resorted in other ways, such as according to how recently the ad appeared or how close (based on zip code area) the apartment is to your job in Century City.

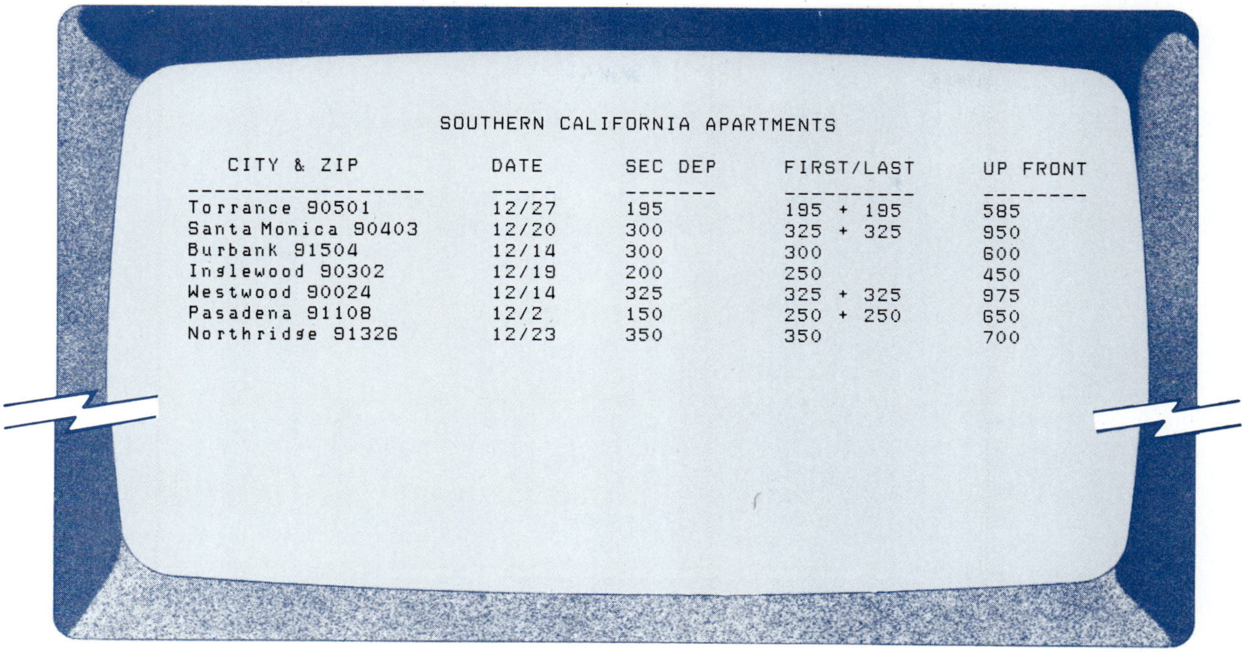

SOUTHERN CALIFORNIA APARTMENTS

CITY & ZIP	DATE	SEC DEP	FIRST/LAST	UP FRONT
Torrance 90501	12/27	195	195 + 195	585
Santa Monica 90403	12/20	300	325 + 325	950
Burbank 91504	12/14	300	300	600
Inglewood 90302	12/19	200	250	450
Westwood 90024	12/14	325	325 + 325	975
Pasadena 91108	12/2	150	250 + 250	650
Northridge 91326	12/23	350	350	700

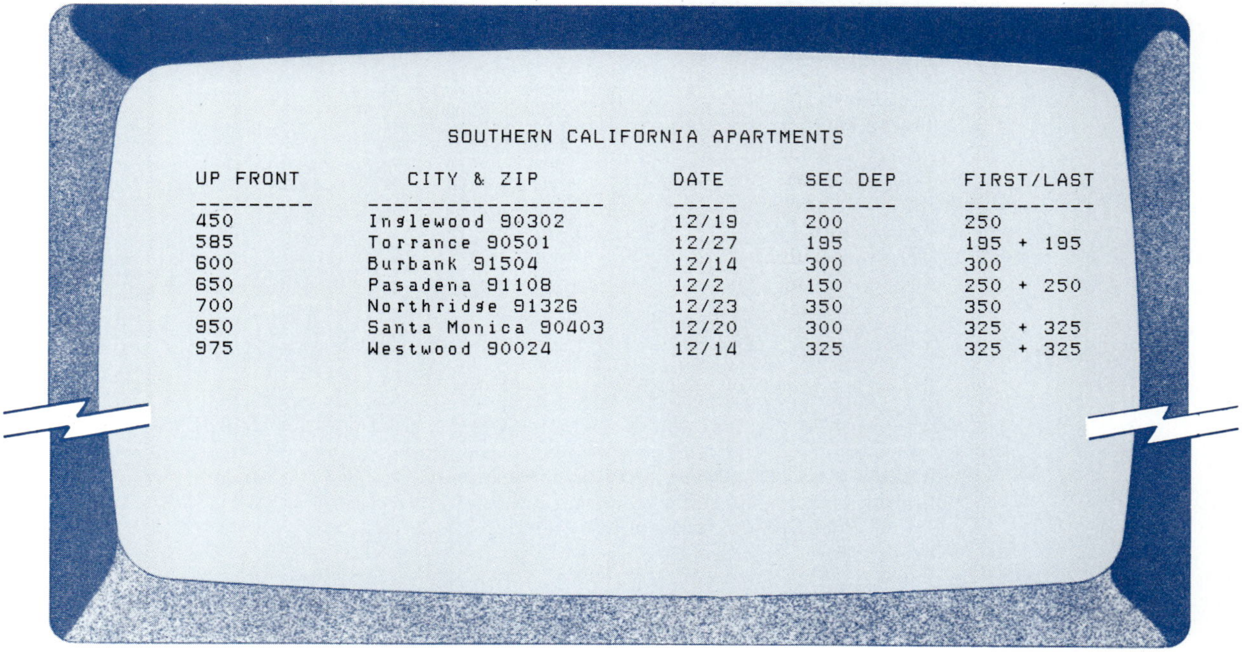

SOUTHERN CALIFORNIA APARTMENTS

UP FRONT	CITY & ZIP	DATE	SEC DEP	FIRST/LAST
450	Inglewood 90302	12/19	200	250
585	Torrance 90501	12/27	195	195 + 195
600	Burbank 91504	12/14	300	300
650	Pasadena 91108	12/2	150	250 + 250
700	Northridge 91326	12/23	350	350
950	Santa Monica 90403	12/20	300	325 + 325
975	Westwood 90024	12/14	325	325 + 325

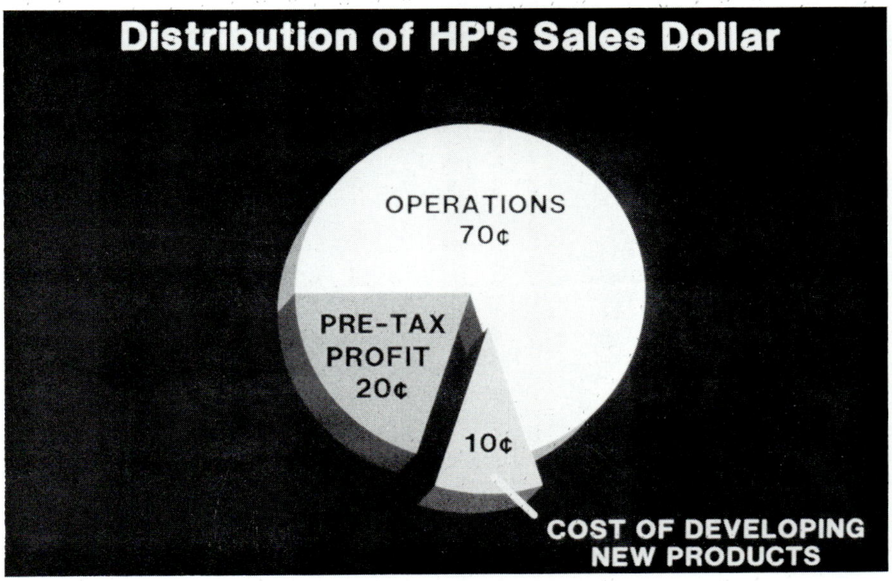
Distribution of HP's Sales Dollar
OPERATIONS
70¢
PRE-TAX
PROFIT
20¢
10¢
COST OF DEVELOPING
NEW PRODUCTS

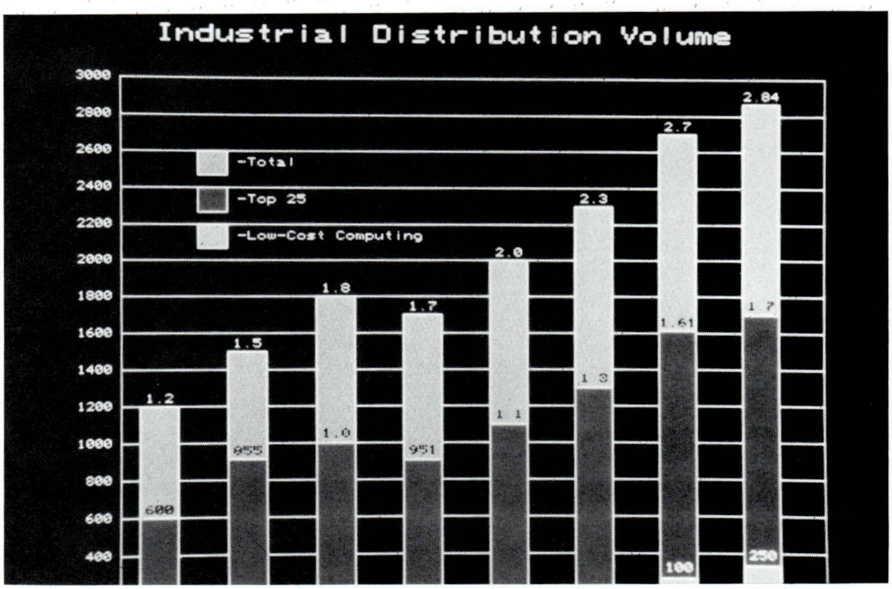
Industrial Distribution Volume
3000
2800
2600
2400
2200
2000
1800
1600
1400
1200
1000
800
600
400
-Total
-Top 25
-Low-Cost Computing
1.2
600
1.5
955
1.8
1.0
1.7
951
2.0
1.1
2.3
1.3
2.7
1.61
100
2.84
1.7
250

Figure 4-15 **Business graphics.** Analytical graphics, such as pie charts and bar graphs are produced on microcomputers and help users analyze business data.

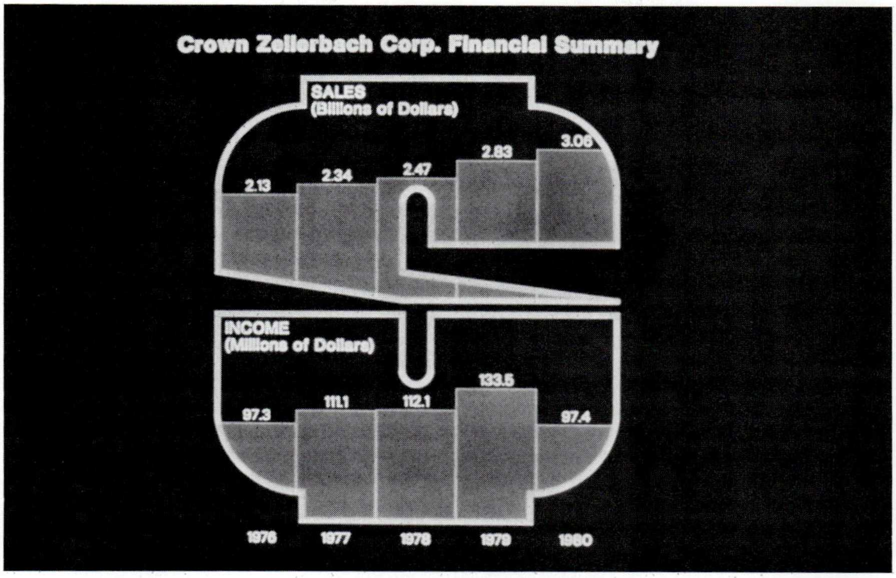
Crown Zellerbach Corp. Financial Summary
SALES
(Billions of Dollars)
2.13
2.34
2.47
2.83
3.06
INCOME
(Millions of Dollars)
97.3
111.1
112.1
133.5
97.4
1976
1977
1978
1979
1980

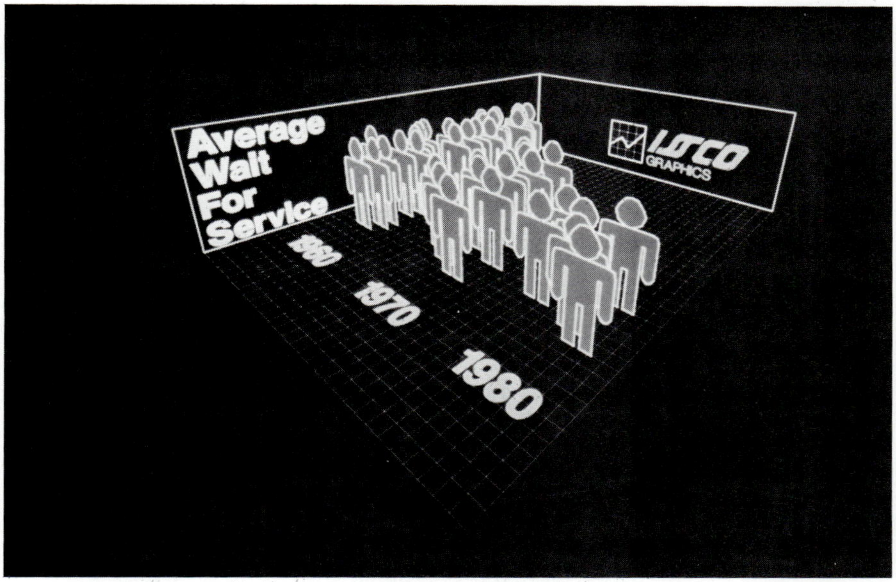
Average
Wait
For
Service
1970
1980
GRAPHICS

Figure 4-15 (continued). Presentation graphics are more sophisticated and are designed to help communicate ideas to others.

people appreciate having business graphics. As the illustrations in Figure 4-15 show, charts and graphs can convey meaning far more quickly than numbers can. For special presentations, you can also use animation to communicate your ideas. And, as we will see, some integrated software packages allow you to take statistical information you have generated from spreadsheets and present them in visual form. Other uses of business graphics are shown in our color portfolios.

Business computer graphics can be divided into two types:

- Analytical
- Presentation

Analytical graphics help you analyze data you have compiled. Most analytical graphics are part of larger integrated graphics packages, which means they may be fast and convenient to use, but you have less control over what they look like. For instance, you may be confined to drawing pie charts and bar graphs. However, formatting, scaling, and labeling are automatic, so that the program is easy to use. Examples of analytical graphics software are Lotus 1-2-3, PFS:Graph, and VisiTrend/Plot.

Presentation graphics are designed to help you communicate a message to other people. It is one thing to determine the solutions to some problems, it is quite another to convince someone else. Presentation graphics help you sell your ideas to your boss or client. Thus, the requirements become different; you need something to impress—something on the order of what a graphics artist would do for you. A presentation-quality graphics program usually will produce a variety of pie, bar, line, organizational, and other charts and will display them in color or black and white on the video screen or printed out on a printer or on a **plotter**—a printerlike device that produces charts, maps, and drawings in two or three dimensions. With special equipment, slides of computer generated graphics can also be produced for a slide show presentation.

User friendliness is particularly important because most managers do not have the time to learn how to use complicated graphics software. More than this, however, good graphics programs help a person present *effective* graphics. As one specialist in business graphics points out, "the average person is not trained in the graphic arts. If you pick up a blank piece of paper and ask them to create something themselves—forgetting about their drawing skills—they will do a terrible job. They will lay things out badly, the proportions will be bad, they'll select colors that are just outrageous."[3] Good software includes instructions on how to best select and present graphs and charts. And, of course, the more you use business graphics, the better they are apt to become.

PICKING PACKAGES

How to Buy Business Software for a Personal Computer

Companies may write their own programs for their own use, and many of them do, keeping staff or hired programmers busy. But it is quite often much more efficient for a company to buy a software package.

Software packages are available even for large computer systems. In the early 1970s, probably the largest application package was IBM's PARS, or Program for Airline Reservations Systems, and IPARS (International PARS). Other packages are available for inventory control, tax accounting, payroll, and many other commonplace business activities. We describe some of these activities and the software packages in Part 4.

Choosing software packages for a microcomputer is complicated by the fact that there are hundreds of programs offered. In its premier issue, for example, *LIST* magazine, subtitled "the software resource book for personal computer users," presented over 3000 software programs indexed by application, industry, and system. Although many programs are for educational and personal uses, a great many business programs are available in the areas of accounting, business graphics, data processing management, decision support, end-user communications, inventory control, file and mail list management, finance and planning, office administration, personnel, preventive maintenance, product procurement, project management, sales and marketing, small business administration, shipping, and word processing. In addition, there is industry-specific software such as for advertising, banking and finance, medicine and health care, and retail.

The ten key questions you should ask a retailer or software vendor about each software package before you buy, according to *LIST*, are the following:

1. What specific problems does your software package solve?
2. What are the key features and unique benefits of this particular package?
3. What documentation is available?
4. Is there any type of self-paced training available?
5. What happens if I have problems with your software?
6. Do you have any field support available? Telephone support?
7. What kind of warranty do you offer with the software?
8. May I have a list of three users with problems like mine that you have helped solve?
9. What are the specific hardware and software requirements?
   - Media
   - Operating system(s)
   - Memory
   - Computer(s)
10. How much does the package cost?

—*LIST*, Spring 1983

Integrated Packages: Software for Multiple Use

The four kinds of business software we have discussed unquestionably make one's professional work life easier. But there can still be a hassle associated with going from one application to another. Integrated software eliminates this trouble.

Integrated software programs are a collection of programs that work together to accomplish specific objectives. Such software is of two types:

- **Integrated tools,** which are designed to perform a variety of business tasks such as word processing and filing.
- **Integrated applications,** which are designed to perform specific related business tasks such as accounts payable and accounts receivable.

Integrated Tools: Multi-task Business Packages

The president of a St. Louis–based manufacturer of barbecue sauce describes how it used to be before he got an integrated business package:

> If I were typing a letter to a broker . . . and I wanted to check his sales figures for the last three months, I had to shut down WordStar, switch over to VisiCalc, run out his report, shut down VisiCalc, bring WordStar back up, and then try to copy the stuff in. That's a lot of trouble. . . . I had three computers, because they were strictly single-task machines. One was for word processing, one for data-base management, and one for VisiCalc.[4]

The software package that we call the integrated tool is the kind that puts together several programs so that you can do a variety of business tasks without having to have three computers. For instance, Symphony includes programs for word processing, spreadsheet analysis, file management, graphics, and communications. (Symphony is an expanded Lotus 1-2-3, which consists of only spreadsheet analysis, graphics, and limited file management.) The same kind of results are also achieved on integrated hardware-and-software systems, such as Apple's Lisa and Macintosh computers.

An integrated tool, which runs on a microcomputer, allows separate programs to work together by sharing data and information and allows the transfer of data from one program to another. For example, data could be collected by using a file management system to gain access to a data base, then analyzed by using a spreadsheet, summarized in graph form using the graphics program, and finally summarized in a final document created with a word processing program.

Integrated Applications

A different kind of integrated software is a package consisting of several programs, each designed to perform a specific business function and each of which can be used alone, but all sharing a common format.

Integrated applications software programs work together by accessing the same files and using one program's output as the input for another program. A typical package might include programs for accounts payable, accounts receivable, inventory control, payroll records, and sales analysis.

Onward to Programming

As you proceed out to southern California to begin your job with Starfire Film Production Co., think how prepared you will be with all the business tools at hand. A mere few years ago—before Apple Computer introduced its Apple II in 1977 and before VisiCalc made desktop computers so attractive to business people—*none* of these tools were available. That is an indication of how fast technology has revolutionized our lives—and will give you some sense of the changes to come during the rest of your business life.

Why, you might think after reading this, is there any reason for a business person to learn programming? Why, with all the packaged, off-the-shelf software available, does one need to know anything about the intricacies of telling a computer step by step what to do?

The answer is: programming covers a lot more than you probably think. Packaged software will not cover all business applications and there will probably be times when you will want custom-made programs. In addition, you need to be able to understand what programmers do—if you are going to be able to deal with them from a management perspective. Finally, programming is more than just inputting data to a machine; it is a series of *problem-solving techniques* applicable to other facets of business.

We show what we mean in the next chapter.

SUMMARY

- Computers and software can take much of the waste and inefficiency, and some of the boredom, out of work.
- Although computers have been around for over 30 years and have become more powerful at the same time they have become smaller and more accessible, it is recent software that has made them truly useful and accessible to nearly everyone.
- Software development has been explosive; the best sellers, such as WordStar, VisiCalc, SuperCalc, PFS:File, and dBASE II, are intended for general business applications—that is, word processing, filing and manipulating data, financial modeling, and accounting.
- Software is developed by three different sources: (1) *internal programmers*—people employed by companies to do such tasks as developing payroll programs; (2) *software consultants*—also known as third-party suppliers, who are freelancers or employees of consulting firms offering certain types of expertise or temporary personnel solutions to programming problems; (3) *packaged software manufacturers*—people, often called "publishers," who develop programs that are available "off the shelf" to anyone.
- Software packages are the best sellers and have the advantage of being widely tested and mass produced, thus being relatively inexpensive. However, their flexibility is limited and modifications may be impossible.
- Packaged software is being used increasingly in many businesses, thus making it important for people in business to learn how to use it.
- Four of the most important software packages involve (1) word processing, (2) financial spreadsheets, (3) file management, and (4) graphics.
- A **word processor** includes (1) a computer, (2) a keyboard, (3) a CRT screen, (4) a printer, and (5) a word processing program. It can be dedicated (does nothing else but word processing) or be a computer that does word processing in addition to other tasks.
- Word processing is designed to allow the creation, editing, formatting, storing, and printing of text. Some commercial word processing systems are bundled (hardware and software are one unit); others are sold separately (recorded on a floppy disk).
- The **cursor** is a blinking mark that acts as a pointer and indicates the location of the next character to be typed. It can be moved anywhere on the screen.
- A **file** is anything stored as a unit.

- In word processing, one creates text by typing it on the keyboard; the text appears on the screen. Any word that crosses the right-hand margin is automatically moved to the left on the next line down, which is called **automatic carriage return** or **word wrap.**
- Word processing—using WordStar, for example—makes editing, inserting, and deleting text easy using the cursor and the DELETE and INSERT keys. Some programs have an **overtyping** feature, whereby you can simply type over what you have written.
- The **cut and paste** or **block move** feature allows the user to easily move words, phrases, and other material within the text.
- The **search and replace** function instructs the computer to automatically search for and replace, in the entire document, any words the user wants to change.
- **Text formatting** concerns the look of the document, including underlining, margin setting, line centering, and **justification** (evening up the ends of the lines like the type in this book).
- A single keystroke can save a document on a diskette for later use; a couple of keystrokes can print it out.
- Some of the desirable features of word processing programs are as follows: (1) They are screen oriented—editing changes can be seen directly on the screen. (2) The screen is live—text corrections are seen immediately on the screen. (3) They have 80-column screens—the whole page can be seen. (4) They have menus and Help options—a **menu** is a list of commands typed in through the keyboard to make editing, formatting, and other changes; a **Help option** assists the user who does not know what to do next. (5) They have backup capability—a second file is available if the first one is accidentally erased. (6) They have a form letter generator or "mail-merge" feature—the user can merge files. (7) They have a spelling checker—a proofreading program (SpellStar, for example, which works with WordStar) that automatically checks spelling.
- Memory-based word processing systems are able to type only documents that are less than a certain length because most of the program is in the computer memory; disk-based systems allow storage of longer documents, but they are slower than memory-based systems.
- **Windowing (window)**—a split screen—allows the user to look at one file while working on another.
- A **spreadsheet** traditionally was a large sheet of paper divided into rows and columns that accountants and financial analysts used to produce reports. VisiCalc introduced the first electronic spreadsheet in 1979, which marked

the first legitimate business application for microcomputers. VisiCalc was originally programmed to operate on an Apple II; it was followed by SuperCalc, which can run on machines other than the Apple, and by Multiplan and Lotus 1-2-3, both of which are "second generation" and easier to use.

- Electronic spreadsheets are popular because they are simple, flexible, and they have "what-if" capability—a feature that allows the user working with numbers to easily recalculate the results as different variables are changed. They are used for sales projections, expense reports, income and balance sheet preparation, and other numerical problems. Figures can be easily changed, and rows and columns can be inserted and deleted.
- An electronic spreadsheet such as VisiCalc appears on the video screen as a *status section* and a *grid section.* The status section is the top three lines: the entry contents line, the prompt line, and the edit line. The grid section consists of the *column* headings across the top, the *row* headings down the left side, and the *cells* in the middle. The cells are invisible, but each can hold nine spaces or digits. They are designated by their coordinates of column letter and row number.
- Column and row headings are called *labels,* and they must begin with a letter or a word. To enter labels, use the keyboard to move the cursor to the appropriate place and type in the information.
- A *value* is a number contained in a cell. Calculations are done by formulas.
- When working with electronic spreadsheets, the user sees only a part of the sheet; to see both the first column and the last column, one must split the screen.
- There are numerous spreadsheet programs that vary greatly. Following are guidelines to choosing one: (1) *Screen format*—clear presentation and insertion of labels; screen information must be easily edited. (2) *Size of spreadsheet*—is it large enough? Can the spreadsheet be used all at once? (3) *Calculation flexibility*—cell relationships should include not only basic arithmetic operations but any specialized formulas. (4) *File access*—the spreadsheet should be able to interact with files from other programs. (5) *Good* ***documentation***—the instruction manuals should be easy to use, clear, and complete.
- Information-filing systems and filing management are important to businesses; the success of a business is often linked to its having orderly and accessible files. Manual filing systems are inefficient, difficult to organize, and not always easily accessible. However, computerized filing programs—called **data base managers** or **data base management systems (DBMS)**—can facilitate filing and filing management.
- A **data base** is a collection of information, or *integrated* data, that can be used for a variety of applications.

- Graphics is the most effective way to communicate information and ideas for decision making. Charts and graphs can convey meaning far more quickly than numbers can. Some integrated software packages allow the user to take statistical information and present it in visual form. There are two types of business computer graphics: (1) analytical and (2) presentation.
- **Analytical graphics** help the user analyze compiled data. They are usually part of larger integrated graphics packages, which are fast and convenient to use but which offer less control over visual form. Examples of analytical graphics software are Lotus 1-2-3, PFS:Graph, and VisiTrend/Plot.
- **Presentation graphics** are designed to help the user communicate a message to other people; they usually will produce a variety of visual forms and display them in color or black and white on the video screen or printed out on a printer or a **plotter** (a printerlike device that produces charts, maps, and drawings in two or three dimensions).
- Good business graphics programs are "user friendly" and *effective,* and they include instructions on how to best select and present graphs and charts.
- The functions of the four kinds of business software discussed (word processing, financial spreadsheets, file management, and graphics) can be combined into **integrated software programs,** which are a collection of programs that work together to accomplish specific objectives. There are two types of integrated software: (1) *integrated tools,* which combine programs in one package, and (2) *integrated applications,* which combine programs to focus on a particular business activity.
- An integrated tool, which runs on a microcomputer, allows one package of separate programs to work together by sharing data and information and allows the transfer of data from one program to another. An example of integrated-tool software packages is symphony, which includes programs for word processing, spreadsheet analysis, file management, and graphics. (The same kind of results are achieved on integrated hardware-and-software systems, such as Apple's Lisa and Macintosh computers.)
- Integrated applications refer to a package consisting of several programs, each designed to perform a specific business function and each of which can be used alone, but all sharing a common format. Integrated applications software programs work together by accessing the same files and using one program's output as the input for another program.
- Even though packaged software is powerful, efficient, effective, and readily available, business people should still become familiar with programming to be able to devise custom-made programs, to cover all business applications, and to understand what programmers do and deal with them from a management perspective.

KEY TERMS

Analytical graphics, p. 120
Automatic carriage return, p. 97
Block move, p. 97
Cursor, p. 96
Cut and paste, p. 97
Data base, p. 115
Data base management system, p. 114
Data base manager, p. 114
DBMS, p. 115
Documentation, p. 114
File, p. 97
Help option, p. 100
Integrated software programs, p. 122
Justification, p. 100
Menu, p. 100
Mouse, p. 93
Overtyping, p. 97
Plotter, p. 120
Presentation graphics, p. 120
Search and replace, p. 97
Spreadsheet, p. 101
Text formatting, p. 100
Windowing, p. 101
Window, pp. 101, 113
Word processor, p. 93
Word wrap, p. 97

REVIEW QUESTIONS

1. Name the three sources of software development.
2. How does word processing make the creation and editing of documents easy?
3. Describe some of the desirable features of a word processing program.
4. What is VisiCalc? How is it used?
5. Describe the "what-if" capability and its application.
6. What are some of the desirable features to look for in electronic spreadsheets?
7. How would you use a data base manager?

CASE PROBLEMS

Case 4-1: The Electronic Spreadsheet and Managing Cash Flow

One of the most important concepts of business is *cash flow*. You may know what it feels like to be waiting for money to come in while the expenses are piling up. Companies have the same problem. Cash flows into a company at different times than it flows out, so that a company may have to borrow money for the short term while it waits for cash from sales, rents, or whatever to come in.

For example, a farmer may have to borrow money in the spring for seed and fertilizer and make payments for equipment and land throughout the year, but may get no income until crops are harvested and sold in the late summer. It is important, therefore, that the farmer figure out *total* expenses and *total* income in order to know how much to borrow and whether the farm will be profitable that year.[5]

Your assignment: Suppose it is January and you are a farmer with access to an electronic spreadsheet. How would you set up the following categories in order to determine cash flow and profitability? (You can write these categories down on paper also.) The point of this exercise is that theoretically you should be able to go to a banker with your spreadsheet and show how much money you need to borrow. This is the kind of activity that many business people need to do all the time.

The categories are: Projected expenses of $10,000 a month for labor for 12 months; February payment of $40,000 for seed and fertilizer; April payment of $40,000 for equipment; and land payments of $5000 a month for 12 months. That totals $260,000 in expenses. In September, you project you will receive $365,000 in sales, and you will have to set aside $45,000 for taxes. Subtracting expenses and taxes leaves you a net income of $60,000. Now, in January, you currently have $125,000 cash on hand. How much money will you have to borrow per month between now and September? If you pay 15% interest for the total amount that you borrow for the year, how much money will you have left as net income?

Case 4-2: Training Firms for Computers

The following article appeared in the May 4, 1984, *Wall Street Journal* under the headline, "Training Firms for Computers Are Growing":

> It's 9 o'clock Monday morning. Over the weekend, the company president has outfitted each manager's desk with a personal computer, complete with software. The machines are admired, and then the crush of daily business begins.
>
> By 11 A.M. the computers have disappeared under piles of papers and coffee cups. No one knows how to use them, so no one does. . . .
>
> This chain of events—untrained users suddenly confronting sophisticated equipment—happens in a surprising number of corporate offices, according to executives who work in the growing field of computer training. . . .
>
> Growth in microcomputer training, and in the number of trainers, promises to be fast-paced, at least in the immediate future. International Data Corp., a market-research company in Framingham, Mass., estimates there are 50 million potential customers for personal computers in the business market and that more than 3.5 million units have already been sold.
>
> But International Data also estimates that of the potential candidates for the machine, only 8% to 12% are computer-literate.[6]

Your assignment: This is a growth area in which those who have experience can help others who have not had experience. Now that you have read about word processing, explain some of the specific time-saving activities to someone who has not read this chapter.

CHAPTER 5

Application Programming

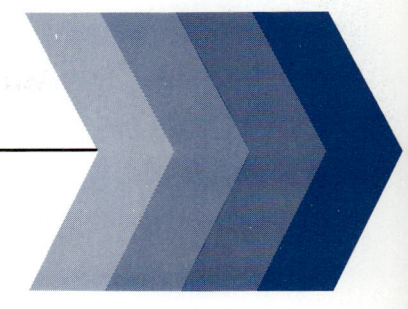

Making the Computer Work for You

Why, if you are interested in a business management career, should you need to know anything about programming?

There are at least three reasons for understanding the programming process:

- Even if you never write a program yourself during your career, you may need to ask programmers to write programs for you. In order to communicate your needs to them and to recognize potential applications of computers, you need to understand the process of programming.
- With the increasing availability of computers, the value of programming skills will certainly continue to increase.
- Finally, programming is more than writing a program. It is a *problem-solving process* in which business users and data processing specialists interact. As the business user half, it is essential that you understand the process.

The importance of understanding programming may be appreciated by a reading of the case study on the next page.

PREVIEW

What Is Programming?

As mentioned in Chapter 3, programming is the means by which we communicate with the computer. A **program** is a series of detailed steps to be completed to solve a problem. These may be thought of as a logical sequence of instructions that direct the computer to perform whatever operations we wish.

CASE STUDY: PROGRAMMING ERROR AND HUMAN LIVES

Is There a Better Way to Write Programs?

The countdown was coming to an end. Lying on their backs in the cockpit of the space shuttle *Columbia,* astronauts John Young and Robert Crippen could see pelicans flying along the beach at Cape Canaveral. Straight ahead the stars had given way to the deep blue of early morning. Within less than an hour they would be the first people to fly the space shuttle into orbit, the first Americans in space in more than five years.

Then, 20 minutes before launch time, warning lights at Mission Control began to flash. Something was wrong with the computer system. The countdown was halted; the computer analysts went to work. They had three hours before the flight would have to be scrubbed.

It became apparent that nothing was physically wrong with the computers. All of the circuits were working. The communication lines were intact. The problem seemed to lie instead in the programs, in the software, that told the computers what to do.

Technicians immediately realized they faced a serious problem. The software on board the space shuttle consists of nearly 500,000 elaborately interwoven instructions. Finding a programming error, a bug, in that web would be like trying to find a single misspelled word in an encyclopedia. Soon the news began to circulate: The maiden flight of the space shuttle would have to be delayed.

"It was precisely the type of error that one would expect," says the Dutch computer scientist Edsger W. Dijkstra (pronounced DIKE-stra). He inhales on his cigarette, then continues. "You see, most of NASA's software is full of bugs."

His eyebrows arch with pleasure, a sure sign that a story follows. "I saw the first moon shot in 1969, when Armstrong, Aldrin, and Collins went to the moon, and shortly thereafter I met Joel Aron of IBM's Federal Systems Division, who I knew had been responsible for a large part of the software. So when I saw Joel at the swimming pool of our hotel in Rome, I said, 'Joel, how did you do it?' 'Do what?' he said. I said, 'Get that software to work okay.' 'Okay?' he said. 'It was full of bugs. In one of the trajectory computations, we had the moon's gravity repulsive rather than attractive, and this was discovered by accident five days before count zero.' "

Dijkstra draws back in his chair, the picture of astonished outrage.

"When I had regained my composure, I said, 'Those three guys, they have been lucky.' 'Oh yes,' Joel said."

For more than 20 years, Dijkstra has been fighting against the kind of programming that inevitably leads to bugs in computer software. To him, the way organizations like NASA program computers is foolhardy at best, perilous at worst. He believes there is another way, a better way. It involves structuring how a person thinks about programming so that programs themselves acquire a firm mathematical basis. The discipline his work has spawned, called structured programming, has been one of the most important advances in computer software of the past two decades.

—Steve Olson,
Science 84, January/February 1984

Computer programs are of two types:

- **Operating system programs** are designed to control and manage the computer's operations, to make the computing machinery operate efficiently. They are not designed to solve particular business or scientific problems. We will discuss operating systems in Chapter 8.
- **Application programs** are designed to perform specific data processing and computational tasks—to do business and scientific problem solving rather than control computer machinery. In payrolls, for instance, such programs are used to record accounting entries, do calculations, and write checks.

Application programming is of particular interest to us since we are less concerned with how a computer works than in using it to solve problems. The software packages we described in Chapter 4 are actual running programs; however, there are occasions when we need customized programs, and these are what we are concerned with here.

Traditional Versus Structured Programming: Individualism Versus Order

Although the word "programming" is often used to mean the writing of statements in a programming language—programmers call this writing **coding**—there is more to it than that. As we suggested above, programming is a *problem-solving procedure.* This procedure has evolved into a discipline with two approaches—traditional and structured.

Traditional Programming. In the old days, programming was a creative and individualized effort, and there were few standards for developing programs. The result of this was events such as that described in the space program at the beginning of this chapter. The emphasis was on the creativity of each programmer to develop programs that would require a minimum of instructions, storage, and computer time. As a result, different programmers frequently used different structure and logic procedures, and many programs employed complex and stylized logic—frequently so intricate that only the original programmer could understand the details (should he or she be able to recall them at all).

The problem became even more acute as the capabilities of the computer increased and it became a widely used business and scientific tool requiring larger, more complex programs. Frequently, as in the space flights, many programmers would be working on one program or a group of related programs. Without strict and formalized standards, this led to problems in modifying and maintaining programs. In addition, serious problems were also apt to develop when a key programmer left the organization.

Structured Programming. To control the problems produced by traditional programming, computer scientists have made a concerted effort to standardize the programming procedure. The result, called structured programming, is as much a philosophy as a programming approach. Structured programming may limit the creativity of individual programmers, but it significantly improves overall programming efficiency because it standardizes the programming process, increases simplicity and reliability, and reduces costs of developing and maintaining programs. In short, **structured programming** may be defined as programming that uses structured design, structured coding, and structured review. We will see what these concepts mean in the following pages.

The Six Steps of the Programming Process

Whichever kind of programming is used, traditional or structured, it follows the same six-step problem-solving approach:

1. Define the problem.
2. Design a solution.
3. Write the program.
4. Test it.
5. Document it.
6. Maintain it.

We will describe these six steps throughout the rest of the chapter.

To help you put these concepts to some use, let us say that by now you have joined Starfire Film Production Company in Century City, California, and are working on the business side of their operation. Mr. Elliott, the president, has the show-business habit of referring to everyone by first name or endearment, but he can be of the bare-knuckles school of business when it comes to cost overruns on pictures. As he explains to you, only about two out of 500 films are sold by their independent producers, such as Starfire, to a major studio distributor for an immediate profit. Usually, the studio gets the picture on a releasing deal and pays the producer back out of money earned, which means the investors in the picture take a long time to get their money back. The upshot is that it is imperative that costs be controlled on a film while it is in production.

Elliott is irate about the way payroll in particular has been handled on some recent Starfire-backed films. There has been a good deal of sloppiness, with overpayments going to several of the cast and crew and late payments to a good many others. One of your initial assignments is to be his personal financial watchdog, as it were, on a new film going into production whose working title is *Rough Cut*. The film crew is going on location shooting in Australia, and planning is critical. There will be over 100 cast and crew members traveling, ranging from major players to a wind-machine operator.

In the past, the payroll system for films on location was maintained by an accountant who operated with a manual system. Sometimes, if the accountant was ill or if there were cast changes, there was difficulty in keeping the payroll system straight. You decide to see if you can set up a payroll procedure using a portable computer that can be used on location. The main thing is to get the paychecks out on time so that morale on the picture will not suffer, thereby contributing to costly production delays.

You meet with a computer programmer and the *Rough Cut* accountant to see what can be worked out. You begin with the first of the six steps, defining the problem.

1. Defining the Problem

Defining the problem, also known as program analysis, involves the following six tasks:

- Specify the objectives of the program.
- Specify the outputs.
- Specify the input requirements.
- Specify the processing requirements.
- Evaluate the feasibility of the program.
- Document the program analysis.

In this stage you want not only to determine the input and output requirements but also to get a sense of how much everything will cost.

Specifying the Objectives of the Program

In order to avoid having the right solution to the wrong problem, we need to be sure we know what the problem actually is. Making a clear statement of the problem depends, of course, on its size and complexity.

If the problem is small and does not involve other systems of instructions, then we can probably state the problem easily and proceed immediately to Step 2, program design. However, most problems interact with an already existing information system (such as the manual system of processing paychecks) or will require a series of programs and so require very complete analysis, meaning careful coordination of people, procedures, and programs. We will discuss such systems analysis and design in detail in Chapter 11, but here let us quickly describe the rest of the program analysis.

In your meeting with the *Rough Cut* accountant and programmer, you agree on the program objective:

Program objective: To develop a computerized payroll system using a portable computer that will print payroll checks on location, replacing the manual system.

Specifying the Outputs

Before you know what should go into a system you need to say what should come out. The best way to specify the outputs is to prepare some output forms that show how the required information will be displayed. The best person to design the output forms is the ultimate user of the information, although forms can also be designed by the program analyst. Both user and program analyst should look the forms over to see that they are useful and have neither too much nor too little detail.

In your *Rough Cut* meeting, you, the programmer, and the accountant agree on the output specifications:

Output specifications: Weekly paycheck.

You then specify the basic format of the paycheck as shown in Figure 5-1. For this first pass, the details are not critical.

Specifying the Input Requirements

Now that you have determined the outputs, you need to define the input and data. To do this, you list the inputs required and the source of the data. For example, in a payroll program, the *inputs* could be employee time sheets and the *source* of the input could be either the employees themselves or their supervisors. You need to be sure that the source of the data is constant—that data will be available in the future when you need it.

At the *Rough Cut* meeting, you agree on the input requirements as follows:

Input requirements: There are two sources of input.

1. *INPUT: Time sheet, with week ending date and hours worked that week*
   SOURCE: Employee's supervisor
   FORMAT: Example shown in Figure 5-2, left
2. *INPUT: Employee data, including pay rate*
   SOURCE: Personnel file
   FORMAT: Example shown in Figure 5-2, right

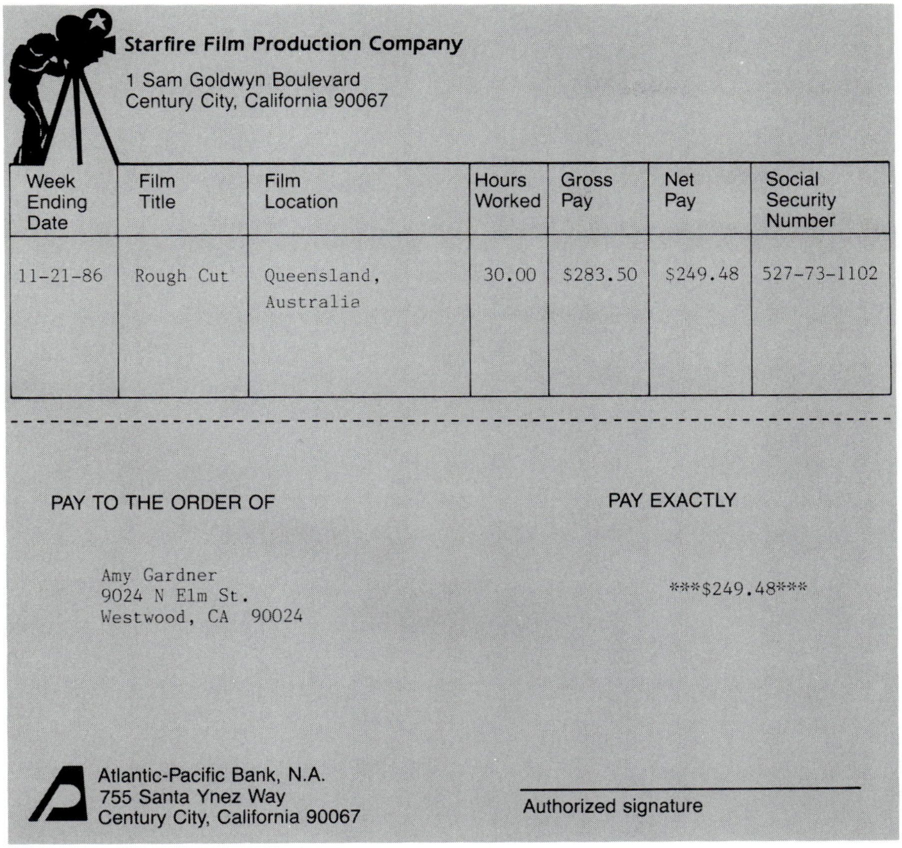

Starfire Film Production Company
1 Sam Goldwyn Boulevard
Century City, California 90067

Week Ending Date	Film Title	Film Location	Hours Worked	Gross Pay	Net Pay	Social Security Number
11-21-86	Rough Cut	Queensland, Australia	30.00	$283.50	$249.48	527-73-1102

PAY TO THE ORDER OF

Amy Gardner
9024 N Elm St.
Westwood, CA 90024

PAY EXACTLY

$249.48

Atlantic-Pacific Bank, N.A.
755 Santa Ynez Way
Century City, California 90067

Authorized signature

Figure 5-1 Weekly paycheck for *Rough Cut* film crew and cast. This shows the output format you wish to produce. In this case the check is for one of the staff members in the sound department on the picture, Amy Gardner, a cableperson, but the format can be used for other staff members also.

Specifying the Processing Requirements

Now you have to determine the processing requirements for converting the input data to output. If the proposed program is to replace or to supplement an existing system, you will want to make a particularly careful evaluation and identification of present processing procedures, noting the logic used and any improvements that could be made. If the proposed system is not designed to replace an existing system, you would be well advised to look over another system in use that addresses a similar problem.

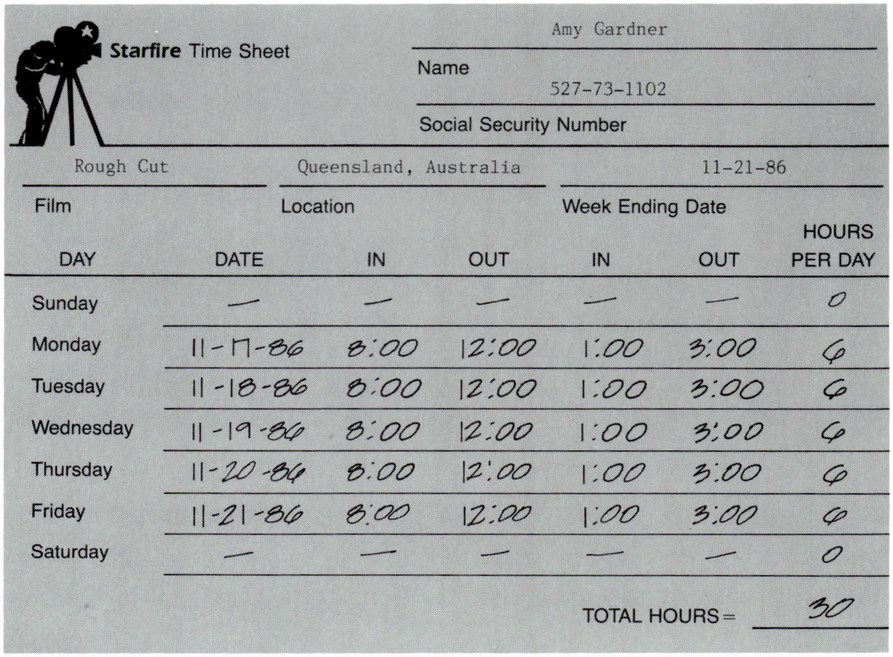

Starfire Time Sheet

Name: Amy Gardner

Social Security Number: 527-73-1102

Film: Rough Cut

Location: Queensland, Australia

Week Ending Date: 11-21-86

DAY	DATE	IN	OUT	IN	OUT	HOURS PER DAY
Sunday	—	—	—	—	—	0
Monday	11-17-86	8:00	12:00	1:00	3:00	6
Tuesday	11-18-86	8:00	12:00	1:00	3:00	6
Wednesday	11-19-86	8:00	12:00	1:00	3:00	6
Thursday	11-20-86	8:00	12:00	1:00	3:00	6
Friday	11-21-86	8:00	12:00	1:00	3:00	6
Saturday	—	—	—	—	—	0

TOTAL HOURS = 30

Figure 5-2 *Rough Cut* payroll input.
Above: Employee time sheet—in this case, a hypothetical one for Amy Gardner. This time sheet would be completed by her supervisor, the Production Manager. *Facing page:* Format for personnel file, source of second input, which includes employee pay rate; specific example of Amy Gardner's personnel file.

In either case, you will want to look for commercially available software that can do the job, so that you will not have to write your own programs. You may not find anything that meets your needs, but if you do, it could greatly reduce the time, cost, and uncertainty of program development.

The programmer advises you and the *Rough Cut* accountant that the processing procedures are uncomplicated. There are a number of commercial software packages available that will fit the bill, but they are more complex than you require and you might as well save the expense. You agree on the following processing requirements:

> *Processing requirements: Paychecks may be produced by multiplying the number of hours an employee works by his or her rate of pay per hour, then calculating deductions to determine net pay, and then printing the payroll check.*

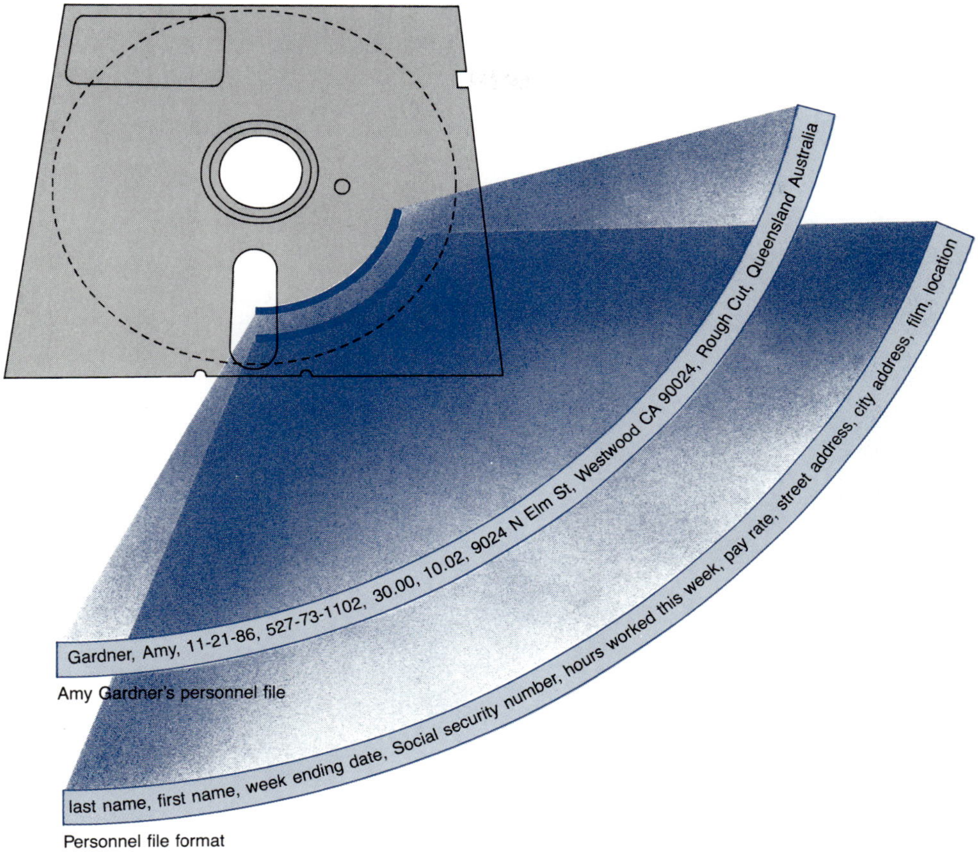
Gardner, Amy, 11-21-86, 527-73-1102, 30.00, 10.02, 9024 N Elm St, Westwood CA 90024, Rough Cut, Queensland Australia
Amy Gardner's personnel file
last name, first name, week ending date, Social security number, hours worked this week, pay rate, street address, city address, film, location
Personnel file format

Evaluating the Feasibility of the Program

Now you need to see if what you have accomplished so far is enough to make a new program feasible. If the program is intended to replace an existing system, you need to determine if the potential improvements outweigh the costs and possible problems. A new computer program, after all, has to be judged like any other new business investment. Thus, evaluating program feasibility is the "go/no go" stage.

The *Rough Cut* accountant does not think the computer system for producing paychecks is worth all the bother. The programmer, however, thinks it would not be that difficult to implement, since the film crew is already packing along a portable computer for other purposes. You break the tie by voting to go ahead:

> *Feasibility: The film crew's portable computer, plus a simplified payroll program, will be an adequate on-site payroll system. Costs to develop the program will be less than purchasing a packaged program.*

Documenting the Program Analysis

Before concluding the program analysis stage, it is best to write up a document stating the results of this first phase. This document should contain statements on the program's

- Objectives
- Output specifications
- Input requirements
- Processing requirements
- Feasibility

In other words, the document should describe everything you have done so far. In view of Mr. Elliott's intense interest in *Rough Cut*'s profitability, you decide this is an especially good idea.

2. Designing a Solution

You know you have a problem and have identified it in the program analysis stage. Now you need to plan a solution to meet the objectives you specified there. This second stage is called the **program design** stage; it consists of designing a solution.

Structured program design is a method of designing a computer program in such a way as to minimize complexity. Among the tools used in this stage are:

- Top-down program design
- Structure charts
- HIPO charts
- Flowcharts
- Pseudocode

Whether to use all or only some of these tools is up to the programmer. We will describe them below.

Top-Down Program Design

Top-down program design is a structured design technique in which the programmer, having determined the outputs to be produced and inputs required, identifies the major processing steps that the program must perform. These major processing steps are called program **modules.** A module is a set of logically related program statements.

The modules for the *Rough Cut* payroll problem are shown in Figure 5-3. Notice that there are three modules in this example:

- **Control Module:** The module labeled *PAYROLL PROCESSING* is called the *control module;* this main module controls the operation of the other two, *READ DATA* and *CALCULATE PAY AND PRINT PAYCHECK.*

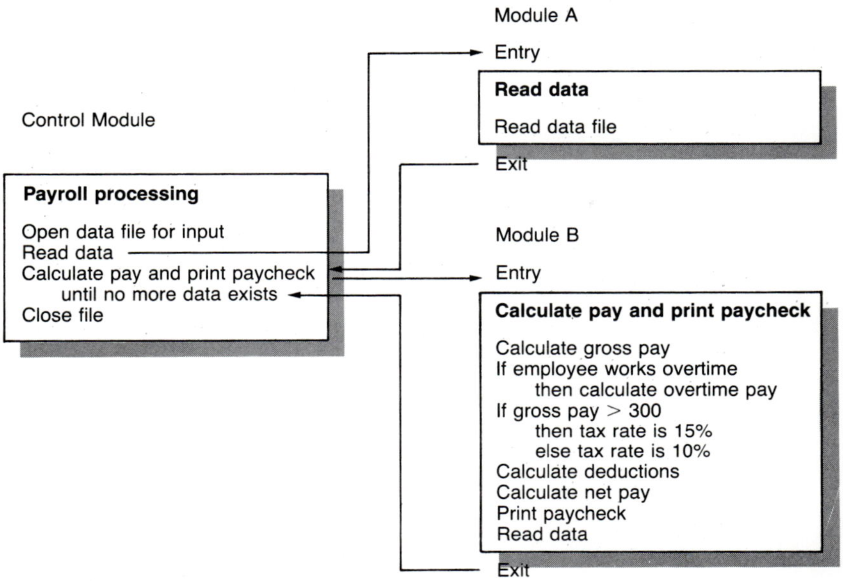
Module A
Entry
Read data
Read data file
Exit
Control Module
Payroll processing
Open data file for input
Read data
Calculate pay and print paycheck
until no more data exists
Close file
Module B
Entry
Calculate pay and print paycheck
Calculate gross pay
If employee works overtime
then calculate overtime pay
If gross pay > 300
then tax rate is 15%
else tax rate is 10%
Calculate deductions
Calculate net pay
Print paycheck
Read data
Exit

Figure 5-3 Top-down design. This example for the *Rough Cut* movie payroll shows the three principal program modules and their functions. Notice how the control module transfers to the Module A entry point, reads the data, then exits and transfers back to the control module. It then transfers to the module B entry point, makes all the calculations and prints the paycheck, reads the data, then exits and transfers back to the control module. The sequence is then repeated for another employee's wage data and paycheck.

- **Module A:** The *READ DATA* module is concerned with the inputs—the word "data" represents two items of data: number of hours worked, and wage rate per hour.
- **Module B:** The module called *CALCULATE PAY AND PRINT PAYCHECK* specifies the processing requirements and the output required—that is, the paycheck.

Top-down design has some rigid rules:

- Each module can have only *one entry point and one exit point,* so that the logic flow of the program is easy to follow.
- When the program is **executed**—programmer talk for "run through the computer"—it must be able *to move from one module to the next*

in sequence until the last module has been executed. Thus, in Figure 5-3, program control moves from Control Module to Module A, back to Control Module, then to Module B until no more data exists, then back to Control Module to close the file.

- Each module should be *independent and should have a single function.* For example, a module that is used to compute withholding tax should not also be used to compute pension benefits. If a module is independent, it can be easily changed later without having to change other modules.
- Each module should be of *manageable size*—have no more than 50 program instructions—*in order to make the design and testing of the program easier.* Module B in Figure 5-3, for instance, has only seven program instructions.

The top-down design is demonstrated more readily in the structure chart shown in Figure 5-4.

Computer Programming: What's in It for You?

Today, businessmen with plenty of other things to do with their time are studying the art of programming and taking advantage of the wide variety of software, books, and specialized computers. Some of these people are driven by pure curiosity, others by an inability to find software that meets their needs, and still others by the belief that learning to program will give them a competitive edge.

The curiosity angle is easy to figure. After you've been working on a personal computer for some time, it's natural to wonder how it works. Programming, the means by which you put a computer through its paces, goes a long way toward satisfying this curiosity.

It's also easy to understand how people can become frustrated by the idiosyncrasies of commercial software, or by an inability to find a commercial program that exactly meets individual needs. It's been said that you can't write a job description for any job worth doing. That implies that any challenging job is unique, making it difficult for a manufacturer who wants to sell thousands of copies of his program to supply a tool that fits the unique requirements of such jobs. It also suggests that the person doing such a job is unique, thinks uniquely, and works in a unique way. That may be why you can read a glowing software review, only to find when you buy the program that its command structure and the way it works don't seem logical and natural to you. Learning to program helps solve these problems, since you'll be able to write applications programs tailored to fit your needs and preferences.

Finally, there's the possibility that knowing how to program will give you an edge in business. Understanding more about computers than can be learned solely by using commercial applications programs may enhance your value to a company.

—Paul Bonner,
Personal Computing, August 1983

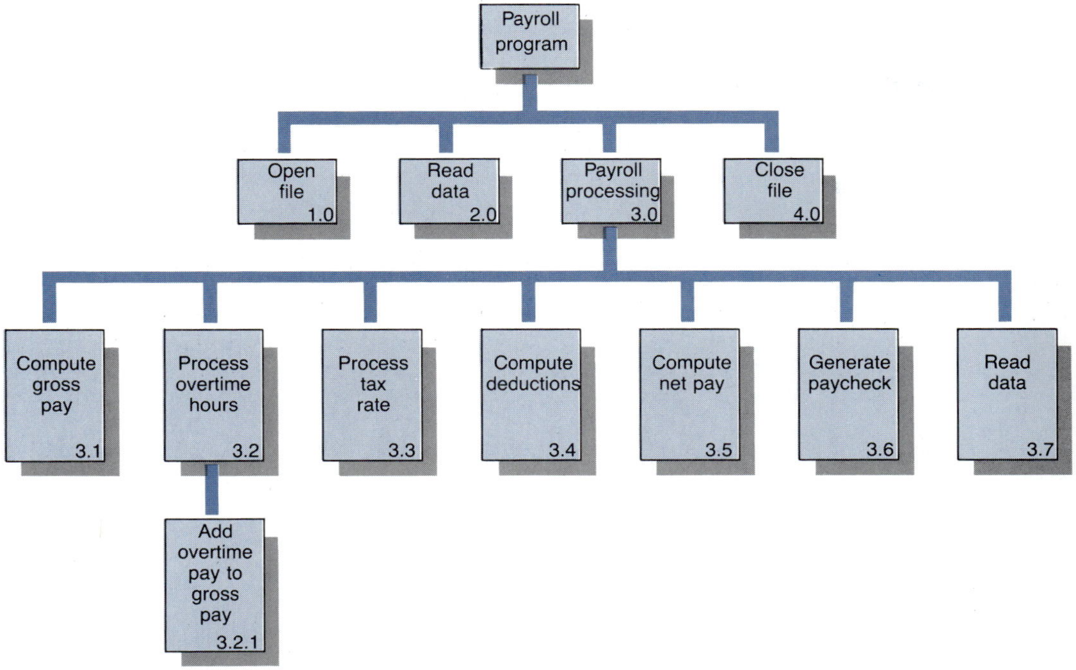
Payroll program
Open file 1.0
Read data 2.0
Payroll processing 3.0
Close file 4.0
Compute gross pay 3.1
Process overtime hours 3.2
Process tax rate 3.3
Compute deductions 3.4
Compute net pay 3.5
Generate paycheck 3.6
Read data 3.7
Add overtime pay to gross pay 3.2.1

Figure 5-4 Structure chart. This is a hierarchical graphical representation of the *Rough Cut* payroll program. A structure chart is also called a visual table of contents. The numbers in the boxes, or modules, refer to more detailed diagrams of these functions. Note that boxes 1.0 and 4.0 correspond to the control module in Figure 5-3, box 2.0 corresponds to Module A, and box 3.0 and its offspring correspond to Module B.

Structure Charts

A **structure chart,** shown in Figure 5-4, is a graphical description of the hierarchy of independent modules used in a structured program. The top level of the chart gives the name of the program—*PAYROLL PROGRAM,* in Figure 5-4. The next level breaks the program down into its major processing steps; in Figure 5-4, these are *OPEN FILE, READ DATA, PAYROLL PROCESSING,* and *CLOSE FILE.* Each of these second-level modules can then be subdivided further into smaller modules, as we have done with the *PAYROLL PROCESSING* module in Figure 5-4.

The numbers within the modules, such as 1.0, refer to more detailed diagrams of these functions.

HIPO Charts

HIPO—pronounced *high*-poh—stands for *H*ierarchy plus *I*nput-*P*rocess-*O*utput. Consisting of a package of diagrams that describes the structured program from general to particular, it is primarily a visual tool.

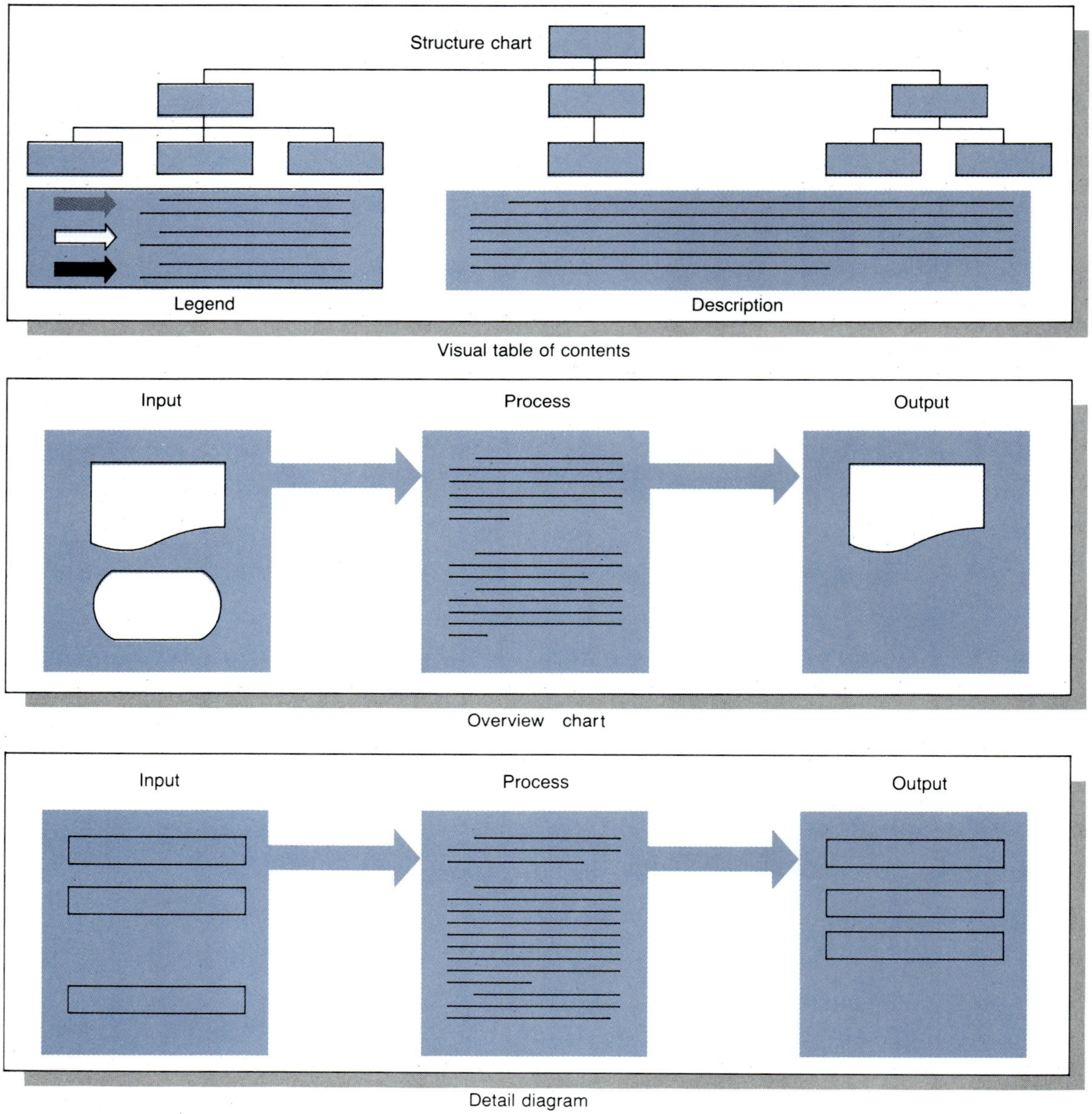
Structure chart
Legend
Description
Visual table of contents
Input
Process
Output
Overview chart
Input
Process
Output
Detail diagram

Figure 5-5 A HIPO package. Notice that this consists of three different kinds of diagrams: a structure chart, or visual table of contents; an overview chart; and a detail diagram.

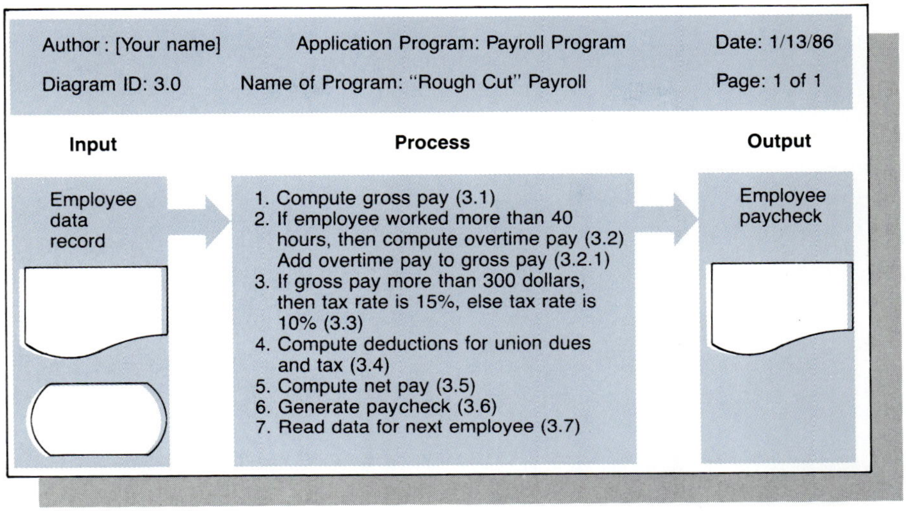
Author : [Your name]
Application Program: Payroll Program
Date: 1/13/86
Diagram ID: 3.0
Name of Program: "Rough Cut" Payroll
Page: 1 of 1
Input
Process
Output
Employee data record
1. Compute gross pay (3.1)
2. If employee worked more than 40 hours, then compute overtime pay (3.2) Add overtime pay to gross pay (3.2.1)
3. If gross pay more than 300 dollars, then tax rate is 15%, else tax rate is 10% (3.3)
4. Compute deductions for union dues and tax (3.4)
5. Compute net pay (3.5)
6. Generate paycheck (3.6)
7. Read data for next employee (3.7)
Employee paycheck

Figure 5-6 **Overview chart.** This second-level chart in a HIPO package shows the details of Module 3.0 in the *Rough Cut* payroll problem presented in the structure chart of Figure 5-4.

A HIPO package consists of three separate diagrams, as represented in Figure 5-5:

- A **visual table of contents,** which is the same thing as a structure chart, but with a short description and a legend describing what some symbols such as arrows mean.
- An **overview chart,** which shows, from left to right, the inputs, processes, and outputs of a particular module in the visual table of contents. An actual overview chart is shown in Figure 5-6. This chart, you will notice, is an elaboration of module 3.0 in Figure 5-4.
- A **detail diagram,** which looks like the overview chart in format, but is used to represent a finer level of detail, presenting the particulars of the functions to be performed and the data items required.

Most programming problems using a HIPO chart use only the visual table of contents and the overview chart; only large programs use the third level, the detail diagram.

Flowcharts

One of the most widely used devices for designing programs is the **flowchart,** which graphically presents the logic needed to solve a programming problem. There are two types of flowcharts: system and program.

A **system flowchart** depicts the way data in various forms moves through the stages of input, processing, output, and storage. A system

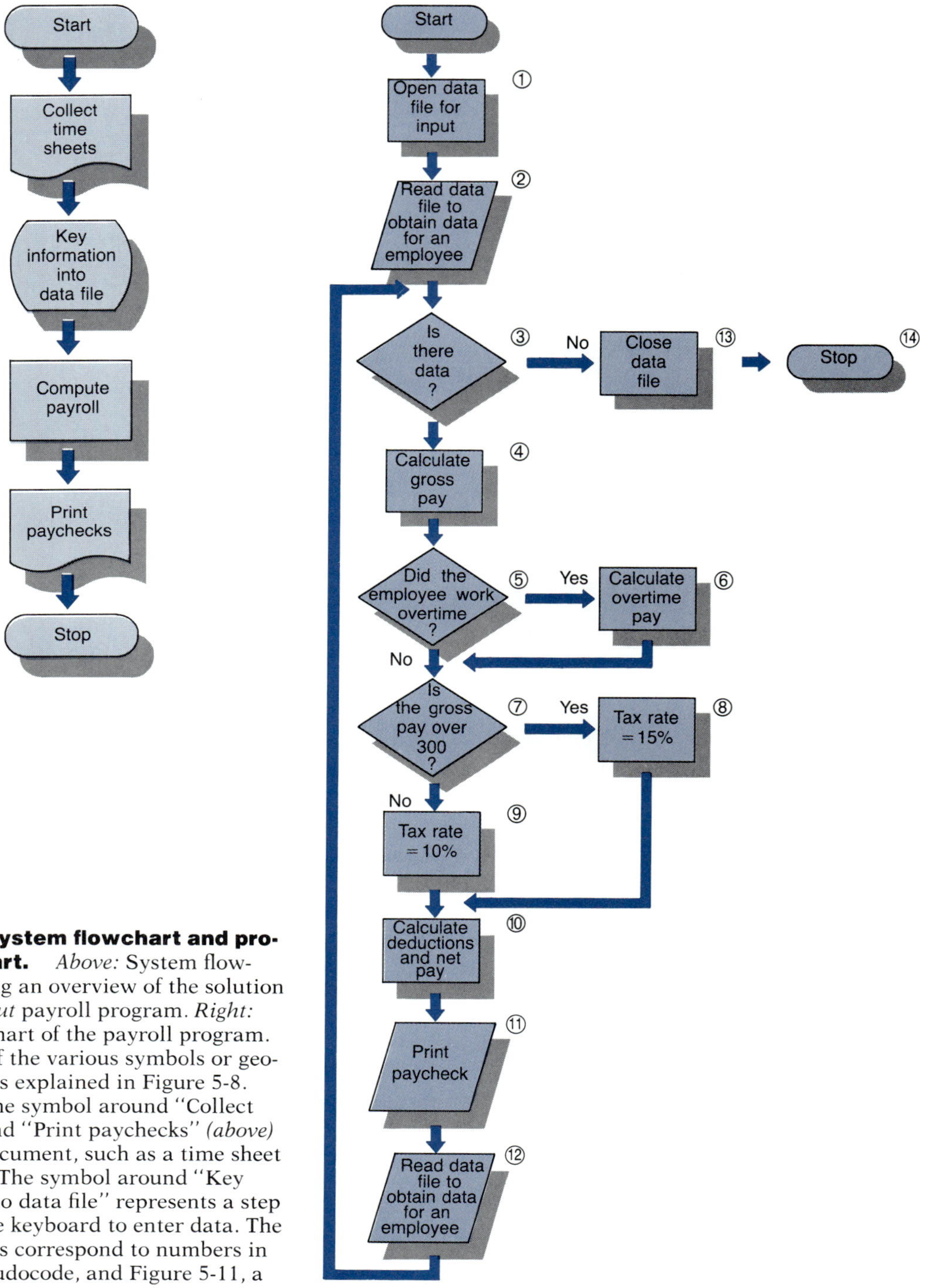
Start
Collect time sheets
Key information into data file
Compute payroll
Print paychecks
Stop
Start
Open data file for input
Read data file to obtain data for an employee
Is there data ?
No
Close data file
Stop
Calculate gross pay
Did the employee work overtime ?
Yes
Calculate overtime pay
No
Is the gross pay over 300 ?
Yes
Tax rate = 15%
No
Tax rate = 10%
Calculate deductions and net pay
Print paycheck
Read data file to obtain data for an employee

Figure 5-7 System flowchart and program flowchart. *Above:* System flowchart presenting an overview of the solution to the *Rough Cut* payroll program. *Right:* Program flowchart of the payroll program. The meaning of the various symbols or geometric shapes is explained in Figure 5-8. Additionally, the symbol around "Collect time sheets" and "Print paychecks" *(above)* represents a document, such as a time sheet or a paycheck. The symbol around "Key information into data file" represents a step that utilizes the keyboard to enter data. The circled numbers correspond to numbers in Figure 5-9, pseudocode, and Figure 5-11, a program listing.

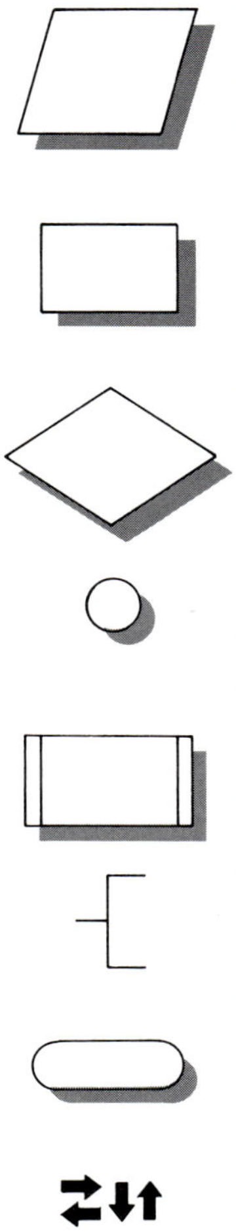

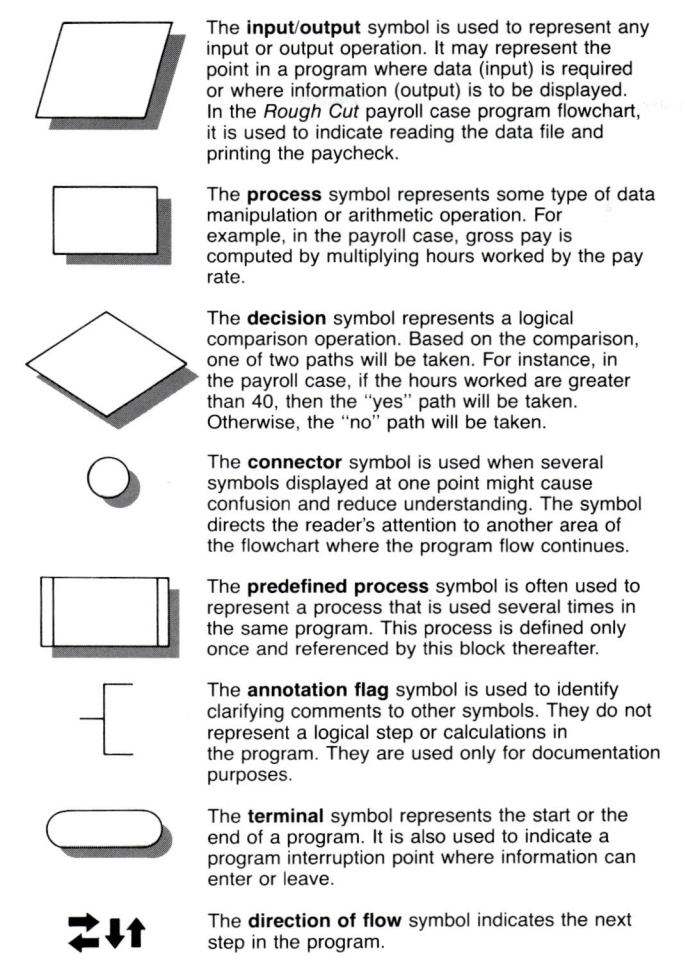

The **input/output** symbol is used to represent any input or output operation. It may represent the point in a program where data (input) is required or where information (output) is to be displayed. In the *Rough Cut* payroll case program flowchart, it is used to indicate reading the data file and printing the paycheck.

The **process** symbol represents some type of data manipulation or arithmetic operation. For example, in the payroll case, gross pay is computed by multiplying hours worked by the pay rate.

The **decision** symbol represents a logical comparison operation. Based on the comparison, one of two paths will be taken. For instance, in the payroll case, if the hours worked are greater than 40, then the "yes" path will be taken. Otherwise, the "no" path will be taken.

The **connector** symbol is used when several symbols displayed at one point might cause confusion and reduce understanding. The symbol directs the reader's attention to another area of the flowchart where the program flow continues.

The **predefined process** symbol is often used to represent a process that is used several times in the same program. This process is defined only once and referenced by this block thereafter.

The **annotation flag** symbol is used to identify clarifying comments to other symbols. They do not represent a logical step or calculations in the program. They are used only for documentation purposes.

The **terminal** symbol represents the start or the end of a program. It is also used to indicate a program interruption point where information can enter or leave.

The **direction of flow** symbol indicates the next step in the program.

Figure 5-8 Symbols used in flowcharting.

flowchart presents an overview, not the details, of the solution to the problem. A **program flowchart** presents the detailed sequence of steps needed to solve the problem. Program flowcharts are frequently used to visualize the logic and steps in processing. Figure 5-7 presents both a system flowchart and a program flowchart for the *Rough Cut* payroll problem.

There are only a few standard flowchart symbols necessary to solve almost any programming problem. These are explained in Figure 5-8.

Pseudocode

An alternative or supplement to flowcharts, **pseudocode** is a narrative rather than graphical form of describing structured program logic. It allows the program designer to focus upon the *logic* of the program and not on the details of programming or flowcharting.

A pseudocode to a program, says one writer, "is as beneficial as a sentence outline is to a research paper." Just as an outline contains enough specifics to ensure that you will not overlook any pertinent details when you are drafting your research paper, so a pseudocode will contain enough specifics to define what information or calculations need to be performed within all the major "outline" areas—the modules.[2]

As a manager, you may find pseudocode helpful because it allows you to get a preview of the program before the programmer actually starts putting it into flowchart or code form.

Figure 5-9 presents some pseudocode for the *Rough Cut* problem.

Document Program Design

At the end of the program design stage, a formal document should be prepared to guide future users. Often HIPO charts are used to document the program design. How long and detailed the document is depends on the size and complexity of the program. How important the document is also varies. If the program is so specialized as to be used only once, it will deserve a different kind of document than that of a typical business program that is to be used over and over.

3. Writing the Program

Writing the program is called coding. In this step, you use the logic you developed in the program design stage to actually write the program. This coding stage is, as we mentioned, what many people mean when they say "programming," but it really is only one of the six steps.

What programming language should you use for a program? BASIC? Pascal? COBOL? FORTRAN? We will defer this question to the next chapter, when we discuss several programming languages. Here we will discuss what makes a good program regardless of the language used.

What Makes a Good Program?

As in other categories of life, there are many ways to get to the same place. Traditional styles of programming *can* yield correct results just as structured programming can. But why take extra time, make extra mistakes, and produce a program that your successors may or may not be able to figure out after you have moved on?

Here are some of the qualities of a good program:

- It should be easily readable and understandable by people other than the original programmer.
- It should be efficient, increasing the programmer's productivity.

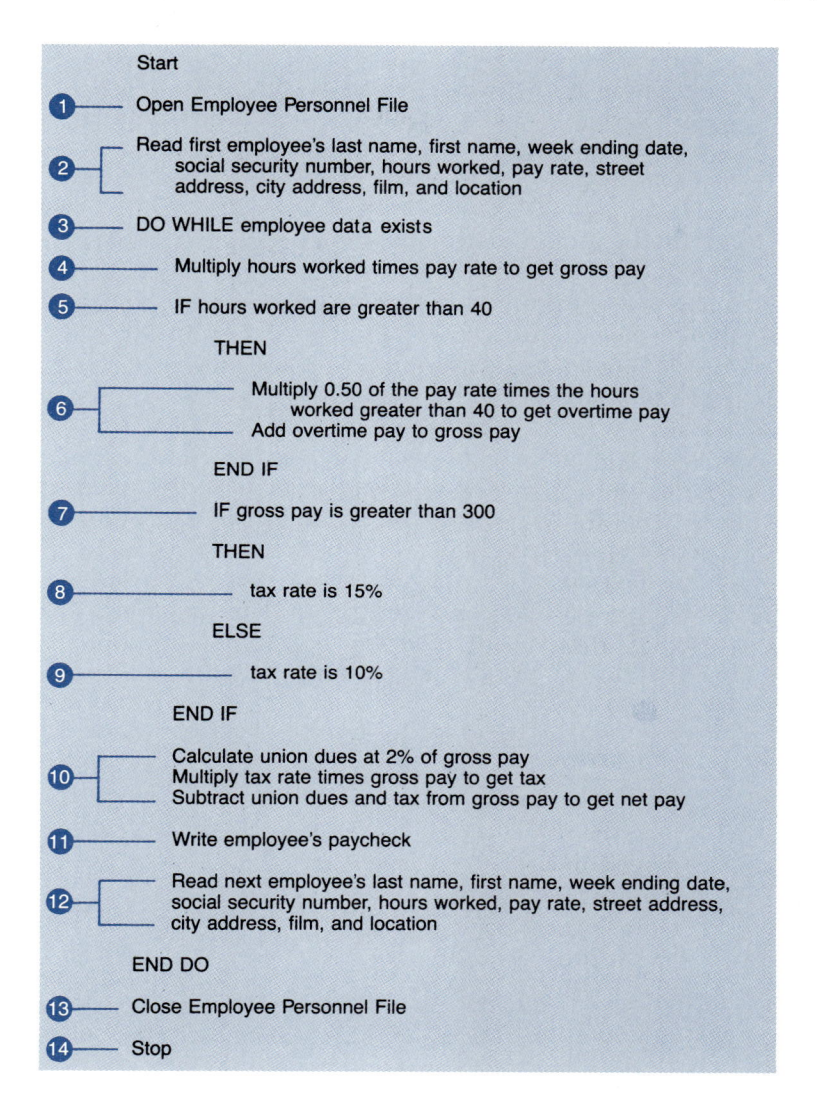

```
      Start
(1)   Open Employee Personnel File
(2)   Read first employee's last name, first name, week ending date,
          social security number, hours worked, pay rate, street
          address, city address, film, and location
(3)   DO WHILE employee data exists
(4)       Multiply hours worked times pay rate to get gross pay
(5)       IF hours worked are greater than 40
              THEN
(6)               Multiply 0.50 of the pay rate times the hours
                      worked greater than 40 to get overtime pay
                  Add overtime pay to gross pay
              END IF
(7)           IF gross pay is greater than 300
              THEN
(8)               tax rate is 15%
              ELSE
(9)               tax rate is 10%
          END IF
(10)      Calculate union dues at 2% of gross pay
          Multiply tax rate times gross pay to get tax
          Subtract union dues and tax from gross pay to get net pay
(11)      Write employee's paycheck
(12)      Read next employee's last name, first name, week ending date,
          social security number, hours worked, pay rate, street address,
          city address, film, and location
      END DO
(13)  Close Employee Personnel File
(14)  Stop
```

Figure 5-9 Pseudocode. This example shows how the *Rough Cut* payroll could be expressed in narrative rather than graphical form. DO WHILE means the computer should continue to *do* the processing *while*—that is, so long as—the conditions apply; namely, that "more employees exist" for whom paychecks must be made up. When that condition no longer exists, the program is instructed to END DO—that is, stop processing. Note that IF a certain condition exists, THEN certain steps must follow (or ELSE certain other steps must follow), until the condition no longer exists, at which point the computer is instructed to END IF. The IF and THEN would be expressed in a flowchart as the diamond-shaped decision symbol. The circled numbers correspond to the relevant portions of the program flowchart in Figure 5-7 and the actually coded program shown in Figure 5-11.

- It should not take excessive time to process or occupy any more computer memory than necessary.
- It should be reliable, able to work under all reasonable conditions.
- It should be able to detect unreasonable or erroneous conditions and indicate them to the programmer or operator.

Three factors that help make programs efficient are: (1) the statements can be arranged into patterns that enhance readability; (2) the variables—**variables** are symbolically named entities to which may be assigned a value or values—used are carefully and descriptively named; and (3) comments can be inserted into the program to document the logic patterns used.

As Mr. Elliott's right-hand person on the *Rough Cut* payroll project, you are particularly interested in anything that holds costs down. Thus, for instance, you would probably want the program to screen out any obvious errors in input data. For instance, except for the salaries of the top stars, you would not want the wage rate per hour incorrectly input at $300 per hour. The program should catch obvious and common errors of this sort, although, of course, it cannot catch everything. You also want the program to be easily maintained and updated by other programmers, since you hope the same program can be used on other Starfire productions.

Structured Coding: Avoiding "Spaghetti Code"

This is a very important discussion, for it has to do with the very nature of the logic of writing programs. Structured coding has been developed to take much of the guesswork out of programming, to assist programmers to produce programs of quality on a regular basis.

Once you have done your top-down design, breaking down the principal modules into lower-level functional modules, you can then proceed to write *any* program using a combination of three—and just these three—basic logic structures:

- Sequence
- Selection
- Loop

These three structures, shown in Figure 5-10, work as follows:

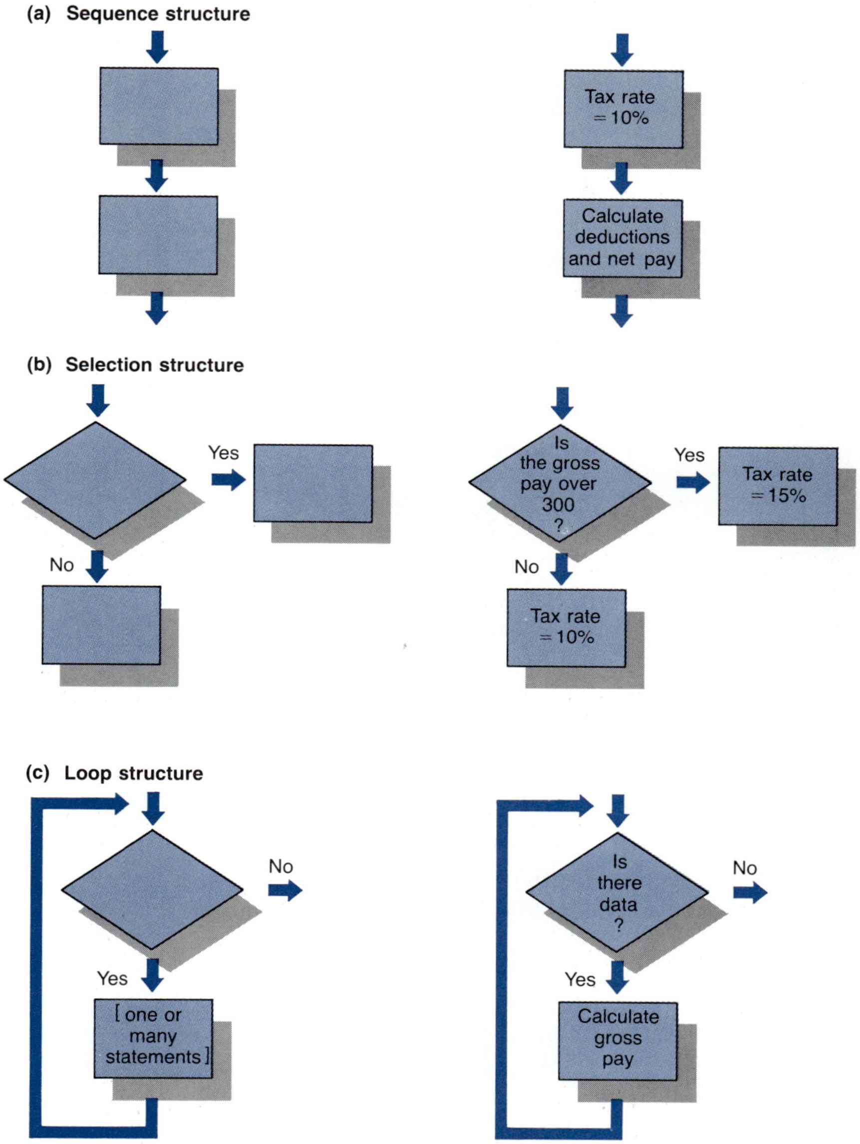
(a) Sequence structure
Tax rate = 10%
Calculate deductions and net pay
(b) Selection structure
Yes
No
Is the gross pay over 300 ?
Yes
Tax rate = 15%
No
Tax rate = 10%
(c) Loop structure
No
Yes
[one or many statements]
Is there data ?
No
Yes
Calculate gross pay

Figure 5-10 Sequence, selection, and loop logic structures. The examples at right are taken from the *Rough Cut* payroll flowchart in Figure 5-7.

Sequence Structure. The **sequence structure**—also known as *simple sequence*—is easily defined: it is simply *one program statement followed by another.* An example for the payroll program, where the sequence structure is used to calculate deductions, is shown in Figure 5-10(a).

Selection Structure. The selection structure occurs when a decision has to be made. It may be defined as: *a test must be made, and the outcome determines the choice of one of two paths to follow.* The selection structure was used in the payroll example to decide whether an employee's tax rate was 10% or 15%, as shown in Figure 5-10(b).

The selection structure is also known as an **IF-THEN-ELSE structure,** because that is how you would formulate the problem when making the decision or test. For example, in our program, you could say, "IF gross pay is over $300, THEN tax rate is 15%, ELSE tax rate is only 10%."

Loop Structure. The **loop structure**—also known as an *iteration structure*—may be defined as: *a process may be repeated as long as a certain condition remains true.* The structure is called a loop because the program loops around again and again. We see this in the *Rough Cut* program example in which the loop structure is used to process the payroll; see Figure 5-7. The program will continue to loop repeatedly until the answer to the question in the first selection structure ("Is there more data?") is no, not yes—in other words, until there are no more employees to figure weekly wages for. Then the program will close the data file and stop.

The loop structure is also known as a **DO UNTIL** structure in the principal form in which the loop is used. This is a handy way of thinking about the loop structure while you are writing a program. For example, in our payroll case, you could express the loop as: "DO process the payroll program UNTIL there is no more data to process." A variation is the **DO WHILE** structure. For example, in our payroll case, you could express the loop as: "DO process the payroll program WHILE there are employees whose time cards need processing."

Although other logic sequences exist, any program can be written with just these three.

Having worked through the logic of the program in structured form, you are now in a position to actually write it or code it—assuming you know what programming language to write it in. Since the *Rough Cut* film crew is taking a portable computer with them and since most portable computers run the language known as BASIC, you ask the programmer to code it in BASIC. This program is shown in Figure 5-11. We will describe this in more detail in Chapter 6, along with a discussion of other programming languages.

FLASHBACK: BEFORE STRUCTURED PROGRAM DESIGN

A Bowl of Spaghetti

The best way to show why structured coding is important is to go back to the "Sage of Software," as he has been called, Edsger Dijkstra. In 1968, Dijkstra published a letter in the *Communications of the ACM* (Association for Computing Machinery), which appeared under the heading, "Go To Statements Considered Harmful." The GO TO (often expressed as GOTO) is a transfer of control within a program: the program is told to go to another line in the program. In his letter, Dijkstra contended that the GOTO statements were overused to the point where a program could be compared to a bowl of spaghetti. That is, if you drew a line from each GOTO statement in a program to the statement to which it transferred, the result would be a picture that looked like a bowl of spaghetti. Since then, people have referred to a program that uses a lot of GOTOs as "spaghetti code."

Two years before Dijkstra's letter, the *Communications of the ACM* had also published a paper by C. Bohm and G. Jacopini that proved mathematically that any problem solution could be constructed using only three basic logic structures—the ones referred to in the text under the names *sequence, selection,* and *loop.* It is noteworthy that these three structures have remained unchanged since they were proposed in 1966.

Edsger Dijkstra.

The first major project using structured programming was a large undertaking done for the *New York Times,* the results of which were published in 1972. The task was to automate the newspaper's vast clipping file in such a way that a user could, from a list of index terms, browse through summaries of the paper's articles, automatically retrieve on microfiche the text of any article, and display it on a terminal. The project involved 83,000 lines of code, took 22 calendar months, and involved 11 person-years, yet it came in ahead of schedule and under budget—and with only 21 errors during the five weeks of acceptance testing. Only 25 additional errors appeared during the first year of the system's operation—an unheard-of record in the days of spaghetti code. Since then, structured programming has gained wide acceptance.

```
100 OPEN 'EMP.DAT' FOR INPUT AS FILE #1
110 INPUT #1, N1$, N2$, W1$, S1$, H1, P1, A1$, A2$, F$, L$
120 IF N1$ = 'END OF FILE' THEN 310
130   LET G1 = H1 * P1
140   IF H1 <= 40 THEN 170
150   LET O1 = (.50 * P1) * (H1 - 40)
160   LET G1 = G1 + O1
170   IF G1 > 300 THEN 200
180   LET T = .10
190   GOTO 210
200   LET T = .15
210   LET U1 = .02 * G1
220   LET T2 = T * G1
230   LET N3 = G1 - U1 - T2
240   PRINT : PRINT : PRINT : PRINT : PRINT : PRINT
250   PRINT W1$, F$, L$, H1, G1, N3, S1$
260   PRINT : PRINT
270   PRINT N2$, N1$
280   PRINT A1$, N3
290   PRINT A2$
300 GOTO 110
310 CLOSE #1
320 END
```

Figure 5-11 BASIC program for *Rough Cut* payroll program. The circled numbers correspond to the pertinent portions of the flowchart in Figure 5-7 and pseudocode in Figure 5-9.

The program has been written, so you are now ready to run it and test it on the computer.

4. Testing the Program

Testing means running the program and fixing it if it does not work, or **debugging** it (getting the errors or bugs out), as programmers call it. Let us consider two types of bugs or errors—syntax errors and logic errors.

A **syntax error** is a violation of the rules of whatever programming language you are writing in. For example, if you are trying to print a line and are writing in the BASIC language, you need to use the output statement PRINT. If you write PRRINT, it is a syntax error.

A **logic error** occurs when you have used an incorrect calculation or left out a programming procedure. If you forgot to write in a procedure for computing overtime pay in the *Rough Cut* example, that would be a logic error. The program would still produce paychecks, but some would be wrong.

There are a number of ways by which syntax and logic errors are weeded out.

Structured Walkthroughs

A **structured walkthrough** is a formal review process designed not only to verify computer code but also to evaluate the documentation and the design of the program. In this process, a coded program is submitted to a review team of three or four programmers, including the one who produced the code. After the review, the program's overall completeness, accuracy, and quality of design are discussed.

Typically, the program is put through **desk-checking,** a phase similar to proofreading, in which the entire program is reviewed, statement by statement, for syntax and logic errors. Following this, the program is further checked by manually tracing the program—that is, by checking every instruction with sample data (both correct and incorrect) manually through the program.

Structured walkthroughs are more than just attempts to check a particular coded program. Their purpose also is to help standardize the design and coding process and produce error-free coding. It has been found to be an effective technique to identify programming errors and to increase programmer productivity.

Checking for Syntax Errors

In the next stage, the program is sent to the computer. Using a translator program, the computer attempts to convert each coded program statement from the programming language in which it was written (BASIC, COBOL, or whatever) into a form the computer will accept, a form known as **machine language,** the lowest level of computer language. (This process is discussed further in Chapter 6.) Before the program can be executed, it must be entirely free of any syntax errors. Typically, these syntax errors are readily identified by the computer when it attempts to translate the program.

Checking for Logic Errors

After all syntax errors have been corrected and the program code has been successfully translated into machine language, the program can be tested for logic errors, usually using a set of test data designed to test thoroughly all aspects of the program. The test data should cause each program statement to execute at least once. Both the tested output and the sequence of operations are compared against a manual desk check.

Program Verification Document

When the program has been tested and corrected, it is now a production program and ready for use. A **program verification document** should be prepared that lists the final program, discusses the checking and testing procedures used, and presents the test data.

The Importance of Documentation

With programmers changing jobs as frequently as every one to two years, it becomes impossible to live without documentation. The days of the "lifers" are gone—those loyal employees who spend their entire careers in one company. At the same time, nearly every DP [data processing] manager has made the mistake of watching the one person who knows the system inside and out walk off the job, leaving no morsel of documentation behind.

The ability of users and operators to interface with the system is determined, in large part, by the documentation provided. And users' documentation needs grow as more activity and control shift their way. Users must have the tools to understand and interact with systems to perform effectively.

—Nancy B. Lerner, Irv Brownstein, and Wallace W. Smith, *Computerworld*, March 29, 1982

5. Documenting the Program

Although program documentation is presented here as the fifth stage in the programming process, it has been an ongoing practice since the beginning. The importance of program documentation is sometimes minimized; it cannot be overstated, however, for programs intended for frequent use in business applications. Without proper documentation, it is very difficult for a programmer, even the original programmer, to update and maintain a program.

The final document should contain the following information:

- **Program analysis document,** with a concise statement of the program's objectives, outputs, inputs, and processing procedures.
- **Program design document,** with detailed flowcharts and other appropriate diagrams such as HIPO charts.

- **Program verification document,** outlining the checking, testing, and correction procedures along with a list of test data and solutions.
- **Log** used to document future program revision and maintenance activity.

6. Maintaining the Program

After the program has been fully tested and has become operational, it typically will require occasional maintenance to modify or update it. This activity is so commonplace that many organizations have specialists called maintenance programmers.

Maintenance is particularly important in the payroll application since tax-related computations must have the tax percentages and the like changed annually or whenever the government changes the tax basis.

Moving on to Languages

This concludes the six steps of applications programming. In the next chapter, we will discuss the languages of principal interest to business users.

SUMMARY

- Business managers need to understand the programming process for three reasons: (1) They must communicate programming needs to hired programmers and understand the program applications. (2) With the increasing availability of computers, the value of programming skills increases. (3) Programming is a *problem-solving process* in which business users and data processing specialists interact.
- There are two types of computer programs: (1) **operating system programs,** which are designed to efficiently control and manage the computer's operations, and (2) **application programs,** which perform specific data processing and computational tasks—to do business and scientific problem solving.
- Programming is more than **coding**—the writing of statements in a programming language; it is a problem-solving procedure that can be approached in two ways: (1) traditional and (2) structured.
- **Traditional programming** refers to early programming—that is, creative and individualized, with few standards. Different programmers used differ-

ent structure and logic procedures—often complex and stylized—that were difficult for others to understand. Lack of strict and formalized standards led to problems in modifying and maintaining programs.

- **Structured programming** is standardized programming. By using structured design, structured coding, and structured review, it increases program simplicity and reliability and reduces costs of developing and maintaining programs.
- All programming processes follow the same six steps: (1) Define the problem. (2) Design a solution. (3) Write the program. (4) Test it. (5) Document it. (6) Maintain it.
- Defining the problem—**program analysis**—involves six tasks: (1) Specify the objectives of the program. (2) Specify the outputs. (3) Specify the input requirements. (4) Specify the processing requirements. (5) Evaluate the feasibility of the program. (6) Document the program analysis (provide statements on the preceding five tasks).
- The second step of the programming process is the **program design** stage, during which a solution to the problem is designed. **Structured program design** minimizes complexity; it uses one or more of the following tools: (1) top-down program design, (2) structure charts, (3) HIPO charts, (4) flowcharts, and (5) pseudocode.
- **Top-down program design** is a structured design technique in which the programmer, having determined the outputs to be produced and the inputs required, identifies the major processing steps, called **modules** (logically related program statements). This type of design has some rigid rules: (1) Each module can have only one entry point and one exit point. (2) When the program is **executed** (run through the computer) it must be able to move from one module to the next in sequence until the last module has been executed. (3) Each module should be independent and should have a single function. (4) Each module should be of manageable size to make the design and testing of the program easier.
- A **structure chart** is a graphical description of the hierarchy of independent modules used in a structured program.
- A **HIPO** chart, which stands for *H*ierarchy plus *I*nput-*P*rocess-*O*utput, is a package of three diagrams that describe the structured program from general to particular. The three diagrams are (1) a **visual table of contents,** which is a structure chart with a short description and explanations of symbols; (2) an **overview chart,** which shows, from left to right, the inputs, processes, and outputs of a particular module in the visual table of contents; and (3) a **detail diagram,** which represents a finer level of detail than the overview chart and which is used only for large programs.
- **Flowcharts,** which are widely used for designing programs, graphically present the logic needed to solve a programming problem. There are two types of flowcharts: (1) system and (2) program.

Summary continues on p.159

Corporate Report 2

The Software Industry: Inside Look at a Software Development Firm

730
ASK

According to legend, computer-related businesses begin in a garage. Indeed, computer makers Hewlett-Packard and Apple Computer actually did. But Sandra Kurtzig, the founder of ASK Computer Systems, Inc., had no garage. When she started the company in 1972, it was in an apartment bedroom.

Launched on an investment of $2000 with the idea of providing part-time work while Sandra raised two small children, today ASK is a major software company with more than 400 employees and over $65 million in 1984 sales, and is headquartered in an attractive one-story, garden-style office complex in Los Altos, California.

Management Information Systems for Manufacturing Companies

Sandra Kurtzig *(behind desk)* is now ASK's chief executive officer and chairman of the board, having in 1984 turned over her duties of president to Ron Braniff *(lower right)*. Ms. Kurtzig started out developing computer software that allowed weekly newspapers to keep track of their newspaper carriers. Now ASK offers integrated computer software—management information systems to help companies run their manufacturing operations more efficiently.

There are essentially three parts to ASK's operation:

- **Software development:** The MANMAN® (manufacturing management) family of products, shown in the drawing at the end of this Corporate Report, consists of software developed for the major functional areas of a manufacturing company: marketing, engineering, production, and finance.
- **Timesharing network:** Under the name ASKNET,® the company runs a remote processing service, with a national telecommunications network through which manufacturing companies can use the MANMAN software on ASK's computers.
- **User training and support:** Training classes for users of ASK products are provided at several locations nationwide.

Software Development

Software development begins with brainwork—perhaps at a cluttered desk (in the photo below, note the flowchart in the binder), at a meeting of a project development group, or in a group sitting on the carpet doing shop-floor control models. These are the problem-definition and design stages in which, after consultation with customers and programmers, the problems are analyzed and solutions proposed. Next comes writing and testing of the program, which involves the use of a computer. The software documentation is then written up with the help of a technical writer, who can put instructions about the software into language users can understand.

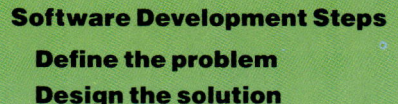

Software Development Steps

- **Define the problem**
- **Design the solution**
- **Write the program**
- **Test the program**
- **Document the program**
- **Maintain the program**

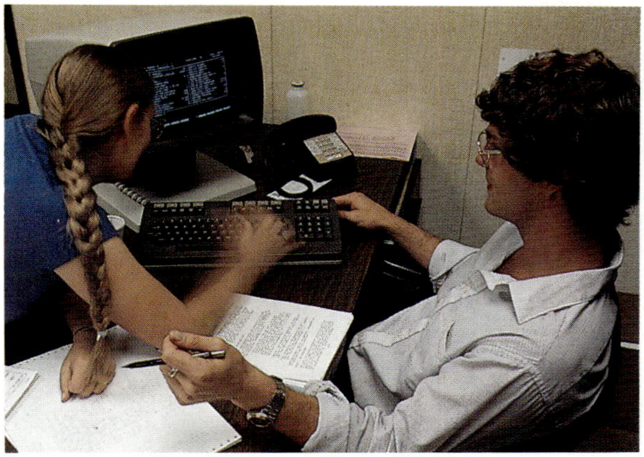

Telecommunications and Hardware

ASK's management information system is available to customers in three ways:

- As a turnkey system—"Turnkey" means customers buy the hardware and software together from ASK and simply "turn the key on" to use it. No special adaptations are required. ASK

buys Hewlett-Packard 3000 or Digital Equipment Corp. VAX minicomputers and resells them.

- On a licensed software-only basis—This is for manufacturers that already have HP3000 computers or DEC's VAX minicomputers. They are licensed to use ASK software only for themselves; it may not be distributed or resold.
- Through ASK's remote processing service—Manufacturers have their own terminals linked via telecommunication networks to ASKNET, an on-line remote processing service with the hardware located in the network's command center in ASK's Los Altos headquarters. This benefits small, fast-growing manufacturing companies that do not yet want to invest in data processing equipment or personnel.

Some of the hardware and telecommunications equipment is shown on these two pages. *Opposite page, right:* ASKNET's command center, on which two technicians are working; note the circuit board on the floor in front of them. *Middle left:* Foreground view of hardcopy and softcopy terminals, background view of two Digital Equipment Corp. minicomputers. *Middle right:* View of Hewlett-Packard minicomputer; operator at left is mounting a tape reel on a magnetic tape drive. *Lower right:* Lifting the suction-cup handle on the floor reveals cables linking computers with peripheral and telecommunications equipment. *This page, top:* A magnetic tape drive. *Middle:* Lock-boxes for security of magnetic tapes, to prevent damage from fire. *Bottom:* Operator removing printout from a printer.

User Education and Support

Many software development companies find that customer support is an ongoing requirement. All provide user manuals—documentation—and most provide consultation by phone or visits to the customer. ASK also provides training classes for users of its management information system, as shown in the top three photos on this page. There are seven education centers throughout the country, which

offer a series of twenty-one courses, including lectures, handbooks, case studies, and hands-on experience. The courses give users the theory and practice they need to know to understand MANMAN.

Opposite page:

The customer-support department, which offers telephone consultation to customers, is shown below. Members of ASK's corporate communications department, shown meeting lower right, are responsible for advertising, public relations, trade shows, collateral materials, and sales incentive trips.

Pioneers in Undersea Systems
Sippican

HEWITT CUSTOM SOAPS.
THEY'LL ADD A NEW DIMENSION
TO YOUR BUSINESS.

HI-TEK
KEYBOARDS

ASK customers. Three of ASK's 750 customers are represented here. *Top:* Sippican Ocean Systems is an oceanographic products manufacturer based in Marion, Massachusetts. It has been using the MANMAN system since 1979. *Middle:* Hewitt Soap Company, located in Dayton, Ohio, is a manufacturer of specialty soap products. Hewitt has been an ASK customer since 1981. *Bottom:* Hi-Tek Corporation is a keyboard manufacturer located in Garden Grove, California. The company has been using MANMAN since 1982.

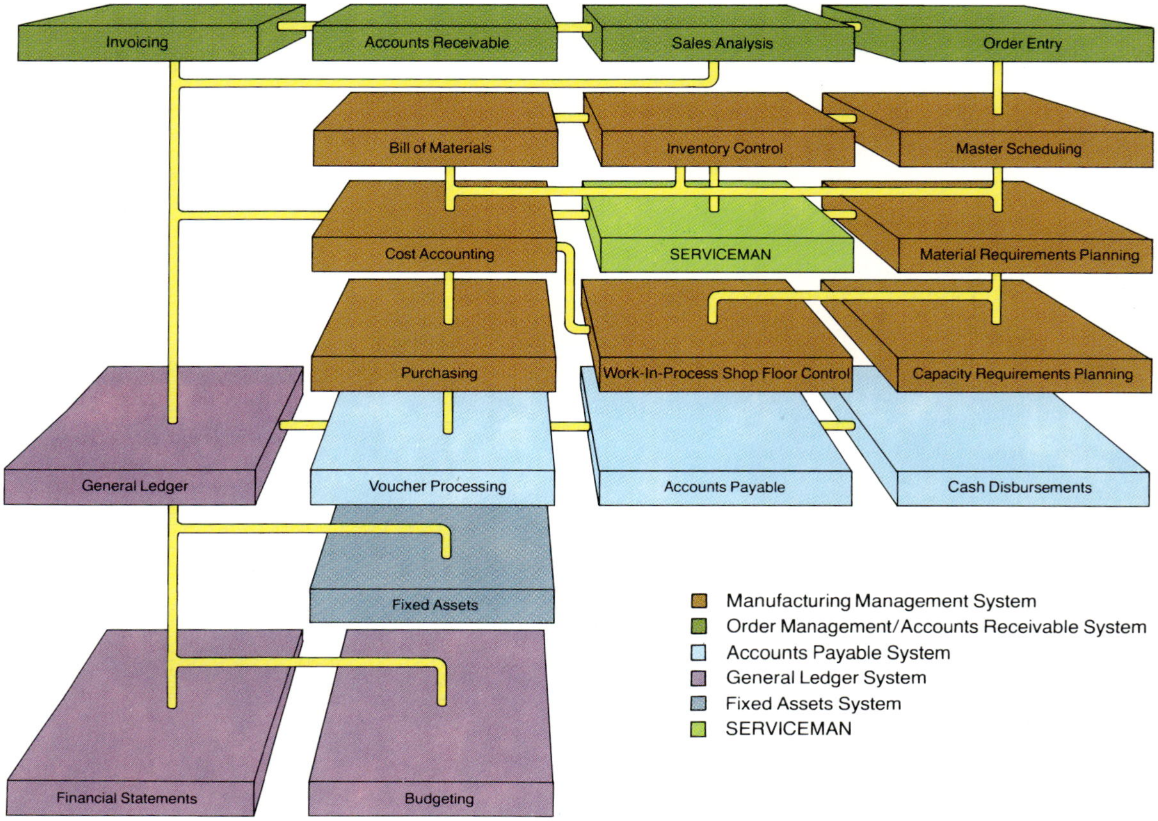
Invoicing
Accounts Receivable
Sales Analysis
Order Entry
Bill of Materials
Inventory Control
Master Scheduling
Cost Accounting
SERVICEMAN
Material Requirements Planning
Purchasing
Work-In-Process Shop Floor Control
Capacity Requirements Planning
General Ledger
Voucher Processing
Accounts Payable
Cash Disbursements
Fixed Assets
Financial Statements
Budgeting
Manufacturing Management System
Order Management/Accounts Receivable System
Accounts Payable System
General Ledger System
Fixed Assets System
SERVICEMAN

Management Information System. Short for "Manufacturing Management," ASK calls this series of programs or management information systems MANMAN. This particular kind of management information system (MIS) is designed to help manufacturers deal with problems such as controlling costs without reducing customer service, meeting delivery dates without pushing labor or machines into overtime, and keeping inventory levels high enough to meet changes in market demand but low enough to avoid excessive carrying costs. The MISs link all resources of a company through common data bases that reflect up-to-the-minute status of every operation. The system is "integrated," meaning that those who use the information—shop people, managers, vice presidents—are accessing the source data from a common data base. All the modules tie together in the system, so that the user only need enter the data once.

End of the day.

- A **system flowchart** shows the way data in various forms moves through the stages of input, processing, output, and storage; it presents a general overview of the solution to the problem. A **program flowchart** presents the detailed sequence of steps needed to solve the problem.
- **Pseudocode** is a narrative rather than a graphical form of describing structured program logic. It focuses on the logic of the program rather than on the details of programming or flowcharting.
- A formal document should be prepared at the end of the program design stage to guide future users.
- The third step of the programming process—writing the program, or **coding**—uses the logic developed in the design stage.
- A good program should (1) be easily readable and understandable by people other than the original programmer; (2) be efficient, increasing the programmer's productivity; (3) not take excessive time to process or occupy more computer memory than necessary; (4) be reliable, able to work under all reasonable conditions; and (5) be able to detect unreasonable or erroneous conditions and indicate them to the programmer or operator.
- In an efficient program, (1) the statements can be arranged into patterns that enhance readability; (2) the **variables** (symbolically named entities to which may be assigned a value or values) used are carefully and descriptively named; and (3) comments can be inserted into the program to document the logic patterns used.
- Structured coding—developed to take much of the guesswork out of programming—can be used to write *any* program using a combination of three basic logic structures: (1) sequence, (2) selection, and (3) loop.
- **Sequence structure**, also known as *simple sequence,* is simply one program statement followed by another.
- **Selection structure,** or **IF-THEN-ELSE structure,** occurs when a decision has to be made, and the outcome determines the choice of one of two paths to follow—IF this is true THEN do this command; IF not true, do ELSE.
- **Loop structure,** or iteration structure, refers to a process that may be repeated as long as a certain condition remains true. This is also known as a **DO UNTIL structure**—DO command UNTIL there is no more data to process. A variation of this is the **DO WHILE structure**—DO command WHILE there is data to process.
- The fourth step of the programming process is testing the program, or **debugging** it, which means running the program and fixing it if it does not work. Debugging involves two types of errors: syntax errors and logic errors. A **syntax error** is a violation of the rules of whatever programming language is being used. A **logic error** is the use of an incorrect calculation or the omission of a programming procedure.

- A **structured walkthrough,** used to weed out syntax and logic errors, is a formal review process designed not only to verify computer code but also to evaluate the documentation and the design of the program. In this process, a review team checks the program's completeness, accuracy, and quality of design. The program is put through **desk-checking,** during which it is reviewed statement by statement for syntax and logic errors. Following this, the program is traced by manually running both correct and incorrect sample data through it. Structured walkthroughs also help standardize the design and coding process.
- To eliminate additional syntax errors, the program is sent to the computer, which attempts to convert (translate) each coded program statement from the programming language in which it was written into a form the computer will accept—known as **machine language,** the lowest level of computer language.
- To eliminate additional logic errors, a set of test data will be run that has been designed to test thoroughly all aspects of the program.
- The fifth step in the programming process, documenting the program, actually starts at the beginning of the process. It is very important for programs intended for frequent use in business applications. Without a proper **program verification document,** it is difficult for a programmer to update and maintain a program.
- The final document should contain the following information: (1) Program analysis document, with a concise statement of the program's objectives, outputs, inputs, and processing procedures; (2) program design document, with detailed flowcharts and other appropriate diagrams; (3) program verification document, outlining the checking, testing, and correction procedures along with a list of test data and solutions; (4) a log used to document future program revision and maintenance activity.
- The sixth step in the programming process, maintaining the program, is required to modify or update the program. This is usually done by maintenance programmers.

KEY TERMS

Application program, p. 133
Coding, p. 133
Debugging, p. 154
Desk-checking, p. 155
Detail diagram, p. 145
DO UNTIL structure, p. 152
DO WHILE structure, p. 152
Executed, p. 141
Flowchart, p. 145
IF-THEN-ELSE structure, p. 152
HIPO, p. 143
Logic error, p. 154
Loop structure, p. 152
Machine language, p. 155
Module, p. 140
Operating system program, p. 133
Overview chart, p. 145
Program, p. 131

Program analysis, p. 156
Program design, pp. 140, 156
Program flowchart, p. 145
Program verification document, p. 155
Pseudocode, p. 147
Sequence structure, p. 152
Structure chart, p. 143
Structured program design, p. 140
Structured programming, p. 134
Structured walk-through, p. 155
Syntax error, p. 154
System flowchart, p. 145
Top-down program design, p. 140
Traditional programming, p. 133
Variable, p. 150
Visual table of contents, p. 145

REVIEW QUESTIONS

1. Why should someone planning a business management career learn about computer programming?
2. How does structured programming differ from traditional programming?
3. What are the six steps of the programming process?
4. Describe the process of program analysis.
5. What are the two types of flowcharts, and how are they used?
6. What makes a good program?
7. Describe how a program is debugged and checked for errors.
8. Why is program documentation important, and what information should it contain?

CASE PROBLEMS

Case 5-1: A Program for Billable Time

Professionals such as lawyers, accountants, or advertising executives must keep a careful accounting of their time so they can charge clients correctly. Sometimes this can be done with paper and pencil or time cards and calculators, but as your enterprise gets larger and your clients multiply, it can get to be a real hassle. As an article in *Personal Computing* puts it, "In most service-oriented organizations, there are typically a lot of employees recording little bits of time which have to be accumulated and summarized at the end of a month. This type of business usually has either a limited number of clients, each having a lot of projects, or a lot of clients and a limited number of projects." In addition, the article points out, "Most of these service-oriented firms (such as advertising agencies) bill their clients on a per-hour basis. A particular kind of work, done by, say, a high-level employee, costs the client more than if it was done by a lower-level employee. Consequently, the firm must carefully track not only the amount of time, but the level of time spent on each part of a client's particular job."[3]

Suppose you are running an advertising agency, with different clients who have different products, and with two levels of employees within your agency—"creative" (such as copywriters and artists) and "account managers," the latter charging half again as much as the former for their hourly work. When you look at this, you can see it is not greatly different from the *Rough Cut* payroll application. You can identify your clients as Client A, Client B, and so on; the products whose ad campaigns you are working on as A-1, A-2, and so on; and the employees in your shop as Creative-1, Creative-2, Account Manager-1, Account Manager-2, and so on.

Your assignment: Using the programming steps outlined in this chapter, see if you can solve the problem of writing a general program with which to keep track of billable time.

Case 5-2: Saving for College

Sometimes when you are learning a new method of problem solving, it helps to try it out on a problem for which you already know the answer. We will do this here.

Let us suppose you are a banker who is trying to interest parents in beginning a savings plan to help put their children through college. A single year of room, board, and tuition costs $4500 at a state university and more than $12,000 at some private colleges and universities. If inflation continues, it will, of course, cost even more in the future.

Table 5-1 Saving for College

	Estimated Total College Cost		Savings Needed per Month through College	
Child's Age	*State*	*Private*	*State*	*Private*
3	$56,700	$94,500	$ 83.87	$139.79
6	46,440	77,400	98.72	164.53
9	37,800	63,000	118.89	198.14
12	30,600	51,000	149.38	248.97
15	25,200	42,000	208.35	347.25

Table 5-1 (which assumes college expenses will rise 7% a year and that savings will earn 10% a year) shows how much a family must save every month, depending on the age of the child.[4]

Your assignment: See if you can construct a flowchart, much like a simple version of the flowchart shown in Figure 5-7(b), in which the program reads the file for children of the different ages shown in the table and then shows the alternative monthly amounts to be saved for a state institution versus a private institution.

CHAPTER 6

READY FOR COMMANDS
AUX TRAY SELECTED
READY FOR COMMANDS
"ON-LINE" INPUT IS WAITING FOR DATA
"ON-LINE" INPUT IS RECEIVING DATA
RESUMING OUTPUT.
OUTPUT PROCESSING HAS CAUGHT-UP WITH INPUT PROCESSING
READY FOR COMMANDS
HAS COMPLETED INPUT PHASE
RESUMING OUTPUT.
HAS COMPLETED PRINTING.
READY FOR COMMANDS
READY FOR COMMANDS
"ON-LINE" INPUT IS WAITING FOR DATA
"ON-LINE" INPUT IS RECEIVING DATA

Programming Languages

The Different Ways of Communicating with the Computer

P R E V I E W

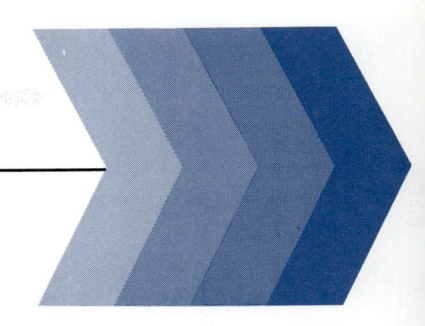

English has become one of the important international languages of business. But an American traveling on business in, say, the Far East quickly discovers that English is not enough outside the hotels and executive suites. If, on your way to Australia for the *Rough Cut* location shoot, you find yourself with a couple of days' layover in Tokyo, you will soon discover that to get around the city and make yourself understood in local shops and restaurants, you will need a translator.

Computers are the same way: You speak English, but their local dialect is machine language, which in printed form is apt to be an incomprehensible page after page of ones and zeros. How can you communicate with the computer?

Levels of Language

The solution to communicating with the computer is to develop a third language—a language that can be understood by both you and the computer. This is what a **programming language** is—a set of rules that provides a way of instructing the computer to perform certain operations.

The choice of programming language—step 3 of the programming process in Chapter 5—is, however, an important one. There are over 150 programming languages in existence—and these are just the ones that are still being used; we are not counting the ones that, for one reason or another, are considered obsolete. How do you know whether to use JOVIAL instead of HEARSAY, DOCTOR instead of STUDENT, COBOL instead of SNOBOL? Actually, it is not as difficult as it looks because certain languages are used for

CASE STUDY: A LOOK INSIDE A SOFTWARE HOUSE

Who Grows the Software?

For the would-be software buyer, the choice is staggering, and it's no wonder that most users settle for a few well known names. In fact, computer dealers themselves are overwhelmed with options. Facing a 40-hour training session to really master a system, they tend to stick with the tip of the iceberg, stocking only a limited number of popular programs. . . .

It's therefore not surprising that a few software programs have attracted most of the limelight. Such highly visible products as WordStar and VisiCalc have become high-tech-household names, launching an armada of imitators.

Despite the harsh competition, however, the market is still not saturated with good ideas. Newer companies operating in the free market traditions of hard work, gumption, and innovation keep starting up, and sometimes flourish. They are typically managed by a youthful crew and financed for a song when compared to the costs of manufacturing computer hardware.

Take Silicon Valley Systems, a software house starting to burst through the walls of its Belmont, California location. Founder and president Nathan M. Schulhof denies he's obsessed by the business, but confesses to thinking about it even in the more intimate moments of his personal life. A behavioral scientist by training, with a leaning

towards Freud, Schulhof turned software vendor in 1980, specializing in programs for Apple. . . .

According to Schulhof, it is service coupled with programmer genius that constitute what the best software houses are actually selling—the disk itself, after all, only costs a few dollars. Software development, on the other hand, is dependent on the talents of a programmer who can cost upwards of $50 an hour, raising the initial investment well into the six figures.

To produce its first product, a word processing package [called The Word Handler], Schulhof conducted his own headhunting to recruit Lenny Elekman, a programmer with extensive minicomputer experience and two word processing systems already under his belt. Schulhof's offer was modest: "Give me blind obedience and nine months of your life, and I'll make you a wealthy man."

Who could resist? Lenny was locked up in a motel with his Apple, and within the promised gestation period he delivered the goods. The company was launched, and Elekman turned in his room key for more luxurious quarters. The two are still working together.

Actually, as any programmer would tell you, it wasn't that simple. The act, or perhaps the art, of programming involves issuing a set of very small, very specific instructions to the computer, which in fact turns out to be a remarkably stupid device. Even with "higher level" languages such as the familiar BASIC, the program operates on a simplistic level: IF this THEN do that; ADD these; GO do this for a while and come back again. What passes for intelligence on the machine's part is actually forethought by the programmer—writing enough commands to cover all contingencies, especially the unexpected. For ultimately it is a living, breathing, and marvelously inconsistent human being who must interact with all this rigorous logic.

To make Elekman's job even more complex, commercial programs such as his are almost always written in a "lower level" language that more closely reflects the inner workings of the machine. The payoff is machine efficiency—the less translating a computer has to do, the faster it can operate. Unfortunately, machine (or assembly) language is even more incremental than its higher level counterparts, with a tremendous number of commands required.

The final program listing—called the source code—is the size of a novelette. "It takes concentration, dedication, and infinite care to handle that kind of detail," says Elekman. "The process is very much analogous to writing a book."

—Bart Eisenberg,
LIST, Spring 1983

certain disciplines. In this chapter, we will deal only with those of primary interest to people in business—BASIC, COBOL, PL/I, and RPG. We will also describe some languages that have scientific applications—FORTRAN, Ada, and Pascal.

First, however, we need to discuss the notion of levels of language. Programming languages are said to be lower or higher, depending on whether they are closer to the language the computer itself uses (lower, which means 0s and 1s, as we shall explain) or to the language that people use (higher, which means more English-like). In this chapter we shall consider three levels of language:

- Machine language
- Assembly language
- High-level language

The high-level languages—such as BASIC and COBOL—are the ones used to code applications programs, so we shall emphasize them. The closer the level is to humans, the more it is described as a "user-friendly" language. (The term "user-friendly," as we mentioned, is one used a great deal throughout the computer industry. While it describes an ideal—that a piece of equipment or software should be easy for an untrained person to use, it also appears frequently in manufacturers' ads—and what ad is not trying to be friendly?)

Machine Language: Binary Spoken Here

We think of computers as being quite complicated, but actually their basis is very simple: they rest on the concept of electricity being turned "on" and "off." From this on/off, yes/no, two-state system, sophisticated ways of representing data have been constructed using the binary system of numbers. The **binary system** is based on two digits—0 and 1. By contrast, the decimal system that we all use is based on ten digits—0 through 9. The numbers 1, 2, and 3 in the decimal system are represented in the binary system as 0001, 0010, and 0011, respectively. Letters of the alphabet are also represented as numbers: in one system, the letter A is represented as 1000001. Commas, semicolons, and other special characters are also represented as bunches of 0s and 1s.

In the early days of computers, with machines such as the ENIAC, which used vacuum tubes, one could actually see the tubes lit up or unlit, corresponding to the 1/0 binary state—the switch was either on or off. In addition, in those early days there was no such thing as software. There was only hardware with electrical on/off switches. Whenever a program was to be run, all the switches had to be set—sometimes

as many as 6000 switches for a single program. Then for the next program the switches had to be reset, a process that might take weeks. Were we to try the same thing today with the *Rough Cut* payroll program, it might require three to four times as many switches.

Since those days, machine switches have been replaced by machine programming—programs with statements consisting of 0s and 1s that electrically set the switches, with 0 representing off and 1 representing on. This has made changing from one program to another considerably easier.

Still, programming directly in **machine language**—the lowest level of programming language, in which information is represented as 0s and 1s—is *very* tedious and time-consuming. As a programmer, you must keep track of a tremendous amount of detail. Moreover, you must understand the technical operations of the computer.

In the *Rough Cut* payroll program the gross pay was calculated by multiplying the number of hours worked by the pay rate. Six lines of machine code are required to perform this multiplication, one line of which looks like this:

```
11110010 01110011 1101 001000010000 0111 000000101011
```

Clearly, working with this kind of code is not for everybody.

Programming in machine code has one advantage over programming at other language levels—namely, its execution is very fast and efficient because the computer can accept the machine code as is (higher-level languages must be converted to machine code before they are usable). However, besides the complexity and sheer tedium involved in working at this level, there is a severe disadvantage to machine language: there is no single standard machine language. Rather, there are machine *languages*. The languages are machine dependent, which means that programs written in machine language for one computer model will not, in all likelihood, run on a different model computer. Although the machine language for a particular computer is supplied by the manufacturer, few application programs are written in machine languages.

Let us be grateful, then, as you worry about getting your back-up payroll program up and running for Mr. Elliott, that you do not live at a time when your programmer has to do all the coding and debugging in 0s and 1s.

Assembly Languages: Programming with Abbreviations

It became clear early on that working with 0s and 1s could turn people into ciphers themselves. In the 1950s, to reduce programming complexity and provide some standardization, assembly languages were developed. **Assembly languages,** also known as **symbolic languages,** use abbreviations or mnemonic codes—codes more easily memorized—to replace the 0s and 1s of machine languages.

Actually, assembly languages do not replace machine languages. In fact, for an assembly language program to be executed, it must be converted to machine code.

What does assembly language look like? The machine language statement presented above—

11110010 01110011 1101 001000010000 0111 000000101011

—could be expressed in an assembly language statement as:

PACK 210(8,13),02B(4,7)

However, for this assembly statement to be executed, it must be translated into the machine statement, because the computer can recognize only 0s and 1s.

Assembly language code is very similar in form to machine language code. In fact, the first assembly languages had a one-to-one correspondence—15 assembly statements, for example, would be translated into 15 machine statements. This one-to-one correspondence was still so laborious, however, that assembly language instructions called **macro instructions** were devised, which offered a one-to-many correspondence to machine code. That is, one line of assembly language code would correspond to many lines of machine language code.

Assembly languages offer several advantages:

- They are more standardized and easier to use than machine languages.
- They operate very efficiently, although not as efficiently as machine languages.
- They are easier to debug because programs locate and identify syntax errors.

However, there are still some disadvantages:

- The programs frequently are quite long.
- Though less abstract than machine languages, assembly language programs are still complex.
- Though more standardized than machine languages, assembly languages are still machine-dependent.

Despite such drawbacks, assembly programs are still widely used, primarily because of their efficiency. They are also used for custom-made application programs designed to run on a particular computer model—for instance, a payroll program for a specific computer.

Contemplating the fact that someone else is going to have to be able to use your *Rough Cut* payroll program, you decide not to work in assembly language. You want a program written in a language that is a little more user-friendly.

Let us step up to high-level languages.

High-Level Languages: More User Friendliness

High-level languages further assisted programmers by reducing the number of details of the computer operations they had to specify so that they could concentrate more on the logic needed to solve the problem. To see this, you need only look at Figure 6-1, in which the same instruction—calculate gross pay—is expressed in three different ways: in the high-level language known as COBOL, in assembly language, and in machine language. Here we see that the six lines of 0s and 1s of machine language can be expressed in COBOL in a single line of English (or almost English): MULTIPLY HOURS-WORKED BY PAY-RATE GIVING GROSS-PAY ROUNDED (that is, "rounded off").

A **high-level language,** then, is an English-like programming lan-

Figure 6-1 Why people like high-level languages. In this comparison, a single line of an English-like high-level language, COBOL, is expressed in its equivalent in an assembly language and a machine language.

COBOL

```
MULTIPLY HOURS-WORKED BY PAY-RATE GIVING GROSS-PAY ROUNDED
```

Assembly

```
PACK  210(8,13),02B(4,7)
PACK  218(8,13),02F(4,7)
MP    212(6,13),21D(3,13)
SRP   213(5,13),03E(0),5
UNPK  050(5,7),214(4,13)
OI    054(7),X'F0'
```

Machine

```
11110010 01110011 1101 001000010000 0111 000000101011
11110010 01110011 1101 001000011000 0111 000000101111
11111100 01010010 1101 001000010010 1101 001000011101
11110000 01000101 1101 001000010011 0000 000000111110
11110011 01000011 0111 000001010000 1101 001000010100
10010110 11110000 0111 000001010100
```

guage (at least in English-speaking countries; elsewhere in the world they are written in other human languages). High-level languages have many advantages over machine and assembly languages:

- As we just demonstrated, the program statements resemble English and hence are easier to work with.
- Because of their English-like nature, less time is required to program a problem.
- Once coded, programs are easier to understand and to modify.
- The programming languages are machine-independent.
- A program may run on different computers.

However, high-level languages still have some disadvantages compared to machine and assembly languages:

- Programs execute more slowly.
- The languages use computer resources less efficiently.

Compilers and Interpreters: Translating from High to Low

For a high-level language to work on the computer, it must be translated into machine language. There are two kinds of translators—*compilers* and *interpreters*—and high-level languages are called either *compiler languages* or *interpreter languages.*

In a **compiler language,** a translation program is run to convert the programmer's high-level language program, which is called the **source code,** into a machine language code. This translation process is called a **compiling run.** The machine language code is called the **object code** and can be saved and run (executed) either immediately or later. The execution of the object code is called a **production run.** The most widely used compiler languages are COBOL and FORTRAN.

In an **interpreter language,** a translation program converts each program statement to machine code just before the program statement is to be executed. Translation and execution occur immediately, one after another, one statement at a time. Unlike the compiler languages, no object code is stored and there is no compiling run, only a production run. This means that in a program where one statement is executed several times (like reading an employee's payroll record) that statement is converted to machine language each time it is executed. The most frequently used interpreter languages are BASIC and Pascal.

Compiler languages are better than interpreter languages in that they can be executed faster and more efficiently once the object code has been obtained. On the other hand, interpreter languages do not need to create object code and so are usually easier to develop—that is, to code and test. Interpreter languages are frequently used for **interactive programming,** the kind of programming in which the user and the computer carry on a dialogue—that is, interact—with each other.

Languages for General Problems and Specific Problems

High-level languages are also classified according to whether they solve general problems or specific problems. General-purpose programming languages are called **procedural languages.** They are languages such as BASIC, COBOL, FORTRAN, and Pascal, which are designed to express the logic—the procedure—of a problem. Because of their flexibility, procedural languages are able to solve a variety of problems.

High-level languages designed to solve specific problems are known, naturally, as **problem-oriented languages.** The most "user-friendly" of the high-level languages, they are intended primarily to help people who are not programmers gain access to a data bank, such as airline reservations personnel needing flight and ticket information. People using such languages need not be concerned with solution procedures so much as with the input and output. An example of a problem-oriented language is RPG.

Problem-oriented languages are often referred to as **fourth-generation languages.** This follows the idea that programming languages were developed in generations:

- Machine languages—first generation
- Assembly languages—second generation
- Procedural languages—third generation
- Problem-oriented languages—fourth generation

Let us turn now to a description of the principal high-level languages. They and their applications are shown in Table 6-1, page 176. We will first describe languages important in business, then describe others that you may encounter in a business career.

The Languages of Business

If you are already involved in programming a microcomputer, you are probably working in BASIC. Originally intended for educational use, this programming language also has become useful in business and science. The most widespread language for business applications is COBOL, but you will probably also encounter PL/I and RPG. Let us discuss each of these below.

BASIC: For Beginners and Micro-computerists

It is highly likely the first programming language you will use will be BASIC. Developed in 1964 at Dartmouth College with college students specifically in mind, **BASIC**—short for *B*eginner's *A*ll-purpose *S*ymbolic *I*nstruction *C*ode—is by far the most popular computer language and is

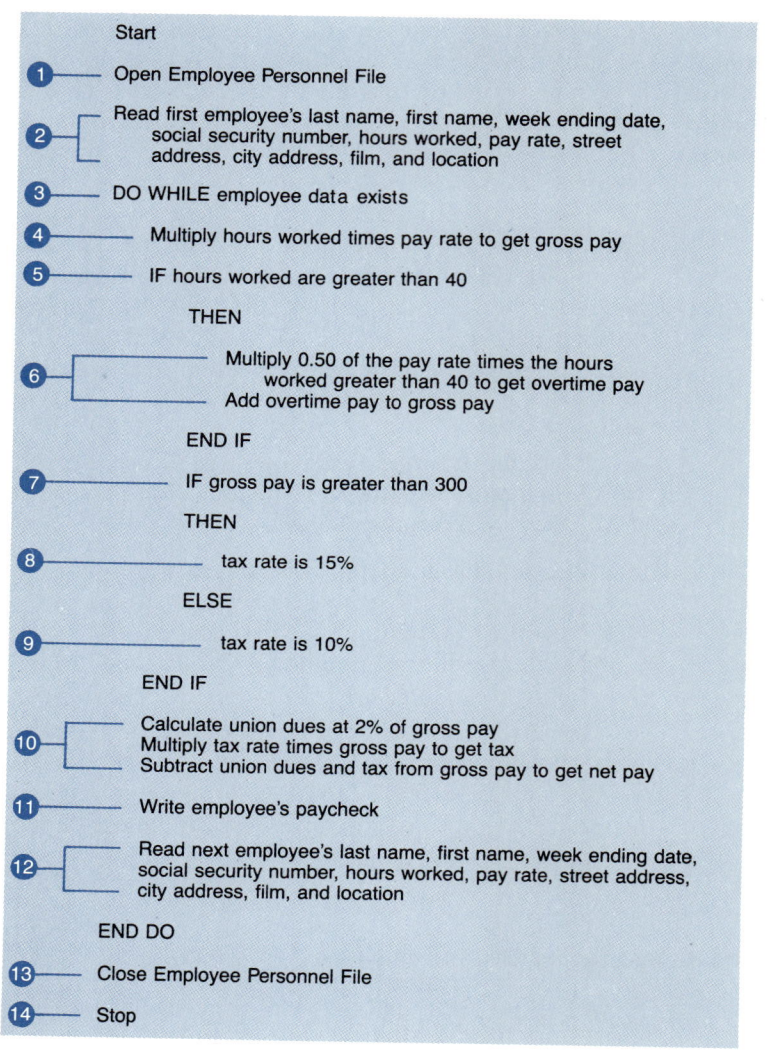

```
     Start
(1)  Open Employee Personnel File
(2)  Read first employee's last name, first name, week ending date,
         social security number, hours worked, pay rate, street
         address, city address, film, and location
(3)  DO WHILE employee data exists
(4)      Multiply hours worked times pay rate to get gross pay
(5)      IF hours worked are greater than 40
             THEN
(6)              Multiply 0.50 of the pay rate times the hours
                     worked greater than 40 to get overtime pay
                 Add overtime pay to gross pay
             END IF
(7)          IF gross pay is greater than 300
             THEN
(8)              tax rate is 15%
             ELSE
(9)              tax rate is 10%
         END IF
(10)     Calculate union dues at 2% of gross pay
         Multiply tax rate times gross pay to get tax
         Subtract union dues and tax from gross pay to get net pay
(11)     Write employee's paycheck
(12)     Read next employee's last name, first name, week ending date,
         social security number, hours worked, pay rate, street address,
         city address, film, and location
     END DO
(13) Close Employee Personnel File
(14) Stop
```

Figure 6-2 Flowchart and pseudocode for *Rough Cut* payroll program. The circled numbers refer to major processing functions as translated from the pseudocode and flowchart into a program listing, such as that presented in BASIC, Figure 6-3. The circled numbers also apply to other program listings in this chapter. (Continued on opposite page.)

well suited to the beginning as well as the experienced programmer. It is also an *interactive* language that permits user and computer to communicate with each other directly during the writing and running of programs.

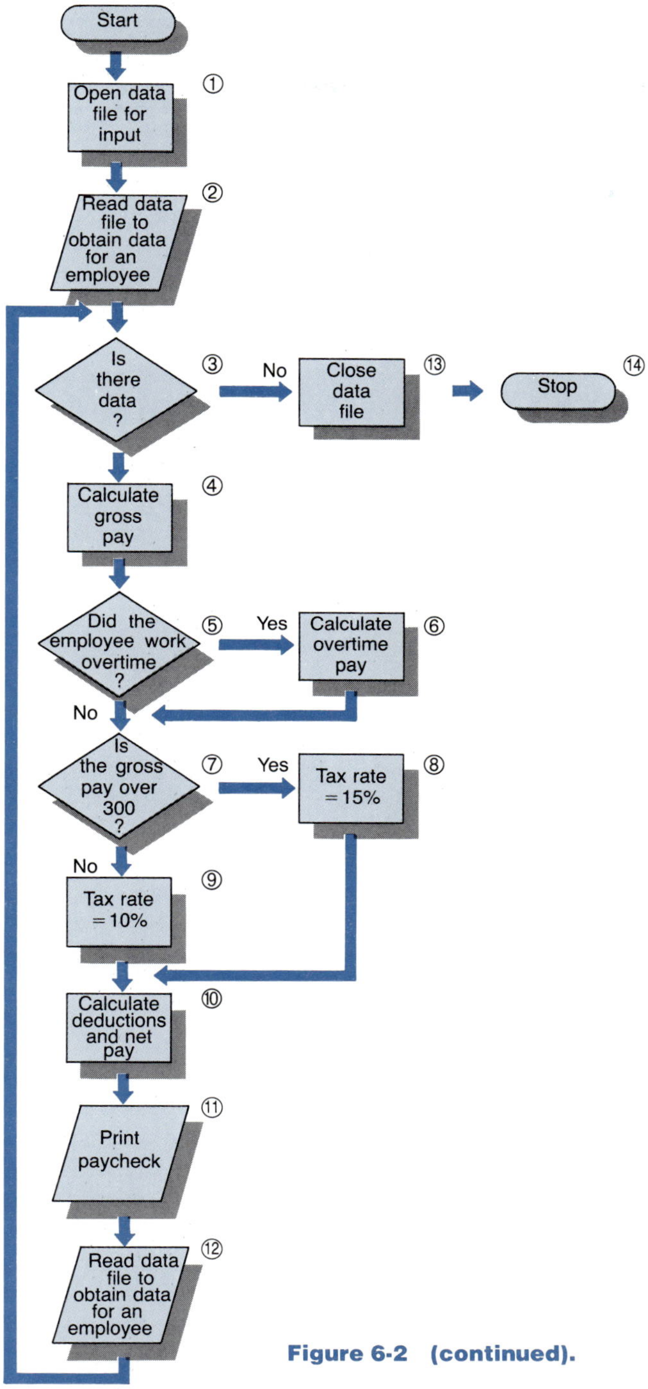
Start
Open data file for input
①
Read data file to obtain data for an employee
②
Is there data ?
③
No
Close data file
⑬
Stop
⑭
Calculate gross pay
④
Did the employee work overtime ?
⑤
Yes
Calculate overtime pay
⑥
No
Is the gross pay over 300 ?
⑦
Yes
Tax rate = 15%
⑧
No
Tax rate = 10%
⑨
Calculate deductions and net pay
⑩
Print paycheck
⑪
Read data file to obtain data for an employee
⑫
(b)

Figure 6-2 (continued).

Table 6-1 **Seven Important Programming Languages**
The languages, the meaning of their abbreviations, the year in which they were developed, and their principal application are given below.

Language	Application
FORTRAN—FORmula TRANSlator (1954)	Scientific
COBOL—COmmon Business-Oriented Language (1959)	Business
PL/I—Programming Language One (1964)	Scientific, business
RPG—Report Program Generator (1964)	Business reports
BASIC—Beginners' All-purpose Symbolic Instruction Code (1965)	Education, business
Pascal—after French inventor Blaise Pascal (1971)	Education, scientific, systems programming
Ada—after Ada, the Countess of Lovelace (1980)	Military, general

Because most microcomputers use BASIC, you can be pretty sure that the one being used by the film crew on location for *Rough Cut* will run a program written in this language. Hence, you instructed your programmer to write the payroll program in BASIC, as shown in Figure 6-3. The circled reference numbers in the program part of the figure refer to the flowchart and pseudocode shown in Figure 6-2 on pages 174 and 175.

BASIC is easy to learn, even for a person who has never programmed before, which is why it has had such commercial success. Entering data is easy, as is the insertion of changes and additions. The original BASIC had a specific syntax, but since 1964 there have been numerous extensions so that there now exist several versions. Like English itself, BASIC has developed into a number of dialects with similar features.

One reasonably standard version of BASIC is presented in the appendix for those interested in doing hands-on programming.

COBOL: The Old-Time Favorite

Developed in 1959, **COBOL**—which stands for *CO*mmon *B*usiness-*O*riented *L*anguage—is the most frequently used programming language in business. Since 1961, this general-purpose compiler language has become a standard feature for nearly all computers used in business information

```
100 OPEN 'EMP.DAT' FOR INPUT AS FILE #1
110 INPUT #1, N1$, N2$, W1$, S1$, H1, P1, A1$, A2$, F$, L$
120 IF N1$ = 'END OF FILE' THEN 310
130     LET G1 = H1 * P1
140     IF H1 <= 40 THEN 170
150     LET O1 = (.50 * P1) * (H1 - 40)
160     LET G1 = G1 + O1
170     IF G1 > 300 THEN 200
180     LET T = .10
190     GOTO 210
200     LET T = .15
210     LET U1 = .02 * G1
220     LET T2 = T * G1
230     LET N3 = G1 - U1 - T2
240     PRINT : PRINT : PRINT : PRINT : PRINT : PRINT
250     PRINT W1$, F$, L$, H1, G1, N3, S1$
260     PRINT : PRINT
270     PRINT N2$, N1$
280     PRINT A1$, N3
290     PRINT A2$
300 GOTO 110
310 CLOSE #1
320 END
```

Figure 6-3 **BASIC.** Program for *Rough Cut* payroll problem. BASIC uses short, cryptic variable names and is very unstructured because of an overabundance of the use of GOTOs.

FLASHBACK

Street BASIC

HANOVER, N.H.—Not since Polish oculist L. L. Zamenhof invented Esperanto [a made-up international human language] has an artificial language attracted as many adherents as BASIC, a computer language.

The language has helped make many computer entrepreneurs rich, but the two Dartmouth College professors who invented it have only benefited by writing a BASIC textbook. Now, they want to perfect their language and, they hope, make some substantial money as well. So, John G. Kemeny and Thomas E. Kurtz are rewriting BASIC and plunging into the vibrant computer marketplace they helped create. . . .

Mr. Kurtz and Mr. Kemeny developed BASIC because they believed, back in 1964, that every educated person should have computer experience. To make computers accessible, the Dartmouth professors did two things. They developed one of the first time-sharing systems, a method for letting people at hundreds of computer terminals use a main computer at the same time, dividing up valuable computer time.

And they developed BASIC—Beginners All-purpose Symbolic Instruction Code. Computer languages of the era, principally FORTRAN, were frustrating to learn because even simple ideas required complex instructions. For example, to print out a number, a programmer had to type in a series of codes. In BASIC, the programmer could simply type PRINT followed by the number, and the computer would do it.

BASIC consists of about 200 words that can be used to tell a computer to perform almost any imaginable task. When the computer recognizes a certain one-word instruction, it must perform a particular operation within its electronic circuits. For example, if a command contains INT, the computer knows it must deal only with integers in that operation. . . .

Dartmouth's BASIC was widely adopted by companies that rented computer time. And when the personal computers came along, starting in 1975, BASIC was the language that was condensed to fit in their small memories. William Gates, the chairman of Microsoft Corp. of Bellevue, Wash., who wrote the first BASIC for a personal computer, says that for beginners "BASIC is great." His company has made tens of millions of dollars adapting BASIC for most personal computers.

Despite its popularity, BASIC is widely criticized by computer scientists. While it works well for short programs, lengthy BASIC programs are generally confusing. Unlike modern structured computer languages, BASIC can't easily be broken up into discrete parts that can then be assigned separately to different members of a team collaborating on a long, complicated program. A command called GOTO enables programmers to write programs that tell computers to jump from one section of the program to another, making it difficult to follow the logic of the program or correct defects. A well-written program in a structured language such as Pascal will be divided into logical blocks, like chapters in a textbook, while a BASIC program is likely to interweave ideas with almost Faulknerian complexity.

Mr. Kurtz, who heads a committee of computer scientists and professionals who are developing a set of standards for all versions of BASIC, says that True BASIC will overcome those problems.

He blames many of BASIC's problems on the many revisions it has gone through. "We don't recognize our own grandchild, as it were," he says. "We're concerned because people are learning street BASIC."

—William M. Bulkeley,
Wall Street Journal,
December 16, 1983

processing, including many personal computers. Indeed, it has been estimated that between 60% and 80% of application programs written for business purposes are written in COBOL.

Thus, for the *Rough Cut* payroll program, you could have had the programmer write it in COBOL, assuming the personal computer being used by the film crew had a COBOL compiler. The result would look like the program shown in Figure 6-4, and the output—the paycheck for cableperson Amy Gardner—would look like that shown in Figure 6-5.

Writing in COBOL is much like writing a paper. You write sentences, which tell the computer which operations to perform. Several sentences dealing with the same operation are grouped into paragraphs, similar paragraphs are grouped into sections, and sections are grouped into a division. As Figure 6-4 shows, there are four divisions, organized in a structural hierarchy:

```
IDENTIFICATION DIVISION.
  PROGRAM-ID. PAYROLL.
  AUTHOR. [YOUR NAME]
****************************************************************
ENVIRONMENT DIVISION.
 CONFIGURATION SECTION.
  SOURCE-COMPUTER. PDP-1170.
  OBJECT-COMPUTER. PDP-1170.
 INPUT-OUTPUT SECTION.
  FILE-CONTROL
    SELECT DATA-FILE ASSIGN TO "EMPL.DAT".
    SELECT PRINT-FILE ASSIGN TO PRINTER.
****************************************************************
DATA DIVISION.
 FILE SECTION.
  FD DATA-FILE
     LABEL RECORDS ARE STANDARD
     DATA RECORD IS DATA-RECORD.
  01 DATA-RECORD                  PICTURE X(115).
  FD PRINT-FILE
     LABEL RECORDS ARE OMITTED
     DATA RECORD IS PRINT-REC.
  01 PRINT-REC                    PICTURE X(133).
 WORKING-STORAGE SECTION.
  01 PROGRAM-FLAG.
     05 MORE-DATA-EXISTS        PICTURE XXX       VALUE 'YES'.
  01 WS-DATA-RECORD.
     05 LAST-NAME               PICTURE X(10)     VALUE SPACES.
     05 FIRST-NAME              PICTURE X(6)      VALUE SPACES.
     05 WEEK-DATE               PICTURE X(8)      VALUE SPACES.
     05 SOCIAL-SECURITY         PICTURE X(11)     VALUE SPACES.
     05 HOURS-WORKED            PICTURE 99V99     VALUE ZEROES.
     05 PAY-RATE                PICTURE 99V99     VALUE ZEROES.
     05 STREET-ADDRESS          PICTURE X(14)     VALUE SPACES.
     05 CITY-ADDRESS            PICTURE X(18)     VALUE SPACES.
     05 FILM-NAME               PICTURE X(15)     VALUE SPACES.
     05 LOCATION-OF-FILM        PICTURE X(25)     VALUE SPACES.
  01 VARIABLES-NEEDED.
     05 GROSS-PAY               PICTURE 999V99    VALUE ZEROES.
     05 OVERTIME-PAY            PICTURE 999V99    VALUE ZEROES.
     05 UNION-DUES              PICTURE 999V99    VALUE ZEROES.
     05 TAX-RATE                PICTURE 999V99    VALUE ZEROES.
     05 TAX                     PICTURE 999V99    VALUE ZEROES.
     05 NET-PAY                 PICTURE 999V99    VALUE ZEROES.
     05 OT-PREMIUM              PICTURE 999V99    VALUE ZEROES.
     05 OT-HOURS                PICTURE 999V99    VALUE ZEROES.
     05 DEDUCTIONS              PICTURE 999V99    VALUE ZEROES.
  01 DETAIL-LINE-ONE.
     05 FILLER                  PICTURE X         VALUE SPACE.
     05 WEEK-DATE-OUT           PICTURE X(8)      VALUE SPACES.
     05 FILLER                  PICTURE X         VALUE SPACE.
     05 FILM-NAME-OUT           PICTURE X(15)     VALUE SPACES.
     05 FILLER                  PICTURE X         VALUE SPACE.
     05 LOCATION-OF-FILM-OUT    PICTURE X(25)     VALUE SPACES.
     05 FILLER                  PICTURE X         VALUE SPACE.
     05 HOURS-WORKED-OUT        PICTURE Z9.99     VALUE ZEROES.
     05 FILLER                  PICTURE X(3)      VALUE SPACES.
     05 GROSS-PAY-OUT           PICTURE $$$$.99   VALUE ZEROES.
     05 FILLER                  PICTURE X         VALUE SPACE.
     05 NET-PAY-OUT1            PICTURE $$$$.99   VALUE ZEROES.
     05 FILLER                  PICTURE X         VALUE SPACE.
     05 SOCIAL-SECURITY-OUT     PICTURE X(11)     VALUE SPACES.
  01 DETAIL-LINE-TWO.
     05 FILLER                  PICTURE X(25)     VALUE SPACES.
     05 FIRST-NAME-OUT          PICTURE X(6)      VALUE SPACES.
     05 FILLER                  PICTURE X         VALUE SPACES.
     05 LAST-NAME-OUT           PICTURE X(10)     VALUE SPACES.
  01 DETAIL-LINE-THREE.
     05 FILLER                  PICTURE X(25)     VALUE SPACES.
     05 STREET-ADDRESS-OUT      PICTURE X(14)     VALUE SPACES.
     05 FILLER                  PICTURE X(20)     VALUE SPACES.
     05 NET-PAY-OUT2            PICTURE $$$$.99   VALUE ZEROES.
  01 DETAIL-LINE-FOUR.
     05 FILLER                  PICTURE X(25)     VALUE SPACES.
     05 CITY-ADDRESS-OUT        PICTURE X(18)     VALUE SPACES.
****************************************************************
```

Figure 6-4 COBOL. Program for *Rough Cut* payroll problem. Circled numbers (see page 180) correspond to the numbers in the flowchart and pseudocode in Figure 6-2. Notice the four divisions (separated by rows of asterisks) and the sections within divisions.

Continued on next page

```
     PROCEDURE DIVISION
       MAIN-PARA.
(1)      OPEN INPUT DATA-FILE
              OUTPUT PRINT-FILE.
(2)      PERFORM READ-DATA-PARA.
         PERFORM PAYROLL-PROCESSING-PARA
(3)          UNTIL MORE-DATA-EXISTS = "NO".
(13)     CLOSE DATA-FILE
               PRINT-FILE.
(14)     STOP RUN.
       READ-DATA-PARA.
         READ DATA-FILE INTO WS-DATA-RECORD
              AT END MOVE "NO" TO MORE-DATA-EXISTS.
       PAYROLL-PROCESSING-PARA.
(4)      MULTIPLY HOURS-WORKED BY PAY-RATE GIVING GROSS-PAY ROUNDED.
(5)      IF HOURS-WORKED GREATER THAN 40
           THEN
(6)            MULTIPLY .50 BY PAY-RATE GIVING OT-PREMIUM ROUNDED
               SUBTRACT 40 FROM HOURS-WORKED GIVING OT-HOURS ROUNDED
               COMPUTE OVERTIME-PAY ROUNDED = OT-PREMIUM * OT-HOURS
               ADD OVERTIME-PAY TO GROSS-PAY
           ELSE
               NEXT SENTENCE.
(7)      IF GROSS-PAY GREATER THAN 300
           THEN
(8)            MOVE .15 TO TAX-RATE
           ELSE
(9)            MOVE .10 TO TAX-RATE.
(10)     MULTIPLY GROSS-PAY BY .02 GIVING UNION-DUES ROUNDED.
         MULTIPLY GROSS-PAY BY TAX-RATE GIVING TAX ROUNDED.
         ADD UNION-DUES, TAX GIVING DEDUCTIONS ROUNDED.
         COMPUTE NET-PAY ROUNDED = GROSS PAY - DEDUCTIONS.
(11)     MOVE WEEK-DATE TO WEEK-DATE-OUT.
         MOVE FILM-NAME TO FILM-NAME-OUT.
         MOVE LOCATION-OF-FILM TO LOCATION-OF-FILM-OUT.
         MOVE HOURS-WORKED TO HOURS-WORKED-OUT.
         MOVE GROSS-PAY TO GROSS-PAY-OUT.
         MOVE NET-PAY TO NET-PAY-OUT1.
         MOVE SOCIAL-SECURITY TO SOCIAL-SECURITY-OUT.
         WRITE PRINT-REC FROM DETAIL-LINE-ONE AFTER ADVANCING 7 LINES.
         MOVE FIRST-NAME TO FIRST-NAME-OUT.
         MOVE LAST-NAME TO LAST-NAME-OUT.
         WRITE PRINT-REC FROM DETAIL-LINE-TWO AFTER ADVANCING 3 LINES.
         MOVE STREET-ADDRESS TO STREET-ADDRESS-OUT.
         MOVE NET-PAY TO NET-PAY-OUT2.
         WRITE PRINT-REC FROM DETAIL-LINE-THREE.
         MOVE CITY-ADDRESS TO CITY-ADDRESS-OUT.
         WRITE PRINT-REC FROM DETAIL-LINE-FOUR.
(12)     PERFORM READ-DATA-PARA.
```

Figure 6-4 (continued).

Figure 6-5 COBOL output. Example of payroll output produced by COBOL program.

```
11-21-86 ROUGH CUT QUEENSLAND AUSTRALIA 30.00   $283.50  249.48  527-73-1102

                      AMY     GARDNER
                      9024 N ELM ST.                  $249.48
                      WESTWOOD CA 90024
```

- The IDENTIFICATION DIVISION presents the name of the program and the programmer. There may be other paragraphs for documentation purposes.
- The ENVIRONMENT DIVISION indicates the computer to be used (in our example, it is a minicomputer called a PDP-1170). The input-output section matches the logical variable names used in the program (such as PRINT-FILE) with the physical input or output device (in this case PRINTER).
- The DATA DIVISION consists of a file section and a working-storage section. This division lists all the data items to be input (including employee names, hours worked, deductions, and the like), describes where the data will be stored within the computer, and gives the format to be used for the output results.
- The PROCEDURE DIVISION contains the actual processing instructions, mirroring the steps mapped out in the flowchart.

Because it has been absorbed so well into the business environment, COBOL clearly must have a number of advantages, and indeed it does:

- It is easy to understand—more so than BASIC, as a comparison of the two programs shows—because of its English-like statements. In business, this is a real advantage, since it allows nonprogrammers to get into a program and follow its logic.
- It is self-documenting, which means that few ongoing comments in the program are needed. This also makes COBOL easy for programmers to learn.
- It can be used for almost any business programming task, and is especially designed to handle business data, such as addresses, dollar amounts, and purchased items.

However, there are also a number of disadvantages:

- It is wordy—precisely because it is so readable—so you cannot write a compact COBOL program, even for a simple task.
- It is not as suited for mathematics as other languages such as FORTRAN.

The American National Standards Institute (ANSI) first standardized COBOL in 1968 and again in 1974, producing a version known as **ANSI-COBOL.** The advantage of standardization is that COBOL is reasonably machine-independent, so that a COBOL program developed for one computer can be run with only slight modifications on another machine for which a COBOL compiler has been developed.

Recently, ANSI has been promoting a new version known as COBOL-8X, a 1980s updating of the 1974 version. The problem is that older COBOL programs will not always run on it; parts of them must be revised.

2 + 2: The BASIC Way, the COBOL Way, the PL/I Way

The long programs shown in the *Rough Cut* payroll examples may seem a bit complicated at this point. How would it seem if we used BASIC, COBOL, and PL/I to perform what is probably one of the first arithmetic operations any of us ever learned—adding 2 + 2? The following shows how:

In BASIC:

```
10 REM THIS IS A PROGRAM TO ADD TWO NUMBERS
20 READ A, B
30 LET X = A + B
40 PRINT X
50 DATA 2, 2
60 END
```

The REM instruction (REM stands for "Remark") tells you what the program is. READ instructs the computer to assign variables A and B the values shown in line 50, the DATA statement; that is, A is 2 and B is 2. Line 30 indicates that X will become the value of the math computation A + B, which is 2 + 2, or 4. When line 40, PRINT, is reached, the value of X, or 4, is displayed. Line 50 has already been dealt with by the statement READ in line 20. Finally, line 60 marks the end of the program.

In COBOL:

```
IDENTIFICATION DIVISION.
   PROGRAM-ID. ADDITION EXAMPLE.
   AUTHOR. [YOUR NAME].
************************************************
ENVIRONMENT DIVISION.
 CONFIGURATION SECTION.
 SOURCE-COMPUTER. PDP-1170.
 OBJECT-COMPUTER. PDP-1170.
**************************************************
DATA DIVISION.
 WORKING-STORAGE SECTION.
```

```
 01 NUMBER-ONE PICTURE 9 VALUE 2.
 01 NUMBER-TWO PICTURE 9 VALUE 2.
 01 ADD-TOTAL  PICTURE 9 VALUE ZERO.
*****************************************************
PROCEDURE DIVISION.
   COMPUTE ADD-TOTAL =
   NUMBER ONE + NUMBER TWO.
  DISPLAY ADD-TOTAL.
  STOP RUN.
```

It is clear that the COBOL version of this exercise may be a lot more readable than the BASIC version, but it is obviously much more wordy—a drawback of even the simplest COBOL programs.

In PL/I:

Intended as a "universal language," useful for both science and business, PL/I would handle the 2 + 2 problem this way:

```
SAMPLE: PROCEDURE OPTIONS (MAIN);
  DECLARE (NUMBER_ONE, NUMBER_TWO, ADD_TOTAL) FIXED DECIMAL(3);
  NUMBER_ONE = 2;
  NUMBER_TWO = 2;
  ADD=,TOTAL = NUMBER_ONE + NUMBER_TWO;
  PUT PAGE LIST(ADD=,TOTAL);
END;
```

For instance, all COBOL languages have **reserved words**—words with exact meanings, such as PROGRAM-ID (see the second line in Figure 6-4). A programmer may not use these words for variable names; **variable names** are names that can be whatever the user or programmer wants, such as PAYROLL. However, COBOL-8X adds some *new* reserved words, which means that if old programs had used them as variable names, they now must be changed—possibly an expensive proposition for a business that has been using these names as variable names all along.

PL/I: For General Purposes

PL/I, which stands for *P*rogramming *L*anguage One, was introduced by IBM in 1964 and promoted as a "universal language"—a compromise between COBOL, which is not especially useful for science and mathematics, and FORTRAN, which (as we shall see) is. PL/I was to general-purpose—neither for business nor science alone but for both. An ANSI committee produced a PL/I standard language in 1976. A version is available for use with small computers.

PL/I has a modular structure. A module can stand alone as a program or become part of a more complex program. This makes the language useful for both novice programmers, who need to learn only a certain part of the language in order to do applications of interest to them, and for expert programmers, who can use all the many options available.

There are several advantages to PL/I:

- The modular structure allows the use of structured programming concepts.
- It has built-in features that can identify and correct common programming errors.
- The language is very flexible, with few coding restrictions: statements can appear in any column, for instance, which is not true of other languages.

Needless to say, however, PL/I has its drawbacks:

- It requires a lot of main storage in the computer, which means it is not usually found in use with minicomputers and microcomputers.
- It has so many options that some people feel it loses its usefulness.
- It is more difficult to learn all parts of PL/I than is the case with COBOL.

Because for many years PL/I was available only on IBM computers, companies worried about finding themselves locked into IBM equipment, with no choice of alternatives. Because, in addition, PL/I did not seem to have tremendous advantages over COBOL for business uses, it did not seem to many people worth the effort of changing languages and risking becoming totally dependent on IBM.

RPG: For Reports

The three languages above are procedure-oriented, designed to allow programmers to write logical sequences of instructions. RPG, a problem-oriented language, is more limited in its uses. Developed at IBM and introduced in 1964, **RPG** stands for *R*eport *P*rogram *G*enerator, and that is what it is designed to do—generate business reports. With minimal training, users can learn to fill out specifications on very detailed coding forms (see Figure 6-6) for such common business applications as accounts receivable and accounts payable, and then produce reports with little effort. The language can also be used for some file updating.

There are several benefits to RPG:

- It is easy to learn and use.

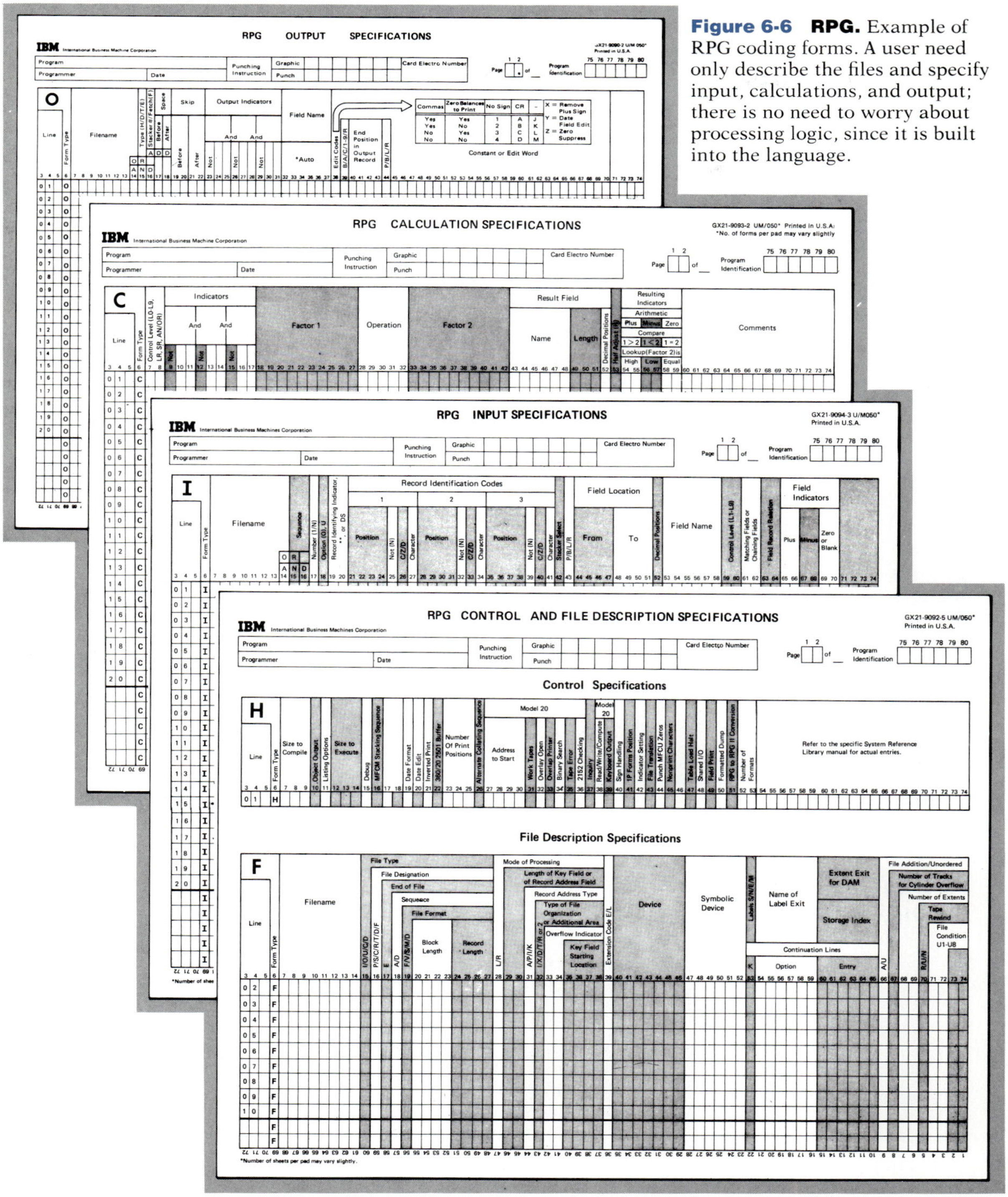
RPG OUTPUT SPECIFICATIONS
RPG CALCULATION SPECIFICATIONS
RPG INPUT SPECIFICATIONS
RPG CONTROL AND FILE DESCRIPTION SPECIFICATIONS
Control Specifications
File Description Specifications

Figure 6-6 RPG. Example of RPG coding forms. A user need only describe the files and specify input, calculations, and output; there is no need to worry about processing logic, since it is built into the language.

- You do not need to remember as many formal rules as you do with other languages.
- It is very efficient for work on large files involving few calculations, for which reports are needed.

As always, the features that make a language useful for some purposes limit its usefulness in others. RPG's drawbacks:

- Originally intended for the limited purpose of making reports and doing some file updating, RPG has evolved into a powerful programming language. Still, programmers wanting more complex logic will usually turn to COBOL or PL/I.
- It cannot be used for scientific applications because of its limited mathematical capability.
- There is no standard RPG (although IBM's versions are as close to standard as any), so that a program written for one computer usually has to be reworked to run on another kind.

An updated version of the language called **RPG II** was introduced in 1970 and extends the language's capabilities. **RPG III** is a modern interactive language that presents the programmer with menus allowing choices of various types of programming specifications.

Other Common Programming Languages

Maybe you will never write a line of code of the following languages. But knowing something about them might be just what will give you that competitive edge in business. After all, you would hate to find yourself in the company of engineers and scientists and confusing COBOL, SNOBOL, ALGOL, and LOGO (the names do sound somewhat alike).

The other principal languages you should be at least conversational with are: FORTRAN, Pascal, and Ada. Some other languages that you may come across are described in the box.

FORTRAN: The Language of Science

FORTRAN—short for *FOR*mula *TRAN*slator—was developed by IBM and introduced in 1954. The first high-level language, **FORTRAN** is a scientific-mathematic language and is still the most widely used language among scientists, mathematicians, and engineers.

By now you would probably have settled on BASIC or COBOL as the language in which to write the *Rough Cut* payroll program, but, if you had asked the programmer to express it as shown in FORTRAN, the result would be as shown in Figure 6-7.

The benefits of FORTRAN are:

- It is more compact than COBOL. Indeed, its brevity and simplicity are the reasons it is so popular.

Some Languages Overheard in Hotel Lobbies

If you were to go to business conventions, depending on which you went to, you might hear one of the following six languages discussed.

ALGOL. Introduced in 1960, ALGOL (for *ALGO*rithmic *L*anguage) has been popular in Europe but never really caught on in the United States. Intended for scientific and mathematical projects, its programs tend to be easy to read, but it has limited input/output capability. It is the forerunner of PL/I, Pascal, and Ada.

APL. Introduced by IBM in 1968, APL (for *A* *P*rogramming *L*anguage) is especially useful for processing tables and arrays—that is, groups of related numbers. However, there are many special characters in this language, so a special keyboard is required. The many special symbols for a large group of operators requires that the APL compiler be rather large, which means the language is apt to be available only on machines with large memories.

LISP. Developed at the Massachusetts Institute of Technology in 1958, LISP is useful for writing programs in artificial intelligence. It is used interactively at a terminal to process characters and words rather than numbers.

Logo. If you are at a convention of school teachers, you may well hear reference to "turtle graphics." This means the teachers are talking about Logo, a dialect of LISP also developed at M.I.T. Logo is used to command a triangular pointer, which is called a "turtle," on a video screen to plot various graphic designs. This variant of Logo, with its simple commands, is useful for teaching some fundamentals of programming to young children.

Smalltalk. This language, which was invented at the Palo Alto (California) Research Center, created by Xerox Corporation, is designed to support an especially visual computer system. A keyboard is used to enter text into the computer, but all other commands are accomplished with the use of a mouse.The principles of Smalltalk were successfully adapted by Apple Computer in their Lisa and Macintosh microcomputers.

SNOBOL. Invented by Bell Telephone Laboratories in the early 1960s, SNOBOL is widely used for manipulating alphanumeric or special characters and has found use in text editors and language processors.

- It is very useful for processing complex formulas, such as those used in science, engineering, and economics. It is even useful for business, if there are not extensive data files.
- Many application programs for scientists and engineers have been written in FORTRAN, and programs written for one computer are usually easily modified for other makes of computers.

And then there are the disadvantages:

- FORTRAN is not as structured as COBOL.
- It is not as able as COBOL to handle large amounts of input and output data.
- It is more difficult to read and understand a FORTRAN program than a COBOL program, which makes it more difficult to change.

```
      INTEGER LNAME(10)
      INTEGER FNAME(6)
      INTEGER WKDATE(8)
      INTEGER SOCSEC(11)
      REAL HOURS
      REAL PAY
      INTEGER STREET(14)
      INTEGER CITY(18)
      INTEGER FILM(15)
      INTEGER LOCAT(25)
      REAL GROPAY
      REAL OTPAY
      REAL UNION
      REAL TAXRT
      REAL TAX
      REAL NETPAY
C
      CALL ASSIGN (99,'EMPLOY.DAT')
      READ(99,10) LNAME,FNAME,WKDATE,SOCSEC,
     &            HOURS,PAY,STREET,CITY,FILM,LOCAT
   10 FORMAT(10A1,6A1,8A1,11A1,F5.0,F5.0,14A1,18A1,15A1,25A1)
C
   20 IF (LNAME(1) .EQ. '#') GO TO 110
         GROPAY = HOURS * PAY
         IF (HOURS .LE. 40) GO TO 30
         OTPAY = (.50 * PAY) * (HOURS - 40)
         GROPAY = GROPAY + OTPAY
   30    IF (GROPAY .GT. 300) GO TO 40
         TAXRT = .10
         GO TO 50
   40    TAXRT = .15
   50    UNION = .02 * GROPAY
         TAX = TAXRT * GROPAY
         NETPAY = GROPAY - UNION - TAX
         WRITE  (7,60)
   60    FORMAT (1H,///////)
         WRITE (7,70) WKDATE, FILM, LOCAT, HOURS, GROPAY, NETPAY, SOCSEC
   70    FORMAT (1H,1X,8A1,1X,15A1,1X,25A1,1X,F5.2,3X,
     &          '$',F6.2,1X,'$',F6.2,1X,11A1,///)
         WRITE (7,80) FNAME, LNAME
   80    FORMAT (1H,25X,6A1,1X,10A1,/)
         WRITE (7,90) STREET, NETPAY
   90    FORMAT (1H,25X,14A1,20X,'$',F6.2,/)
         WRITE (7,100) CITY
  100    FORMAT (1H,25X,18A1)
         READ(99,10) LNAME,FNAME,WKDATE,SOCSEC,
     &               HOURS,PAY,STREET,CITY,FILM,LOCAT
      GO TO 20
  110 END
```

Figure 6-7 FORTRAN. There would probably be no reason to write the *Rough Cut* program in FORTRAN, but if the programmer did so, it would look like this. The circled numbers correspond to the flowchart and pseudocode shown in Figure 6-2. FORTRAN is even more cryptic than BASIC. For example, the formatting and printing in FORTRAN (number 11) is far more difficult to understand than the corresponding code in BASIC, COBOL, and Pascal.

Pascal: The Simple Language

Pascal was named after the 17th-century French mathematician and philosopher Blaise Pascal and was developed in the mid-1970s. It has become quite popular in computer science educational programs in the universities of Europe and now the United States. Its principal significance is that it was developed to take advantage of structured programming concepts.

A Pascal version of our payroll program is shown in Figure 6-8. Although it looks more like a COBOL program than either the BASIC or FORTRAN variations, it actually is more closely related to the BASIC version, for it is relatively easy to learn and is frequently available on microcomputer systems.

The benefits of Pascal are:

- It is simpler to learn than other languages because you need to know only a few rules of coding to write some simple programs.
- It is excellent for scientific applications use.
- It has excellent graphics capabilities.

And the drawbacks:

- It has limited input and output capabilities so it is not apt to have serious business uses, at least at present, although it has had some acceptance in industry.

Ada: Possible National Standard

Presented late in 1980, **Ada** is named for Lady Ada Augusta, the Countess of Lovelace, who, as we mentioned in an earlier chapter, earned the title of "the first programmer" for her work with Charles Babbage in the 19th century. Ada was developed under the sponsorship of the U.S. Department of Defense and originally was intended to be a standard language for weapons systems. However, it has not only military applications but commercial ones as well.

The advantages of Ada are:

- It has more general input and output capability than Pascal, and so is more apt to find favor in industry.
- It is a structured language, with a modular design that allows pieces or modules of a large program to be written and tested separately before the entire program is put together.
- It has features that permit the compiler to check for errors before the entire program is run, so that it is easier to write error-free programs.

The drawbacks of Ada are as follows:

- Although some experts believe Ada is easy to use, others think it is too complex.

```
PROGRAM PAYROLL (INPUT, OUTPUT, EMPDAT);
{--------------------------------------------------------------------------}

   TYPE
        CHARARRAY        = ARRAY [1..25] OF CHAR;
{--------------------------------------------------------------------------}

   VAR
          EMPDAT            : TEXT;
          LASTNAME          : CHARARRAY;
          FIRSTNAME         : CHARARRAY;
          WEEKDATE          : CHARARRAY;
          SOCIALSECURITY    : CHARARRAY;
          HOURSWORKED       : REAL;
          PAYRATE           : REAL;
          STREETADDRESS     : CHARARRAY;
          CITYADDRESS       : CHARARRAY;
          FILMNAME          : CHARARRAY;
          LOCATIONOFFILM    : CHARARRAY;
          GROSSPAY          : REAL;
          OVERTIMEPAY       : REAL;
          UNIONDUES         : REAL;
          TAXRATE           : REAL;
          TAX               : REAL;
          NETPAY            : REAL;
{--------------------------------------------------------------------------}

PROCEDURE READFILE (VAR EMPDAT : TEXT);
   BEGIN
      READLN(EMPDAT, LASTNAME, FIRSTNAME, WEEKDATE, SOCIALSECURITY,
             PAYRATE, STREETADDRESS, CITYADDRESS, FILMNAME, LOCATIONOFFILM)
   END;
{--------------------------------------------------------------------------}

PROCEDURE COMPUTEPAYROLL
                         (VAR LASTNAME          : CHARARRAY;
                          VAR FIRSTNAME         : CHARARRAY;
                          VAR WEEKDATE          : CHARARRAY;
                          VAR SOCIALSECURITY    : CHARARRAY;
                          VAR HOURSWORKED       : REAL;
                          VAR PAYRATE           : REAL;
                          VAR STREETADDRESS     : CHARARRAY;
                          VAR CITYADDRESS       : CHARARRAY;
                          VAR FILMNAME          : CHARARRAY;
                          VAR LOCATIONOFFILM    : CHARARRAY);
```

Continued on next page

Figure 6-8 Pascal. The *Rough Cut* program written in Pascal would look like this. Circled numbers correspond to those in Figure 6-2. Pascal is structured and easy to understand. Pascal procedures are modules of the program and are independent of each other, leading to good structured techniques.

- Ada has also been called too unwieldy and inefficient.
- Its size may hinder its use on microcomputers, although the development of more powerful microcomputer chips may obviate this concern.

```
    BEGIN
(3)   WHILE (LASTNAME <> 'END OF FILE     ') DO
        BEGIN
(4)       GROSSPAY := HOURSWORKED * PAYRATE;
(5)       IF HOURSWORKED > 40.00
            THEN
              BEGIN
(6)             OVERTIMEPAY := (0.50 * PAYRATE) * (HOURSWORKED - 40.00);
                GROSSPAY := GROSSPAY + OVERTIMEPAY
              END;
(7)       IF GROSSPAY > 300
            THEN
(8)           TAXRATE := 0.15
            ELSE
(9)           TAXRATE := 0.10;
(10)      UNIONDUES := 0.02 * GROSSPAY;
          TAX := TAXRATE * GROSSPAY;
          NETPAY := GROSSPAY - UNIONDUES - TAX;
(11)      WRITELN;
          WRITELN;
          WRITELN;
          WRITELN;
          WRITELN;
          WRITELN;
          WRITELN (WEEKDATE:9, FILMNAME:17, LOCATIONOFFILM:26,
                HOURSWORKED:3:2, '    $', GROSSPAY:3:2, ' $', NETPAY:3:2,
                ' ', SOCIALSECURITY:12);
          WRITELN;
          WRITELN;
          WRITELN (FIRSTNAME:31, ' ', LASTNAME:11);
          WRITELN (STREETADDRESS:39, '                         $', NETPAY:3:2);
          WRITELN (CITYADDRESS:40);
(12)      READFILE(EMPDAT)
        END
    END;

 {----------------------------------------------------------------------------}

 BEGIN {MAIN PROGRAM}
(1) RESET(EMPDAT, 'E.DAT');
    READFILE(EMPDAT); (2)
    COMPUTEPAYROLL(LASTNAME, FIRSTNAME, WEEKDATE, SOCIALSECURITY,
              HOURSWORKED, PAYRATE, STREETADDRESS, CITYADDRESS,FILMNAME, LOCATIONOFFILM);
(13) CLOSE(EMPDAT)
 END. {MAIN PROGRAM} (14)
```

Figure 6-8 (continued).

At present, it is probably too early to tell what its acceptance will be, although since Ada is required by the Department of Defense on military computers, we will no doubt be hearing more about it.

From Software to Hardware

We turn now from a discussion of software to a discussion of hardware. Why study software *before* hardware? The first piece of advice most experts give about buying a microcomputer is: Choose software before hardware. This kind of advice could apply to the selection of larger computer systems as well. The computer is valueless to us unless it can use the *right kind* of software for our needs.

Now we have some sense of how we can tell the computer what we want to do, using the right kind of software package or programming approach and programming language. In Part 3, let us look next at the machines at our disposal.

SUMMARY

- To communicate with the computer, one uses a **programming language,** which can be understood by both the user and the computer. A programming language is a set of rules that provides a way of instructing the computer to perform certain operations.
- There are more than 150 programming languages, not counting obsolete ones; those of primary interest to people in business are BASIC, COBOL, PL/I, and RPG. FORTRAN, Ada, and Pascal are important for scientific applications.
- Programming languages are said to be lower or higher, depending on whether they are closer to the language of the computer (machine language) or the language of the user (in this case, more English-like).
- The **binary system** is a sophisticated way of representing data; it is based on two digits—0 and 1—that represent the turning off and on of electricity. All programming is based on the binary system.
- There are three levels of programming language: (1) machine language, (2) assembly language, and (3) high-level language. "User-friendly" language is close to human language.
- **Machine language** is the lowest form of programming language; information is represented as 0s and 1s, and it is very tedious and time-consuming to use. There is no single standard machine language, which means that such a language is machine dependent. However, its execution is fast and efficient because the computer can accept the machine code as is.
- **Assembly languages,** also known as **symbolic languages,** were developed to reduce programming complexity and provide some standardization. These languages use abbreviations or mnemonic codes to replace the 0s and 1s of machine languages. Assembly language must be converted to machine code to be executed. The assembly language program is called a **source program;** the machine language program is an **object program.**

- **Macro instructions** are assembly language instructions devised to offer a one-to-many correspondence to machine code, meaning that one assembly statement can be translated into many machine statements.

- Assembly languages have several advantages: (1) They are more standardized and easier to use than machine languages. (2) They operate efficiently. (3) They are easy to debug because programs locate and identify syntax errors. They also have some disadvantages: (1) The programs are often long. (2) They are still complex. (3) They are still machine dependent.

- **High-level languages** are used to code applications programs; they are humanlike ("user-friendly") programming languages that allow programmers to concentrate on the logic needed to solve the problem. These languages have several advantages over machine and assembly languages: (1) Their statements resemble human languages (English, in this case) and thus are easier to work with. (2) Because they resemble human languages, less time is required to program a problem. (3) Once coded, programs are easier to understand and to modify. (4) The programming languages are machine independent. (5) A program may run on different computers. High-level languages also have some disadvantages: (1) Programs execute more slowly. (2) The languages use computer resources less efficiently.

- A high-level language must be translated into machine language to work on the computer. There are two kinds of translators—*compilers* and *interpreters*—and high-level languages are called either *compiler languages* or *interpreter languages*.

- In **compiler language,** a translation program is run to convert the programmer's high-level language program, called the **source code,** into a machine language code, called the **object code.** The translation process is called a **compiling run;** the execution of the object code is a **production run.** The most widely used compiler languages are COBOL and FORTRAN.

- In **interpreter language,** a translation program converts each program statement to machine code just before the program statement is to be executed. Translation and execution occur immediately. In this case, there is no compiling run, only a production run. The most frequently used interpreter languages are BASIC and Pascal. Interpreter languages are frequently used for **interactive programming,** the kind of programming in which the user and the computer carry on a dialogue.

- High-level languages are also classified according to whether they solve general problems (procedural languages) or specific problems (problem-oriented languages).

- **Procedural languages** are general-purpose programming languages such as BASIC, COBOL, FORTRAN, and Pascal, which express the logic, or procedure, of a problem. They are flexible and can solve a variety of problems.

- **Problem-oriented languages,** the most "user-friendly" of the high-level languages, are designed to solve specific problems and are intended primarily to help nonprogrammers gain access to a data bank. (RPG is a problem-oriented language.) These languages are also known as **fourth-generation languages,** which refers to the idea that programming languages were developed in generations: (1) machine language—first generation; (2) assembly language—second generation; (3) procedural language—third generation; (4) problem-oriented language—fourth generation.

- **BASIC**—*B*eginner's *A*ll-purpose *S*ymbolic *I*nstruction *C*ode—was developed in 1964 at Dartmouth College with the intent to provide every educated person with computer experience; it is the most popular computer language and can be used by beginners as well as experienced people. BASIC is an *interactive,* procedure-oriented language that permits user and computer to communicate with each other directly. Most microcomputers use BASIC.

- **COBOL—***CO*mmon *B*usiness-*O*riented *L*anguage—is a general-purpose, procedure-oriented compiler language developed in 1959; it is the most frequently used programming language in business. Writing in COBOL is like writing a paper: one writes sentences that tell the computer which operations to perform. Sentences are grouped into paragraphs, paragraphs into sections, and sections into one of four divisions: (1) The IDENTIFICATION DIVISION presents the name of the program and the programmer (other paragraphs may be used for documentation purposes). (2) The ENVIRONMENT DIVISION indicates the computer to be used. (3) The DATA DIVISION comprises a file section and a working-storage section; it lists all the data items to be input, describes where the data will be stored, and gives the format to be used for the output results. (4) The PROCEDURE DIVISION contains the actual processing instructions, mirroring the steps mapped out in the flowchart.

- COBOL has several advantages: (1) It is easy to understand—even more so than BASIC. (2) It is self-documenting. (3) It can be used for almost any business programming task. COBOL also has some disadvantages: (1) It is wordy. (2) It is not well suited for mathematics. (3) It is not as speedy as other languages. All COBOL languages have **reserved words**—words with exact meanings that cannot be used for **variable names**—which can stand for whatever the user or programmer wants.

- **ANSI-COBOL,** a standardized version of COBOL produced by the American National Standards Institute, is reasonably machine independent. The newest ANSI-COBOL, COBOL-8X, will not always run older ANSI-COBOL programs because of the addition of new reserved words.

- **PL/I**—*P*rogramming *L*anguage One—was introduced by IBM in 1964 as a "universal language"—a compromise between COBOL and FORTRAN to apply to both scientific-mathematic problems and general purposes. ANSI produced a PL/I standard language in 1976. PL/I is a procedure-oriented language with a modular structure in which a module can stand alone as a program or become part of a more complex program. It is useful for both novice and expert programmers. PL/I has several advantages: (1) Its modular structure allows the use of structured programming concepts. (2) It has built-in features that can identify and correct common programming errors. (3) It is very flexible, with few coding restrictions. It also has some disadvantages: (1) It requires a lot of main storage in the computer. (2) It has so many options that some people think it loses its usefulness. (3) It is more difficult to learn than COBOL.

- **RPG**—*R*eport *P*rogram *G*enerator—introduced by IBM in 1964, is a problem-oriented language that is fairly limited in its uses: it is designed to generate business reports. RPG has several advantages: (1) It is easy to learn and use. (2) Its use does not involve the memorization of many formal rules. (3) It is very efficient for work on large files involving few calculations. It also has some disadvantages: (1) Its logic is not as complex as COBOL's or PL/I's; thus it is not as powerful. (2) It has limited mathematical capability. (3) There is no standard RPG.
- **FORTRAN**—*FOR*mula *TRAN*slator—was introduced by IBM in 1954 as the first high-level language. It is the most widely used scientific-mathematic language. FORTRAN has several advantages: (1) It is more compact than COBOL. (2) It is very useful for processing complex formulas. (3) Many application programs for scientists and engineers have been written in FORTRAN. It also has some disadvantages: (1) It is not as structured as COBOL. (2) It is not as able to handle large amounts of input and output data. (3) It is more difficult to read and understand, and thus harder to change.
- **Pascal**—developed in the mid-1970s and named after the 17th-century French mathematician and philosopher Blaise Pascal—takes advantage of structured programming concepts. It is relatively easy to learn and is frequently available on microcomputer systems. Pascal has several advantages: (1) It is simpler to learn than other languages. (2) It is excellent for scientific and systems uses. (3) It has excellent graphics capabilities. Pascal's main drawback is that it has limited input and output capabilities, so it is not apt to have serious business uses.
- **Ada**—developed under the sponsorship of the U.S. Department of Defense and named for Lady Ada Augusta ("the first programmer")—was originally intended to be a standard language for weapons systems, although it also has commercial applications. Ada has several advantages: (1) It has more general input and output capability than Pascal. (2) It is a structured language, with a modular design that allows pieces or modules of a large program to be written and tested separately before the entire program is put

together. (3) It permits the compiler to check for errors before the entire program is run. It also has some disadvantages: (1) Some people think it is too complex. (2) It has been called unwieldy and inefficient. (3) Its size may hinder its use on microcomputers, although the development of more powerful microcomputer chips may obviate this concern.

- **ALGOL**—*ALGO*rithmic *L*anguage—was introduced in 1960 and is intended for scientific and mathematical projects. Its programs tend to be easy to read, but it has limited input/output capability. It is the forerunner of PL/I, Pascal, and Ada.
- **APL**—*A P*rogramming *L*anguage—was introduced by IBM in 1968 and is useful for processing tables and arrays (groups of related numbers). There are many special characters in this language, and a special keyboard is required. This language is apt to be available only on machines with large memories.
- **LISP** was developed at the Massachusetts Institute of Technology in 1958 to write programs in artificial intelligence.
- **Logo,** a version of which is known as "turtle graphics," was developed at M.I.T. as a dialect of LISP. It is used to command a triangular pointer, called a "turtle," on a video screen to plot graphic designs. Logo is useful for teaching some fundamentals of programming to young children.
- **Smalltalk** was invented at the Palo Alto (California) Research Center, created by Xerox Corporation. It is designed to support an especially visual computer system. Most commands are accomplished with the use of a mouse. The principles of Smalltalk were adapted by Apple Computer in their Lisa and Macintosh computers.
- **SNOBOL** was invented by Bell Telephone Laboratories in the early 1960s and is widely used for manipulating alphanumeric or special characters. It has found use in text editors and language processors.

KEY TERMS

REVIEW QUESTIONS

1. Describe the different levels of programming languages.
2. What system does machine language use to represent data?
3. What are some of the advantages of assembly language?
4. Why are problem-oriented languages considered to be the most "user-friendly"?
5. How are assembly and high-level languages translated into machine language?
6. Name the four generations of computer languages.
7. Name some languages that would perform well for scientific and mathematical applications. Why?
8. Name some languages that would perform well for business applications. Why?

CASE PROBLEMS

Case 6-1: COBOL or Ada?

COBOL became the dominant programming language for business in great part not only because the Department of Defense (DOD) made a great effort to develop the language to standardize computer languages but also because it specified the use of COBOL in many contracts it awarded. Today COBOL is perhaps the most widespread programming language in the world. In the early 1970s, DOD developed Ada as a uniform, all-purpose programming language to control runaway software costs and to simplify the use of hardware. Will it become the language of the future? A February 6, 1984, article in *Computerworld* described the pros and cons this way:

> Proponents of Ada see it as an advancement in the art of programming, because the new language allows use of application programs on any computer model, making programmers independent of computer hardware. Ada language is supported by IBM and Intel Corp., which gives it a lot of credibility.
>
> On the other hand, because it is so comprehensive, it is not among the most user-friendly computer languages. Its critics believe it will never become widely used by the programming community. But if Ada is to save billions for DOD, the reluctance of present software suppliers who stand to lose lucrative contracts is expected. . . .
>
> Since DOD is the largest software consumer in the world, its preference for Ada is being closely watched by software companies who see a new business bonanza in Pentagon programs such as these. Some even believe that Ada will affect more software professionals during the 1980s than COBOL did in the 1960s and 1970s.[1]

Your assignment: Let us say you already are working in a management-trainee position for a defense contractor. Most of the present programming is still done in COBOL, and it is part of your job to communicate with programmers. Since you already are working full time, it is difficult for you to take more than one night course, but you are determined to take at least one—in programming. Let us assume you have taken BASIC. Now you can take either COBOL or Ada. Which one would you take and why?

Case 6-2: A Turn Toward Turing?

There is one programming language we did not mention in the text: Turing. Named in honor of Alan Turing, a brilliant British mathematician and computer theorist, **Turing** is a general-purpose language developed in 1983 at the University of Toronto by Jim Cordy, Richard Holt, and J. N. P. Hume. According to a February 20, 1984, article in *Computerworld*, Holt said Turing is "simpler than BASIC, more powerful and elegant than either Pascal or PL/I and offers debugging, portability and modular programming capabilities that outstrip all three." Most important, Turing, unlike Pascal and PL/I, uses modular programming techniques, said Holt, which allow a building-block approach to system design and maintenance and ensures accuracy and flexibility. As a general-purpose language, Turing is useful for basic data processing, microcomputer, and scientific applications. However, Holt admitted that at present Turing is not as good as COBOL for large file processing applications such as those used for business data processing.[2]

Your assignment: One of the decisions you may well face in the future is whether a business or installation you are working for should convert to a more efficient programming language than the one it has been using for some time. Consider the following: Would you use Turing if you were working for a scientific research-and-development laboratory? If not Turing, then what? Would you use Turing for a payroll program for a microcomputer to be carried on location by a movie company? If not Turing and not BASIC, then what? Would you consider converting to Turing if you were working for a large insurance company that already had thousands of program statements written in COBOL?

Part 3

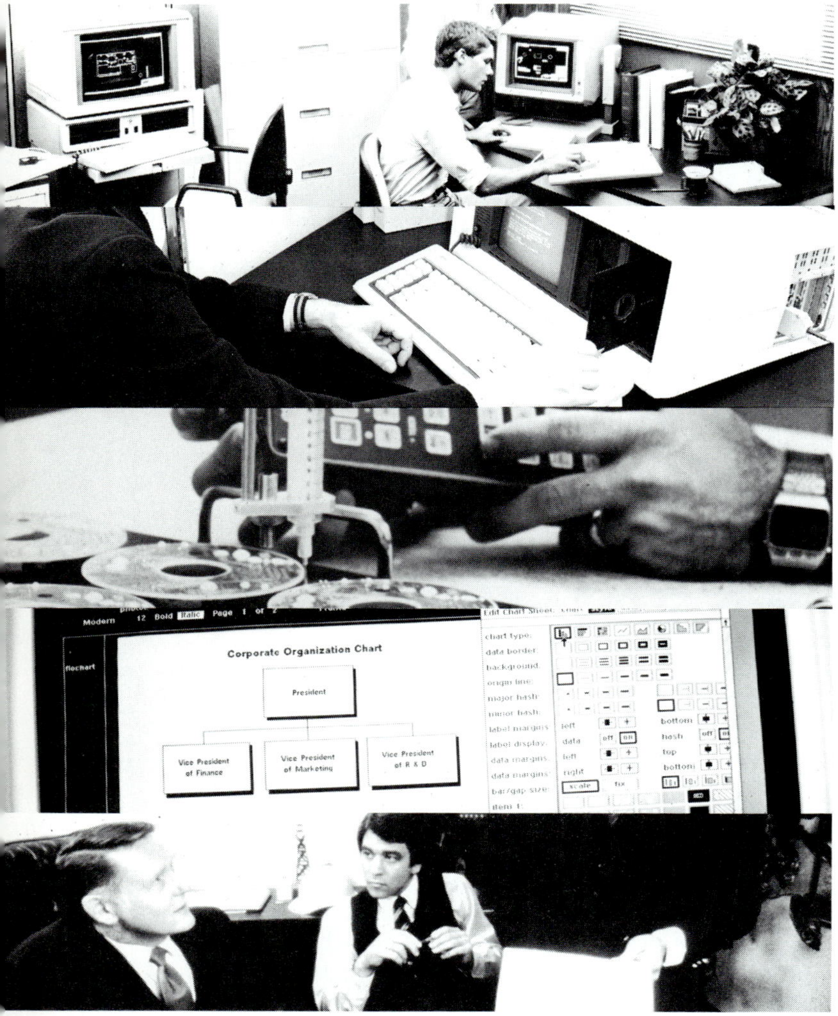

Corporate Organization Chart
President
Vice President of Finance
Vice President of Marketing
Vice President of R & D

The Uses of Hardware

Being a good manager isn't enough any more. You have to manage differently. Because of rapidly changing technology, quick market saturation, and unexpected competition, succeeding in business—particularly a high-tech business—may be harder than ever today, says *Fortune* writer Susan Fraker. Thus, a new management technique is called for. "The skills that make up the new technique—call it high-speed management—aren't easy to master," she says. "But learning them is becoming increasingly imperative."[1]

The heart of Fraker's analysis is that product life cycles are getting shorter. Whereas the market for refrigerators took over 30 years to mature, the market for microwave ovens has taken about ten years. Calculators at Hewlett-Packard went through 23 models in eight years. Microcomputers came seemingly out of nowhere in 1977, quickly multiplied into 150 to 200 models, and just as quickly saw an industry shakeout that left fewer micro manufacturers in the field.

Do rapid product cycles mean that the types of hardware that we are about to study in this part—input and output, central processing unit, storage, networks—will also shortly become obsolete? The answer is both yes and no. To see why, turn the page.

CHAPTER 7

Input and Output

Problems In, Solutions Out

PREVIEW

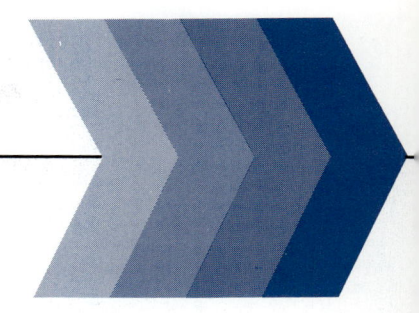

"Being educated is what is left over when everything else is forgotten," writes the famous psychologist B. F. Skinner. Being educated in this sense is what we hope you will be after you have finished reading this chapter. The hardware you are starting to read about here will someday be forgotten because it will change dramatically during your lifetime. Indeed, some of the equipment is changing even as you read this.

But there are at least two good reasons for reading this chapter anyway, reasons that will have an important bearing on your business career:

- Many of the *concepts* that we describe will remain true even as the equipment changes. This means both hardware concepts and business concepts, as the case study on the next page shows.
- In point of fact, many executives—particularly data processing managers—are working with what one writer describes as "ancient hardware—technology that is pushing 20 years old." Classics such as IBM's 360 and 370 lines of mainframe computers, he says, "still make up 10% of the domestic IBM installed base."[1]

This, then, is what we mean by being educated: you will need to come away from this part of the book prepared for anything—for dealing with the cutting edge of technology sooner than you think and for muddling through with equipment that industry watchers wrote off years ago.

Input and Output: Data into Information

"Satisfaction guaranteed or your garbage back," says the slogan on the scavenger truck. Input and output operate in essentially

CASE STUDY: CREATING A NEW WAY TO INPUT

High-Speed Management for the High-Tech Age

"High-speed management," according to Susan Fraker, consists of thinking constantly about new products and then backing the thinking with investment—fast. Besides a fat research-and-development budget, she says, such management requires continuous close contact with customers, careful monitoring of the competition, smart marketing and manufacturing, and "impeccable timing." The following shows how computer maker Hewlett-Packard used the technique of staying in touch with its customers to come up with a new way to input data.

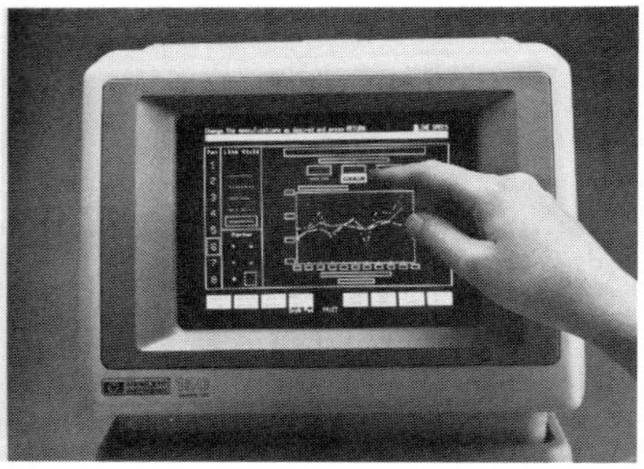

"Stay close to the customer"—the advice comes straight out of the best-seller *In Search of Excellence.* No company, high tech or low, can afford to ignore it. "Successful companies always ask what the customer needs," says William P. Sommers, a Booz Allen executive vice president. "Even if they have strong technology, they do their marketing homework." Hewlett-Packard, which used to design scientific instruments by asking the guy on the next bench what kind of device he would like, now asks its customers. H-P's personal computer division even ran focus groups—in which potential customers sit around and talk about their needs and interests—to see what computer buyers wanted. Focus groups? At Hewlett-Packard? "We'd never heard of them," admits Edward McCracken, H-P's executive in charge of business development. "But in using them we discovered overwhelming support for our touch screen." With this device, the computer user can give directions to the machine simply by touching a spot on the screen's face. "The popularity of the touch screen was contrary to what many of us at the company expected," McCracken says. "I grew up typing. I didn't want a touch screen." When its customers spoke, Hewlett-Packard listened. Instead of making touch screens an option on the HP150 [microcomputer] as planned, the company made them standard.

—*Susan Fraker,*
Fortune, March 5, 1984

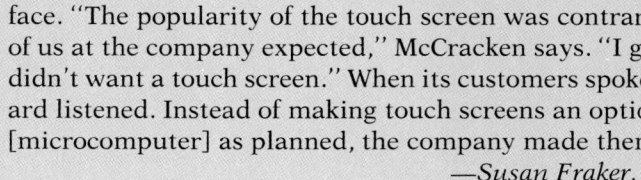

the same way. Programmers use the acronym **GIGO**—short for "Garbage In, Garbage Out"—to mean that the quality of the information that comes out is no better than the quality of the data put in.

Data consists of letters, numbers, symbols, shapes, colors, temperatures, sounds, or other raw material. For the computer to convert these to information, the data must be made available in *machine-readable* form. That is the purpose of the input devices to be described here—to convert the stuff of life into forms the computer can handle.

The computer processes the raw data into information, but that information is still only machine-readable until output devices convert it to a form people can use. Actually, the forms of output are practically limitless. Although some of the output devices that we will describe in this chapter may sometime become obsolete, it is an important principle that a computer can operate *any* machine that can be run by electricity. As one writer put it, giving free rein to the possibilities:

> Computers can activate printers, picture screens, lawn sprinklers, musical instruments, jukeboxes, music synthesizers, rocket launchers, atomic weapons, electric trains, cameras, water pistols, puppets, exhibits, theater lights, fish feeders, cattle gates, movie projectors, bells, whistles, klaxons, foghorns and chimes.[2]

In this book, however, we are less concerned with rocket launchers and puppets than we are with such business-related output devices as video terminals and printers.

We shall now describe the most important input devices. In the second half of the chapter we shall describe output devices. No single computer system has all the possible different types of input and output devices. Some of the devices are designed for special applications and are ineffective in other applications.

To show you how useful this equipment probably will be in your business future, let us imagine that you have left Starfire Film Production Company for a career in international banking. (You found that the business side of movie making was as crazy as the creative side.) You have moved to Atlantic-Pacific Bank, headquartered in Boston and with offices in the United States and Canada. You begin in the Boston office with a job that is essentially an internship; it allows you to move around and become familiar with different parts of the bank's operation. As you are about to discover, input and output are a great deal of what banking is all about.

Input: Batch versus Transaction Processing

There are two basic methods of handling data:

- Batch processing—in which data is saved up and input at one time, as a batch
- Transaction processing—in which data is not saved up but input as it is created, as transactions happen

Let us see how these work.

Batch Processing

In **batch processing,** the data is originally recorded on a source document such as a payroll time sheet, as in the *Rough Cut* payroll example in the last chapter. The data from the source documents is then accumulated and input to the computer in a batch all at one time, as was the case at the end of the week for everyone working on the *Rough Cut* film.

Transaction Processing

With **transaction processing,** data is input to the computer as soon as it is created—that is, at the time of a transaction. For example, many department stores use cash registers that are directly connected to the store's computer. When you buy a sweater on credit at such a store, the sales clerk records the sale on the cash register, which immediately notifies the store's central computer to post the purchase against your charge account for later billing, updates the clothing department's sales figures, and advises higher management of decreasing inventory (by one unit, at least) in sweaters. Transaction processing is also called **real-time processing,** because a transaction is processed fast enough that the results can come back and be of use immediately. It is also called **on-line processing,** because it works by having the user's terminal directly connected to—"on line" with—the computer.

Batch and Transaction Processing at the Bank

In your new job with Atlantic-Pacific Bank, you find both batch and transaction processing in operation. *Batch processing* is used to service those customers in a branch bank who hate to stand in line at a teller window to make deposits to their checking accounts. Instead, they put their cash, checks, and deposit slips in an envelope and drop them into the convenient No-Wait Deposit box in the bank's lobby. That evening, bank personnel open all the envelopes and key the deposits into the bank's computer, all in one batch—that is, in one session.

Transaction processing takes place when customers make withdrawals at the automatic teller machines. When they punch in the numbers to withdraw cash from their checking or savings accounts, the machine will provide them with a slip of paper telling them the amount withdrawn and their new account balance—an instant process.

Some kinds of input equipment will work only for batch and some only for transaction processing, but many will work for both. Let us consider the various categories.

Taking It All In: Keyboard versus Direct Entry

In general, input devices receive data in one of two ways:

- By keyboard entry
- By direct entry

In *keyboard entry,* data is input to the computer *after* the transaction that produced the data has taken place. Also, someone copies, using the keyboard, the data from its original source document. This is the case with the no-wait deposits; someone at the bank scoops up all the checks, cash, and deposit slips from the No-Wait Deposit box at the end of the day and keys them into the computer to record them in people's checking or savings accounts.

In *direct entry,* data is made into machine-processable form at the time the transaction is being made. No one has to enter the data manually through a keyboard later. You see this with oil company credit cards. When you paid for your gas while traveling for Starfire, you charged it on a Shell, Texaco, or similar credit card. A service station attendant would run your credit card through an imprinting device, which would imprint your credit card number on an invoice slip. Although the attendant wrote up the transaction with a pen on the slip, he or she also recorded the date, dollar amount, and dealer with the imprinting device, which produced machine-readable numbers. You kept the invoice slip, but the dealer sent a carbon copy to the oil company's accounting department. At the end of the month, someone in the accounting department collected all the imprinted copies of all your transactions and put them directly into a machine that automatically read the machine-readable numbers on the slips and computed the total amount you owed; no retyping or keying was required.

If you have ever tried to haggle with a store about a "computer error" in your bill, you know what true frustration is. Most mistakes, however, are not computer errors but *people* errors: someone probably keyed in the wrong data. Thus, you can already see why there is a trend toward less keying of data and more use of direct entry: it not only saves on labor, because data has to go through fewer hands; for the same reason, it also saves on errors.

HISTORY OF THE INFORMATION AGE

Hollerith and the Punched-Card Revolution

Technology often advances by the adoption of ideas from unlikely quarters. The analytical engine of Charles Babbage (see box, p. 67), for instance, used a concept devised by Frenchman Joseph Jacquard for weaving textiles. Jacquard, noting the repetitious nature of the task required of weavers working on looms, devised a stiff card with a series of holes punched in it. The card blocked certain threads from entering the loom and let other threads go on to complete the weave. Babbage realized that the punched-card system could also be used to control the order of calculations in the analytical engine, and the device was incorporated in his machine. The Babbage/Jacquard idea, kept alive in Lady Ada Byron's notes, finally found utility in the United States in the 1890 census.

America in the late 19th century burgeoned with a growing population of new immigrants from Europe, so large a mass yearning to breathe free that as a consequence the census of 1880 required seven and one-half years to tabulate, since all counting had to be done by hand. Realizing that it faced the danger of not completing a census before having to do the next one (the U.S. Congress requires a census of the country's population every ten years), the Census Bureau held a competition to find a new method of counting.

Many ideas were submitted, but three were chosen as final contenders: William Hunt's system of colored cards, Charles Pidgin's system of color-coded tokens, and Herman Hollerith's electronic tabulation machine (although opinion was against the latter, because machines were still regarded with considerable suspicion). A final test, involving a count of the population of St. Louis, Missouri, however, yielded the following results: Hunt's system—55 hours; Pidgin's system—44 hours; Hollerith's machine—$5\frac{1}{2}$ hours. The Census Bureau accordingly adopted the Hollerith electric tabulator, and as a result, an official count

Herman Hollerith and his tabulating machine. This electrical tabulator and sorter was used to process punched cards.

of the 1890 population (62,622,250) was announced only six weeks after the census was taken.

Like the Jacquard cards, Hollerith's punched cards involved stiff paper with holes punched in specific places, representing data to be processed. In the machine, rods passing through the holes completed an electrical circuit, causing a counter to advance one unit. The difference between Babbage's and Hollerith's machines, however, was crucial: Babbage's was mechanical and physically incapable of operating with precision; Hollerith's was *electrical.*

Hollerith realized that there was a commercial need for the rapid tabulation of figures and statistics, and in 1896 he left the Census Bureau to found the Tabulating Machine Company. The company was successful in selling services to railroads and other clients, including the government of Czarist Russia. In 1924, the successor to this company merged with two others to form the International Business Machines Corporation, known today as that giant of the computer industry, IBM.

Next history installment: **From Electromechanical to Electronic Computers: Aiken to ENIAC,** p. 279.

Let us consider the input devices and recording material used for keyboard entry and direct entry.

Keyboard Entry

In keyboard entry, data is recorded on either of two kinds of *media* or materials:

- *Paper* media, such as punched cards
- *Magnetic* media, such as cassette, diskette, tape, or hard disk

Except for the keyboards used for paper media, the keyboard entry device most commonly used is the computer terminal. Let us look at the paper and magnetic media first and then the types of computer terminals.

Punched Cards

Punched cards, shown in Figure 7-1, were the first form of input used for computers, and they are still used in a number of places principally because they are there—the equipment for using them was bought and paid for years ago.

Punched cards are stiff paper cards punched with holes that represent data. The holes are punched using a **keypunch machine,** which has a typewriterlike keyboard. After a stack of cards has been punched, it is taken to a **card reader,** which translates the card holes into electrical impulses, which in turn are input to the computer.

There are several difficulties with having punched cards. They take a lot of space to store. There is a lot of waste involved in keypunching;

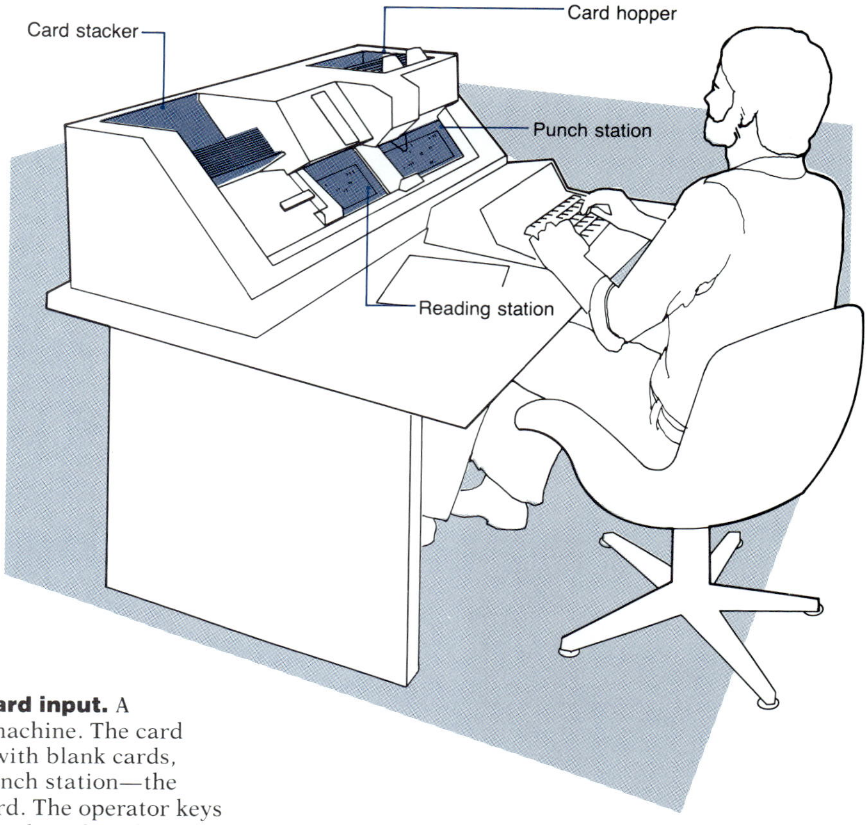
Card hopper
Card stacker
Punch station
Reading station

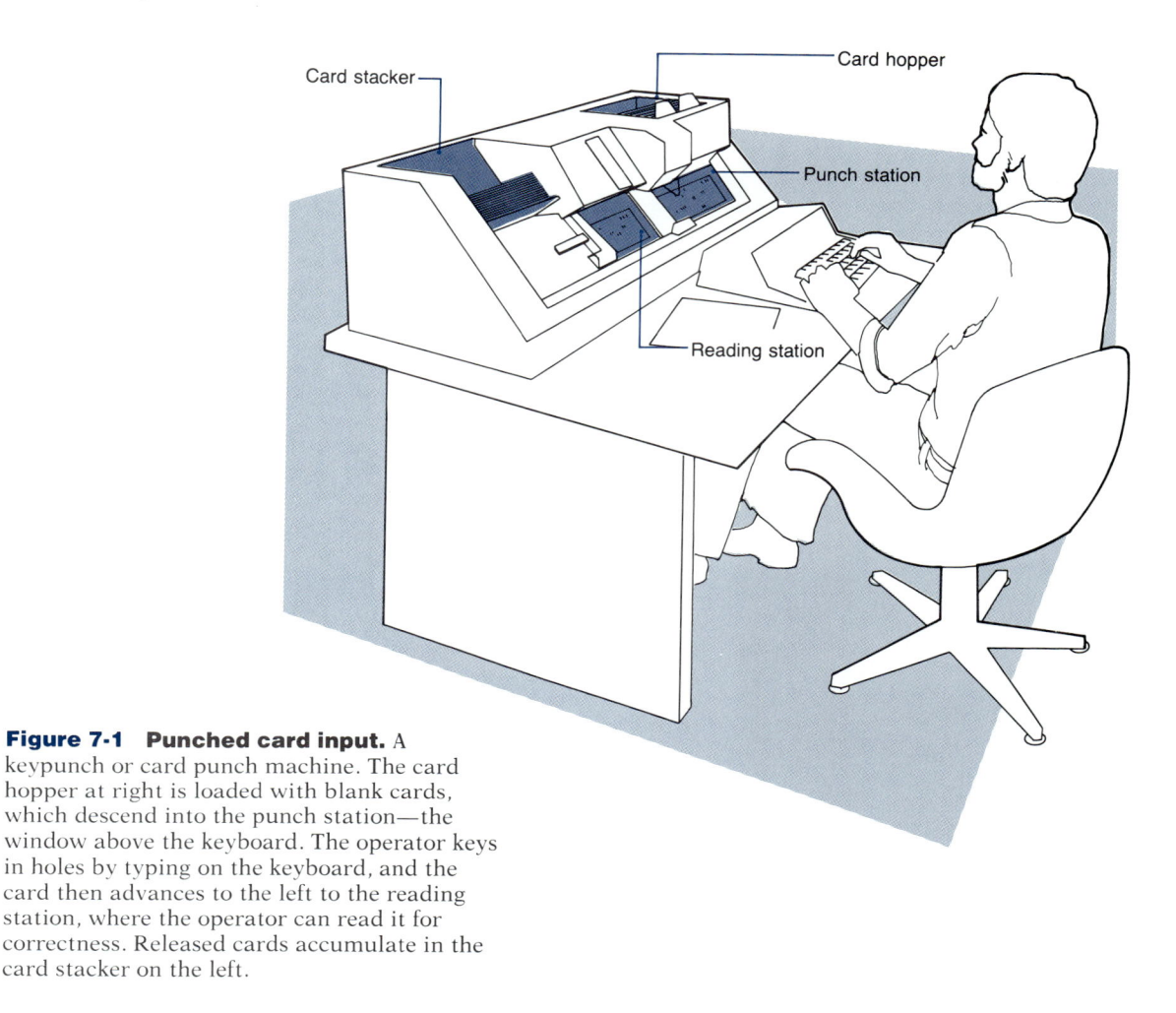

Figure 7-1 Punched card input. A keypunch or card punch machine. The card hopper at right is loaded with blank cards, which descend into the punch station—the window above the keyboard. The operator keys in holes by typing on the keyboard, and the card then advances to the left to the reading station, where the operator can read it for correctness. Released cards accumulate in the card stacker on the left.

when you make a mistake, you cannot just backspace, you have to throw the card away and start over. The cards are heavy. It is easy to drop them. Compared to other media, they are slow to process. Finally, there are so many intermediate steps involved—copying from source documents, punching cards, taking cards to the card reader, and so on—that there are a lot of places where errors can be introduced. In any case, the steps require a lot of time, which, of course, makes the process expensive. The warning DO NOT FOLD, SPINDLE, OR MUTILATE, which used to appear on the punched cards in college registration materials, may mean nothing nowadays, but an entire generation of students came to resent these words as an attempt to impose computerization on their lives. In most

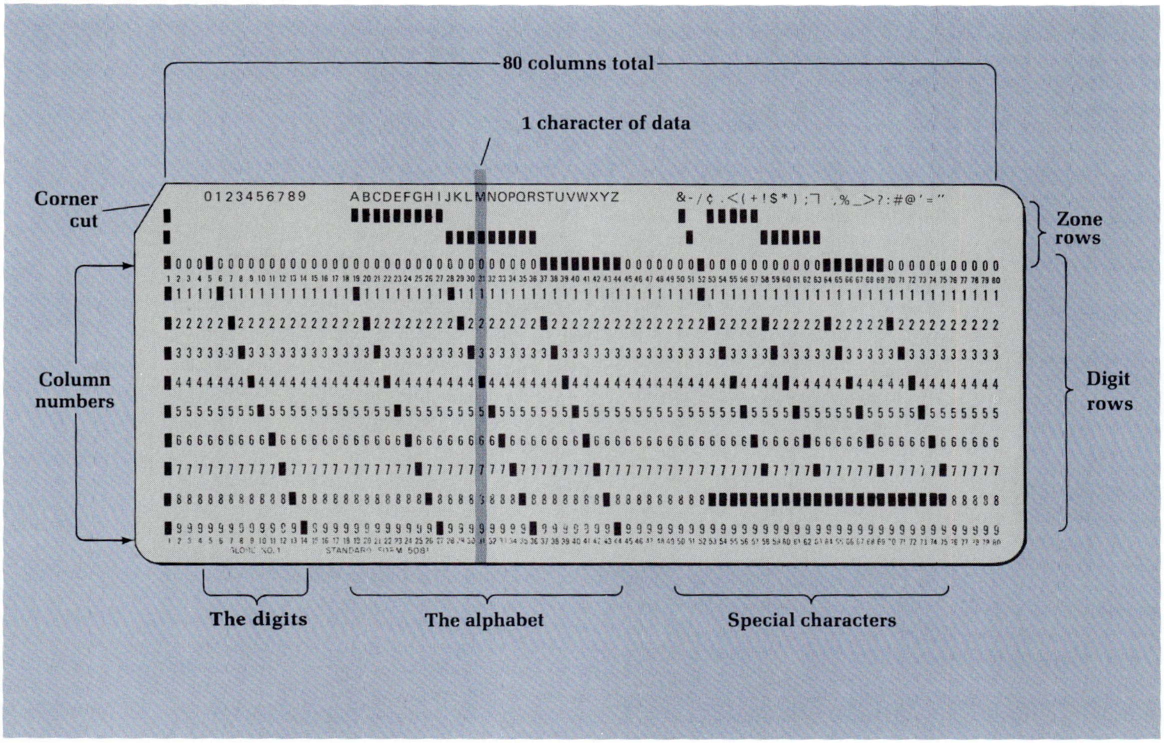
80 columns total
1 character of data
Corner cut
Zone rows
Column numbers
Digit rows
The digits
The alphabet
Special characters

Figure 7-1 (continued). A punched 80-column card. Each digit, letter, or special character is represented by a unique combination of punched holes. One character of data—the letter *M* is highlighted here—is represented by two punched holes in particular rows. Keypunched cards are placed in a card reader; light passing through the punched holes causes electronic signals representing data to be sent to the computer.

places, however, cards are being phased out in favor of the more efficient magnetic media, which we will now describe.

Magnetic Media

Data on paper cards is represented by punched holes. Data on magnetic media, such as tape or disk, is represented by magnetized spots. The three popular devices used for magnetic keyboard entry are:

- Key-to-diskette
- Key-to-tape
- Key-to-disk

Examples of these three kinds of devices are shown in Figure 7-2.

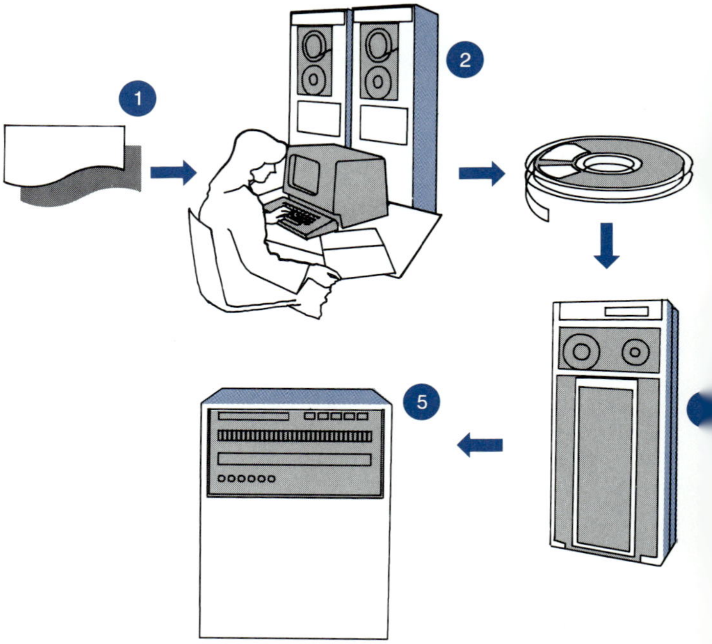
1
2
5

Figure 7-2 Three kinds of magnetic media input devices. *Top left*: Key-to-diskette device. The flexible or floppy disk, shown being inserted by this textbook editor into a disk drive, is a popular input medium for word processors. *Top right*: Key-to-tape or key-to-disk input. The input process is the same, but the magnetic media are different. Magnetic tape drives and disk drives are shown in the background. People shown are data entry operators in the centralized data processing center for San Francisco–based Wells Fargo Bank. *Near right*: Key-to-tape device and input steps. The operator keys information from ❶ source documents on ❷ a key-to-tape device, which records information on ❸ magnetic tape in the form of magnetized spots. Later the tape will be removed by hand and mounted on ❹ a magnetic tape reader, which reads the magnetized spots and converts them to electrical impulses of data, which are sent to ❺ the computer. *Middle right*: Key-to-disk device and input steps. Note there are usually several operators simultaneously. The operator copies from ❶ source documents on ❷ a key-to-disk device, which then sends data directly to ❸ a computer, which then sends it to ❹ a magnetic disk. *Far right*: Key-to-disk with microcomputer. Note detachable keyboard.

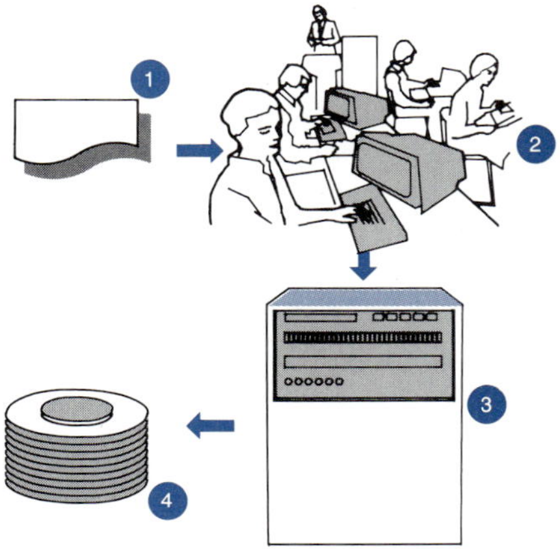
1
2
3
4

You probably already know about the **key-to-diskette device** if you have sat down at a microcomputer. It is a machine by which you key in data through the keyboard onto a floppy disk or diskette. Special-purpose computers such as word processors are also key-to-diskette devices.

A key-to-tape device and a key-to-disk device can look the same as far as the person sitting at the keyboard is concerned: both consist of videoscreens and keyboards. The differences lie in the type of magnetic medium that data is being recorded on. The **key-to-tape devices** use recording tape—in cassette, cartridge, or reel form—similar to the audio tape used in stereo tape players. The **key-to-disk devices** use a magnetic recording disk that is somewhat like a long-playing record that has concentric grooves rather than continuous grooves. We talk about both tape and disk in more detail in Chapter 9.

Magnetic media have several advantages over punched cards:

- They can be used over and over again, by recording over previous data. (Punched cards can be used only once.)
- They are easier to correct, for the same reason.
- The input devices are quieter. The machines in a keypunch room make an incredible racket, so much so that many keypunch operators wear earplugs.
- The input devices are also more reliable, since they are electronic rather than mechanical—hence have fewer moving parts to break down.
- Of great importance, magnetic media take less storage space. A closetful of punched cards can be stored on a few reels of tape.
- Most important, the data can be accessed faster by the computer.

Computer Terminals

The most popular keyboard entry device bar none is the computer terminal. For starters, terminals may be either cathode ray tube terminals (CRTs) or hard-copy terminals, depending on whether the words and numbers you type appear on a screen or on paper (Figure 7-3). Terminals may also be classified according to their capabilities as either dumb, smart, or intelligent terminals. Let us examine these characteristics of terminals further.

CRT Terminals. A **cathode ray tube terminal,** which everyone calls a **CRT terminal,** is a terminal with a keyboard and a CRT, or televisionlike screen. In computer jargon, **hard copy** is paper output—that is, a computer printout; **soft copy** is output on a computer screen. A CRT terminal thus is also called a soft-copy terminal.

A walk through the airport en route to your new Atlantic-Pacific Bank job shows CRT terminals galore. These are the devices that ticket sellers use at the airline counters to check on your reservation. They are

Figure 7-3 **Terminals.** *Top*: A CRT terminal and keyboard. This is for the IBM PC. *Bottom*: A portable hard-copy, or teleprinter, terminal. This battery-powered Texas Instruments Silent Model 707 is especially suited for people in insurance, sales, and real estate.

in the corridors and lounges in the form of arcade video games. They are at the car rental desks for determining what cars in the fleet are on hand for you to take out. And at the bank itself, CRT screens are everywhere: they are the windows through which the bank watches the ebb and flow of money.

As an input device, the CRT screen has several advantages:

- It is compact and inexpensive.
- It allows erroneous data to be corrected easily.
- It allows files to be updated on the spot and allows access to these files.

And it has some disadvantages:

- It does not make a permanent record of any transaction (unless a printer is added).
- Some people have difficulty adjusting to reading and editing on a screen instead of paper—although this problem usually disappears with use.

What to Look for in a CRT Screen

CRT screens vary in size, clarity, and number of characters that can fit on a line. They also vary in color; usually the background is black, but the characters may be in white, green, or amber. Some CRTs are also full-color.

Depending on the software, most screens also permit the following features:

- **Scrolling:** This allows you to move lines up and down on the screen, as though you were reading a scroll or reading the words of a song rolling past on a player-piano's piano roll.
- **Paging:** This allows you to flip through a file full of data a screen (or "page") at a time.
- **Highlighting:** This allows you to highlight or emphasize a portion of the text, such as by underscoring, brightening, blinking letters, or **reverse video**—in which brightness and darkness are reversed.
- **Split screens:** Sometimes two pages or screen images may be displayed side by side, as you see done in televised football games when kicker and receiver, for instance, are shown at the same time.

Hard-Copy Terminals. A keyboard with a printer attached is called a **hard-copy terminal** or **teleprinter.** Now, at whatever location the terminal happens to be, you can make a permanent paper record of the data input or the information output. The convenience is akin to that of your adding up numbers on a calculator that produces a paper tape: if you make a mistake, you can look back at the tape to see what it was—a mistake that can easily get by you if you are just using a regular pocket calculator (as you may have noticed when balancing your checkbook).

The hard-copy terminal has the advantage of producing a permanent record. However, it also has two disadvantages:

- The printing process makes it slightly slower than the CRT terminal.
- It can be quite noisy, although recently developed printers are quieter.

Dumb, Smart, and Intelligent Terminals. By themselves, the two types of terminals above are called **dumb terminals;** they cannot do any processing of their own but must be connected to a computer in order to do so. All dumb terminals do is provide a keyboard for data entry and a CRT screen and/or printer for information output.

Smart terminals—also referred to as **interactive terminals**—can be simple input or output devices to a computer located elsewhere (a mainframe or minicomputer), but they also have a microprocessor and primary storage that allows you to do some processing—calculations, editing, input modification—before the data is sent on to the computer. However, you cannot do any programming with a smart terminal.

An **intelligent terminal** includes a microcomputer that allows users to do programming as well as to input and receive data from a larger computer. At a minimum, an intelligent terminal includes a keyboard, electronics to convert data to machine-readable code, communication equipment such as a telephone line and modem, an output device such as a CRT, a processing unit, internal storage to do some data processing, software consisting of a programming language and editing programs, and secondary storage such as magnetic disk.

If you have a microcomputer, such as an IBM PC or Apple IIe, it can become a smart terminal for a mainframe just by the addition of a link that connects it by telephone to the larger computer. Atlantic-Pacific Bank, you find out, has taken a leaf from the marketing strategy of West Coast–based Bank of America and launched a program of home banking, whereby bank customers can use their home computers as smart terminals to connect with the bank's mainframe. This allows users to pay bills, move funds from one account to another, and otherwise do a limited amount of over-the-phone banking.

Direct Entry

There are certain basic skills without which one can be somewhat handicapped in living in the 20th century—reading, for instance (although one out of five adults in the U.S. cannot read this sentence), and elementary mathematics. Learning to drive a car may give you more freedom. And so may learning to type. The keyboard probably will always be with us, and it will become more important as computers become more commonplace instruments.

However, because keyboard entry depends on human skills and because to err is human, direct data entry has become more and more attractive. **Direct entry** is a form of input that does not require data to be keyed by someone reading from a source document. Direct entry creates machine-processable data right on paper or magnetic media or feeds it directly into the computer's CPU, thus eliminating the possibility of errors being introduced in the keying process. Clearly, then, direct entry represents the wave of the future.

The most popular direct-entry devices are:

- Magnetic-ink character recognition
- Optical-character recognition
- Optical-mark recognition
- Digitizers
- Point-of-sale terminals
- Touch-tone devices
- Light pens
- Mice
- Speech recognition devices

We will describe these below. No doubt you already are aware of many of them.

Magnetic-Ink Character Recognition

Abbreviated **MICR,** which is pronounced "miker" to rhyme with "biker," **magnetic-ink character recognition** is a method of machine-reading characters made of ink containing magnetized particles. Developed by the banking industry in the 1950s to make it easier to process checks, the system uses the futuristic-looking kind of numbers you see printed at the bottom of your checks, as shown in Figure 7-4.

"What do the MICR check numbers mean?" you ask on the first day of your new job at Atlantic-Pacific Bank. Although it is not the only application, check processing is by far the most common use of MICR, you are told. Examine the check and machines shown in Figure 7-4. All blank checks have a check routing symbol so that the checks can be routed back to a particular bank. The routing code consists of both the

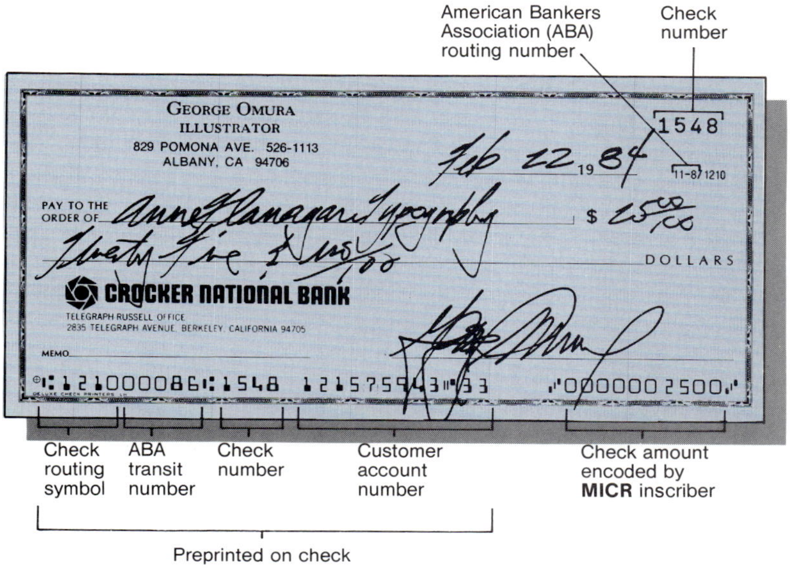
American Bankers Association (ABA) routing number
Check number
GEORGE OMURA
ILLUSTRATOR
829 POMONA AVE. 526-1113
ALBANY, CA 94706
1548
11-8/1210
PAY TO THE ORDER OF
$
DOLLARS
CROCKER NATIONAL BANK
TELEGRAPH RUSSELL OFFICE
2835 TELEGRAPH AVENUE BERKELEY, CALIFORNIA 94705
MEMO
Check routing symbol
ABA transit number
Check number
Customer account number
Check amount encoded by MICR inscriber
Preprinted on check

Figure 7-4 Magnetic-Ink Character Recognition. *Top:* The meaning of the symbols on your check. Note that the MICR characters in the lower right-hand corner of the check are put there by the bank after the check is cashed; hence, the numbers *should* correspond to the amount for which you wrote the check. *Lower left:* A magnetic-character inscriber. This machine is used to inscribe magnetic numbers in the lower right-hand corner of each check after it comes to the bank for processing. *Lower right:* A MICR reader/sorter. This machine processes checks with MICR numbers, reading them at the rate of 750–1500 characters per minute, and sorting the checks into different compartments.

NCR

transit number and the account number printed on the checks. After a check is cashed, the amount of the check is keyed (inscribed) manually by the bank in the lower right-hand area of the check. The check is then cleared through the Federal Reserve System by using a MICR reader/sorter, which reads and verifies the magnetic-ink characters. The data is then sent directly to a computer for processing or to an external storage device at one of the Federal Reserve Banks. The checks are next sorted by bank number, routed to the appropriate home bank via the transit number, and then to the customer's account via the account number.

The advantages of the MICR system over other systems are that:

- The codes can be read by both machines and people.
- It is fast, accurate, and automatic.
- The amount of human involvement—and hence human error—is reduced.

However, there are still two disadvantages:

- The MICR system is limited to only 14 characters.
- There is still some manual keying required— namely, at the point when the amount must be inscribed in MICR characters on the bottom right-hand corner of each check.

Optical-Character Recognition

Developed by the U.S. Postal Service in hopes of speeding mail sorting, the direct-entry technology known as **optical-character recognition,** abbreviated **OCR,** consists of special characters—letters, numbers, and special symbols—which can be read by a light source that converts them into electrical signals that can be sent to the computer for processing. The Postal Service hoped that the system would allow postal patrons to write addresses or zip codes in OCR, which could then be read by machine. However, it found the variations in handwriting insurmountable. Nevertheless, OCR that uses *preprinted* characters has found many uses. This means that *someone* must key the characters to begin with, but once they are on the document—most commonly retail price tags, cash register receipts, utility bills, and phone bills—they need not be keyed again for entry into the computer.

Although some OCR devices can read characters printed by people, most cannot; they read a standard typeface, the most common of which is shown in Figure 7-5.

The most popular OCR input device is the hand-held **wand reader,** as shown in Figure 7-5. The wand reflects light on the printed characters, and the reflection is converted by photoelectric cells to machine-readable code. You often see sales clerks in department stores use the wand to read retail tags and send data to the store's computer for billing and

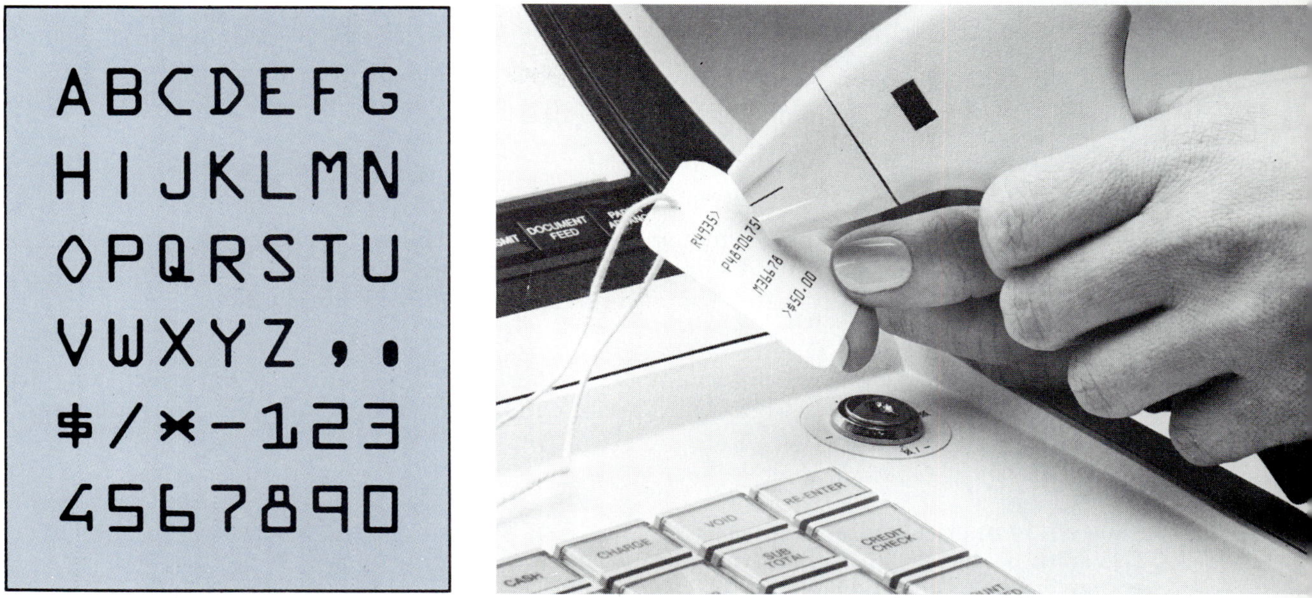
ABCDEFG
HIJKLMN
OPQRSTU
VWXYZ,.
$/*-123
4567890
DOCUMENT FEED
$50.00
RE-ENTER
VOID
CHARGE
CASH
SUB TOTAL
CREDIT CHECK

Figure 7-5 Optical-character recognition. *Left*: A standard OCR typeface. *Right*: A wand reader, a hand-held photoelectric scanning device that can read OCR characters.

merchandise-reordering purposes.

The advantages of OCR are:

- It has all of the benefits of MICR plus it has a larger set of characters—42 instead of 14.
- Using a wand reader does not require *any* manual keying of data.
- Data is electronically transferred from source document to computer.

The drawback, however, is that:

- OCR wand readers can recognize only a special set of characters.

Optical-Mark Recognition

Abbreviated **OMR, optical-mark recognition** is also known as mark-sensing; an OMR device senses the presence or absence of a mark. You see this form of direct entry used in tests such as the College Board's Scholastic Aptitude Test and the Graduate Record Examination, in which the test taker answers multiple-choice questions by filling in little boxes on a form with a special pencil. The answer sheet is then graded by an

OMR machine that uses a light beam to recognize the marks and convert them to electric signals that can be processed by the computer. Advantages of OMR are:

- No manual keying of data.
- Low cost.

The disadvantages are:

- Strict format specifications—special forms and pencils must be used.
- Limited applications for business purposes—very little flexibility in that all potential responses must be anticipated.

Digitizer

One of the more interesting forms of direct entry, a **digitizer** is a device that, as Figure 7-6 shows, can be moved over a drawing or photograph

Figure 7-6 Digitizer. This device, which the man at left is guiding with his right hand, can be moved over drawings or photographs, converting them to data that can be stored in a computer or presented on a CRT screen or paper. Here Bell Laboratories engineers are using the digitizer in the computer-aided design of integrated circuits. The circuit's layers are shown in different colors on the CRT screen.

and convert it to digital data. The digital data can then be stored in a computer, represented on a CRT screen, or printed out on paper. The principle behind the device is that each part of the drawing represents a point on a horizontal and vertical axis (that is, a pair of X-Y coordinates); thus, any given point can be identified. Indeed, there may be 1000 points per square inch. Digitizers are useful for map-making.

Point-of-Sale Terminals

Abbreviated **POS, point-of-sale** terminals (see Figure 7-7, page 224–225) represent the new evolution in cash registers. Seen often in grocery and department stores, a POS terminal consists of a keyboard for entering data, a CRT screen or digital display area for displaying dollar amounts, and a printer for printing out the list of items and prices for the customer.

Some POS terminals are also **bar-code readers**—photoelectric scanners that read the **bar codes** or vertical zebra-striped marks or bars printed on many products (see Figure 7-7). Supermarkets and other retail stores use a bar code system called the Universal Product Code (UPC). The bar code identifies the product to the store's computer, which stores the latest price on the product. The computer automatically tells the cash register or POS terminal what the price is and prints the price and the product name on the customer's receipt.

POS terminals offer several advantages:

- The skill level of sales clerks and supermarket checkers need not be as high as for those working in stores without POS systems.
- Checkout is faster.
- Current sales and inventory information is maintained automatically.

But, of course, there are some disadvantages:

- Back-up systems are required, because if there is computer failure, the POS devices fail, too.
- The equipment is expensive.
- Some states require that prices be stamped on the merchandise, since bar codes cannot be read by customers. This means stores must do double duty on price marking—putting prices in the store's computer that correspond to the bar codes and stamping prices or putting price stickers on the cans and boxes.

Touch-Tone Devices

One of the things you discover about working for Atlantic-Pacific Bank is that credit is a subject bankers care a lot about. There are many occasions when merchants need to check credit instantaneously, and a touch-tone device is a way to help them do it. A **touch-tone device** is an instrument that sends data over ordinary telephone lines to a central computer. An example (see Figure 7-8) is a **card dialer,** which reads a customer's credit card, checks the customer's creditworthiness over the phone with a computer, and reports the results to the local merchant.

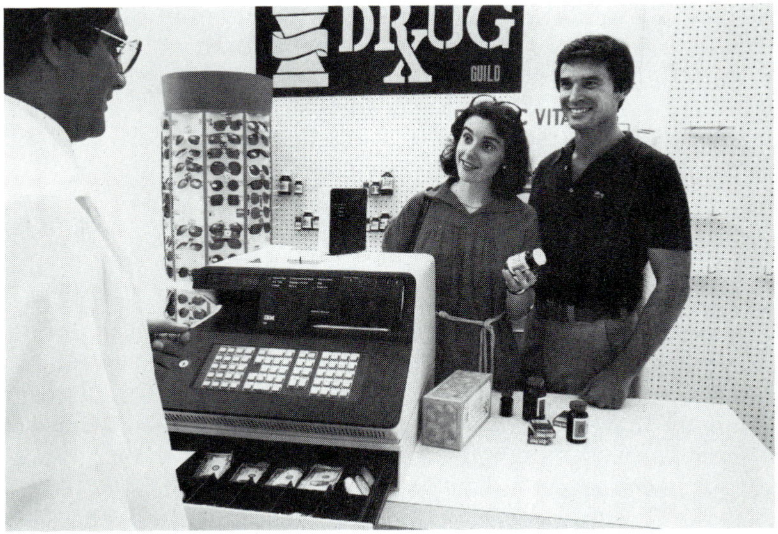

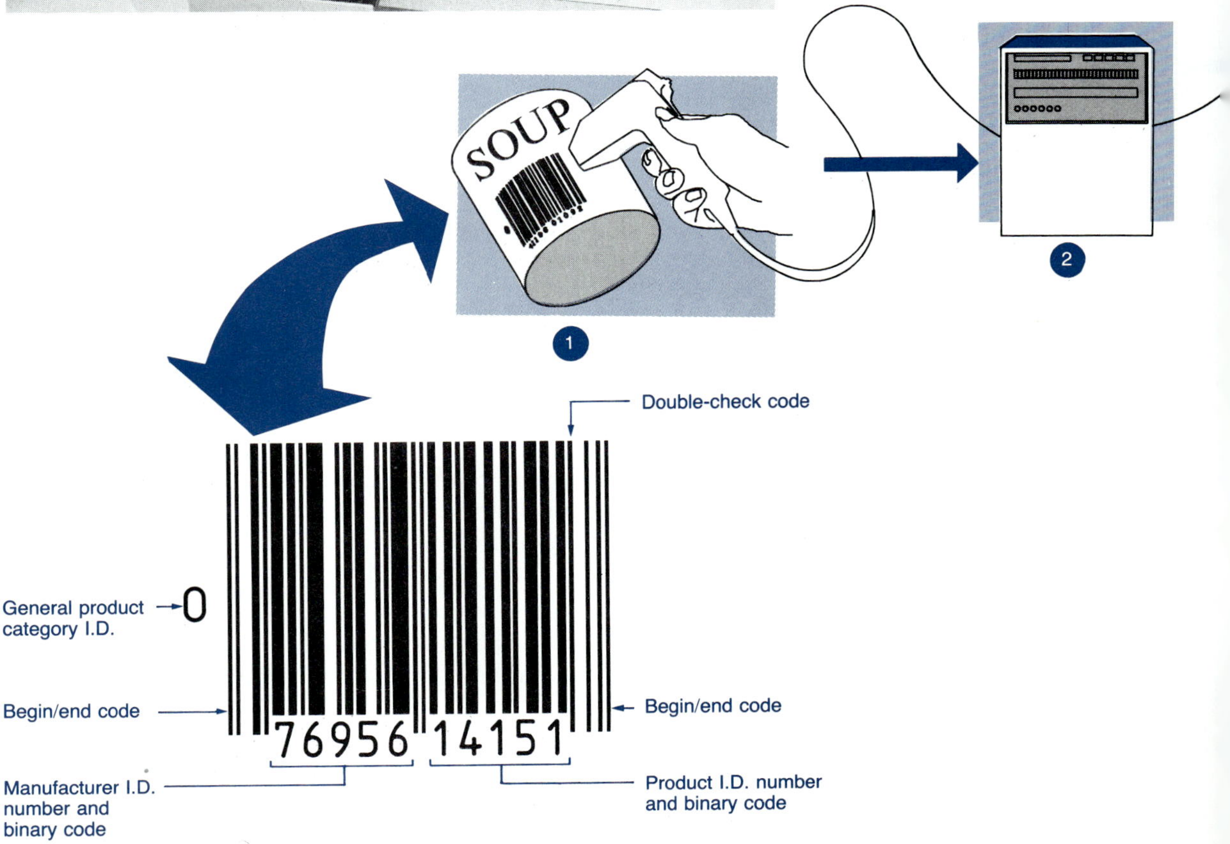
SOUP
1
2
Double-check code
General product category I.D.
0
Begin/end code
Begin/end code
76956 14151
Manufacturer I.D. number and binary code
Product I.D. number and binary code

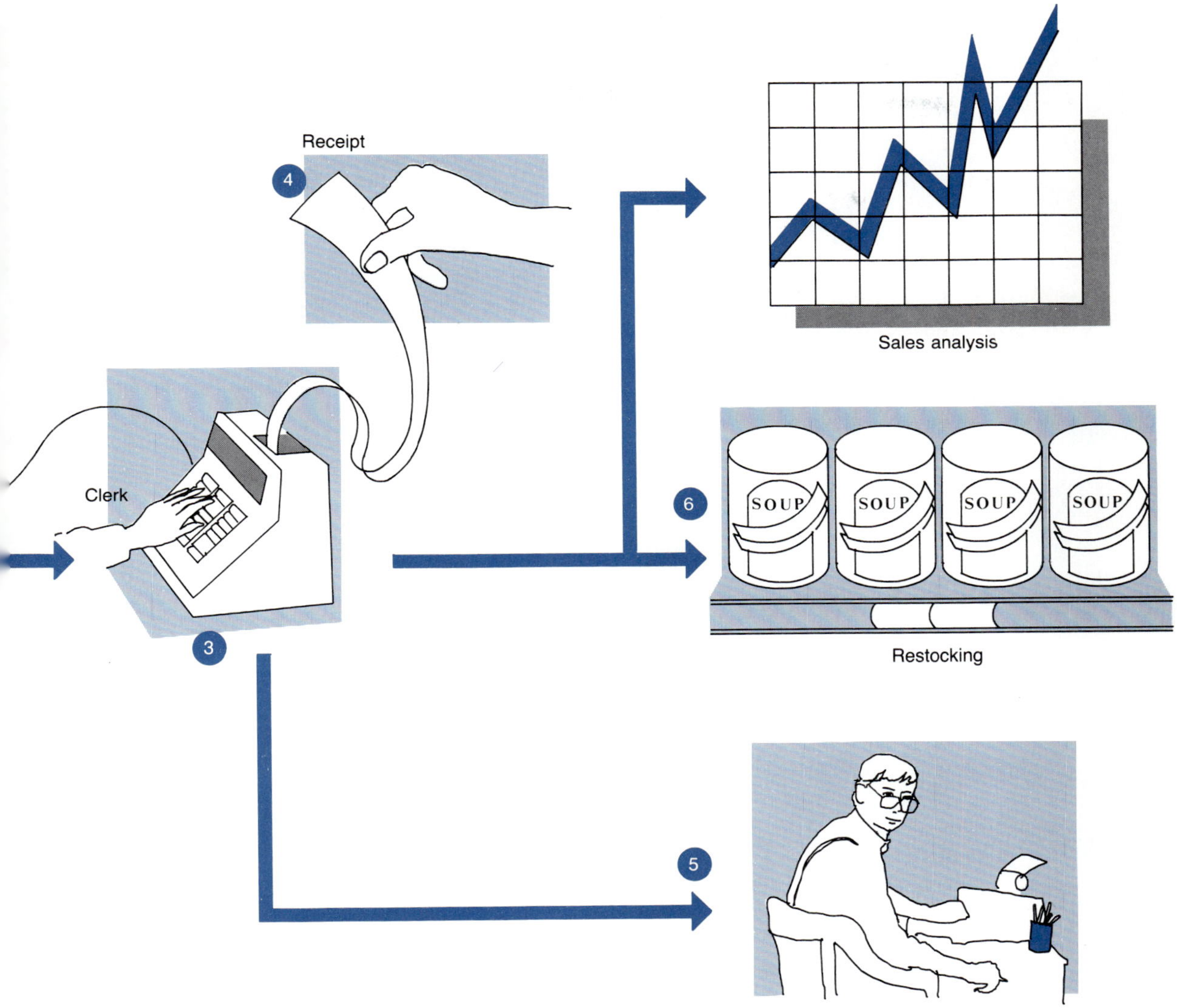
Receipt
4
Clerk
3
Sales analysis
6
SOUP
SOUP
SOUP
SOUP
Restocking
5
Accounting

Figure 7-7 Point-of-sale terminal. *Top left*: A standard POS terminal, used to enter sales data. These terminals are found in many retail stores, such as drug stores. *Bottom left*: Example of bar code—the Universal Product Code used on retail products. *Middle left and above*: What bar code readers do in the supermarket. The supermarket checker moves the grocery product's bar code ❶ past the bar-code reader, which reads it with a light beam and sensor. The price and description of the item, which is stored in ❷ the computer system, is sent to ❸ the POS terminal, where it is ❹ printed out as a receipt for the customer. The information from the POS terminal is also used by the store, on the one hand, ❺ for accounting purposes and, on the other hand, ❻ for restocking store inventory and for analyzing which products sell better than others.

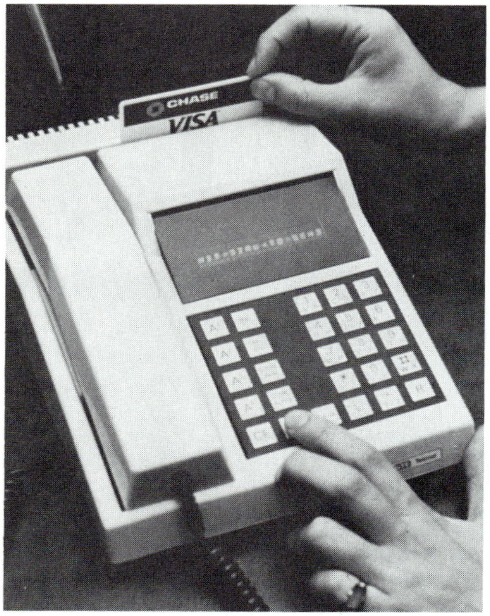
CHASE
VISA

Figure 7-8 A card dialer. A credit card check is being performed over telephone lines.

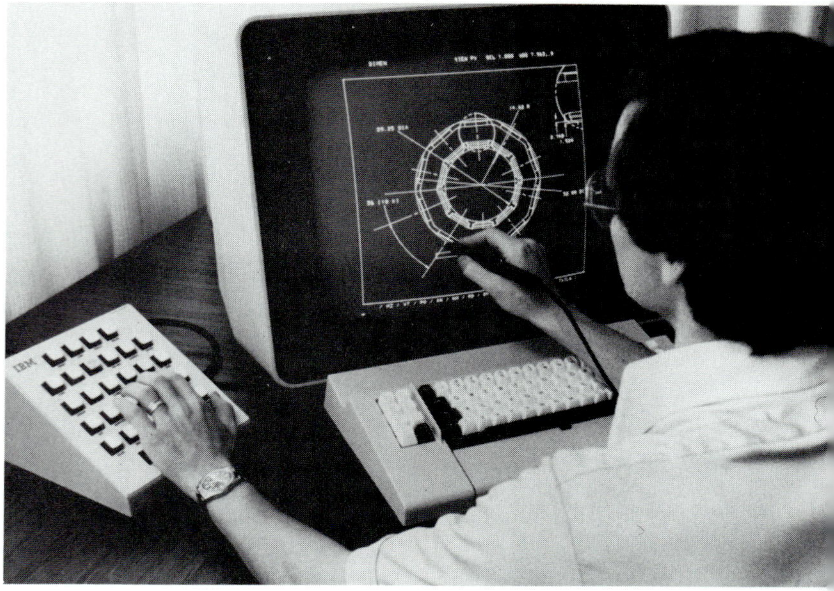
IBM

Figure 7-9 Light pen. When a pen with a light-sensitive cell at the end is placed against the screen of this graphic display terminal, it closes a photoelectric circuit, enabling the terminal to identify the point on the screen. Data may also be entered through keyboards.

Light Pens

Used in designing products from blue jeans to airplanes, a **light pen** consists of a light-sensitive penlike device which, when placed against the CRT screen of a particular kind of terminal, closes a photoelectric circuit that identifies the X-Y coordinates to the computer. This allows the user to create a drawing right on the screen. Figure 7-9 shows an example of a light pen developed for personal computers.

Mice

We described the mouse briefly in Chapter 4, but to repeat: A **mouse** is a direct-entry input device with a ball on the bottom and attached with a cord to a computer terminal (see Figure 7-10). When rolled on the table top, the mouse directs the location of the cursor or pointer on the screen. The pointer can then be used to draw pictures on the screen or point to a particular instruction.

Speech-Recognition Devices

This is the voice of the future, the ultimate data-entry device. **Speech-recognition devices** or **voice-recognition systems** (Figure 7-11) convert the spoken word into a numeric code, which is matched against a code

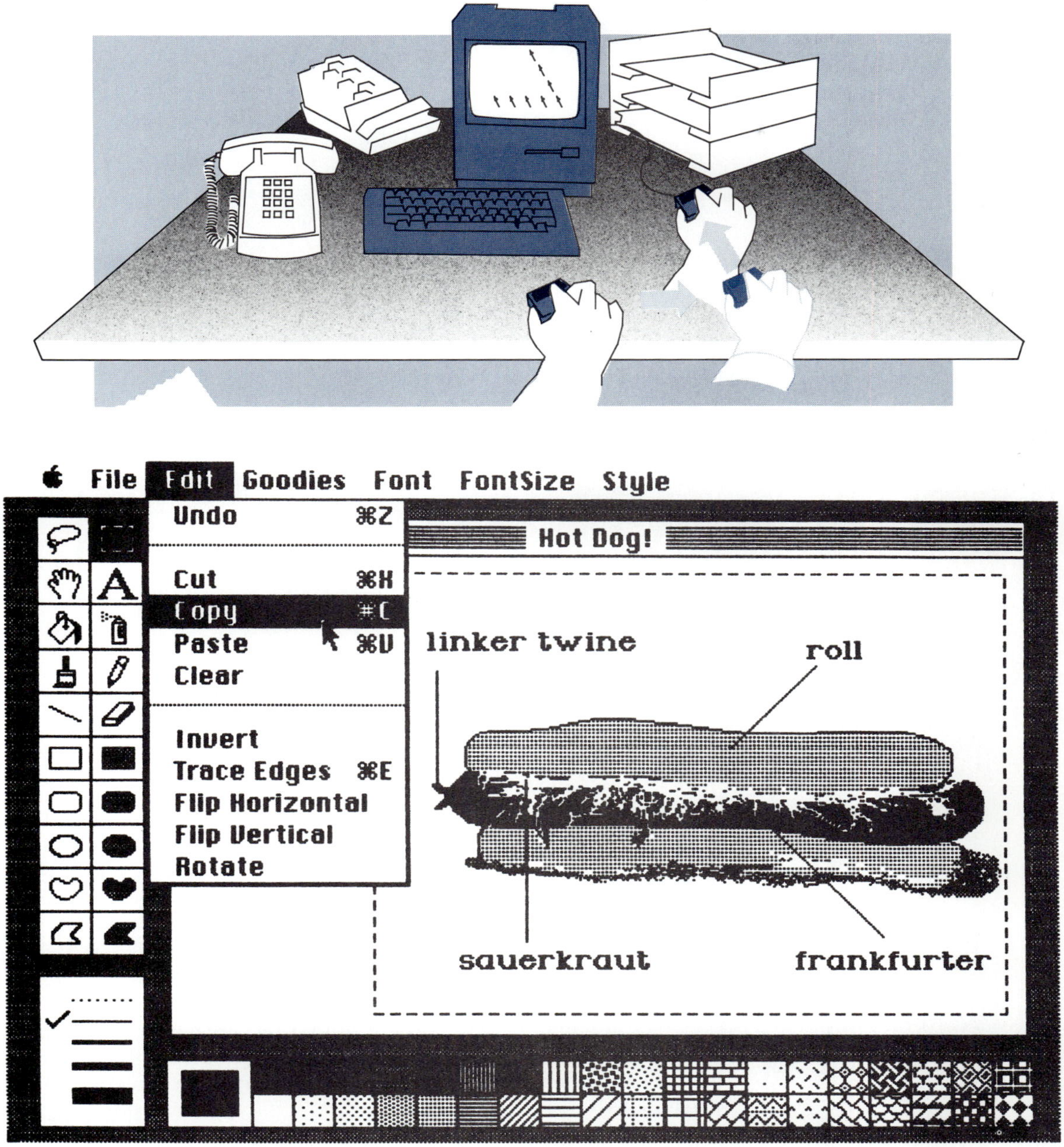
File
Edit
Goodies
Font
FontSize
Style
Undo ⌘Z
Cut ⌘X
Copy ⌘C
Paste ⌘V
Clear
Invert
Trace Edges ⌘E
Flip Horizontal
Flip Vertical
Rotate
Hot Dog!
linker twine
roll
sauerkraut
frankfurter

Figure 7-10 **Mouse.** *Top*: Movement of the mouse on the desk top makes a corresponding movement of the cursor on the CRT screen. *Bottom*: The screen of an Apple Macintosh computer. Note the symbols (called *icons*) along the left side, which represent various "brush strokes" and artist's options. The mouse's cursor (the arrow) may be used to select one of these options and then to create drawings or different type styles on the screen.

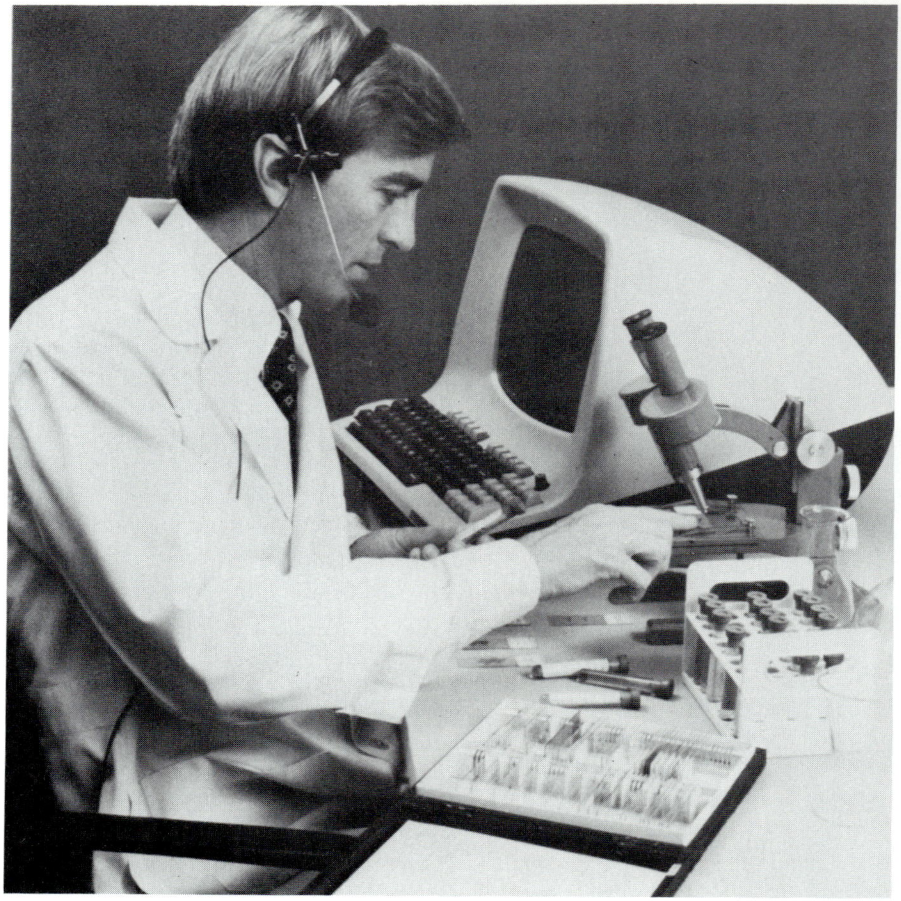

Figure 7-11 Speech recognition device. The system frees an operator's hands for other activities, as might be required of someone working with a microscope.

stored in a minicomputer. You speak a word into the microphone, the word is displayed on the screen for your visual verification, and you confirm that the input is correct.

The state of the art of speech recognition has been described as follows:

> Machines are already being produced that recognize voices in a primitive way. And experts are confident that they will be able to build computers able to comprehend the human voice and carry out sophisticated spoken instructions.
>
> A number of products are being introduced that have an ability, however crude, to recognize spoken words. They are used already by quality inspectors in factories and baggage handlers in airports. Computers in video games can respond to shouted commands; personal computers understand such spoken orders as "store" and "copy."

> Some of these devices, however simple-minded they are at the moment, represent the initial consumer applications of what is considered a promising but extremely elusive technology.[3]

Most speech-recognition systems operate by being "trained" to the user's voice. That is, they match the operator's spoken word to patterns previously stored in the computer. Systems that are "speaker-independent"—that can recognize the same word spoken by many different people—can be built by sampling how several people say the same word and storing several patterns for each word, but the vocabularies must be restricted. Moreover, it is difficult to build systems to recognize continuous speech, since people normally run their words together.

The advantages of voice-recognition devices are as follows:

- Input is very controlled, with great accuracy.
- Input is readily verified and corrected.
- The user's hands are free to perform tasks other than keying data.
- There are numerous potential applications.

The disadvantages are:

- Such systems are expensive.
- Vocabulary is limited.
- Speed of entry is slow.

Automatic Teller Machines

A specialized form of input device for transaction processing, **automatic teller machines,** abbreviated **ATMs,** are those wonderful devices you see on the outside of bank walls and in shopping malls (see Figure 7-12). ATMs allow you to withdraw funds even in the middle of the night, assuming you meet three criteria: you have a credit-cardlike ATM card, which you insert into a slot in the machine; you have a secret code number, which you punch in on the ATM keyboard; and you have enough funds in your checking account to cover the withdrawal. The ATM also allows you to make deposits, loan payments, and charge card payments and to borrow money against a bank credit card. ATMs can be installed at numerous locations since all are connected to the bank's main computer.

At Atlantic-Pacific Bank, you discover to your surprise that many people actually *prefer* doing bank business with an ATM rather than a human teller. (It is less embarrassing to learn you have insufficient funds from an ATM than from a person, after all.) There are other advantages also:

24 HOUR BANK
ENVELOPES

Figure 7-12 Automatic teller machine. *Right*: An ATM mounted on the wall of a bank. *Below*: How an ATM works. Customer ❶ inserts special ATM card into slot, ❷ keys in his or her personal identification number, ❸ pushes button identifying transaction, such as cash withdrawal, ❹ indicates amount, ❺ lifts door and removes money, ❻ removes card and paper record of transaction.

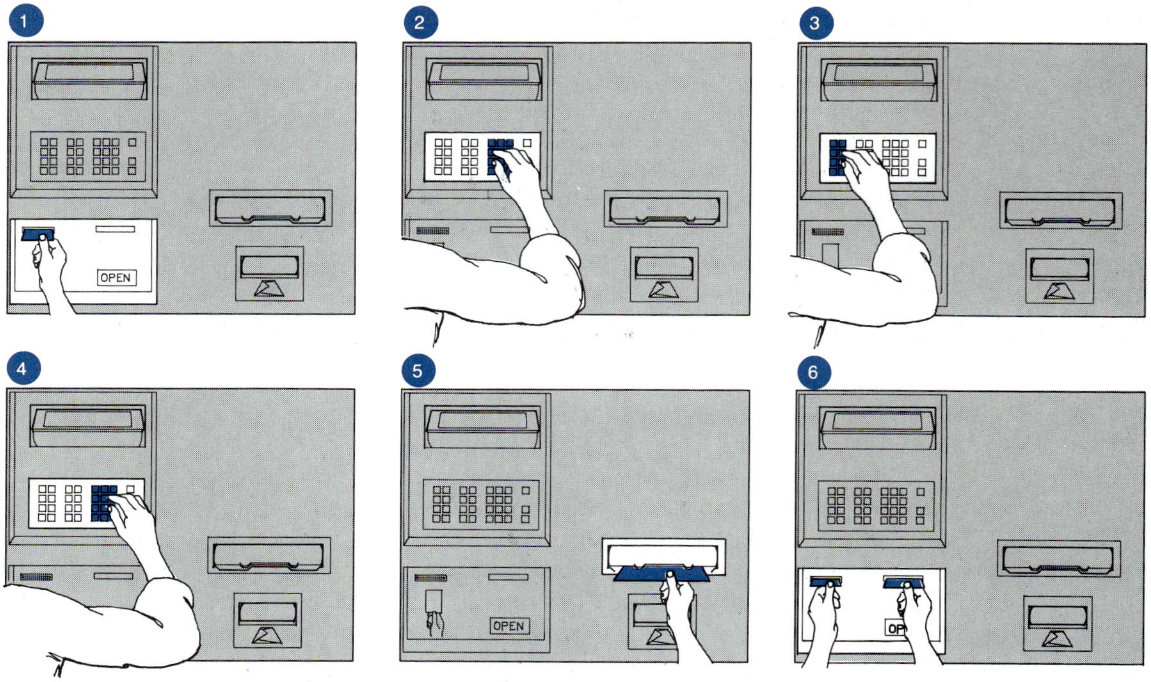
1
OPEN
2
3
4
5
OPEN
6

- As mentioned, service is available to customers 24 hours a day without increased bank employee costs.
- A lot of routine banking tasks can be accomplished with fewer manual errors.

But inevitably there are some disadvantages:

- The system may fail—and there may be no backup in the form of humans who can help process transactions using paper.
- An ATM can run out of money at night or on weekends.
- There are security problems—ATMs have been broken into, stolen cards have been used, and people have been mugged near ATMs.
- The reduced interaction with bank employees may have a negative effect on customer relations.

This concludes our discussion of input. Now let us consider the other side of the story—output.

The Evolving Credit Card

The automatic teller machine is not the only way in which machines and credit cards have replaced human beings in tedious but straightforward business exchanges. The following stories show how credit cards may be used not just to reduce labor costs but to improve service. As the last story makes clear, however, there are also downside risks to credit cards.

The Age of "Hoteltronics"

One of the more time-consuming aspects of hotel visits is the hassle of check-in and check-out. In the hotel of the future, that will be handled by computer.

For example, the new NCR 1810 Self-Service Terminal will soon start popping up in hotel lobbies.

The terminal does check-in and check-out procedures automatically. The unit is similar in appearance to a bank-automated money machine with a TV-type screen and slots for inserting a credit card and issuing paper printouts.

Wells Fargo Bank
VISA
VALID FIRST DAY OF 01/80 GOOD THRU LAST DAY OF 12/80 VISA
JOSEPH H JOHNSON

Insert a major credit card and the "user-friendly" computer starts to work. It displays complete reservation information: name, length of stay, size of room requested and rate per night. If all the details are correct, the guest presses a button and a printed confirmation is issued.

When it is time to check out, the guest simply inserts the major credit card again to review all charges on the display screen. If the bill is correct, he pushes the appropriate button, a copy of the bill is issued by the machine and the amount owed charged to his credit card. . . .

There are those who fear the new electronic age will turn hotels into cold, super-efficient storage facilities for travelers. The proponents of "Hoteltronics" argue that the computer age will improve service in their industry, not eliminate it. By freeing people from the drudgery of menial tasks, there will be more time to polish personal service. . . .

—Christopher Lofting, *Journal of Commerce*, reprinted in *San Francisco Sunday Examiner & Chronicle*, February 26, 1984

The Medical "Smart Card"

BLOIS, France—Imagine walking around with your entire medical history—records of every doctor visit, prescription and treatment you ever had—in your back pocket.

This is exactly what people here will be doing, thanks to smart card technology. Smart cards resemble credit cards, but in addition to a magnetic signature band, they contain an embedded programmable microprocessor equipped with logic and memory. Originally developed by Honeywell Bull SA for retail and banking applications, they are now breaking new ground with the medical application. . . .

The first program in the project will be launched early this year with the school children of Blois, a small city southwest of Paris. Minister for Social Affairs Pierre Beregovy said the smart cards will be distributed in the school system to maintain individual vaccination records.

To support the program, card readers will be issued to all schools and physicians in the region. A card reader can display and update a card holder's entire permanent file.

"Ultimately, we hope that an individual health card could be created for every member of the population," Beregovy said. "This would lead to improved health care by reducing delays in treatment, eliminating duplicate medical tests and ensuring correct medical care." . . .

To ensure that privacy is maintained in the use of the smart cards, all medical applications will be supervised by the National Commission for Computer Technologies and Civil Liberties, Beregovy noted. Furthermore, the cards feature built-in security devices that make them especially well suited to medical applications. . . .

So far, smart cards have been adopted by French university students as portable school records; they're being used to make direct-billing phone calls from special French phone booths; and to make direct-billing purchases at many of France's retail stores. Smart cards are also scheduled to become a part of the French pay-TV network.

—Susan Blakeney, *Computerworld*, February 27, 1984

ATMs, Credit Cards, and Criminal Abuse

WASHINGTON—The Department of Justice warned yesterday that the increasing use of automatic teller machines and other means of electronic financial transactions are "potentially fertile for criminal abuse."

Techniques for robbing the systems have already cropped up, and they are expected to increase. They range from the dynamiting of an ATM to a cardholder's withdrawing funds and then claiming that he had nothing to do with the transaction, the department's Bureau of Justice Statistics said in a special report.

Of the machine that was dynamited, the report said, "Unfortunately for the attackers, the money was destroyed along with the automatic teller." . . .

Even though bank officials may be skeptical of a cardholder's disclaiming any knowledge of a withdrawal that had been made from his account, federal law makes it difficult for the officials to reject such a claim. If a bogus loss is reported within two business days, the law makes the cardholder responsible for only the first $50 of losses. . . .

As automatic tellers proliferate, bankers have grown sensitive about increasing fraud experienced recently by credit card companies, which jumped almost 50 percent in the four years from the beginning of 1979 through the end of 1982, the report said.

Loss per $1000 of credit card volume climbed from $1.13 in 1979 to $1.67 in 1982, and loss per transaction nearly doubled, from 4.2 cents to 7.9 cents. The report said that it is generally believed that the mounting credit card fraud losses result from "counterfeiting techniques used by syndicated criminal enterprises working with corrupt merchants."

So far, ATM losses do not approach those suffered by the credit card companies, the bureau said.

This could be the result of the added safeguards built into ATMs, such as requirements that a personal identification number be entered before each transaction and that daily withdrawals be limited, the report said.

—*Los Angeles Times,* Ronald J. Ostrow, February 20, 1984

Output: The Results of Processing

Output is what we are all impatient to receive, of course. It is, we hope, the solution to the problems we have input to the computer. The solutions are now inside the computer in machine-readable form; the purpose of output devices is to make them people-readable.

As we mentioned, output devices represent an ever-growing list, but we shall describe only those of principal interest to people in business. The two most popular are:

- Terminals
- Printers

However, there are several others that we shall also examine:

- Plotters
- Computer output microfilm
- Audio-response devices
- Robots

Terminals

Terminals, particularly cathode ray tube (CRT) terminals, are the real windows on the computing process. To the usual clutter on an executive's desk—telephone, calendar, pen-and-pencil set, family photographs—now in many cases must be added the green or amber luminescence of the CRT terminal.

There are three principal types of terminals:

- Alphanumeric
- Graphic
- Flat panel display

Alphanumeric Terminals

Alphanumeric terminals are so called because they display alphanumeric output—that is, letters, numbers, and special characters such as $, ?, and *. These are the kinds of terminals you frequently see on secretaries' desks for word processing, on travel agents' desks for making plane and hotel reservations, and on stockbrokers' desks for reading stock prices. They look like television screens (9- or 12-inch) and some offer 80 characters per line, with 24 lines visible at one time. We showed an example of an alphanumeric terminal back in the top part of Figure 7-3.

As you are finding out at Atlantic-Pacific, banks are full of these terminals, and there are many advantages:

- They are relatively inexpensive.
- They are quite reliable.
- The format of the output on the screen can be varied widely.
- Training cost for users is small.
- Information can be transferred rapidly to the screen via telephone lines (at up to 960 characters per second) or by direct lines (at up to 55,000 characters per second).

There are a few disadvantages:

- No hard copy is available, although the addition of a printer can eliminate this problem.
- The screen size limits the amount of information that can be displayed at any one time.

Graphics Terminals

As shown in the color photographs in this book, computer output in graphics form can be spectacular, and this method of presenting information has come into its own in a major way. One might be tempted to scoff at the notion of business people spending their time drawing "pretty pictures," but the research is pretty hard-headed on this point: In one famous study, Hewlett-Packard found that whereas people could absorb words and numbers at up to 1200 words per minute they could absorb numeric information displayed in graphic form at the equivalent of up to *40 million* words per minute. This statistic makes it graphically clear, as it were, why **graphics terminals**—terminals that can display both alphanumeric and graphic data such as charts and maps—are no longer used just by scientists and engineers but have been embraced by business people as well. They simply make it easier to do business.

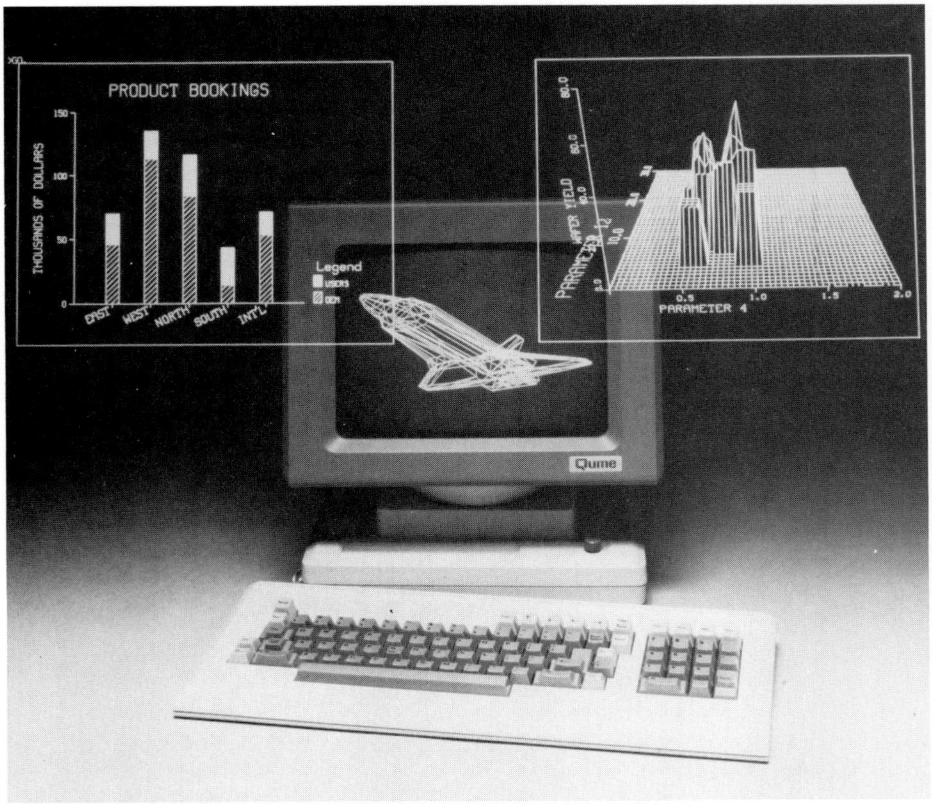
PRODUCT BOOKINGS
THOUSANDS OF DOLLARS
EAST
WEST
NORTH
SOUTH
INT'L
Legend
PARAMETER 4
Qume

Figure 7-13 Three levels of graphics. Graphics terminals have three levels of complexity in graphics. *Left*: Two-dimensional graphics such as bar graphs. *Right*: Two-dimensional angle forms. *Middle*: Three-dimensional graphics such as might be used in product design; the airplane fuselage shown here can be rotated on the screen, allowing aircraft designers to see all sides.

As Figure 7-13 shows, there are three levels of complexity in graphics produced:

- **Two-dimensional graphics,** the simplest level, consist of pie, line, and bar graphs, the kind of graphics discussed with personal computer software back in Chapter 4.
- **Two-dimensional angle forms** are the kind of graphics found in such uses as topographic maps.

- **Three-dimensional graphics** are used in product design, since they allow designers to turn the object on the screen to look at it from different perspectives.

Two particular uses of computer graphics that you are apt to come across in business go under the abbreviations of CAI and CAD/CAM. **CAI** stands for **computer-assisted instruction,** whereby the computer is used to help teach instructional materials. CAI may take the form of simulation, demonstration, tutorial, or drill and practice. Although more often found in schools, it is a method of instruction also found in company training programs. Railroads, for instance, have found it is cheaper—and certainly safer—to teach prospective locomotive engineers using simulation than to send them out on an actual diesel.

CAD/CAM stands for **computer-aided design/computer-aided manufacturing.** CAD is used by engineers, architects, and others to design products, buildings, and manufacturing processes. Two- and three-dimensional pictures can be shown on the screen, combined with other drawings, rotated, enlarged, reduced, and otherwise manipulated. CAM is used to physically manufacture products; for example, a CAD-developed program for a particular piece of clothing may be fed to a garment-cutting machine which will cut cloth to the exact fit—and will cut thousands of copies of the same thing. A new variant on CAD/CAM is **computer-assisted engineering (CAE),** in which graphics are used to assist in developing such complicated products as airplanes.

The advantages of graphics terminals are:

- They can present information in easily grasped form.
- They can present it quickly and reliably.

The disadvantages are:

- Graphics software is expensive (though decreasing in cost).
- No hard copy is available unless a printer or plotter (to be discussed later in the chapter) is added; color slides and prints of the graphics can be made with special photographic equipment.

Flat Panel Displays

Most terminals use the same technology as TV sets—a long cathode ray tube—to project images on a screen. As a result, they are quite bulky, which makes them not very portable. A recent advance, **flat panel displays** are alphanumeric or graphics terminals that use a liquid crystal display (LCD) or an electroluminescent substance that glows when electrically charged. Figure 7-14 shows an example of one of these terminals.

The advantages of flat panel displays over CRTs are considerable:

- They are more compact—hence more portable.
- They have lower power consumption.

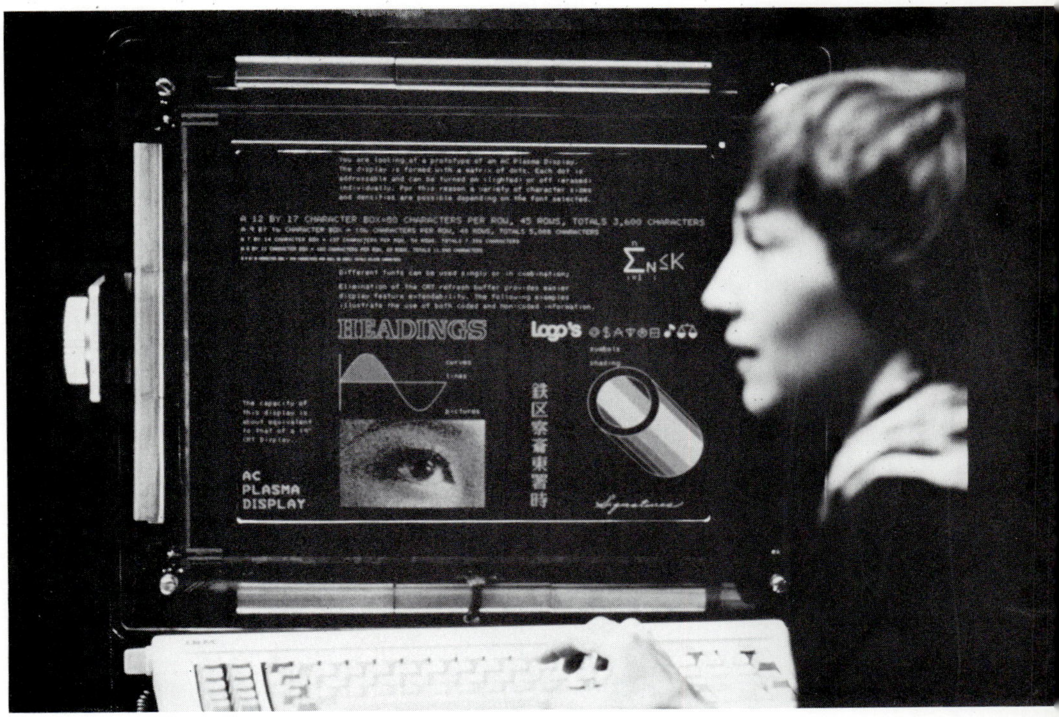
HEADINGS
logo's
AC
PLASMA
DISPLAY

Figure 7-14 **Flat panel display.** This screen allows for clearer images and is more compact and portable than the standard CRT terminal.

- They have greater daylight visibility.
- They have longer expected life.

However, they do have their disadvantages:

- They cost more than conventional terminals.
- They are somewhat fragile.
- Their reliability is uncertain at present because the technology is still in its developmental stage.

Despite their drawbacks, the outlook for flat panel displays—especially for special applications—is positive.

Printers: Putting It on Paper

Terminals and the "soft copy" they produce are fine as far as they go. But what if you want hard copy?

There are many reasons you might want paper output. In word processing, of course, paper output is *the* result you want. The need for presentation graphics is another reason for wanting printed output. And, of course, you cannot cash a paycheck that only appears on a CRT screen; to get hard currency, you need that check as hard copy. Finally, there are many legal reasons you might want a record on paper. As movie mogul Sam Goldwyn is supposed to have said, "A verbal contract isn't worth the paper it's printed on."

Hard copy is produced by printers and plotters, but here we will deal with **printers,** those machines that produce printing or graphics on paper. Printers are classified according to:

- Speed
- Print quality
- Printing method

Speed. Printers may print a *character at a time*—such printers are called **serial printers**—or a *line at a time.* Printers may be as slow as 600 characters per minute for some home-computer printers to as fast as 21,000 lines per minute for some laser printers.

Print Quality. Printers may be *draft quality* or *letter quality.* **Dot matrix printers** construct a character by using a matrix of pins (see Figure 7-15). This, you notice, follows the principle of those time-and-temperature signs you see hanging in front of some of Atlantic-Pacific's branch banks: the same matrix or grid may be used to construct a variety of characters. Although some dot matrix printers can print letter-quality images, the result of many dot matrix printers is that they produce a somewhat fuzzy appearance—acceptable for certain kinds of work, such as writing internal memos to your boss, but not for impressing customers of the bank.

Letter-quality printers produce printed characters that resemble those produced by an office typewriter. The "letter quality," in fact, means they are able to produce print that *is* of good enough quality to write letters, for instance, to bank customers. Letter-quality printers are generally more expensive than dot matrix printers.

Printing Method. Printers can be either *impact printers* or *nonimpact printers.* An **impact printer** forms characters by physically striking a type device—a hammer—against inked ribbon to form characters on paper; in other words, it is like a typewriter. **Nonimpact printers** form characters by using heat, lasers, photography, or ink spray, often on a special kind of electrostatic or sensitized paper. Because there is no physical

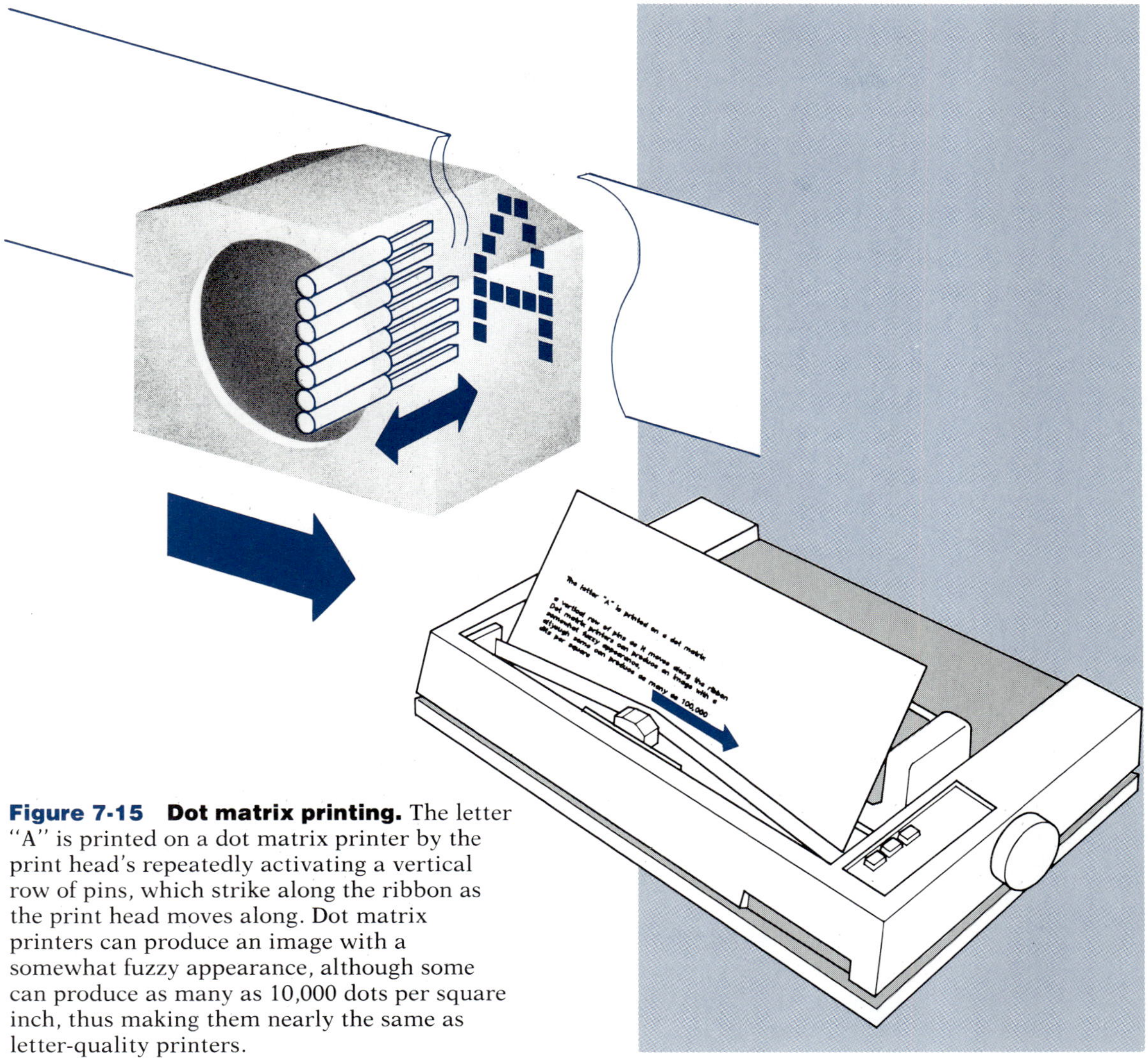

Figure 7-15 Dot matrix printing. The letter "A" is printed on a dot matrix printer by the print head's repeatedly activating a vertical row of pins, which strike along the ribbon as the print head moves along. Dot matrix printers can produce an image with a somewhat fuzzy appearance, although some can produce as many as 10,000 dots per square inch, thus making them nearly the same as letter-quality printers.

contact between printer and paper, nonimpact printers are quieter than impact printers.

The types of impact and nonimpact printers are described below.

Impact Printers

There are five basic designs for impact printers—chain, band, drum, matrix, and daisy wheel. The differences between these designs is the manner in which the characters are transferred from the type elements to the paper.

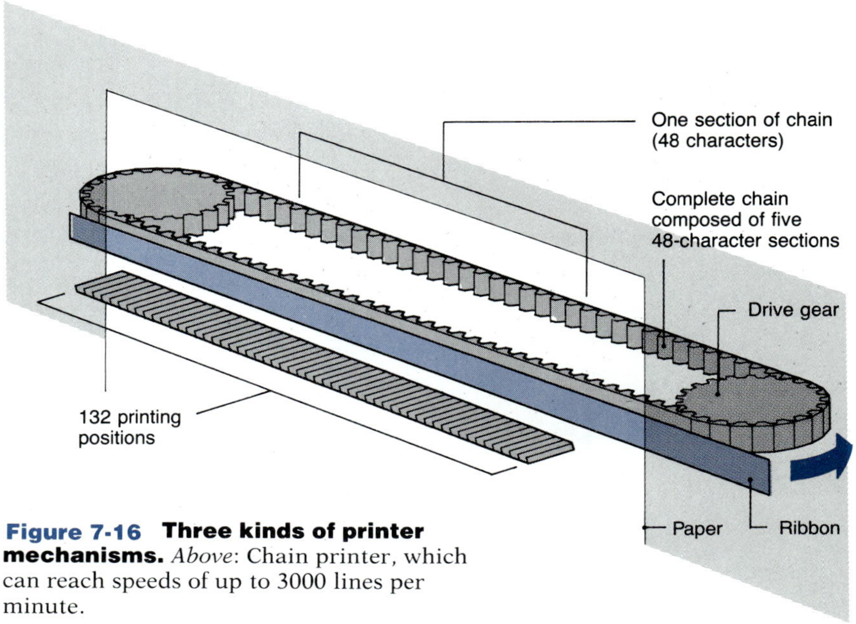
One section of chain (48 characters)
Complete chain composed of five 48-character sections
Drive gear
132 printing positions
Paper
Ribbon

Figure 7-16 Three kinds of printer mechanisms. *Above*: Chain printer, which can reach speeds of up to 3000 lines per minute.

Chain. A **chain printer** consists of several sets of characters connected together on a printing chain which, like a bicycle chain (see Figure 7-16), revolves in front of the paper. Hammers are aligned with each position, and when the appropriate character passes by, each hammer strikes the paper and ribbon against it. An advantage of chain printers is that the chains can be changed for different type fonts or styles.

Band. A **band printer** (Figure 7-16) operates somewhat like a chain printer. Also called a *belt printer*, a band printer uses a horizontally rotating band. The characters on the band are struck by hammers through the paper and ribbon. Band printers too have a variety of type fonts available.

Drum. The **drum printer** is a line printer in which embossed characters are wrapped around a cylinder or drum, as shown in Figure 7-16. Each band around the drum consists of one each of the 64 different characters the printer is able to print. The number of bands on the drum equals the number of characters the printer is able to print on one line. For example, a drum with 132 bands will be used with a 132-character printer. One entire revolution of the drum is required to print each line. Print hammers opposite each print band strike the paper against the proper character as it goes by.

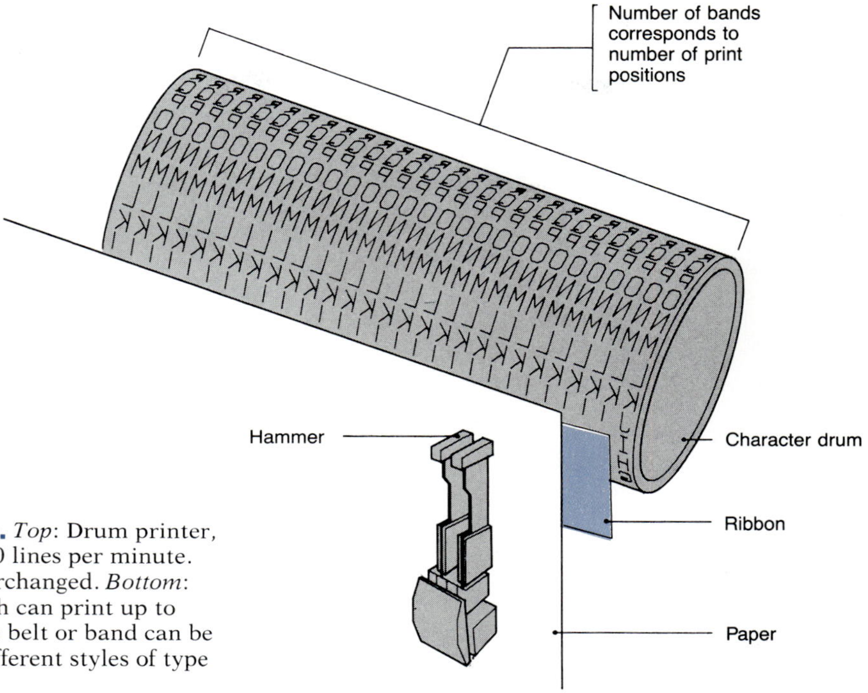
Number of bands corresponds to number of print positions
Hammer
Character drum
Ribbon
Paper

Figure 7-16 (continued). *Top*: Drum printer, which can print up to 3000 lines per minute. Type styles cannot be interchanged. *Bottom*: Belt or band printer, which can print up to 2000 lines per minute. The belt or band can be changed easily to make different styles of type available.

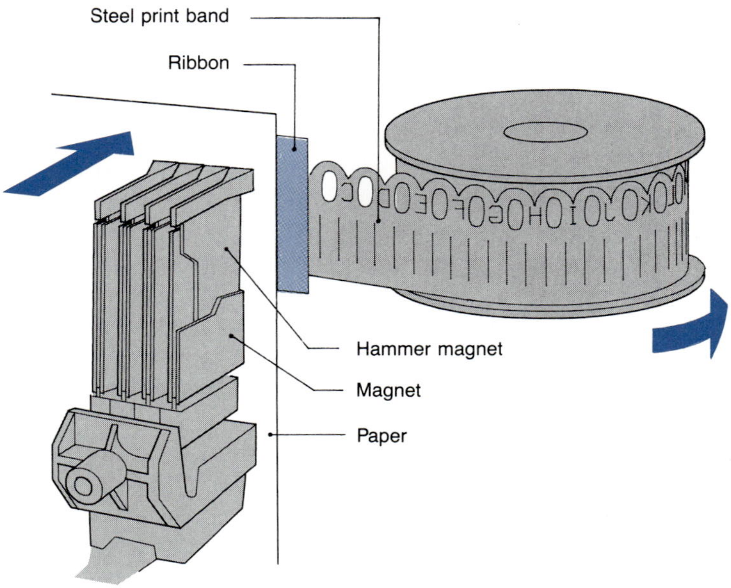
Steel print band
Ribbon
Hammer magnet
Magnet
Paper

Matrix. As mentioned, in the **matrix printer** or the dot matrix printer, the characters are formed by arranging dots closely together. Typically, such printers are character-at-a-time devices. Often, matrix printers are **bi-directional**; that is, the print head first moves to the right, printing out a line, then moves to the left, printing out the next line. It is not like a typewriter, which prints every line starting at the left. The great advantage of dot matrix printers is that they can print any shape instructed by the software—not just letters and numbers.

Daisy Wheel. In the **daisy-wheel printer,** the print mechanism consists of a removable wheel with a set of spokes, each containing a raised character (see Figure 7-17). The wheel rotates to align the correct character, which is then struck with a hammer. Although noisier and slower than dot matrix, daisy-wheel printers are used for professional correspondence because they produce letter-quality type.

Variations of the daisy-wheel printer are the *ball printer,* which has the characters on a ball that rotates to the appropriate letter, and the *thimble printer,* which has a pivoting head to locate the appropriate letter.

Nonimpact Printers

As mentioned, nonimpact printers do not strike the paper to form characters. They are therefore much quieter than impact printers and, because of fewer moving parts, generally more reliable. We will examine six types of nonimpact printers—electrostatic, magnetic, ink-jet, xerographic, laser, and thermal, some of which are shown in Figure 7-18.

Electrostatic. The **electrostatic printer** operates by depositing invisible charges on the paper's surface in the shape of characters. The paper is then passed through a toner containing ink particles of the opposite charge. The ink adheres to the paper only at the charged locations. Electrostatic printers are very reliable because of their few moving parts; however, toner and special electrostatic paper are an extra cost.

Magnetic. The **magnetic printer** is like the electrostatic printer in that characters are formed by electric charges. However, the charges are not deposited directly onto the paper; they go to a moving belt that passes through the toner, picks up the ink, and then transfers the ink to the paper. The advantage of this process is that special paper is not required; however, magnetic printing is slower than electrostatic printing because of the extra processing step.

Ink Jet. An **ink-jet printer** actually sprays small droplets of ink onto the surface of the paper at a very rapid rate. The print is letter quality, and a wide variety of colors is available. The printer has begun to gain in popularity because it is able to duplicate color directly from the CRT for color graphics.

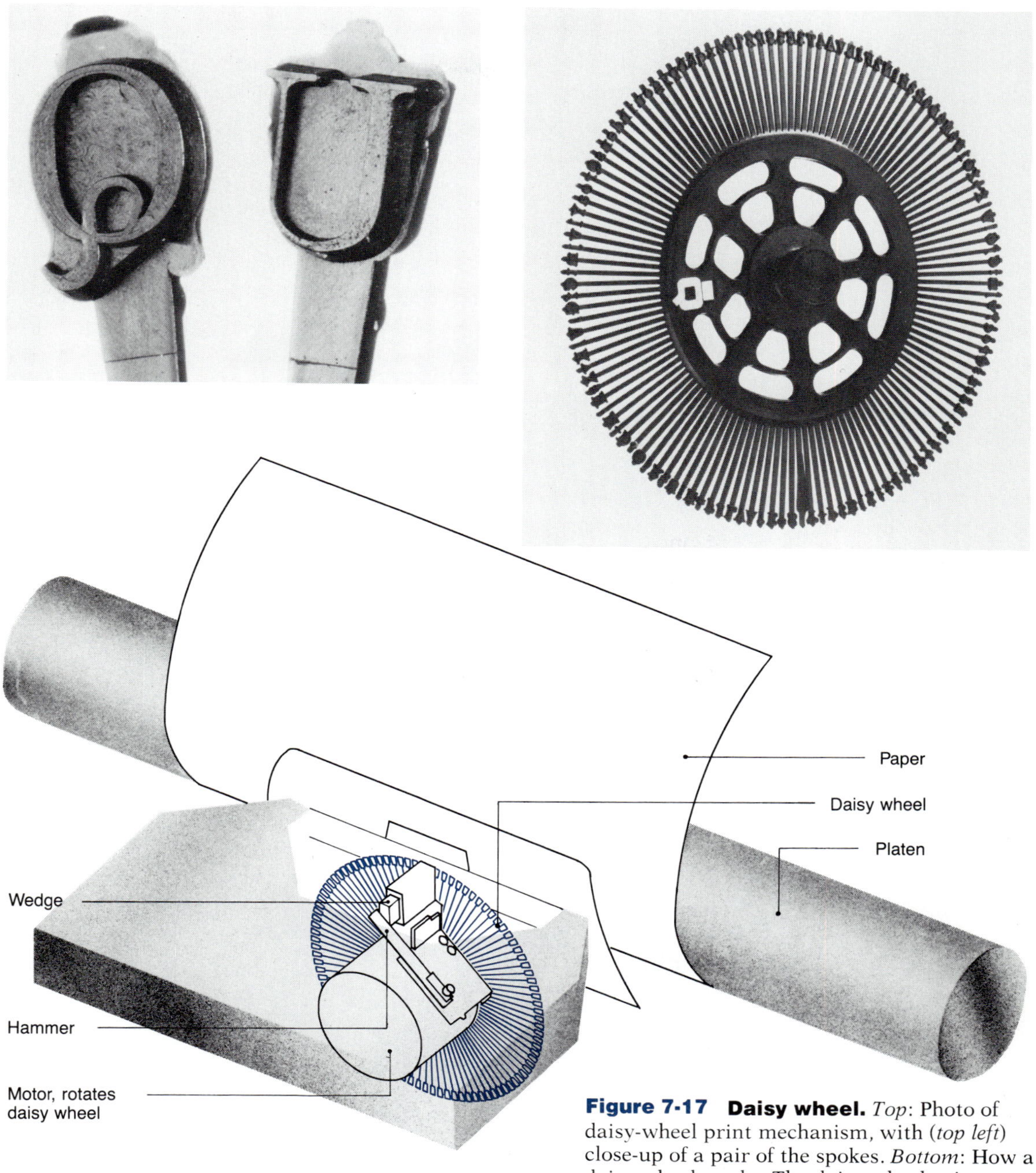
Paper
Daisy wheel
Platen
Wedge
Hammer
Motor, rotates daisy wheel

Figure 7-17 **Daisy wheel.** *Top*: Photo of daisy-wheel print mechanism, with (*top left*) close-up of a pair of the spokes. *Bottom*: How a daisy wheel works. The daisy wheel spins to bring the desired spoke into position. A hammer then hits the wedge, which strikes the spoke against the ribbon.

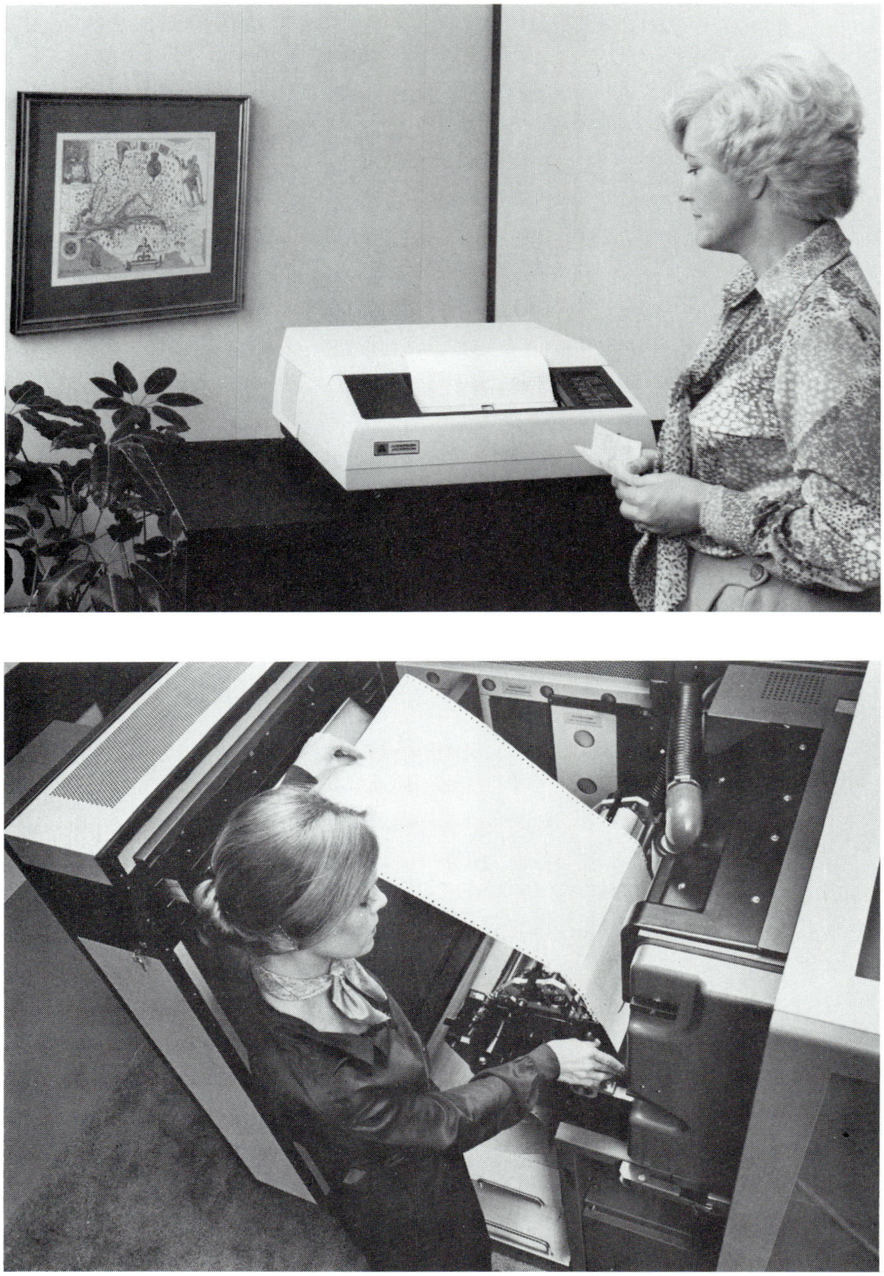

Figure 7-18 Nonimpact printers. *Top*: Ink-jet printer produced by Anderson-Jacobson. *Bottom*: Sperry laser printer.

Xerographic. Developed by Xerox Corporation, the **xerographic printer** combines computer and Xerox office copier technology. Characters are formed on a drum as in a Xerox photocopying machine, the drum is treated with a toner, and characters are then transferred to paper. The printer can be operated not only directly from a computer but also off-line from magnetic tape or disk storage. Although very fast and producing very high quality print, the printer is quite expensive.

Laser. The **laser electrographic printer** creates characters on a drum, utilizing a laser beam light source. The characters are then treated with a toner and transferred to paper. Laser printers produce very high quality images but are very expensive.

Thermal. The **thermal printer** creates characters by converting electrical impulses to heat energy, which is then transferred to special heat-sensitive paper using a dot matrix print head. Thermal printers are inexpensive and reliable; though they require no ribbon, they do require special paper.

Plotters: Drawing Machines

Plotters are special-purpose output devices used to reproduce hard-copy drawings—bar charts, engineering drawings, maps, even three-dimensional illustrations. There are two types of plotters—flatbed and drum, as shown in Figure 7-19.

The **flatbed plotter,** also called a **table plotter,** is one in which paper is held stable and a pen or pens of different colors, controlled by a computer program, move about on the surface. Some flatbed plotters are quite large.

In the **drum plotter,** the pen or pens are held stationary and the paper is rolled on a drum.

The primary advantage of these devices is their ability to produce consistently accurate drawings very quickly—at least compared to human-artist counterparts. (Actually, they operate quite slowly, at least when they are attached to microcomputers.) Their disadvantages are the limited availability of software and the development costs associated with creating appropriate software, although this is changing.

Computer Output Microfilm

Banking is an industry that depends on records, but imagine all the records being on paper. How many warehouses would be required to

Getty

Figure 7-19 **Plotters.** *Left*: Flatbed plotter. *Middle and right*: Two types of drum plotters. Plotters are also available in desk-top models. Note (*middle*) four pens of different colors which inscribe image on paper.

store all the loan applications and check records? Paper may be the easiest form for people to use, but it takes a lot of space. What produces output that costs less than paper, can store the equivalent of a 210-page report on a 4-by-6-inch sheet, and is 20 times faster than a high-speed printer? The answer is computer output microfilm, as shown in Figure 7-20, p. 248.

A **computer output microfilm** or **COM** system consists of a computer to produce original documents or images and a recording machine to prepare the microfilm, miniature photographic images. If the microfilm is produced directly from the computer, it is called "on-line," if produced from magnetic tape, it is called "off-line."

Microfilm may be produced on a roll of film (16, 35, or 105 millimeter) or on a 4-by-6-inch sheet called **microfiche,** often called "fish." To read microfilm requires a microfilm reader, such as the kinds you see in libraries. Banks use COM to record checks that have been depos-

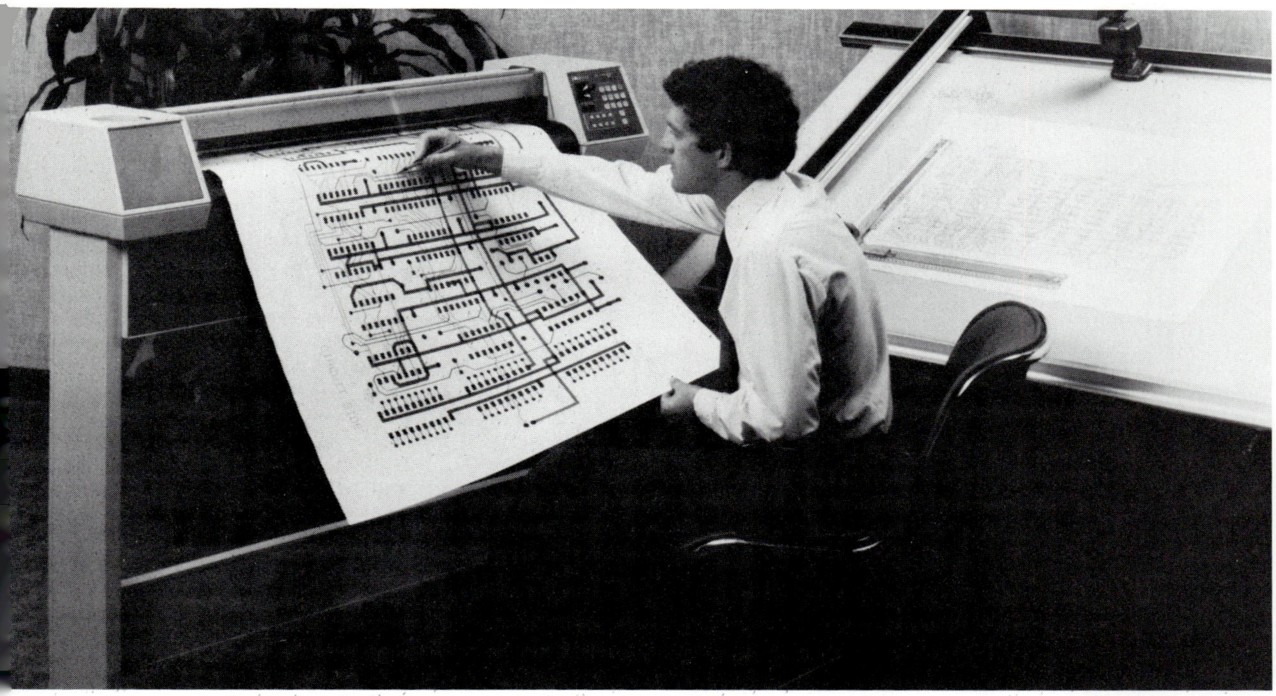

ited, since the original checks are usually returned to the payers (although many banks are trying to get out of the business of returning cancelled checks).

Although there are the many advantages of storage capability, fast retrieval, and ability to store graphics and figures, microfilm has disadvantages in that it requires special equipment for viewing and for producing hard-copy documents. It also cannot be updated on the same sheet or roll. Nonetheless, it has been found to be economical in situations requiring a very high volume of documents to be reproduced or a large number of documents to be stored and maintained.

Audio-Response Devices

Audio-response or **voice-output devices** make sounds that seem like human voices but actually are prerecorded vocalized sounds. Voice output is not nearly as difficult to engineer as voice input, and indeed by now you

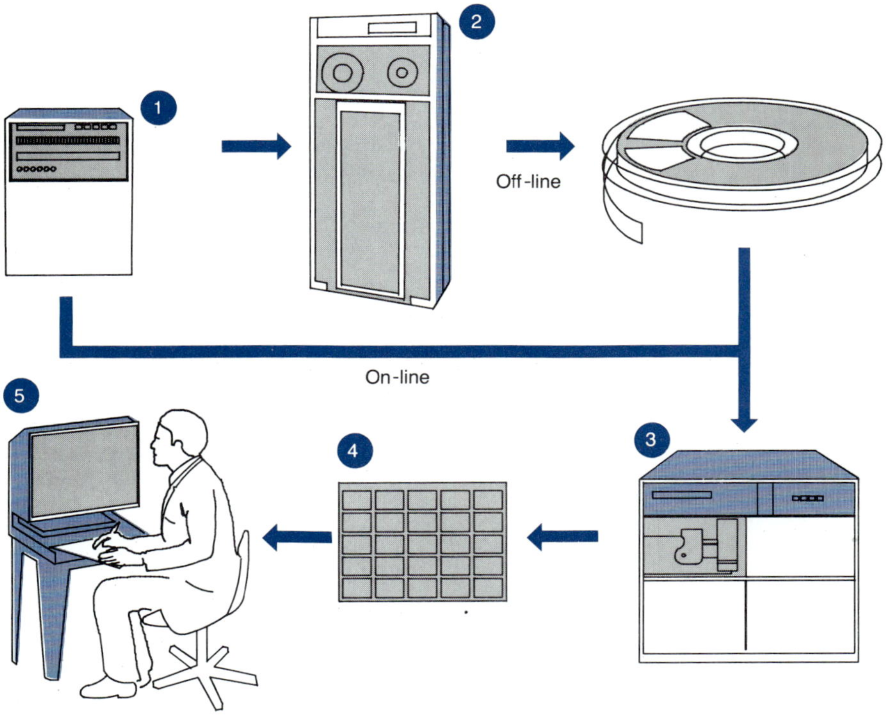
1
2
Off-line
On-line
5
4
3

Figure 7-20 **Computer output microfilm.** This illustration shows COM off-line and on-line. In the *off-line* version, the data comes directly off ❶ the computer and onto ❷ magnetic tape on a tape drive. The data on the tape is then run through ❸ a microfilm recorder. In the *on-line* version, the data goes directly from ❶ to ❸. The microfilm recorder converts the data to images stored on microfiche. After the microfiche is ❹ developed, it may be viewed on ❺ a microfilm viewer or CRT.

may be aware of several situations in which such "voices" are used—in cars, in airports, for some of those voices that sound like telephone operators when you misdial and are asked "to hang up and dial your call again."

Robots: Computer Automation in the Factory

Want a robot built to order? A Colorado company will make you one in the shape of a milk carton that can talk and move. Or, if you prefer, you may have a furry robot that can ride a tricycle.

Are these the kinds of robots that are going to be important in the future? Actually, these are purely for entertainment and are only one variety. **Robotics**—the study of the design, construction, and use of robots—is a serious engineering field, one that becomes more important as wages go up and the cost of technology goes down.

Unlike standard assembly-line machines, which are designed to perform one function, **robots** have two qualities that make them flexible. They are *multifunctional,* which means they are able to do more than one task, and they are *reprogrammable,* which means they can be reprogrammed to carry out many kinds of tasks. These two characteristics mean that, unlike traditional kinds of machinery, robots are not as apt to become obsolete.

There are four areas of robotics (see Figure 7-21), as explained below.

- **Large industrial robots:** These are computer-controlled tools used on factory assembly lines to perform skills previously performed by human beings, such as welding or paint spraying. Although automatic machinery has been in use for years on production lines, industrial robots are far more versatile. Most robots operate by electronic impulses through a claw, but others use hydraulic pressure for heavy work.
- **Small industrial robots:** These highly reprogrammable systems generally handle objects up to 20 pounds. These include machine vision systems—robots that "see" with television-camera vision systems—which can be used for parts inspection, product identification, and robot guidance. Other robot systems operate by touch, measuring sizes and shapes, temperature, hardness, and so on.
- **Mobile robots:** These are the kind that people think of when they hear the word "robot"—namely, peoplelike machines that can roll around and talk. Some can also serve drinks at cocktail parties and do vacuuming (up to a point), and there is a great deal of discussion about building robots for household tasks. Some have called these machines "showbots"; they are not true robots since they are not multifunctional and reprogrammable. At present, home robots are probably at about the state where home computers were five years ago. These robots have some use in offices as mailmobiles.
- **Artificial intelligence or expert systems:** This is the most promising and awesome area of all. **Artificial intelligence (AI)** is the field of study concerned with exploring tasks for computers to do that previously were reserved for human intelligence, imagination, and intuition. A 1983 report by the National Research Council predicted that AI "would affect the circumstances of human life profoundly." It went on: "It would surely create a new economics, a new sociology and a new history. If artificial intelligences can be created at all, there is little reason to believe that they could not lead swiftly to

20
18
16

the construction of superintelligences able to explore significant mathematical, scientific or engineering alternatives at a rate far exceeding human ability."[4] Already, artificial intelligence has created what are known as **expert systems,** computer programs that essentially copy the knowledge—both textbook knowledge and tricks of the trade—of human experts in a particular field. There are expert diagnostic systems in medicine and a computer system called Prospector that aids geologists in mineral exploration. We will come back to this aspect of robotics in more detail in the final chapter of this book.

The Thinking that Goes Into It

In between input and output is a great deal of "thinking"—the calculations that the computer must make to turn problems into solutions, data into information. In the next chapter, we will show in detail how this is done.

Figure 7-21 Three areas of robotics. *Far left*: Industrial robots line the automotive assembly line at a Chrysler plant in Detroit; these robots perform welding operations. *Near left*: A machine vision system. General Motors engineers have developed computer vision systems that allow robots to locate parts that are overlapping or partly obscured. A television camera mounted in the apparatus at the rear views the moving conveyor belt below it, and the computer forms a digitized picture of the part (*inset*). The computer goes through a series of recognition techniques and, when it makes a match with a similar part already in its program, it advises the robot arm where the part will be on the belt so that it may pick it up. *Below*: A mobile robot used to deliver interoffice mail. The device moves slowly along a preprogrammed course; office workers leave their desks to exchange mail.

SUMMARY

- Although hardware may change radically, the concepts it embodies may not, and the old hardware may not rapidly be replaced with the new; therefore, managers must be prepared to work with both old equipment and new technology.
- **GIGO** is an acronym for "Garbage In, Garbage Out," which means that the quality of information that comes out of a computer is no better than the quality of the data put in.
- *Data* is the raw material (letters, numbers, symbols, shapes, colors, sounds, etc.) that must be converted into *machine-readable* form for the computer to process into information.
- Input devices convert data into machine-readable information.
- Output devices convert the information to a form people can use. These devices are almost limitless in form, because a computer can operate any machine (output device) that can run on electricity.
- No one computer system has all the possible different types of input and output devices.
- The two basic methods of handling data (input) are (1) **batch processing,** in which data is collected on source documents and then accumulated and input all at one time (as a batch), and (2) **transaction processing,** in which data is input as it is created (as transactions happen).
- Transaction processing is also called **real-time processing,** because a transaction is processed so fast that the results can be used immediately, and **on-line processing,** because the user's terminal is directly connected to ("on line" with) the computer.
- Some input equipment works only for batch processing, some only for transaction processing, and some for both.
- Input devices receive data either by keyboard entry or by direct entry.
- In **keyboard entry,** data is input to the computer *after* the transaction that produced the data has taken place; someone copies, using the keyboard, the data from its source document. In **direct entry,** data is made into machine-processable form at the time the transaction is made. Because people do the keying, errors may occur during keyboard entry; thus the trend is toward more use of direct-entry input devices.
- Keyboard entry records data on two kinds of *media,* or materials: (1) paper media, such as punched cards, and (2) magnetic media, such as cassette, diskette, tape, or hard disk. Except for paper media, the computer terminal is the most commonly used keyboard entry device.

- **Punched cards**—the first form of input used for computers—are stiff paper cards punched with holes that represent data. The holes are punched using a **keypunch machine.** A **card reader** translates the card holes into electrical impulses, which are then input to the computer.
- The use of punched cards involves several difficulties: (1) They take up a lot of space. (2) If the keypuncher makes a mistake, the card must be thrown away. (3) The cards are heavy. (4) They are relatively slow to process. (5) Errors can be introduced at any of the many intermediate steps involved in processing punched cards. (6) The process is expensive. In general, the use of cards is being phased out.
- Data on **magnetic media** is represented by magnetized spots. The three popular devices used for magnetic keyboard entry are (1) **key-to-diskette,** by which one keys in data through the keyboard onto a floppy disk or diskette, (2) **key-to-tape,** and (3) **key-to-disk.** The key-to-tape device is similar to key-to-disk but uses recording tape—cassette, cartridge, or reel—to receive the data input, whereas the key-to-disk device uses a magnetic recording disk.
- Magnetic media have several advantages over punched cards: (1) They can be reused. (2) They are easier to correct. (3) The input devices are quieter. (4) The devices are also more reliable (they are electronic rather than mechanical, so there are fewer moving parts to break down). (5) They take less storage space. (6) The data can be accessed faster by the computer.
- The computer terminal is the most popular keyboard entry device. It can be a **cathode ray tube (CRT) terminal** or a **hard-copy terminal;** it can also be a **dumb,** a **smart,** or an **intelligent terminal.**
- **Hard copy** is paper output (computer printout); **soft copy** is output on a computer screen.
- A **cathode ray tube (CRT)** terminal is a terminal with a keyboard and a CRT, or televisionlike, screen; it is also called a soft-copy terminal. As an input device, the CRT has several advantages: (1) It is compact and inexpensive. (2) It allows erroneous data to be corrected easily. (3) It allows files to be updated on the spot and allows access to these files. Its disadvantages include: (1) It makes no permanent record of transactions. (2) The screen is difficult for some people to read.
- A **hard-copy terminal,** or **teleprinter,** is a keyboard with a printer attached. The hard-copy terminal has the advantage of producing a permanent record; however, it also has two disadvantages: (1) The printing process makes it slower than the CRT terminal. (2) It can be noisy.
- Both the CRT terminal and the hard-copy terminal are **dumb terminals**; they cannot do any processing of their own but must be connected to a computer. Dumb terminals provide only a keyboard for data entry and a CRT screen and/or printer for information output.

- **Smart terminals,** or **interactive terminals,** can be simple input or output devices to a computer located elsewhere, but they also have a microprocessor and primary storage that allows some processing before the data is sent to the computer. However, programming cannot be done with a smart terminal.
- **Intelligent terminals** include a microcomputer that allows users to do programming as well as to input and to receive data from a larger computer. An intelligent terminal includes at least a keyboard, electronics to convert data to machine-readable code, communications equipment, an output device, a processing unit, internal storage for data processing, software consisting of a programming language and editing programs, and secondary storage.
- The most popular direct-entry devices are (1) magnetic-ink character recognition, (2) optical-character recognition, (3) optical-mark recognition, (4) digitizers, (5) point-of-sale terminals, (6) touch-tone devices, (7) light pens, (8) mice, and (9) speech recognition devices.
- **Magnetic-ink character recognition (MICR)** is a method of machine-reading characters made of ink containing magnetized particles. It was developed in the 1950s by the banking industry to make check processing easier. MICR has several advantages: (1) The codes can be read by both machines and people. (2) It is fast, accurate, and automatic. (3) Human involvement—and thus human error—is minimized. Its disadvantages are (1) that it is limited to only 14 characters and (2) that some manual keying is still required (for example, when the MICR characters are inscribed on a check).
- **Optical-character recognition (OCR)** was developed by the U.S. Postal Service to assist in mail sorting. It consists of special characters (letters, numbers, and symbols) which can be read by a light source that converts them into electrical signals that can be sent to the computer for processing. The special characters are preprinted, thus someone must initially key the characters; however, they are not keyed again for data entry into the computer. The most common OCR input device is the hand-held **wand reader,** which reflects light on the printed characters, whose reflection is converted by photoelectric cells to machine-readable code. OCR has several advantages: (1) It has all the benefits of MICR plus a larger set of characters (42). (2) Using a wand reader does not require any manual keying of data. (3) Data is electronically transferred from source document to computer. Its main disadvantage is that OCR wand readers can recognize only a special set of characters.
- **Optical-mark recognition (OMR),** also known as *mark-sensing,* senses the presence or the absence of a mark, such as those made by a pencil on a special preprinted examination form. The advantages of OMR are (1) that it requires no manual keying of data and (2) that it is inexpensive. Its disadvantages are (1) that strict format specifications (for example, special forms and pencils) must be used and (2) that it has limited business applications.

Summary continues on p. 255

→ Emergency

Corporate Report 3

The Health Care Industry: Inside Look at a Modern Hospital

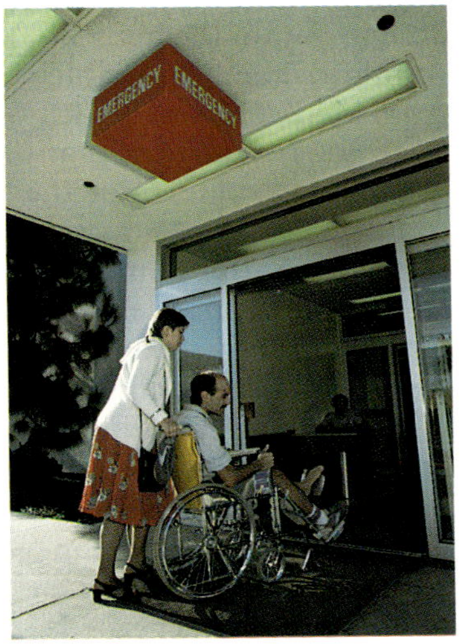
EMERGENCY
EMERGENCY

Not long ago hospitals did not know how much it cost to treat a patient. The emphasis was strictly on quality of medical care. Then in 1983 the federal government began to hold down costs on Medicare—medical payments for the elderly, which account for over a third of hospitals' incomes. Now health-care institutions are being paid only a fixed amount for each specific illness, and no more. Thus, today's hospital administrator must operate as people in other businesses have for years: managing for cost-effectiveness. This is where the Information Age has come to hospitals. Computers are used not only to track the course of each patient and each disease, but also the health-care treatments and procedures of each doctor, since physicians' decisions determine most hospital costs.

In addition, computers are used in medical treatment, as this Corporate Report demonstrates. The setting is El Camino Hospital, a progressive health-care institution in Mountain View, California. The hypothetical patient, his knee damaged in a sports injury, is being wheeled through the emergency entrance by his wife.

End of the Story

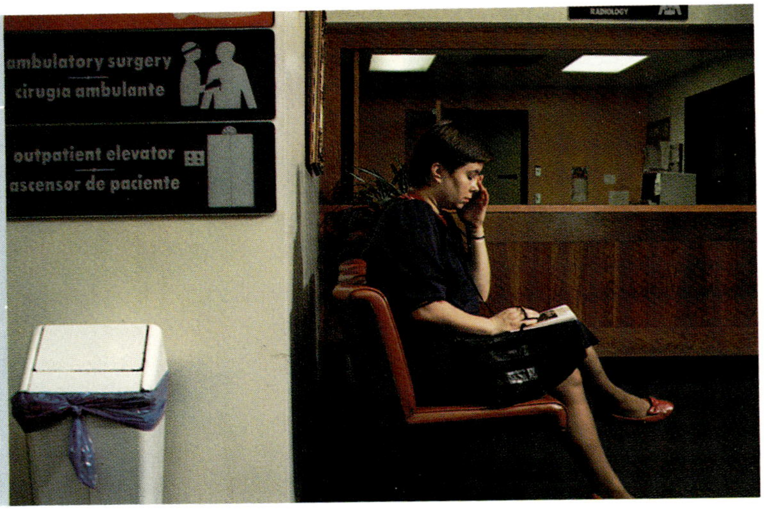
ambulatory surgery
cirugia ambulante
outpatient elevator
ascensor de paciente

Throughout the patient's knee surgery, his wife has been waiting for the good news that finally comes: word from the doctor that the operation was successful and that her husband will be discharged soon. In time, he is wheeled out of the hospital—from beginning to end his stay and his recovery managed by the tools of the computer age.

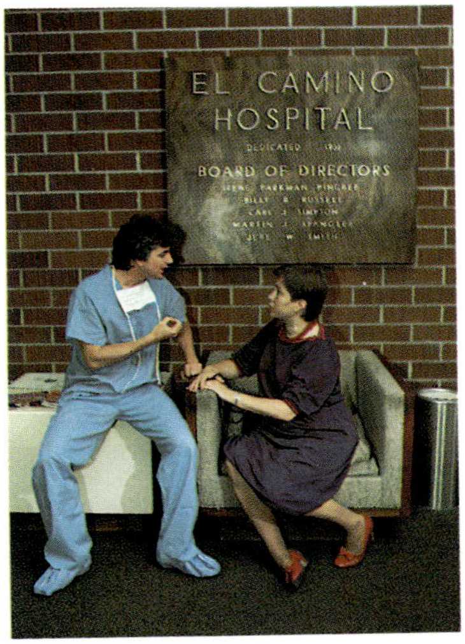
EL CAMINO
HOSPITAL
BOARD OF DIRECTORS

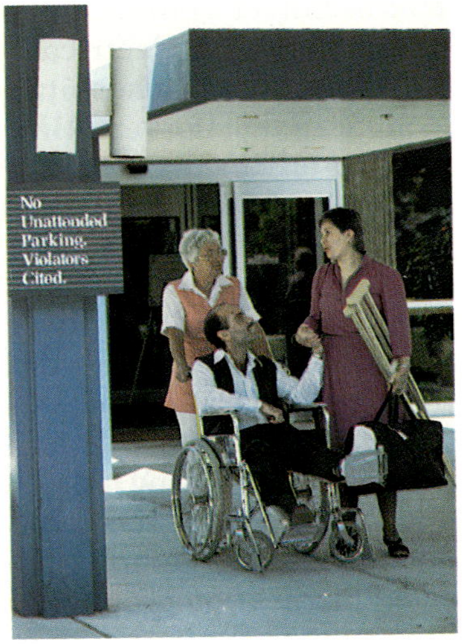
No
Unattended
Parking.
Violators
Cited.

→ Emergency

Corporate Report 3

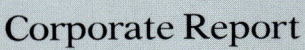

The Health Care Industry: Inside Look at a Modern Hospital

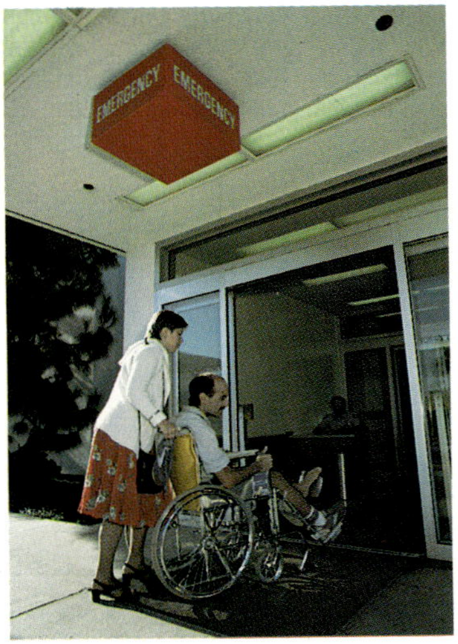
EMERGENCY EMERGENCY

Not long ago hospitals did not know how much it cost to treat a patient. The emphasis was strictly on quality of medical care. Then in 1983 the federal government began to hold down costs on Medicare—medical payments for the elderly, which account for over a third of hospitals' incomes. Now health-care institutions are being paid only a fixed amount for each specific illness, and no more. Thus, today's hospital administrator must operate as people in other businesses have for years: managing for cost-effectiveness. This is where the Information Age has come to hospitals. Computers are used not only to track the course of each patient and each disease, but also the health-care treatments and procedures of each doctor, since physicians' decisions determine most hospital costs.

In addition, computers are used in medical treatment, as this Corporate Report demonstrates. The setting is El Camino Hospital, a progressive health-care institution in Mountain View, California. The hypothetical patient, his knee damaged in a sports injury, is being wheeled through the emergency entrance by his wife.

Admissions and Record-keeping

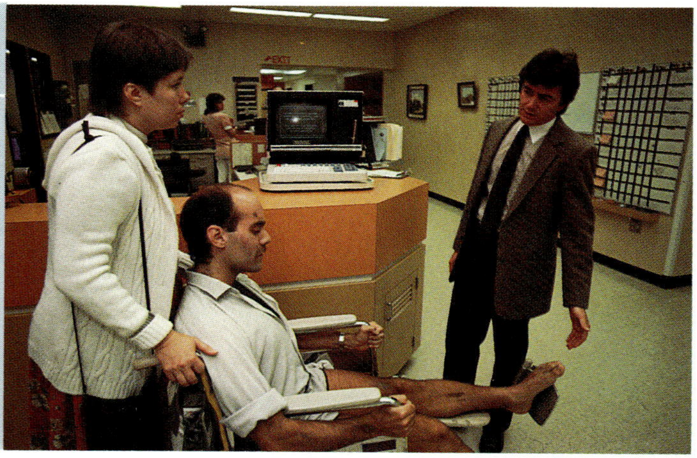

After being met in the emergency room by the patient's physician, the pair go to the admitting desk, where the clerk creates a new file on the patient, using a keyboard and light pen on a CRT screen for data entry. The file will include not only the patient's complaint but also financial and medical insurance data about him. Hospitals have used computers for years for maintaining patient information, insurance records, and hospital inventories.

Under new ways of handling information, hospitals are changing their medical records systems so that in some cases they are even combining them with accounting departments, in order to make sure they are able to obtain the highest reimbursements possible from Medicare and health insurers. In addition, many are trying to determine the patterns of illnesses as soon as possible after admissions so that they can ascertain what kinds of tests and procedures to order and the optimal length of patient stay, with the aim of delivering quality care without the hospital's incurring financial losses. Obviously, then, the job of medical records administrator—who directs systems for storing and retrieving patient records, keeps medical statistics for government agencies, and assists the medical staff in evaluating patient care—is an important one.

Hardware Behind the Scenes

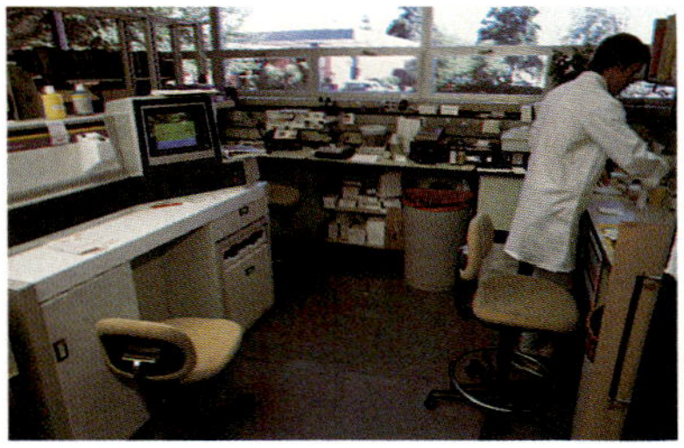

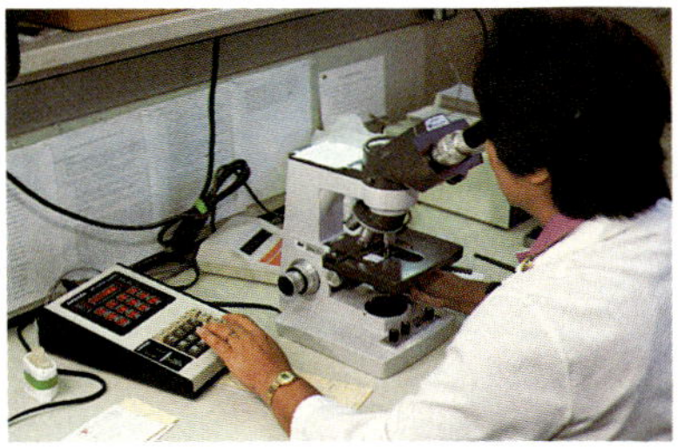

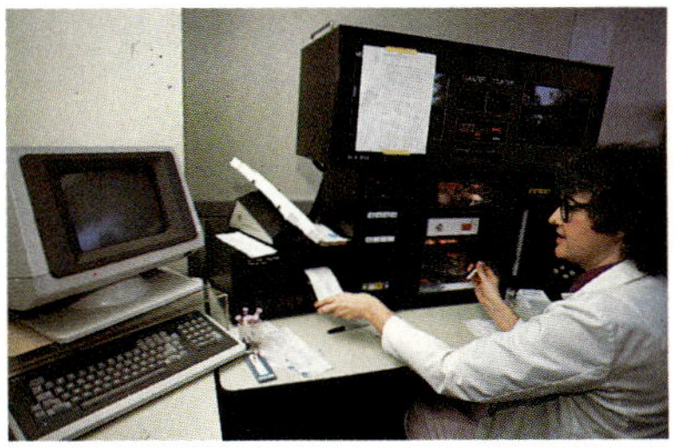

While the patient is being moved to a hospital bed, the doctor confers with the nurse near the computer at the nursing station. Computers help nurses by allowing them more easily to perform the clerical work that used to keep them away from patients. Test results, doctors' orders for laboratory work, diet, and medication, and other nursing instructions are entered into the computer, making this information more accessible than when orders were hand-carried throughout the hospital.

There are many areas in a hospital that a patient never sees. A blood test ordered by the physician is drawn and sent to the laboratory. At El Camino Hospital, computers are used extensively in the lab for analysis of blood and other specimens.

Computers for Cross-Checking

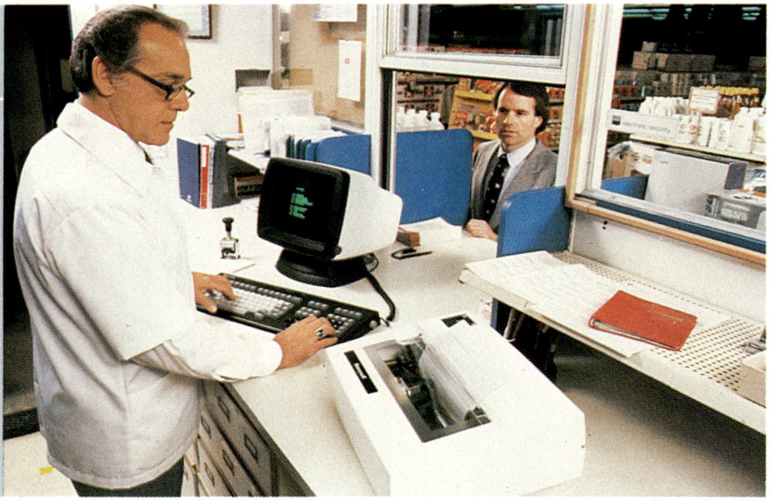

Many hospitals also use the computer to keep an inventory on medications and other supplies, using light pens and bar-code scanners, as shown here. Pharmacists are making especially interesting uses of computers and information management. When a computer indicates a potential danger from a drug or drug combination for a particular patient, it will alert the hospital staff so that the physician may adjust the medication order. This means that before a drug is administered to the patient, the computer can test for proper dosage, effects when mixed with other drugs, allergic reactions, and influence of drugs on lab tests.

Our patient has now had the benefit of several diagnostic tools, including X-rays and other tests of the damaged leg. The physican, after consulting with other specialists, is ready to specify treatment. The recommendation is for surgery on the knee.

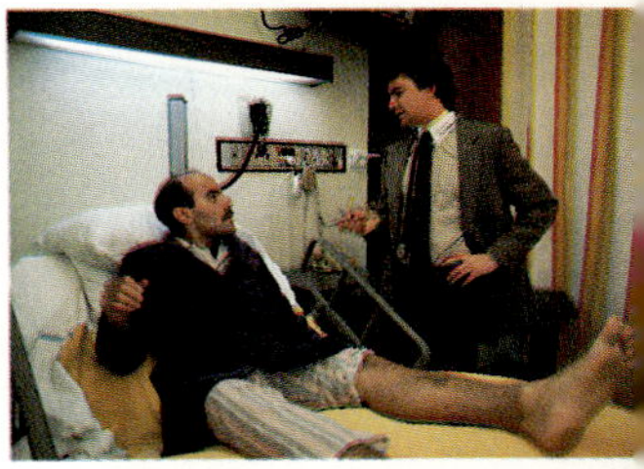

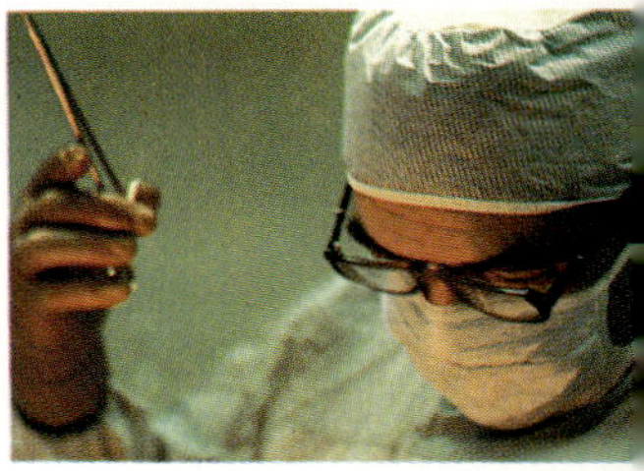

Health Care Administration: Big Growth Area

- 7000 hospitals
- 10,000 clinics
- 13,000 clinical laboratories
- 22,000 nursing homes
- 60,000 pharmacies
- 100 national or international health product corporations and 5000 smaller companies

With these numbers, as reported by Ellen Barlow in *Business Week's Guide to Careers* (Spring/Summer 1984), no wonder that health care is a $390 billion industry, surpassed only by agriculture and construction in number of employees. Among the changing trends, one of them is that more hospitals are for-profit organizations than in the past and there is increased competition for patient dollars. Thus, the field is filled with more opportunities for people other than physicians, especially professional health care administrators. Job openings for such administrators will increase 57% over the next decade, according to the U.S. Department of Labor.

The well-equipped administrator will have an advanced degree in business administration or health and will have studied financial analysis and management theory. Particularly critical is a knowledge of management information systems and information processing, since hospitals use computers not only to aid in medical diagnosis and treatment but also to track patients from admission until discharge and for billing, payroll, facility scheduling, and other matters. Health care administrators direct all the supporting activities of a hospital, from personnel and equipment to fund raising and community education programs.

Well-paying jobs are also available with health insurers, nursing homes and home health care providers for the elderly, manufacturers of health-related products, and pharmaceutical companies.

Today's High-Tech Medicine

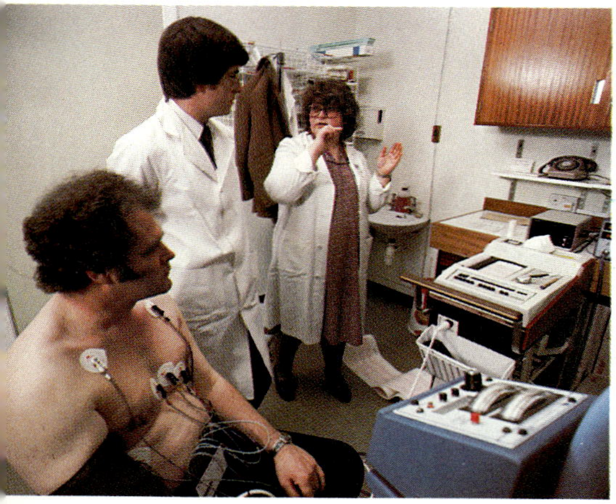

Computers are involved in a great many aspects of medicine besides those shown so far. Although not all of these may be available at El Camino Hospital, the following examples show some of the health-related benefits offered by today's high-tech medicine.

Top row: If our patient's knee had been so badly injured as to require surgical implantation of a prosthesis—an artificial knee—that item would itself have been generated by computer, using computer-aided design *(left)*. The highly polished prostheses for hip implants *(right)* are made in this manner.

Middle row: Heart patients are assisted with computerized stress tests and by monitoring devices for coronary care units.

Top row, next page: For cancer patients, doctors use medical imaging systems to locate brain tumors. The CAT scan (CAT stands for computerized axial tomography) has revolutionized radiology, producing a slice or cross-sectional image of the body. The CAT rotates about the subject "taking pictures" from every angle. Computers analyze and refine the data from the image-making machine. The picture produced at right shows the human brain.

Middle and lower right: Computers are also used in patient education and preventive medicine, as shown in these two pictures: one shows a patient taking a self-paced test on heart-attack risk factors, the other gives instruction in CPR, using a mannequin.

Lower left: Even the hospital itself can be designed with the aid of computers, using engineering graphics. This architect's building design shows the electrical outlets for part of a hospital.

Some of the most exciting medical advances using computers are difficult to illustrate. In time, computers may be used to help doctors make diagnoses and manage treatment. Already there are programs such as CADUCEUS, which offers internists consulting help, and ONCOCIN, which helps doctors manage complicated medication programs for cancer patients.

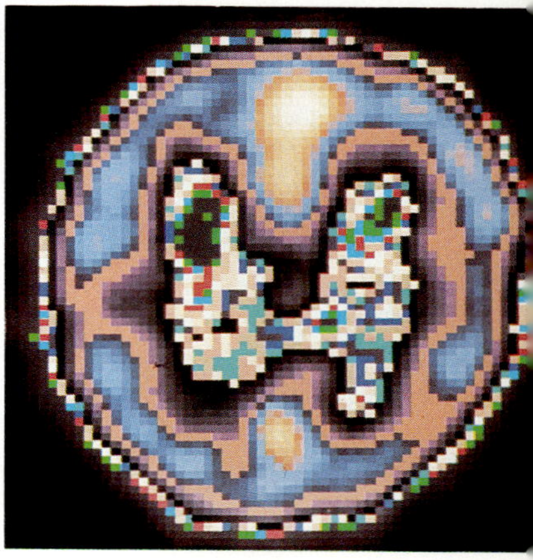

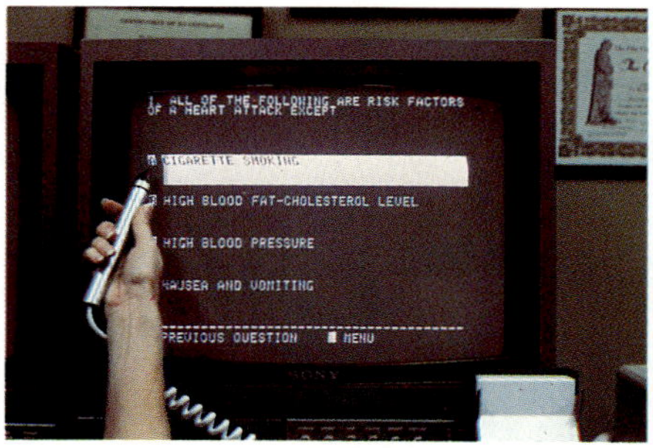
1. ALL OF THE FOLLOWING ARE RISK FACTORS OF A HEART ATTACK EXCEPT
CIGARETTE SMOKING
HIGH BLOOD FAT-CHOLESTEROL LEVEL
HIGH BLOOD PRESSURE
PREVIOUS QUESTION
MENU

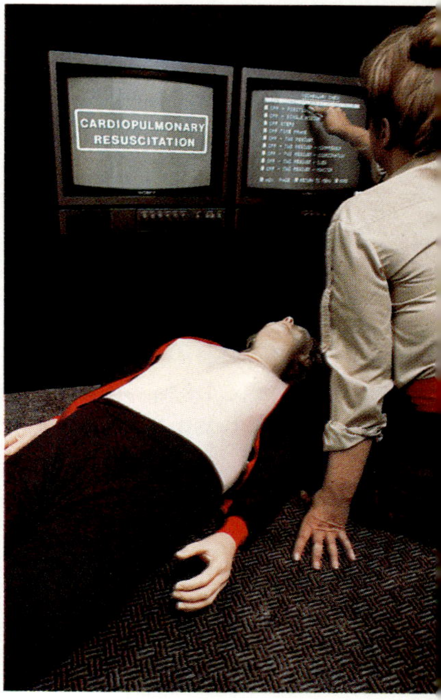
CARDIOPULMONARY RESUSCITATION

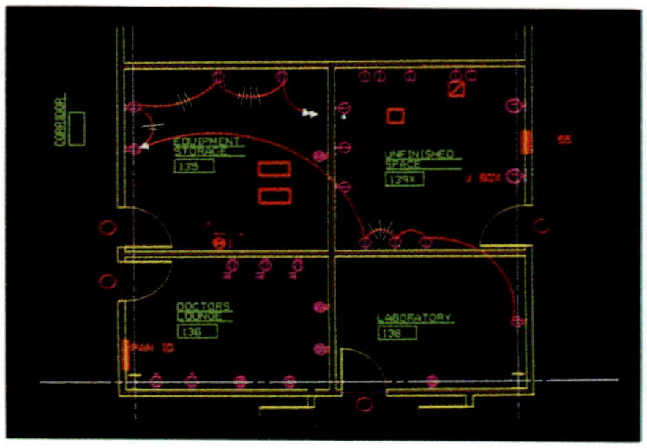
EQUIPMENT STORAGE
UNFINISHED SPACE
LABORATORY

End of the Story

ambulatory surgery
cirugia ambulante
outpatient elevator
ascensor de paciente

Throughout the patient's knee surgery, his wife has been waiting for the good news that finally comes: word from the doctor that the operation was successful and that her husband will be discharged soon. In time, he is wheeled out of the hospital—from beginning to end his stay and his recovery managed by the tools of the computer age.

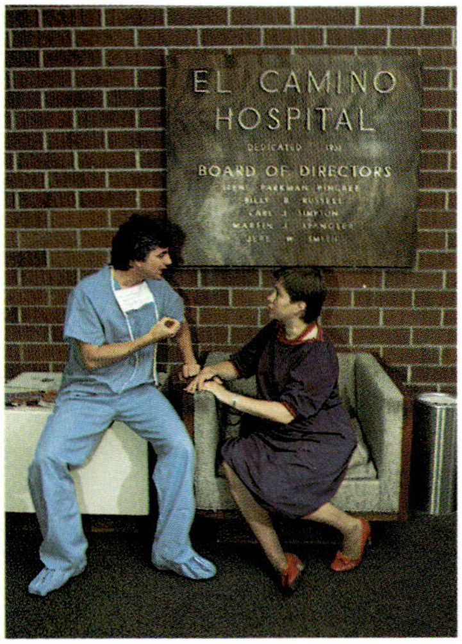
EL CAMINO
HOSPITAL
BOARD OF DIRECTORS

No
Unattended
Parking.
Violators
Cited.

- A **digitizer** is a device that can be moved over a drawing or photograph to convert the picture to digital data, which can then be stored in a computer, displayed on a CRT screen, or printed out on paper.
- **Point-of-sale (POS) terminals** represent the new evolution in cash registers. They consist of a keyboard for entering data, a CRT screen or digital display area for displaying dollar amounts, and a printer for providing a list of items and prices for the customer. Some POS terminals are **bar-code readers**—photoelectric scanners that read the **bar codes** (zebra-striped vertical marks or bars) printed on many products. POS terminals have several advantages: (1) Their use enables stores to hire less skilled sales clerks and checkers. (2) Checkout is faster. (3) There is better credit control. (4) Current sales and inventory information is maintained automatically. The disadvantages include: (1) Back-up systems are required in case the computer, and thus the POS devices, fails. (2) The equipment is expensive. (3) Stores may have to do double duty on price marking, because some states require that prices be stamped on the merchandise for customers to read.
- A **touch-tone device** is an instrument that sends data over ordinary telephone lines to a central computer (for example, a **card dialer** reads a customer's credit card, checks the customer's credit status, and reports the results to the local merchant).
- A **light pen** consists of a light-sensitive penlike device that, when placed against the CRT screen of a particular kind of terminal, closes a photoelectric circuit that identifies the X-Y coordinates to the computer. This allows the user to create a drawing right on the screen.
- A **mouse** is a direct-entry device with a ball on the bottom and attached with a cord to a computer terminal. When rolled on the table top, the mouse directs the location of the cursor or the pointer on the screen to draw pictures or give commands.
- **Speech-recognition devices,** or **voice-recognition systems,** convert the spoken word into a numeric code, which is matched against a code stored in a minicomputer. Then when one speaks into the microphone, the word is displayed on the screen for verification. Speech-recognition devices are the ultimate data-entry devices. Already machines are being produced that recognize voices, but they are primitive. They usually operate by being "trained" previously to the user's voice. Systems that are "speaker-independent"—that can recognize the same word spoken by many different people—can be built, but it is difficult to do so and the vocabularies are limited. Voice-recognition devices have several advantages: (1) Input is accurately controlled. (2) Input is readily verified and corrected. (3) The user's hands are free to perform tasks other than keying. (4) There are numerous potential applications. The disadvantages are that (1) such systems are expensive, (2) their vocabulary is limited, and (3) the speed of entry is slow.
- A specialized form of input device for transaction processing that is neither purely keyboard nor purely direct entry is the **automatic teller machine**

(ATM). The ATM has the advantages of (1) making banking services available to customers 24 hours a day without increased bank employee costs and (2) completing many routine banking tasks without many manual errors. However, if the system fails there may be no backup to help process transactions using paper. Other disadvantages are that the ATM can run out of money at night or on weekends, that it introduces several types of security problems, and that it reduces human interaction, which may have a negative effect on customer relations.

- The purpose of output devices is to make the solutions to computer input people-readable. The two most popular output devices are *terminals* and *printers.* Others are plotters, computer output microfilm, audio-response devices, and robots.
- Terminals—mainly cathode ray tube (CRT) terminals—are the windows on the computing process. There are three principal types of terminals: *alphanumeric, graphic,* and *flat panel display.*
- **Alphanumeric terminals** display alphanumeric output (letters, numbers, and special characters). They look like 9- or 12-inch television screens. These terminals have many advantages: (1) They are relatively inexpensive. (2) They are reliable. (3) The format on the screen can be varied widely. (4) The training cost for users is small. (5) Information can be transferred rapidly to the screen via telephone lines or by direct lines. However, with alphanumeric terminals, no hard copy is available (unless a printer is added) and the screen size limits the amount of information that can be displayed at one time.
- **Graphics terminals** can display both alphanumeric *and* graphic data, which is significant because research has shown that people can absorb numeric information displayed in graphic form much faster than in nongraphic form. There are three levels of complexity in graphics produced: (1) *two-dimensional graphics,* the simplest level, which consist of pie, line, and bar graphs; (2) *two-dimensional angle forms,* such as those found in topographic maps; and (3) *three-dimensional graphics,* which are used in product design because they allow designers to turn the object to be viewed from different perspectives.
- Two common business uses of computer graphics are **computer-assisted instruction (CAI)** and **computer-aided design** or **manufacturing (CAD/CAM)** (**computer-assisted engineering,** or **CAE,** is a variant). In CAI the computer is used to present instructional materials. It may take the form of simulation, demonstration, tutorial, or drill and practice. CAD is used by engineers, architects, and others to design products, buildings, and manufacturing processes. With CAD, two- and three-dimensional pictures can be shown on the screen, combined with other drawings, rotated, enlarged, reduced, and otherwise manipulated. CAM is used to physically manufacture products. The advantages of graphics terminals include: (1) They can present information in easily grasped form. (2) They can present information quickly and

reliably. Their disadvantages are (1) that graphics software is expensive and (2) that no hard copy is available unless a printer or plotter is added.

- **Flat panel displays** are alphanumeric or graphics terminals that do not use a cathode ray tube to project images on the screen; instead they use a liquid crystal display (LCD) or an electroluminescent substance that glows when electrically charged. The advantages of flat panel displays over CRTs are that (1) they are more compact and portable, (2) they consume less power, (3) they have greater daylight visibility, and (4) they have greater expected longevity. Their disadvantages are that (1) they cost more than conventional terminals, (2) they are somewhat fragile, and (3) their reliability is currently uncertain.
- Printers produce hard copy. They are classified according to *speed, print quality,* and *printing method.*
- Printers may print a character at a time **(serial printers)** or a line at a time; they may be as slow as ten characters per second (some home-computer printers) or as fast as 21,000 lines per minute (laser printers).
- Printers may be *draft quality* or *letter quality.* **Dot matrix printers** construct characters by using a matrix of pins; these characters usually appear a bit fuzzy, although some dot matrix printers can print letter-quality images.
- **Letter-quality printers** produce printed characters that resemble those produced by an office typewriter. They are generally more expensive than dot matrix printers.
- Printers can be either *impact printers* or *nonimpact printers.* An **impact printer** forms characters by physically striking a type device (a hammer) against inked ribbon to form characters on paper (like a typewriter). **Nonimpact printers** do not strike paper to form images; instead they form characters by using heat, lasers, photography, or ink spray, often on electrostatic or sensitized paper. Because there is no physical contact between printer and paper, nonimpact printers are quieter than impact printers. Also, because they have fewer moving parts, nonimpact printers are generally more reliable.
- There are four basic designs for impact printers: (1) *chain,* (2) *drum,* (3) *matrix,* and (4) *daisy wheel.*
- A **chain printer** consists of several sets of characters connected on a printing chain that revolves in front of the hammer. When the appropriate character passes by, the hammer strikes the paper and ribbon against it. The chains can be changed for different type fonts or styles. A **band printer** ("belt printer") operates similarly to a chain printer in that it uses a horizontally rotating band; the characters on the band are struck by hammers through the paper and ribbon.
- A **drum printer** is a line printer in which embossed characters are wrapped around a cylinder or drum. Each band around the drum consists of one each of the 64 different characters the printer is able to print; the number of

bands on the drum equals the number of characters the printer is able to print on one line. One entire revolution of the drum is required to print each line.

- A **matrix** or **dot matrix printer** forms characters by arranging dots closely together. Matrix printers are often **bi-directional;** that is, the print head first moves to the right, printing out a line, then moves to the left, printing out the next line. Dot matrix printers can print any shape instructed by the software—not just letters and numbers.
- In the **daisy-wheel printer,** the print mechanism consists of a removable wheel with a set of spokes, each containing a raised character. The wheel rotates to align the correct character, which is then struck with a hammer. These printers are noisier and slower than dot matrix printers, but they do produce letter-quality type. Variations of the daisy-wheel printer are the *ball printer* and the *thimble printer.*
- Among the types of nonimpact printers are *electrostatic, magnetic, ink jet, xerographic, laser,* and *thermal.*
- The **electrostatic printer** operates by depositing invisible charges on the paper's surface in the shape of characters. The paper is passed through a toner containing ink particles of the opposite charge, and the ink adheres to the paper only at the charged locations. These printers are very reliable; however, they require special paper.
- The **magnetic printer** also form characters by using electrical charges; however, the charges go to a moving belt that passes through the toner, picks up the ink, and transfers the ink to the paper. Magnetic printing is slower than electrostatic printing, but it does not require special paper.
- An **ink-jet printer** sprays small droplets of ink rapidly onto the surface of the paper. The print is letter quality, and many colors are available.
- The **xerographic printer** was developed by the Xerox Corporation. It combines computer and Xerox office copier technology. Characters are formed on a drum, the drum is treated with a toner, and characters are transferred to paper. This printer can be operated either from a computer or from magnetic tape or disk storage. It is very fast and produces high-quality print; however, it is very expensive.
- The **laser electrographic printer** creates characters on a drum using a laser beam light source. The characters are then treated with toner and transferred to paper. These printers produce very high quality images but are very expensive.
- The **thermal printer** creates characters by converting electrical impulses to heat energy that is transferred to special heat-sensitive paper using a dot matrix print head. Although these printers require special paper, they are inexpensive and reliable.

- **Plotters** are special-purpose output devices used to reproduce hard-copy drawings. The two types of plotters are *flatbed* and *drum*. The **flatbed plotter**—also called a **table plotter**—holds the paper still and allows a pen or pens of different colors, controlled by computer, to move about on the surface. The **drum plotter** holds the pens stationary and the paper rolls on a drum. These devices' main advantage is their ability to produce consistently accurate drawings very quickly. Their disadvantages are the limited availability of software and the high costs associated with developing it.
- A **computer output microfilm (COM)** system consists of a computer to produce original documents or images and a recording machine to prepare microfilm (miniature photographic images). The microfilm is called "on-line" if it is produced directly from the computer; it is called "off-line" if it is produced from magnetic tape. Microfilm can be in roll form or sheet form (called **microfiche**). To read microfilm requires a microfilm reader. Microfilm has several advantages: (1) It increases storage capability. (2) The information on it can be quickly retrieved. (3) It can store graphics and figures. (4) It is economical when used to process a large number of documents. Its disadvantages are (1) that it requires special equipment for viewing and for producing hard-copy documents and (2) that it cannot be updated on the same sheet or roll.
- **Audio-response** or **voice-output devices** make sounds that seem like human voices but are prerecorded vocalized sounds. They are much easier to engineer than voice-input devices.
- **Robotics** is the study of the design, construction, and use of robots. It is a serious engineering field that is becoming increasingly important. **Robots** have two qualities that make them flexible: (1) they are *multifunctional,* which means that they can do more than one task, and (2) they are *reprogrammable,* which means that they can be reprogrammed to carry out many kinds of tasks.
- There are four areas of robotics: (1) **Large industrial robots:** computer-controlled tools used on factory assembly lines to perform tasks previously performed by human beings. (2) **Small industrial robots:** reprogrammable robots that handle objects up to 20 pounds and that can "see" using television-camera vision systems so they can be used for inspection, identification, and guidance functions. (3) **Mobile robots:** peoplelike machines that can roll around and talk and perhaps perform a few functions. These are not true robots because they are not multifunctional and reprogrammable. (4) **Artificial intelligence:** the field of study concerned with exploring tasks computers do that previously were reserved for human intelligence, imagination, and intuition. This is the most promising and awesome area of robotics. Artificial intelligence has already created **expert systems,** which are computer programs that essentially copy the knowledge of human experts in a particular field.

KEY TERMS

Alphanumeric terminal, p. 234
Artificial intelligence, p. 249
Audio-response device, p. 247
Automatic teller machine (ATM), p. 229
Band printer, p. 240
Bar-code reader, p. 223
Batch processing, p. 206
Bi-directional, p. 242
Card dialer, p. 223
Card reader, p. 209
Cathode ray tube (CRT) terminal, p. 214
Chain printer, p. 240
Computer-aided design (CAD), p. 236
Computer-aided manufacturing (CAM), p. 236
Computer-assisted engineering (CAE), p. 236
Computer-assisted instruction (CAI), p. 236
Computer output microfilm (COM), p. 246
Daisy-wheel printer, p. 242
Digitizer, p. 222
Direct entry, pp. 207, 218
Dot matrix printer, p. 238
Drum plotter, p. 245
Drum printer, p. 240
Dumb terminal, p. 217
Electrostatic printer, p. 242
Expert system, pp. 249, 250
Flatbed plotter, p. 245
Flat panel display, p. 236
GIGO, p. 205
Graphics terminal, p. 234
Hard copy, p. 214
Hard-copy terminal, p. 217
Impact printer, p. 238
Ink-jet printer, p. 242
Intelligent terminal, p. 217
Interactive terminal, p. 217
Key-to-disk device, p. 214
Key-to-diskette device, p. 214
Key-to-tape device, p. 214
Large industrial robot, p. 249
Laser electrographic printer, p. 245
Letter-quality printer, p. 238
Light pen, p. 226
Magnetic-ink character recognition (MICR), p. 218
Magnetic printer, p. 242
Matrix printer, p. 242
Microfiche, p. 246
Mobile robot, p. 249
Mouse, p. 226
Nonimpact printer, p. 238
On-line processing, p. 206
Optical-character recognition (OCR), p. 220
Optical-mark recognition (OMR), p. 221
Plotter, p. 245
Point-of-sales (POS) terminal, p. 223
Printer, p. 238
Punched cards, p. 209
Real-time processing, p. 206
Robotics, p. 249
Serial printer, p. 238
Small industrial robot, p. 249
Smart terminal, p. 217
Soft copy, p. 214
Speech recognition device, p. 226
Table plotter, p. 245
Teleprinter, p. 217
Thermal printer, p. 245
Touch-tone device, p. 223
Transaction processing, p. 206
Voice-output device, p. 247
Voice-recognition system, p. 226
Wand reader, p. 220
Xerographic printer, p. 245

REVIEW QUESTIONS

1. Describe how the computer transforms raw data into usable information using input and output devices.
2. What are some of the most commonly used input and output devices?
3. What is the difference between batch processing and transaction processing?
4. Direct entry is more reliable than keyboard entry. Why?
5. Describe the differences among dumb, smart, and intelligent terminals.
6. How are printers classified, and what are some of the kinds of printers available?
7. How can color graphics be reproduced on hard copy by computer?
8. Describe some of the ways robotics can affect industry.
9. What is artificial intelligence?

CASE PROBLEMS

Case 7-1: Taking the Lead with Robots

Japan currently dominates the industrial robot industry, producing 65 percent of the world's robots. Many of these robots are shipped to the United States. The August 6, 1984, issue of *Fortune*, however, reports an instance of robots traveling the other way—from the United States to Japan. American Robot Corp. of Pittsburgh signed a seven-year agreement to sell the design and parts of its robot (called Merlin) to Daikin Industries of Osaka, which will manufacture the robot for sale in Asia. The reason the Japanese like Merlin is that "it has fewer moving parts than most other robots. They also like its computer, software, the UNIX system developed by Bell Labs to control voice and data communications. With UNIX, customers can expand from a single robot to a factory full of robots that can talk to each other."[5]

Your assignment: Some experts, such as Glenn Seaborg, director of the Lawrence Hall of Science in Berkeley and 1952 winner of the Nobel prize in Chemistry, believe the United States robotics industry will make significant gains in the future because of its leadership in robots that can sense, see, and think.[6] Pick some manufacturing or service industry that you know something about (if only second hand). With that industry in mind, what kind of task would you like to try to robotize? What would the robot have to be able to do? In what markets, both domestic and international, might the robot sell?

Case 7-2: Being an Entrepreneur

Where do most jobs come from? According to a Dun & Bradstreet Corporation survey, a third of the new jobs for 1984 were expected to come from very small companies—those with 20 or fewer workers—which provide the bulk of the nation's employment.[7] (Big employers, those with 25,000 or more workers, were expected to provide only 7 to 8% of the new jobs.)

Small firms often have a more entrepreneurial bent than large firms do. Being an entrepreneur is often associated with a willingness to take risks in pursuit of business opportunities, although economist Paul Hawken disagrees. Entrepreneurs, he says, see a market, idea, or product that others do not or that others discount, but to entrepreneurs the need is obvious. "There is no risk because they are totally identified with the end result," says Hawken. "They are not studying the market, they *are* the market. . .What an entrepreneur will then do is try to identify every possible risk and obstacle that could prevent him or her from achieving that goal, and eliminate as many as possible."[8]

Entrepreneurs are no longer inventors like Thomas Edison or industrial geniuses like Henry Ford. They are often young, unconventional, and wary of large, bureaucratized institutions. Among the new entrepreneurs are Apple Computer founders Steven Jobs, 29, and Stephen Wozniak; David Liederman, chief of David's Cookies stores; and Marc Lieder, 21, who founded Powercard/USA, a service providing small companies with discounts on office equipment, insurance, and so on. Women are also among the forefront of today's entrepreneurs, as exemplified by Veronica Napoles, a corporate design consultant; Heather Evans, maker of high-fashion dresses for executive women; and Sandra Kurtzig, head of ASK Computers Systems.

Entrepreneurship is not without risk. For every three businesses that start, two will fail, and nearly half that fail do so in the first five years. But, as a *New York Times* article points out, failure does not have the price that it used to—some entrepreneurs, such as Adam Osborne, founder of Osborne Computer Corp., which went bankrupt, have picked themselves up and started over again—with new financial backing.[9]

Entrepreneuring has changed the character of business schools and big business. As you may be finding yourself, many college and university business departments and graduate schools of business are now being called upon to offer courses in entrepreneurship. Large corporations are now turning to "intrepreneuralism"—giving corporate incentives to innovators.

Your assignment: No company, large or small, necessarily has a divine vision that leads to success, which is why some companies sponsor competing projects for the same goal. Look back over this chapter and determine which of the input and output devices interest you. Then see how they might be linked to a possible business of interest to you. Your best bet is not to look for a business to go into but to do something that satisfies a personal passion, that is close to home. As Hawken says, "Don't try to figure out the market—be it."

CHAPTER 8

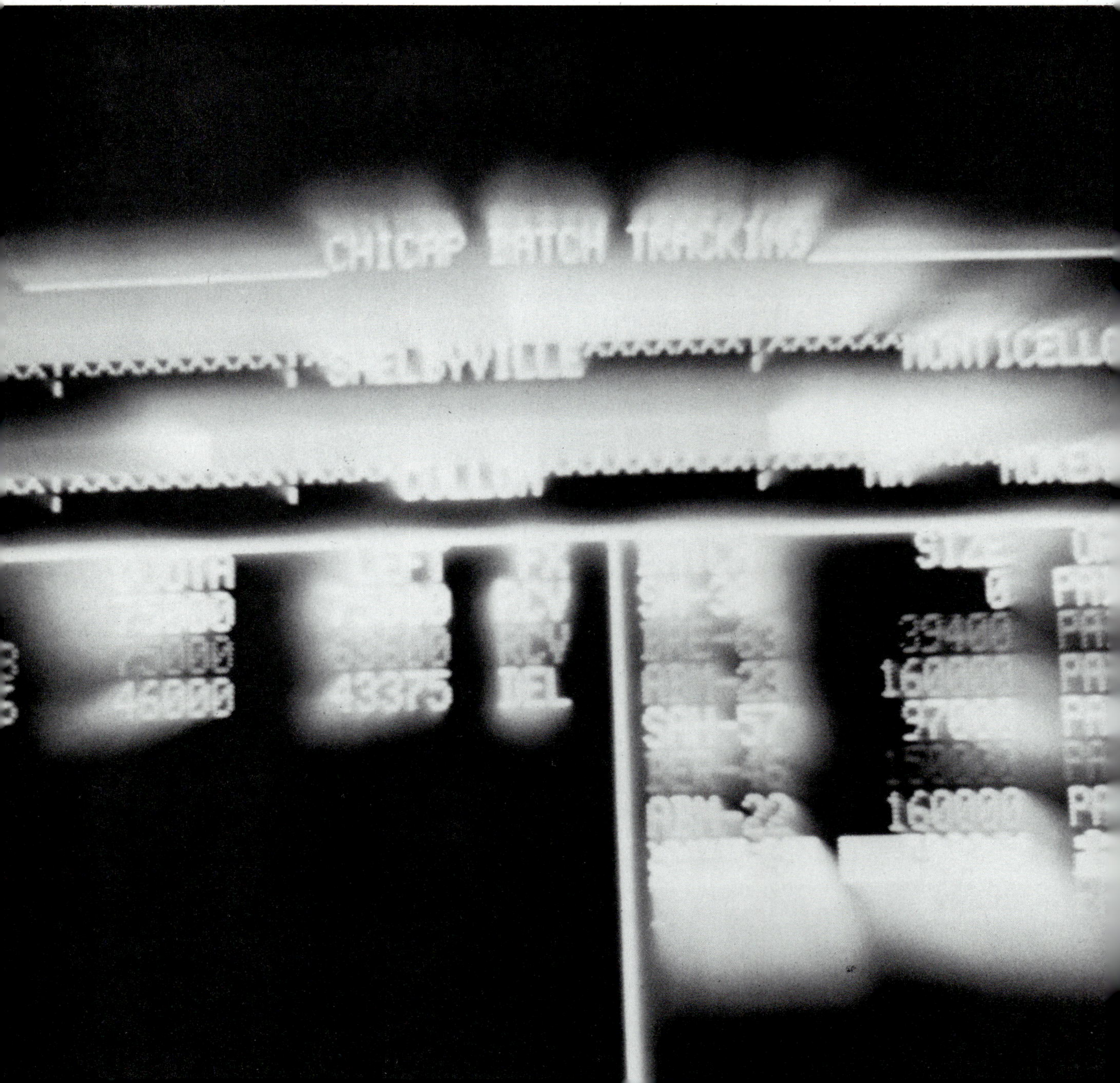

Processors and Operating Systems

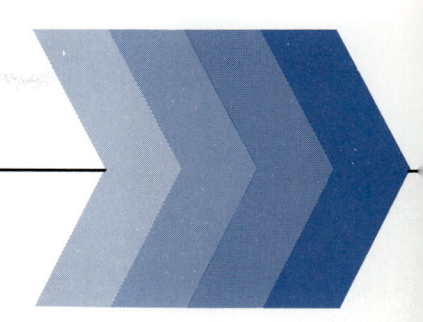

Report from Behind the Scenes

Perhaps one of the strongest quests in life is for power. You seek power, in the personal sense, not necessarily to dominate other people but to enhance your ability to control events, to have more flexibility to do things, to have a wider range of skills and choices. The computer gives us power, for it expands our ability to do all these things. "What the lever was to the body," says Charles P. Lecht, author of *The Waves of Change,* "the computer system is to the mind."

P R E V I E W

Computer Power to the People

Power is a word often used to describe how well computers provide this leverage. When people speak of the power of computer *hardware,* they usually mean in a specific sense—namely, how much data can its internal memory hold and how quickly can data be processed? When they speak of the power of computer *software,* they usually mean, how flexible is it? How much can it do?

In this chapter, we will describe the two critical things you need to know about most computers which give them—and therefore you—their power. The first is the *central processing unit,* which is part of the hardware; the second is the *operating system,* which is important system software. Whereas in Chapter 7 we described how application programs and data could be converted into machine-readable form by input devices, here we need to show how hardware and software actually process data.

In your new job with Atlantic-Pacific Bank you are in a position to appreciate how important computer processing speeds are, as

CASE STUDY: THE NEED FOR FAST PROCESSING

Banks and the Holiday Rush

NEW YORK—With Christmas less than a week away, banks here are stockpiling clean, crisp bills for their customers to hand out as job-well-done tips to New York's legion of superintendents, doormen, and parking garage attendants.

But in other ways, banks in the Big Apple began preparations for the Christmas crush a long time ago.

"Our planning year is based on the Christmas rush. If we can get past Christmas, we can relax in January," said Alan Silberstein, senior vice-president of retail operations at Chemical Bank here.

For the banks' systems managers, this means new computer equipment has to be in place, tested and broken in well before Thanksgiving. The Christmas shopping season begins the day after America's fall feast and runs until the day of Christmas Eve, according to banking executives. . . .

Business is particularly brisk in at least two areas: remittance processing and credit card transactions.

Remittance processing is up during December, according to William W. Shine, senior vice-president of operations and systems for Chase Manhattan Bank. Shine speculated that customers increase the number of payments on their charge card accounts in order to boost the amount of credit they have available to them for Christmas presents.

Credit card transactions are heavier in the 30 days between Thanksgiving and Christmas than at any other time during the year. These strain the banks' computer systems for both processing the sales tickets and authorizing the purchase to the merchant, according to Shine.

"Christmas purchases are in large measure made by plastic," Shine pointed out. The reason for this seems obvious: Christmas shoppers do not want to know how much they are spending until after the Christmas spirit has worn off.

In preparation for the heavy volume of charge account activity, the banks must purge their computer storage disks just prior to Thanksgiving. This gives them more room for the flood of shopping data to come.

—David Myers, *Computerworld*, December 19, 1983

the case starting on the opposite page makes clear. In banking more than in most businesses, time literally means money—and the time lost in processing checks and credit card transactions because of slow computers is not time a bank willingly gives up.

Processor and Memory: The Central Processing Unit

How much data does a computer actually hold in its internal memory? (This is the memory inside the machine itself, not the external disk or tape memory.) Peter Laurie, in *The Joy of Computers*, points out that an eight-bit microcomputer, which is what the popular Apple II is, for instance, has 65,536 memory locations inside it. Each memory location stores one number, letter, or special character. If the contents of *each* of these memory locations were written out on an ordinary index card, and all those cards were laid end to end, they would stretch for about six miles.[1] This would reach from the southern tip of Manhattan Island,

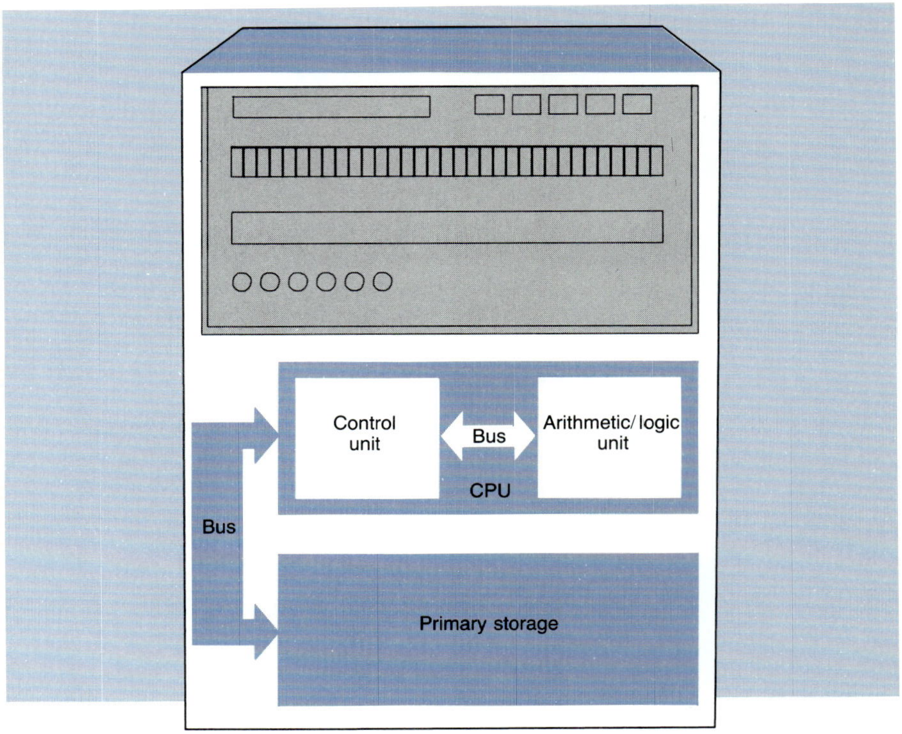
Control unit
Bus
Arithmetic/logic unit
CPU
Bus
Primary storage

Figure 8-1 The central processor. The central processing unit (CPU) has two parts—the control unit and the arithmetic/logic unit. Primary storage is temporary storage for data instructions at the time the program is being executed. Note that the three components are joined by a bus.

New York, to the middle of Central Park. For the newer 16-bit machines, the cards would cover more than 100 miles. Says Laurie:

> Imagine having to run up and down such an array, picking up a card here, reading it, rushing off over the horizon to read the one it referred to, tear back, pick up two more and doing the sums they commanded on the trot. This is not an unreasonable analogy because no computer ever does anything that you could not do with pencil and paper. It just does it a lot faster and more accurately—so much so, in fact, that it can give a quantum jump in work possibilities.[2]

As Figure 8-1 shows, the memory is considered part of the central processing unit. The **central processing unit,** which you will nearly always hear referred to as the **CPU,** is hardware that interprets and executes program instructions and communicates with the input, output, and external storage devices. The CPU has been compared to the human brain; however, the brain can hold up to 3 billion pieces of information at one time compared to a computer's 16 million pieces. It also consumes very little energy, whereas a computer may produce enough energy to heat a house. On the other hand, the computer can send information at speeds of 654,000 feet per second (compared to the brain's 350 feet per second) and is certainly easier to repair when something goes wrong.

The Three Parts of the CPU

The CPU consists of three components, which are shown in Figure 8-1 and which are described below:

- The controller
- The arithmetic/logic unit
- Primary storage

Note, in Figure 8-1, that the communications among these three units are made through physical connections known as a **bus.**

The Controller. Like a traffic cop, the **controller**—also known as the **control unit**—directs and coordinates the rest of the system in carrying out program instructions. It also tells input devices when additional input is needed and notifies output devices that information is available for output.

SPERRY UNIVAC 90/60

Console. The array of switches and lights, which indicates the status of processing occurring in the computer, is less dramatic on most recent models of computers. However, the Sperry Univac 90/60 is still being used in many places.

The controller does not store data or programs—that is done by the primary storage unit, as we shall see. But the control unit assigns and records the locations within the storage unit where data and programs are stored. As each statement in the computer program is input, the control unit also interprets that statement and directs the other two CPU components.

Arithmetic/Logic Unit. The **arithmetic/logic unit,** abbreviated **ALU,** is the part of the CPU that calculates and compares data, based on instructions from the controller. Because the ALU controls the speed of calculations and because speed is a very important concern of computer users, it receives a great deal of attention from computer-design engineers.

The two operations performed by the ALU are arithmetic operations and logical operations. *Arithmetic operations* consist of the four standard mathematical calculations—addition, subtraction, multiplication, and division. *Logical operations* consist of the three common comparison operations; in comparing numbers the ALU will find that one is equal to (=), less than (<), or greater than (>) the other.

Primary Storage Unit. As we mentioned earlier in the book, the **primary storage unit** is also called **memory, main storage,** or **internal storage,** and it is that part of the CPU that holds (1) data for processing, (2) instructions for processing (the program), and (3) processed data waiting to be output. (Secondary or auxiliary storage—which we shall describe in the next chapter—consists of external storage such as magnetic disk or magnetic tape.)

Computer Processing Speeds

If a computer has two reasons for being, they are that it is able to process great quantities of data and that it works extremely quickly. An instruction may be executed on a small computer in less than a **millisecond,** which is one-thousandth of a second. Many computers can execute an instruction in microseconds—a **microsecond** is one-millionth of a second. Supercomputers are approaching the **nanosecond** range—one-billionth of a second. To give you a sense of how short a nanosecond is, if a nanosecond were equal to one minute, then a minute would be equal to 1900 years.

How Data Is Stored

Primary storage consists of thousands of memory locations. Each such location has an *address*—a number—just like the box numbers on mailboxes in the post office. Unlike P.O. boxes, however, each memory location stores only one instruction or piece of data. The controller manipulates the data and instructions by referring to the locations (addresses)—for example, "Multiply the contents of location 1 times the contents of location 2 and put the results in location 3." The locations always stay the same, but new data and new instructions may be placed in them. Just as when new letters are put in a mailbox, the address does not change, only the contents. An important point: Obviously, there must be *enough* locations in primary storage to hold both data and instructions, otherwise the program will not work—which explains why some microcomputers have memories that are too small (have too little capacity) to handle complicated programs and data.

An example of how data and instructions are manipulated is given in the box below.

HOW PRIMARY STORAGE WORKS

A Problem of Interest

Of considerable interest to bankers is interest, the profit on money loaned. If you sit down with your Lotus 1-2-3 or other spreadsheet on your computer at Atlantic-Pacific Bank and compute alternative interest rates for alternative amounts of money loaned for alternative lengths of time, all such data and instructions must be manipulated by the central processing unit. This suggests, by the way, why you need a computer with a fairly large capacity in memory: it must have room to hold not only the program, such as Lotus 1-2-3 or VisiCalc, but also all the data or numbers you are working with.

Let us suppose you are not using packaged software but are writing the program yourself to compute the interest rate. As an inducement to get people to borrow more, Atlantic-Pacific Bank offers a lower interest rate on larger loan amounts. Thus, let us say for the sake of this exercise that the bank charges a regular interest rate for loans up to $1000 and half that interest rate as a special interest for any amounts beyond $1000. (Actually, if you can find a deal like this, grab it! No bank would really do this.) Let us say you already have a program written for calculating interest on loans up to $1000. If you wrote a program in pseudocode for calculating interest on loans over $1000, it would look like this:

```
IF loan is greater than 1000
  THEN
        multiply 0.50 of the regular
      interest rate times the amount
      greater than 1000 to get special
      interest
        add special interest to regular
      interest
  END IF
```

We will say that the regular interest rate is 20%.With the bank's special deal, the borrower of $1500 will have to pay 20% of $1000, or $200, in interest on the first $1000 borrowed. On the additional $500, the borrower will have to pay interest at half the regular interest rate, or 10%. Thus, interest on the additional $500 will be $50 (the result of .10 × $500). In all, the borrower will have to repay $250 in interest plus the $1500 the bank loaned, for a total of $1750. (Actually, computations of interest are usually more complicated than this.)

How do these numbers get handled inside the computer? Take a look at the illustration. The computer goes through the following steps:

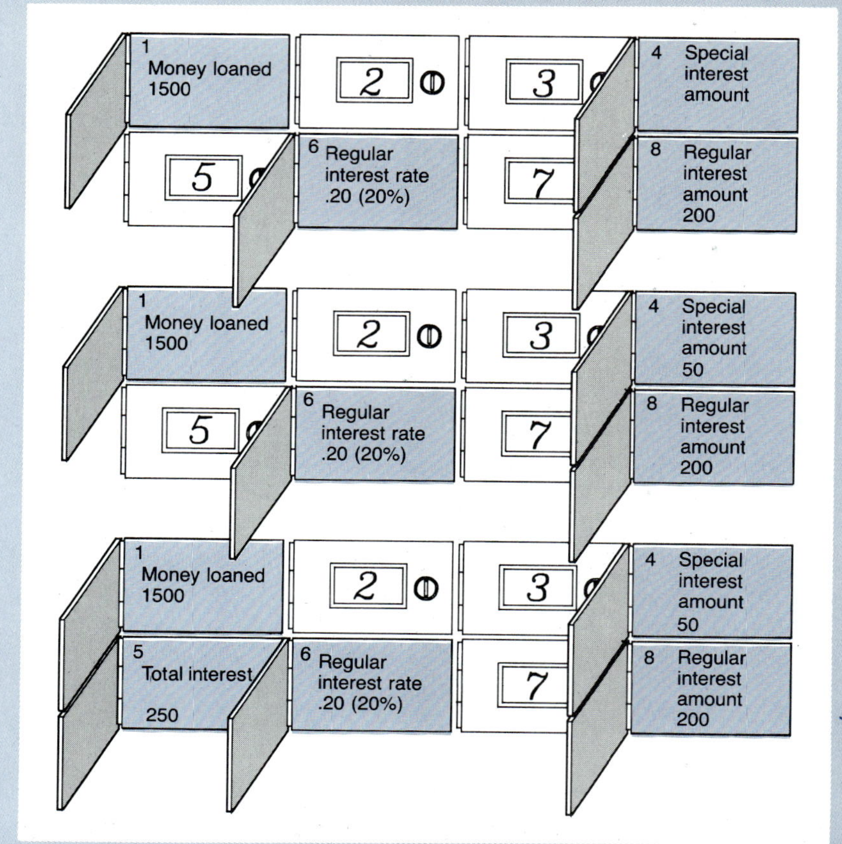
1
Money loaned
1500
2
3
4 Special interest amount
5
6 Regular interest rate .20 (20%)
7
8 Regular interest amount 200
1
Money loaned
1500
2
3
4 Special interest amount 50
5
6 Regular interest rate .20 (20%)
7
8 Regular interest amount 200
1
Money loaned
1500
2
3
4 Special interest amount 50
5
Total interest
250
6 Regular interest rate .20 (20%)
7
8 Regular interest amount 200

1. The controller reads the statement, "IF loan is greater than 1000" from the program in primary storage—actually, this would be expressed as "IF data in address 1 is greater than 1000"—and the controller would then tell the ALU to make the logical comparison (that is, see if the loan amount is greater than 1000). The ALU answers yes. The controller then moves to the THEN statement.
2. The controller reads the statement, "multiply 0.50 of the regular interest rate times the amount greater than 1000 to get special interest" from primary storage. (The computer would actually express this as "multiply 0.50 times the data in address 6 times the data over 1000 in address 1 to provide data for address 4.") The controller contacts the ALU to make the calculation, which it does, first determining "0.50 times regular interest rate" and storing the answer,

10, in the ALU, then determining "money loaned minus 1000" and storing that answer, 500, in the ALU. The controller then contacts the ALU to calculate ".10 times 500," which the ALU does and returns the answer of 50 to the controller. The controller then stores this answer in primary storage in address 4, Special Interest Amount.

3. The controller reads the next statement, "add special interest to regular interest" from primary storage. (This can be expressed as "add data from address 4 to data in address 8, to provide data in address 5.") The ALU calculates this and returns the answer, 250, to the controller, which stores it in address 5—total interest.

This example is greatly simplified because each memory address would actually contain only one instruction. Moreover, the data and instructions would not be readable in English but in machine language—that is, 0s and 1s.

Binary Business: How Electricity Represents Data

To the standard measures by which we live—of currency, weather, distance, and so on—we must now add another for the Information Age: that of computer storage capacity. As mentioned, if the microcomputer you are using does not have enough storage, for example, it may not be able to do everything you want. Storage capacity is principally expressed using the letter *K*, which can be thought of as representing 1024 characters. (We will describe this in more detail in a moment.) When you buy software, you may see listed on the package—as on *The Home Accountant*, for example—"Hardware requirements: 64K IBM PC . . . ," which means the program is designed to run on an IBM Personal Computer with at least 64K of storage capacity. That is, the computer must be able to hold at least 64 × 1024, or 65,536 characters of data.

On and Off

But how, you may wonder, does such data get represented in the computer? You can think of a computer as consisting of a long series of switches—each either turned on or off. This on/off corresponds to electricity being turned on or off or a magnetic field being positive or negative. Indeed, in the early days of computers, one could actually see the light in vacuum tubes go on and off.

The two states of on and off can be represented by the **binary system** of numbers—that is, a number system using only the two digits 0 and

Two by Two: Binary Numbers

Presumably because our ancestors had ten fingers, our numbering system is decimal, or base ten. Our counting system, then, is based on some obvious physical characteristics. But the world is full of other characteristics for which we often use such names as "couple," "pair," "duet," and "twins." Counting by twos is called the binary numbering system. Since computers use electricity, which has two states—"on" and "off"—they must use the binary system. In order for us to do business, we must convert decimal numbers to binary on input to the computer.

Binary numbers are manipulated the same way as decimal numbers. The difference is that binary has only 0 and 1 whereas decimal has ten numbers, 0 through 9. However, when adding the 1s in binary, you carry the 1s to the top of the left column—a maneuver familiar to you in adding columns of decimal numbers. In binary, then, 1 + 1 equals 10 (this is 2 in decimal); 1 + 1 + 1 equals 11 (3 in decimal) and 1 + 1 + 1 + 1 equals 100 (4 in decimal) as the following shows:

$$\begin{array}{r} 1 \\ +1 \\ \hline 10 \\ +\ 1 \\ \hline 11 \\ +\ 1 \\ \hline 100 \end{array}$$

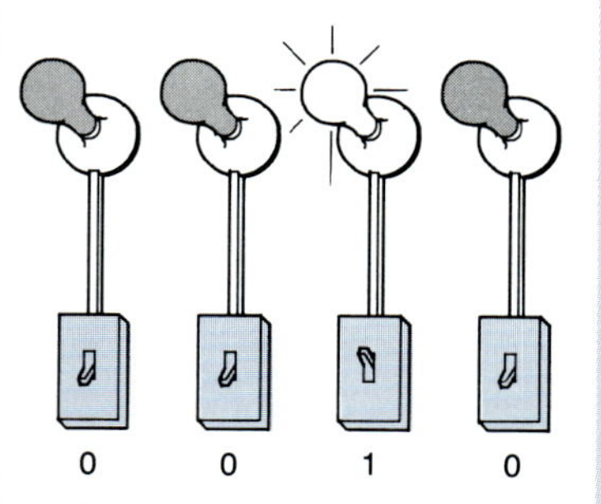
0
0
1
0

Here are the numbers 0 through 9 in base ten as written in base two:

Base ten	*Base two*	*Base two with preceding zeros added*
0	0	0000
1	1	0001
2	10	0010
3	11	0011
4	100	0100
5	101	0101
6	110	0110
7	111	0111
8	1000	1000
9	1001	1001

The zeros added in front of each base two number do not change the meaning of the number (just as, in decimal, 0015 is the same as 15). When working with computers, every column must be filled with something, because electricity is either off (0) or on (1).

Continuing, we see that decimal numbers 10 through 16 are as follows in binary:

Base ten	*Base two*
10	1010
11	1011
12	1100
13	1101
14	1110
15	1111
16	10000

Clearly, numbers in the binary system can get long very quickly. For instance, the decimal number 5000 is the binary number 1001110001000.

Binary bulbs. The decimal number 2, which is 0010 in binary, could be expressed with on and off light bulbs, with "on" for 1 and "off" for 0.

1. (The decimal system that we all are accustomed to, by contrast, uses 10 digits—0, 1, 2, 3, 4, 5, 6, 7, 8, 9.) In the binary system, the 0 can be represented in the computer by the off state and the 1 by the on state.

When applied to computers, each 0 or 1 in the binary system is called a **bit** (which stands for *bi*nary digi*t*). Because bits alone cannot represent numbers, letters, and special characters, they are combined into groups of four to eight bits called **bytes** (pronounced "bites"). Each byte, or group of zeros and ones, represents one character of data—that is, a letter, digit, or special character (such as ? or $).

The letter **K,** the unit of capacity of primary storage, stands for **kilobytes,** which is 1024 bytes. On large computers, primary storage may be expressed in **megabytes,** or millions of bytes ("mega" means million). Some manufacturers even speak of **gigabytes**—billions of bytes. Microcomputers may range from 4K (for pocket size) to 512K or more—there being more "more" every year. Minicomputers may range up to a megabyte and mainframes to 16 megabytes or more.

Bytes into Codes

Combinations of bits—that is, of 0s and 1s—can be used to represent the complete alphabet, the decimal numbers 0 through 9, and special characters. There are different sets of combinations or coding schemes, the most common being:

- Four-bit binary coded decimal (BCD)
- Extended Binary Coded Decimal Interchange Code (EBCDIC)
- American Standard Code for Information Interchange (ASCII)

The three are compared in Figure 8-2. Let us take a look at these.

Binary Coded Decimal.

Popular with the first computers, **binary coded decimal (BCD)** is frequently used today to code numeric data. It consists of 0s and 1s grouped into units of four bits each. For example, the decimal number 4196 is represented by the four digits 4, 1, 9, and 6, each written in binary (base two):

	0100	0001	1001	0110
=	4	1	9	6

The problem with this code is that it runs out of new combinations in each four-bit sequence very quickly, since there are only 16 possible combinations of 0s and 1s in each four-bit unit. Ten combinations are needed to represent the decimal digits 0 through 9, leaving only six combinations—clearly not enough to represent the 26 characters of the alphabet and special characters needed.

Extended Binary Coded Decimal Interchange Code.

By expanding the byte from four bits to eight, it is possible to represent alphabetic and special characters as well as numeric. The **Extended Binary Coded Dec-**

Character	BCD	EBCDIC	ASCII
A		1100 0001	100 0001
B		1100 0010	100 0010
C		1100 0011	100 0011
D		1100 0100	100 0100
E		1100 0101	100 0101
F		1100 0110	100 0110
G		1100 0111	100 0111
H		1100 1000	100 1000
I		1100 1001	100 1001
J		1101 0001	100 1010
K		1101 0010	100 1011
L		1101 0011	100 1100
M		1101 0100	100 1101
N		1101 0101	100 1110
O		1101 0110	100 1111
P		1101 0111	101 0000
Q		1101 1000	101 0001
R		1101 1001	101 0010
S		1110 0010	101 0011
T		1110 0011	101 0100
U		1110 0100	101 0101
V		1110 0101	101 0110
W		1110 0110	101 0111
X		1110 0111	101 1000
Y		1110 1000	101 1001
Z		1110 1001	101 1010
0	0000	1111 0000	011 0000
1	0001	1111 0001	011 0001
2	0010	1111 0010	011 0001
3	0011	1111 0011	011 0011
4	0100	1111 0100	011 0100
5	0101	1111 0101	011 0101
6	0110	1111 0110	011 0110
7	0111	1111 0111	011 0111
8	1000	1111 1000	011 1000
9	1001	1111 1001	011 1001

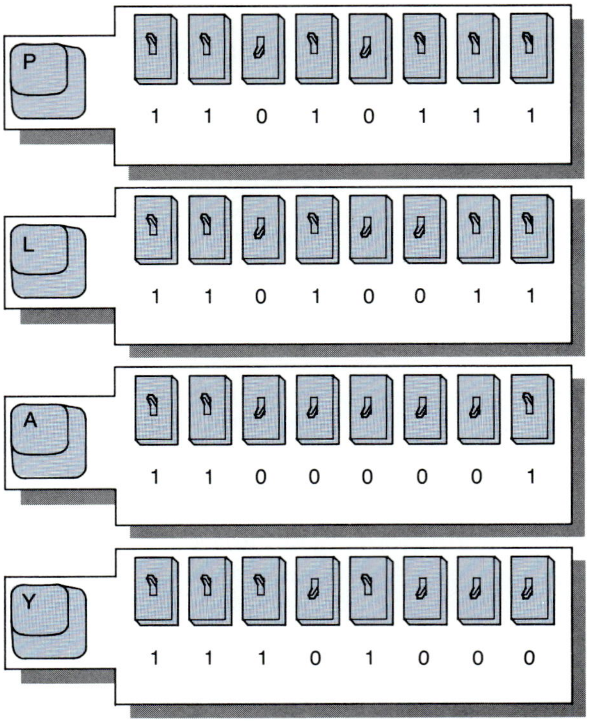
P
1 1 0 1 0 1 1 1
L
1 1 0 1 0 0 1 1
A
1 1 0 0 0 0 0 1
Y
1 1 1 0 1 0 0 0

Figure 8-2 Three computer coding schemes: BCD, EBCDIC, ASCII. These are binary representations for letters and numbers; special characters are also included (not shown). The bits—0s and 1s—may be thought of as "off" and "on" switches, as in the word "PLAY" shown above expressed in EBCDIC.

imal Interchange Code, abbreviated **EBCDIC** (pronounced "*eb*-see-dick") not only allows alphabetic characters but also allows them in uppercase and lowercase. One of the two most popular eight-bit codes used, EBCDIC was developed by IBM and is used in most IBM computers, as well as in machines produced by other manufacturers.

The eight bits—which, as mentioned, are usually referred to as a *byte*—are divided into two parts, the first four bits being called **zone bits** and the second four bits being called **numeric** or **digit bits.** The combination of zone bits with numeric bits allows for 256 possible arrangements. (If only six bits are used, only 64 arrangements are possible—not enough to cover numbers, special characters, and upper- and lowercase alphabets.) Note, for instance, that both the following have the same numeric bits but different zone bits, so that one byte can represent a letter and the other a number:

Byte		
Zone bits	*Numeric bits*	
1100	0010	= B
1111	0010	= 2

American Standard Code for Information Interchange. The second most popular eight-bit code, the **American Standard Code for Information Interchange** is usually referred to by its abbreviation, **ASCII** (pronounced "*as*-key"). ASCII is frequently used in data communications, nearly always in microcomputers, and in several large computers.

Note in Figure 8-2 that a byte represented in ASCII consists of seven bits (rather than eight, as in EBCDIC), allowing for 128 possible arrangements—fewer than the 256 possible combinations of EBCDIC. Because some computers are designed for eight-bit rather than seven-bit codes, an eight-bit version of ASCII has been developed called **ASCII-8.**

The Parity Bit: Tip-off to Errors

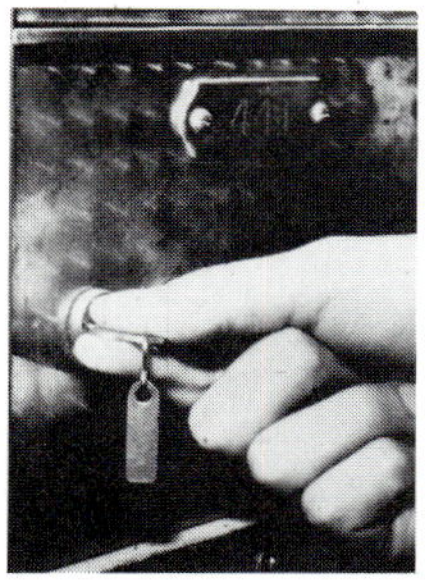

To err is not just human, although too often the expression "computer error" is simply a cover-up for human mistakes. Dust, static electricity, high humidity, and other factors can affect the sending of data to and through a computer. Obviously, at Atlantic-Pacific Bank, which transmits a lot of financial information through communications lines, errors in transit can mean substantial losses. Although the computer typically cannot tell you the exact error, frequently it can tell you that there *is* one. The way the computer detects errors is through the use of a parity bit, which is used in transmission of data.

A **parity bit,** also called a **check bit,** is simply an additional bit attached to the byte. That is, in EBCDIC, it would be a ninth bit, as shown in Figure 8-3. (In ASCII, the extra bit would be an eighth bit.) The addition of this extra bit allows the computer to detect errors.

Notice that if you add up the number of 1s in a byte, the total will be either odd or even (1100 0001 has three 1s and therefore is odd, 1100 0011 has four 1s and so is even). In an *even parity* format, the extra parity bit is set to either 0 or 1 in order to make the number of 1s an even number. Thus, for the EBCDIC letter A, which is 1100 0001 and which is odd, a parity bit of 1 is added so that the nine-bit sequence is 1 1100 0001,

	Parity bit			
EBCDIC letter A	1	1100	0001	Even—four 1s
EBCDIC letter C	0	1100	0011	Even—four 1s
Error in EBCDIC letter C	0	1100	0010	Odd—three 1s (last 1 dropped)

Figure 8-3 **The parity bit.** This is an example of an even parity format. The parity bit is always such that the nine-bit sequence is even. If any one of the 1-bits is missing, the computer will display an error message to the computer operator.

making the number of 1s even. Any time a nine-bit sequence shows up in the computer as odd, the computer will display an error message, so that the computer operator can take corrective action.

An *odd parity* format is the reverse of even parity—the parity bit is set to make the number of 1s odd. Odd parity is used on some systems. Either way, the parity bit is not infallible in catching errors—after all, suppose *two* 1s were missing from 1 1100 0001 in an even parity system? But it has been shown to be very effective in detecting the majority of coding errors.

Storage Designs

The storage capacity of a computer is part of the design of the computer. There are three types of designs:

- Word-addressable
- Character-addressable
- Byte-addressable

These describe what will fit into each storage location or address.

Word-Addressable. In a **word-addressable** design, each address stores a fixed number of characters—for example, a single data item such as BAKER or a single program instruction such as ADD, as expressed in binary numbers. A computer **word** consists of the number of bits that constitute a common unit of information, as defined by the computer system. The length of the word depends on the computer system. Earliest microcomputers had eight-bit word sizes, but minicomputers and some microcomputers have 16-bit words. Mainframes and some minicomputers have 32, supercomputers have 64, and some very large machines have 128-bit words. In general, the larger the word size, the more powerful the computer, because the computer can transfer more information at a time. Word-addressable design is common in large, powerful computers used for scientific calculations. Although this kind of design makes for efficient computation, it is not efficient allocation of storage.

Character-Addressable. In a **character-addressable** design, each address stores a single character. This means that an item of data or a program instruction could require several storage locations. Character-addressable storage is common in microcomputers. It is characterized by lower efficiency for calculations but higher efficiency in storage allocations.

Byte-Addressable. The third design type, **byte-addressable** storage, can store data in either manner—by character or by word—according to instructions written in the computer program. There are two versions of byte-addressable storage. A *fixed version* design is commonly used for scientific applications; a *variable version* design is used for business applications. Byte-addressable design is most frequently used with large computers that service both scientific and business applications.

HISTORY OF THE INFORMATION AGE

From Electromechanical to Electronic Computers: Aiken to ENIAC

For over 30 years, Thomas J. Watson, Sr., one of the supersalesmen of the 20th century, ran International Business Machines Corp. (IBM) with an autocratic hand. As a result, the company that emerged as a successor to Herman Hollerith's Tabulating Machine Company (see p. 208) was highly successful at selling calculators to business.

It was only natural, then, that a young Harvard associate professor of mathematics, Howard H. Aiken, after reading Charles Babbage and Ada Byron's notes and conceiving of a modern equivalent of Babbage's analytical engine, should approach Watson for research funds. The cranky head of IBM, after hearing a pitch for the commercial possibilities, thereupon gave Aiken $1 million. As a result, the Harvard Mark I was born.

Nothing like the Mark I had ever been built before. Eight feet high and 55 feet long, made of streamlined steel and glass, it emitted a sound that one person said was "like listening to a roomful of old ladies knitting away with steel needles." Whereas Babbage's original machine had been mechanical, the Mark I was electromechanical, using electromagnetic relays (not vacuum tubes) in combination with mechanical counters. Unveiled in 1944, the Mark I had enormous publicity value for IBM, but it was never really efficient. The invention of a truly *electronic* computer came from other quarters.

Who is the true inventor of the electronic computer? In 1974, a federal court determined, as a result of patent litigation, that Dr. John V. Atanasoff was the originator of the ideas required to make an electronic digital computer actually work. However, some computer historians dispute this court decision, attributing that designation to Dr. John Mauchly. The background is as follows.

In the late 1930s, Atanasoff, a professor of physics at what is now Iowa State University, spent time trying to build an electronic calculating device to help his students solve complicated mathematical problems. One night, while sitting in an Illinois roadside tavern, after having driven 189 miles to clear his thoughts, the idea came to him for linking the computer memory and associated logic. With the help of a graduate student, Clifford Berry, and using vacuum tubes,

Howard Aiken. The inventor of the Mark I is shown at left.

Thomas J. Watson, Sr. The "Old Man" of IBM, he gave Aiken the funds with which to develop the Mark I.

The Mark I. This magnificent-looking and—for the times—streamlined machine was the first electromechanical computer. It may be seen in the Smithsonian in Washington, D.C.

John V. Atanasoff. As a young man, he and Clifford Berry developed the components of the first electronic digital computer.

The ABC. The Atanasoff-Berry Computer.

he built the first digital computer that worked electronically. The computer was called the ABC, for "Atanasoff-Berry Computer."

During the years of 1940–41, Atanasoff met with Mauchly, who was then a professor with the Moore School of Electrical Engineering at the University of Pennsylvania. Mauchly had been interested in building his own computer and there is a good deal of dispute as to how much of Atanasoff and Berry's ideas he might have utilized. In any case, in 1942 Mauchly and his assistant, J. Presper Eckert, had been asked by American military officials to build a machine that would rapidly calculate trajectories for artillery and missiles. The machine they proposed, which would cut the time needed to produce trajectories from 15 minutes to 30 seconds, would employ 18,000 vacuum tubes—and all of them would have to operate simultaneously.

This machine, called ENIAC—for Electronic Numerical Integrator and Calculator—was worked on 24 hours a day for 30 months and was finally turned on in February 1946, too late to aid in the war effort, of course. A massive machine that filled an entire room, it was able to multiply a pair of numbers in about 3 milliseconds, which made it 300 times faster than any other machine.

There were a number of drawbacks to ENIAC—including serious cooling problems because of the heat generated by all the tubes and, more importantly, ridiculously small storage capacity. Worst of all, the system was quite inflexible. Each time a program was changed, the machine had to be rewired. This last obstacle was overcome by the Hungarian-born mathematical genius Dr. John von Neumann.

The holder of degrees in chemistry and physics, a great storyteller, and a man with total recall, von Neumann was a member of the Institute for Advanced Study in Princeton, New Jersey. One day in 1945, while waiting for a train in Aberdeen, Maryland, a member of the ENIAC devel-

John von Neumann. The Hungarian-born mathematical genius who helped originate the stored program concept.

The ENIAC. Co-inventors J. Presper Eckert, Jr. (*left*) and John W. Mauchly (*center*) are shown with the first fully working electronic computer. The ENIAC occupied 1500 square feet of space.

opment team, Herman Goldstine, ran into von Neumann, who was then involved in the top-secret work of designing nuclear weapons. Since both men had security clearances, they were able to discuss each other's work, and von Neumann began to realize that the difficulties he was having in the time-consuming checking of his advanced equations could be solved by the high speeds of ENIAC. As a result of that chance meeting, von Neumann joined the ENIAC team as a special consultant.

When the Army requested a more powerful computer than ENIAC, von Neumann responded by proposing the EDVAC (for Electronic Discrete Variable Automatic Computer), which would utilize the stored program concept. That is, instead of people having to rewire the machine to go to a different program, the machine would, in less than a second, "read" instructions from computer storage for switching to a new program. Von Neumann also proposed that the computer use the binary numbering system (the ENIAC worked on the decimal system), to take advantage of the two-state conditions of electronics ("on" and "off" to correspond to 1 and 0).

Mauchly and Eckert and others at the Moore School of Electrical Engineering set out to build the EDVAC, but the first computer using the stored program concept was actually the EDSAC, built in 1949 at Cambridge University in England. One reason that EDVAC was delayed was that Eckert and Mauchly founded their own company in 1946 to build what would ultimately be called the UNIVAC computer.

Next history installment: **From UNIVAC to AT&T**, p. 354.

The Upward Curve of Storage Technology

As we shall see, we stand on the verge of some technological breakthroughs in storage technology. But the machines with which you will no doubt be working in the next couple of years will not use "state-of-the-art" technology, and so we should discuss the present kinds of storage first. The most common storage devices today use two forms of technology:

- Magnetic core
- Semiconductor

We will describe these and then consider three possible future technologies:

- Bubble memory devices
- Josephson junction technology
- Biochips

Magnetic Core Storage

A technology that is fading away but is still present in many of today's mainframe computers—including some still in production—**magnetic core storage** consists of pinhead-sized rings strung like beads on intersecting wires, as shown in Figure 8-4. Electricity runs through the wires and magnetizes the cores to represent bits. Many cores are strung together, creating a screen 6 by 11 inches called a core plane; such planes are stacked one above the other to create the computer memory.

The biggest advantage of magnetic core memory is that it is **non-volatile.** That is, the magnetized cores will retain their charge even when the power supply to the computer is shut off. Magnetic core storage is also fairly fast and safe. However, as the cost of other forms of storage, such as semiconductor, goes down, magnetic core storage becomes less attractive.

Semiconductor Storage

Semiconductors—also known as **integrated circuits** and **silicon chips**—are complete electronic circuits made out of silicon, the second most common element in the earth's crust. The chip may be less than one-eighth inch square and have hundreds of electronic components on it. Although semiconductors have the disadvantage of losing data once the power to them is turned off—they are **volatile**—they have spectacular advantages:

- **They are small.** A semiconductor is half the size of your thumbnail, yet contains the power of an old room-sized ENIAC computer and can hold a thousand times more data than a single magnetic core. Despite the size of a microcomputer, if you open it up you will find

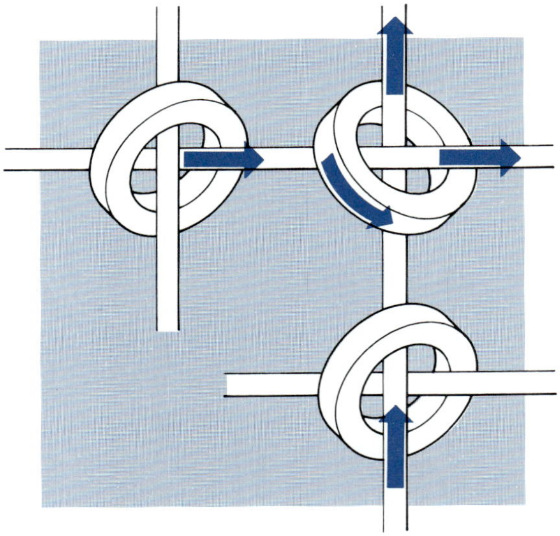

Figure8-4. Magnetic core memory. *Left:* A Woman holds up a magnetic core memory, which measures 6 by 11 inches. Such magnetic core memories are now being supplanted by quarter-inch-square silicon chips, shown being held by tweezers. *Above:* Magnetic cores, each a few hundredths of an inch in diameter, are mounted on wires. When electricity is passed through the wire on which a core is strung, it can be magnetized as "on" to represent 1 or "off" to represent 0 in the binary system.

there is only a single chip for a CPU, and you will have to look hard to find it, it being less than one-half inch square. Nevertheless, a 64K chip, which is very common, can store 65,536 bytes or characters of data.

- **They are economical.** Because of mass production methods, a semiconductor can be bought for a few dollars—an incredible buy, considering its power. They also have extremely low power requirements.
- **They are reliable.** Producers put them through a rigorous "burning in"—testing—so that chips rarely fail, perhaps once in 33 million hours of operation.

An example of a 512K chip is shown in Figure 8-5. Several different sized chips are available. IBM has designed a chip that can store one megabit—a little more than one million bits, or the equivalent of 100 pages of double-spaced typed text.

research i
nd fas
nsf
t future, w

Figure 8-5 A 512K chip. This is magnified several times. One such chip, half the size of a thumbnail, may power the calculations in a microcomputer.

RAM and ROM, PROM and EPROM

There are several different types of chips, which are referred to by their initials: RAM, ROM, PROM, EPROM. These represent different types of semiconductor storage.

RAM. Standing for **random-access memory**, the letters **RAM** are very common in conversations about microcomputers. RAM refers to storage in which data and programs not only can be obtained from primary storage but also can be put into it. When you hear of a 64K RAM microcomputer, then, it means that you can put 65,536 bytes or characters of data and programs into it.

ROM. An abbreviation for **read-only memory**—the word "read" means you can retrieve data—**ROM** describes chips in which programs are built into the primary storage at the factory and cannot be changed by you, the user. You can read them, but not alter them. You find this particularly, for instance, in calculators that have a square-root function. ROMs are often also called **firmware** because they contain programs that are "firm"—they cannot be altered.

PROM. Short for **programmable read-only memory, PROM** chips are another kind of firmware which can be programmed once and only once. They are like ROM in that the contents cannot be altered. They are custom-made by the manufacturer to meet particular customer needs and have the advantage of being able to operate faster than typical application programs written in a high-level language.

EPROM. EPROM chips are simply erasable PROM firmware; **EPROM** stands for **erasable, programmable read-only memory.** The erasure requires a special process involving ultraviolet light, making accidental erasing unlikely.

More Bang for the Byte: Increasing CPU Efficiency

Computer efficiency has been increased by improvements in the way data is moved, both within the CPU and to and from it. This has been accomplished in three ways:

- Registers
- Control units
- Channels

Registers. The CPU has primary storage, of course, but it also has some special-purpose storage devices called registers. **Registers** act as temporary holding locations for instructions and data, but they are not part of primary storage. There are different types of registers, among them:

- An **accumulator,** located in the ALU, which holds accumulated data.
- A **storage register,** which holds data that is to be sent to or taken from primary storage and which is also in the ALU.
- An **instruction register,** which is located in the controller and which is used to decode instructions.
- An **address register,** also located in the controller, which holds the address of a location containing data called for by an instruction.
- A **general register,** which has varied uses such as for arithmetic and addressing.

Not all computers have registers, but most do, though perhaps not all those listed above. The main advantage of registers, as we mentioned, is speed. They can operate very quickly in manipulating instructions or data or in performing computations, as directed by the CPU.

Control Units. The control units we are talking about are not the same as the controller in the CPU. They are located as part of an input or output device or are located between the CPU and such devices. The purpose of **control units** is to reduce the CPU time spent waiting to receive input data or output information. The device is important because the typical CPU operates ten times faster than its accompanying input and output devices. A control unit enhances the efficiency of the CPU by supplying a temporary storage or **buffer** area for data waiting to be input to the CPU or information awaiting output. The control unit gathers data from an input device and sends it to the CPU at speeds much faster than the input devices. It outputs information the same way. Control units are typically part of an input terminal where input is done a character at a time. A buffer collects the data one character at a time until it reaches capacity, then, as soon as the CPU is ready for the data, empties its contents at a rapid rate.

Channels. Also designed to reduce CPU time waiting for inputting of data and outputting of information, **channels** may be part of the CPU or outside it as a small, separate computer located near the CPU. Channels are of two types, selector and multiplexor. A **selector** services only one input or output device; a **multiplexor** services several. Selectors are used with high-speed devices such as tape drives and disk drives; multiplexors are used with lower-speed devices, such as terminals.

In Memory of the Future

Is there any point in having *more* powerful CPUs when we already have such powerful supercomputers? Indeed there is: information technologies are what advanced countries have to sell, and there is worldwide competition not just among companies but among entire nations. The Japanese are well aware of this, as are many European countries. As we will see in the last chapter of this book, the fields of artificial intelligence and expert systems require more computer power.

Computer and semiconductor makers have been exploring new ways of making speedier processors with new technologies, among them bubble memories and Josephson junctions. Some companies are also scrambling to develop a new approach to building computers known as parallel processing (see box, p. 288). And a number of scientists are inquiring into the possibility of building so-called "biochips," using genetic engineering to replace today's inorganic silicon chips with computers made of organic materials.

Bubble Memories. A **magnetic bubble memory** (see Figure 8-6) uses magnetic "bubbles" or spots on a thin layer of magnetic film. When a uniform magnetic field is applied, the bubble forms. The absence of a bubble represents a 0, its presence a 1, which provides the binary basis for representing data. The advantage of the bubble memory is that it has much more capacity than present semiconductors and also is nonvolatile, so that it retains data even when the current is turned off.

Although bubble memory was first introduced by Bell Laboratories

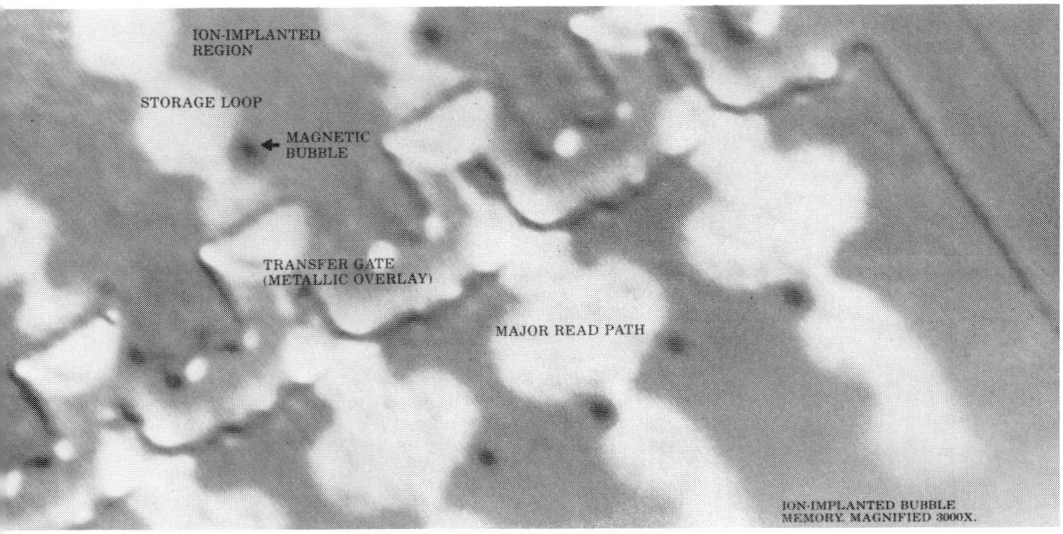
ION-IMPLANTED
REGION
STORAGE LOOP
MAGNETIC
BUBBLE
TRANSFER GATE
(METALLIC OVERLAY)
MAJOR READ PATH
ION-IMPLANTED BUBBLE
MEMORY. MAGNIFIED 3000X.

Figure 8-6 Magnetic bubble memory. This part of a bubble memory chip is magnified 3000 times. Individual bubbles are visible as dark dots.

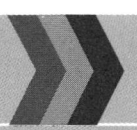

Reinventing the Computer

A wave of technological change is poised to sweep over the computer industry. Faster and cheaper computers will allow users to do things they can't today—operate a typewriter by voice, for example. Companies and nations alike will face the opportunities and dangers that always accompany a major innovation. The stakes are high: the new technology will affect all information-age businesses, ranging from electronic mail networks to computer manufacturing. . . .

The transformation will be based on one fundamental idea: that the way to speed up computers is to divide the labor among many inexpensive data-processing devices rather than continue the present quest for ever faster single processors made with ever more exotic materials and techniques. Called parallel processing, the new approach is analogous to mass-producing shoes with unskilled labor on assembly lines instead of handcrafting them with skilled workmen. . . .

Today's supercomputers are too slow for many potential tasks. Some jobs now take weeks or months—for example, simulating the airflow around an entire airplane in flight. Users have identified additional applications that would take hundreds or thousands of times longer; one would create a minutely detailed three-dimensional model of a fusion reactor's interior at work.

Unfortunately, performing these tasks will be impractical as long as computer makers stick with the present dominant design—the "von Neumann architecture," named for the Hungarian-American genius John von Neumann, who helped develop it near the end of World War II. In the von Neumann approach a single main processing unit calls forth programmed instructions and data from memory in sequence, manipulates the data as instructed, and either returns the results to memory or performs other operations (see illustrations). With only one processor at work, the pace of computation is set by the speed of the processor's electronic circuits. . . .

A formidable barrier is what IBM's eminent computer scientist John Backus . . . has identified as the "von Neumann bottleneck." That is the single channel along which data and instructions must flow between a conventional com-

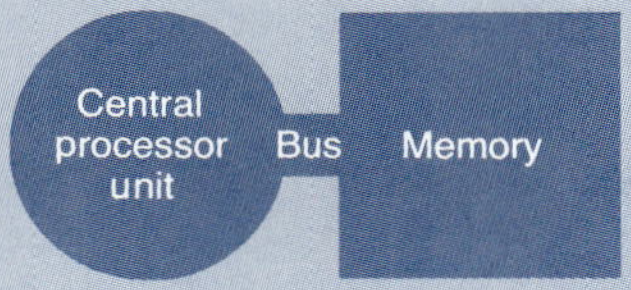
Central processor unit
Bus
Memory

Oldest: The ultimate coarse-grained architecture is the von Neumann machine, with one main processor and memory bank. Instructions from the processor and data from memory flow back and forth through the bus, which limits processing speed.

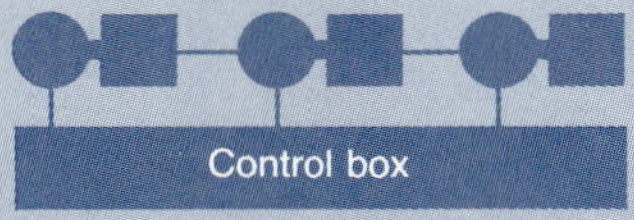
Control box

Newer: Intermediate-grain computer architectures have few powerful processor-memory units under the control of a central computer (the control box). Each processor can work alone on a job or with other processors.

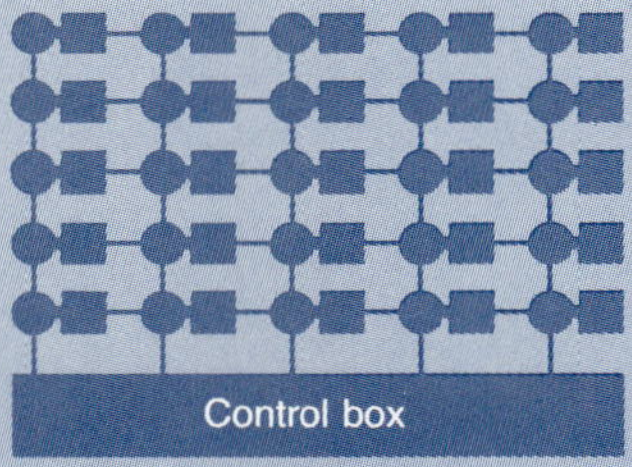
Control box

Newest: Fine-grained architectures use many processors. The latticelike arrangement resembles that of the Connection Machine under development at Thinking Machines Corp. Columbia University has mounted a "Non Von" project—that is, not von Neumann—and proposes an architecture with a million processors arranged in a branching, treelike structure.

puter's central processor and its memory. Like a constriction in a pipe feeding raw material to a factory, the von Neumann bottleneck can limit the pace of production.

The faster, smarter, cheaper alternative to von Neumann's architecture, many designers agree, is parallel processing. The latent advantages of parallelism have long been recognized; even von Neumann was impressed by discoveries in the 1940s about how animal brains process information in a parallel manner. Had electronic hardware not been so costly in his day, he might have designed a machine more like a brain.

That economic constraint no longer applies. A technology called VLSI (for "very large-scale integration") makes it possible to reproduce computer circuits with hundreds of thousands of transistors on a single tiny silicon chip almost as easily and cheaply as printing pages of a book. This capability affords designers a tantalizing way around the von Neumann bottleneck: put many processors on a single chip. Processors could operate simultaneously on different parts of a problem and even specialize in performing particular operations at great speed. Another type of parallelism, called active or associative memory, can immensely speed up certain computing tasks, such as retrieving information from data bases, by eliminating the role of the central processor in searching through memory. In essence, each piece of data would be stored with its own tiny processor, smart enough to respond when a centralized computer calls for that item. . . .

Some proponents of parallelism hope that it will make possible machines that learn things on their own—computers able to do jobs no programmer knows how to tell them to do.

—Tom Alexander,
Fortune, March 5, 1984

in 1966, it has never realized its earlier promises because of cost and production problems, although it is presently being used in some special applications. It may yet become a major storage technology of the future, however. Indeed, Intel has developed a bubble memory chip that stores four million bits of information.

Josephson Junctions. Named for British researcher and Nobel prize winner Brian Josephson, **Josephson junctions** consist of a device that can change bits from 0 to 1 ten times faster than any present chip. The reason for this is that the circuits are cooled to within a few degrees of absolute zero (−400 degrees Fahrenheit), so that the usual hindrances to electron flow are diminished. However, this is an expensive process, and recently IBM has scaled back its Josephson junction development.

Biochips. No prototypes have yet been built, but scientists and engineers have proposed that **biochips**—organic molecules or genetically engineered proteins—could conceivably be produced. Their advantages, according to one writer, are "vastly increased densities of computing elements, and entirely new styles of data processing, suited to such high-level tasks as pattern recognition and context-dependent analysis."[3] Two types of biochips have been contemplated—*digital* biochips in which organic molecules would turn the flow of electrons on and off, like today's silicon chips, and *analog* biochips, in which protein enzymes would be capable of graded responses and so provide other forrns of computation presumably not based on a binary system of representing data. Will such biological circuitry indeed come about? There are many research steps to take, none of which have yet been taken. Stay tuned to the 21st century.

Let us now turn from hardware and the processor/memory to software and the operating system.

Operating Systems: Orchestra Conductors for Software

A lot of housekeeping goes on during the operation of a computer, housekeeping that would be a nuisance if you, the user or programmer, had to do it all yourself. What takes it out of your hands is the **operating system,** a set of programs that allows the computer system to direct its own resources and operations, much as an orchestra conductor directs an orchestra (see Figure 8-7).

Among the tasks the operating system will take care of are: coordinating the flow of data to and from the CPU and from input and output devices, assigning and recalling memory addresses, reporting on the sizes of files, preventing multiple users from getting into each other's

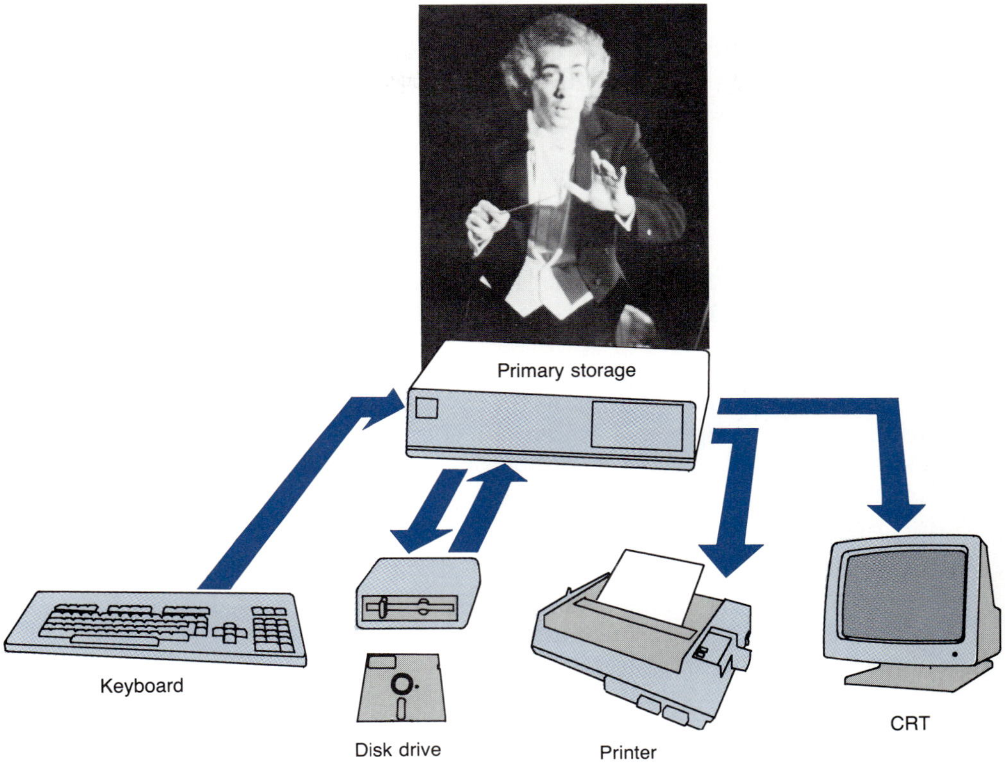
Primary storage
Keyboard
Disk drive
Printer
CRT

Figure 8-7 The operating system as orchestra conductor. A collection of programs within the computer, the operating system for a microcomputer controls the system's operations: input from the keyboard, recording of data on or retrieving of data from the disk in the disk drive, output to a CRT, or printing to a printer.

files, preventing one person from writing data into a file at the same time another person is reading data from it, and allowing one user to send a message to another.

In general, then, an operating system has three purposes:

- It controls computer system resources.
- It executes computer programs.
- It manages data.

Why is it important for a prospective business manager to know anything about something as seemingly technical as operating systems? There are some good reasons for becoming familiar with this subject—the principal one being that the kind of operating system you choose has a lot to do with the kind of computers available to you and the kinds of available software, particularly in microcomputers.

An operating system can be categorized into two types of programs, as Figure 8-8 shows:

- Control-oriented programs
- Processing-oriented programs

Control-Oriented Programs: The Uses of the Operating System

Control-oriented programs are concerned with the overall management of the computer system. The master program, known as the **supervisor program,** is located principally in primary storage (see Figure 8-8). Like an orchestra conductor, it controls the entire operating system and calls upon other operating system programs located in secondary storage when they are needed.

Among the functions of the control-oriented programs are to allow:

- Batch processing.
- Multiprogramming—scheduling of multiple jobs.
- Multiprocessing—concurrent execution of multiple programs.
- Virtual storage—storage of a very large program in both primary storage and disk storage.

Batch Processing. A major control function of the operating system is to schedule one job to follow another automatically without human intervention. The running of **jobs**—user programs—one after another is batch processing. An application programmer prepares identifiers marking the beginning and ending of each job, which are interpreted by the operating system.

Multiprogramming. In the old days, computers would read a single program into primary storage and operate on that program exclusively until it was done—a type of processing known as **serial processing.** However, because a computer's CPU operates faster than its input and output units, this meant the CPU was not being used a good deal of the time. In **multiprogramming,** more than one program is executed concurrently (see Figure 8-9). "Concurrently" is not the same as "simultaneously," because one program will be operated on by the CPU while the other is held in primary storage, then the programs are switched; however, because they are both processed during the same period of time (the same 15 minutes, for instance), the CPU is not idle and different users get their

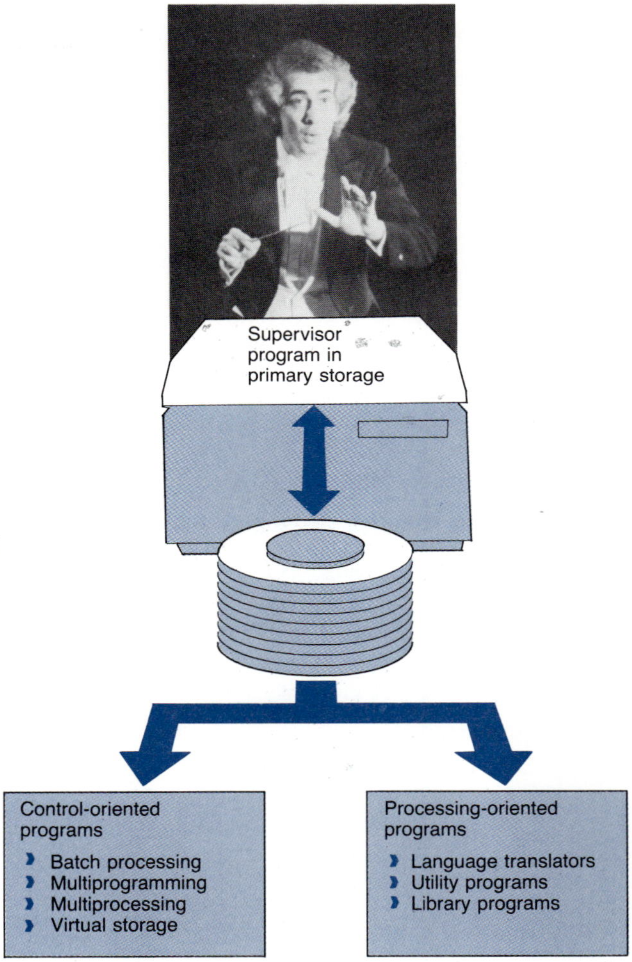
Supervisor program in primary storage
Control-oriented programs
Batch processing
Multiprogramming
Multiprocessing
Virtual storage
Processing-oriented programs
Language translators
Utility programs
Library programs

Figure 8-8 Control-oriented and processing-oriented programs. Two uses of the operating system.

programs run in ample time. Multiprogramming is often used for batch programs such as payroll, accounts receivable, financial planning, sales and marketing analyses, and quality control.

Multiprocessing. Whereas with multiprogramming only one program can be executed at any one time in the CPU, with **multiprocessing** more than one program can be executed simultaneously in computers that consist of two or more independent CPUs linked together for coordinated

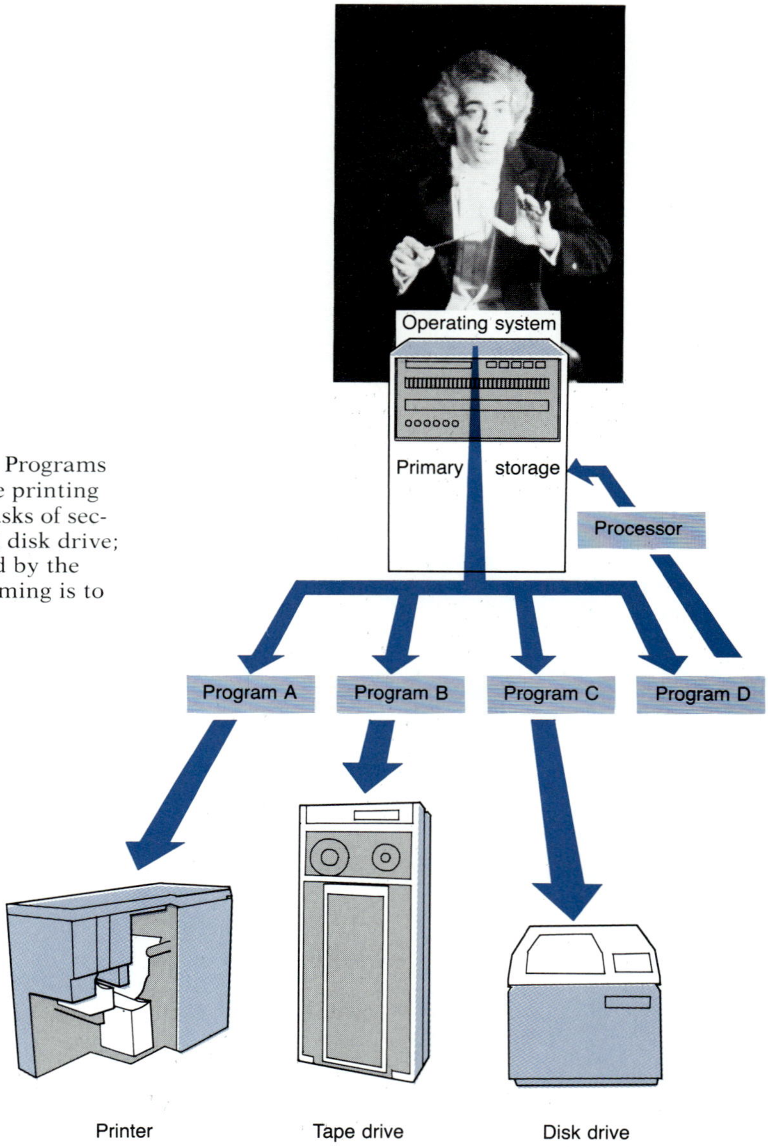
Operating system
Primary storage
Processor
Program A
Program B
Program C
Program D
Printer
Tape drive
Disk drive

Figure 8-9 Multiprogramming. Programs are executed concurrently, with one printing out while other programs handle tasks of secondary storage from tape drive and disk drive; a fourth program is being processed by the CPU. The purpose of multiprogramming is to keep the CPU from being idle.

operation. Indeed, the CPUs can work together on the same program as well as on different programs.

Because the job of scheduling and mediating the tasks of the input and output units and the independent CPUs is so complex, some multiprocessing systems combine a large CPU called the *host computer* with a small CPU called a *front-end processor*. The job of the front-end processor is to handle the tasks of inputting data from different input devices, which allows the host computer to concentrate on processing complicated applications programs.

Sometimes two large CPUs are combined to work independently on small jobs and work together on large, complex jobs.

Virtual Storage. For many years, if you were a programmer you had to limit the size of your application programs to the size that would fit into the CPU and its primary storage. If you had a very large program, you were required to break it up into smaller programs and run them one at a time. To alleviate this problem, virtual storage was developed. With **virtual storage,** you can store part of the program on a secondary storage device—specifically disk storage—and bring it into primary storage for execution as needed. Since only part of the program is in storage at any one time, the amount of primary storage needed for a program is minimal.

Virtual storage can be implemented by *paging, segmentation,* or a combination of both. **Paging** means that a program is broken up into blocks of the same size—generally 2K or 4K bytes—which fit into spaces of corresponding size in primary storage. In **segmentation,** a program is broken up into different-size blocks—which could be 30K, 20K, and 10K—which are then distributed throughout primary storage in locations not necessarily next to each other; the operating system keeps track of the locations of the segments throughout the primary storage.

Processing-Oriented Programs

Processing programs are operating system programs designed to simplify processing operations and to reduce the time and cost of program preparation. Three of the most widely used types of processing programs are (refer back to Figure 8-8):

- Language translators
- Utility programs
- Library programs

Language Translators. A program written in COBOL, BASIC, or other high-level language needs to be translated into machine language; this is the task of a **translator program.** If you are using a high-level language, the translator program is called a **compiler** or, sometimes, an **interpreter.** If you are using an assembly language, the translator is called an **assembler.**

Utility Programs. Sorting, merging, updating, and transferring of data from one input device to an output device are repetitive tasks that are easily handled by prewritten, standard programs. These programs are called **utility programs,** and they are used for converting files from one form to another (such as from tape to disk) and for sort/merge operations (such as sorting out data on files and merging it with other files).

Library Programs. Supplied by the computer manufacturer or a software firm or written by the user, **library programs** contain frequently used programs or subroutines. They are written in machine language for faster execution time.

UNIX, CP/M, and MS-DOS: Operating in Business with Operating Systems

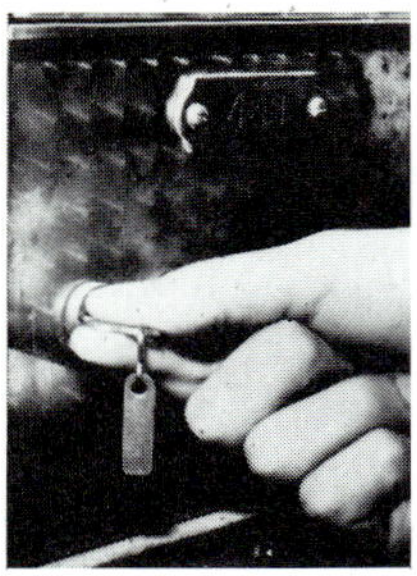

Atlantic-Pacific Bank is facing the same problems as nearly every other large corporation. What kinds of microcomputers should they buy? Should they tie into the bank's mainframes? And—since the bank wants users of microcomputers to be able to trade data and software back and forth directly—what kind of operating system should it favor?

In the old days, when a company bought or leased a computer, the operating system came with it. Unfortunately, if you bought an IBM, the chances were very good its operating system was not compatible with one that would run on a Hewlett-Packard or Honeywell or other computer. Now, however, computer users are interested in **generic operating systems**—operating systems that work with more than one manufacturer's computer system. There are several operating systems available, but let us consider three of the most popular:

- UNIX
- CP/M
- MS-DOS

As Figure 8-10 shows, in 1983, the leading business operating systems for microcomputers were CP/M and MS-DOS. These two operating systems were mainly designed for single users of 8-bit and 16-bit microcomputers. But, points out one observer, with the growing power of microcomputers, some of which are capable of running mainframe applications, and with the computer industry on the verge of creating 32-bit microcomputers, there is a good chance that UNIX may become more of an industry standard.[4]

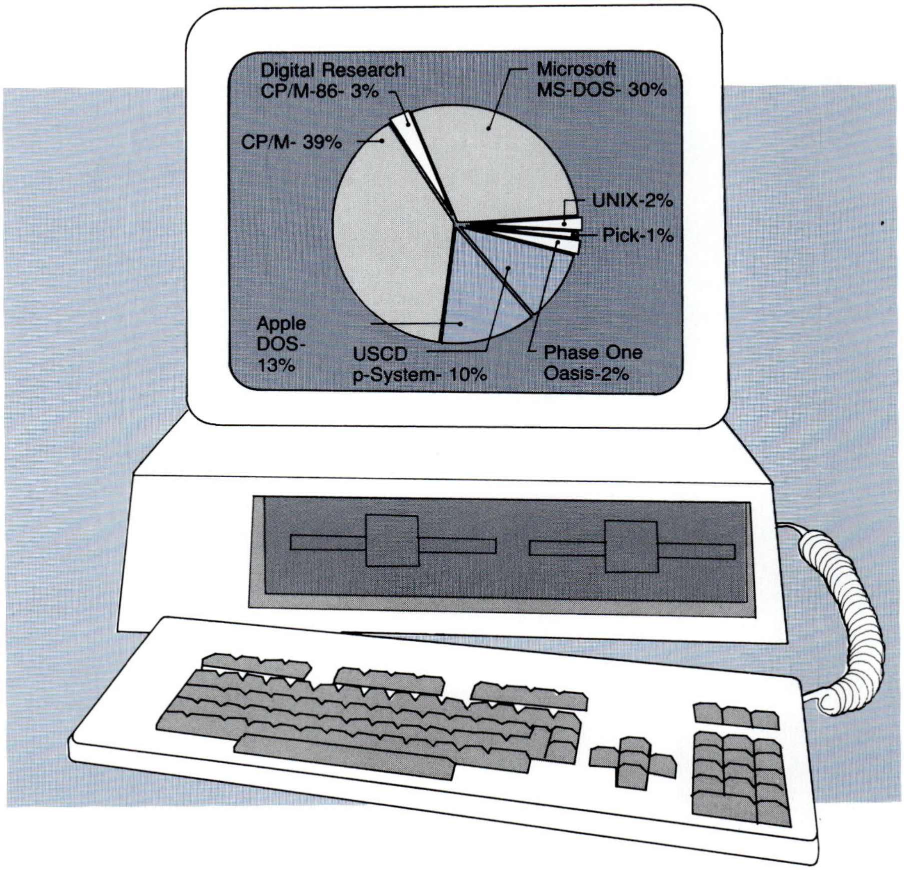
Digital Research
CP/M-86- 3%
Microsoft
MS-DOS- 30%
CP/M- 39%
UNIX-2%
Pick-1%
Apple
DOS-
13%
USCD
p-System- 10%
Phase One
Oasis-2%

Figure 8-10 Market share of operating systems. This shows the market share for 1983 of business operating systems for microcomputers.

UNIX: The AT&T Standard

Developed in 1971 by Dennis Richie and Ken Thompson of Bell Laboratories and available under license from Western Electric, **UNIX** is a very sophisticated multiprogramming, time-sharing operating system that was originally designed for minicomputers but now runs on mainframes and is being pushed for microcomputers.

UNIX has become popular principally because AT&T for many years licensed the system to universities for a nominal fee, as a result of which many computer science students became accustomed to it. As they became professional programmers they urged acceptance of UNIX in industry.

Aisle 5000
VALUE SETS US APART
codex
codex
codex
codex

What kind of computers to buy? One of the most important trade shows is the National Computer Conference, held annually. With hundreds of hardware and software products exhibited, a walk through the show can be an overpowering experience.

Although the system is not without faults, it appears likely that UNIX will become a standard for microcomputers, for the reason that 32-bit micros are expected to replace the present generation of 8- and 16-bit micros, and UNIX is probably the most popular operating system for 32-bit computers. It is noteworthy, however, that when AT&T announced its own microcomputer in summer of 1984, it did not choose to use UNIX as its operating system but rather MS-DOS and PC-DOS—the standards used by IBM.

CP/M

Written by Gary Kildall in 1973 and produced by Digital Research, Inc., of Pacific Grove, California, **CP/M** stands for Control Program/Microcomputers and was designed for 8-bit microcomputers, although there is now a version (CP/M-86) available for 16-bit micros. By virtue of its longevity, there is now a great deal of software available that will run with CP/M only. Many manufacturers—such as IBM, Apple, and Tandy-Radio Shack—offer it as an alternate operating system for their microcomputers.

MS-DOS

By a stroke of bad luck, Gary Kildall of Digital Research was away when IBM executives came calling in 1980 to discuss buying an operating system for their soon-to-be-announced IBM Personal Computer. IBM thereupon went back to the person who had recommended Kildall, a young man named William Gates of Microsoft Corp. of Bellevue, Washington. Gates and Microsoft then proceeded to help IBM create its **MS-DOS,** which stands for Microsoft Disk Operating System. With about 100 companies licensed to use it, MS-DOS has become the standard operating system for 16-bit microcomputers. Microsoft has also developed its own version of UNIX, which it calls XENIX.

Even More Storage

We have described primary storage at length in this chapter, as well as the mechanisms of the operating system that make primary storage operate at peak efficiency. However, with the enormous amounts of information that must be dealt with in the business world, it is clear that more than primary storage is needed. In the next chapter we will explore computer storage external to the CPU.

SUMMARY

- The **central processing unit (CPU)** is hardware that interprets and executes program instructions and communicates with the input, output, and external storage devices. The CPU has three parts: (1) the controller, (2) the arithmetic/logic unit, and (3) primary storage. The communications among these three units are made through a **bus.**
- The **controller,** or **control unit,** directs and coordinates the other units in carrying out program instructions. It also tells input devices when additional input is needed and notifies output devices that information is available for output. The controller does not store data but assigns and records the locations within the storage unit where data and programs are stored.
- The **arithmetic/logic unit (ALU)** calculates and compares data, based on instructions from the controller. The ALU controls the speed of calculations and thus is extremely important to computer users and computer-design engineers. The ALU performs two operations: *arithmetic operations,* which consist of the four standard mathematical calculations—addition, subtraction, multiplication, and division—and *logical operations,* which consist of the three common comparison operations—equal to (=), less than (<), and greater than (>).
- The **primary storage unit—also called memory, main storage,** or **internal storage**—holds (1) data for processing, (2) instructions for processing, and (3) processed data waiting to be output.
- Small computers may execute an instruction in less than a **millisecond** (one-thousandth of a second). Many computers can execute an instruction in **microseconds** (one-millionth of a second). Supercomputers work close to the **nanosecond** range (one-billionth of a second).
- Primary storage consists of thousands of memory locations. Each location has an *address*—a number like a post office box number. Each memory location stores only one instruction or piece of data. The controller manipulates the data and instructions by referring to the locations. The locations

always stay the same, but new data and new instructions may be placed in them—the address does not change, only the contents.

- All computers start with the notion of two states: on and off. On/off corresponds to electricity being turned on and off or a magnetic field being positive or negative. These two states are represented by the **binary system** of numbers, which uses only the digits 0 ("off") and 1 ("on"). Each 0 and 1 in the binary system is called a **bit** (*bi*nary digi*t*). Bits alone cannot represent letters, numbers, and special characters, so they are combined into groups of four to eight bits called **bytes.** Each byte represents one character of data.
- The letter *K*, the unit of capacity of primary storage, stands for **kilobyte,** which is 1024 bytes. On large computers, primary storage may be expressed as **megabytes** (millions of bytes) or even **gigabytes** (billions of bytes).
- To represent the alphabet, the decimal numbers 0 through 9, and special characters, bytes are commonly combined in three different ways (coding schemes): (1) four-bit binary coded decimal (BCD), (2) Extended Binary Coded Decimal Interchange Code (EBCDIC), and (3) American Standard Code for Information Interchange (ASCII).
- **Binary coded decimal (BCD),** popular with the first computers, is used frequently today to code numeric data. It consists of 0s and 1s grouped into units of four bits each. This code runs out of new combinations in each four-bit sequence very quickly, since there are only 16 possible combinations of 0s and 1s in each four-bit unit. Thus, it does not provide enough combinations to represent both the decimal digits and all the characters of the alphabet.
- **Extended Binary Coded Decimal Interchange Code (EBCDIC)**, developed by IBM, consists of units of eight bits each, which enable it to represent both alphabetic and numeric, as well as special characters—and the alphabetic characters in both uppercase and lowercase. The eight bits (one byte) are divided into two parts: the first four are **zone bits** and the second four are **numeric,** or **digit, bits.** The combination of zone bits with numeric bits allows for 256 possible arrangements.
- The **American Standard Code for Information Interchange (ASCII),** the second most popular code after EBCDIC, is frequently used in data communications, nearly always in microcomputers, and in several large computers. In this code, a byte consists of seven bits, allowing for 128 possible arrangements (an eight-bit version, called **ASCII-8,** has been developed).
- Computer errors are detected through the use of a **parity bit,** also called a **check bit,** which is an additional bit attached to the byte that allows the computers to tell whether a 1-bit in the byte has been lost. If a bit has been lost, the computer will signal a data error to the operator. In an *even parity* format, the extra parity bit is set to either 0 or 1 to make the number of 1s an even number. Any time a nine-bit sequence shows up in the computer as odd, the computer will display an error message. An *odd parity* format is the reverse of even parity—the parity bit is set to make the number of 1s odd.

Although it is not infallible, the parity system is very effective in detecting the majority of coding errors.

- There are three types of computer storage-capacity designs: (1) word-addressable, (2) character-addressable, and (3) byte-addressable.
- In a **word-addressable** design, each address stores a fixed number of characters called a computer **word,** which consists of the number of bits that constitute a common unit of information, as defined by the computer system. The length of the word depends on the system. In general, the larger the word size, the more powerful the computer. Word-addressable design is common in large, powerful computers used for scientific calculations. Although it makes for efficient computation, it is not efficient allocation of storage.
- In a **character-addressable** design, each address stores a single character, which means that an item of data or a program instruction could require several storage locations. Commonly used in microcomputers, this design is characterized by lower calculation efficiency but greater storage-allocation efficiency.
- In **byte-addressable** design, data can be stored in either manner—by character or by word—according to instructions written in the computer program. There are two versions of byte-addressable storage: *fixed version,* which is commonly used for scientific applications, and *variable version,* which is used for business applications. Byte-addressable design is used most frequently with large computers that service both scientific and business applications.
- The most common storage devices today use two forms of technology (1) magnetic core and (2) semiconductor.
- **Magnetic core storage,** which is becoming obsolete, consists of pinhead-sized rings strung like beads on intersecting wires with electricity running through them that magnetizes the cores to represent bits. Many cores are strung together, creating a 6-by-11-inch screen called a *core plane.* Such planes are stacked one above the other to create the computer memory. The biggest advantage of magnetic core memory is that it is **nonvolatile,** which means that the magnetized cores will retain their charge even when the computer's power supply is shut off. This form of storage is also fairly fast and safe but is becoming more expensive than other forms of storage.
- **Semiconductors**—also called **integrated circuits** and **silicon chips**—are complete electronic circuits made out of silicon. These chips are very small (several sizes are available) and have hundreds of electronic components on them. Although they are **volatile** (they will lose data when the power to them is turned off), they have some important advantages: (1) They are small—about half the size of a thumbnail—but very powerful and can hold a thousand times more data than a single magnetic core. (2) They are economical and have low power requirements. (3) They are reliable.

- There are several types of chips, representing different types of semiconductor storage: RAM, ROM, PROM, and EPROM.
- **RAM—random-access memory**—refers to storage in which data and programs can not only be obtained from primary storage but also can be put into it.
- **ROM—read-only memory**—describes chips in which programs are built into the primary storage at the factory and cannot be changed by the user; they can be "read"—meaning that data can be retrieved—but they cannot be altered. ROM is also called **firmware.**
- **PROM—programmable read-only memory**—is a kind of firmware that can be programmed only once—then the contents cannot be altered. It is custom-made by the manufacturer and can operate faster than typical programs written in a high-level language.
- **EPROM—erasable read-only memory**—is erasable PROM firmware. The erasure requires a special process involving ultraviolet light that makes accidental erasure impossible.
- **Registers** act as temporary, special-purpose holding locations for instructions and data; they are not part of primary storage. There are different types of registers: (1) **accumulators,** located in the ALU, which hold accumulated data, (2) **storage registers,** which hold data that is to be sent to or taken from primary storage, also located in the ALU, (3) **instruction registers,** which are located in the controller and which are used to decode instructions, (4) **address registers,** also located in the controller, which hold the address of a location containing data called for by an instruction, and (5) **general registers,** which have varied uses. Most computers have registers, whose main advantage is speed.
- **Control units** (not the same as the controller in the CPU) are part of an input or output device and are located between the CPU and the device. Their purpose is to increase CPU efficiency by supplying it with a temporary storage or **buffer** area for data waiting to be input or information awaiting output, thus reducing the wait time. Control units gather data from an input device and send it to the CPU much faster than the input device. They output information the same way. These units are typically part of an input terminal.
- **Channels** also reduce CPU waiting time for inputting of data and outputting of information. They may be part of the CPU or outside it. There are two types of channels: selector and multiplexor. **Selectors** service only one input or output device and are used with high-speed devices such as tape drives and disk drives; **multiplexors** service several input or output devices and are used with lower-speed devices, such as terminals.
- A **magnetic bubble memory** uses magnetic "bubbles," or spots, on a thin layer of magnetic film. When a uniform magnetic field is applied, the bubble forms. The absence of a bubble represents a 0, its presence a 1. Bubble

memory, first introduced by Bell Laboratories in 1966, has much more capacity than semiconductors and is also nonvolatile. Although it is currently being used in some special applications and may become more important in the future, cost and production problems have prevented it from realizing its earlier promises.

- **Josephson junctions,** named for British researcher Brian Josephson, consist of a device that, through the use of cooled circuits, can change bits from 0 to 1 ten times faster than any present chip. This is an expensive process whose development has been scaled back.
- Although no prototypes have been built, **biochips**—organic molecules or genetically engineered proteins—could conceivably be produced. Two types of biochips have been contemplated: *digital,* in which organic molecules would turn the flow of electrons on and off, and *analog,* in which protein enzymes would be capable of graded responses and so provide other forms of computation not based on a binary system of data representation.
- The **operating system** is the set of programs that allows the computer system to direct its own resources and operations. It (1) coordinates the flow of data to and from the CPU and from input and output devices, (2) assigns and recalls memory addresses, (3) reports on the size of the files, (4) prevents multiple users from getting into one another's files, (5) prevents one person from writing data into a file at the same time another person is reading data from it, and (6) allows one user to send a message to another. An operating system has three purposes: (1) controlling computer system resources, (2) executing computer programs, and (3) managing data. The two types of operating systems are (1) control-oriented programs and (2) processing-oriented programs.
- **Control-oriented programs** are concerned with the overall management of the computer system. The master program—also called the **supervisor program**—is located principally in primary storage. Control-oriented programs allow several functions: (1) batch processing, (2) multiprogramming, (3) multiprocessing, and (4) virtual storage.
- **Batch processing** refers to the running of **jobs**—user programs—one after another without human intervention.
- **Multiprogramming** is the opposite of **serial programming**—the old type of processing in which a computer would read a single program into primary storage and operate on that program exclusively until it was done (the CPU was not being used much of the time). In multiprogramming, more than one program is executed concurrently (not simultaneously, however). In this case, the CPU is not idle. Multiprogramming is often used for batch processing.
- In **multiprocessing** more than one program can be executed simultaneously in computers that consist of two or more independent CPUs linked together for coordinated operation. The CPUs can work together on the same program

or independently on different programs. Some complex multiprocessing units combine a large CPU called the *host computer* with a small CPU called a *front-end processor.* The front-end processor handles the tasks of inputting data from different input devices, which allows the host computer to concentrate on processing complicated applications programs.

- **Virtual storage** was developed to allow programmers to run very large programs at one time. With virtual storage, one can store part of the program on a secondary storage device (disk storage) and bring it into primary storage execution as needed. Virtual storage can be implemented by (1) **paging,** meaning that a program is broken up into same-size blocks that fit into spaces of corresponding size in primary storage, (2) **segmentation,** in which a program is broken up into different-size blocks that are distributed throughout primary storage in locations not necessarily next to each other and that are tracked by the operating system, or (3) a combination of both.
- **Processing programs** are operating system programs designed to simplify processing operations and to reduce the time and cost of program operation. The three most widely used types of processing programs are (1) language translators, (2) utility programs, and (3) library programs.
- **Language translators** are **translator programs** that translate high-level languages and assembly languages into machine language. A **compiler,** or **interpreter,** translates high-level languages; an **assembler** translates assembly language.
- **Utility programs** are prewritten, standard programs that convert files from one form to another and perform sort/merge operations. They handle many repetitive tasks such as sorting, merging, updating, and transferring of data from an input device to an output device.
- **Library programs** contain frequently used programs or subroutines; they are written in machine language for fast execution.
- **Generic operating systems** are operating systems that work with more than one manufacturer's computer system. Three of the most popular generic systems are CP/M, MS-DOS, and UNIX, the last of which is used less frequently than the first two.
- **UNIX,** developed in 1971 by Bell Laboratory researchers, is a very sophisticated multiprogramming, time-sharing operating system originally designed for minicomputers but now used with mainframes and increasingly with microcomputers. For years, AT&T licensed this system to universities.
- **CP/M,** written in 1973, stands for Control Program/Microcomputers and was designed for eight-bit microcomputers, although there is now a version for 16-bit micros. A great deal of software runs with CP/M, and many computer manufacturers offer it as an alternate operating system.
- **MS-DOS,** which stands for Microsoft Disk Operating System, was developed for IBM and has become the standard operating system for 16-bit microcomputers.

KEY TERMS

Accumulator, p. 286
Address register, p. 286
American Standard Code for Information Interchange (ASCII), p. 277
Arithmetic/logic unit, p. 270
Assembler, p. 295
Batch processing, p. 292
Binary coded decimal (BCD), p. 275
Binary system, p. 273
Biochip, p. 290
Bit, p. 275
Buffer, p. 287
Byte, p. 275
Byte-addressable, p. 279
Central processing unit (CPU), p. 268
Channel, p. 287
Character-addressable, p. 279
Check bit, p. 277
Compiler, p. 295
Controller, p. 269
Control-oriented program, p. 292
Control unit, p. 269, 286
CP/M, p. 298
Digit bits, p. 276
Erasable, programmable read-only memory (EPROM), p. 286
Extended Binary Coded Decimal Interchange Code (EBCDIC), p. 275
Firmware, p. 285
General register, p. 286
Generic operating system, p. 296
Gigabyte, p. 275
Instruction register, p. 286
Integrated circuit, p. 283
Internal storage, p. 270
Interpreter, p. 295
Josephson junction, p. 290
Kilobyte, p. 275
Language translator, p. 295
Library program, p. 296
Magnetic bubble memory, p. 287
Magnetic core storage, p. 283
Main storage, p. 270
Megabyte, p. 275
Memory, p. 270
Microsecond, p. 270
Millisecond, p. 270
MS-DOS, p. 298
Multiplexor, p. 287
Multiprocessing, p. 293
Multiprogramming, p. 292
Nanosecond, p. 270
Nonvolatile, p. 283
Numeric bit, p. 276
Operating system, p. 290
Paging, p. 295
Parity bit, p. 277
Primary storage unit, p. 270
Processing program, p. 295
Programmable read-only memory (PROM), p. 286
Random-access memory (RAM), p. 285
Read-only memory (ROM), p. 285
Register, p. 286
Segmentation, p. 295
Selector, p. 287
Semiconductor, p. 283
Silicon chip, p. 283
Storage register, p. 286
Supervisor program, p. 292
Translator program, p. 295
Virtual storage, p. 295
UNIX, p. 297
Utility program, p. 296
Volatile, p. 283
Word-addressable, p. 278
Zone bit, p. 276

REVIEW QUESTIONS

1. Name the three components of the CPU and describe their functions.
2. How is data stored within primary storage?
3. What does the letter *K* represent?
4. What are the three principal computer codes?
5. How does the parity bit work?
6. Describe the types of storage designs.
7. Describe one of the technologies available to increase CPU efficiency.
8. What is bubble memory? What are Josephson junctions?
9. What are the three purposes of an operating system?
10. What is a generic operating system?

CASE PROBLEMS

Case 8-1: Multiuser Computer Systems and the Microcomputer

As we have seen, microcomputers put processing power on millions of desks. But, as the *Wall Street Journal* (August 6, 1984) has reported, some companies have stopped buying microcomputers and are now buying multiuser systems. A multiuser system consists of "a powerful microcomputer connected to several terminals and a hard disk, which stores the company's data. This way, several workers can use the same computer, sharing information on the disks without having to copy it separately for each computer."[5]

Many small businesses find a multiuser system less expensive and more useful than a collection of unconnected microcomputers. Multiuser computers were available during the 1970s, but their cost was relatively high (more than $30,000) and they required customized software. Now systems are available for under $10,000. On the other hand, as the *Journal* points out, too many people using a multiuser system may slow it down, users worry that their private files may be read by others, a system breakdown will idle several users (not just one), and large companies can use a mainframe or minicomputer to link various employees.

Your assignment: Suppose you are working for a real estate management company that must keep track of hundreds of tenants in several large apartment buildings. You have some peak-load periods, such as the beginning of every month, when rents are due. You also have to keep track of security deposits, expenses for repairs, salaries for building managers and gardeners, and payments to banks for building mortgages. You presently have a staff of six who need to use computers, but the business is growing. You could buy each person a personal computer with hard disk for about $5000 each. You could buy a multiuser system for a $7000 base price for one person, plus $1200 for each additional terminal. You could buy a $50,000 minicomputer, with $20,000 worth of software, which would keep pace with a growing business. What kind of system should you get?

Case 8-2: Choosing Operating Systems—E Pluribus UNIX?

There are presently only 700 applications programs to run with UNIX System V, the latest UNIX operating system, announced by AT&T in February 1984. This compares with an estimated 10,000 applications programs available to run on CP/M and more than 5000 for Tandy-Radio Shack's TRS DOS operating system.

Users choosing an operating system frequently consider only applications and costs, but there is more to it than that. More and more, it is important that systems integrate with each other. As one writer puts it, "Word processors must be compatible with photocomposers; microcomputers need to exchange information with minicomputers, mainframes and other microcomputers; many unlike systems will send messages to each other through electronic mail networks; computers, word processors and other information products may share common facilities, such as electronic filing, laser printing or communications processors."[6]

If at present there is a lack of applications software based on UNIX, says Rick Cook in *CAP* (September 1984), that which does exist is more usable than that for CP/M and TRS DOS, especially for business applications.[7] Moreover, AT&T is counting on UNIX gaining wide acceptance because it can handle multiple tasks simultaneously and run on machines ranging from personal computers to mainframes.

Your assignment: The next generation of microcomputers, says one software market researcher in *Business Week* (April 16, 1984), "will run multiple operating systems, with no single one grabbing a stranglehold like MS/DOS [operating system for the IBM PC] had throughout 1982 and 1983."[8] Let us suppose, however, that you are running a construction company that handles several construction jobs for the military, and you are having to use an outside computer firm to meet government requirements. You could make considerable immediate savings if you brought the government-required computing activities in-house, but the programs you want only run with CP/M at present. You also want to be able to do all those other activities mentioned previously for which UNIX is best suited. What should you do?

CHAPTER 9

Storage and File Organization

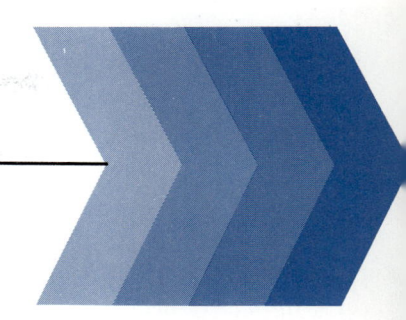

Facts at Your Fingertips

PREVIEW

Empty out your wallet, desk, and safe deposit box, if any. How many personal paper documents do you have in your possession? About 40?

This may not sound like much. But if you consider that is the number for each man, woman, and child in the United States, it works out to 887 billion paper documents stored in various personal, business, and archival files—the number estimated by Strategic, Inc., a San Jose, California, research firm.

The soaring cost of managing paper documents is obviously one of the reasons for going electronic—for storing files in a computer system. Indeed, says Strategic, Inc., although microcomputers tend not to employ major innovations in storage technology, they are having a profound effect on data storage, for they are allowing relatively inexperienced computer users to set up their own electronic files, often replacing paper filing systems.[1]

The storage capability of microcomputers is creating a revolution on the personal and professional level. A new type of storage technology, videodisc, is the vision of the future, as the case study shows.

Secondary Storage: The Electronic Library

Figure 9-1 shows the four basic hardware components of a microcomputer system—input, CPU, output, and secondary storage. The first three could convert data into machine-readable form, process it, and output information in people-readable form, and do it all

CASE STUDY: THE STORAGE REVOLUTION

New Look in Videodiscs

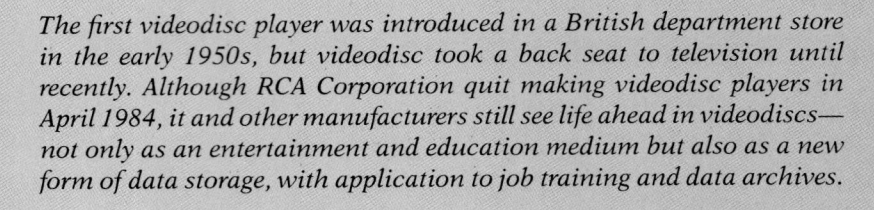

The first videodisc player was introduced in a British department store in the early 1950s, but videodisc took a back seat to television until recently. Although RCA Corporation quit making videodisc players in April 1984, it and other manufacturers still see life ahead in videodiscs—not only as an entertainment and education medium but also as a new form of data storage, with application to job training and data archives.

Because the videodisc offers frame-by-frmae advance, some corporations feel it's the ideal medium for technical training. Westinghouse Corporation has designed an interactive system (using Pioneer players and Apple II computers) to teach the basics of aircraft maintenance. Some frames have no text whatsoever (for example, a picture of what tools are needed to perform a certain task). . .

Using the same hardware as Westinghouse does, Caterpillar Tractor Company of East Peoria, Illinois, is preparing videodiscs to teach its employees how to maintain the company's awesome earth-moving machinery. In the old days, Caterpillar's training material was assembled from print, photographs, and videotape. "The videodisc is a really effective blend of those three media," says Clint Moewe, a Caterpillar development engineer. "And unlike videotape, the optical discs just never wear out." . . .

The optical-encoded videodisc has been a godsend for organizations that need to catalog vast amounts of data or visual material. The microfilm era has ended rather abruptly for many museums, art galleries, laboratories, and government agencies because, as one New York City curator notes, "every painting in New York's Metropolitan Museum can be cataloged on a single optical disc." . . .

"The videodisc industry will really blossom when producers start mass-marketing database discs," says Mark Heyer, Sony's manager of interactive products. "This might turn out to be the biggest market of all."

Officials at the Lister Hill Center in Bethesda, Maryland, would certainly concur with Heyer. For many years the center produced and distributed sets of medical indexes that were three to four feet thick. Today it stores this information in digital form on a videodisc master that can be used to make thousands of copies for subscribers.

—Jane Wollman,
Popular Computing, April 1983

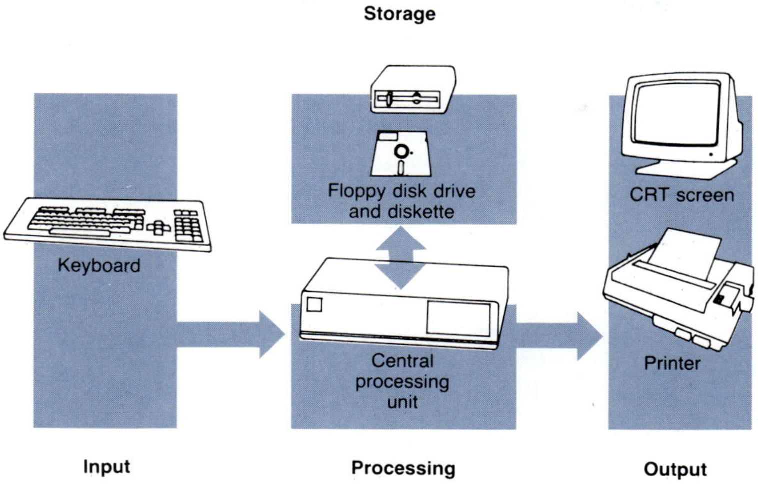
Storage
Floppy disk drive and diskette
CRT screen
Keyboard
Central processing unit
Printer
Input
Processing
Output

Figure 9-1 The four hardware components of a computer system. Although the system needs only input, CPU, and output in order to operate, the fourth component—secondary storage—is the one that expands its usefulness, particularly for business people, who must sort through numerous files.

without the fourth component, secondary storage. However, as you can quickly appreciate if you have used a personal computer, this very much limits what you can do. Indeed, for business uses, secondary storage is indispensable. Until the technology is drastically changed, it seems unlikely that a computer could be built that was large enough to hold all the customer records of Atlantic-Pacific Bank, say, inside the computer itself.

The Advantages of Secondary Storage

Although primary storage can process data faster, secondary storage has a number of advantages:

- **Economy:** It is more economical to store data on magnetic media than in a filing cabinet or most certainly in primary storage.
- **Capacity:** There is much more capacity in secondary storage than in primary storage—indeed, "off-line" storage is practically unlimited.
- **Security:** Data is usually stored in secondary storage so that it is safe from tampering by unauthorized people or from natural hazards and degradation.

As we have seen, primary storage, also known as **internal storage,** is the storage within the CPU. **Secondary storage**—also called **external**

storage or **auxiliary storage**—consists of storage outside the computer itself. There are two types of secondary storage: *direct access* and *sequential access*.

These three alternative forms of storage may be arranged in a hierarchy, with faster speed of access at the top and larger capacity at the bottom, as follows:

- **Primary storage:** This storage within the CPU is the fastest in terms of the computer accessing stored data; however, the capacity for storing data is the most limited. The cost per unit of data stored is also the most expensive of the three categories.
- **Direct access storage:** This form of secondary storage is slower than primary storage but faster than sequential access storage, as we shall explain. However, it is also more expensive than sequential access storage.
- **Sequential access storage:** The bottom of the hierarchy, this form of secondary storage is quite slow, but it has unlimited capacity and is the least expensive.

We have described primary storage in Chapter 8. Let us now consider the two types of secondary storage—direct access and sequential access.

Direct Access Storage

Direct access storage requires an input device that is directly connected to the CPU; that is, it is said to be **on-line,** making the stored data available to the CPU at all times. Such devices are called **direct access storage devices (DASDs).**

An example of direct access media is a magnetic disk, like the diskettes used with a personal computer. With a disk, as we will explain, it is far easier to go directly to the file you want. It is as though you move the record arm on your stereo directly to the song on the LP record you want to play instead of having to listen to all the songs preceding the one you really want to hear. As mentioned, direct access storage is less expensive and has greater capacity than primary storage; however, it is not nearly as fast.

Sequential Access Storage

Sequential access storage is **off-line;** the data in this kind of storage is not accessible to the CPU until it has been manually loaded onto an input device. An example of sequential access media is a reel of tape: records are stored in sequence—alphabetically, say—one after the other. A stack of punched cards is another example of sequential media.

A reel of tape can hold a great deal of data, perfect for many purposes of a bank. The problem, however, is that if you are looking for a customer name far into the alphabet—O'Leary or Williams, say—you have to run the tape past all the earlier files first, a relatively slow process.

Being outside the CPU and not directly connected to it, sequential access storage is much slower than either primary storage or direct access storage. However, it has much greater—indeed, unlimited—capacity and is considered to be more secure because it is stored off-line and not directly accessible to anyone who has gained access to a computer's CPU.

The two forms of secondary storage are described in more detail below. In general, direct access uses magnetic disk and sequential access uses magnetic tape.

Sequential Access Storage: The Uses of Magnetic Tape

As mentioned, in sequential processing, files of data are stored one after the other and access to the files is the same way—one after the other, starting with the first file and examining all successive ones until you find the right one.

The two principal sequential access storage devices are magnetic tape devices and magnetic disk devices; we will concentrate on the first one here.

Magnetic Tape Devices

The most common medium for sequential access storage, **magnetic tape**, consists of plastic tape of the sort you see on reel-to-reel stereo tape recorders. Indeed, a pitch made by some home computer companies is that you can save money on your computer system by using an audio tape recorder, if you already have one, as a storage device; a special cable connection is required. Such cassette tapes are usually 200 feet long and can record 200 characters to the inch.

The reels used with minicomputers and mainframes, on the other hand, take tape that is a half inch wide, nearly half a mile long (2400 feet), and capable of storing 1600 characters to the inch. This book could be stored on only the first 25 feet of one of these tapes. The devices on which such tapes are run are called **magnetic tape drives** or **magnetic tape units** (see Figure 9-2). Often about the size and shape of a refrigerator, these machines consist of two reels—a **supply reel** and a **take-up reel,** as shown in the illustration—along with a read/write head and an erase head. In computer parlance, **read** means to retrieve data from, **write** means to record data on. (Read is like playing a tape recorder, write is like recording on it.) The **read/write head,** then, is an electromagnet that *reads* magnetized areas on the tape (which represent data), converts them into electrical signals, and sends them to the CPU. It *writes*—that is, records—data on the tape from the CPU. If there is previous data on the tape, it also erases that data, using the **erase head,** as it writes the new data.

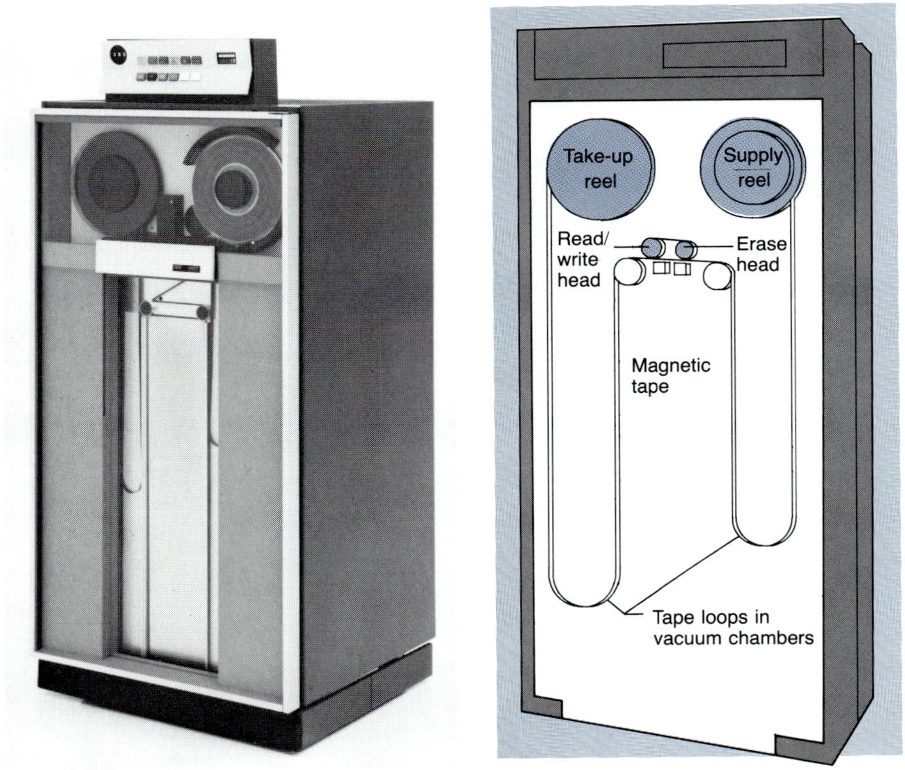
Take-up reel
Supply reel
Read/ write head
Erase head
Magnetic tape
Tape loops in vacuum chambers

Figure 9-2 Magnetic tape storage. *Top*: A magnetic tape drive, with parts labeled. Tapes are always protected by glass from outside dust and dirt. *Bottom*: Magnetic tape reel and tape, with read/write head. There may be up to 2400 feet of tape on a reel of this size. Electrical current passes in one direction to read data, in the other direction to write it.

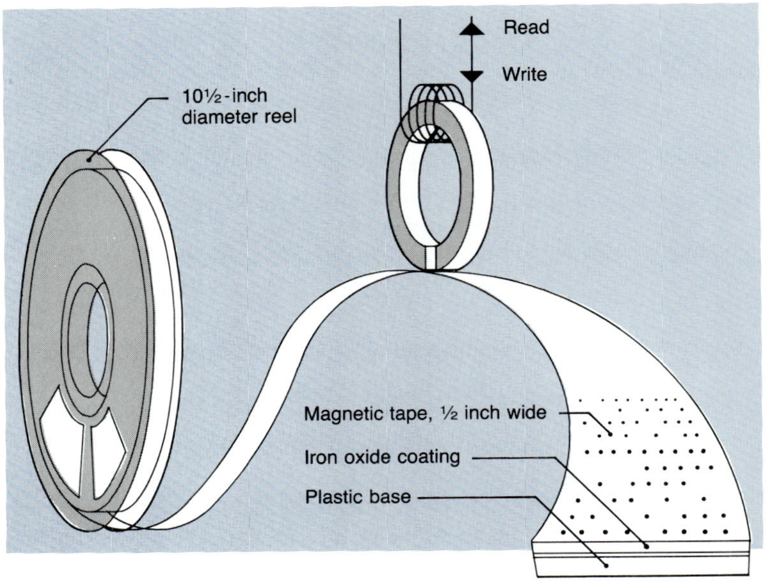
Read
Write
10½-inch diameter reel
Magnetic tape, ½ inch wide
Iron oxide coating
Plastic base

What Do You Call Data?

Until now we have been using the terms of raw data, such as "characters," "records," and "files," somewhat loosely. It is time now for some definitions:

- A **character** is a letter, number, or special character (such as $ or #).
- A **field,** which is made up of one or more related characters, contains an item of data. For example, an Atlantic-Pacific Bank customer would have a name field, a street address field, a city field, a state field, a zip code field, and an account number field.
- A **record** is a collection of related fields. Thus, one bank customer's name, address, city, state, zip code, and account number would make up a record.
- A **file** is a collection of related records. Thus, all the data about customers on the Christmas Savings Plan list would be a file.
- A **data base** is a collection of interrelated data, a systematic or structured organization of files available for central access and retrieval. A data base allows specific data items to be retrieved for specific applications—for instance, all bank customers living in a particular zip code area for notification that an automatic teller machine has just been installed in the branch bank in their neighborhood.

The terms field and record are illustrated in Figure 9-3. We will describe data base, which is a fairly complex concept, in Chapter 13.

Figure 9-3 How data is organized. Whether on a reel of tape (as shown here) or a magnetic disk, data is organized into characters, fields, records, and files. A *character* is an individual letter, member, or special character; a *file* is a group of related records.

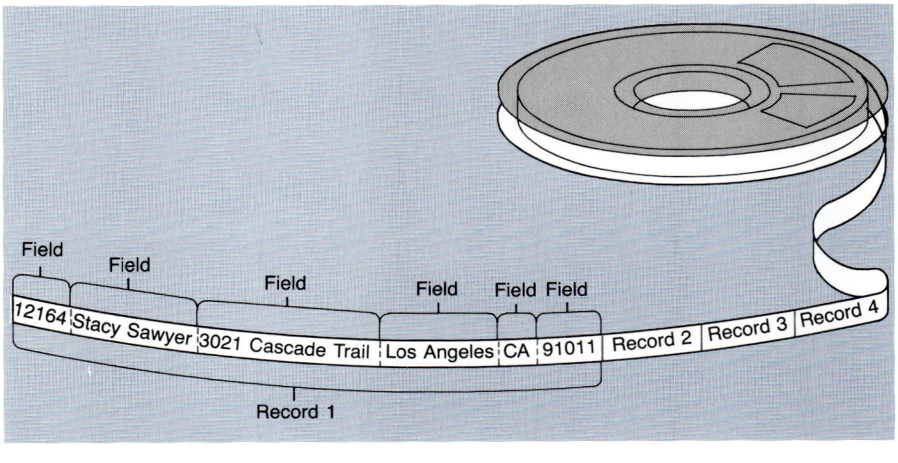
Field
Field
Field
Field
Field
Field
12164
Stacy Sawyer
3021 Cascade Trail
Los Angeles
CA
91011
Record 2
Record 3
Record 4
Record 1

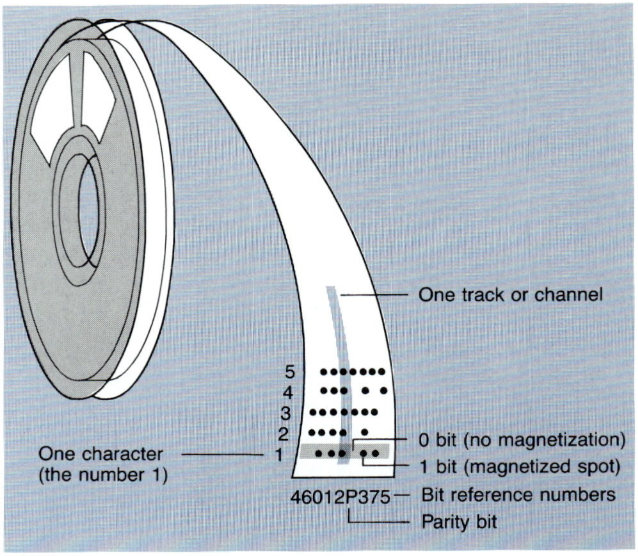
One track or channel
5
4
3
2
1
One character
(the number 1)
0 bit (no magnetization)
1 bit (magnetized spot)
46012P375
Bit reference numbers
Parity bit

Figure 9-4 How data is represented on magnetic tape. This shows how the numbers 1 through 9 are represented in EBCDIC code, using a combination of 1-bits (magnetized spots) and 0-bits (no magnetization). The parity bit—shown here near the middle of the tape, which is where it usually appears—is used to represent an odd parity system. If a 1-bit were missing, the parity bit system would signal the computer that the parity was even—and that something was wrong. (Incidentally, if you look in the EBCDIC table in Figure 8-2, you will see that the number 1 is represented as 1111 0001. However, the bits do not appear in that order on the tape here—they are in the order indicated by the bit reference numbers: 0, 1, 2, 3, 4, 5, 6, 7. The letter *P* stands for parity bit.)

How Data Is Represented on Tape

As mentioned, data is represented on tape by invisible magnetized spots, the presence or absence of a spot corresponding to a 1-bit or a 0-bit. Perhaps the most common way of organizing data, as Figure 9-4 shows, is a nine-track code. That is, the tape is divided into nine tracks or channels that run the length of the tape. Each row across the nine tracks represents a single EBCDIC character plus a parity bit, as shown in Figure 9-4.

Blocking

When data is written onto a tape, it is usually divided into logical records—for example, checking account records. However, some room is usually left between records for stopping space, since you cannot stop a tape exactly where you want; like a car when the brakes are hit, the tape will skid a bit. These spaces, shown in Figure 9-5, are called **interrecord gaps (IRGs).** A typical space is three-fifths of an inch long.

If each record is short, then a large number of interrecord gaps will be required, which means much of the tape—indeed, as much as half—will be blank. In such cases, some of the records will be pulled together and the interrecord gaps will be eliminated and replaced by **interblock gaps (IBGs),** gaps between blocks of records (see Figure 9-5). **Blocking** is the activity of putting records together into blocks.

Getting It on Tape: Benefits and Drawbacks

As Figure 9-6 shows, reels of magnetic tape are often maintained in **tape libraries**—special rooms made safe from forces that might disturb the magnetization and therefore data, forces such as static electricity, heat,

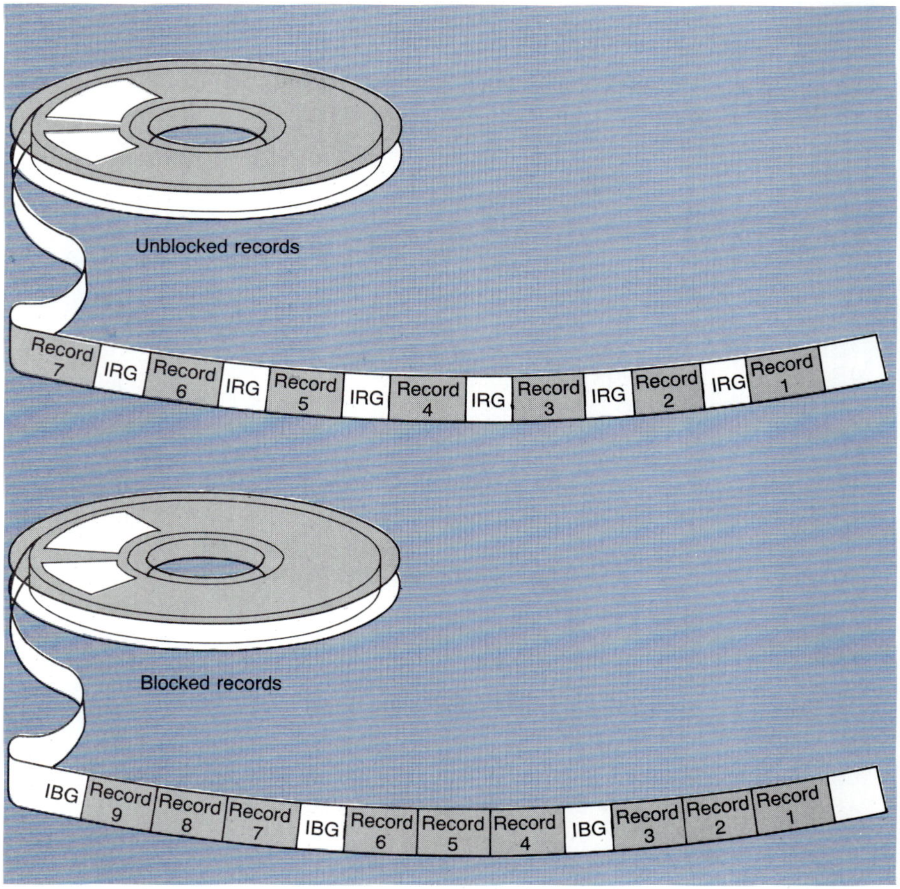
Unblocked records
Record 7
IRG
Record 6
IRG
Record 5
IRG
Record 4
IRG
Record 3
IRG
Record 2
IRG
Record 1
Blocked records
IBG
Record 9
Record 8
Record 7
IBG
Record 6
Record 5
Record 4
IBG
Record 3
Record 2
Record 1

Figure 9-5 Blocking. *Top*: Spaces between records on this tape are called interrecord gaps (IRGs); these spaces are about three-fifths of an inch long. *Bottom*: When short records are grouped together into blocks of several records in order to minimize blank spaces on the tape, the spaces between blocks are called interblock gaps (IBGs).

and dust. The existence of such libraries suggests the first two of five advantages of tape:

- It can hold a lot of data in compact space.
- It is portable. It is easily mailable. (Try mailing 240 boxes of punched cards, at 2000 cards per box—the equivalent of one 2400-foot reel of tape.)
- It is not expensive, costing less than $15 per reel.
- It can hold records of different lengths.
- Tape can be erased and reused.

Figure 9-6 Keeping track of tapes. *Left*: A tape library. This special room keeps tapes safe from dust, heat, static electricity, and other forces that might disturb the magnetization on the tapes. *Right*: Tape librarians keep track of the locations of magnetic tapes.

The fact that tape is an off-line storage medium, however, poses some drawbacks:

- It does not give fast access to data, since the tape must be manually mounted on a tape drive by an operator.
- It is relatively slow. It can only access data sequentially, which means, as previously stated, you must go through all preceding records before you come to the record you want.
- It can be physically damaged by dust, heat, and tearing and, of course, by people touching it or dropping it.

Direct Access Storage: The Uses of Magnetic Disk

Magnetic disk is another form of sequential access storage, but it is far better for direct access storage—which magnetic tape cannot be. A **magnetic disk** can be of two forms:

- Flexible or "floppy" disk
- Solid or hard disk

Flexible Disk

You may already be familiar with this kind of disk from working with personal computers. Made of a thin film of plastic with metal oxide and encased within a sleeve of nonremovable paper or plastic (see Figure 9-

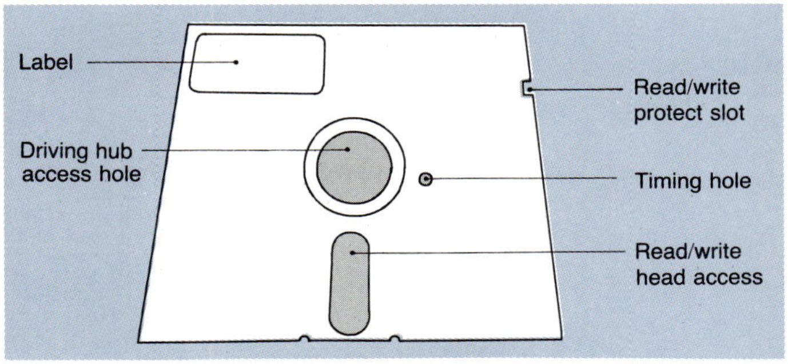
Label
Read/write protect slot
Driving hub access hole
Timing hole
Read/write head access

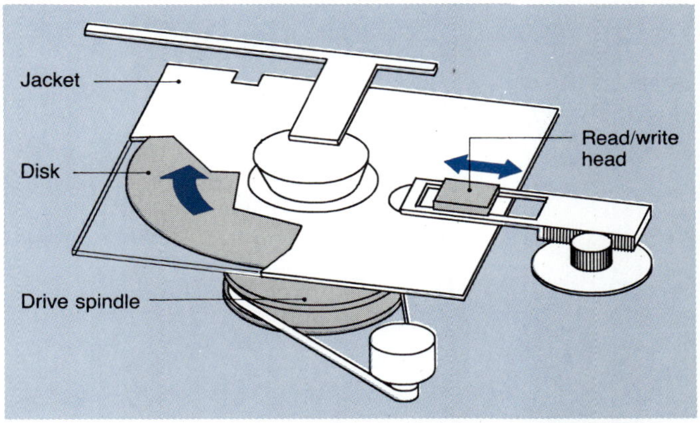
Jacket
Read/write head
Disk
Drive spindle

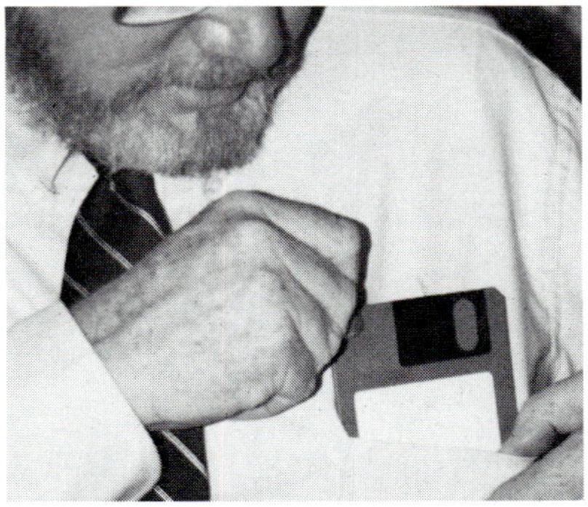

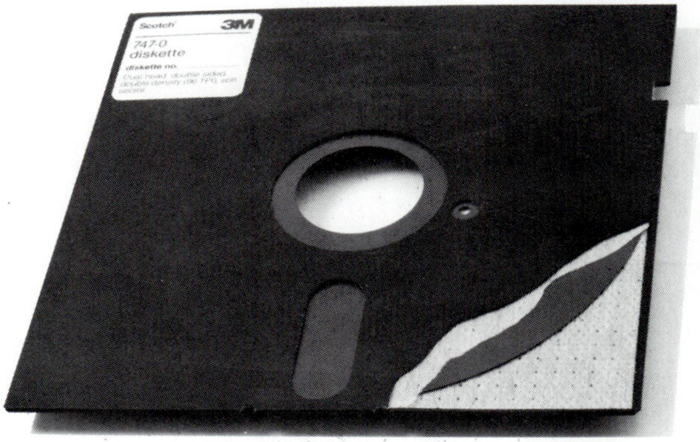
Scotch
3M
747-0
diskette

Figure 9-7 Diskettes. *Bottom right:* A 5¼-inch minifloppy, or "floppy disk," shown with part of protective jacket removed. Parts are labeled at top left. *Top left and right:* Disk drive for 5¼-inch flexible disk. The read/write head is able to move across the disk, giving it access to information anywhere on the disk. This is known as "random access." *Above:* A 3¼-inch microfloppy, small enough to fit in a shirt pocket.

7), **flexible disks**—more often spoken of as **diskettes, floppy disks,** or "**floppies**"—are used principally with microcomputers. Originally manufactured as 8 inches in diameter, they are now generally 5¼ inches in size (called **minifloppies**) and, for computers like Apple's Macintosh, 3¼ inches (**microfloppies**), as well as some other sizes of between 3 and 4 inches.

Flexible disks are inserted into a **disk drive** (see Figure 9-7), a mechanical machine with a spindle in it. A read/write head within the

Floppy Disk Handling and Storage Tips

People have been known to pin their floppy disks to a refrigerator door with a magnet and to leave their disks on their car dashboards in the sun. More subtly, they have taken disks on trips on subways and been surprised to find data disappeared when they tried to use the disks. (Subways are electrically motored and create magnetic force fields capable of erasing electronic data stored on disks.) Diskettes require tender loving care. The following are some tips from Maxell, a manufacturer of floppy disks.

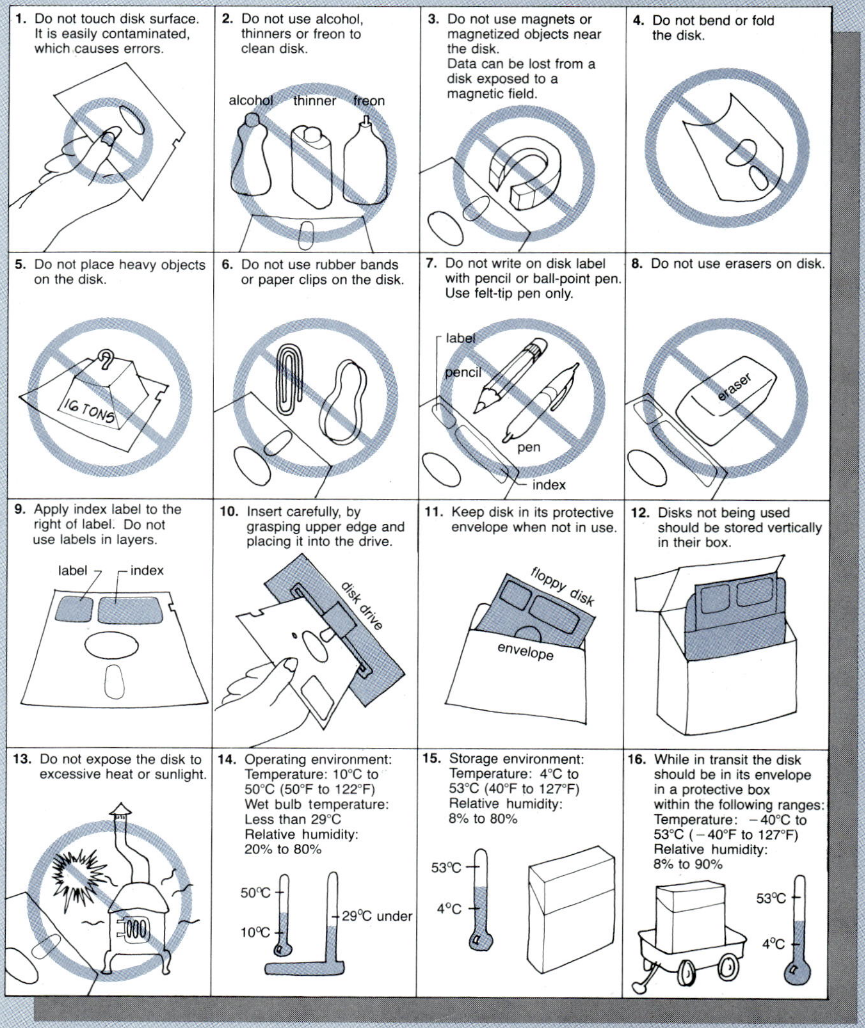
1. Do not touch disk surface. It is easily contaminated, which causes errors.
2. Do not use alcohol, thinners or freon to clean disk.
alcohol
thinner
freon
3. Do not use magnets or magnetized objects near the disk. Data can be lost from a disk exposed to a magnetic field.
4. Do not bend or fold the disk.
5. Do not place heavy objects on the disk.
16 TONS
6. Do not use rubber bands or paper clips on the disk.
7. Do not write on disk label with pencil or ball-point pen. Use felt-tip pen only.
label
pencil
pen
index
8. Do not use erasers on disk.
eraser
9. Apply index label to the right of label. Do not use labels in layers.
label
index
10. Insert carefully, by grasping upper edge and placing it into the drive.
disk drive
11. Keep disk in its protective envelope when not in use.
floppy disk
envelope
12. Disks not being used should be stored vertically in their box.
13. Do not expose the disk to excessive heat or sunlight.
14. Operating environment: Temperature: 10°C to 50°C (50°F to 122°F) Wet bulb temperature: Less than 29°C Relative humidity: 20% to 80%
50°C
10°C
29°C under
15. Storage environment: Temperature: 4°C to 53°C (40°F to 127°F) Relative humidity: 8% to 80%
53°C
4°C
16. While in transit the disk should be in its envelope in a protective box within the following ranges: Temperature: −40°C to 53°C (−40°F to 127°F) Relative humidity: 8% to 90%
53°C
4°C

Figure 9-8 Three types of solid disks. *Top left*: Made for microcomputers, this is an example of a hard disk, a 5¼-inch Winchester disk. *Top right*: A sealed data module, which has disk, access arm, and read/write head sealed within it. Used with minicomputers, the entire unit is removable. *Bottom*: A disk pack containing more than one disk. This IBM 3350 disk pack, introduced in 1977, is nonremovable. Other kinds of disk packs are removable.

disk drive retrieves data from and records data on the disk. In a flexible disk system, the read/write head actually makes contact with the rotating disk.

Solid Disk

Made of rigid metal coated with a metal oxide, **solid disks** are seen in the following forms, as shown in Figure 9-8:

- As an 8- or 5¼ -inch disk permanently mounted for use with a microcomputer.
- As a 14-inch disk also permanently mounted in a disk drive unit for use with a larger computer system. The entire unit may be removable.
- As stacks of 14-inch disks in a disk pack. Some disk packs are removable, others are not.

Let us first describe the hard disks that are used with microcomputers, since these are becoming more popular and you may find yourself using them also. Then we will consider how hard disks work, for they are not simply the same as your stereo and LP record.

Hard Disk for Microcomputers

Developed by IBM in 1973, hard disk drives use a disk formed from aluminum and coated with a magnetic recording medium. Unlike floppy disks, the hard disk drive is a **sealed data module**—it has disk, access arms, and read/write head sealed inside it, and the read/write heads, instead of riding directly on the disk, float on a cushion of air over the disk surface. The technology for the data module is commonly called **Winchester technology.** A hard disk drive for a microcomputer is shown in Figure 9-8.

Although hard disk drives are far more expensive than floppy disk drives and are more sensitive to cigarette smoke and other adverse environmental conditions, they can store far more information. An 8-inch hard disk drive can hold 20 megabytes of information—equivalent to about 400 pages—as opposed to half a megabyte on one 8-inch floppy disk. Moreover, a hard disk drive can transfer information up to ten times faster than floppy disk drives can—a fact you can appreciate if you are trying to load a lot of text into your computer for word processing or data for your electronic spreadsheet.

Disk, Disk Pack, and Disk Drive

Unlike a phonograph record, the tracks on a disk (whether flexible or hard) are not a single spiral that moves the arm from the outside to the center. Rather, as Figure 9-9 shows, they are a series of closed (concentric) circles. A hard disk has 200 to 800 of these tracks, which, incidentally, are invisible to the naked eye.

Data is read from or written on the disk by a disk drive unit containing an **access arm** (see Figure 9-9), which moves a read/write head over a particular track. With solid disk, the access arm does not actually touch the disk; rather, it floats above the surface, just close enough to detect the magnetized data. Sometimes this close tolerance can cause serious problems: a piece of dust, for instance, can stick to the read/write head and scratch the disk—an event known as a **head crash.** When this happens, the data can be lost and the disk is no longer usable.

Although many disk drives have only one access arm, some are constructed to accept **disk packs,** which consist of several disks assembled together, like a stack of phonograph records but with space between the disks. The space allows the access arms to move in and out, each with two read/write heads—one to read the disk surface above it, one to read the disk surface below it (see Figure 9-9). The disk pack has 11 disks with 20 recording surfaces; the top and bottom are not used because they are more apt to be damaged when the disk pack is being mounted on the

Track 199
Track 000

MEMOREX
MARK XIII

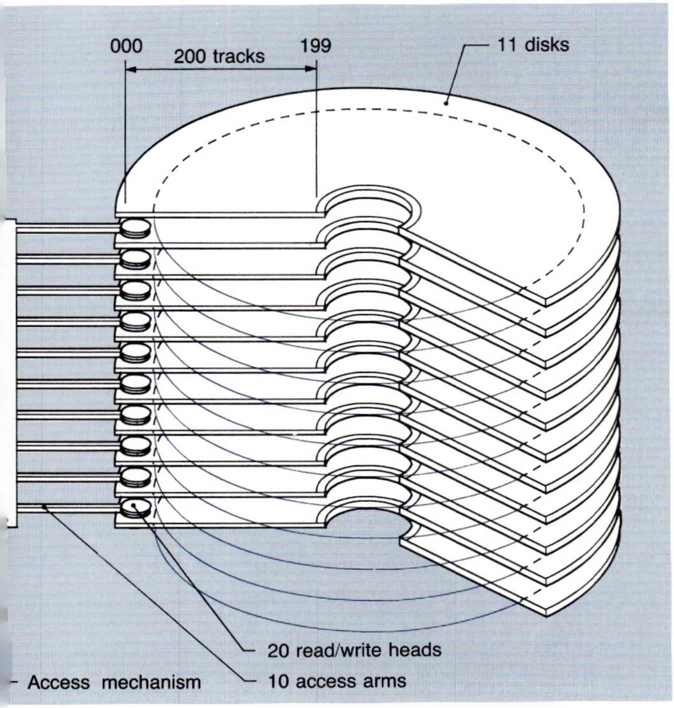
000
200 tracks
199
11 disks
20 read/write heads
Access mechanism
10 access arms

Figure 9-9 Disk, disk pack, and access arms. *Top left*: Surface of a disk. Each of the 200 circles is a closed track. The circles cannot be seen with the naked eye. *Top right*: This disk pack (shown from top and side) has 11 disks or metal platters, providing 20 surfaces for recording. *Bottom*: In this disk pack of 11 disks, the ten access arms each have two read/write heads. The ten access arms move simultaneously, slipping between the disks, but only one read/write head operates at one time. The top disk has data only on its bottom side, and the bottom disk has data only on its top side.

disk drive. All access arms move at the same time; however, only one of the 20 read/write heads is activated at any one time.

Access time to locate data on hard disks is 10 to 100 milliseconds (a millisecond is one-thousandth of a second), compared to 100 to 600 milliseconds on flexible disks. **Access time**—the time between when the computer requests data from a secondary storage device and when the transfer of data is completed—consists of four factors: seek time, head switching, rotational delay, and data transfer.

Seek time is the time it takes an access arm to get into position over a particular track. **Head switching** is the activation of a particular read/write head over a particular track and surface. **Rotational delay time** is the time for the particular record to be positioned under the read/write head. **Data transfer** is the time for the transfer of data from disk track to primary storage. The average access time for most disk drives is less than 25 milliseconds—fast, but not nearly as fast as the actual processing speeds of computers, which are measured in microseconds or nanoseconds.

Disk Addressing: Two Approaches

In order for access arms to find data on a disk, the exact address of the data must be known. (This is not something you have to worry about personally; it is handled by the operating system.) There are two approaches to disk addressing:

- Cylinder method
- Sector method

Cylinder Method. Used with solid disk packs, the **cylinder method** uses a vertical method of addressing, as shown in Figure 9-10. Because all access arms move simultaneously, they therefore all move to the same track (called a cylinder here) on all 20 surfaces at once. Thus, data can be addressed by the track (or cylinder) number, the disk surface, and the record number on that track on that disk surface. This is shown in Figure 9-10 (top).

Sector Method. Used with flexible disks and single disks (and sometimes with multiple disks), the **sector method** divides the surface of a disk into pie-shaped sectors, as shown in Figure 9-10 (bottom). Data addresses then consist of the track number and sector number.

Putting Data on Disks: Benefits and Drawbacks

It might seem from the foregoing that magnetic disk has it all over magnetic tape, and indeed there are a number of advantages:

- Disks can be used for both sequential and direct processing.
- Disks can be on-line—connected directly to the CPU at all times, thereby greatly reducing access time and allowing data files to be updated immediately.

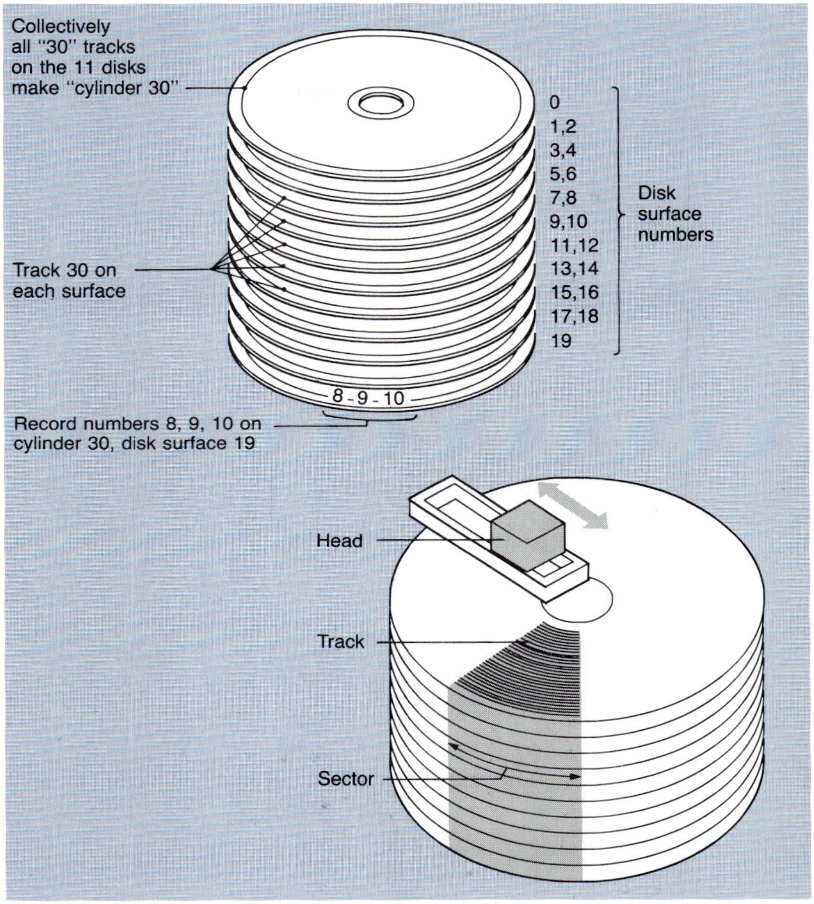
Collectively all "30" tracks on the 11 disks make "cylinder 30"
0
1,2
3,4
5,6
7,8
9,10
11,12
13,14
15,16
17,18
19
Disk surface numbers
Track 30 on each surface
8-9-10
Record numbers 8, 9, 10 on cylinder 30, disk surface 19
Head
Track
Sector

Figure 9-10 Methods of disk addressing. *Top*: Cylinder method of data organization. If there are 200 tracks on a single surface, there are 200 cylinders in the disk pack. *Bottom*: Sector method of data organization.

- People using disk storage can interact with stored information immediately and get rapid responses to their inquiries.
- Files stored on disk can be linked by software so that several files can be updated at once from a single transaction.

Nevertheless, there are still some disadvantages:

- Sequential processing with disk is actually slower than it is with tape for many applications.
- Disks are 25 times more expensive than tape.

- When files are updated on disks, the original files are destroyed—which is not the case with tape. (A tape and new updates will be merged to create a new tape, but the old tape is kept unchanged.)
- Tapes are more secure than disks from access by unauthorized persons because they are off-line storage.

Mass Storage

Mass storage devices combine the low-cost, high-capacity advantages of magnetic tape with the on-line advantages of magnetic disk, yet the technology resembles neither. As Figure 9-11 shows, **mass storage devices** consist of honeycombed storage compartments containing data cartridges. Each data cartridge is about 2 inches in diameter by 4 inches long and contains a 771-inch long piece of magnetic tape.

Storage is relatively slow—retrieval takes seconds rather than milliseconds—because it takes a few seconds for the device to find the particular cartridge called for by the CPU and another few seconds to transfer data from the mass storage device to magnetic disk and then to the CPU. However, mass storage is still faster than the time required to mount a tape reel on a tape drive. Moreover, storage capacity is tremendous: the IBM 3850, for instance, can store the equivalent of a library of 400,000 volumes. This kind of storage is only required, however, for applications such as those that might be conceived by the Census Bureau or the Internal Revenue Service, organizations that deal with millions of files.

Future Storage: Optical Disks and Other Marvels

An exciting development in external storage is **optical disk** or **videodisc technology,** which uses the same engineering as optical disk recordings of audiovisual performances for playback on television—that is, laser recording systems (see Figure 9-12, page 328). In this technology, a light beam burns tiny holes into the surface of the disk; the holes are arranged to represent numbers, letters, and colors. Optical disks are inexpensive, can hold a great deal of data—in fact, one low-cost disk can replace 25 reels of magnetic tape—and are a natural for direct access storage. However, optical disks are not reusable as magnetic tape and disk are.

Other developments in secondary storage include chip-mounted devices—that is, devices made out of solid-state electronic chips:

K31 009 197

Figure 9-11 **A mass storage device.** *Top*: This IBM 3850 Mass Storage System consists of honeycomblike cells, each of which holds a cartridge 2 inches in diameter by 4 inches long and with a 771-inch long strip of magnetic tape. A single cartridge can store 50 million bytes. *Bottom*: Two data cartridges are compared in size to a standard disk pack.

Figure 9-12 Optical disk storage. *Top*: An optical disk can replace 200,000 traditional library cards, such as those found in the card catalogs in libraries. Optical disk has been replacing library cards at the Library of Congress. *Bottom*: Mirror writing/reading: how an optical disk system works. Using mirrors, a point of light or heat from a laser beam is focused to create—write—a minuscule 0- or 1-bit, formed by one of three methods: etching the disk surface, creating a gas bubble in a lower layer, or changing the disk from light-reflecting to transparent. For reading, the read laser is focused on the marks.

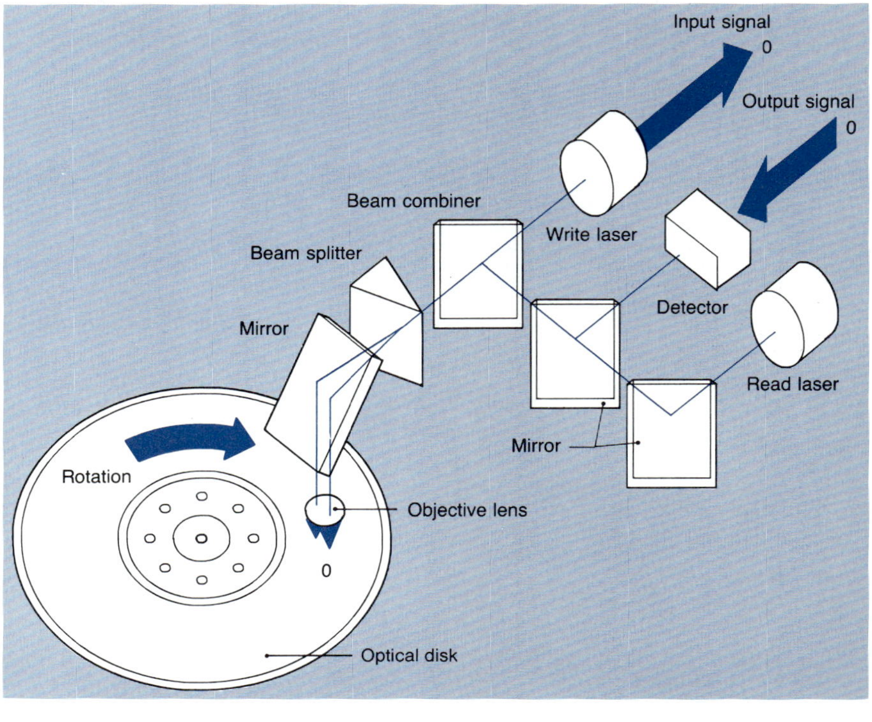
Input signal
0
Output signal
0
Beam combiner
Write laser
Beam splitter
Detector
Mirror
Read laser
Mirror
Rotation
Objective lens
0
Optical disk

- **Bubble memory,** discussed in the last chapter, has few moving parts and potentially great reliability.
- The **charged couple device,** also chip-mounted, is more than 100 times faster than the bubble, smaller, and cheaper to produce. However, it is also slower and it is volatile—it loses data when the power is turned off.

File Organization

Whatever kind of machines or media are used to store data, there must be some way of putting it in order. Let us consider how this is done.

Three Ways to Organize Files

There are two basic types of files—master and transaction.

- A **master file** is a complete file containing all records current up to the last update.
- A **transaction file** is a file containing *recent* changes to records that will be used to update the master file.

There are three ways in which these types of files may be organized:

- Sequential files
- Direct files
- Index sequential files

There is also a fourth way of organizing files—by data base filing system—but, as mentioned, we shall describe this later. Here we will look at the first three.

Bank of tapes. The computer room of the Exchange Bank in Santa Rosa, California, holds several magnetic tape drives, along with a library of computer tapes. Banks are big users of magnetic tape storage because back-up storage is so important.

Sequential File Organization

Sequential files are stored one after another in ascending or descending order, as determined by their record keys. A **key** is a particular field of a record that is usually chosen as an identifier of that record. The key may be a number, such as your social security number—this is a very common identifier—or it may be alphabetic, such as your last name. To find a record in a sequential file, the computer starts at the beginning of the file and checks each record's key until it finds the one you want.

The most commonly used media for sequential files is magnetic tape, although magnetic disk and punched cards are also used. Sequential files are often used for applications that require periodic updates of a large number of records—that is, where updates are *batched* together for processing—such as payroll, billing, and preparation of customer accounts. At Atlantic-Pacific Bank, for instance, it is used to update customer loans.

To update a sequential file, the old master file and the transaction file are input together as data, along with an update program. The result, as Figure 9-13 shows, is a new master file. The old master file and transaction file are kept as backups in case the system fails and the new master file has to be re-created.

The advantages of sequential file processing are several:

- It is well suited to a number of business applications, such as payroll and billing.
- It is the best kind of file organization for uses where there are frequent and large updates.
- It can use magnetic tape, which is inexpensive and has large storage capacity.

But there are some disadvantages:

- The entire master file must be read to update it—even if only the very last record on the file needs to be changed.
- Records must be carefully sequenced according to their keys, which requires time.
- If there is an unanticipated inquiry, it is difficult to locate a particular record.

Direct File Organization

If the number of records to be updated is small and if updated transactions arrive irregularly, direct access processing is better than sequential processing, for this method allows you to update your files whenever you want and get a status report whenever you want that will be as up to date as your last transaction.

With **direct file organization,** you can go directly to the record you want. You do not have to sequence files by key nor do the records need to be stored one after the other; they can be distributed in seemingly random fashion. Direct file organization requires, however, that the data

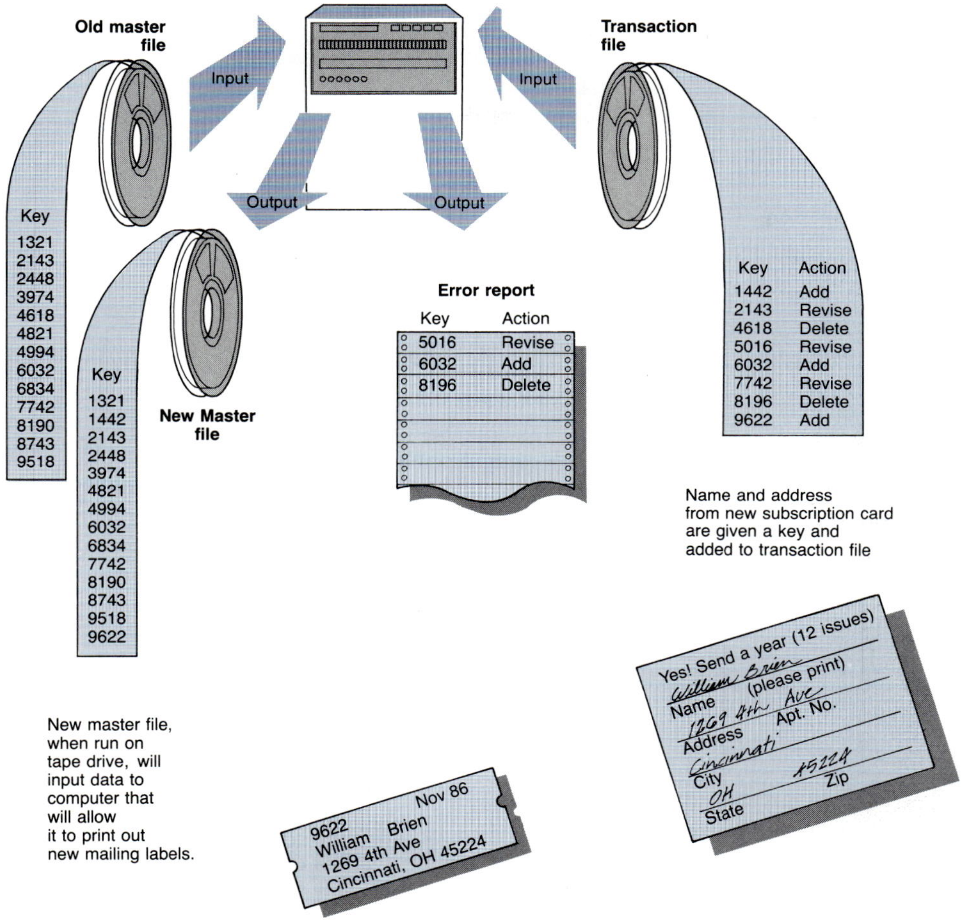
Old master file
Input
Input
Transaction file
Output
Output
Key
1321
2143
2448
3974
4618
4821
4994
6032
6834
7742
8190
8743
9518
Key
1321
1442
2143
2448
3974
4821
4994
6032
6834
7742
8190
8743
9518
9622
New Master file
Error report
Key Action
5016 Revise
6032 Add
8196 Delete
Key Action
1442 Add
2143 Revise
4618 Delete
5016 Revise
6032 Add
7742 Revise
8196 Delete
9622 Add
Name and address from new subscription card are given a key and added to transaction file
Yes! Send a year (12 issues)
Name (please print)
Address Apt. No.
City Zip
State
New master file, when run on tape drive, will input data to computer that will allow it to print out new mailing labels.
Nov 86
9622
William Brien
1269 4th Ave
Cincinnati, OH 45224

Figure 9-13 Sequential file organization. Sequential updating of magazine subscription list. Each key here represents an entire subscriber's magazine label—name, address, zip code, and date of expiration. The old master file consists of records of all the subscribers until last month, when subscription changes came in. The changes are reflected in the transaction file and consist of additions (new subscribers), deletions (cancellations or expirations), and revisions (changes of address, usually). Records for both transaction file and master file must be in order by key, perhaps arranged from low numbers to high, before the updating can be done. (This means the numbers on the transaction tape actually had to be presorted.) During processing, the computer reads records from the transaction and master files and takes action on whichever of the two keys is lower in number. If the master file record key is lower, there is no change. If the master file record is higher, the transaction is added to the master file. If the keys are the same, the record in the master file should be revised or deleted. As the processing proceeds, a new master file is produced which incorporates all the changes from the transaction file. An error report is also produced that calls attention to deletions and revision of names that do not exist or additions that were already in the master file—perhaps because of mistakes by magazine subscription agencies. The updated master file is used to produce new subscription labels every month in time for the magazine's latest mailing.

be stored on a direct access storage device such as a magnetic disk. In addition, you must, of course, have a way of finding the records, which means that there must be a scheme for maintaining the addresses of all the records.

There are two ways of maintaining addresses for direct file organization:

- Directory approach
- Transformation approach

The Directory Approach. In the directory approach to addressing, every time data is stored on the direct access storage device an entry is made automatically into a table called the **directory.** The directory is located on the storage medium and records reference numbers—which are keys for the records stored on the disk—and their corresponding storage addresses, which are the locations of the complete record for each key. When you want to find a particular record, the computer finds that record's key in the directory and then the address corresponding to that key.

The Transformation Approach. In the **transformation** approach to direct file organization, some arithmetic calculation is used with the key field which produces the address of the desired record. For example, suppose the direct access storage device has a three-digit storage address and suppose the key to the record you want is a particular year. One transformation process would be to take the year, divide it by the closest prime number, and only save the remainder. The record corresponding to that year will be stored in an address equal to this remainder plus 1.

Although these methods of finding a record sound complicated, they have some important benefits. The advantages of direct file organization are:

- Transactions can be used to update master files directly from terminals. There is no need to batch transactions, as in sequential file processing.
- Several files can be updated simultaneously.

But there are some drawbacks:

- Because the updating is done on the original file, the previous master file is lost. Therefore, there is no backup master file available in case something goes wrong.
- More users have access to the master file through their terminals. Consequently, there is a greater chance of data being deliberately or accidentally altered, so security of information is therfore reduced.

Index Sequential File Organization

The above two kinds of file organization—sequential and direct—clearly have their place. As we mentioned, sequential is better when a master file needs periodic updates with a relatively large volume of updates. Direct is better if there are irregular updates and the volume of updates is small.

In some cases, however, file updates can be batched, but there is an ongoing need to get to records rapidly for data inquiries. At Atlantic-Pacific Bank, for instance, the daily deposits are batched to create a transaction file, which is then used at the end of the banking day to update the master file of checking-account balances. However, throughout the day, customers occasionally want to know what their account balances are. Although a sequential file organization would be suitable for updating account balances, it would be too inefficient to allow tellers to search for an individual depositor's account balance. The answer: index sequential file organization.

A compromise between sequential and direct, **index sequential file organization** stores records in a file in sequential order, but the file also contains an index. The index lists the key to each record stored and the corresponding disk address for that record. The index works like the index in the back of a book. For instance, to find "bubble memory," you could start at page 1 and read until you came to the word "bubble"—that would be sequential processing. Or you could go to the back of the book to the index and look up "Bubble memory" and the page number given and then go the right place. In much the same way, the computer can use an index sequential file organization to locate records in an index sequential file. A further example of how this works is given in Figure 9-14.

The advantages of index sequential file organization are as follows:

- It allows efficient processing of large batch updates.
- It permits you to retrieve data quickly and efficiently.

The disadvantages are:

- The method makes less efficient use of storage than other methods.
- Access to particular records is slower than it is with direct file organization.
- The hardware and software required to carry out this method are more expensive than that required for other methods.

On to the Wired World

This discussion of secondary storage may seem unduly technical for what might be useful in a business career. However, as we will see in Chapter 13, it is the development of computer storage that has permitted

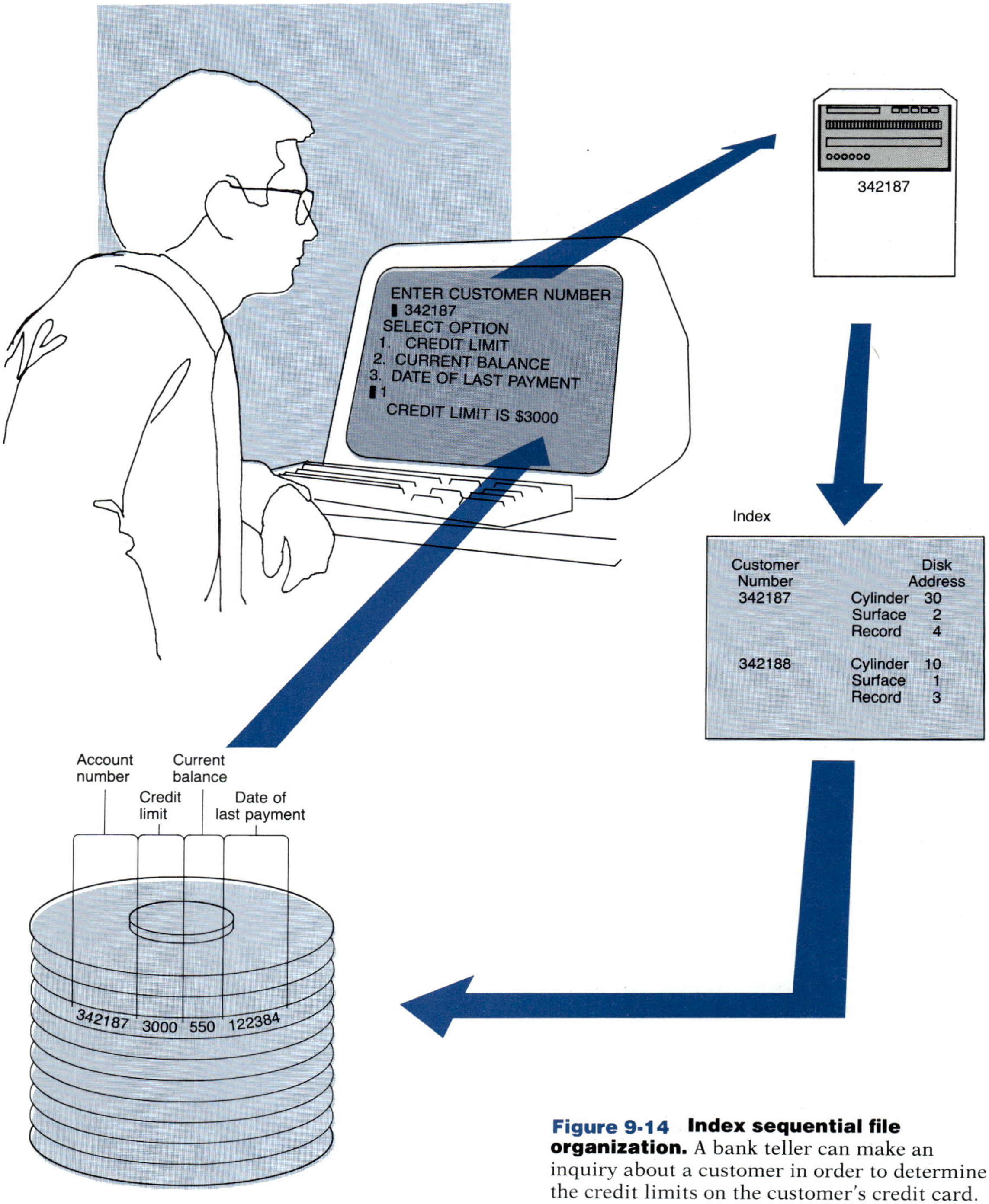
ENTER CUSTOMER NUMBER
342187
SELECT OPTION
1. CREDIT LIMIT
2. CURRENT BALANCE
3. DATE OF LAST PAYMENT
1
CREDIT LIMIT IS $3000
342187
Index
Customer Number
Disk Address
342187
Cylinder 30
Surface 2
Record 4
342188
Cylinder 10
Surface 1
Record 3
Account number
Current balance
Credit limit
Date of last payment
342187
3000
550
122384

Figure 9-14 Index sequential file organization. A bank teller can make an inquiry about a customer in order to determine the credit limits on the customer's credit card.

one of the most fascinating information resources for managers—huge data bases that can be manipulated for many different uses.

But having large *amounts* of information available is only one part of the picture. It is also important to make the information *accessible.* This is where networking and data communications come in—the subject of the next chapter.

SUMMARY

- The soaring cost of managing paper documents is an important reason for using electronic storage. The availability of such storage can also create huge data bases that can be manipulated for many purposes.
- **Secondary storage,** also known as **external storage** or **auxiliary storage,** is storage outside the computer itself. It is indispensable because it is unlikely that all the records of a large corporation, for example, could be stored inside the computer itself (called **primary storage** or **internal storage**).
- Although primary storage can process data faster, secondary storage has several advantages: (1) It is more economical. (2) It has greater storage capacity. (3) The data it stores is generally safe from tampering and natural hazards.
- There are two types of secondary storage: *direct access* and *sequential access.* In order of speed and cost of use, after primary storage—which is the fastest, most limited, and most expensive of the three types of storage—is **direct access storage. Sequential access storage** is the slowest form of storage, but it has unlimited capacity and is the least expensive.
- Direct access storage requires an input device, called a **direct access storage device (DASD),** that is directly connected to the CPU, thereby keeping the stored data **on-line** (available to the CPU at all times). A **magnetic disk** is an example of direct access storage media.
- Sequential access storage is **off-line** (the data is not accessible to the CPU until it has been loaded onto an input device). Examples of sequential access storage media are a reel of **magnetic tape** and a stack of punched cards.
- Magnetic tape, the most common medium for sequential access storage, consists of plastic tape like that on reel-to-reel tape recorders. The devices that run the tapes are called **magnetic tape drives** or **magnetic tape units.** These machines consist of two reels—a **supply reel** and a **take-up reel**—plus a **read/write head** and an **erase head.** (**Read** means to retrieve data from, and **write** means to record data on. The read/write head reads magnetized areas on the tape—which represent data—converts them into electrical signals, and sends them to the CPU. It also writes, or records, the data on the tape from the CPU. If necessary, it erases old data using the **erase head.**)

- In referring to data, certain terms are used: A **character** is a letter, number, or special symbol. A **field** is made up of one or more characters and contains an item of data. A **record** is a collection of related fields. A **file** is a collection of related records. A **data base** is a collection of interrelated data, a systematic or structured organization of files available for central access and retrieval.
- Data is represented on tape by invisible magnetized spots, the presence or absence of a spot corresponding to a 1 or 0 bit. The most common way of organizing data is by a nine-track code.
- When data is written onto a tape, it is usually divided into logical records. There are usually spaces left between records, and these are called **interrecord gaps (IRGs).** A typical space is three-fifths inch long. If each record is short, there will be many interrecord gaps, which means that much of the tape will be blank. To save space, the records can be pulled together and the interrecord gaps can be replaced by **interblock gaps (IBGs),** which are gaps between blocks of records. **Blocking** is the activity of putting records together into blocks.
- Reels of magnetic tape are often maintained in **tape libraries,** which are special rooms designed to protect the tape from forces that might disturb the magnetization, such as static electricity, heat, and dust.
- Magnetic tape has five advantages: (1) It can hold a lot of data in compact space. (2) It is portable and easily mailable. (3) It is inexpensive. (4) It can hold records of different lengths. (5) It can be erased and reused. Because tape is an off-line storage medium, it poses some drawbacks: (1) It does not provide fast access to data because the reel must be manually mounted. (2) It is relatively slow because it can only access data sequentially. (3) It can be physically damaged by dust, heat, tearing, and by people touching or dropping it.
- **Magnetic disk** is generally used for direct access storage, and it can be either flexible ("floppy") or solid (hard).
- **Flexible disks**—also called **diskettes, floppy disks,** or "**floppies**"—are made of plastic and encased within a nonremovable paper or plastic sleeve. They are used principally with microcomputers. Originally 8 inches in diameter, they are now usually 5¼ inches in size **(minifloppies)** or 3¼ inches **(microfloppies)**. Flexible disks are inserted into a **disk drive**, where a read/write head contacts the rotating disk and retrieves data from and also records data on the disk.
- **Solid disks** are made of rigid metal and can be (1) an 8- or 5¼-inch disk permanently mounted for use with a microcomputer, (2) a 14-inch disk permanently mounted in a disk drive for use with a larger computer system, or (3) a stack of 14-inch disks in a disk pack.
- A hard disk drive is a **sealed data module**—it has disk, access arms, and read/write head sealed inside it, and the read/write head floats on a cushion

of air over the disk surface. The technology for the data module is commonly called **Winchester technology.** Hard disk drives are more expensive than floppy disk drives and are more sensitive to environmental conditions, but they can store more information and transfer information faster.

- Data is read from or written on the disk by a disk drive unit containing an **access arm,** which moves a read/write head over, not on, a particular track (one of a number of concentric circles) on the disk. If something sticks to the read/write head—dust, for example—it may scratch the disk and cause a **head crash,** ruining the disk and losing the data.
- Many disk drives have only one access arm, but some can accept **disk packs,** which consist of several disks assembled together with space between them. The spaces accommodate a series of access arms, each with two read/write heads—one to read the disk surface above it and one to read the surface below it.
- **Access time** is the time between when the computer requests data from a secondary storage device and when the transfer of data is completed. It consists of four factors: (1) seek time, (2) head switching, (3) rotational delay, and (4) data transfer.
- **Seek time** is the time it takes an access arm to get into position over a particular track. **Head switching** is the activation of a particular read/write head over a particular track and surface. **Rotational delay** is the time for the particular record to be positioned under the read/write head. **Data transfer** is the time for transfer of data from disk track to primary storage.
- For access arms to find data on a disk, the exact address of the data must be known. The two approaches to disk addressing are (1) the cylinder method and (2) the sector method. The **cylinder method** is used with solid disk packs; it employs a vertical method of addressing. The **sector method** is used with flexible disks and, generally, with single disks; it divides the surface of a disk into pie-shaped sectors.
- Magnetic disks have several advantages: (1) They can be used for both sequential and direct processing. (2) They can be on-line, thereby reducing access time and allowing immediate file updating. (3) People using disk storage can interact with stored information immediately and get rapid responses. (4) Files stored on disk can be linked by software. The disadvantages include: (1) Sequential processing with disk is usually slower than it is with tape. (2) Disks are more expensive than tape. (3) When files are updated on disks, the original files are destroyed, which is not the case with tape. (3) Tapes are more secure than disks from unauthorized access because they are off-line storage.
- **Mass storage devices** use their own technology to combine the low-cost, high-capacity advantages of magnetic tape with the on-line advantages of magnetic disk. They consist of honeycombed storage compartments con-

taining data cartridges. These devices are slower than disk but faster than tape, and they have tremendous storage capacity.

- **Optical disk** or **videodisk technology** uses the same engineering for external storage as optical disk recordings—that is, laser recording systems. Optical disks are inexpensive, can hold much data, and can be used for direct access storage. However, they are not as reusable as magnetic tape and disk are.
- Some solid-state electronic chip-mounted devices have also been developed for secondary storage: for example, **bubble memory** and the **charged couple device.**
- Files are usually organized. There are two types of files and three ways of organizing them. A **master file** is a complete file containing all current records. A **transaction file** contains recent changes to records that will be used to update the master file. These files can be organized sequentially, directly, or sequentially with an index.
- **Sequential files** are stored one after another in ascending or descending order, as determined by their record keys. A **key** is a particular field of a record that is usually chosen as an identifier of that record. It can be numeric or alphabetic, and it allows the computer to find the file you want. Magnetic tape is generally used for sequential files. This type of file is commonly used for applications that require periodic updates of a large number of records. Sequential files have several advantages: (1) They are well suited to many business applications. (2) They are the best kind of file organization where frequent and large updates are necessary. (3) They can use magnetic tape, which is inexpensive and has large storage capacity. Their disadvantages include: (1) The entire master file must be read to update a sequential file. (2) Records must be carefully sequenced according to their keys, which is time consuming. (3) When there is an unanticipated inquiry, it is difficult to locate a particular record.
- **Direct file organization** is used when the number of records needing to be updated is small and when updated transactions arrive irregularly. In direct file organization, files are not sequenced by key or stored one after the other; distribution can be random, and one can go directly to the record one wants. However, data must be stored on a direct access storage device such as a magnetic disk pack, and there must be some system for maintaining the address of all the records. This can be done in two ways: by directory approach or by transformation approach.
- The **directory approach** uses a table called a **directory** to record entries that are automatically made in the table every time data is stored on the direct access storage device. The directory is on the storage medium, and it records reference numbers (keys) and corresponding storage addresses. The computer uses the record's key in the directory to find the stored file you want.

- The **transformation approach** to direct file organization uses some arithmetic calculation with the key field to produce the address of the desired record.
- Direct file organization has some advantages: (1) Transactions can be used to update master files directly from terminals. (2) Several files can be updated simultaneously. The disadvantages include: (1) Because the updating is done on the original file, the previous master file is lost. (2) Because more users have access to the master file through their terminals, there is a greater chance that data might be altered.
- **Index sequential file organization** is a compromise between sequential and direct file organization. It stores files in sequential order, but the file also contains an index that lists the key to each record stored and the corresponding disk address for that record. Its advantages include: (1) It allows efficient processing of large batch updates. (2) It can retrieve data quickly and efficiently. This system also has several disadvantages: (1) It makes less efficient use of storage than other methods because the index must also be stored. (2) Access to particular records is slower than it is with direct file organization. (3) The necessary hardware and software are more expensive than those required for other methods.

KEY TERMS

Access arm, p. 322
Access time, p. 324
Auxiliary storage, p. 312
Blocking, p. 316
Bubble memory, p. 329
Character, p. 315
Charged couple device, p. 329
Cylinder method, p. 324
Data base, p. 315
Data transfer, p. 324
Direct access storage, p. 312
Direct access storage device (DASD), p. 312
Direct file organization, p. 330
Directory, p. 332
Directory approach, p. 332
Disk drive, p. 319
Diskette, p. 319
Disk pack, p. 322
Erase head, p. 313
External storage, p. 311, 312
Field, p. 315
File, p. 315
Flexible disk, p. 319
Floppy, p. 319
Floppy disk, p. 319
Head crash, p. 322
Head switching, p. 324
Index sequential file organization, p. 333
Interblock gap (IBG), p. 316
Internal storage, p. 311
Interrecord gap (IRG), p. 316
Magnetic disk, p. 318
Magnetic tape, p. 313
Magnetic tape drive, p. 313
Magnetic tape unit, p. 313
Mass storage device, p. 326
Master file, p. 329
Microfloppy, p. 319
Minifloppy, p. 319

Off-line, p. 312
On-line, p. 312
Optical disk, p. 326
Primary storage, p. 312
Read, p. 313
Read/write head, p. 313
Record, p. 315
Rotational delay time, p. 324
Sealed data module, p. 322
Secondary storage, p. 311
Sector method, p. 324
Seek time, p. 324
Sequential access storage, p. 312
Sequential file organization, p. 330
Solid disk, p. 321
Supply reel, p. 313
Take-up reel, p. 313
Tape library, p. 316
Transaction file, p. 329
Transformation approach, p. 332
Videodisc technology, p. 326
Winchester technology, p. 322
Write, p. 313

REVIEW QUESTIONS

1. How does secondary storage differ from primary storage? What advantages does it offer?
2. Compare sequential access storage to direct access storage. What types of technology does each type of storage use? What are the advantages and disadvantages of each?
3. How is data represented on tape?
4. What is meant by the term *blocking?*
5. Describe how a disk pack operates.
6. What is mass storage?
7. Describe one of the three methods of file organization.

CASE PROBLEMS

Case 9-1: Bits and Bites—Computers in Restaurants

Because people like to eat—and to eat out, when they can afford it—the food service industry is expanding. McDonald's opens 500 new restaurants every year, and Kentucky Fried Chicken and Burger King continue to expand throughout the world. Adults eat out on the average of three times a week and would like to eat out more, and so thousands of small-business people are encouraged to start up new eateries. As business writer Milton Moskowitz points out, starting a restaurant does not take a lot of capital, running one does not require an advanced degree, and the market potential is enormous.[2] Still, the restaurant business is a perilous business, and the failure rate is extremely high.

One restaurant owner who has done well is Washington Redskins' football star Joe Theismann, who uses a computer to help in managing his restaurant in Bailey's Crossroads, Virginia (as well as to keep track of fan mail). According to an August 6, 1984, story in *Computerworld*, the Fortune 32:16 multiuser microcomputer is used by five employees, including the restaurant manager, the kitchen manager, and the office manager. Besides recording several thousand transactions, averaging about $20 each, in the general ledger each week, the management has found the computer useful for keeping track of which areas of sales—food and beverage—are most profitable, what method of payment customers are using (cash or credit card), and variables such as the cost of goods to help establish pricing. The restaurant seats 200 patrons.[3]

Your assignment: Suppose you are installing a computer system for a chain of 20 restaurants. For this you will need something larger than a microcomputer, although you could have a microcomputer in each restaurant as a terminal connected via telephone lines to the central computer. As is the case with Joe Theismann, you will be recording thousands of transactions and will be analyzing them for different purposes. Consider the pros and cons of the different storage systems discussed in this chapter as applied to your needs.

Case 9-2: A Little Insurance—Hard Disk versus Floppy Disk

A hard disk (Winchester disk) for your microcomputer may cost as much as the computer itself. Yet, according to David Gabel in *Personal Computing* magazine (August 1984), the cost of a 10Mbyte hard disk works out to only one-tenth the per-kilobyte cost of floppy disk storage.[4] Many users who convert to hard disk do not want to go back to floppies; hard disk is 10 times faster, makes much more data available, and in other ways is much more convenient (no more searching through file boxes for floppy disks, for example).

Besides the expense, there are some disadvantages, however. Some software, says Gabel, cannot be put on hard disk by any legal means. In addition, you have to consider backing up the information that is on hard disk, since even Winchester disk drives can fail. The backup might consist of a floppy disk or reel-to-reel tape, the kind that, once you get them running, just keep on going; they do not start-stop like regular magnetic tape drives.

Your assignment: As an independent insurance agent, you would find a microcomputer a definite asset, and not just to remind you of clients' birthdays. You could use it to store data on clients, policy changes, payment dates, and so on. You could also use a spreadsheet to show prospective clients the various kinds of policy options. Once you build your business to a certain level, you may find it a headache to have to keep track of a lot of floppy disks. On the other hand, even with a hard disk, you may find yourself using floppies anyway for backup purposes, because risking failure of your hard disk is risking loss of your business. Discuss whether or not you ought to buy a hard disk system for your business.

CHAPTER 10

Networks and Data Communications

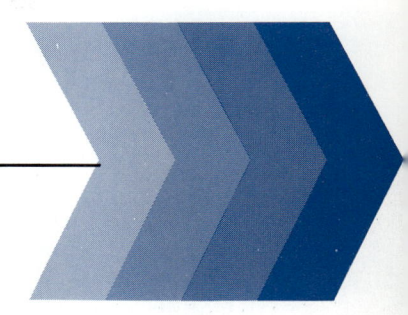

Bringing Us Together

Inventions often come about because of attempts to get an edge on the competition. The direct dial telephone—in which calls are placed directly, without the assistance of an operator—was invented by an Indiana undertaker in 1889 who had the strongest of reasons for eliminating reliance on operators: one of the local operators was the wife of his main rival, and he was convinced she was deliberately diverting calls for undertakers to her husband's funeral parlor.

Without the direct dial telephone there could probably be no long-distance computer communications. But for a long time, computer systems and communications systems were separate industries. The industry that developed COBOL had little to do with the industry that developed cable. Then, somewhere in the late fifties and early sixties, as Figure 10-1 (pages 346–347) shows, the two industries began to fuse.

The merger became particularly evident in 1984, when American Telephone & Telegraph—forced by the U.S. Department of Justice to divest itself of regional telephone companies in return for being allowed to enter the computer business—announced a line of several computer products. A few weeks earlier, IBM announced it had joined forces with broadcasting network CBS and nationwide retailer Sears, Roebuck & Co. in the formation of a joint venture in the videotex business, as the case study on the next page describes. **Videotex** is the sending and receiving of words and pictures to at-home video screens so that people can do shopping, banking, and other tasks from their living rooms. Thus, AT&T, the communications giant, and IBM, the computer giant, seem pitted to do battle in the two-way electronic services field. There could be no clearer example of how different is the new world of the Information Age.

PREVIEW

CASE STUDY: SHOPPING AND BANKING FROM HOME

New Moves to Videotex

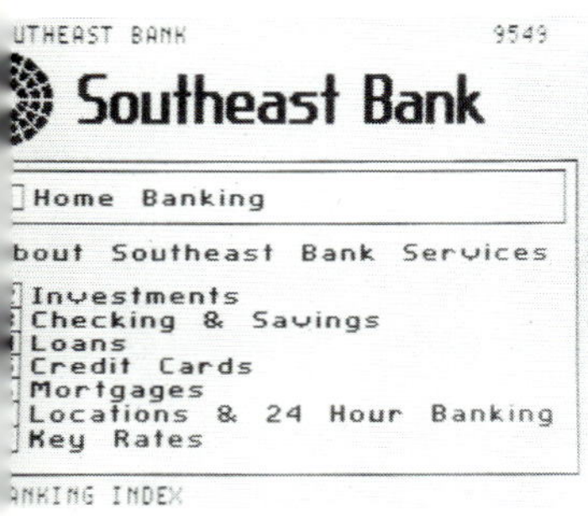
UTHEAST BANK 9549
Southeast Bank
Home Banking
bout Southeast Bank Services
Investments
Checking & Savings
Loans
Credit Cards
Mortgages
Locations & 24 Hour Banking
Key Rates
ANKING INDEX

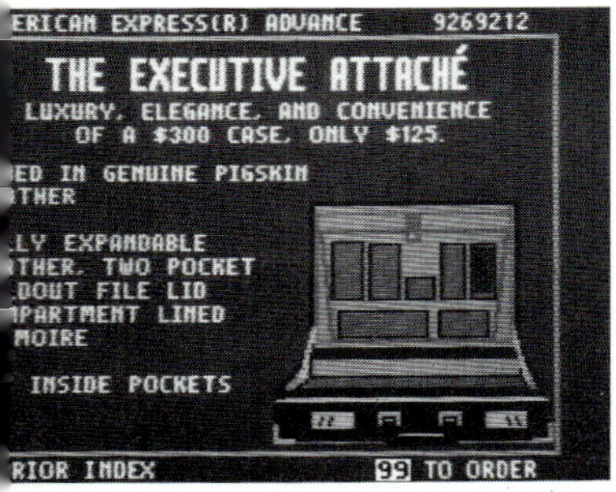
ERICAN EXPRESS(R) ADVANCE 9269212
THE EXECUTIVE ATTACHÉ
LUXURY, ELEGANCE, AND CONVENIENCE
OF A $300 CASE. ONLY $125.
ED IN GENUINE PIGSKIN
THER
LY EXPANDABLE
THER. TWO POCKET
DOUT FILE LID
PARTMENT LINED
MOIRE
INSIDE POCKETS
RIOR INDEX
99 TO ORDER

Though profits may be years away, a host of firms are betting tens of millions that Americans are eager to use their TV sets and computers to shop and bank from home.

Media moguls, bankers, retailers and others are gambling on videotex, a relatively new technology that allows users to call up shopping catalogs, bank statements, stock quotes, news and an array of other data on their TV's or computer monitors. Videotex customers can also make purchases, pay bills and even play videogames with other subscribers—all from their living rooms. . . .

Many see enough potential in videotex to justify big risks. Gartner Group, a consulting firm, predicts that annual U.S. revenues for videotex subscription and usage charges will reach 14 billion dollars by 1992, compared with just 500 million in 1982. Operators will reap billions more from ads and fees assessed for purchases consummated over their systems.

Says John Farnsworth of Chemical Bank, which offers Pronto, a videotex home-banking service, in the New York City area: "We believe this will be a multibillion-dollar industry, reach significant penetration in U.S. households and allow banks to operate less expensively. To us, it's an absolute winner." . . .

Behind the optimism of videotex supporters is the growing popularity of personal computers, which some experts feel will be found in 45 million U.S. households by 1990. Videotex is bound to flourish, observers say, as more and more computer owners buy modems—devices that permit computer-to-computer communication over telephone lines.

The center of attention today is Knight-Ridder's Viewtron, which does not require a computer. Instead, customers buy a special terminal, called Sceptre, that is made by Knight-Ridder's partner in the venture, American Telephone & Telegraph. . . .

Once Sceptre is hooked up to phone line and TV, the user simply presses a key to call Viewtron, then types in access codes. Subscribers can receive Viewtron's offerings in one of two ways: By selecting from a "menu" of 14 broad topics such as news, shopping, health and classified ads, or by typing in such key words as "weather" or "financial news" for a more specific subject.

—Manuel Schiffres,
U.S. News & World Report, February 13, 1984

Telecommunications and Computers

Videotex is only one of the services possible within the field of **data communications,** an all-encompassing term that refers to the way in which data is transmitted from one location to another, whether it is a letter borne by Pony Express or a telephone call beamed by satellite. Data communications includes anything that has the four elements of sender, transmission line, message, and receiver. This, of course, would describe you and a caller having a conversation over a telephone line, but it also describes the communications between parts of a computer system when input and output units, processor, and storage devices are spread out in dispersed locations. Working for Atlantic-Pacific Bank, you are in a position to see how important data communications is to banking. From ATMs to credit-checking to keeping up with changing foreign-exchange rates, banking today depends on data communications.

Telecommunications is a form of data communications, specifically communicating at a distance using either electromagnetic signals, such as those in telephone, radio, or television, or light energy, such as that in optical fiber lines. **Teleprocessing** combines the words "telecommunications" and "data processing" and means data processing at a distance; a teleprocessing system consists of terminals connected to a central computer by communication lines. Quite often telecommunications and teleprocessing are in the form of a **network,** an interconnected system of computers and/or peripheral devices at remote locations. There are various kinds of networks, and, as we shall see, the whole idea of networks is one of the most exciting things to come along in recent years, for it expands the uses of computers considerably.

Whether telephone or computer system, a telecommunications system has three basic parts:

- Communications interface—the sending and receiving instruments
- Transmission—the communications channel
- Communications processing—devices to enhance communications

Let us show how these work.

Sending a Message: Communications Interfaces

Before you can send a message as voice, video, data, or whatever, you need some sort of device at your end of the communications line that will convert your ideas into the signal to be transmitted. A telegraph key is one example of such a **communications interface,** a telephone handset is another, a microphone is still another.

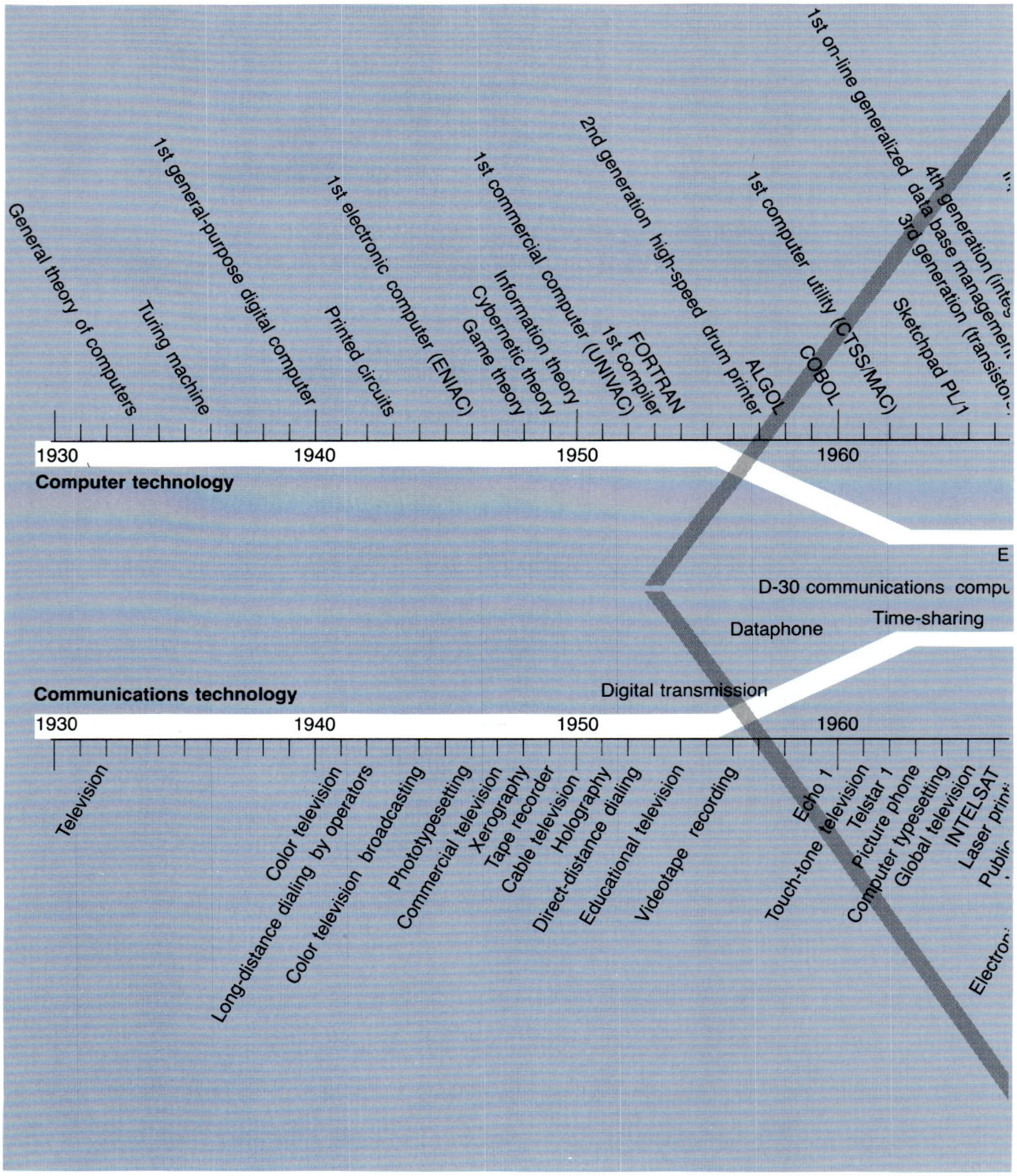
General theory of computers
Turing machine
1st general-purpose digital computer
Printed circuits
1st electronic computer (ENIAC)
Game theory
Cybernetic theory
Information theory
1st commercial computer (UNIVAC)
1st compiler
FORTRAN
2nd generation high-speed drum printer
ALGOL
1st computer utility (CTSS/MAC)
COBOL
1st on-line generalized data base management
3rd generation (transistor
Sketchpad PL/1
1930
1940
1950
1960
Computer technology
D-30 communications
Dataphone
Time-sharing
Digital transmission
Communications technology
1930
1940
1950
1960
Television
Color television
Long-distance dialing by operators
Color television broadcasting
Phototypesetting
Commercial television
Xerography
Tape recorder
Cable television
Holography
Direct-distance dialing
Educational television
Videotape recording
Touch-tone television
Echo 1
Telstar 1
Picture phone
Computer typesetting
Global television
INTELSAT

Figure 10-1 The information environment. The two industries of computers and communications fuse together.

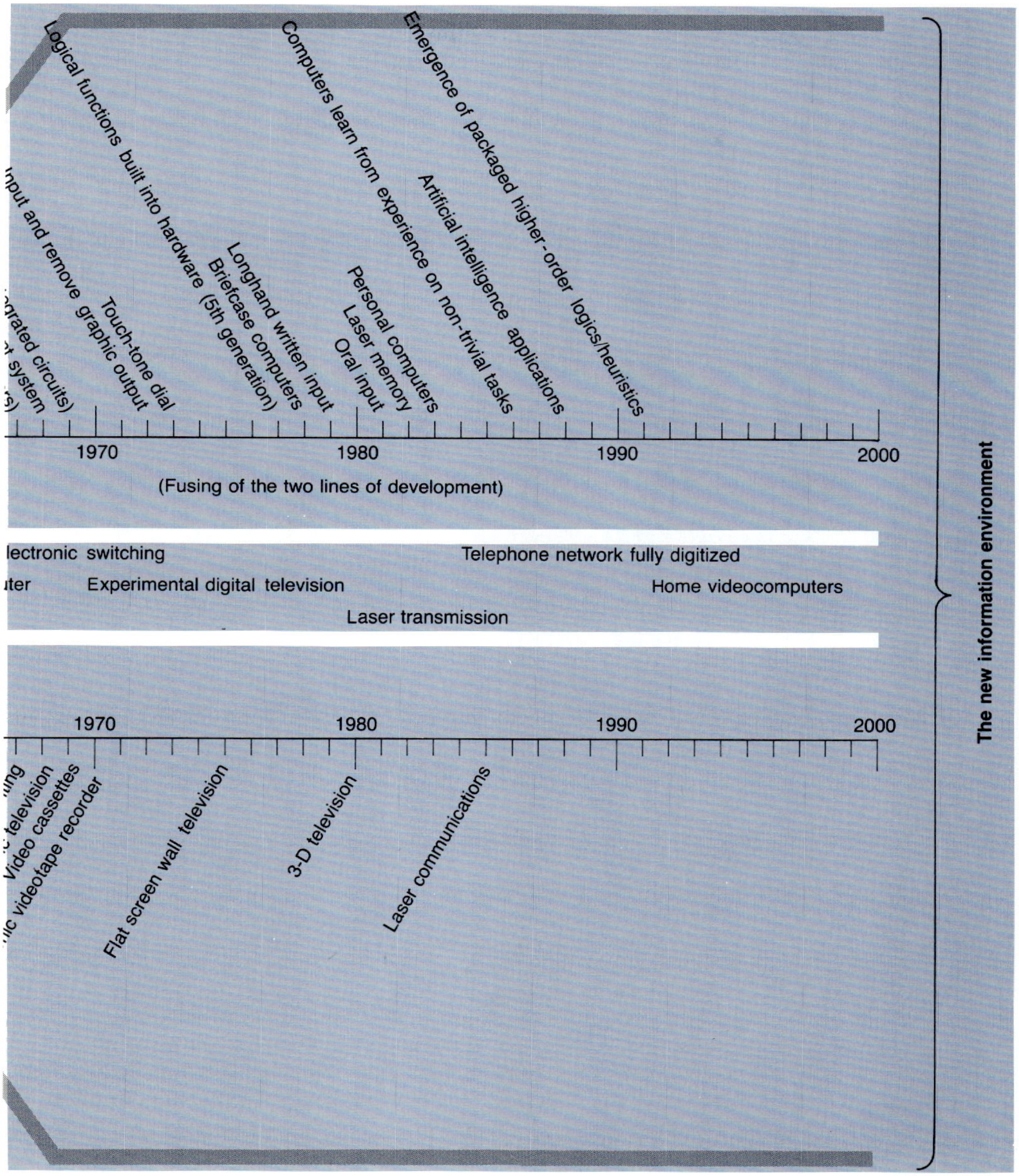
Logical functions built into hardware (5th generation)
Computers learn from experience on non-trivial tasks
Emergence of packaged higher-order logics/heuristics
Artificial intelligence applications
Input and remove graphic output
Touch-tone dial
Longhand written input
Briefcase computers
Personal computers
Laser memory
Oral input
1970
1980
1990
2000
(Fusing of the two lines of development)
lectronic switching
Telephone network fully digitized
ıter
Experimental digital television
Home videocomputers
Laser transmission
1970
1980
1990
2000
Video cassettes
videotape recorder
Flat screen wall television
3-D television
Laser communications
The new information environment

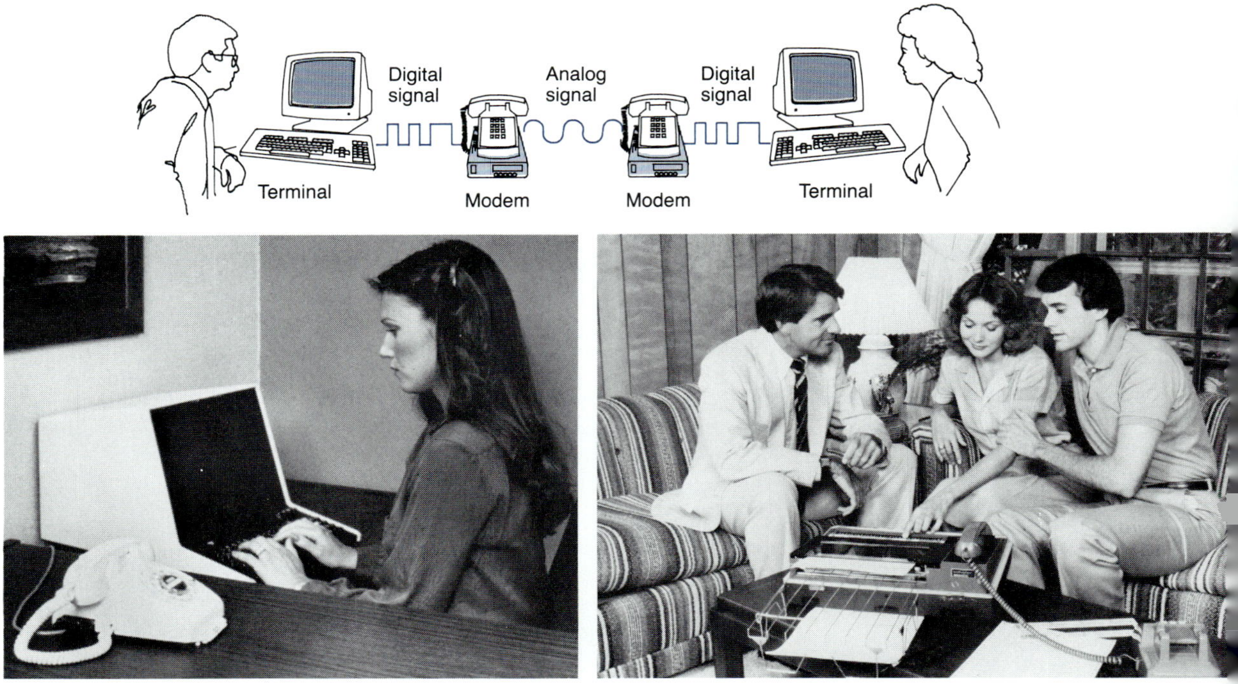
Digital signal
Analog signal
Digital signal
Terminal
Modem
Modem
Terminal

Figure 10-2 **Digital to analog and back.** *Top*: A modem converts the digital signal's pulse and absence of a pulse into the analog signal of the telephone, which has a wider range of frequencies in order to accommodate the human voice. A modem at the receiving end converts the analog signal back into the digital signal for use by the second computer. *Bottom left:* A modem. What is there to see here? Note the attachment on the side of the telephone. There are different types of modems. Onboard modems are in the computer housing and not visible to the user. Stand alone modems are located in a box separate from the computer. *Bottom right:* An acoustic coupler. This style of modem allows a standard telephone handset to be placed in the cradle. Here an insurance salesman uses a computer-with-modem to help this couple with their financial-planning questions. The answers are obtained via telephone from the insurance company's data base.

Here we are principally concerned with sending computer data. Because of the extensive telephone network already in place throughout this country and the world, a great deal of computer communications is over telephone lines. The telephone was built for voice transmission, which requires an **analog signal**—an electronic signal that will represent a range of frequencies. However, most input and output devices and most CPUs will send and receive only **digital signals**—which are merely the presence or absence of an electronic pulse.

The device that converts digital signals to analog and the reverse is a **modem,** the tool for communications interface. *Modem* is short for "*mo*dulate/*dem*odulate"; **modulation** is the name of the process of converting from digital to analog and **demodulation** from analog to digital. Sometimes the modem has a cradle that will accept a standard telephone handset; this is called an **acoustic coupler** (see Figure 10-2). The speed with which information is sent is expressed in **bits per second (bps).** Because of industry standardization, only a few different bps speeds are used for personal computers. They include 300, 1200, 2400, 4800, and 9600 bps.

Not all computer communications must be converted from digital to analog and back. In computer systems where input, output, CPU, and secondary storage are all reasonably close together—within the same building, say—data can be transmitted digitally through special cables.

The Communication Channel: Transmission

The communication channel, like a freeway or turnpike for cars, is the route along which data is transmitted. Telecommunications **transmission** is described by four characteristics:

- Direction of flow of data
- Communication lines or data roadways
- Speed of data transmission
- Sequencing

Direction of the Flow of Data

There are three directions or modes of data flow in a telecommunications system, as shown in Figure 10-3:

- Simplex
- Half-duplex
- Full-duplex

Simplex. Like a one-way street, **simplex** transmission allows data to travel in one direction only. Some terminals or processors are send-only or receive-only. Some POS terminals, for example, are send-only; some printers are receive-only devices.

Simplex transmission is not frequently used in telecommunications systems today, and it is generally used only when the terminal or processor requires it.

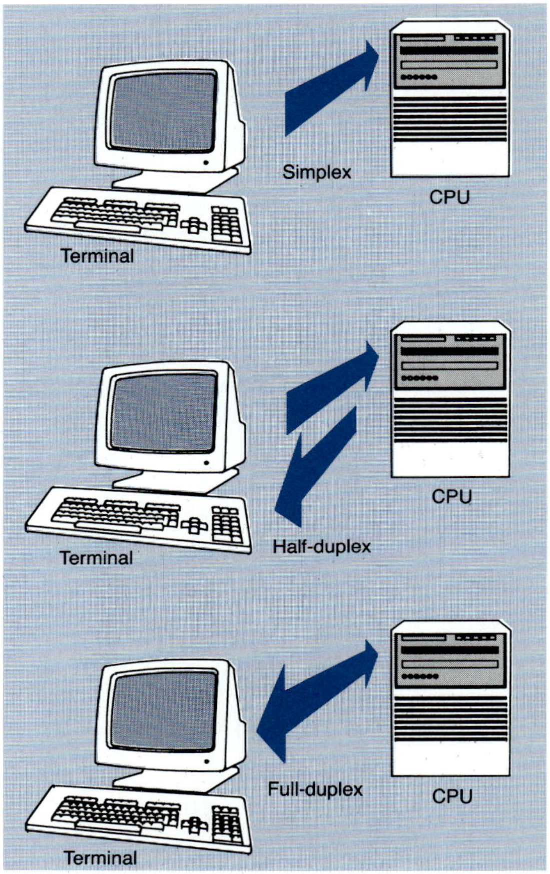
Simplex
CPU
Terminal
Half-duplex
CPU
Terminal
Full-duplex
CPU
Terminal

Figure 10-3 Three kinds of transmission lines. *Top*: Simplex—one-way flow of data. *Middle*: Half-duplex—one-way-at-a-time flow of data in either direction. *Bottom*: Full-duplex—simultaneous two-way flow of data.

Half-Duplex. In **half-duplex** operation, transmission is in both directions, but not simultaneously. Sometimes called "one way at a time" transmission, half-duplex is by far the most common type of transmission operation. In half-duplex communications, data flows only in one direction at any one time, like traffic on a one-lane bridge or two people having a very polite conversation. For example, a POS terminal may transmit sales data to a distant CPU, and then the CPU may respond by acknowledging the receipt of that data.

Half-duplex transmission requires terminals or processors that can both send and receive messages. In addition, the transmission lines must be able to operate in either direction. The process of reversing the direction of transmission is called **overhead** and requires a certain amount

Text continues on p. 351

CORPORATE REPORT 4

The Information Industry: Inside Look at a Computer Magazine Publisher

The Information Age of computers has spawned a need for information *about* computers and how to use them. As a result, there are about 600 computer periodicals worldwide. As the chart on the next right-hand page indicates, 16 of the top 25 magazines are related to personal computers—and all but five of them were started within the last decade.

A member of CW Communications/Inc. group, the world's largest publisher of computer-related information, PC World Communications is a San Francisco publisher of two magazines: *PC World*, for users of the IBM Personal Computer, and *Macworld*, for users of the Apple Macintosh computer. Located in what was formerly a soap factory—some of the old soap vats have even been converted to offices, as shown here—PC World Communications uses computers extensively in the production of its magazines, for telecommunications, and for other office activities.

The Making of a Magazine

On these and the following pages, we show how computers are used in the production of *Macworld* magazine. There are essentially two processes: the writing and editing process is illustrated in the strip of pictures along the top of this page; the art and production process is shown at the top of the right-hand page.

above: PC World Communications was founded by David Bunnell (shown with his son at the keyboard), a personal computer industry pioneer who worked at the first company that offered microcomputer kits by mail, MITS, based in Albuquerque in the mid-1970s. Publisher Bunnell often consults with in-house writers about article ideas, although ideas also come from outside freelancers. Staff writers, like the woman shown talking on the telephone, prepare their stories directly on the computer, either an IBM PC or a Macintosh. Diskettes containing finished articles are then sent to the copyediting department—an area of frenetic activity during the monthly's publishing deadline.

above: An overview of the *Macworld* offices, including the production department, which uses computers for scheduling and budgets. The production manager and staff discuss the requirements for meeting the issue's deadline. A page-by-page layout of the issue indicates placement of articles, artwork, and advertising. At far right, a designer does preliminary sketches of a magazine page.

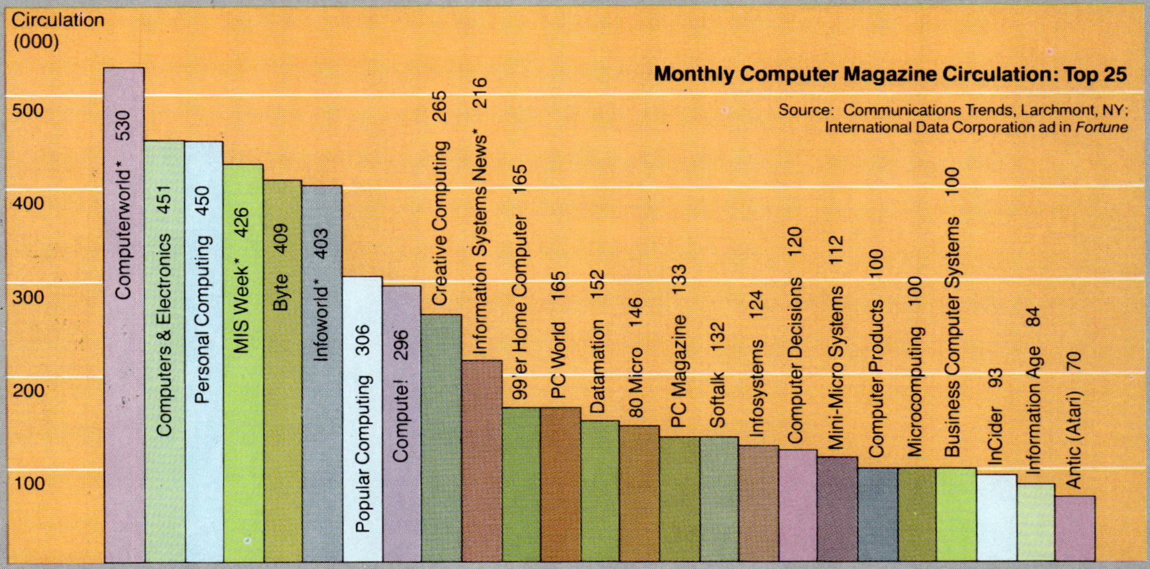

Circulation (000)
500
400
300
200
100
Monthly Computer Magazine Circulation: Top 25
Source: Communications Trends, Larchmont, NY; International Data Corporation ad in *Fortune*
Computerworld* 530
Computers & Electronics 451
Personal Computing 450
MIS Week* 426
Byte 409
Infoworld* 403
Popular Computing 306
Compute! 296
Creative Computing 265
Information Systems News* 216
99'er Home Computer 165
PC World 165
Datamation 152
80 Micro 146
PC Magazine 133
Softalk 132
Infosystems 124
Computer Decisions 120
Mini-Micro Systems 112
Computer Products 100
Microcomputing 100
Business Computer Systems 100
InCider 93
Information Age 84
Antic (Atari) 70

*Weekly and biweekly magazines calculated by taking 1983 distribution and dividing by 12.

above: Copyeditors edit writers' diskettes for spelling, punctuation, and clarity, using Macintosh and IBM PC computers. Members of the editorial department confer over progress of moving stories through their department. A final edited disk is then given to a keyboard operator, who sends it via telecommunications to a typesetting shop in another part of the city. A normal article takes 2 to 3 minutes to send via phone lines. The typesetter later delivers back (by messenger) typeset articles that the magazine's art staff can paste up into "camera-ready copy" that can be printed.

MACWORLD
September/October 1984 $4.00
The Macintosh Magazine
MacDraw, the Mac's Electronic Drafting Set
Enter the $22,000 Macworld Art Contest!
Meet the Macintosh Game Wizards
The Imagewriter and Beyond
Chart and Multiplan Team Up

above: The art director uses a Macintosh computer with a mouse to create artwork for a story the magazine is running about an electronic drafting program (MacDraw); the drawing shows a sketch of the San Francisco Zoo's Primate Discovery Center, which is featured with the article and on the issue's cover *(see below)*. Artwork is printed out on a printer. The production manager confers with the staff about the schedule of the magazine. Far right: a production artist pastes up a page of type and artwork. The "book," as the magazine is called, is now ready to go to the printer.

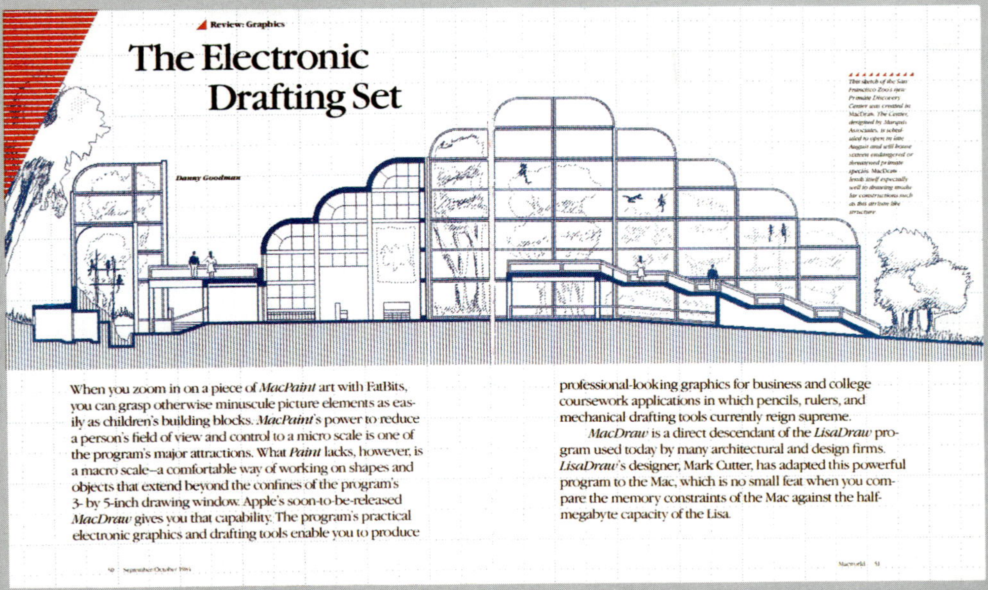

Review: Graphics

The Electronic Drafting Set

Danny Goodman

This sketch of the San Francisco Zoo's new Primate Discovery Center was created in MacDraw. The Center, designed by Marquis Associates, is scheduled to open in late August and will house sixteen endangered or threatened primate species. MacDraw lends itself especially well to drawing modular constructions such as this atrium-like structure.

When you zoom in on a piece of *MacPaint* art with FatBits, you can grasp otherwise minuscule picture elements as easily as children's building blocks. *MacPaint*'s power to reduce a person's field of view and control to a micro scale is one of the program's major attractions. What *Paint* lacks, however, is a macro scale–a comfortable way of working on shapes and objects that extend beyond the confines of the program's 3- by 5-inch drawing window. Apple's soon-to-be-released *MacDraw* gives you that capability. The program's practical electronic graphics and drafting tools enable you to produce professional-looking graphics for business and college coursework applications in which pencils, rulers, and mechanical drafting tools currently reign supreme.

MacDraw is a direct descendant of the *LisaDraw* program used today by many architectural and design firms. *LisaDraw*'s designer, Mark Cutter, has adapted this powerful program to the Mac, which is no small feat when you compare the memory constraints of the Mac against the half-megabyte capacity of the Lisa.

50 September/October 1984

Macworld 51

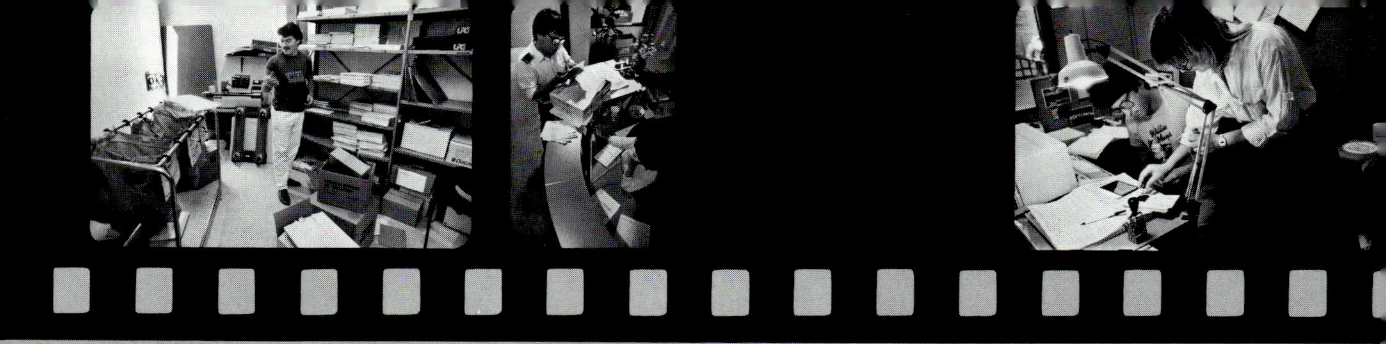

Communications: Old Ways, New Ways

Just as the production of the magazine is a combination of old-fashioned hand work and computer automation and just as the offices themselves are a fascinating mix of old and new, so are PC World's methods of communication: tomorrow has not yet quite arrived, and yesterday is not yet completely past.

Information comes and goes in that time-honored method—via U.S. Postal Service mail bags. It also is handled by messengers and overnight delivery services such as Federal Express. But it would be surprising if a member of the CW Communications group—which publishes overseas editions

MACWORLD
Picture-Perfect Macintosh Charts
The Lisa 2 Connection
Macintosh Goes to College
Working with a Single-Drive Mac

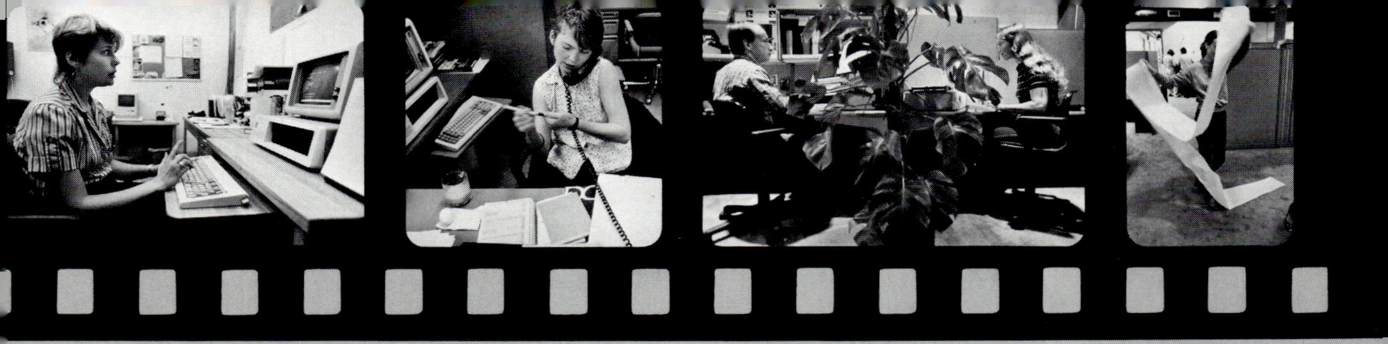

of *Computerworld* from Australia to Germany—did not do some sort of electronic exchange of information.

This is in fact what the people shown above are doing. A good deal of contact with the parent company in Framingham, Massachusetts, is handled by telecommunications, including accounting matters. A news digest is sent simultaneously to a number of CW Communications publications via computers connected to the Tymshare network. An electronic mailbox allows PC World to share messages with a number of sister publications.

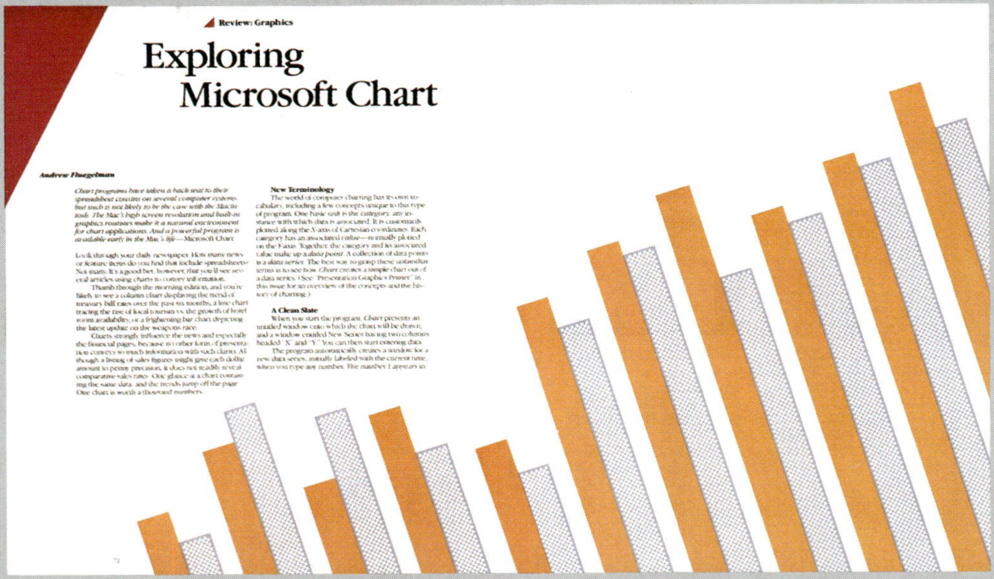

Review: Graphics

Exploring Microsoft Chart

Andrew Fluegelman

Chart programs have taken a back seat to their spreadsheet cousins on several computer systems, but such is not likely to be the case with the Macintosh. The Mac's high screen resolution and built-in graphics routines make it a natural environment for chart applications. And a powerful program is available early in the Mac's life—Microsoft Chart.

Look through your daily newspaper. How many news or feature items do you find that include spreadsheets? Not many. It's a good bet, however, that you'll see several articles using charts to convey information.

Thumb through the morning edition, and you're likely to see a column chart displaying the trend of treasury bill rates over the past six months, a line chart tracing the rise of local tourism vs. the growth of hotel room availability, or a frightening bar chart depicting the latest update on the weapons race.

Charts strongly influence the news and especially the financial pages, because no other form of presentation conveys so much information with such clarity. Although a listing of sales figures might give each dollar amount to penny precision, it does not readily reveal comparative sales rates. One glance at a chart containing the same data, and the trends jump off the page. One chart is worth a thousand numbers.

New Terminology

The world of computer charting has its own vocabulary, including a few concepts unique to this type of program. One basic unit is the *category*: any instance with which data is associated. It is customarily plotted along the X-axis of Cartesian coordinates. Each category has an associated *value*—normally plotted on the Y-axis. Together, the category and its associated value make up a *data point*. A collection of data points is a *data series*. The best way to grasp these unfamiliar terms is to see how *Chart* creates a simple chart out of a data series. (See "Presentation Graphics Primer" in this issue for an overview of the concepts and the history of charting.)

A Clean Slate

When you start the program, *Chart* presents an untitled window onto which the chart will be drawn, and a window entitled New Series having two columns headed "X" and "Y." You can then start entering data.

The program automatically creates a window for a new data series, initially labeled with the current time, when you type any number. The number 1 appears in

Keeping Up

Anyone involved with computers—and this will probably include you—finds that keeping up is an ongoing task. Formal education opens the door, but the continual changes in software, hardware, and systems require that one keep current. Although conventions, workshops, and seminars are three ways of keeping up, the easiest way is the one we have shown here—with computer magazines.

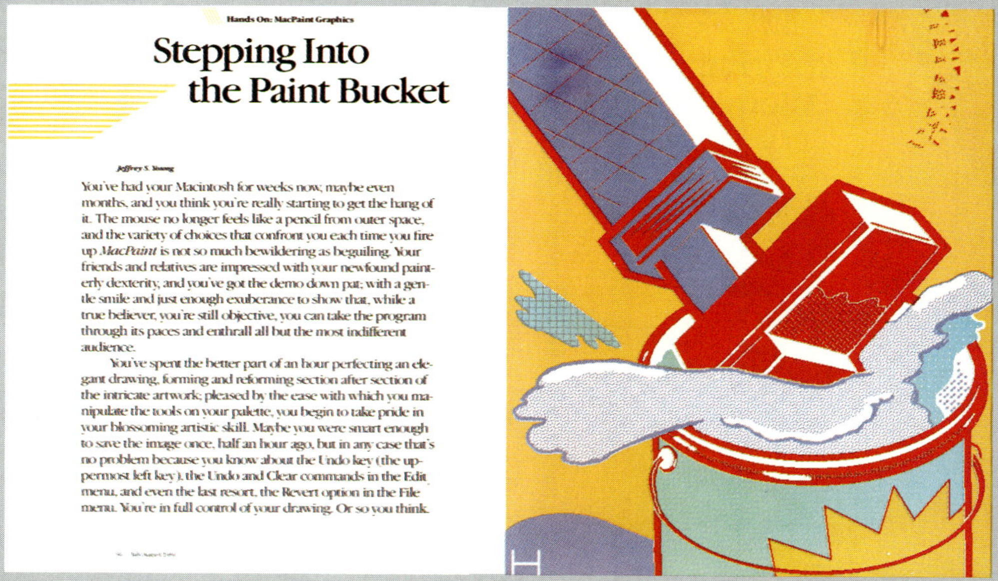

Hands On: MacPaint Graphics

Stepping Into the Paint Bucket

Jeffrey S. Young

You've had your Macintosh for weeks now, maybe even months, and you think you're really starting to get the hang of it. The mouse no longer feels like a pencil from outer space, and the variety of choices that confront you each time you fire up *MacPaint* is not so much bewildering as beguiling. Your friends and relatives are impressed with your newfound painterly dexterity, and you've got the demo down pat; with a gentle smile and just enough exuberance to show that, while a true believer, you're still objective, you can take the program through its paces and enthrall all but the most indifferent audience.

You've spent the better part of an hour perfecting an elegant drawing, forming and reforming section after section of the intricate artwork; pleased by the ease with which you manipulate the tools on your palette, you begin to take pride in your blossoming artistic skill. Maybe you were smart enough to save the image once, half an hour ago, but in any case that's no problem because you know about the Undo key (the uppermost left key), the Undo and Clear commands in the Edit menu, and even the last resort, the Revert option in the File menu. You're in full control of your drawing. Or so you think.

of **turnaround time,** such as 20 to 200 milliseconds—time that can be significant if a large number of direction reversals occur.

Full-Duplex. Sometimes called "two-way operation," **full-duplex** transmission is just that; like cars on a two-lane two-way street, data can be transmitted back and forth simultaneously. It is clearly the fastest of the three forms of transmission because not only is data moving both ways at the same time, but the turnaround time is eliminated.

Despite its obvious advantage, full-duplex transmission is not yet widely used because coordination is more difficult: not only must the transmission line be able to handle bidirectional flow of data, but the terminals and processors at each end must also be able to send and receive messages simultaneously. Nevertheless, full-duplex transmission promises to be the technology of the future.

Important Connections: Data Roadways

There are three major roadways or transmission media through which data can be made to flow:

- Wire cable
- Microwave
- Fiber optics

These are shown in Figure 10-4, pages 352–353.

Wire Cable. The oldest and still most common transmission line, **wire cable** is a major part of the nation's telephone system. Originally, telephone lines were simply pairs of copper wires strung between poles. Later these wire pairs were improved upon by the development of cables in which several hundred pairs of wires were bundled together to form a single cable. A more recent improvement is **coaxial cable,** in which multiple wires are replaced by a single solid core. You are apt to see coaxial cable used to link parts of a computer system located on one site.

Microwave. A more recent development, **microwave transmission** consists of high-frequency waves that travel in straight lines through the air rather than through wires. Because the waves cannot bend with the curvature of the earth, they are relayed via antennas placed on the tops of buildings—including those of banks—and mountains and located usually every 25 to 35 miles. More than half of the telephone system is now made up of microwave technology.

Communications satellites in space, orbiting 22,000 miles above the earth, are also used as microwave relay stations because they rotate at the precise point and speed above the equator that makes them appear stationary to microwave transmitters on the ground. Among the dozens

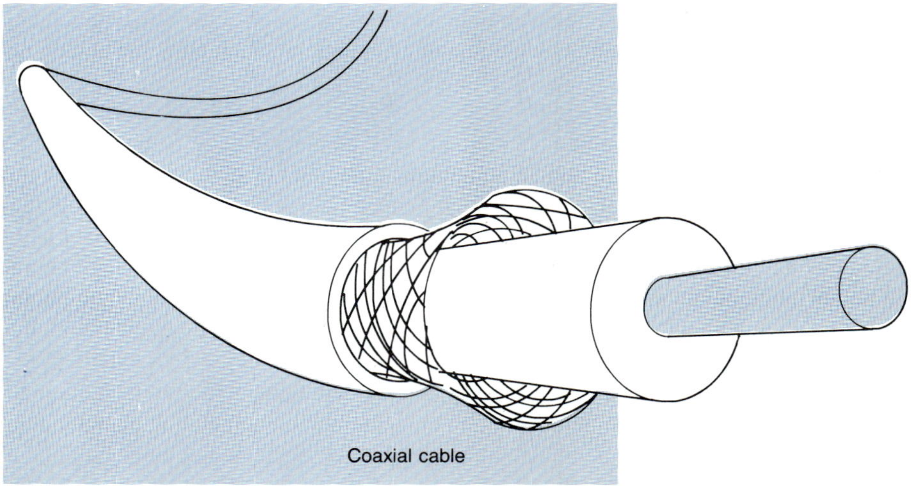
Coaxial cable

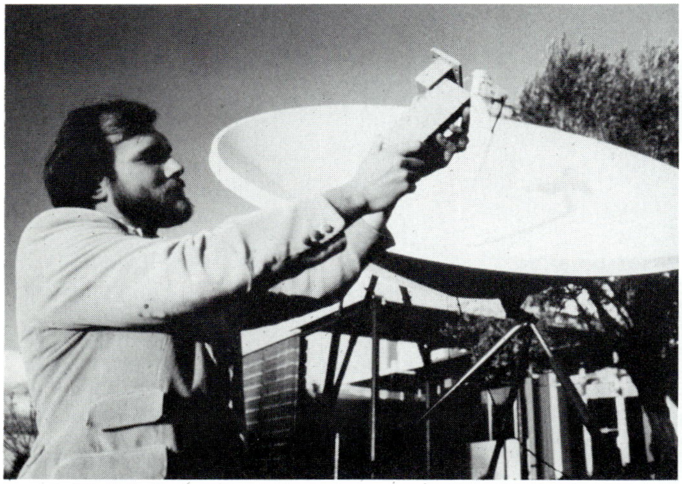

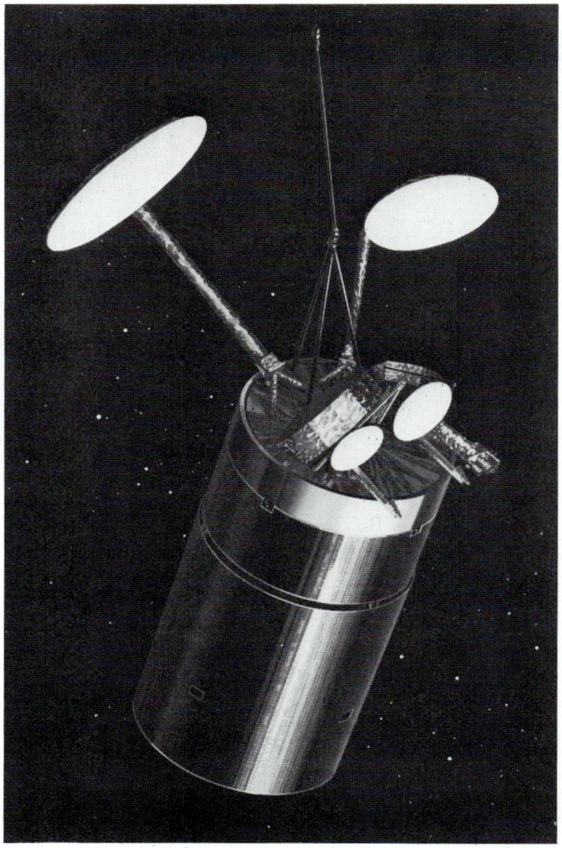

Figure 10-4 Three kinds of communication lines. *Top:* Coaxial cable. *Above left:* Microwave dish-shaped antenna. *Right:* INTELSAT VI communications satellite. With antenna system unfolded and aft solar panel extended, it stands nearly 39 feet high. *Opposite page:* Fiber optics. Hairlike glass fibers *(top left)* carry voice, television, and data signals, using a new technology called lightwave communication. Honeycombs of crystal within the cable *(top right)* hold fibers in precise alignment. *Bottom:* Fiber optic cable routes link parts of New York and New Jersey.

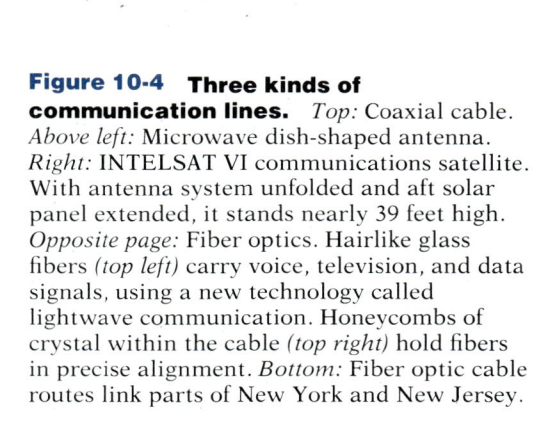

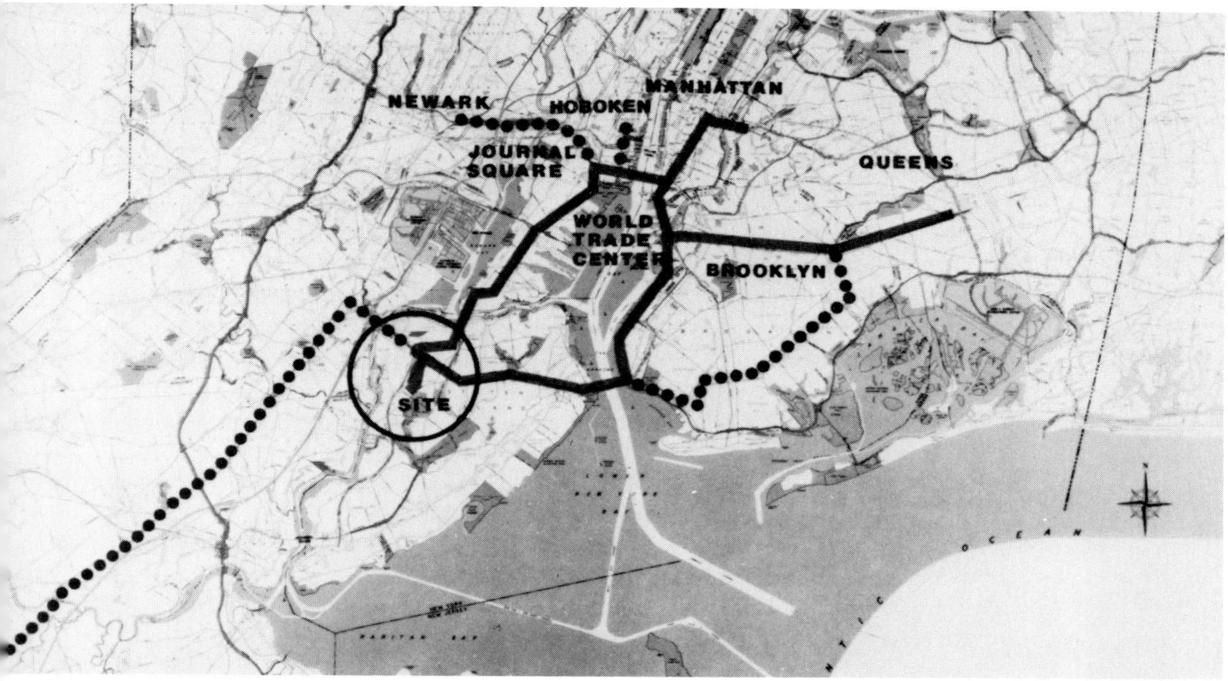
NEWARK
HOBOKEN
MANHATTAN
JOURNAL SQUARE
QUEENS
WORLD TRADE CENTER
BROOKLYN
SITE

HISTORY OF THE INFORMATION AGE

From UNIVAC to AT&T

It is hard to believe now that people used to refer to a computer as "Univac," but this is the name by which it probably first came to public attention. UNIVAC was the name that Presper Eckert and John Mauchly gave to their Universal Automatic Computer, on which they began work in 1946, fresh from their work on ENIAC (see p. 282). In 1949, Remington Rand acquired the company, and the first UNIVAC became operational at the Census Bureau in 1951.

However, it was the next year, a presidential election year, that the public really came to know the term UNIVAC. During vote counting the night of the 1952 election, UNIVAC surprised CBS network executives by predicting—after analyzing only 5% of the vote counted—that Eisenhower would defeat Stevenson. Of course, since then, computers have been used extensively by television networks to predict election outcomes.

UNIVAC was also the first computer used for data processing and record keeping by a business organization, installed by General Electric in Louisville, Kentucky, in 1954. Also in that year, IBM's 650 mainframe computer was first installed, an upgrade of the company's punched card machines. Because business people were already used to punched card data processing, the IBM 650 was readily accepted by the business commmunity, thus giving IBM a substantial foot in the door to the computer market, an advantage it still enjoys today.

In Chapter 1 we described the movement of computers from vacuum tubes (1951) to transistors (1959) to integrated circuit (1965). By 1960, a number of companies had entered the computer market, among them Control Data Corporation (CDC) and National Cash Register (NCR), which are still in competition, and General Electric, which is not.

of satellites now orbiting the globe and handling voice, video, and data communications are those launched by **INTELSAT,** short for *In*ternational *Tel*ecommunications *Sat*ellite Consortium. INTELSAT began with the Early Bird satellite in 1965 and now forms a worldwide communications system of over 100 countries. It accounts for most long-distance international communications. The United States representative to the consortium is **COMSAT** (*Com*munications *Sat*ellite Corporation).

Other satellite systems include those owned by RCA, the Americom system, which was the first to offer domestic communications service via satellite; Western Union, which launched its Westar system in 1974; AT&T, which leases satellites from COMSAT and has plans to launch its own; Satellite Business Systems, which began operating in 1981 and was put together by IBM, Aetna Life and Casualty Insurance Company, and COMSAT; and American Satellite Company, developed by Fairchild Industries and Continental Telephone Company, which leases satellite usage from Western Union.

In 1964, after reportedly spending a spectacular $5 billion, IBM announced an entire new line of computers called the System/360, so called because they covered "360 degrees" of a circle. That is, the System/360 came in several models and sizes, with about 40 different kinds of input and output and secondary storage devices, all compatible so that customers could put together systems tailor-made to their needs and budgets. The System/360 was a resounding success and repaid IBM's investment many times over.

But in the 1960s and 1970s, competitors to IBM saw holes they could fill. Large mainframe computers began to be supplemented by minicomputers, such as those made by Digital Equipment Corporation (DEC), Data General Corporation, and Hewlett-Packard. Cray, formed by Seymour Cray, began developing the supercomputer. A former IBM employee named Gene Amdahl marketed his Amdahl 470V/6, which was one and one-half times as fast as a comparable IBM computer, yet cost less and occupied only a third the space. Besides General Electric, RCA also tried to penetrate the mainframe computer market, but later withdrew. Of the original mainframe makers, the survivors today are IBM, NCR, Sperry-Univac, Burroughs, and Honeywell—and IBM has about 70% of the mainframe market.

In the 1970s, the volatile computer industry was thrown into an uproar when the microprocessor was invented, pointing the way to the relatively inexpensive microcomputer. Led by products from Tandy–Radio Shack, Apple, Commodore, Atari, and Texas Instruments, the microcomputer market has been the battleground of over 150 different computer manufacturers—among the most recent being those two industrial giants, IBM and AT&T.

IBM introduced its IBM PC (for Personal Computer) in the summer of 1981, and immediate-

The UNIVAC. J. Presper Eckert points out to newsman Walter Cronkite a printout from UNIVAC during the 1952 presidential election.

The IBM System/360. This $5 billion system helped IBM control 70% of the market for mainframe computers.

ly zoomed to the top in microcomputer sales—not surprising, considering IBM's long-term presence in the computer industry and its strength as a marketing-oriented organization. American Telephone & Telegraph, on the other hand, which used to be thought of as Ma Bell or "the Phone Company," was forced by the U.S. Government to divest itself of 22 local Bell operating companies (regrouped into seven regional holding companies) and to allow competition from other long-distance telephone services, such as MCI, GTE's Sprint, and Allnet Communications. In return, the government permitted AT&T to enter the computer market, but the question in many observers' minds was whether AT&T could relinquish the habits of a monopoly and become an aggressive marketing force in a highly competitive business. The announcement of AT&T's personal computer, the PC6300, in June 1984 was the company's opening gun. The strategy is to approach office automation from the company's historic base in communications, so that AT&T products can be linked together for both computing and communicating.

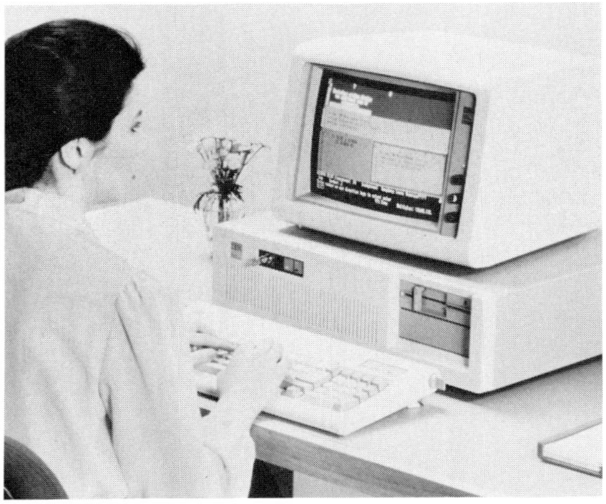

IBM personal computer AT. This personal computer was announced in August 1984.

AT&T personal computer. The PC6300 was announced in June 1984.

Fiber Optics. One of the most exciting new communications technologies is **fiber optics,** in which data is transmitted as pulses of light through tubes of glass half the diameter of a human hair. Among the many advantages of fiber optics are that the materials are lighter and less expensive than wire cables, more flexible than microwave and not limited to line-of-sight transmission, and faster and more reliable at transmitting data than the other communications materials. However, fiber optics are limited in the distance over which information may be transmitted.

Speed of Data Transmission

Nearly any kind of message can be converted into analog form for transmission, but different messages require different numbers of bits. A burglar alarm signal may take 40 bits, a typical interoffice memo 3000 bits, a newspaper-quality photograph 100,000 bits, and a high-quality photograph 2 million bits. Obviously, then, the *speed* with which a communications line can transmit data becomes important for certain kinds of purposes.

As mentioned, data transmission rates are measured in bits per second (bps). Each kind of communication line has a certain speed or capacity for transmitting that information; this is called the **bandwidth** of that medium. Some of the bandwidths are as follows:

- **45–150 bps:** Called **narrowband,** this is the lowest-grade pathway. It is used for telegraph lines and for low-speed data terminals.
- **1800 bps:** Called **voice grade,** this bandwidth is for the standard telephone line.
- **9600 bps:** This speed is available for special leased lines that are frequently used to support high-speed terminals connected to CPUs.
- **230,400 bps:** The highest quality transmission line, this is the **wideband** or **broadband** channel. It is used to support CPU-to-CPU communications.

Modes of Transmission: Asynchronous and Synchronous

Data can be transmitted in two modes, or sequences:

- Asynchronous—one character at a time
- Synchronous—groups of characters at a time

Asynchronous Transmission. Data travels down the transmission line the way people travel down the highway in a bus—in a group. In **asynchronous transmission,** data is sent and received one character at a time and each character, which is composed of seven or eight bits, is preceded by a "start" bit and followed by a "stop" bit. This is illustrated in Figure 10-5. The advantage of asynchronous transmission is that the data can be transmitted at any time that is convenient for the sender.

In order for a transmission to be successful, there must be a line **protocol,** a set of rules for the exchange of information between sender

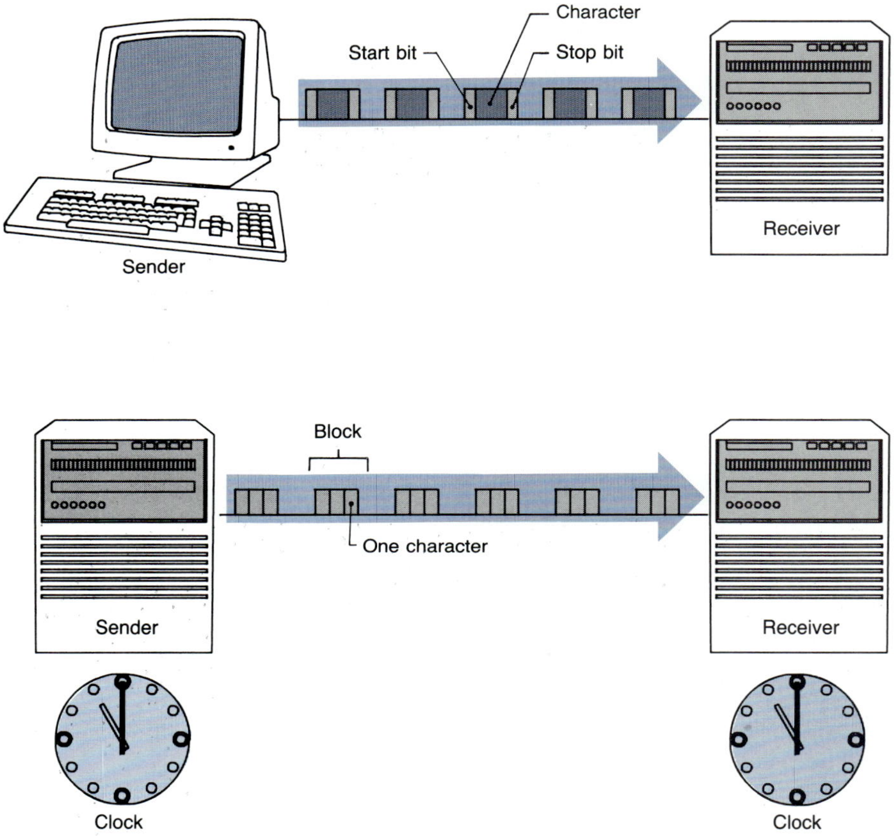
Character
Start bit
Stop bit
Sender
Receiver
Block
One character
Sender
Receiver
Clock
Clock

Figure 10-5 Asynchronous and synchronous transmission. *Top*: Asynchronous transmission. Note that each character is preceded by a start bit and followed by a stop bit. *Bottom*: Synchronous transmission. This kind of transmission requires a carefully controlled clock in order for the receiver to recognize or accept the message transmitted by the sender.

and receiver. The protocol in asynchronous transmission is that the start and stop bits indicate to the receiver the arrival of data. This type of protocol is often used for terminals with slow speeds.

Synchronous Transmission. In this mode, data is sent without start and stop bits. For the data transmission to be accepted by the receiver, however, sender and receiver must be synchronized by a carefully controlled clock (see Figure 10-5, bottom). That is, the blocks of characters are sent and received in a timed sequence. This type of transmission requires more expensive equipment than does the first kind, but data is transmitted faster.

Communications Processors

Communications processors resemble computer CPUs in that they have similar circuitry, have memories, and can be programmed, but their purpose is limited: to enhance data communications between two points. Communications processors fall into three broad categories (although there is some overlap):

- Message switchers
- Multiplexers and concentrators
- Front-end processors

Message Switchers

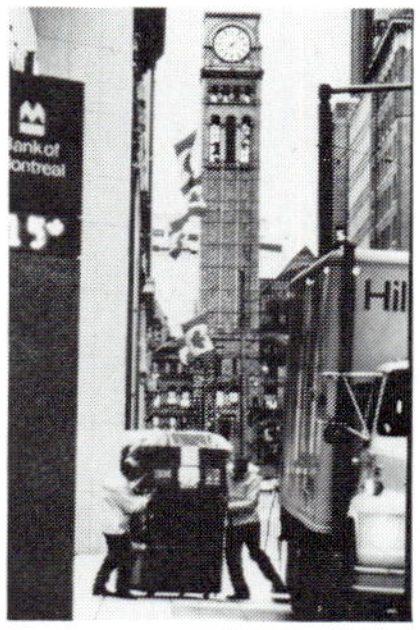

Atlantic-Pacific Bank's mainframe is in the Boston headquarters, but it is connected to three terminals in another branch bank across the state in Pittsfield. This is not an unusual arrangement; it makes sense for a single CPU to serve several terminals since the CPU operates at much greater speeds than the terminals do. As Figure 10-6 shows, there are two ways to connect the terminals to the CPU:

- Use three long-distance lines for the three terminals.
- Use a *single* long-distance line to connect all three terminals and have a switching device called a message switcher at the Pittsfield branch bank.

A **message switcher** is a processor that receives data messages from terminals, determines their destination, and routes them one at a time to the CPU. It distributes messages coming from the CPU to the appropriate terminal.

The advantage of a message switcher, of course, is that it reduces long-distance transmission costs, since only a single line is needed. Although only one terminal at a time can communicate with the CPU, message switchers are efficient with low-speed terminals that are used intermittently at remote sites.

Multiplexers and Concentrators

Like a message switcher, a multiplexer allows several terminals to use one line to communicate with a CPU; however, it allows the terminals to send their messages *simultaneously*. A **multiplexer,** in other words, collects messages from various senders and transmits them along a broadband channel at very high speeds to the receiver.

A **concentrator** is essentially a smart multiplexer: it can be programmed, has more processing capability, and is more flexible than a multiplexer.

Multiplexers and concentrators are frequently used at terminal sites with large input and output requirements.

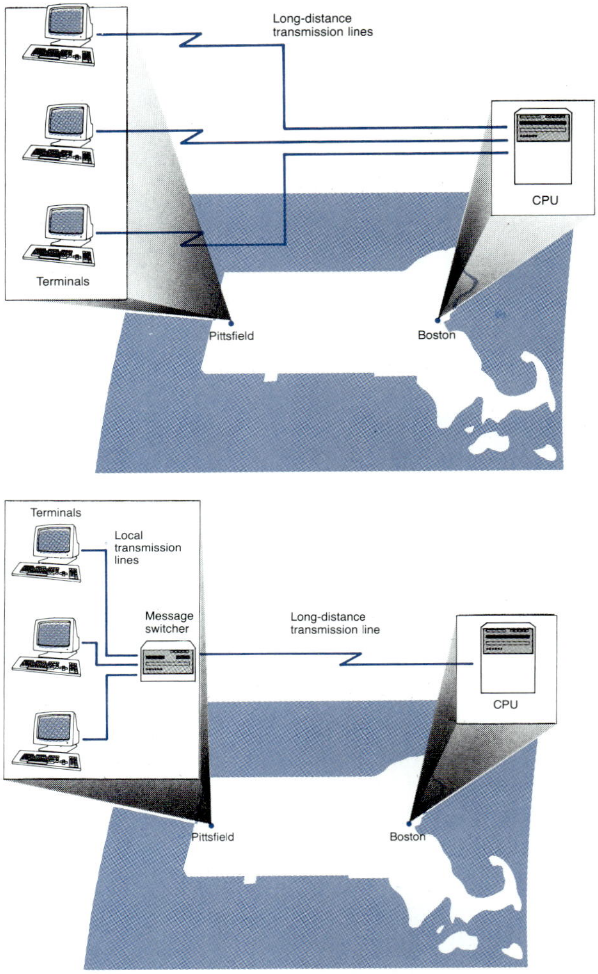
Long-distance
transmission lines
CPU
Terminals
Pittsfield
Boston
Terminals
Local
transmission
lines
Message
switcher
Long-distance
transmission line
CPU
Pittsfield
Boston

Figure 10-6 With and without a message switcher. *Top*: Each terminal has its own long-distance line connecting it to the CPU in Boston. *Bottom*: A single long-distance line connects the CPU to the three terminals in Pittsfield, but a message switcher in Pittsfield is used to distribute incoming messages from the CPU and to pick up outgoing messages.

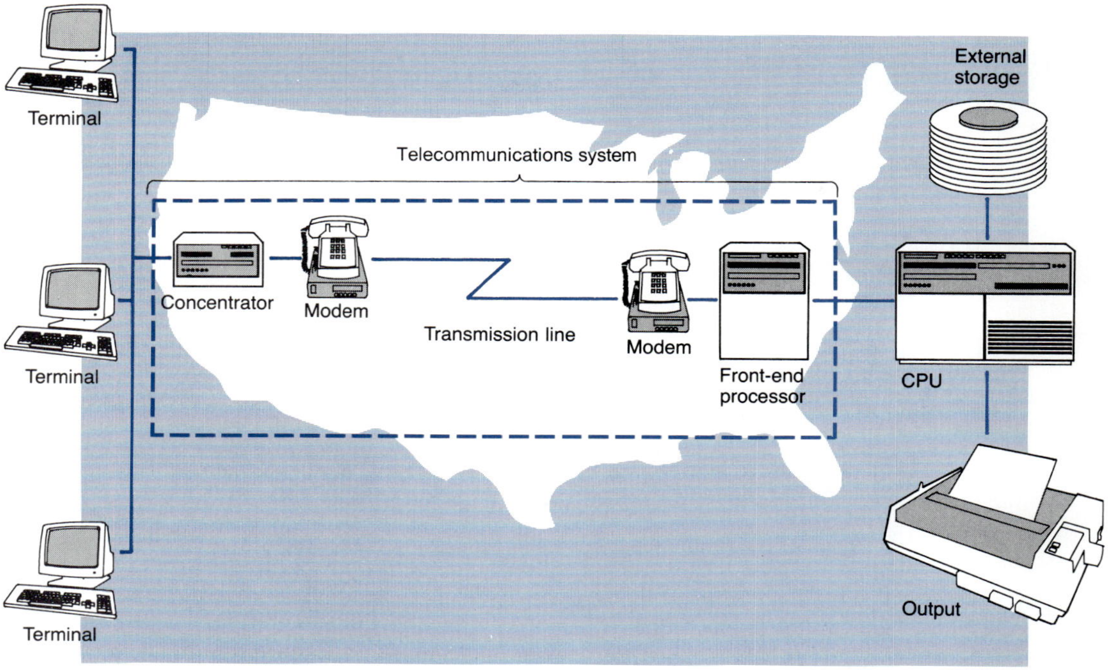
Terminal
Terminal
Terminal
Telecommunications system
Concentrator
Modem
Transmission line
Modem
Front-end processor
External storage
CPU
Output

Figure 10-7 How a telecommunications system works. Terminals are linked to concentrators, which are microcomputers or minicomputers used for communications purposes. The computer's digital signal is changed to an analog signal by the sending modem, then changed back to digital by the receiving modem. The front-end processor is a micro- or minicomputer that relieves the central computer of some of its communications tasks.

Front-End Processors

A **front-end processor** is located at the site of the CPU or the host computer and its purpose is to relieve the central computer of some of the communications tasks, leaving it free for processing applications programs.

Here we can see that communications processing and data processing equipment are nearly alike. Indeed, front-end processors *are* computers: they have some identical circuitry and perform many of the operations that data processing equipment performs. The only difference between the two kinds of equipment is their purpose.

An example of how these several communications devices work is shown in Figure 10-7.

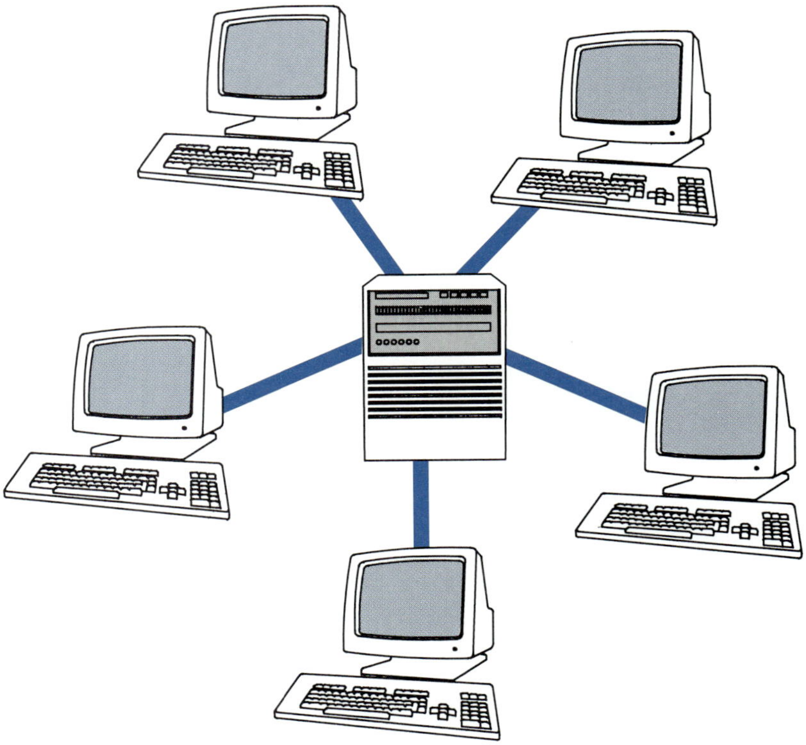

Networks

A **network** is simply a telecommunications system that connects two or more computers and their peripheral devices. The most common networks are:

- Star network—used in time sharing
- Ring network—used in distributed data processing
- Hierarchy

These are shown in Figure 10-8. The points in a network are called **nodes** and the lines joining them are called **arcs.**

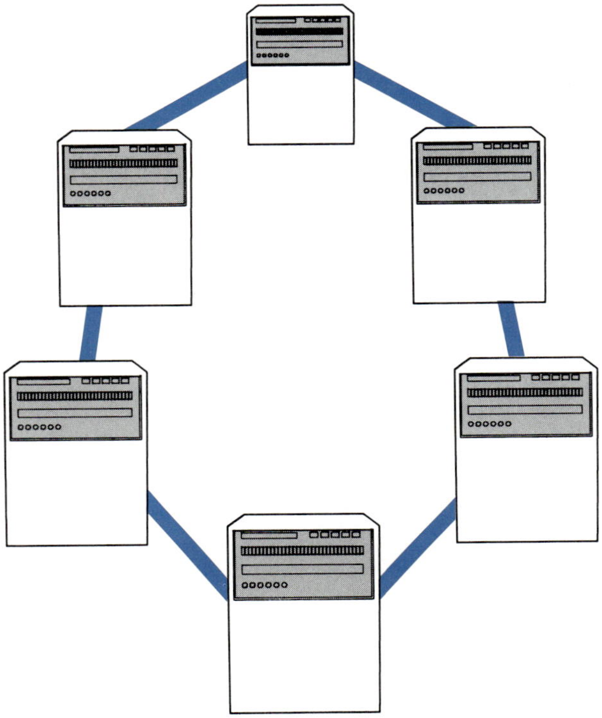

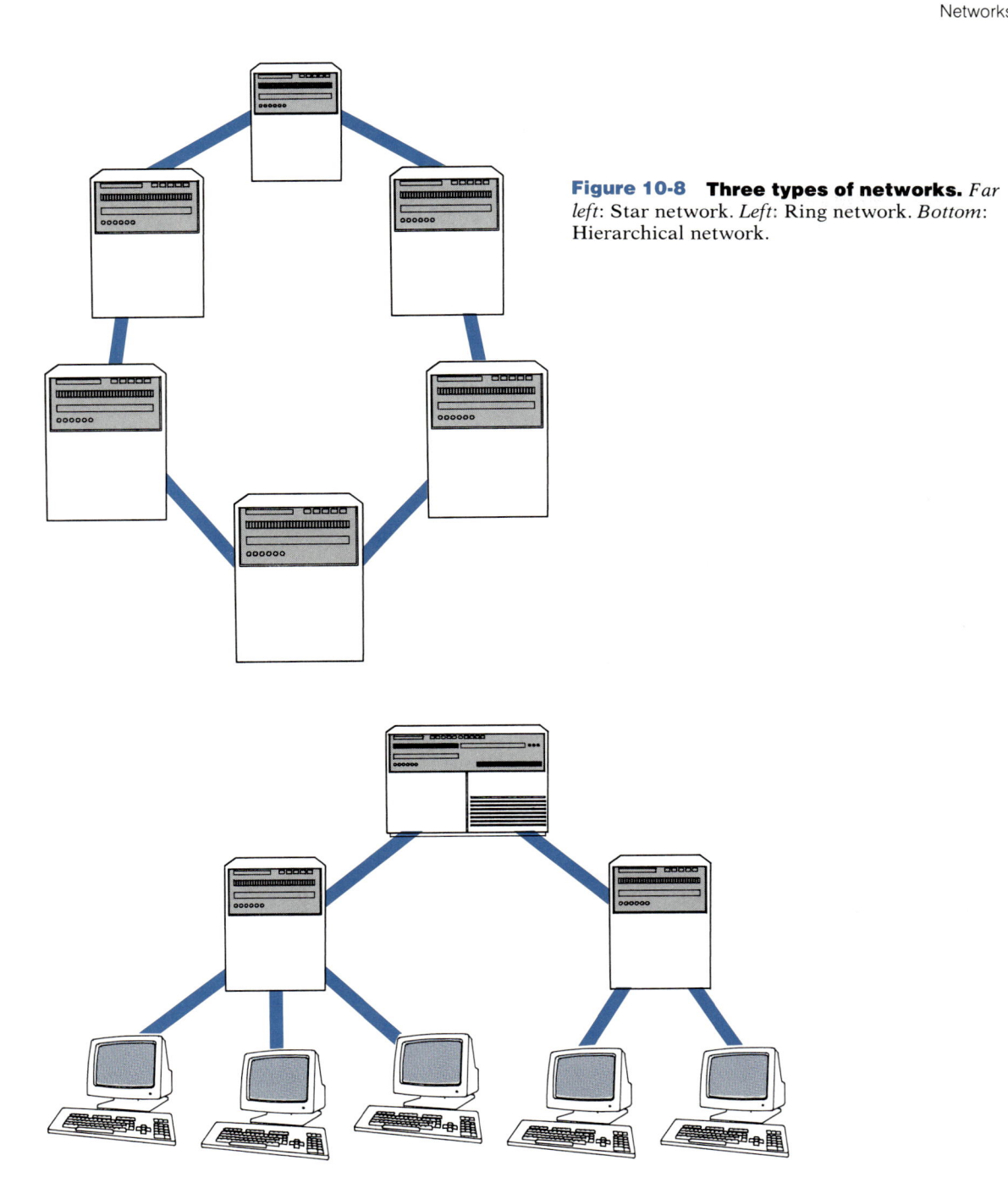

Figure 10-8 **Three types of networks.** *Far left*: Star network. *Left*: Ring network. *Bottom*: Hierarchical network.

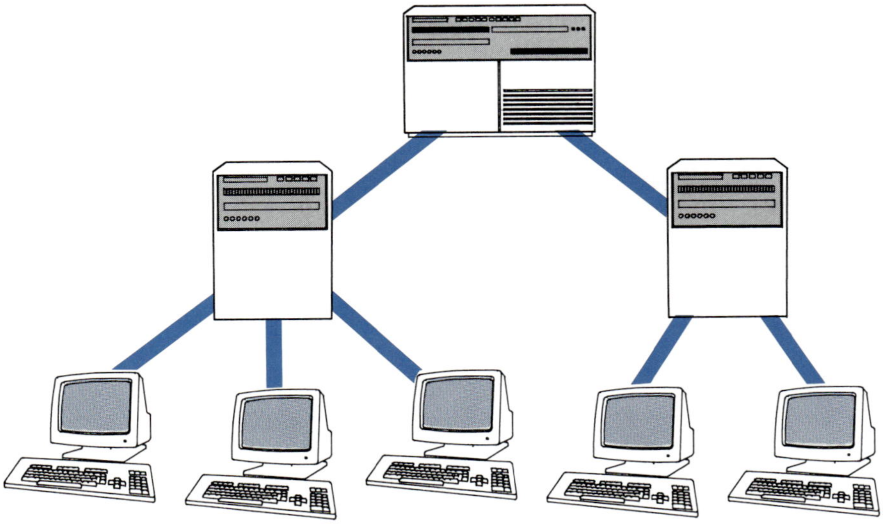

Star Networks: Time Sharing

The **star network** consists of one or more small computers or peripheral devices connected to a large host computer or CPU. Many organizations use the star network or a variation of it in a **time-sharing system,** in which several users are able to share a common central processor.

In a time-sharing setup, each terminal receives a fixed amount of the central CPU's time, called a **time slice.** If you are sitting at a terminal and cannot complete your task during the time slice, the computer will come back to you to allow you to do so. Actually, because the CPU operates so much faster than terminals, you will probably not even notice the CPU's being away.

By establishing time sharing, many people in a large organization can use a centralized computing facility. Time sharing can also be purchased from an outside service, and is an economical way to operate for a small company that cannot afford its own large computer.

The advantages of time sharing are:

- It allows economical allocation of an expensive resource, the CPU.
- It allows geographically dispersed users access to a large, powerful system.

The disadvantages are:

- Communications costs—particularly the cost of long-distance telephone lines—can be high for users in remote locations.
- Because the system is being shared with others, there is a possibility that data will not be secure.

Ring Networks: Distributed Data Processing

The **ring network**—which, as Figure 10-8 shows, can be as simple as a circle of point-to-point connections of computers at dispersed locations, with no central host computer—is appropriate for distributed data processing systems. A **distributed data processing system** is a decentralized computer system in which computers do their own processing in various locations but are connected to each other, usually via telephone lines. This linkage allows the computers to share processing loads, programs, data, and other resources. Typically the computers are minicomputers.

The advantages of distributed data processing are:

- Processing requirements and demands are shared among several computers.
- People at local sites have independence and control over their own computer resources.

The disadvantages are:

- There may be communication problems between CPUs, especially if they are made by different manufacturers.

- There may be problems in keeping data secure—that is, in keeping unauthorized people from seeing it.
- More skilled programmers and computer operators are required because there are more computer operations than in a time-sharing or centralized operation.
- Tighter organizational control is required of all computing facilities.

Hierarchical Networks

As Figure 10-8 shows, the **hierarchical network** somewhat resembles the star network. It consists of several computers linked to a central host computer or CPU, but these other computers may also play host to smaller computers. For instance, the host at the top of the hierarchy may be a mainframe; the ones below it may be minicomputers. These computers may be used to gain access to large data bases and to assist lower-level computers (such as microcomputers and terminals) with sophisticated computations.

SWIFT networks. An international association of banks in Belgium, SWIFT stands for Society for Worldwide Interbank Financial Telecommunications. Member banks—most are in Western Europe, but there are some as far away as the United States, Canada, Chile, and Japan—use their network of computers to transfer money between branches.

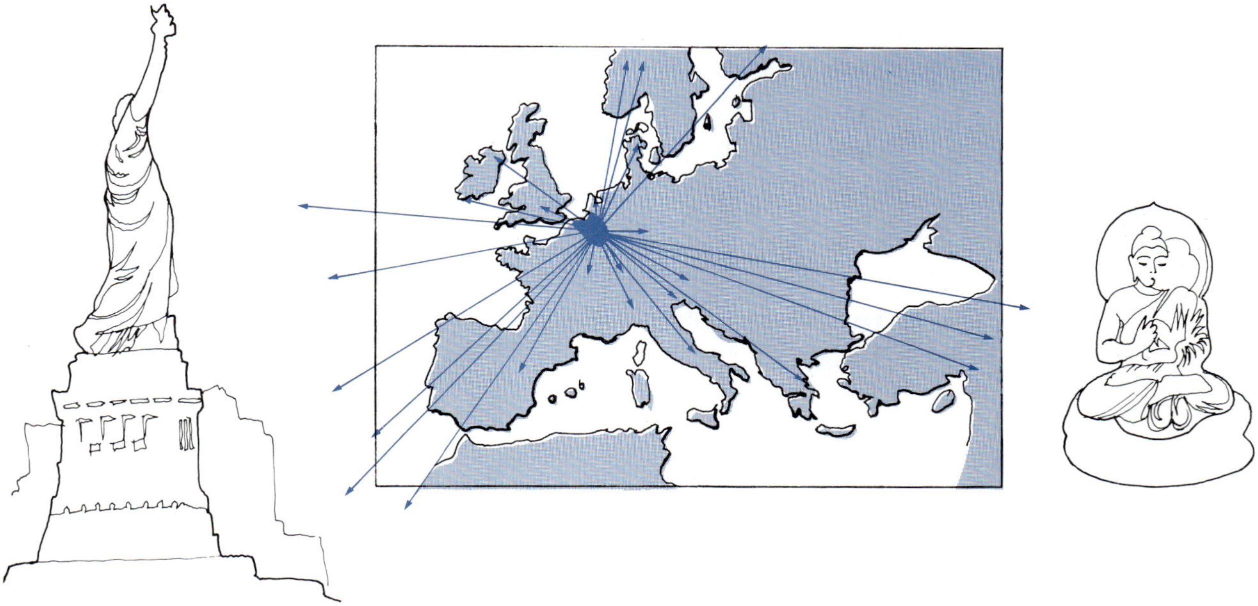

Networks and Geographical Dispersion

An organization the size of Atlantic-Pacific Bank will have several kinds of networks. On the one hand, you may find you need to communicate with another microcomputer down the hall in another office. On the other hand, the bank may wish to move money electronically around the world through several time zones throughout the night in order to take advantage of the most favorable interest rates in different parts of the world.

The types of networks are as follows:

- **Local area networks:** Using copper wire, coaxial cable, or optical fiber, **local area networks (LANs)** are networks in which all the computers and terminals are located in the same offices or buildings—for instance, several buildings on a college campus.
- **Metropolitan area networks:** Using microwave, optical fiber, copper wire, and perhaps **cellular radio**—radio phones in cars—**metropolitan area networks (MANs)** are usually created by a local telephone company to serve customers in the same city.
- **Wide area networks:** Abbreviated **WANs, wide area networks** make use of microwave relays and satellites to reach users over long distances in the same country. Examples of such networks in the United States are Tymnet, Telenet, and Uninet.
- **International networks:** Reaching clients outside the country, an **international network** uses coaxial cables and/or satellites. Examples are Western Union and RCA.

Installing a Network: Owning versus Renting

Atlantic-Pacific Bank, NA, is a big organization with many branches. Should it have its own network or rent parts of it from the outside? You have three choices:

- A private network
- A vendor's network
- A value-added network

Private Network. Atlantic-Pacific could design and install its own network; this is a **private network.** The advantages are:

- The network will custom fit your organization's needs.
- Security of data and operations will be tighter—this is of particular importance for a bank—because no outside organization will have direct access to the network.

The disadvantages are:

- A private network may be expensive.
- Your organization will have to assume total responsibility for the design, installation, and operation of the network—a task for which

Teleconferencing. Improved networking systems will permit better teleconferencing, such as the services offered by AT&T (*top*) and Western Union.

it may be difficult to find people, since data communications is a rather specialized occupation.

Vendor Network. If you decide not to have a private network, you could have a **vendor network,** in which an outside company furnishes all the hardware, software, and protocols—everything except the transmission line. The transmission line would be furnished by a **common carrier,** an organization such as AT&T or Western Union, which has been approved by the Federal Communications Commission and state regulatory agencies to offer communications services to the public. One well-known vendor network is IBM's Systems Network Architecture, better known as SNA. Introduced in 1974 as a standard way of connecting IBM host computers to terminal networks, SNA has been enhanced over the years so that it now can support a wide variety of hosts and peripheral devices.

The advantages of using a vendor network are:

- Outside expertise is available to design, install, and operate the network, so you need not hire staff of your own.
- Security of data and operations can still be controlled because the network is not shared with other users.

Disadvantages are:

- Vendor networks are still more expensive than alternatives.
- You do not have complete control over the network.

Value-Added Network. Whereas the vendor in a vendor network provides everything but the transmission line itself, the vendor of a **value-added network (VAN)** leases communication lines from a common carrier and then enhances (improves the value of) these lines by adding improvements such as error detection and faster response time. A value-added network also allows communications within your own organization as well as between user organizations.

The advantages of a value-added network are:

- It requires only a small initial investment.
- The responsibility for designing, installing, and operating the network remains outside your organization.
- Charges are based on usage—you pay only for the services you use.
- You can communicate with other users outside your organization.

The disadvantages are:

- You have no control over the network itself.
- Because you are sharing resources with other companies, security of your data and operations may be a concern.

ISDN: Planetwide Communications

The initials **ISDN**—for **Integrated Services Digital Network**—describe something that is not here yet but perhaps will be by 1990. Its effects are awesome to contemplate. As one writer puts it:

Facsimile. Facsimile ("fax") machines transmit both text and pictures, using telephone lines. Facsimile machines have been used for some time—for instance, by the Associated Press wire service to transmit photographs to member newspapers—but this digital facsimile unit by Exxon Office Systems is smaller and less expensive than most.

Suppose that telephone numbers were like Social Security numbers, good for a lifetime. No matter where you lived, or how often you moved, dialing the number permanently assigned to you would always ring your telephone. Or suppose that wherever you were, you could reach, say, the nearest Holiday Inn by tapping the telephone buttons marked H-O-L-I-D-A-Y-I-N-N.

Such feats—and many others—are becoming technically possible, as telephones and computers grow more alike. Indeed, as telephones make increasing use of the digital technology once found only in computers, the world's communications companies are fashioning a grand design for tomorrow's telephones known as the Integrated Services Digital Network, or ISDN.[1]

ISDN reflects the hope of many people that as most major countries build digital networks for computer communications over the next few years—networks that will replace the analog telephone networks—computer and telephone communications will be integrated with each other.

This means that the planning for such networks must occur now—as indeed it is—otherwise, the systems of the various countries will be incompatible with each other.

Clearly, ISDN would change the nature of both the communications and the computer industries. A telephone bought in the United States could also work in England. A computer could communicate with any other computer. A person could make a telephone call and communicate with a computer on the same line and at the same time. Information could be obtained from a distant computer as quickly as from one's own microcomputer.

It could also change the nature of publishing—and videotex, the subject we came in on at the beginning of this chapter. As the above writer points out:

> Despite years of experiments with videotex, most people prefer books, magazines and newspapers because reading a video screen is slow and eye-straining. ISDN could correct these shortcomings, which are a function of the rate at which information is sent to the screen. By sending data more than 200 times faster than today's videotex systems, ISDN would allow letters and numbers to be as crisp in video as in print. And scanning information on a screen could be done as rapidly as flipping pages in a book.[2]

SUMMARY

- **Data communications** refers to the way in which data is transmitted from one location to another; it includes anything that has the elements of sender, transmission line, message, and receiver, such as the different parts of a computer system in different locations. **Videotex** is a form of data communications that allows words and pictures to be sent and received on at-home video screens.
- **Telecommunications** is a form of data communications that uses electromagnetic signals or light energy over distance (such as telephone, radio, and television signals). **Teleprocessing** combines telecommunications and data processing; it means data processing at a distance. A teleprocessing system consists of terminals connected to a central computer by communication lines. Telecommunication and teleprocessing systems are often in **network** form—an interconnected system of computers and/or peripheral devices at remote locations.
- A telecommunications system has three parts: (1) communications interface, (2) transmission, and (3) communications processing.
- **Communications interface** comprises the sending and receiving instruments, such as telegraph keys and telephone handsets. Because of the extensive telephone network already in place in this country, much computer

communication is over telephone lines. The telephone uses an **analog signal**—an electronic signal that will represent a range of frequencies—for voice transmission. However, most input and output devices and most CPUs will send and receive only **digital signals**—which are the presence or absence of an electronic pulse.

- A **modem** (short for *mo*dulate/*dem*odulate) is the device that converts digital signals to analog signals, and vice versa. **Modulation** is the process of converting from digital to analog signals, and **demodulation** converts analog signals to digital ones. An **acoustic coupler** is a cradle that allows the modem to accept a standard telephone handset.
- The speed at which information is sent is expressed in **bits per second (bps).** The speeds used for personal computers are 300, 1200, 2400, 4800, and 9600 bps.
- Telecommunications **transmission,** the second part of a telecommunications system, is described by four characteristics: (1) direction of flow of data, (2) communication lines, or data roadways, (3) speed of data transmission, and (4) mode of transmission, or sequencing.
- The three directions, or modes of data flow are (1) simplex, (2) half-duplex, and (3) full-duplex. **Simplex** transmission allows data to travel in one direction only. Some terminals are send-only or receive-only. Simplex transmission is not frequently used in telecommunications systems today—generally only when the terminal or processor requires it. **Half-duplex** transmission, sometimes called "one way at a time transmission," is in both directions, but not simultaneously. This type of transmission, which is the most common kind of transmission operation, requires terminals or processors that can both send and receive messages, and the transmission lines must be able to operate in either direction. **Overhead** is the process of reversing the direction of transmission, which requires a certain amount of **turnaround time. Full-duplex** transmission, sometimes called "two-way operation," works in both directions simultaneously. It is the fastest of the three forms of transmission, but it is not yet widely used because coordination is difficult and it requires special equipment.
- There are three major kinds of communications lines, or data roadways: (1) wire cable, (2) microwave, and (3) fiber optics. **Wire cable** is the oldest and most common transmission line and is a major part of the American telephone system. Wires are sometimes bundled together to form a single cable. A **coaxial cable** replaces multiple wires with a single core. **Microwave** transmission consists of high-frequency waves that travel in straight lines through the air rather than through wires; the waves are relayed via antennas placed about 25 to 35 miles apart. More than half the American telephone system is now made up of microwave technology. **Communications satellites** are also used as microwave relay stations. **INTELSAT** (*In*ternational *Tel*ecommunications *Sat*ellite Consortium) has launched many of these satellites and

accounts for most long-distance international communications. The United States representative to the consortium is **COMSAT** (*Com*munications *Sat*ellite Corporation). **Fiber optics** is a new communications technology that transmits data as pulses of light through tubes of glass half the diameter of a human hair. Fiber optics materials are lighter and less expensive than wire cables; more flexible than microwave and not limited to line-of-sight transmission; and faster and more reliable than the other communications materials. However, fiber optics are limited in the distance over which information may be transmitted.

- Because different messages require different numbers of bits, the speed of transmission of data is important for certain purposes. Each kind of communication line has a certain speed or capacity for transmitting information; this is called the **bandwidth. Narrowband** (45–150 bps) is the lowest-grade pathway and is used for telegraph lines and low-speed data terminals. **Voice grade** (1800 bps) is the bandwidth used for the standard telephone line. The speed of 9600 bps is available for special leased lines that are frequently used to support high-speed terminals connected to CPUs. The **wideband,** or **broadband,** channel (230,400 bps) is the highest quality transmission line and is used to support CPU-to-CPU communications.

- The mode of transmission, or sequencing, of data can be **asynchronous** (one character at a time) or **synchronous** (groups of characters at a time). In asynchronous transmission, seven- or eight-bit characters are sent or received one at a time, preceded by a "start" bit and followed by a "stop" bit. The data can be transmitted at any time that is convenient for the sender. The **protocol,** which is a set of rules for the exchange of information between sender and receiver, in asynchronous transmission, is the start and stop bits that indicate to the receiver the arrival of data. In synchronous transmission, data is sent without start and stop bits, but the sender and the receiver must be synchronized by a clock, which means that the blocks of characters are sent and received in a timed sequence. Synchronous transmission requires more expensive equipment than asynchronous transmission, but the former transmits data faster than the latter.

- Communications processors (the third part of a telecommunications system) have circuitry similar to CPUs and memories, and they can be programmed. However, their purpose is limited: to enhance data communications between two points. Communications processors fall into three broad categories, with some overlap: (1) message switchers, (2) multiplexers and concentrators, and (3) front-end processors.

- A **message switcher** is a processor that receives data messages from terminals, determines their destination, and routes them one at a time to the CPU. It distributes messages coming from the CPU to the appropriate terminal. Message switchers have the advantage of reducing long-distance transmission costs, because only one line is needed. These switchers are efficient with low-speed terminals that are intermittently used at remote sites. Only one terminal at a time can communicate with the CPU.

- A **multiplexer** allows several terminals to use one line simultaneously to communicate with a CPU. It collects messages, puts them in order, and transmits them along a broadband channel. A **concentrator** is a multiplexer that can be programmed and that has increased processing capability and greater flexibility. Multiplexers and concentrators are frequently used at terminal sites that have large input and output requirements.

- A **front-end processor** is located at the site of the CPU or the host computer; it relieves the central computer of some of the communications tasks, leaving it free for processing application programs. Communications processors are computers in themselves; they differ from data processors in their purpose.

- A **network** is a telecommunications system that connects two or more computers and their peripheral devices. The most common networks are (1) star networks, (2) ring networks, and (3) hierarchies.

- A **star network** consists of one or more small computers or peripheral devices connected to a large host computer or CPU. Star networks are often used in a **time-sharing system,** in which several users are able to share a common central processor by receiving a **time slice,** which is a fixed amount of CPU time allotted to the user's terminal. Time sharing can be established within a single organization or purchased from an outside service. Its advantages are (1) that it allows economical allocation of an expensive resource and (2) that it allows geographically dispersed users access to a large, powerful system. Its disadvantages are (1) that communications costs can be high for users in remote locations and (2) that data may not be secure.

- A **ring network** is a **distributed data processing** system, which is a decentralized computer system in which connected computers do their own processing in various locations, usually via telephone lines. This linkage allows the computers, typically minicomputers, to share processing loads, programs, data, and other resources. Distributed data processing has several advantages: (1) Processing requirements and demands are shared among several computers. (2) People at local sites are independent and have control over their own computer resources. Its disadvantages include: (1) There may be communication problems between CPUs. (2) Data may not be secure. (3) More skilled programmers and computer operators are required because there are more computer operations than in a time-sharing, or centralized, operation. (4) Tighter organizational control is required of all computing facilities.

- **Hierarchical networks** resemble star networks. They consist of several computers linked to a central host computer or CPU, but these computers may also play host to smaller computers.

- **Local area networks (LANs)** use copper wire, coaxial cable, or optical fiber to connect all the computers and terminals located in the same offices or buildings.
- **Metropolitan area networks (MANs),** usually created by a local telephone company, use microwave, optical fiber, copper wire, and perhaps **cellular radio** (mobile radio phones) to serve customers in the same city.
- **Wide area networks (WANs)** use microwave relays and satellites to reach users over long distances in the same country.
- **International networks** use coaxial cables and/or satellites to reach clients outside a country.
- A **private network** is a company's own network. Its advantages are (1) that it will custom fit the organization's needs and (2) that the security of data and operations will be tight. Its disadvantages are (1) that it may be expensive, and (2) that the organization will have to assume total responsibility for the design, installation, and operation of the network.
- In the case of a **vendor network,** an outside company furnishes all the hardware, software, and protocols, but not the transmission line, which is furnished by a **common carrier**—an organization that has been approved by the Federal Communications Commission and state regulatory agencies to offer communications services to the public. The advantages of a vendor network are (1) that outside expertise is available to design, install, and operate the network and (2) that the security of data and operations can still be controlled because the network is not shared with others. Its disadvantages are that (1) it is expensive and (2) the user does not have complete control over the network.
- A **value-added network (VAN)** is like a vendor network; however, in this case the leased communications lines are enhanced by adding improvements such as error detection and faster response time. A value-added network also allows communications within an organization as well as between user organizations. Its advantages are as follows: (1) It requires only a small initial investment. (2) The responsibility for designing, installing, and operating the network remains with the outside service. (3) Charges are based on usage. (4) The user can communicate with other users outside the organization. Its disadvantages include: (1) The user has no control over the network. (2) Because the user is sharing resources with other companies, data and operations may not be secure.
- **Integrated Services Digital Networks (ISDN)** may be available by 1990. These computer communications networks will use digital technology to replace analog telephone networks. This technology will allow a computer to communicate with any other computer, a telephone bought in one country to work in any other country, and a person to make a phone call and use the same line at the same time to communicate with a computer; it will also change the nature of publishing and improve videotex systems. Plan-

ning is now in progress to make these systems compatible—even among countries.

KEY TERMS

Acoustic coupler, p. 349
Analog signal, p. 348
Arc, p. 362
Asynchronous transmission, p. 357
Bandwidth, p. 357
Bits per second (bps), p. 349
Broadband channel, p. 357
Cellular radio, p. 366
Coaxial cable, p. 351
Common carrier, p. 367
Communications satellite, p. 351
Communications interface, p. 345
Communications processor, p. 359
COMSAT, p. 354
Concentrator, p. 359
Data communications, p. 345
Demodulation, p. 349
Digital signal, p. 348
Distributed data processing system, p. 364
Fiber optics, p. 357
Front-end processor, p. 361
Full-duplex transmission, p. 351
Half-duplex transmission, p. 351
Hierarchical network, p. 365
Integrated Services Digital Network (ISDN), p. 368
INTELSAT, p. 354
International network, p. 366
Local area network (LAN), p. 366
Message switcher, p. 359
Metropolitan area network (MAN), p. 366
Microwave transmission, p. 351
Modem, p. 349
Modulation, p. 349
Multiplexer, p. 359
Narrowband, p. 357
Network, p. 345, 362
Node, p. 362
Overhead, p. 350
Private network, p. 366
Protocol, p. 357
Ring network, p. 364
Simplex transmission, p. 349
Star network, p. 364
Synchronous transmission, p. 358
Telecommunications, p. 345
Teleprocessing, p. 345
Time-sharing system, p. 364
Time slice, p. 364
Transmission, p. 349
Turnaround time, p. 351
Value-added network (VAN), p. 368
Vendor network, p. 367
Videotex, p. 343
Voice grade, p. 367
Wide area network (WAN), p. 366
Wideband channel, p. 351
Wire cable, p. 351

REVIEW QUESTIONS

1. Name the three basic parts of any telecommunications system.
2. What is the function of a modem? Define digital and analog signals.
3. What is half-duplex transmission?

4. Describe the three major data roadways.
5. How is the speed of data transmission measured?
6. What is the difference between asynchronous and synchronous transmission?
7. Describe the operations of one type of communications processor.
8. What is a time-sharing network? A distributed data processing system?
9. Compare the advantages of a vendor network with the advantages of a private network.

CASE PROBLEMS

Case 10-1: Using the Present While Waiting for the Information Age

Despite the claims of the futurists, the Information Age has not arrived just yet. There are a great many bottlenecks, such as the old-fashioned telephone network now in existence, which has limited ability to handle information—low-cost information can be transmitted to personal computers at only 120 characters per second, slightly faster than what most people comfortably read, but the IBM PC, for example, can receive 5 million characters per second.[2] In addition, of course, there are a great many people who do not *have* personal computers—your great aunt, perhaps. The term "Information Age" is premature. This fact has some implications for electronic mail.

Electronic mail applies to any communications service that permits the transmission and storage of messages by electronic means. This includes the telex machine, widely used since World War I and operated by Western Union, which leases telex lines to subscribers. It also includes facsimile ("fax") machines, which transmit both text and photographic images. The future, however, lies with the computer-mailbox services, in which a personal computer is used to send a message over telephone lines to a central computer, which then transmits it to the recipient's personal computer.

At present, says an August 20, 1984, *Fortune* article, the situation in computer-mailbox services "is akin to that in the early days of the telephone; both the sender and the recipient must subscribe to the same service, and until it has plenty of subscribers there will be little incentive to subscribe."[3] MCI is one company that is trying to expand electronic mail. With MCI Mail, the sender must have a personal computer (or telex, word processor, or electronic typewriter with a memory) linked to a telephone in order to send an electronic letter, but the letter is sent to a special high-speed laser printer at a regional center, which prints it out; the letter is then hand-delivered—at its fastest, about four hours—either through the U.S. mail or by courier service. This is an example of mixing the new technology with the old. Federal Express offers ZapMail, a service that is less demanding of the user and that allows graphics and already-typed material to be transmitted. In this process, the sender's document is picked up by courier and taken to a Federal Express office, where it is "faxed" to another Federal Express office, then delivered by courier to the recipient.

Your assignment: The Information Age may not have entirely arrived just yet, but the next few years will be pivotal and there will be major changes. The trick is to anticipate trends. Both MCI and Federal Express are trying to bridge the present and the future, not an easy undertaking. Look back over this chapter—and the preceding three chapters on hardware. Can you think of ways of using the present—present transportation, consumer habits, people's expectations, and so on—linking them with new communications technology, and applying them to certain kinds of enterprise?

Case 10-2: Avoiding Local Area Turmoil in LANs

Local area networks (LANs) have been around since the mid-1970s, but there have been conflicts as to what technologies are best. The result, says one observer quoted in *Business Week* (May 14, 1984), is that the LAN market "is better known as local area turmoil."[4] Some LANs are made by computer manufacturers that connect only their equipment, others work with a variety of equipment. Standards have begun to evolve, but manufacturers must still come together to agree on protocols, the coding and formats that permit computers to communicate with each other. Perhaps the closest to being an industry standard is Ethernet, marketed by Xerox Corporation; however, it is relatively expensive.

When considering whether to install a LAN, says John M. Allswang in *CAP* (April 1984), you want to know how your business or office will actually change when it is implemented. Will current software work under the network? Are all printers available to all users via software control? Is there a mail facility for storing messages and sending them from one user to another? Can any user send jobs to another station if that station is not currently in use? What do employees have to learn?[5]

Your assignment: Suppose you were the dean of a small technical college that is expanding onto a brand-new campus. You are to consult with the architect about the best kind of facilities, and you are to specify the kind of features you want in a LAN that will be wired into all the offices, dormitories, classrooms, and laboratories. What kind of requirements would you state?

Part 4

Corporate Organization Chart
President
Vice President of Finance
Vice President of Marketing
Vice President of R & D
chart type:
data border:
background:
origin line:
major hash:
minor hash:
label margins:
label display:
data margins:
data margins:
bar/gap size:
left
bottom
data
off
on
hash
left
top
right
bottom
scale
fix

Business Information Systems

"Although we continue to think we live in an industrial society," writes futurist John Naisbitt, "we have in fact changed to an economy based on the creation and distribution of information."[1]

This has tremendous significance for anyone contemplating a career in business during the next 20 years. The amount of scientific and technical information now doubles every $5\frac{1}{2}$ years, but with more powerful information systems and more scientists, the doubling could increase to 20 months, according to one estimate. And with mass-produced knowledge the driving force in our economy, computer skills will be needed in up to 75% of all jobs by 1990.[2] Indeed, a key question, says the president of Honeywell Information Systems, is whether workers can learn to "relate the computer to their jobs on their own initiative," without having to turn constantly to a computer professional for help.[3]

The four chapters that follow describe the kinds of computer-based business information systems with which the successful manager must become familiar, from systems concerned with detailed record keeping to systems that assist in making decisions at the executive level. After a discussion of how systems analysis and design works, we describe three levels of systems: *operations information systems,* which help an organization keep track of its material, money, employee, and facility resources; *management information systems,* which provide managers with structured reports; and *decision support systems,* which help executives analyze and make decisions about complicated problems.

CHAPTER 11

Systems Analysis and Design

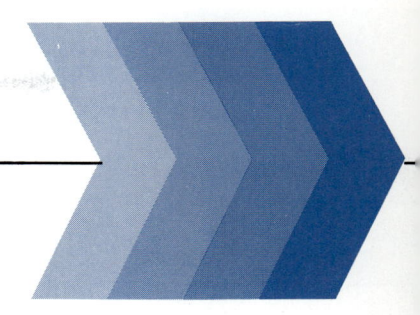

Putting Things in Order

PREVIEW

Two signs that the world's way of doing business has moved on while many people were looking elsewhere:

On April 24, 1984, the *New York Times* reported that—four years shy of its centennial—a venerable department store, Bugbee's of Putnam, Connecticut, had closed. Once an eastern Connecticut landmark, Bugbee's was more than a source of clothing, it was a place of shared experiences and rituals. The death of Bugbee's, said the *Times,* symbolized for many people "the continuing fragmentation of communal life in small towns such as Putnam, towns once largely self-sufficient that have been transformed into satellites of larger cities."[1] The times changed, in other words, and Bugbee's was unable to keep up with them.

Across the country on the same day, a writer in the *San Francisco Chronicle* pointed out that the rest of the world has moved on beyond the United States in a much more important way—in adopting the metric system of weights and measures, a system that makes much more sense than the "English" system of pounds, feet, gallons, and so on that we use. "Only a handful of countries, none of them major except for the U.S., still persist in using the archaic systems of weights and measurements," he writes. "We are one with only Burma, Brunei [a dot on the north coast of Borneo], and Liberia in insisting on being pound foolish and footloose. Even Britain, from which we took our system, has converted to metrics."[2] What, we must ask, will be the future of the United States if it refuses to go along with the rest of the world's changes?

Whatever enterprise you are in, there are quite often better ways of working. The trick is to identify when changes are needed and what those changes should be. The following case study shows a company that had a problem—a backlog amounting, in some instances, to 64 years' worth of items in stock—that it resolved by finding a better system. In this chapter, we describe a valuable tool

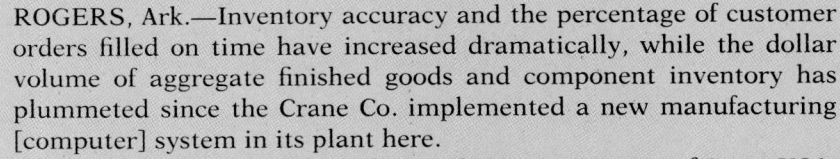

CASE STUDY: ELIMINATING A 64-YEAR SUPPLY

Closing the Valve on Inventory Mistakes

ROGERS, Ark.—Inventory accuracy and the percentage of customer orders filled on time have increased dramatically, while the dollar volume of aggregate finished goods and component inventory has plummeted since the Crane Co. implemented a new manufacturing [computer] system in its plant here.

CRANE

Crane, a division of the Valves and Fittings Division of Crane USA, manufactures bronze, stainless steel and iron valves. Before Crane implemented the new software package, all of its manufacturing records were kept on cards and updated by hand. Workers pulling parts for a rush order sometimes forgot to account for them on the card file. And if a card was lost, the entire record was lost.

Mistakes caused huge inventory buildups at Crane. Often the purchasing department reordered an item simply because a vendor was giving a price break. "The inventory was unreal," Mirian Von Struble, purchasing manager, explained. "There was a 64-year supply on some things. And there were always missing items. We had no control."

In addition, she said, parts were not inspected as they were received from vendors. "We spent many hours just retooling parts so we could use them," said Bill Wells, machine shop general foreman.

In 1979 Crane USA approved a plan to implement a Material Requirements Planning II system at the plant here. . . .

Under the new procedures, products would no longer be built without an engineering bill of material and specific manufacturing standards. "We can now provide accurate bills of material that truly represent the way the product is supposed to be built," Joe Weber, engineering manager, maintained.

The parts stockroom was another department where new procedures were implemented. "Now, there's only one way to put the inventory in and one way to take it out," [software evaluator] Robert Holiman said.

The receiving department also made changes. Employees are now issued drawings of each part ordered, and parts that do not match specifications are quickly rejected. As a result, suppliers no longer send unsatisfactory parts, Holiman said.

Plant Manager Russell Dutton said the change has had a ripple effect on the rest of the company. "In the assembly department, there are always matched sets of parts when they begin assembling a product," he said.

And in purchasing, according to Von Struble, "We're able to respond to the needs of production much faster now."

Crane's inventory has shot up to 95% accuracy, and the percentage of customer orders filled on time has doubled. Holiman, who became materials manager for Crane when implementation was complete, said Crane reduced its aggregate finished goods and component inventory from \$8.5 million to less than \$5.1 million in two years.

—*Computerworld,*
January 30, 1984

for the manager's toolkit, a collection of techniques for identifying and solving problems called systems analysis and design.

Systems Analysis and Design: What It Is, Why We Need It

All businesses, small or large, have information systems—even Bugbee's department store when it first opened in 1888 as a store for "dry and fancy goods." An **information system** includes people, procedures, inputs, outputs, and processing, all working together to produce accurate and timely information. Information must flow successfully into the firm from the outside and also flow successfully within the firm. Thus, an information system must link and coordinate the various departments within the company (see Figure 11-1).

Systems analysis and design is the process of analyzing a company's information system and designing improvements. It is basically a problem-solving procedure, consisting of five steps:

Marketing
Production
Information system
Accounting and finance
Research and development

Figure 11-1 A centralized business information system. This illustration, which appeared earlier in the book as Figure 3-8, shows that the four principal functional departments of a business organization draw on the same flow of information.

1. Identifying a company's business information needs and determining the feasibility of meeting those needs.
2. Evaluating the effectiveness of the company's present information system and specifying the new information requirements in detail.
3. Formulating alternative information systems and recommending one system.
4. Implementing the new information system.
5. Maintaining the new information system.

Systems analysis and design requires close cooperation of computer specialists and the users of the information to be produced by the system.

Let us suppose that on your job at Atlantic-Pacific Bank one day you received a phone call from Greg Douglas, an executive you met on a plane while traveling. He told you on the phone that he had recently been promoted to chief executive officer (CEO) of a stylish clothing manufacturer that calls itself Know-wear, because it specializes in designing and manufacturing clothes for collegians and young professionals—people in "knowledge work." The company is bleeding, he said, the money going out faster than it is coming in. It earned no profits last year and is on a certain path to bankruptcy—unless he can turn it around. Despite a good reputation, it has lost touch with its market, the young knowledge professionals. Perhaps, he said, you might be of help because you seem closer to that market. Also, he has been impressed with your background in computers. Your job would be to act as an assistant to the CEO, working on his pet projects. Mr. Douglas explains that your first assignment would be to determine whether computers could help Know-wear bail out of its difficulties.

Even on your first day on the job you can appreciate the importance of good procedures for information flow within the company. Know-wear's Production department must set its clothing production schedules on the basis of orders and predicted sales provided by the Marketing department. And, obviously, the Production department needs to be informed if any current order is cancelled or if sales forecasts are revised.

But, like most companies, Know-wear must also continually react to changes in the outside business and political environment. The company's information systems must monitor and adapt to price-cutting by competitors, the emergence of new synthetic fabric materials, government regulations, and many, many other events.

When Companies Need Systems Analysis and Design

Companies may go along for years using the same methods for gathering and handling business information. What would make them want to do things differently?

Changes in company information systems come about because of changes inside or outside of the company itself. For example:

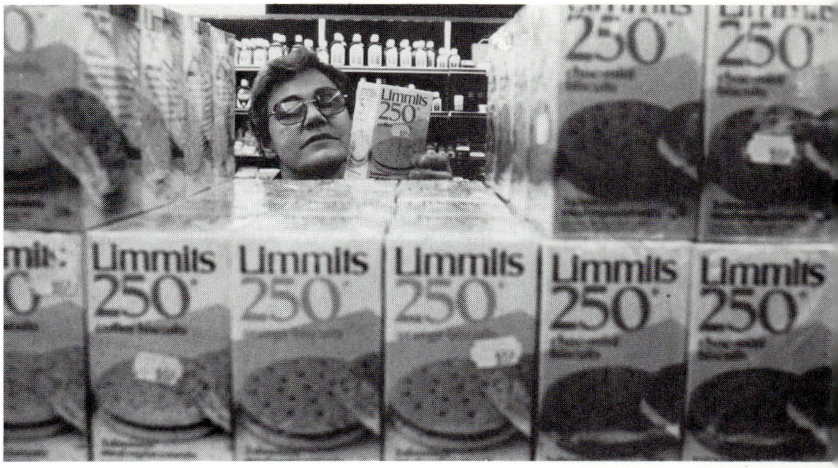

JCPenney
TSC
EXPRESS

All-purpose problem-solving. Systems analysis and design is a problem-solving procedure that may be applied to many different kinds of businesses and different facets of a business. Examples could be inventory problems in a book warehouse, retail distribution of dietary products, scheduling and workflow in an engineering-drawing department, and routing of truck deliveries for maximum effectiveness. The five steps of the procedure are identifying a business's information needs and feasibility, evaluating present information systems, formulating alternative information systems and recommending one, implementing the new information system, and maintaining the system. These five steps are called the systems life cycle.

- **Organizational growth:** As a company grows, so does its demand for timely information. A company with 100 employees, for example, has a much greater need for a computerized payroll system than does a company with only ten employees.
- **Better, cheaper technology:** As computer hardware and software decrease in cost and increase in capabilities, a company is better able to justify their acquisition.
- **Change in corporate structure:** The acquisition (taking over) of one company by another or merging of two companies can change a corporation's structure and hence the information system. For

example, when two organizations merge, their respective information systems must also be merged, which usually requires modifications or even the creation of a new system.

- **Change in government regulations:** A change in privacy laws, for instance, can change the way a corporation is allowed to handle employee personnel records.
- **New business opportunities:** Companies may see new ways of making money that require changes in their information systems. For example, when banks saw it was good business to install 24-hour automatic teller machines, they had to change their deposit and withdrawal information systems.

There are other reasons why a company might need to revise its information system, and many of them can be quite far-reaching. Whatever the cause, however, before a new information system can be installed, one course of action is indicated: systems analysis and design.

Why Should You Be Involved?

Setting up a computerized information system is going to require the help of experts, most particularly a **systems analyst**—an information specialist with specific expertise in systems analysis, design, and implementation. If a computer-based information system is being installed or changed, the systems analyst will most likely be assisted by programmers.

It is tempting sometimes to think that the "experts" understand your needs better than you do—especially if they seem to understand the mysteries of computers and data processing and you do not.

That is precisely why you should be involved.

After all, it is *you,* the user, who will have to live with the results of the new information system after the systems analyst and programmers have left. Moreover, it is highly likely that it will be you, the user, who initiates the request for systems analysis and design because you will be the one who has perceived that the present information system is not working as well as it should.

It takes the combined efforts of user, systems analyst, and programmers to develop a successful computer-based information system. The user is able to describe his or her needs and evaluate the worth of alternative information systems. The systems analyst works with the user and the programmers to analyze, design, and implement new information systems. The programmers do the technical work required.

But you, the user, are key: the ultimate success of the information system depends more on your perceptions and capabilities than on anyone else's. To be successful in business today, then, you need to understand the systems approach and the procedures for systems analysis and design.

Today's business organization can be very complex. You cannot expect (as, unfortunately, too many managers have) to simply bring in a computer system and have it be effective. An information specialist needs special tools with which to study a business and decide how best to use a computer-based information system. The best known tool is the systems approach.

According to the **systems approach** to problem solving, a problem can be approached as a system broken down into subsystems. For example, an information system consists of the following five subsystems: people, procedures, inputs, outputs, and processing. Thus, if an information system is to be studied, each one of these subsystems must be studied. The problem can be analyzed in smaller parts and then the parts can be brought back together to arrive at a solution. (The systems approach is derived from systems theory, which is discussed in the box on pp. 387–390.)

Systems Theory

As we mentioned earlier, there are all kinds of systems: biological, political, theological, mechanical, and so on. There is a system to nearly everything—to the relationship of the 52 bones in the foot, to the irrigation of a farmer's field, to the exchange of currency between nations. As we noted back in Chapter 3, a system is defined as a collection of interrelated parts that work together for a common purpose. The fact that a system does not seem to be working very well does not change the fact that it is nevertheless a system.

The Makings of a System

In the systems theory there are six important concepts:

- **Inputs** are the elements that enter the system from outside it.
- The **processor** is the part that operates on the inputs to transform them into something else.
- **Outputs** are the products of the processing.
- **Feedback** is communication back to the system, either from within the system or from outside it.
- The **environment** is the world outside the system.
- The **boundary** is the separation line between the system and the environment.

The figures on the next two pages illustrate these six concepts. Note that the inputs and outputs act as the connections—the interfaces—between the system and the environment.

Feedback is used to modify the system's operations, according to communications from the effects of the output. Depending on the kind of feedback, a system can be closed or open. Closed systems are those in which the feedback is only from within the system. Open systems are those in which feedback is from outside the system. Systems that have both internal and external feedback are classified as open systems, such as those shown in the figures on the next page.

Computer Systems and Subsystems

By themselves, these abstract concepts may not seem to mean much. Since we have spent a great deal of time studying computers, let us show how the concepts of a system relate to a computer.

Consider the computer system shown in the bottom figure, p. 388. The *input* device is a terminal. Instructions, in the form of data and pro-

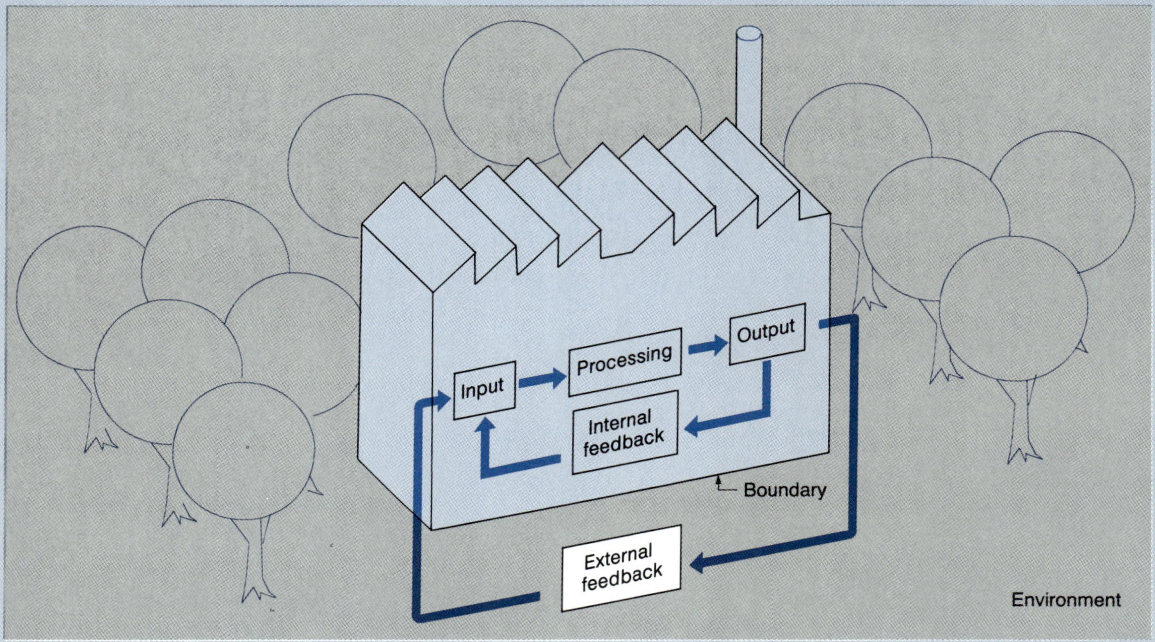
Input
Processing
Output
Internal feedback
Boundary
External feedback
Environment

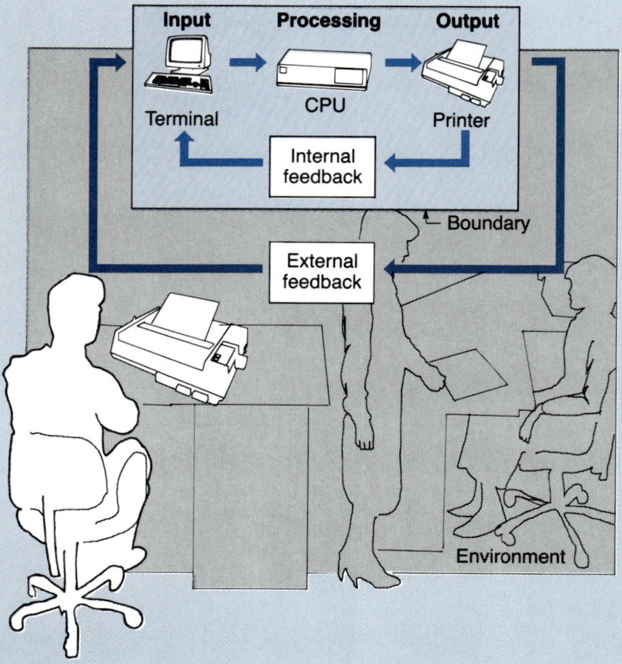
Input
Processing
Output
Terminal
CPU
Printer
Internal feedback
Boundary
External feedback
Environment

The elements of a system. *Above:* The concepts illustrated here make up the principal elements of a system: *input, processing, output, environment, boundary,* and *feedback.* A system situated in an environment can be compared to a factory standing in a field. Note that there are two feedback loops. The one contained within the system is an internal feedback loop. The one going through the environment outside the system is an external feedback loop. *Left:* System concepts can be applied to a computer system consisting of a terminal, CPU, and printer. *Opposite:* A business firm exists as a *system* in an environment of suppliers, customers, government regulators, and competitors. From the environment it draws inputs of employees, materials, facilities, and money. It produces outputs of finished goods and services for customers and, if successful, profits for itself. The processing part of the firm consists of four *subsystems* or functional departments: Marketing, Accounting and Finance, Production, and Research and Development.

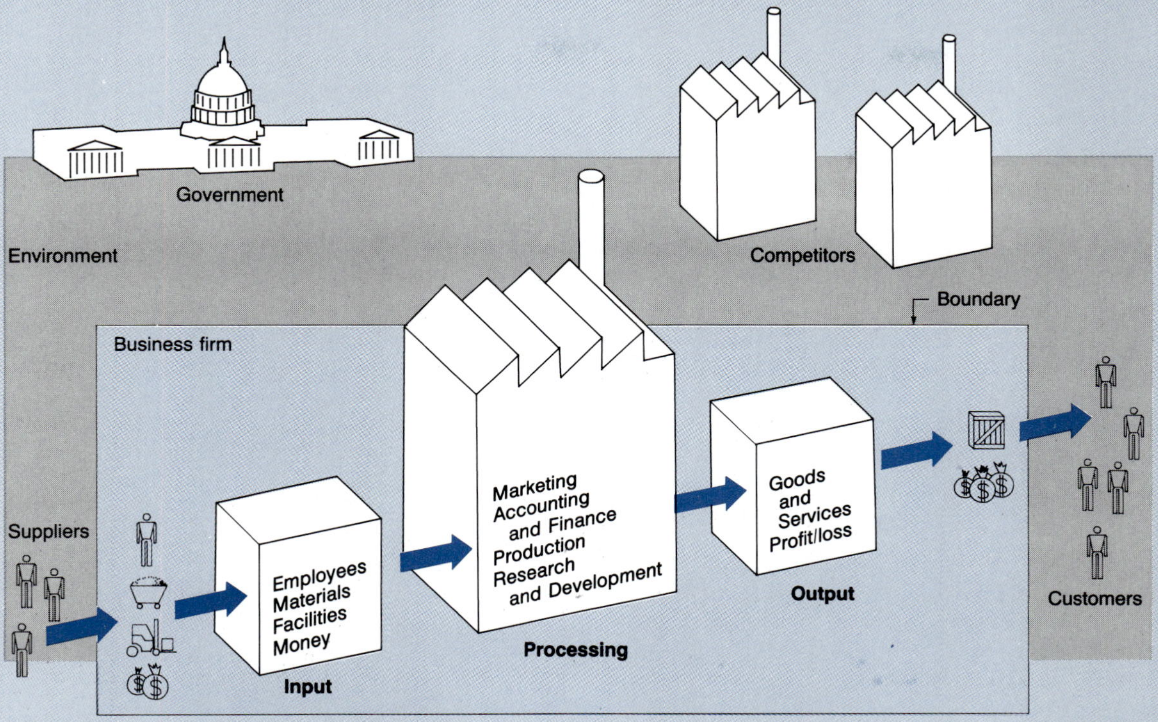
Government
Environment
Competitors
Boundary
Business firm
Suppliers
Employees
Materials
Facilities
Money
Input
Marketing
Accounting
and Finance
Production
Research
and Development
Processing
Goods
and
Services
Profit/loss
Output
Customers

grams, come from a person in the *environment* (an office, say), outside the computer system's *boundaries*. The input unit accepts data and programs and transmits them to the central processing unit, the CPU. *Processing* of the program and data is done by the CPU to produce information. This information is transmitted to the printer, an *output* unit.

This system represents an open system because it has two feedback loops. The *external feedback loop* consists of someone looking at the information produced by the printer and, if necessary, using the terminal to make modifications in the data or the program. The *internal feedback loop* consists of the computer's operating system, which "orchestrates" the activities of the computer. For instance, after one data processing job has been completed, the operating system instructs the input device to begin handling the next job.

This computer system can also be viewed as a collection of *subsystems*. For instance, the CPU can be considered a subsystem with three parts—the arithmetic/logic unit (ALU), the control unit, and primary storage. The printer is also a subsystem consisting of input (information from the CPU), processing (the actual printing), output (the completed computer printout), and feedback. The feedback devices tell the printer's input unit when a report has been completely printed out. They also signal when the printer is out of paper so a human operator can refill it.

Let us further extend the concept of system. The computer system we have just described can be part of a much larger and more complex business information system. That is, the computer can be considered a *subsystem* that facilitates the flow of information throughout the *system* of the business organization.

Business Information Systems

A business organization does not exist by itself, of course; it, too, is part of a larger economic system, as shown in the figure on page 389. As part of the larger system, a firm draws the inputs of employees, materials, facilities, and money from the outside environment. The company processes these items into outputs of goods and services to sell to customers, and it is hoped that profits are one of the outputs also. The environment in which the firm must operate includes not only suppliers and customers but also government regulators and competitors, among other things.

We can also look at the firm as being made up of several subsystems. As we saw back in Chapter 3, each subsystem consists of a *functional area*, which can be a department of a company—namely, Marketing, Accounting and Finance, Production, and Research and Development. In turn, each functional area has its own input, processing, and output. For example, the Production department at Know-wear receives inputs of customer orders as well as sales forecasts. The managers of the Production department use this information to develop production schedules for the processing of cloth into clothing. The goal is to produce enough output—clothing—to satisfy customer demands while minimizing inventory costs—that is, the costs of maintaining and warehousing the clothing.

All the subsystems or functional departments of an organization make up a system with two common goals—to produce goods and services and to produce a profit. Information from various subsystems is input to other subsystems, so there is an information system that ties together and coördinates the departments. Although each department has specific goals, the information system interrelates them and focuses them on the two main goals of the organization as a whole—to produce goods and services and to make a profit.

Information and the Systems Life Cycle

To develop a computer-based information system you must have a careful analysis of the complex system of your business organization. At Know-wear, each department's activities must be carefully coordinated with those of every other, or the company's goals of producing goods and getting profits will not be met. Advertising and sales promotions within Marketing must be coordinated with manufacturing and inventory scheduling within Production. If Production must expand its manufacturing facilities as a result of Marketing's forecast of increased demand for a particular line of Know-wear clothes, then the Accounting and Finance department must be alerted so that it can borrow or otherwise obtain the funds for Production's expansion. Marketing's perception of future customer demands must be fed to Research and Development if that department is to have the time to plan and develop new products.

All this information swapping and movement need not be computer-based, and of course in the past it was not. People simply called or sent memos to each other. However, the computer can do a lot of this more efficiently, thereby increasing productivity.

It is important to note, however, that not every present manual method of handling information needs to be computerized. Thus, the objective of systems analysis and design is not to replace every manual information channel but rather to identify which ones need improving and then to design better ways of providing information support. These new systems may or may not be computer-based.

Systems analysis and design is not supposed to just happen every now and then. It should be an ongoing activity, so that a company's information systems are being continually reevaluated and modified. Systems analysis and design uses a process called the **systems life cycle** (or *systems development cycle*), which, as Figure 11-2 shows, consists of five principal steps:

1. **System investigation**—in which information needs are identified and the feasibility of meeting those needs is determined.
2. **System analysis**—in which the existing information flow is analyzed and new information requirements are specified in detail.
3. **System design**—in which alternative information systems are designed and a preferred design recommended.
4. **System implementation**—in which new hardware and software are developed and tested, personnel are trained, and any necessary redesign accomplished.
5. **System maintenance**—in which the information system is monitored and evaluated and, if necessary, modified.

These five steps are described throughout the rest of this chapter.

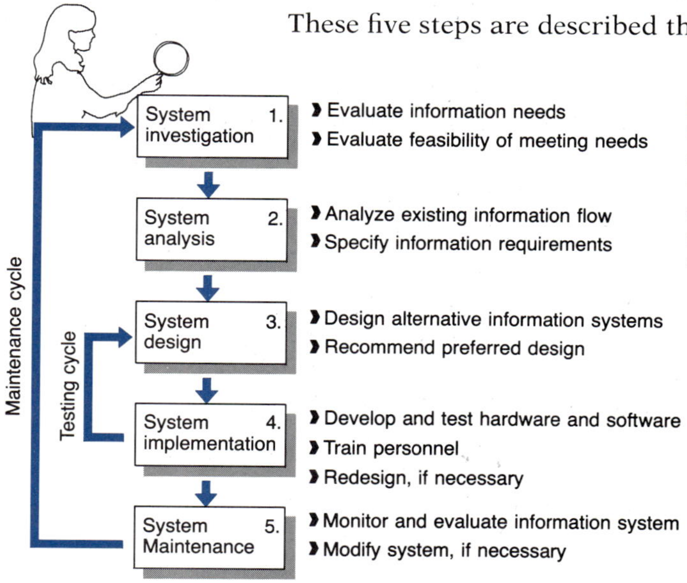
System investigation 1.
System analysis 2.
System design 3.
System implementation 4.
System Maintenance 5.
Maintenance cycle
Testing cycle
Evaluate information needs
Evaluate feasibility of meeting needs
Analyze existing information flow
Specify information requirements
Design alternative information systems
Recommend preferred design
Develop and test hardware and software
Train personnel
Redesign, if necessary
Monitor and evaluate information system
Modify system, if necessary

Figure 11-2 The systems life cycle. The five steps of investigation, analysis, design, implementation, and maintenance, along with their feedback loops, make up the activity of systems analysis and design, which a business should apply to its information systems on an ongoing basis.

1. System Investigation: What Is Not Working Right?

In any company there probably will be more projects proposed for systems analysis and design than can be undertaken. You discover this very quickly at Know-wear. As the first step in your assignment to determine whether a computer system can help Know-wear, you spend your first few days on the job talking to people in the various departments about the Know-wear information processing system, which is a manual system. You are quickly inundated with complaints. The vice-president of Marketing thinks the sales reports come out so late that they are practically useless. The Production vp thinks the inventory control system is a mess. Mr. Douglas feels the accounts receivable system is not working—the money is not coming in fast enough from customers.

With so many problems obvious at the outset, you recommend to Mr. Douglas that Know-wear hire a systems analyst. At first Mr. Douglas balks at spending money on another salary, but he agrees once you explain what a systems analyst does and how much money could be saved with a properly designed information system. He puts you in charge of hiring the analyst and being the liaison between the analyst and Know-wear employees.

After you hire the analyst, the first step is a **system investigation** of each proposed project to define the problem and evaluate the feasibility of solving the problem within an affordable budget and schedule. This means that someone or some collection of people must decide what proposed projects deserve further study, which ones are the most important, and what resources of money, people, and time may be required for each project. The point now is not to come up with a detailed design for a new system. Rather, the point is to evaluate the need for and feasibility of a new or revised system. These findings will be described at the end of this stage in a formal written document called a **system study charter.**

The steps in a system investigation are:

- Define the problem.
- Propose two or three alternative information systems.
- Evaluate the feasibility of the alternative systems and recommend one alternative.
- Write a system study charter.

In many ways, system investigation is a mini-version of a complete system analysis and design. The purpose of this step, though, is just to get an idea of the scope of the problem and solution so that management can decide if they want to invest in continuing the project.

Defining the Problem

To discover the problem or problems in an information system, the current system must be examined. A brand-new information system will be useless if it does not address existing problems, but the true problems are often hidden below the complaint, "This job is driving me crazy!" Thus, a **system needs survey** should be conducted to determine the problems in information flow and the needs of information users. This investigation will be continued in more detail in the system analysis stage if management decides to continue the study. The **system needs survey** report must be specific, clear, and easily understood. It should specify *what* information is needed, *who* needs it, *where, when,* and *why*. It should also define the problems in the current system.

For large information systems, a systems analyst may be the one to conduct the system needs survey. If so, the users of the system should be involved; indeed, the users' contributions and support are essential to the project's success. Even with the best intentions in the world, there may be misunderstandings between users and systems analysts. Users may talk the language of their trade, and systems analysts may use computer jargon. In addition, users frequently describe problems as symptoms of difficulties. Know-wear's sales manager, for instance, says that inventories are so low for a certain line of clothing that she cannot fill customer orders quickly enough, when the real problem is that sales cannot be predicted accurately enough to allow the Production department to schedule the assembly of sufficient quantities.

Let us say that you and the systems analyst decide to look at Know-wear's problem in accounts receivable for your first system investigation. Accounts receivable is that arm of the Accounting and Finance department that sends invoices to customers and keeps track of payments. At Know-wear, money is not coming in fast enough from customers—that is, retail clothing stores. The problem does not seem to be the customers' fault so much as a paperwork tie-up at Know-wear, but that is what you have to investigate.

You start by looking at the present accounts receivable system at Know-wear. When you talk to the accounts receivable manager, he tells you that the department is going through a temporary busy period, but everything will be caught up soon. He does admit, however, that the monthly report on overdue accounts is usually late and out of date. Thus, when he calls customers to inquire about invoices that the report shows as unpaid, he often finds the customers saying they *have* paid. After several telephone calls back and forth, the Know-wear manager must sheepishly admit that the invoices have been paid. Thus, he has succeeded only in creating ill will with those customers.

As you talk to other personnel in the Accounting and Finance department, you discover that morale is quite low. The accounting clerks feel overworked. You and the systems analyst notice stacks of paperwork piled up on desks with notes such as "To be processed," "To be filed," and "Miscellaneous." Managers in other departments also complain that the reports they receive from Accounting and Finance are late and out of date.

After analyzing the current flow of information, you and the systems analyst agree that the accounts receivable system has serious problems, but you also suspect that these problems extend to the entire sales, order entry, and accounting system. This will require further investigation if the accounts receivable project gets the go-ahead for further analysis. You summarize your preliminary findings in parts 1 and 2 of the system study charter, shown in Figure 11-3.

Developing Alternative Solutions

Now that you have some idea of what the problems are, you can come up with some preliminary solutions. As we said earlier, the goal at this point is not to design a completely new information system but just to come up with a few possible plans so management—specifically, Mr. Douglas—will have some idea of the scope of the project. The alternative solutions suggested now are developed from the systems analyst's training and experience.

The Know-wear systems analyst proposes three possible solutions: (1) Hire more accounting clerks and further analyze the present manual system to design a more efficient manual system. (2) Introduce a computer-based accounts receivable system. (3) Introduce a computer-based information system that would encompass all sales, order entry, and accounting procedures. These proposals are presented in part 3 of the system study charter (Figure 11-3).

Evaluating Feasibility

Are the proposed solutions really feasible? The answer to this question has three parts:

- Economic feasibility
- Technical feasibility
- Operational feasibility

Let us consider these.

Economic Feasibility. What is the *net cost/benefit?* What is the *rate of return?*

Benefits include increased sales, reduced operating costs, better customer goodwill because of improved service, and better management decisions because of improved quality of information. *Costs* include money spent on the new system and possibly lost customer goodwill because of interruptions in normal operations when a new information system is being phased in. The **net cost/benefit** is the expected benefit minus the expected cost. The **rate of return** is the ratio between estimated benefits and estimated costs.

To compare proposed alternative systems, specific cost estimates must be made. In many cases this is hard to do, especially when the costs and benefits are intangible, such as customer goodwill. This is where the systems analyst's experience is valuable.

SYSTEM STUDY CHARTER

PROJECT: Accounts Receivable, Know-wear, Inc.

1. PRESENT INFORMATION SYSTEM

The present Know-wear accounts receivable department uses a manual system. Personnel include one manager, one assistant manager, six accounting clerks, and one secretary. The department produces invoices upon notification that goods have been shipped to customers. The department also keeps track of payments made on invoices, producing several reports for use of managers (see next section).

2. SYSTEM NEEDS SURVEY

In discussions with accounting personnel and users of accounting information, it was determined that the following reports are needed:

What	Who	Where	When	Why
Report on customers with overdue accounts	Accounts receivable manager	Accounts receivable office	Monthly	To monitor the amounts customers owe the company
Report on dates orders taken and dates orders filled	Order entry manager	Order entry office	Monthly	To monitor the time lag between order entry and actual shipping
Report on goods shipped and billed for each customer	Marketing manager	Sales office	Weekly	To keep abreast of actual sales to customers

These reports are currently being generated, but managers complain that the reports are usually late and out-of-date. The problem appears to be that the accounts receivable department is not set up to handle the volume of work it has. We suspect, however, that the problem extends to the entire sales, order entry, and accounting system. Further investigation of these problems will be required.

1 (continued)

Figure 11-3 The system study charter. This report summarizes the system investigation for the Know-wear accounts receivable project.

3. PROPOSED ALTERNATIVE INFORMATION SYSTEMS

Objectives of the alternative information systems:

To produce invoices in a timely manner after goods have been shipped; to keep accurate and up-to-date records of payments; to produce reports for managers that are accurate, up-to-date, and produced on time.

Alternative proposals:

1. Hire more accounting clerks and further analyze the present manual system to design a more efficient manual system. (No matter what course of action is pursued, the accounts receivable department should be given temporary help right away so they can catch up on their backlog.)

2. Introduce a computer-based accounts receivable system.

3. Introduce a computer-based information system that would encompass all sales, order entry, and accounting procedures.

4. FEASIBILITY OF PROPOSAL #3

A. Economic feasibility (Note: All costs are very rough estimates and are subject to change):

Costs:

	1987	1988	1989	1990
Tangible costs:				
Systems analyst's salary	$30,000	$32,000		
Programmers' salary	10,000	18,000		
Additional systems support personnel			$100,000	$40,000
Intangible costs:				
Potential lost customer goodwill during transition period		15,000		
Total expected costs:	$40,000	$65,000	$100,000	$40,000

Benefits:

	1987	1988	1989	1990
Tangible benefits:				
Reduction in clerical salaries by normal attrition (3 clerks at $13,000)	0	0	$39,000	$39,000

2

Figure 11-3 (continued)

Added profits from more sales and fewer lost sales due to improved customer service	0	20,000	50,000	50,000
Intangible benefits:				
Improved quality of decisions by use of more timely and relevant information	0	10,000	25,000	25,000
Total expected benefits:	0	$30,000	$114,000	$114,000

Cost/Benefit Analysis:

	1987	1988	1989	1990
Benefits	0	$30,000	$114,000	$114,000
Costs	40,000	65,000	100,000	40,000
Net, yearly	-$40,000	-$35,000	$ 14,000	$ 74,000
Net, cumulative	-$40,000	-$75,000	-61,000	13,000

The improved system should recover all costs within two years after being put into operation.

Net cost/benefit for 1989 = expected benefit - expected cost
($30,000 + $114,000) - ($105,000 + $100,000)
=-$61,000

Net cost/benefit for 1990 = expected benefit - expected cost
($144,000 + $114,000) - ($205,000 + $40,000)
= $13,000 This number is positive so is a good net cost/benefit.

B. Technical feasibility:

Specialized personnel such as systems analysts and programmers are needed. Their supply is sufficient, so availability should not be a problem.

Hardware could be purchased or leased, with leasing the preferred alternative at the beginning until the system is deemed to be successful. Software may be easily purchased, but may have to be modified before it can be used in the system.

C. Operational feasibility:

Users must be kept abreast of all developments in the new system since only their acceptance and use of the system will lead to a successful system.

3

Figure 11-3 (continued)

5. POTENTIAL PROBLEMS

Cost: Final system cost could exceed the estimates presented here.

Time schedule: More time may be needed to develop and implement the new system.

6. SYSTEM DEVELOPMENT SCHEDULE

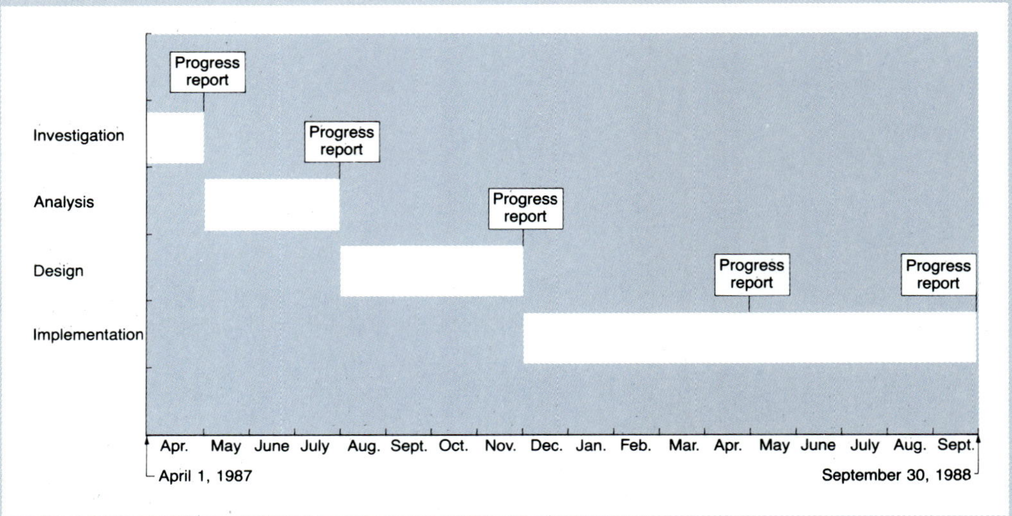
Progress report
Progress report
Progress report
Progress report
Progress report
Investigation
Analysis
Design
Implementation
Apr. May June July Aug. Sept. Oct. Nov. Dec. Jan. Feb. Mar. Apr. May June July Aug. Sept.
April 1, 1987
September 30, 1988

7. RECOMMENDATION

My recommendation is to pursue the development of a new information system (proposal #3) because the problems in the order entry/accounts receivable process will probably increase and the payoff from the new system should be rapid.

4

Figure 11-3 (continued)

Technical Feasibility. What hardware, software, and people are required? Are they available? How reliable is the necessary hardware and software? The uncertainties in developing a computer-based information system can be reduced if the company already has thoroughly tested hardware and software or if they can be easily purchased.

Operational Feasibility. How acceptable will the proposed system be to users and management? If potential users are resistant or indifferent, the system may not be used. If higher management does not support the project, its chances of success are low. Are there any external constraints, such as government regulations or specific customer requirements? If either insiders or outsiders are constrained in some way, you have to weigh just how operational the system will be.

The feasibility report of the Know-wear systems analyst is presented in part 4 of the system study charter (Figure 11-3). For the sake of brevity, we present only the feasibility report for the third alternative proposal—a computer-based information system that would include all sales, order entry, and accounting procedures. The systems analyst concludes that this project is feasible on all three counts—economically, technically, and operationally.

The System Study Charter

The **system study charter** is the formal document that summarizes the first step in the systems life cycle—systems investigation. Along with system study charters for other projects, it will be used by management to decide which information system project to pursue.

The system study charter should include the following:

1. A brief description of the present information system, identifying the users and describing the information provided.
2. A summary of the system needs survey. This should describe the users' current and future information needs and inadequacies in the present system to meet those needs. This is where the problem is defined.
3. A summary of the proposed alternative information systems. This should include a short, clear, and precise statement of the objectives of the proposed systems.
4. A report on the feasibility of the proposed projects.
5. A statement of any potential problems. The systems analyst for Know-wear, for instance, points out that final cost estimates could exceed those presented here as could the time estimates for developing and implementing the system.
6. A development schedule, also known as a Gannt chart, for the proposed system. This should estimate the time, equipment, and people required. For the remaining four stages of the systems analysis and design of Know-wear's accounts receivable project, the systems analyst estimates that the entire project will take about a year and a half, if management approves it. The systems analyst has scheduled a progress report at the end of each stage and an interim progress report during implementation, the final stage (see Figure 11-3, part 6).
7. Go/No go recommendations. These should include recommendations to pursue or not pursue the project and give a short statement of justifications. "My recommendation," writes the Know-wear sys-

tems analyst, "is to pursue the development of a new information system because the problems in the order entry/accounts receivable process will probably increase and the payoff from the new system should be rapid."

The system investigation for Know-wear's accounts receivable project is summarized in the system study charter shown in Figure 11-3. Next, you and the systems analyst conduct a system investigation of Know-wear's inventory control system, as requested by the Production department's vice-president.

2. System Analysis: What Needs to Be Done?

Management—including the CEO, Mr. Douglas—examines the system study charters you and the systems analyst have prepared. You explain how a comprehensive computer-based information system could solve many of the problems plaguing various departments at Know-wear, so Mr. Douglas gives the green light to proceed with the second stage of the project. This second stage, **system analysis,** is concerned with collecting and analyzing data about the present and future information needs of prospective users.

System analysis asks, "What needs to be done?" However, it is not concerned with the *design* of a new or alternative information system—that comes in stage 3—only with making a detailed analysis of the existing system and developing the *requirements* for an improved information system, which are described in a system requirements report.

Structured system analysis has a top-down approach, which is consistent with the philosophy of structured programming. That is, the systems analyst begins by examining the flow of information starting with upper-level management and moving down through the organization's hierarchy.

There are three steps in the system analysis stage:

- Gathering data.
- Analyzing the data.
- Writing the system requirements report.

You will see how these are developed as you watch the Know-wear systems analyst at work.

Data Gathering

You have already seen the gathering of some preliminary facts in stage 1. Now you need to add detail. Data gathering is primarily concerned with determining how the present information system operates. Although there are numerous sources of data, let us look at four of the most common:

Figure 11-4 An organization chart. Charts like this one indicate the titles of an organization's executives and the lines of authority.

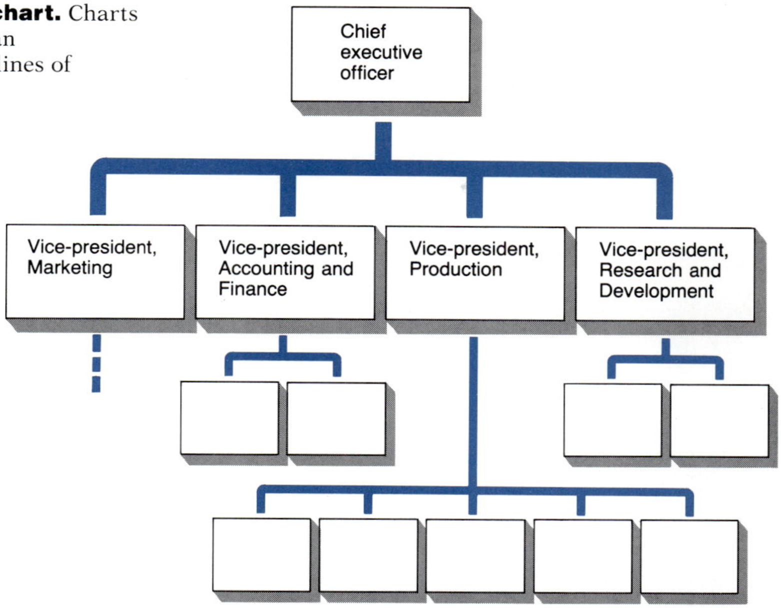
Chief executive officer
Vice-president, Marketing
Vice-president, Accounting and Finance
Vice-president, Production
Vice-president, Research and Development

- Written documents
- Interviews
- Questionnaires
- Observation

Written Documents. Written documents may consist of organization charts, flowcharts, and other written materials.

An **organization chart** is a drawing that indicates the positions, by title, and lines of authority within an organization (see Figure 11-4). Since they represent the formal lines of communication and flow of information, such charts are valuable in giving the systems analyst a top-down perspective. The organization chart for Know-wear, Inc., allows the analyst to see which people and departments are affected by the present information system and might be affected by changes in that system.

Flowcharts are also valuable to an analyst for describing the current information system. System flowcharts describe what input devices are used, what files have been created or are accessible, and what people receive written information. Program flowcharts and HIPO (Hierarchy plus Input-Process-Output) charts also may be of value in showing the logic of the current information system. More on this below.

Besides organization charts and flowcharts, a systems analyst should look at any other written documents relating to the system under study: reports, forms, procedures manuals, and so on.

Interviews. The analyst cannot work just from paper. Personal **interviews** (see box) with key people in the organization will undoubtedly yield important data, for they often will define the actual flow as opposed to the intended flow of information. The analyst asks users of the current Know-wear accounts receivable system how well it is performing—that is, what information is and is not provided.

Tips for Interviewing

The expression "Garbage in, garbage out" also applies in systems analysis: The results of your analysis can be no better than the information that has gone into it. Information comes not only from paper but from interviews—and there are right ways and wrong ways to conduct an interview. The following are some tips:

- **Plan your questions beforehand.** You may vary from them during the interview, but you should not try to "wing it"—that is, go in unprepared. Do your homework, determining the questions for which you need answers, the people probably best able to answer them, and the *specific* questions that the *specific* individual being interviewed can address.
- **Establish proper rapport with the interviewee.** This means, above all, respect his or her time. Ask for an appointment, arranging your schedule to fit that of the person being interviewed. Dress and behave in a businesslike manner, avoiding office gossip and discussion of personal problems. Avoid technical jargon. Use your best small-talk abilities (without going on at length) to comment on the weather, the interviewee's office, and so on, in order to put the subject at ease. Do not go on the offensive so that the subject feels threatened; on the other hand, do not try to overdo it with flattery. Talk straight. Thank the subject for the interview and ask if you may contact him or her later to clarify any questions.
- **State the problem and focus the questions.** Identify yourself, state the purpose of the interview, and share the problem definition. Identify the managers who authorized the system analysis. Have your first question ready, or perhaps use an open question, such as: "The office procedures manual states that copies of the customer order should go to other departments besides yours, but I'm not sure I understand which ones. Can you explain how this works?" Follow up with specific questions, focusing on particular details of concern. Concentrate not only on how things work but why they work as they do.
- **Get the information.** You should listen carefully to the answers, observing the respondent's body movements and voice inflection to help you evaluate the responses. Take notes on key points, but do not record every word, since you must listen to the subject and be prepared to ask follow-up questions. Make a written summary of the interview as soon as possible, concentrating on the key issues. Share the summary with the respondent and allow him or her to correct mistakes or make adjustments. Do follow-up interviews, if necessary.

Questionnaires. Although personal interviews are generally more effective, **questionnaires** also are frequently used because they cost less and allow the analyst to obtain more responses in a shorter time. An analyst may find out from questionnaires how frequently people use the present information system, the time required to use it, and special equipment and personnel requirements. Questionnaires have drawbacks, however. Some people will not fill them out no matter what the inducements. People are also wary of putting on paper opinions for which they think they may be held accountable later. And, of course, answers to questionnaires may be highly biased.

Observation. Observation is always valuable, but it should not be done secretly. Arrangements should be made with the work unit's supervisor, and the analyst should let people know they are under observation. Sometimes the analyst may actually join the people being observed; this is known as participant observation. The point of observation is to see how information flows from person to person, who interrelates with whom, and how information comes into and leaves the group.

Analyzing the Data

If data gathering is to define what is being done, analysis is to determine why certain procedures are being used and look for better ways of doing them. Of the several tools used in this step, the three most common are:

- System flowcharts
- Grid charts
- Checklists

Here is how they work.

System Flowcharts. As we discussed in Chapter 5, *program flowcharts* are primarily used by programmers to write application programs; their purpose is to specify the details of a problem for ease in coding. **System flowcharts,** by contrast, are used to represent information flow within a system by focusing upon input and output operations. The standard input and output symbols and standard process symbols for system flowcharts are shown in Figure 11-5. Because they present a macro view or overview, system flowcharts are a valuable tool for system analysis and design.

Grid Chart. A **grid chart,** also called an **input/output chart,** is often used in analysis to show the relationship between input and output documents. Figure 11-6, for example, shows the relationship between forms (input) and reports (output). A sales order is used for producing a sales report, a purchase order for an inventory report, and so on. Horizontal rows represent input documents (such as a purchase order); vertical rows represent the output documents. An "X" at the intersection of

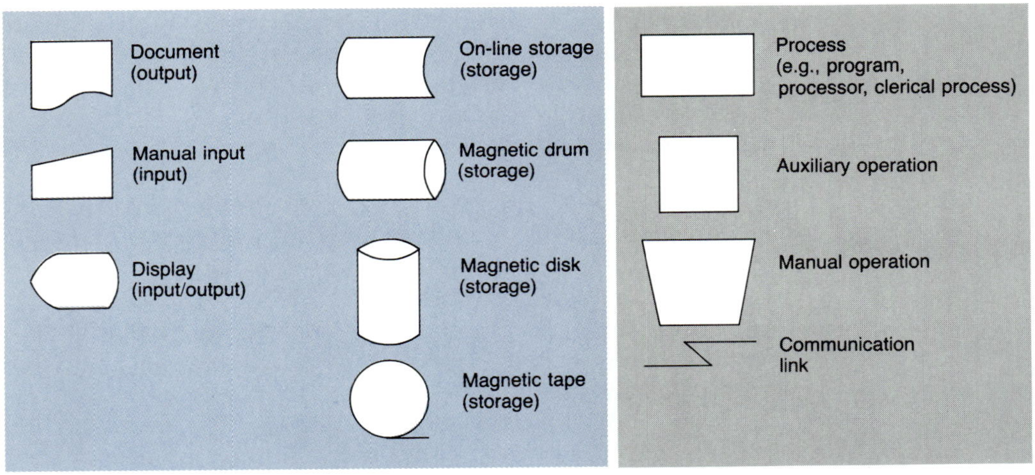
Document
(output)
Manual input
(input)
Display
(input/output)
On-line storage
(storage)
Magnetic drum
(storage)
Magnetic disk
(storage)
Magnetic tape
(storage)
Process
(e.g., program,
processor, clerical process)
Auxiliary operation
Manual operation
Communication
link

Figure 11-5 System flowchart symbols. *Left:* Input, output, and storage symbols. *Right:* Process symbols. These symbols are used by systems analysts rather than programmers; their purpose is to represent information flow within a system.

Forms (input) \ Reports (output)	Sales report	Inventory report	Payroll report	Financial report
Sales order	X			
Purchase order		X		
Time card			X	
Paycheck			X	
Check voucher				X

Figure 11-6 Grid chart. This chart indicates the relationship of input documents to output reports. For instance, time cards and paychecks are needed as the input to produce a payroll report.

a row and column means that the input document is used to create the output document. Thus, if you look down a column for an output document, the chart indicates all the input documents needed to produce it.

- ☐ 1. Are the tasks and responsibilities for the current information system clearly defined and assigned?
- ☐ 2. Are the policies and procedures of the current information system understood and followed by the employees?
- ☐ 3. Does each procedure in the current information system achieve its intended objective?
- ☐ 4. Are there unnecessary delays in obtaining and/or processing data in the current information system?
- ☐ 5. How easily does the current information system adapt to change and growth?
- ☐ 6. Can reports be easily prepared from the files and documents presently in use?
- ☐ 7. Are the channels of information flow clearly defined?
- ☐ 8. Are policies and security well established?

Figure 11-7 **Checklist.** This is an example of a checklist of questions that systems analysts and users can use to address important issues in the analysis step. The questions listed here are fairly general but can be made specific to the particular project under analysis.

Checklist. A checklist of questions is frequently used to ensure that the user and systems analyst address key issues when they are evaluating the present system. An example is shown in Figure 11-7.

Now comes the time to tie together the results of the systems analysis stage in a report—the system requirements report.

The System Requirements Report

The **system requirements report** describes the findings of the system analysis. It ensures that users and the systems analyst agree on the details of the current system and on the need for a new or improved information system. Since the report is prepared for higher management, it should be written to ensure their continued interest and support.

The system requirements report has five sections:

- A statement of scope and objectives.
- A description of the present information system.
- An estimate of system requirements.
- A revised system development schedule.
- A request to management for authorization to proceed.

Let us see what these look like, using the Know-wear project. The complete system requirements report for the Know-wear system analysis stage is shown in Figure 11-8.

SYSTEM REQUIREMENTS REPORT

PROJECT: Accounts Receivable, Know-wear, Inc.

1. SCOPE AND OBJECTIVES

Scope:

The project extends from the point the customer order is obtained from the customer, to the shipment and invoice leaving for the customer, to the receipt of payment from the customer.

Objectives:

1. To reduce the average time between the receipt of the customer order and the shipping of the ordered products.

2. To reduce the average time for response to a customer inquiry concerning order status.

3. To reduce the billing error rate.

2. DESCRIPTION OF PRESENT INFORMATION SYSTEM

Overview diagram of present sales and order management system:

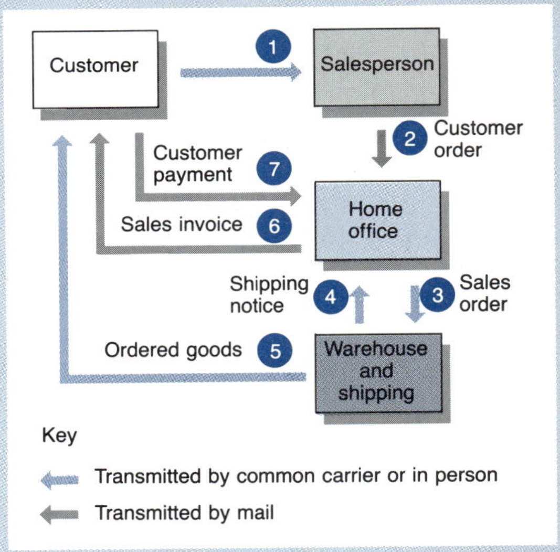
Customer
1
Salesperson
2 Customer order
Customer payment 7
Sales invoice 6
Home office
Shipping notice 4
3 Sales order
Ordered goods 5
Warehouse and shipping
Key
Transmitted by common carrier or in person
Transmitted by mail

1 (continued)

Figure 11-8 The system requirements report. This report draws together the conclusions of stage 2, system analysis, of the Know-wear project.

HIPO diagram of present sales and order processing system:

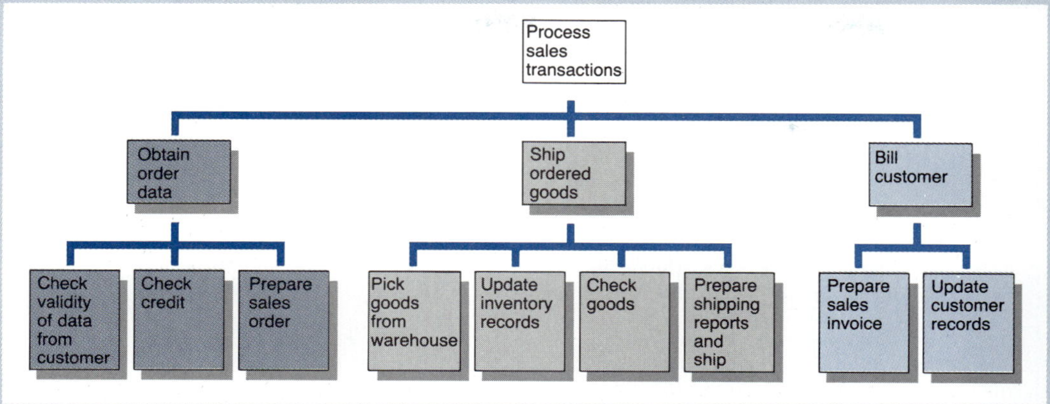
Process sales transactions
Obtain order data
Ship ordered goods
Bill customer
Check validity of data from customer
Check credit
Prepare sales order
Pick goods from warehouse
Update inventory records
Check goods
Prepare shipping reports and ship
Prepare sales invoice
Update customer records

Overview diagram of present sales and order processing system:

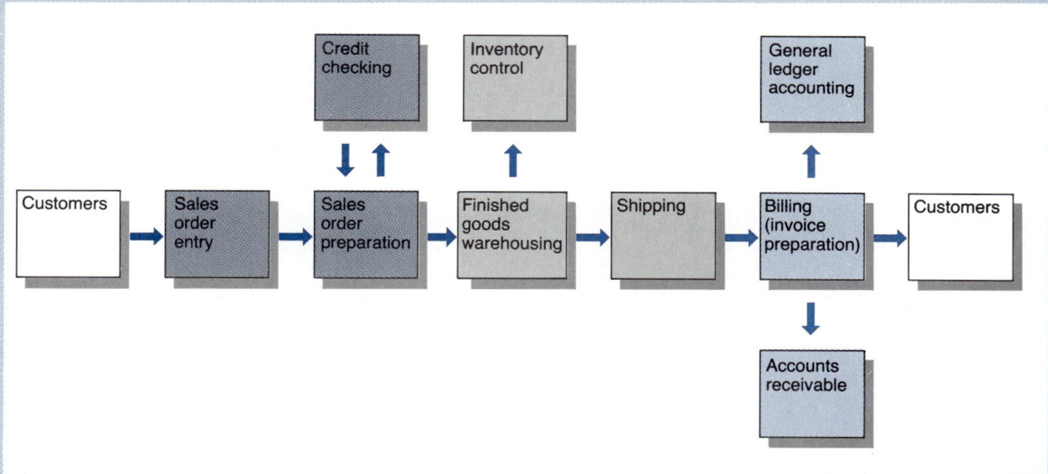
Credit checking
Inventory control
General ledger accounting
Customers
Sales order entry
Sales order preparation
Finished goods warehousing
Shipping
Billing (invoice preparation)
Customers
Accounts receivable

Users:

Billing Department, Accounts Receivable Department, Sales Order Department, Cash Receipts Department, Credit Department, Sales Office, Shipping Department.

Problems:

1. The past few years the rate of sales growth has been declining.

2

(continued)

2. Net income has fallen from $57 million last year to $47 million this year. Another drop in net income is expected next year.

3. Costs of sales and operating costs have been rising faster than sales.

4. Average time required to fill a customer order has become long and many promised delivery dates are being missed.

<u>Inadequacies of present system</u>:

1. Using mail to process customer orders slows down the process and leads to delivery dates being missed.

2. Too few clerks are employed for the amount of paperwork that is being done. Overworked clerks make errors in processing customer orders and in preparing monthly statements.

3. Credit checks cause excessive delays in processing.

<u>Information provided by present system</u>:

1. Order entry function produces a customer invoice.

2. Accounts receivable function produces an account statement.

3. SYSTEM REQUIREMENTS

1. Capacity: Average of 700 customer orders daily, with a peak of 1000.

2. Response time for telephone or in-person inquiries: one minute or less.

3. Accuracy: No more than one processing error per 1000 transactions.

4. Delivery reliability: 98% of promised delivery dates are met.

<u>Feasibility of changing current information system</u>:

Based on expected costs and benefits, the system should pay off within two years of operation, so it should be economically feasible. It also should be technically feasible since the computer hardware and software should be available for use. As for operational feasibility, that can only be assured when the users show their acceptance of the system and management gives full support to the system development project.

3

Figure 11-8 (continued)

4. REVISED SYSTEM DEVELOPMENT SCHEDULE

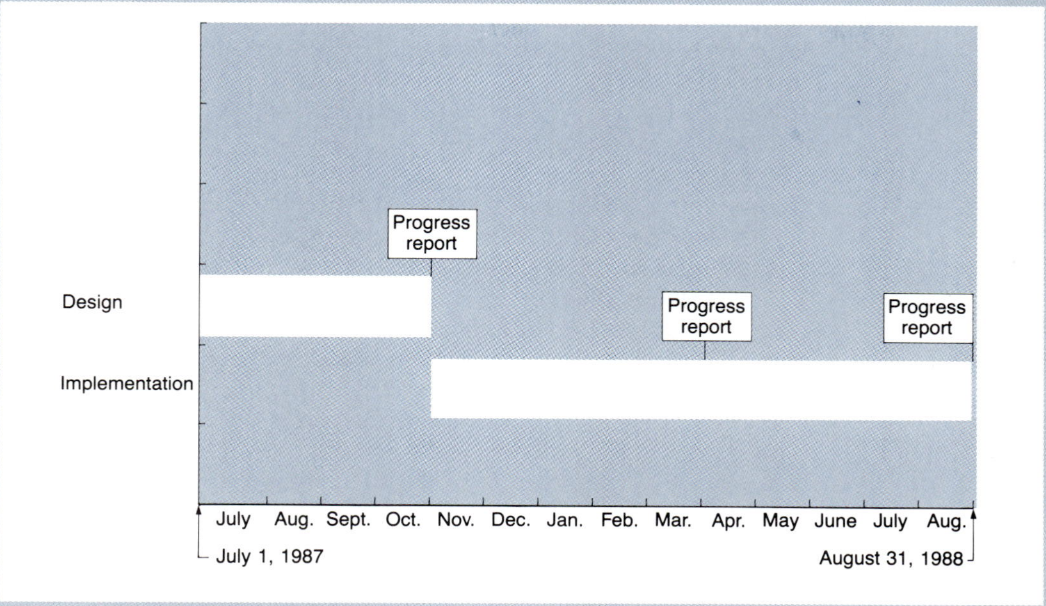
Progress report
Design
Progress report
Progress report
Implementation
July Aug. Sept. Oct. Nov. Dec. Jan. Feb. Mar. Apr. May June July Aug.
July 1, 1987
August 31, 1988

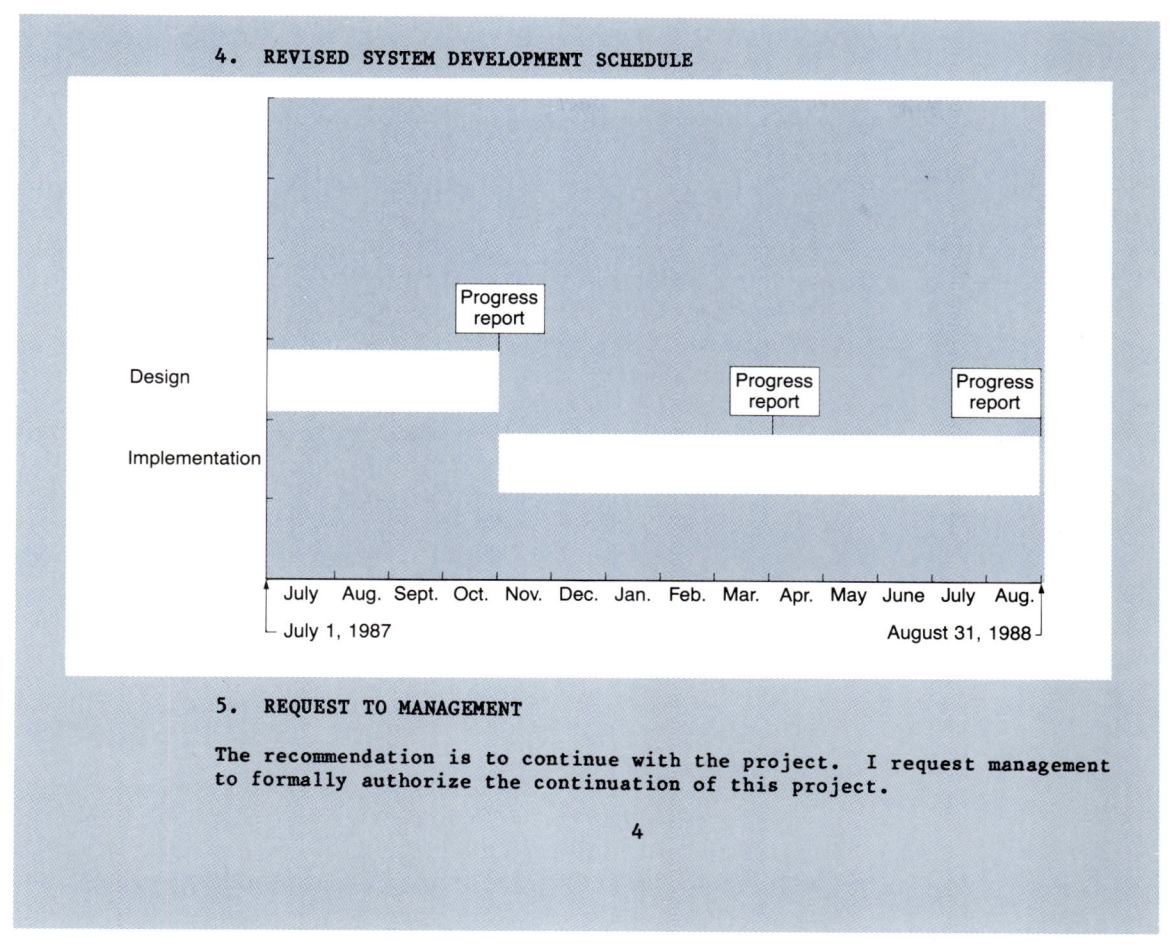

5. REQUEST TO MANAGEMENT

The recommendation is to continue with the project. I request management to formally authorize the continuation of this project.

4

Figure 11-8 (continued)

1. Scope and Objectives. This is simply a detailed statement of the scope and objectives of the system analysis study. The CEO of Knowwear, you will recall, was concerned about the amount of paperwork involved in accounts receivable and the delays in money coming in. But, as you and the systems analyst have determined, there is more to it than that. As part 1 in Figure 11-8 shows, the objectives have been broadened so that delays in money coming in from customers cannot be separated from concerns such as shipping time, meeting of promised delivery dates, quicker response to customer inquiries, and reduced billing error rates. In other words, the project extends, as the system analyst writes, "from the point the customer order is obtained from the customer, to the shipment and invoice leaving for the customer, to the receipt of payment from the customer."

2. Description of Present Information System. This second section of the system requirements report describes the current information flow, the procedures used, and any problems—and opportunities—that exist. Here is where some artwork helps, such as overview diagrams and HIPO diagrams.

Part 2 of the system requirements report for Know-wear includes three drawings (see Figure 11-8):

- An overview diagram of how the present sales and order system works, showing how people and materials move from place to place. (Accounts receivable cannot be separated from the sales process—late customer payments are often a reflection of sales order foul-ups.)
- A HIPO diagram of the present sales and order processing system. HIPO, let us recall, stands for *H*ierarchy plus *I*nput-*P*rocess-*O*utput and HIPO diagrams are a set of diagrams that graphically describes functions from general level to detailed level.
- An overview diagram of the present sales and order processing system, showing how paperwork flows through the system.

Part 2 of the system requirements report also has some text that describes the following important facts (see Figure 11-8, part 2):

- Who the users of the present information system are—seven departments, from Billing to Shipping.
- What the problems of the present information system are—decline in sales growth and net income, rise in sales and operating costs and in the time required to fill customer orders.
- The inadequacies of the present system—use of mail to process customer orders, too few clerks to handle the paperwork of orders, delays in processing because of credit checks of customers.
- The information provided by the present system—invoices and account statements.

3. System Requirements. This third section of the system requirements report is an estimate of the resources required. It also indicates what the systems analyst and users believe to be the feasibility of changing over from the present information system.

Figure 11-8, part 3, shows what you and the systems analyst have determined is necessary for a new Know-wear system. You want the system to be able to handle 700 customer orders a day from dress shops and clothing stores, with a capacity for 1000. You also want the response time for telephone inquiries to be a minute or less. Processing must be accurate and promised delivery dates must be met. You conclude that such a system can become feasible within two years.

4. System Development Schedule. This fourth part of the system requirements report is a tentative schedule for completing the project, as shown in Figure 11-8, part 4. Note that you and the systems analyst were able to complete the system analysis stage in a shorter time than you anticipated in the development schedule in Figure 11-3 (part 6), partly because you built enough time into your original estimate to allow for surprises and delays.

5. Request to Management. This final step of the system analysis stage includes the recommendation that the project be continued. It is a formal request by the systems analyst for authorization to continue with the project.

3. System Design: How Should a New System Work?

Mr. Douglas gives you and the systems analyst permission to proceed—to design a new information system. Now you are no longer looking at the present system, for **system design** focuses on creating and specifying a new information system to meet current and future needs. Thus, you need to restate the scope and objectives of the project somewhat from what you indicated in the system analysis stage. The system design scope and objectives are shown in part 1 of Figure 11-9; you might wish to compare them with the scope and objectives given back in part 1 of Figure 11-8.

There are three steps in the system design stage:

- Design of alternative systems.
- Selection of the best alternative.
- Preparation of a system design report.

Designing Alternative Systems

System design can be very simple, particularly for information systems that do not interact with other information systems within the organization. For most information systems, however, there are trade-offs between costs and efficiency, making system design a complex task. Costs are how much time and money will be required to create the system. Efficiency is how quickly and accurately the system can collect data, convert it to information, and distribute it to users. Usually, though not always, the most efficient system is the most expensive.

Still, a good way to begin system design is simply to ignore the costs and create the best information system imaginable. Although the result may be economically impractical, the approach has the effect of stimulating design inventiveness. Moreover, out of this exercise, affordable design alternatives probably will emerge.

SYSTEM DESIGN REPORT

PROJECT: Accounts Receivable, Know-wear, Inc.

1. SCOPE AND OBJECTIVES

Scope:

The project extends from the point the customer order is obtained from the customer, to the shipment and invoice leaving for the customer, to the receipt of payment from the customer.

Objectives:

1. To reduce the average time between the receipt of the customer order and the shipping of the ordered products so at least 98% of promised delivery dates are met.

2. To reduce the average time for response to a customer inquiry concerning order status to less than one minute.

3. To reduce the billing error rate from one error per 50 transactions to one error per 1000 transactions.

2. ALTERNATIVE SYSTEM DESIGNS

Alternative #1:

Salespeople will be equipped with computer terminals and customer orders will be transmitted to the home office computer via a data communications system. Sales orders will be communicated to the warehouse via a data communications system, which will also be used to transmit shipping notices back to the home office. Ordered goods, invoices, and customer payments will be transmitted by common carrier or mail as before. Invoices will be generated by the home office computer system, however, and customer payments will be entered into the computer. Reports for managers will be generated by the computer system. Customer service representatives will have on-line access to up-to-date information on the status of customer orders and inventory.

1

Figure 11-9 The system design report.
This report summarizes the results of the Know-wear system design study.

<u>System design for Alternative #1</u>:

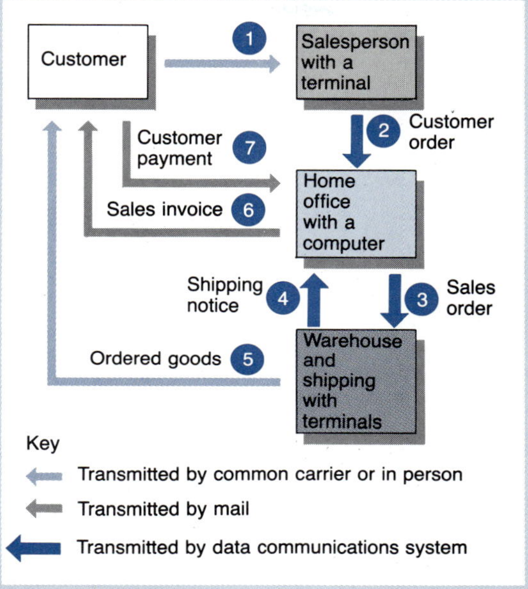
Customer
1
Salesperson with a terminal
2 Customer order
Customer payment 7
Sales invoice 6
Home office with a computer
Shipping notice 4
3 Sales order
Ordered goods 5
Warehouse and shipping with terminals
Key
Transmitted by common carrier or in person
Transmitted by mail
Transmitted by data communications system

<u>Alternative #2</u>:

Goods will be stored at the home office, not in a warehouse at a separate location. This eliminates the need for an expensive data communications connection between the home office and the warehouse.

<u>System design for Alternative #2</u>:

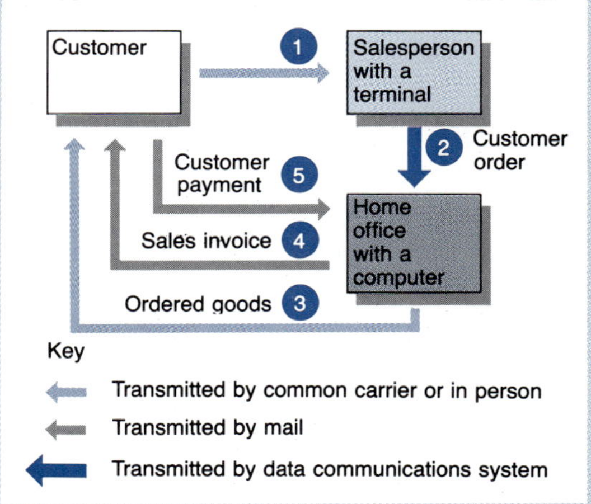
Customer
1
Salesperson with a terminal
2 Customer order
Customer payment 5
Sales invoice 4
Home office with a computer
Ordered goods 3
Key
Transmitted by common carrier or in person
Transmitted by mail
Transmitted by data communications system

Figure 11-9 (continued)

3. ECONOMIC FEASIBILITY FOR TWO ALTERNATIVE DESIGNS

One-time costs:

	#1	#2
System development costs	$ 34,800	$ 32,200
System hardware costs	402,000	327,000
System software costs	47,300	40,000
Total one-time costs:	$484,100	$399,200

Recurring costs:

Information system maintenance	$ 25,000	$ 20,000
Data and information control	26,000	20,000
Information system administration	26,400	20,000
Total recurring costs:	$ 77,400	$ 60,000

Recurring benefits:

Clerical cost savings	$116,000	$120,000
Savings from reduced errors	54,000	46,000
Added sales and other savings resulting from better customer service	200,000	200,000
Total recurring benefits:	$370,000	$366,000

Cost/benefit analysis for Alternative #1:

	1987-1988	1989	1990
Benefits	0	$370,000	$370,000
Costs	$484,100	77,400	77,400
Net, yearly	-$484,100	$292,600	$292,600
Net, cumulative	-$484,100	-$191,500	$101,100

Net cost/benefit for 1989 = expected benefit - expected cost
$370,000 - ($484,100 + 77,400)
= -$191,500

Net cost/benefit for 1990 = expected benefit - expected cost
($370,000 + $370,000) - ($561,500 + $77,400)
= $101,100

Cost/benefit analysis for Alternative #2:

	1987-1988	1989	1990
Benefits	0	$366,000	$366,000
Costs	$399,200	60,000	60,000
Net, yearly	-$399,200	$306,000	$306,000
Net, cumulative	-$399,200	-$93,200	$212,800

3

Figure 11-9 (continued)

```
Net cost/benefit for 1989 = expected benefit - expected cost
                          = $366,000       - ($399,200 + $60,000)
                          = -$93,200

Net cost/benefit for 1990 = expected benefit - expected cost
                           ($366,000 + $366,000) - ($459,200 +$60,000)
                          = $212,800
```

4. PROBABLE EFFECTS OF PROPOSED INFORMATION SYSTEM

The use of computer terminals rather than the mail to deliver customer orders to the home office may increase the chance of a clerical error. Clerks must be well-trained to accept customer orders by computer.

The new software may need to be tailored to the company's specific applications, and problems may result from these alterations.

5. RECOMMENDATION

I recommend that Alternative #2 be chosen since the overall cost of implementation is less. However, the effect of the change from the procedure of using an off-site warehouse in the present system to using an on-site warehouse in Alternative #2 should be taken into consideration before any change is made.

4

Figure 11-9 (continued)

Many of the tools used in structured programming and structured analysis, such as structured design review and walkthroughs, are used to specify the design alternatives. In addition, for each alternative design, the systems analyst should prepare detailed system flowcharts and HIPO charts to document the input, output, and processing requirements, along with clerical, security, and control procedures. Finally, a cost estimate is made for each alternative.

Part 2 of Figure 11-9 shows two alternative system designs developed by you and the systems analyst for a new information system that will reduce shipping time, speed up replies to customer inquiries, and reduce billing errors for Know-wear. The two alternatives are as follows:

- **Alternative #1:** Salespeople equipped with computer terminals will transmit customer orders to the home office computer via a data communications system, which also will transmit sales orders to the warehouse and shipping notices from the warehouse back to the home office. Ordered goods, invoices, and customer payments will be transmitted by common carrier or mail, as before. Invoices will be generated by the home office computer system, however, and customer payments will be entered into the computer. Reports for

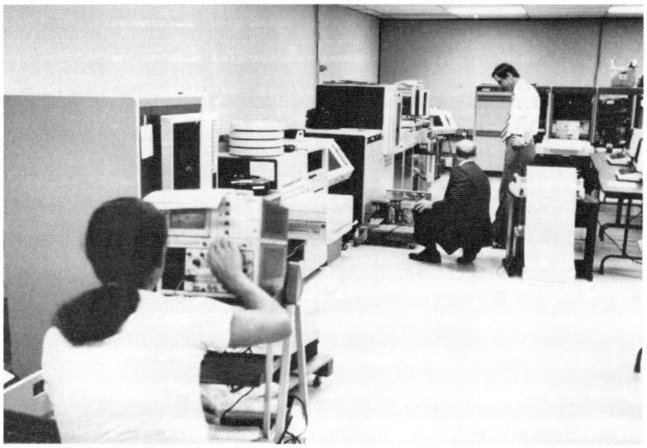

The tasks of system analysis. System analysis begins with gathering data—in part by observation and interviews (*top left and right*). System design (*lower left*) is concerned with designing alternative systems, using detailed system flowcharts and ascertaining cost estimates. In the system implementation stage, two important tasks are hardware acquisition and testing and personnel training.

managers will be generated by the computer system. Customer service representatives will have on-line access to up-to-date information on the status of customer orders.

- **Alternative #2:** In this proposal, goods will be stored at the home office, not in a warehouse in a separate location. This eliminates the need for an expensive data communications connection between the home office and warehouse.

As a glance will show, the first alternative is clearly the more complex and thus the more expensive.

Design Selection

Sometimes the design of information systems is a direct evolutionary process that begins with the ideal information system, as conceived by the users and systems analyst, and is modified until a feasible system emerges. More often, however, alternative systems are developed, each with advantages and disadvantages in efficiency and cost, and management has to make the final choice.

There are several factors to consider in choosing a design, some of the most important being:

- Compatibility
- Flexibility
- Security and control
- Economic feasibility

Compatibility. Is the proposed information system going to fit well within the organization's overall information system? That is, will the part be compatible with the whole? The proposed information system must not only be compatible in hardware and software; that is, in the technical aspects. It must also be compatible with the people using it; it must fit their needs and capabilities.

Flexibility. Can the proposed system be modified or expanded? This is what is meant by flexibility. Of course, the system to be installed will be designed to meet future as well as present information needs, but any dynamic business must allow for changes beyond what can be anticipated at the design stage.

Security and Control. You will want the new information system to be easy to use and gain access to. Unfortunately, the easier it is for authorized people to get into it, the easier it is for unauthorized people also. Thus, the system needs to be designed to control access and ensure security and yet not discourage use. We will have more to say about security in Chapter 16.

Economic Feasibility. To compare the economic feasibility of proposed systems, the systems analyst must prepare a detailed cost/benefit analysis. This means not only a careful evaluation of the costs of hardware, software, and intangibles but also an evaluation of the benefits. With your help, the systems analyst for Know-wear has worked up a careful cost/benefit analysis for the two proposed systems, as shown in part 3 of Figure 11-9.

The System Design Report

As at the end of the other stages, the end of the system design stage requires a report to document the findings. The purpose of the **system design report** is to give management enough background so that they can decide upon the best alternative. The report will include the following information:

1. The scope and objectives of the design study, as we showed for Know-wear in part 1 of Figure 11-9.
2. Two alternative designs for the Know-wear project are shown in part 2 of Figure 11-9. Any additional important details should be included in an appendix to the report or in another document.
3. An economic feasibility report, including costs and benefits, as shown in part 3 of Figure 11-9 for Know-wear.
4. Discussion of the probable effects of the proposed information systems on the organization. This includes not only the effects of infusion of new hardware and software but also the human issues. You and the systems analyst for the Know-wear project call attention to the possibility that use of computer terminals rather than mail to deliver orders to the home office may increase the possibility of clerical errors at first, since clerks must be trained to use the computers. These and other effects are outlined in part 4 of Figure 11-9.
5. The report should recommend one alternative, stating the assumptions and logic behind the recommendation. The report written by the systems analyst for Know-wear reflects the consensus of the two of you that the second alternative should be chosen because the cost of implementation is less. However, the report advises management to consider the fact that an off-site warehouse will not be used in that system whereas it is being used in the existing system (see Figure 11-9, part 5).

The complete system design report for the Know-wear project is shown in Figure 11-9.

4. System Implementation: How Do You Get It Running?

Mr. Douglas signs off on alternative #2. He asks the systems analyst to stay on to implement the project, and he asks you to stay in touch as the liaison for Know-wear.

Figure 11-10 Implementation. Six activities are required to install an information system: software development, hardware acquisition, personnel training, testing, documentation, and conversion.

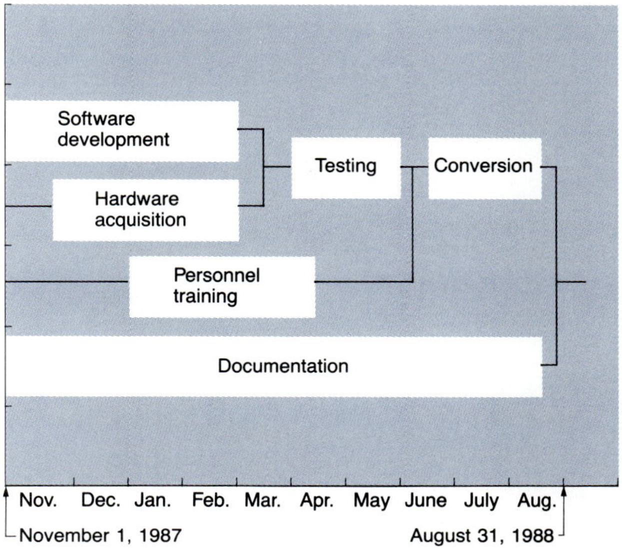
Software development
Hardware acquisition
Testing
Conversion
Personnel training
Documentation
Nov. Dec. Jan. Feb. Mar. Apr. May June July Aug.
November 1, 1987
August 31, 1988

Implementing a recommended design—**system implementation**—has five activities:

- Software development
- Hardware acquisition
- Personnel training
- Testing
- Conversion

These are shown in Figure 11-10 and described below. Note that **documentation**—the written detailed description of the systems analysis and design—is and has been an ongoing process throughout all stages.

Software Development

A computer-based information system, which, of course, is the type you are implementing here, requires computer programs to operate. Typically, the systems analyst works with computer programmers and together they follow the steps described for the programming process in Chapter 5. For simple systems, packaged software may be sufficient.

Software may also be a combination of software packages and of internally developed programs—that is, software developed within the company. The systems analyst must evaluate the available software packages and see which are compatible with the information system being designed. For internally developed programs, each program is usually broken up into independent modules to be developed separately, often by different programmers; they are combined later, under the supervision of the systems analyst.

Hardware Acquisition

Some new information systems being implemented will not require additional hardware, which means that implementation is easier. However, additional equipment often is needed, and the systems analyst has the task of evaluating hardware alternatives and preparing the physical site for the new machines.

Some software packages will operate only on specific kinds of hardware, in which case the software development step will dictate the hardware acquisition. More frequently, software packages will operate on the equipment of different manufacturers, and so the systems analyst must request proposals from different makers and evaluate them. These proposals often will state the alternatives in costs and benefits between leasing equipment and outright purchase.

Before the new hardware arrives, the users and systems analyst must determine the site where it will be installed. Depending on equipment size and space available, preparing the site may or may not be a problem. Some systems, for example, may require more air conditioning or power supply. The systems analyst's role is to determine the site requirements and to stay on top of the schedule for preparing the site.

Personnel Training

Two groups of people will need to be trained—the technical personnel who will develop, operate, and maintain the system, and the system's users and their managers. Training is necessary so that people will understand their responsibility in making the system work.

Some training can begin early, even before equipment is installed. Most early training is to increase the involvement of users in the new system to lessen the shock of adjustment and to nurture a good working relationship between users and technicians.

Once hardware and software are operating, training can be increased. Operating procedures must be understood clearly by both users and technicians.

Testing

With hardware and software in place and training started, you are now in a position to begin **testing**—testing not only of equipment and programs but of operating procedures also. This is when hostilities are apt to emerge, as you discover in the course of implementing Know-wear's new information system. The regular staff of clerks show the fear of being automated out of their jobs as they come face to face with the computer technicians. They begin to complain to you about the system's changing their work patterns, breaking up their work groups, causing them loss of status.

The systems analyst handles all this fairly adroitly, you think, letting employees offer suggestions for improving the system and asking them to provide data for testing. With Mr. Douglas's approval, you offer reassurance that no present worker will lose his or her job. You show how the technical staff will be able to make the users' lives easier, not harder.

During this shake-down phase, software, hardware, and procedures are each tested separately and then combined and tested as a group. The tests consist of feeding dummy or made-up data into the system, following it as it is converted to information, and evaluating the results. The systems analyst monitors this activity and makes (or has programmers make) whatever modifications are needed. Depending on the complexity of the information system involved, testing may take several months. Implementation for the Know-wear project, for example, takes ten months, although not all that time is taken up with testing.

Conversion

Conversion, which follows testing, is the process of changing over from the old information system to the new one. There are four common types of conversions:

- Direct
- Parallel
- Pilot
- Phased

Direct. The most risky type of conversion, the **direct conversion** consists of completely discontinuing the old way of doing things and immediately implementing the new one. This approach should be avoided unless the organization is willing to live without *any* information system should something go wrong with the new one—a distinct possibility with anything untried.

Parallel. In **parallel conversion,** the old and new information systems are operated side by side until the new one has shown its reliability and everyone has confidence in it. The old one is then discontinued. However, it is expensive to operate two systems simultaneously, and so the process should not be continued for long.

Pilot. Under **pilot conversion,** only a part of the organization tries out the new system—one plant may act as a test site, for instance. Before the new system is implemented throughout the organization, it must prove itself at the test site. This approach is less risky than the direct method and less expensive than the parallel method, although it often requires a long installation period in order to convert the whole company to the system.

Phased. In the **phased conversion,** a new information system is implemented over a period of time, gradually replacing the old. Although this avoids the riskiness of some other approaches, it requires a long conversion time.

Mr. Douglas would clearly prefer the last method of conversion for Know-wear. The result would be that everyone—customers, staff, technicians, management—would have a chance to get used to the new system and there would be fewer disruptions and consequent loss of customer goodwill and employee morale. But Know-wear is in financial trouble, and it is important to get the company turned around soon. Mr. Douglas therefore elects the second riskiest option, parallel conversion, with old and new systems operating side by side until everyone has confidence in the new one.

5. System Maintenance: How Do You Take Care of It?

After implementation has been completed, you and the systems analyst go on to other projects. But, once installed, the information system does not just run along by itself, no matter how carefully the implementation stage was handled. All systems, and information systems in particular, are continually changing. As Know-wear grows, its information demands will change. The purpose of **system maintenance,** therefore, is to monitor and evaluate the current operation of the information system and to modify it when necessary.

Some modifications may arise from sudden, unexpected problems, and quick evaluation and changes will be required. Some may be brought about because of less dramatic, gradual changes which may be harder to identify but whose long-term effect is to reduce the system's efficiency.

Many of the latter problems are identified through periodic evaluations called **system audits** or **system reviews.** System audits—the first of which takes place immediately after the information system is successfully implemented—are conducted by a systems analyst who examines the system and asks questions such as the following:

- **Efficiency:** Does the system provide information to its users in an efficient and timely manner?
- **Reliability:** Are the hardware and software reliable and easy to use?
- **Training:** Is the training sufficient and effective?
- **Procedures:** Are the procedures for operating and using the system well documented, and are they being followed?
- **Goals:** Are the original goals and objectives being met?
- **Recommendations:** Are there any recommendations or suggestions for improving the system?

Bedrock for a Computer-Based Business Information System

Why, you might ask, is it necessary to be so *careful?* Is all this patient data gathering and analysis and weighing of alternatives really worthwhile—especially when a company must act quickly to save itself or to take advantage of rapidly changing market conditions?

Sometimes, of course, managers must act decisively and without time to study alternatives—but the risks can be quite great. Moreover, as we have shown in the case of Know-wear, the systems analysis and design is not being used just to study whether to introduce a new product or find the best site for a new plant. As we will see in the next three chapters, it is being used to put in place a whole system of information gathering and processing which can enable a company to act far faster and with more accuracy than it did before.

SUMMARY

- **Systems analysis and design** is the process of examining and improving an information system. It consists of five steps: (1) Identifying a company's business information needs and determining the feasibility of meeting them. (2) Evaluating the effectiveness of the present information system and specifying new requirements. (3) Formulating alternative information systems and recommending one. (4) Implementing and (5) maintaining the new system.
- Changes inside or outside a company may dictate changes in information systems: e.g., organizational growth; better, cheaper technology; change in corporate structure; change in government regulations; new business opportunities.
- Users, a **systems analyst,** and programmers must combine efforts to develop a computer-based information system. Users describe their needs; the systems analyst works with users and programmers to analyze, design, and implement new information systems; the programmers do the technical work required.
- Systems analysis and design uses the **systems approach** to problem solving, in which a problem is looked at as a system that can be broken down into subsystems. Solutions to the problems in the subsystems are then brought together to develop a solution to the overall problem.
- Systems analysis is an ongoing activity; a company's information systems need continual reevaluation and updating. The evaluation process called the **systems life cycle** (or *systems development cycle*) consists of five steps: (1) *System investigation*—in which information needs are evaluated and the feasibility of meeting those needs determined. (2) *System analysis*—in which the existing information flow is analyzed and new information requirements are specified. (3) *System design*—in which alternative information systems are designed and a preferred design recommended. (4) *System implementation*—in which new hardware and software are developed and tested, per-

sonnel trained, and necessary redesign accomplished. (5) *System maintenance*—in which the information system is monitored and evaluated and, if necessary, modified.

- The first step in the systems life cycle is a **system investigation** of each proposed systems design project to help management decide which projects are most important. The steps in a system investigation are: define the problem, propose alternative information systems, evaluate the feasibility of the alternatives and recommend one, write a system study charter.
- A **system needs survey** defines the problem. The system needs survey report must be a specific, clear, and easily understood statement of *what* information is needed, *who* needs it, *where, when,* and *why.*
- In the second step of a system investigation, the analyst develops preliminary alternative solutions to give management an idea of the scope of the project.
- The following factors are considered when evaluating the feasibility of systems project: (1) *Economic:* What is the net cost/benefit? What is the rate of return? (2) *Technical:* What hardware, software, and people are required? (3) *Operational:* How acceptable will the proposed system be to users and management?
- Two common tools for measuring economic feasibility are net cost/benefit and rate of return. **Net cost/benefit** is the expected benefit (e.g., increased sales, reduced costs) minus the expected cost (e.g., money spent, disruptions suffered). **Rate of return** is the ratio between estimated benefits and estimated costs.
- The **system study charter** is the formal document that summarizes the system investigation step in the systems life cycle. It should include the following: (1) A brief description of the present information system. (2) A summary of the system needs study. (3) A summary of the proposed alternative information systems. (4) A feasibility report on the proposed projects. (5) A statement of any potential problems. (6) A development schedule for the proposed system. (7) Go/No go recommendations.
- The second stage of an information systems project, **system analysis,** is concerned with collecting and analyzing data about the present and future information needs of the users. System analysis does not involve the design of a new system, only a detailed analysis of the existing system and the development of requirements for an improved system. There are three steps: gathering data, analyzing the data, and writing a system requirements report.
- Data gathering is primarily concerned with determining how the present system operates. The four most common sources of data are: (1) Written documents. (2) Interviews. (3) Questionnaires. (4) Observation.
- The third stage in the development of an information systems project is **system analysis,** to determine why certain procedures are being used and to look for better ways of doing them. The three most common tools used

in this stage are system flowcharts, grid charts, and checklists.

- **System flowcharts** are used to represent information flow within a system by focusing upon input and output operations. Because they present a macro view or overview, system flowcharts are a valuable tool for systems analysis and design.
- A **grid chart,** also called an **input/output chart,** is used in analysis to show the relationship between input and output documents.
- A **checklist** of questions is used to ensure that the user and systems analyst address key issues when they are evaluating the present system.
- The **system requirements report** describes the findings of the system analysis stage. It ensures that users and the systems analyst agree on the details of the current system and on the need for a new information system. The system requirements report has five sections: (1) a statement of scope and objectives. (2) A description of the present information system. (3) An estimate of system requirements. (4) A revised system development schedule. (5) A request to management for authorization to proceed.
- The stage following system analysis, **system design,** focuses on creating and specifying a new information system to meet current and future needs. The three steps in the system design stage are: design of alternative systems, selection of the best alternative, and preparation of a system design report.
- System design can be very simple or a complex task involving trade-offs between costs and efficiency. For each alternative design, the systems analyst prepares detailed system flowcharts and HIPO charts to document the output, input, and processing requirements, along with clerical, security, and control procedures. Finally, a cost estimate is made for each alternative.
- In choosing a design for an information system there are several factors to consider: compatibility, flexibility, security and control, and economic feasibility.
- A **system design report** documents the findings at the end of the system design stage. The report includes: (1) The scope and objectives of the design study. (2) Two or three alternative designs. (3) An economic feasibility report, including costs and benefits. (4) Discussion of the probable effects of the proposed information systems on the organization. This includes not only the effects of infusion of new hardware and software but also the human issues. (5) A recommendation of one alternative, stating the assumptions and logic behind the recommendation.
- **System implementation** includes five activities: software development, hardware acquisition, personnel training, testing, and conversion.
- Computer-based information systems require computer programs to operate. Software may be internally developed programs and software packages, or a combination of both types of programs.
- If additional equipment is needed to implement a system, the systems ana-

lyst has the task of evaluating hardware alternatives and preparing the physical site for the new machines.

- Two groups of personnel need to be trained—the technical personnel who develop, operate, and maintain the system, and the system's users and their managers.
- After the hardware and software is in place and training started, the new system is ready for **testing,** not only of the equipment and programs but of operating procedures also. During the testing phase, software, hardware, and procedures are each tested separately and then combined and tested as a group. The test consists of feeding dummy data into the system, following it as it is converted to information, and evaluating the results. The systems analyst monitors this activity and makes whatever modifications are needed. Testing can take several months.
- **Conversion,** which follows testing, is the process of changing over from the old information system to the new one. There are four common types of conversions: direct, parallel, pilot, and phased.
- The most risky type of conversion, **direct conversion,** consists of completely discontinuing the old system and implementing the new one. This approach should be avoided unless the organization is willing to live without *any* information system should something go wrong with the new one.
- In **parallel conversion,** the old and new information systems are operated side by side until the new one has shown its reliability; the old one is then discontinued. Since it is expensive to operate two systems simultaneously, the process should not be continued for long.
- Under **pilot conversion,** only a part of the organization tries out the new system—one plant acts as a test site before the new system is implemented throughout the organization. This approach is less risky than the direct method and less expensive than the parallel method, although it requires a long installation period to convert the whole company to the system.
- In **phased conversion,** a new information system is implemented over a period of time, gradually replacing the old. Although this avoids the riskiness of some of the other approaches, it requires a long conversion time.
- The purpose of **system maintenance** is to monitor and evaluate the current operation of the information system and to modify it when necessary. Many problems are identified through periodic evaluations called **system audits** or **system reviews.** System audits are conducted by a systems analyst who examines the system and asks questions such as: (1) *Efficiency:* Does the system provide information to its users in an efficient and timely manner? (2) *Reliability:* Are the hardware and software reliable and easy to use? (3) *Training:* Is the training sufficient and effective? (4) *Procedures:* Are the procedures for operating and using the system well documented, and are they being followed? (5) *Goals:* Are the original goals and objectives being met?

(6) *Recommendations:* Are there any recommendations or suggestions for improving the system?

KEY TERMS

Checklist, pp. 404, 405
Conversion, p. 421
Direct conversion, p. 421
Documentation, p. 419
Flowchart, p. 401
Grid chart, p. 403
Information system, p. 383
Input/output chart, p. 403
Interview, p. 402
Net cost/benefit, p. 394
Organization chart, p. 401
Parallel conversion, p. 421
Phased conversion, p. 421
Pilot conversion, p. 421
Questionnaire, p. 403
Rate of return, p. 394
System analysis, pp. 386, 391, 400
System audit, p. 422
System design, pp. 391, 411
System design report, p. 418
System flowchart, p. 403
System implementation, pp. 391, 418
System investigation, pp. 391, 392
System maintenance, pp. 391, 422
System needs survey, p. 393
System requirements report, p. 405
System review, p. 422
System study charter, pp. 392, 399
Systems analysis and design, p. 383
Systems analyst, p. 386
Systems approach, p. 387
Systems life cycle, p. 391
Testing, p. 420
Written documents, p. 401

REVIEW QUESTIONS

1. Describe two changes that might result in a company's needing to develop a new information system.
2. Why should you be involved in helping the experts set up a computerized information system at the company where you will work?
3. Define the systems approach.
4. What are the five steps of the systems life cycle?
5. What information should be included in a system study charter?
6. Describe one of the common methods of gathering data for system analysis.
7. What is a grid chart?
8. Describe a method of conversion.
9. Outline the process of system implementation.

CASE PROBLEMS

Case 11-1: Systems Analysis and College Registration

There are several pitfalls that can be the undoing of a systems analyst, points out Jerry FitzGerald and his co-authors in *Fundamentals of Systems Analysis.*[3] Among them are:

- Improper definition of the problem by management, which is not redefined by the analyst.
- Excessive ambition by the analyst, which leads him or her to force a favorite solution to the problem.
- A problem solution that is "oriented more toward the technical peculiarities of a computer than to the objectives of the people who will use the system."
- Preoccupation with techniques or equipment rather than the objectives of the problem study.

Being alert to these pitfalls may also serve you well, whether you are using the techniques of systems analysis to deal with a problem or are engaging the services of a systems analyst.

Your assignment: Registering as a student for a new quarter or semester is often tedious, and at some colleges and universities it can be an anxious, exhausting experience, especially for a first-timer. Use the information you learned in this chapter to sketch the flow of steps involved in registering at your college, keeping the above pitfalls in mind. (You may make a separate flow diagram showing preregistration, if you wish.) Include the forms you must fill out, people you must see, and stations to which you must go. After you have done your system investigation and system analysis, can you think of a design for a new system? You probably want to approach this from the standpoint of how you personally can navigate the system better, but you may see ways in which the college could redesign the system to improve it.

Case 11-2: Writing a Request for an Interview

A well-kept secret of the computer age, says Charles J. McDonough, writing in the *Wall Street Journal* (May 21, 1984), is that for each element of computer processing, at least "two distinct segments of human activity are always needed: one before processing and one after. First, some employee has to do something very specific before the computer can do its thing; then when the computer finishes running that program, some employee must do something with the output."[4] The result is that—the computer revolution not withstanding—office employees are still spending most of their working time handling routine pieces of paper. Indeed, says McDonough, the head of a Buffalo, New York, consulting firm, his company has found that "even the most highly computerized offices average four to five detail manual procedures to support each separate accomplishment by the computer." Expansion of computer activities may eliminate certain manual chores, but the paradox is that they require carefully coordinated adjustments in other clerical tasks and new staff instructions. The point is that, no matter how sophisticated office automation may be today, it still must run in conjunction with people. Thus, a systems analyst and a user liaison must be able to relate well to people—both in obtaining information from them and in getting their assistance in implementing a new system.

Your assignment: Suppose, in your role as user liaison at Know-wear, you receive the following draft of a memorandum from the systems analyst, requesting an interview with the manager of the accounts receivable department. Rewrite the memo so that the systems analyst will have a better chance of cordial working relations.[5]

```
I would like for you to come to my office next week sometime to
discuss the very serious problems that you have in your department.
It seems that many of the other managers are upset that their reports
are late and never up-to-date.

I will be discussing the following topics:

1. How many people work for you? What are their salaries?

2. What are the exact duties of each of your employees?

3. Why do they make so many errors?

4. What procedures are followed by the data processing department to
   keep your files up to date?

5. What kinds of reports do the other managers need?

6. How will your staff feel if we automate the entire accounting
   functions and have to lay off the unproductive workers?

I will use this information in coming up with some better ways of
doing the work in your area. I already have some idea of the
changes I would like to see and hope you will agree with them.
If I am not in my office when you come by, please wait, as I will
probably return soon.
```

CHAPTER 12

JOHN DE

Operations Information Systems

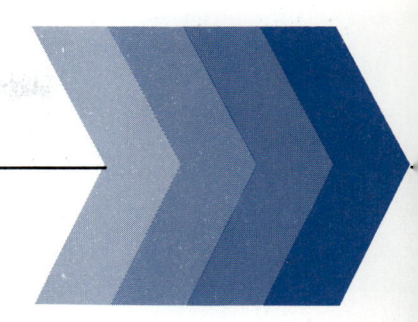

Help for Supervisory Managers

PREVIEW

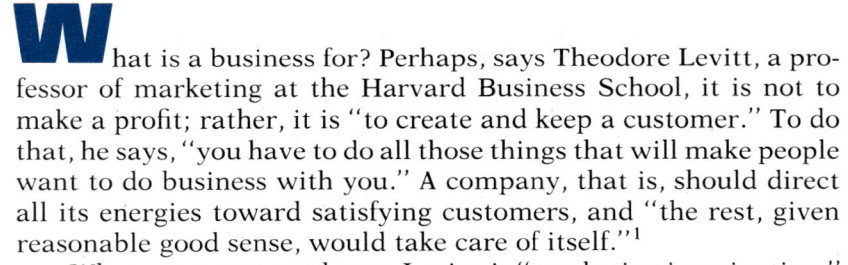

What is a business for? Perhaps, says Theodore Levitt, a professor of marketing at the Harvard Business School, it is not to make a profit; rather, it is "to create and keep a customer." To do that, he says, "you have to do all those things that will make people want to do business with you." A company, that is, should direct all its energies toward satisfying customers, and "the rest, given reasonable good sense, would take care of itself."[1]

What managers need, says Levitt, is "marketing imagination," an understanding that people buy solutions to problems, not things. Customers, then, need to be treated as valued assets, all the more so because it takes so much effort to find customers in the first place that it is not reasonable to ignore them after the sale is made. Even customers that are behind on their payments deserve to be treated well—or certainly fairly, as the case study on the next page shows. And the treatment of customers begins not with top and middle managers but with the lowest level of managers and their employees. Customer relations begin with those prosaic activities of order entry, accounts receivable, and similar clerical tasks. It behooves us, therefore, to see if there are better ways of handling these chores. Here is the logical place to initiate a computer-based information system.

OIS: Keeping Track of Details

As we hinted in the introduction to this part of the book, the **operations information system**—abbreviated **OIS**—is the basis for a computer-based information system, the foundation on which

CASE STUDY: CUTTING DOWN ON BROKEN PROMISES

A Telephone Company Automates Its Billing Process

DALLAS—It tripled its customer base in just three years, but U.S. Telephone, Inc. found that its manual customer accounts collection process could not handle the work load.

"We have cycle billings, 20 cycles a month, and sometimes we didn't get an updated trial balance [a computation of money spent and owed] for six weeks," Chuck Giles, U.S. Telephone's vice president of credit management, recalled. "We could ask a customer for payment, but we couldn't tell him the dollar amount of his most recent invoice."

U.S. Telephone was dissatisfied with its high delinquency rate of 75 to 80 days on the average for 10,000 customers. Even the best collectors managed just 1,800 accounts, with the average carrying 700. U.S. Telephone wanted to raise that average to 3,500.

"Our collectors posted cash and credits manually, then made telephone calls for collections. We were lucky to get a complete trial balance and an updated record every four weeks," Giles said.

Collectors spent $2\frac{1}{2}$ hours each day posting cash and credits in the 75% manual system. Invoices dating back more than a year filled a 10-foot square room.

In 1982, the telecommunications firm installed an IBM 4300 processor with a new accounts receivable package and more than doubled the number of accounts that each collector handled, exceeding even its own goals.

The software it chose was the Accounts Receivable System from Management Science America, Inc. (MSA). . . .

"Today, most of our people are managing 4,000 accounts. Some have been managing more than 6,500," [director of customer information systems Lee] Daly noted. . . .

Delinquency is down from 33% to 16%, he added. The changeover has also allowed the company to improve its method of handling disputed bills. "Being a telephone company," Daly said, "we get calls now and then about bills. You know, 'I didn't make this call to Fargo, N.D.' So we recently installed a change in the system that allows us to dispute one item rather than an entire invoice. If the invoice is for $1,000 and the item in question is for $50, the customer can pay the $950.". . .

Giles noted that since the $50 disputed is set aside, the collectors can treat it as a promise to pay and not constantly review it. "They are only working with broken promises to pay, which saves a lot of time—particularly since they had been looking at all the accounts to determine who paid under the old system," Giles said.

Giles described U.S. Telephone's new accounts receivable package as "essentially paperless," with the collectors completely on-line, reading everything they need on terminal screens.

—*Computerworld*,
May 14, 1984

everything else is built. The purpose of the OIS is to perform processing and produce documents that will help an organization keep track of its resources—materials, money, employees, and facilities. OIS is also known as transaction processing or electronic data processing (EDP).

The word "operations" in an operations information system refers to *clerical* operations—the kind of tasks that clerks do—such as the recording of accounts payable, accounts receivable, and payroll. An OIS takes in the data from such operations and stores them in computer-accessible form. This stored data forms the basis for the other information systems we will discuss in Chapters 13 and 14—management information systems and decision support systems.

Fitting OIS to the Organization

An OIS must fit the structure of the departments within a business organization. As we discussed earlier and as shown in Figure 12-1, these departments or divisions encompass four functional areas:

- **Marketing:** This department is responsible for sales of the product—in the case of Know-wear, clothing. It is the customer's link to the organization.
- **Accounting and Finance:** This department keeps a monetary record of all activities in the organization. It allows people to make an assessment of the organization's well-being with the help of financial statements and daily records.
- **Production:** Production is the organization's main line of activity. It consists of processing the resources that are input to the organization—materials, money, employees, and facilities—and turning out finished goods or services.
- **Research and Development:** Often abbreviated R & D, this department has the task of improving current products and creating new products to meet future customer needs.

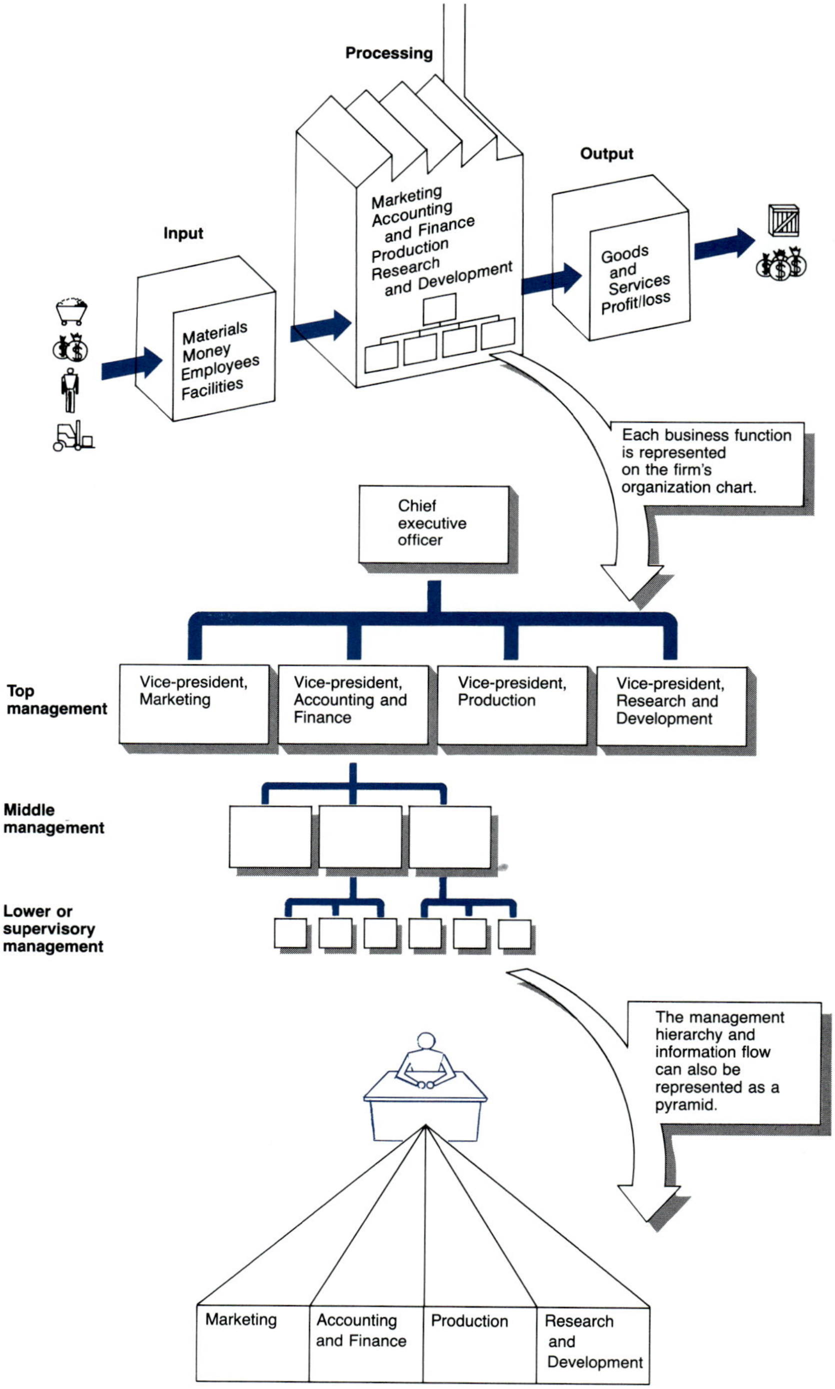
Processing
Input
Output
Materials
Money
Employees
Facilities
Marketing
Accounting
and Finance
Production
Research
and Development
Goods
and
Services
Profit/loss
Each business function is represented on the firm's organization chart.
Chief executive officer
Top management
Vice-president, Marketing
Vice-president, Accounting and Finance
Vice-president, Production
Vice-president, Research and Development
Middle management
Lower or supervisory management
The management hierarchy and information flow can also be represented as a pyramid.
Marketing
Accounting and Finance
Production
Research and Development

Figure 12-1 The organization of a business. *Top:* The four functional areas of a business are shown under Processing. *Middle:* These functional areas are coordinated by a management hierarchy, with each area headed by a vice president who reports to the CEO. *Bottom:* The management hierarchy can be represented another way, as a pyramid, with information flowing up and down the pyramid, from workers to top management and vice versa.

Many firms are organized with departments or divisions corresponding to these four functional areas. Each such area has resources of materials, money, employees, and facilities and each is coordinated by a management hierarchy of supervisory and middle managers under a division head or vice president who reports to the organization's CEO. The result is an organization chart like that we have been showing throughout the book, as repeated in the middle of Figure 12-1. The management hierarchy for these four functional areas can also be thought of as a pyramid; see the bottom of Figure 12-1.

Within each department, most information tends to flow vertically—from top to bottom and from bottom to top, from vice president down to workers and the reverse. Of course, information may flow horizontally, too, such as between departments, but since most flow occurs vertically, information systems must operate the same way.

The structure of an operations information system, therefore, resembles the pyramid arrangment of a management hierarchy, as shown in Figure 12-2. An OIS carries on day-to-day activities, monitoring the inputs—the resources of materials, money, employees, and facilities—as they are processed into outputs of goods and services and profits. This kind of activity, the major function of an OIS, is called **transaction processing.** The OIS uses data files to keep track of what is happening. When organized in an integrated fashion, these data files constitute a data base. This data base describes the operations of the company and provides the basis for the other information systems in the organization, as we will see in Chapters 13 and 14.

Transaction Processing: What It Is, How to Use It

A **transaction** is any action or event dealing with the firm's clients or creditors or with the firm's own resources, anything that needs to be recorded by the organization for later use—a sale, a purchase, a firing, a customer complaint. The purposes of **transaction processing** are:

- To generate outputs, such as invoices, paychecks, and status reports, which will assist the firm in its operations.
- To create a data base to support company-wide decision making and control, as we shall discuss in the next two chapters.

Transaction processing has four activities:

- Data entry
- Data processing
- Data storage
- Output generation

Let us see how these work.

Data Entry. The purpose of **data entry** is to collect necessary data in a way that is cost-effective, error-free, timely, and convenient. Data entry can be done in two ways—manually and automatically.

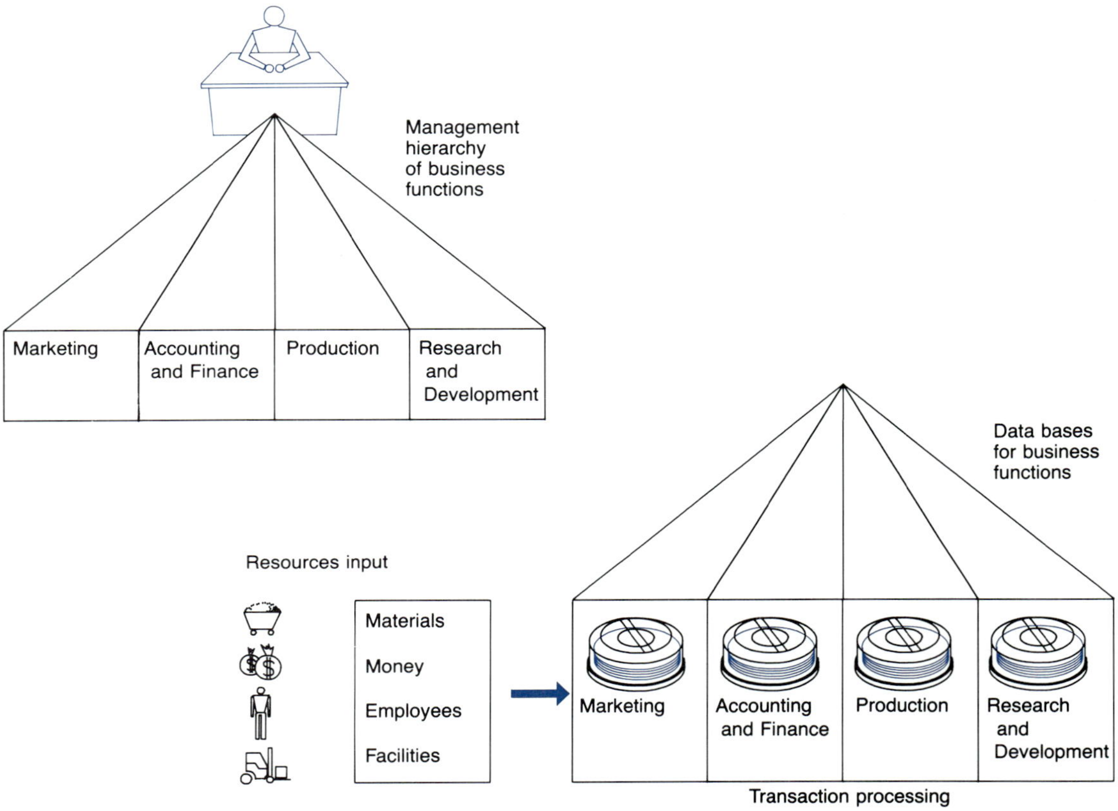
Management hierarchy of business functions
Marketing
Accounting and Finance
Production
Research and Development
Data bases for business functions
Resources input
Materials
Money
Employees
Facilities
Marketing
Accounting and Finance
Production
Research and Development
Transaction processing

Figure 12-2 **Pyramid power.** An operations information system has the same pyramid arrangement as the management hierarchy, with the day-to-day transactions of the business being recorded and stored on data bases, or computerized storage systems. This not only provides a computerized description of such day-to-day business transactions as orders, customer invoices, and paychecks, but also provides the basis for more sophisticated information systems, as will be discussed in Chapters 13 and 14.

Manual data entry is done by a clerk or keyboard operator reading a sales form, purchase order, or other document and converting it into machine-readable form, often by typing on a keyboard. The document that he or she is copying from is called the **source document.**

Automatic data entry is done when the data is already in machine-readable form, such as the bar codes on supermarket products, and can be input directly to the computer by an automatic device such as a bar code scanner or a POS terminal. The automatic way is, of course, faster and more accurate and convenient; you can expect to see more such machines in use in the future—both because they produce many fewer

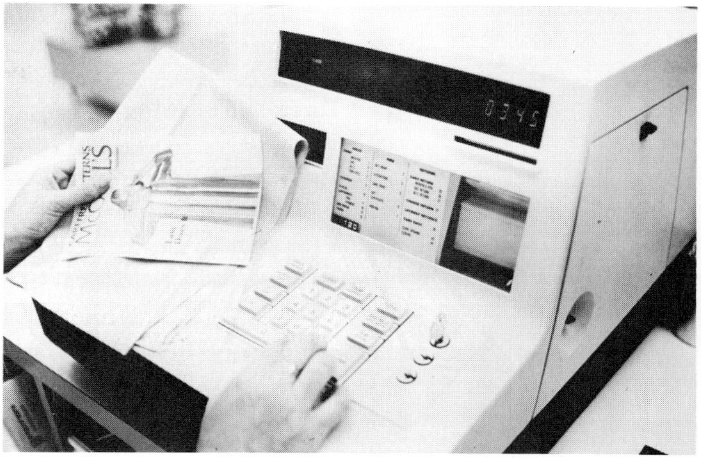

Monarch
SWEET PEAS

Data entry for transaction processing. Data entry can be done either manually or automatically. Examples of manual entry are through keyboards on POS terminals, in which the operator copies from a source document; this is often seen in department stores (*top left and right*). Examples of automatic data entry are bar codes and scanners, seen in grocery stores (*middle left and right*), and hand-held wands, which in factories can gather up-to-the-minute information on employee activity or material movement (*lower left*).

errors and because the cost of data entry operators is increasing while equipment costs are decreasing, as we discussed in Chapter 7.

Data Processing. Data entry and data processing may be coupled in three ways. The main differences are in how accurate they are, how up to the minute, or current, the data is, and how expensive the necessary technology is. The three possible combinations of data entry and data processing are:

- **Batch entry and batch processing:** Here a transaction is stored on a source document, such as a daily time sheet; source documents are then collected, and all such transactions are processed at one time. This is the least expensive method and is appropriate for payroll, accounts payable, and customer billing. However, it is also the least accurate and least current method of processing.
- **Direct entry and batch processing:** Also known as on-line, direct data entry consists of immediately storing a transaction; however, it is not processed immediately. Often the data is stored on magnetic tape or disk. This arrangement is more current than batch entry plus batch processing. Typical applications include inventory control and retail sales, as when grocery sales are recorded on a POS terminal at a supermarket checkout counter; the terminal is connected to the store's computer, which records the transaction on magnetic tape. At the end of the day, sales are processed and inventory updated.
- **Direct entry and direct (immediate) processing:** Here a transaction is entered immediately and processed immediately as it occurs. It is as accurate as the preceding method and even more current. However, the method has disadvantages: equipment is expensive, one must have immediate access to the computer, and if the computer fails, the entire data entry operation must shut down. A typical application is the airline reservations system of most major airlines.

Data Storage. As we discussed in Chapter 9, there are two systems for storing data: file management and data base management. In a *file management system,* files are created for specific applications. They are independent of other files. Thus, files may be created by the Marketing department that cannot be used by the Production department for its purposes. In a *data base management system,* files are created for multiple applications and are integrated. They can be organized logically in various ways and can be accessed by different users.

Originally, operations information systems were built to follow the four functional areas or departments of organizations and to support the applications of those departments. That is, they were file management systems. Now business organizations want their files to be used for broader purposes. Consequently, transaction processing must create data that can be stored such that it can be accessed by many users; in other words, an organization must build a data base management system.

Output Generation. Besides storing data, transaction processing must also create data reports. There are two types of documents:

- Computer-generated documents such as payroll checks or customer invoices, which can be produced more economically and reliably by computer than manually.
- Reports of events, such as transaction listings of customers who have not paid their bills.

The Parts of an OIS

Before the pattern cutters in Know-wear's Production department can go to work, the company must be assured it has money for materials and orders for finished goods. The most common use of an operations information system, therefore, is in the Accounting and Finance department. Often this use is the cornerstone on which the rest of a firm's information systems are built. At Know-wear, for instance, Mr. Douglas is so pleased by the new arrangements for the order entry and accounts receivable information system that he decides to further automate the handling of information within the organization. He asks you, in cooperation with a systems analyst and senior management, to be his liaison in extending the information systems to an OIS at Know-wear.

An accounting and finance OIS consists of seven elements:

- Payroll
- Order entry
- Accounts receivable
- Purchasing
- Accounts payable
- Fixed assets
- General ledger

As Figure 12-3 shows, these elements are the ways the OIS monitors the flow of resources—materials, money, employees, and facilities—within the organization. Specifically:

- **Materials:** This resource is monitored in the *purchasing* and *order entry* functions of the Accounting and Finance department. The raw materials acquisition is tracked in purchasing, and the demand for finished products is recorded in order entry.

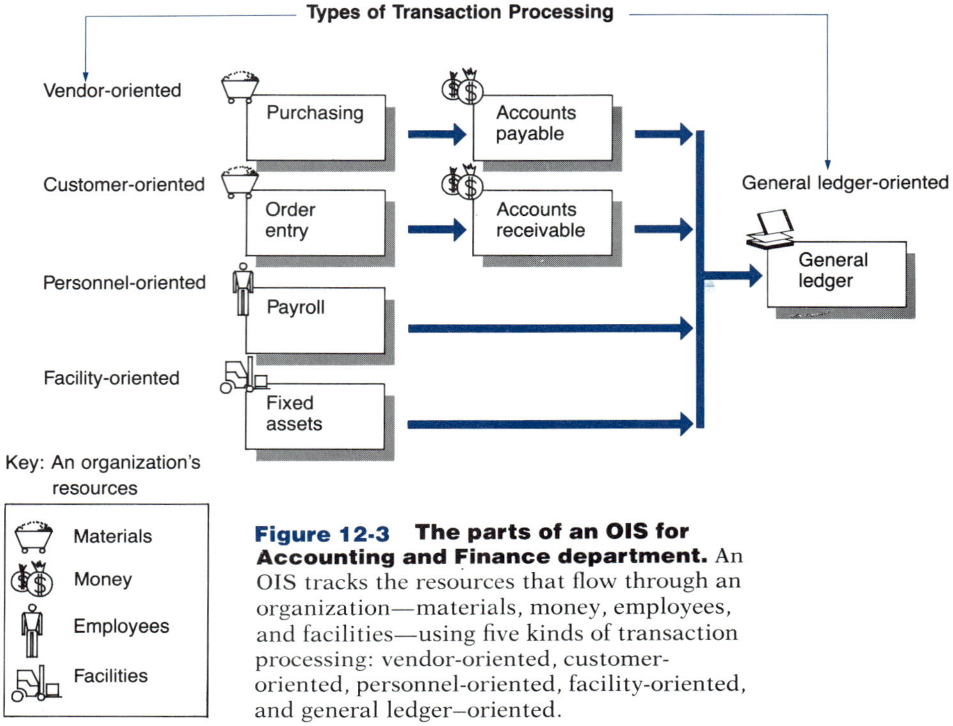
Types of Transaction Processing
Vendor-oriented
Customer-oriented
Personnel-oriented
Facility-oriented
Purchasing
Order entry
Payroll
Fixed assets
Accounts payable
Accounts receivable
General ledger-oriented
General ledger
Key: An organization's resources
Materials
Money
Employees
Facilities

Figure 12-3 The parts of an OIS for Accounting and Finance department. An OIS tracks the resources that flow through an organization—materials, money, employees, and facilities—using five kinds of transaction processing: vendor-oriented, customer-oriented, personnel-oriented, facility-oriented, and general ledger–oriented.

- **Money:** Money is recorded in the *accounts payable* and *accounts receivable* functions. The spending or paying out of money is recorded in accounts payable, and the income or receipt of money is recorded in accounts receivable.
- **Employees:** The people resources are recorded in *payroll,* which calculates employee salaries and wages and issues paychecks.
- **Facilities:** Facilities are recorded in *fixed assets.* **Fixed assets** consist of office equipment, factory equipment, and buildings.

All of these transactions are formally recorded in the *general ledger* of the Accounting and Finance department's OIS.

As we have stated, a business is concerned essentially with taking in resources (input) and converting (processing) them into a final product or service (output) to sell. But the accounting procedures and paperwork required during this conversion or processing stage are not nearly as simple and straightforward. The OIS required to keep track of the transactions being processed is shown in Figure 12-3. Note that the seven elements can be put together into five forms of processing:

- Vendor-oriented processing, which includes purchasing and accounts payable.

- Customer-oriented processing, which includes order entry and accounts receivable.
- Personnel-oriented processing, which includes payroll.
- Facility-oriented processing, which includes fixed assets.
- General ledger–oriented processing.

We will take a look at these five types of transaction processing in the rest of this chapter.

Vendor-Oriented Processing: Buying and Paying for Supplies

Vendors, also known in business as suppliers, are those businesses outside the firm that provide it with raw materials, parts, or services to help the firm assemble or provide *its* products or services. Know-wear, for instance, deals with vendors of fabrics, thread, zippers, buttons, buckles, rivets, and other clothing-related materials. In addition, Know-wear deals with vendors of office supplies, computer equipment, janitorial services, and company cars, among other things.

Whenever an item in inventory runs low—the item can be anything from a carton of pencils to a warehouse full of denim—a request is sent to the Purchasing department, which in turn creates a **purchase order (PO),** a form that identifies the required materials and the vendor to supply them. The original PO is sent to the vendor, and internal copies of the PO are distributed within the firm to confirm that the order has been placed and to document the expected delivery date of the item or items ordered. These copies usually are sent to the originator of the purchase order request and to the firm's Shipping and Receiving department, as well as some others. The copy of the PO sent to the Shipping and Receiving department is called a receiving report.

Upon delivery to the firm's Shipping and Receiving department, the materials should be checked against the receiving report to make sure the correct materials have been delivered. The vendor may also deliver a bill with the goods; this bill, along with a confirmation of the receipt of materials, is sent to the firm's Purchasing and Accounting departments. The Purchasing department notifies the originator of the request that the materials have arrived. The Accounting department records the acquisition of the materials and the bill for their delivery in the general ledger.

In **vendor-oriented processing,** the OIS has two applications, as we saw in Figure 12-3—purchasing and accounts payable—which correspond to the two transactions involved in getting something from a vendor: ordering it and paying for it. Let us see how these work.

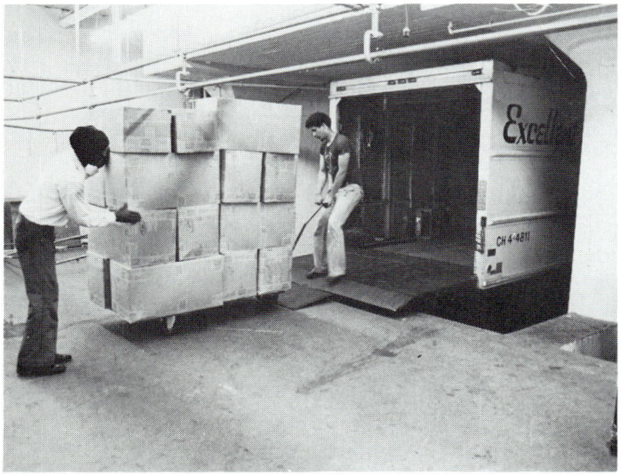

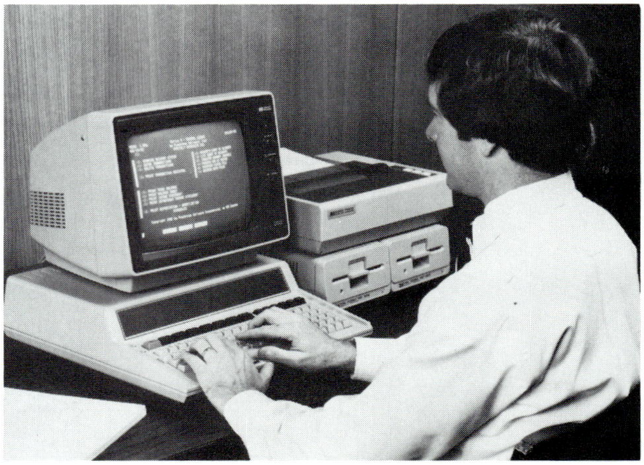

Vendor-oriented processing. Vendors are suppliers outside the firm who provide it with the materials or services to enable it to provide *its* product. When goods are delivered by the vendor to the firm's shipping and receiving department (*left*), the materials must be checked against a copy of the purchase order, called the receiving report. The accounting department records the acquisition of the materials and the bill for their delivery in the part of the OIS known as the general ledger (*right*).

Purchasing

Purchasing is how the paperwork begins. Let us say that Know-wear's Production department is ordering fastening materials for a certain line of outerwear clothing, parkas for the young executive's leisure time. The first transaction is the *request for materials*, which requests in detail the specific materials and the amounts necessary. The request for materials is used to get access to a data base, stored on magnetic disk, which contains the names, addresses, products, and past performances of all of Know-wear's vendors.

Once the best vendor in the data base is identified, the information is used to prepare the *purchase order*. The PO is then mailed to the vendor, the data base is updated to show this fact, and copies of the PO are circulated within the firm. Figure 12-4 shows how the purchase order and receiving report look for one of Know-wear's purchases.

Figure 12-4 (opposite page) Vendor-oriented processing: purchasing. *Top:* An input-processing-output diagram for purchasing. The input is a request for materials, which provides the description of materials to be purchased. Processing consists of checking the request for materials against the company's data base listing its vendors. The output is a purchase order and copies of the purchase order, including a receiving report. Additional output could be a printed general ledger report summarizing new entries. *Middle:* A purchase order from Know-wear for materials needed; this is sent to the vendor. *Bottom:* A receiving report, which is sent to Know-wear's Shipping and Receiving department; copies of the purchase order are also circulated to other departments within Know-wear.

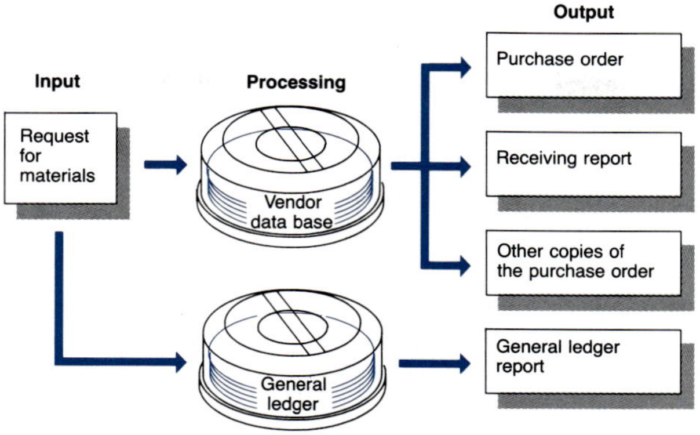
Input
Request for materials
Processing
Vendor data base
General ledger
Output
Purchase order
Receiving report
Other copies of the purchase order
General ledger report

Know-Wear, Inc.
8121 West Bell Road
Springfield, IL 62705

Vendor

Lone Star Buttons & Bows
900 Harrison St.
Dallas, TX 75265

Ship to
Know-Wear, Inc.
8121 West Bell Rd.
Springfield, IL 62705

Purchase order number
1062

Vendor number 017

Purchase order date 7/15/88

Department number	Quantity	Description	Price per unit	Amount
100	15,000	Double slide zippers	$0.18	$2,700.00
110	15,000	Zipper pulls	$0.02	300.00
120	90,000	Snap closures	$0.02	1,800.00
100	30,000	Velcro cuff closures	$0.20	6,000.00
			Total	$10,800.00

Original

Know-Wear, Inc.
8121 West Bell Road
Springfield, IL 62705

Vendor

Lone Star Buttons & Bows
900 Harrison St.
Dallas, TX 75265

Ship to
Know-Wear, Inc.
8121 West Bell Rd.
Springfield, IL 62705

Purchase order number
1062

Vendor number 017

Purchase order date 7/15/88

Department number	Quantity	Description	Date received	Comments
100	15,000	Double slide zippers	7/20/88	
110	15,000	Zipper pulls		Back order expected 7/24/88
120	90,000	Snap closures	7/20/88	
100	30,000	Velcro cuff closures	7/20/88	

Receiving report

Accounts Payable

The second kind of vendor-oriented transaction, **accounts payable** begins with the receipt of materials from the vendor. That is, when the vendor delivers materials ordered, they usually are accompanied by an invoice (bill) for the costs. In the accounts payable application, the Accounting and Finance department accesses the data base of vendors and updates that data base by noting the receipt of materials, pertinent delivery information, and the invoice. The invoice is also used to update the general ledger, whose purpose we shall explain shortly. Periodically, all accounts payable are reviewed to decide which ones are due, and voucher checks are created and mailed as payment to the vendors; the general ledger is also updated. The scheme for this application is shown in Figure 12-5.

Customer-Oriented Processing: Taking Orders and Getting Paid

Vendor-oriented processing concerns acquiring and paying for raw materials. **Customer-oriented processing** focuses on what the firm is in business to do: sell finished products or services. That is, it concerns getting orders from customers for finished goods or services and receiving payment for them.

From the standpoint of business information flow, customer-oriented processing has two activities: order entry and accounts receivable. Let us see how these work.

Order Entry

Remember, we are dealing with information from the standpoint of the Accounting and Finance department, not that of the Marketing department. Marketing is concerned with promoting and selling the product; Accounting and Finance is concerned only with taking orders and collecting money. In this scheme, therefore, the first step is the request for a product by a customer—an order, whether by phone, mail, or personal visit. The customer order is the source document that makes up the input for the **order entry** application. It is used to create internal documents in the company that will result in shipment of the product ordered.

In the case of Know-wear, orders come in from salespeople via the mail (under the old way of doing things) or via the new data communications system. For instance, a purchase order is received from Thriller Threads, a clothing store catering to young professional people. The clothes order is filled from current inventory in the Know-wear warehouse and shipped to the customer by truck. A notice of shipment is mailed to the customer at the same time the product is sent. As Figure 12-6 shows, the customer data base is updated to reflect the shipment

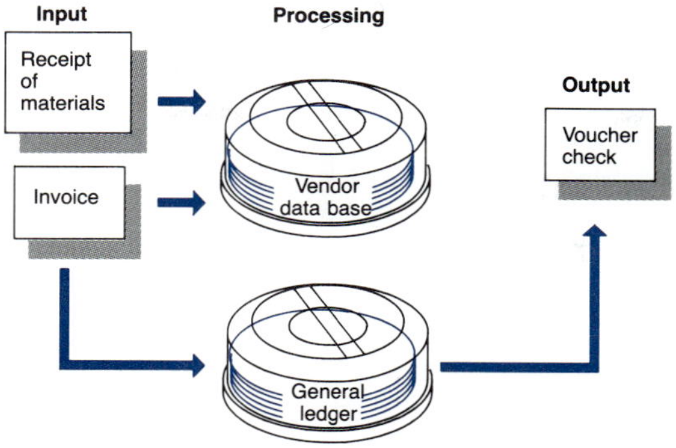
Input
Processing
Output
Receipt of materials
Invoice
Vendor data base
General ledger
Voucher check

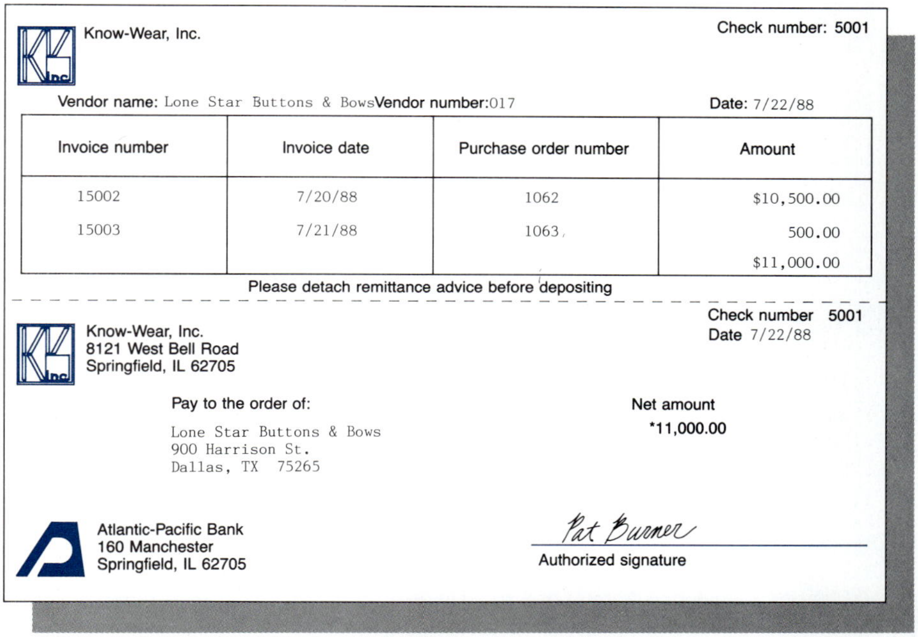

Know-Wear, Inc. Check number: 5001

Vendor name: Lone Star Buttons & Bows Vendor number: 017 Date: 7/22/88

Invoice number	Invoice date	Purchase order number	Amount
15002	7/20/88	1062	$10,500.00
15003	7/21/88	1063	500.00
			$11,000.00

Please detach remittance advice before depositing

Know-Wear, Inc.
8121 West Bell Road
Springfield, IL 62705

Check number 5001
Date 7/22/88

Pay to the order of:

Lone Star Buttons & Bows
900 Harrison St.
Dallas, TX 75265

Net amount
*11,000.00

Atlantic-Pacific Bank
160 Manchester
Springfield, IL 62705

Pat Burner
Authorized signature

Figure 12-5 Vendor-oriented processing: accounts payable. *Top:* The input consists of the receipt of materials and an invoice from the vendor. Processing includes entering data into the vendor data base and updating the general ledger. The output consists of a voucher check for payment issued to the vendor. *Bottom:* Example of a voucher check issued by Know-wear, Inc.

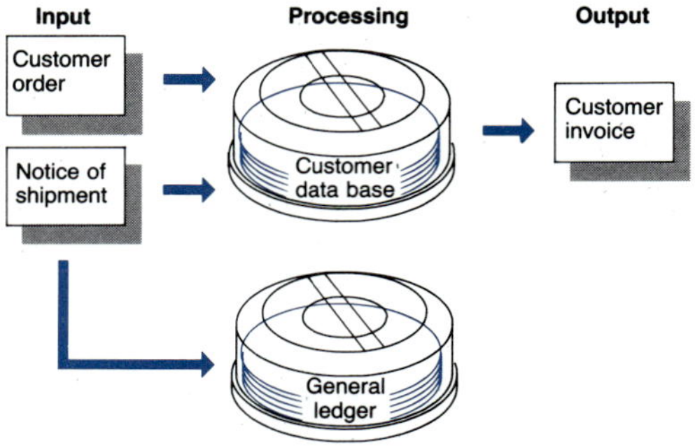
Input
Processing
Output
Customer order
Notice of shipment
Customer data base
Customer invoice
General ledger

Know-Wear, Inc.
8121 West Bell Road
Springfield, IL 62705

Sold to Thriller Threads
350 Townsend
Seattle, WA 98103

Ship To Thriller Threads
350 Townsend
Seattle, WA 98103

Invoice number
14111

Customer number 0025

Invoice date 8/15/88

Order number	Order date	Shipping date	Shipping instructions	Terms	Salesperson
56234	8/10/88	8/15/88	Via truck	2% discount/ 10 days Net/30 days	Marcia Schenk

Quantity ordered	Quantity shipped	Description	Price per unit	Amount
12	12	Parka, large	$35.00	$420.00
5	5	Trench coat, small	58.00	290.00
			Total	$710.00

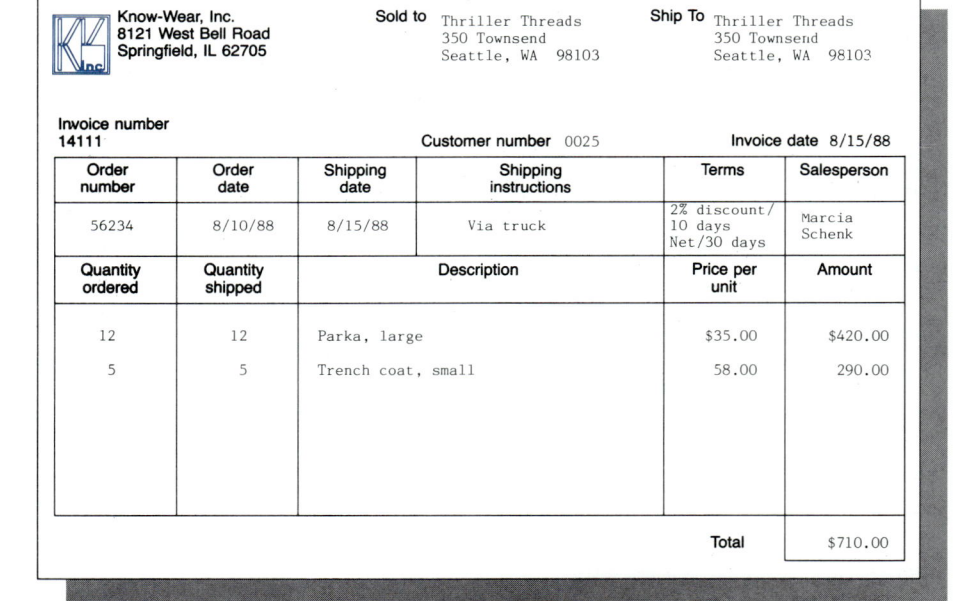

Figure 12-6 Customer-oriented processing: order entry. *Top:* When a customer order is received and the product is shipped, a notice of shipment is sent to the customer. The customer data base is updated to reflect the shipment and the transaction is recorded in the general ledger data base. An invoice is also mailed to the customer. *Bottom:* Example of a customer invoice issued by Know-wear, Inc. to Thriller Threads.

of the goods. In addition, the general ledger is updated to reflect the increased balance due from the customer. Finally, a customer invoice is created and mailed to the customer.

Accounts Receivable

The second OIS application for customer-oriented transaction processing, **accounts receivable** monitors money received from customers in payment for orders filled. As Figure 12-7 shows, when Know-wear receives

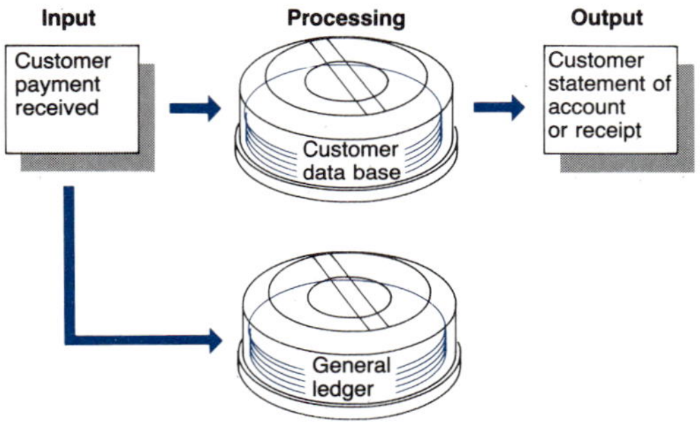
Input
Customer payment received
Processing
Customer data base
Output
Customer statement of account or receipt
General ledger

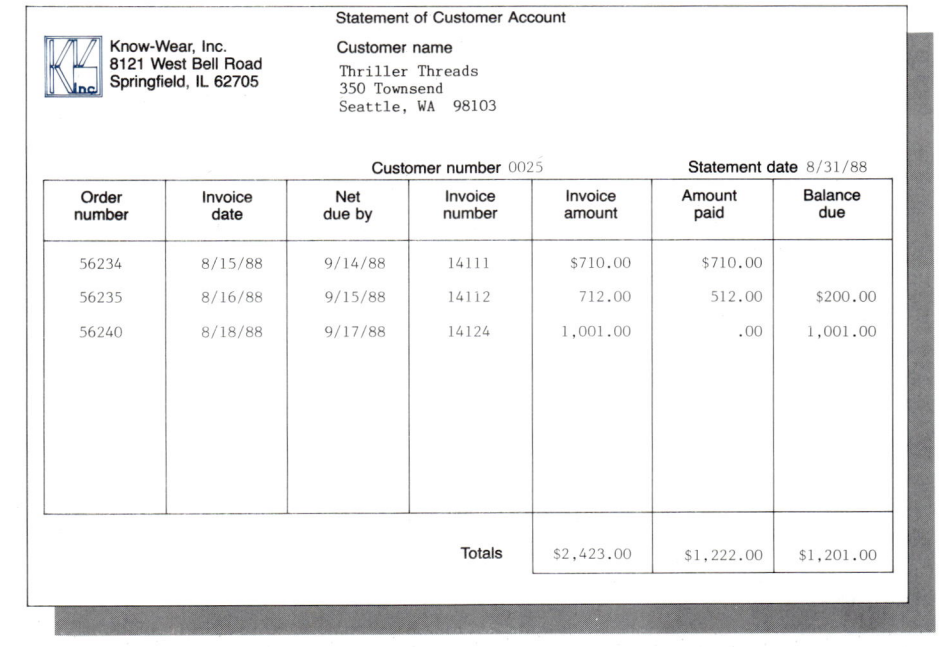

Statement of Customer Account

Know-Wear, Inc.
8121 West Bell Road
Springfield, IL 62705

Customer name
Thriller Threads
350 Townsend
Seattle, WA 98103

Customer number 0025 Statement date 8/31/88

Order number	Invoice date	Net due by	Invoice number	Invoice amount	Amount paid	Balance due
56234	8/15/88	9/14/88	14111	$710.00	$710.00	
56235	8/16/88	9/15/88	14112	712.00	512.00	$200.00
56240	8/18/88	9/17/88	14124	1,001.00	.00	1,001.00
			Totals	$2,423.00	$1,222.00	$1,201.00

Figure 12-7 Customer-oriented processing: accounts receivable. *Top:* When a customer payment is received, the customer data base and general ledger are updated. A customer statement of account or receipt is also mailed. *Bottom:* Example of a statement of account issued by Know-wear to Thriller Threads.

payment from the customer, the customer data base is updated to reflect the change in status of the account. In addition, the general ledger data base is updated to reflect the change in the accounts receivable balance. Finally, the customer is sent a receipt or statement of account to show that payment was received. The customer data base usually is reviewed every month to see which customers are late in payment and to send revised statements of account.

Personnel-Oriented Processing: Paying People

We have shown how vendor-oriented and customer-oriented processing keep track of an organization's material and money resources. **Personnel-oriented processing** concerns monitoring a company's employee resources—in other words, making sure workers and managers are paid the right amount for the jobs they do and the hours they work. Also, deductions are taken from their earnings for taxes and the like.

At Know-wear, employees are paid every two weeks. Hourly workers are paid according to their wage rates and the number of hours worked; salaried workers are paid a fixed amount depending on their positions. The Accounting and Finance department must calculate several deductions from the paycheck: federal, state, and local taxes; social security; union dues, if applicable; and insurance premiums. The company must calculate total (gross) pay and net pay and provide each employee with a paycheck along with an accounting of deductions. It must also keep records for tax and accounting purposes.

The OIS supports personnel-oriented processing through the **payroll** application. The transaction starts, as Figure 12-8 indicates, with the employee time cards, which record the number of hours worked for wage employees and the days worked for salaried employees. Time cards are submitted every pay period—every two weeks at Know-wear—and are used to calculate the resulting payroll. The payroll OIS application takes the employee's identification number (9002, in your case) and uses it to gain access to the payroll data base; it can then determine employees' wage rates or salaries, deductions, and other information necessary to calculate the paycheck. Both the payroll and the general ledger data bases are updated to reflect the latest payroll transactions. The output from the payroll application, of course, consists of paychecks, as shown in Figure 12-8.

Facility-Oriented Processing: Keeping Track of Things

A company's resources include not only materials, money, and employees, but also facilities—that is, things. **Facility-oriented processing** con-

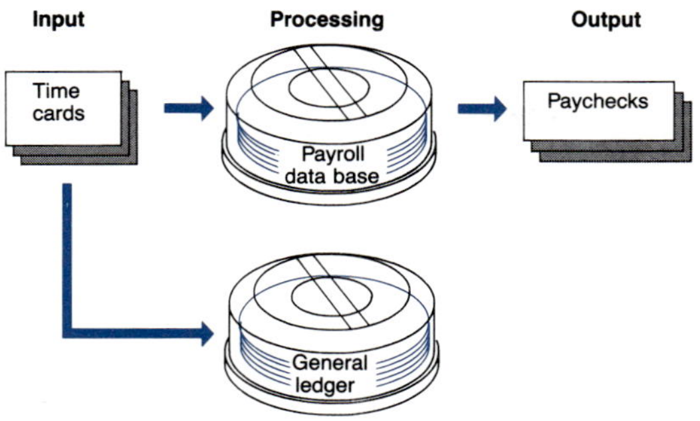
Input
Processing
Output
Time cards
Payroll data base
Paychecks
General ledger

Know-Wear, Inc.
8121 West Bell Road
Springfield, IL 62705

Check number 11123

Date
7/12/88

Pay to the order of: [Your name]

Department no.	Employee no.
120	9002

Pay this amount:
***Eight hundred fifty-six dollars and .20 | $856.20

Atlantic-Pacific Bank
160 Manchester
Springfield, IL 62705

Pat Burner
Authorized signature

Know-Wear, Inc.
Springfield, IL 62705

Employee name
[Your name]

Employee number 9002 Department number 120 Payroll period 6/17/88 through 7/1/88

Items	Current pay period	Year-to-date totals
Total pay	$1,101.22	$14,315.86
Federal withholding tax	111.66	1,451.58
State withholding tax	27.92	362.96
Local withholding tax	12.86	167.18
Social security	73.78	959.14
Insurance	18.80	244.40
Net Pay	$ 856.20	$11,130.60

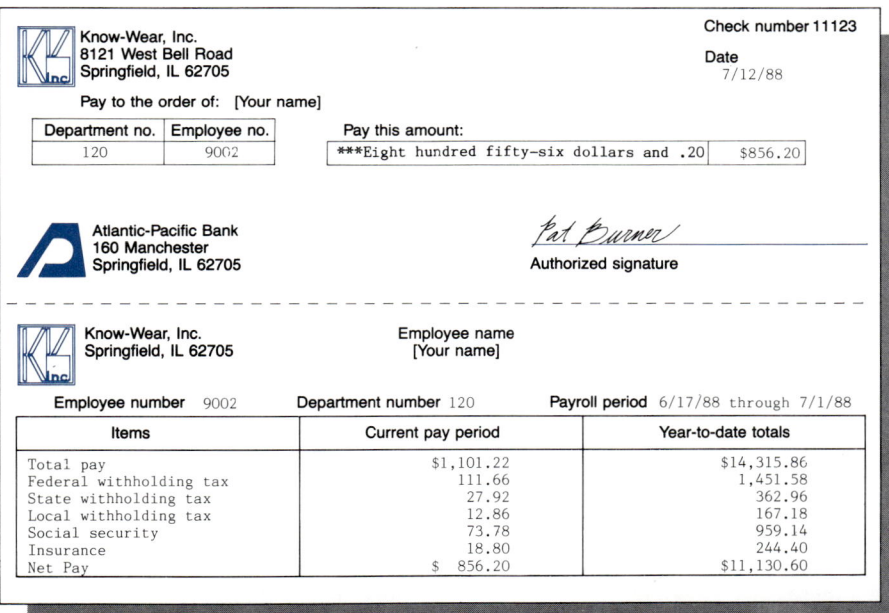

Figure 12-8 Personnel-oriented processing: the paycheck. *Top:* Time cards are the signal to update the payroll data base; simultaneously the general ledger data base is also updated. The output consists of paychecks. *Bottom:* Know-wear paycheck and paycheck stub, which lists deductions from gross pay.

cerns monitoring the acquisition of facilities or fixed assets used by a firm—office equipment, such as word processors and photocopiers; production equipment, such as (for Know-wear) sewing machines and forklift trucks; and buildings.

As Figure 12-9 shows, the fixed asset application for an OIS begins when a fixed asset, such as a building or piece of equipment, is pur-

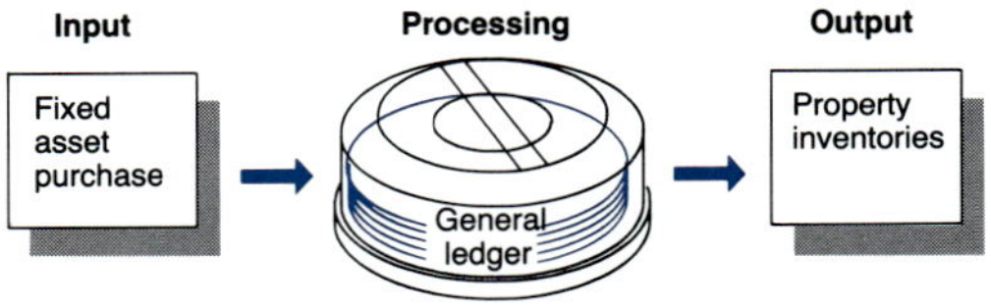
Input
Fixed asset purchase
Processing
General ledger
Output
Property inventories

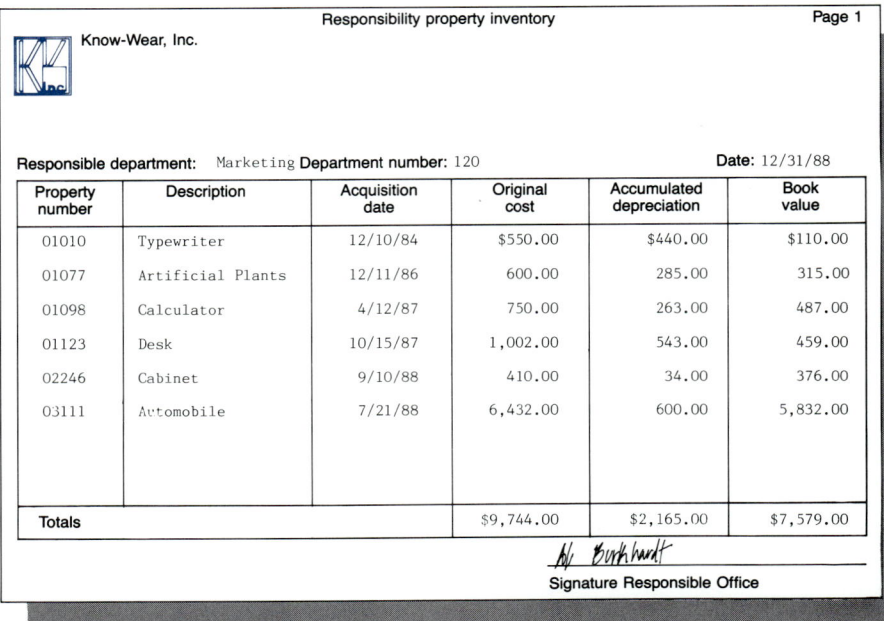

Responsibility property inventory Page 1

Know-Wear, Inc.

Responsible department: Marketing **Department number:** 120 **Date:** 12/31/88

Property number	Description	Acquisition date	Original cost	Accumulated depreciation	Book value
01010	Typewriter	12/10/84	$550.00	$440.00	$110.00
01077	Artificial Plants	12/11/86	600.00	285.00	315.00
01098	Calculator	4/12/87	750.00	263.00	487.00
01123	Desk	10/15/87	1,002.00	543.00	459.00
02246	Cabinet	9/10/88	410.00	34.00	376.00
03111	Automobile	7/21/88	6,432.00	600.00	5,832.00
Totals			$9,744.00	$2,165.00	$7,579.00

Signature Responsible Office

Figure 12-9 Facility-oriented processing: fixed assets. *Top:* Purchase of a fixed asset, such as a typewriter, building, or car, triggers an update of the general ledger data base. The output is a property inventory. *Bottom:* Property inventory of fixed assets that are the responsibility of Know-wear's Marketing department.

chased. This acquisition is recorded through a general ledger entry. The output is a **property inventory,** which describes the fixed assets and states who is responsible for them. The fixed assets described in Figure 12-9 for Know-wear list some items (even including artificial plants) that belong to the Marketing department. For tax purposes, fixed assets are depreciated—that is, they diminish in value over time.

General Ledger—Oriented Processing: The Ongoing Record

We have made many references to the general ledger throughout this chapter. What, exactly, *is* the **general ledger?** It is the data base designed to record all the financial transactions of the business. It consists of a series of entries or statements that are balanced against one another. For example, when Know-wear's Marketing department spends $100 cash on a fake ivy plant, which is a fixed asset (for what could be more fixed than an *artificial* plant?), the general ledger does the following:

- It **debits**—adds—$100 to the financial account known as "fixed assets."
- It **credits**—subtracts—$100 from another financial account known as "cash."

This would be known as a **double entry bookkeeping system,** because a single transaction creates a general ledger entry involving two or more financial accounts whose debit entries equal the credit entries. They would look as follows:

	Debit	Credit
Fixed assets	100	
Cash		100

To check for errors, the Accounting and Finance department periodically—perhaps once a month—runs what are called **trial balances;** that is, all the credits are totaled and all the debits are totaled, and if the two totals are not equal, then a mistake has been made.

As Figure 12-10 shows, the inputs for the trial balance processing consist of all the general ledger entries made in the previous six application areas—purchasing, accounts payable, order entry, accounts receivable, payroll, and fixed assets—plus others that may have been made that are not part of the OIS. The processing consists of totaling the debits and credits, and the output is the trial balance. Figure 12-10 shows what a trial balance might look like for Know-wear at the end of the year. Notice that debits and credits balance—to the penny.

Onward to MIS

An operations information system is the logical beginning for a computer-based information system and is necessary if supervisory managers are to be able to exert operational control over the processes and people for which they are responsible. But what about the people *above* the supervisory level? Can middle managers take advantage of this business information? That is the topic of the next chapter.

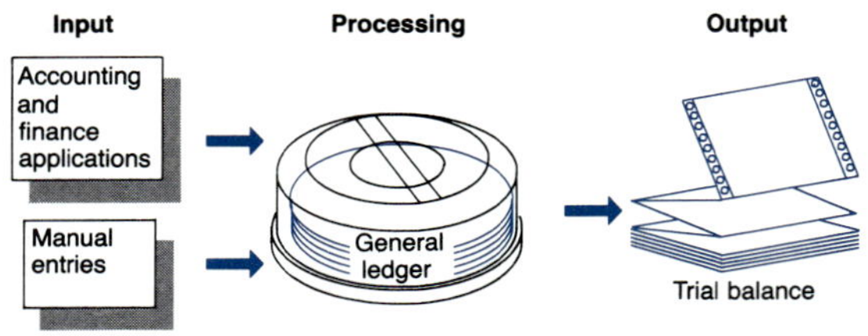
Input
Processing
Output
Accounting and finance applications
Manual entries
General ledger
Trial balance

General ledger trial balance

Know-Wear, Inc.
Springfield, IL 62705

For the year ending 12/31/88

Account number	Account name	Debit	Credit
100	Cash	50,000.00	
101	Accounts receivable	55,000.31	
102	Inventory	68,121.00	
103	Fixed Assets	95,131.00	
104	Buildings	400,100.00	
201	Accounts payable		140,000.31
202	Wages payable		5,428.93
203	Taxes payable		125,000.47
204	Notes payable		134,143.63
301	Retained earnings		100,111.12
401	Sales		230,000.01
502	Marketing expenses	25,121.00	
503	Administrative expenses	23,100.03	
504	Miscellaneous expenses	18,111.12	
	Total	734,684.47	734,684.47

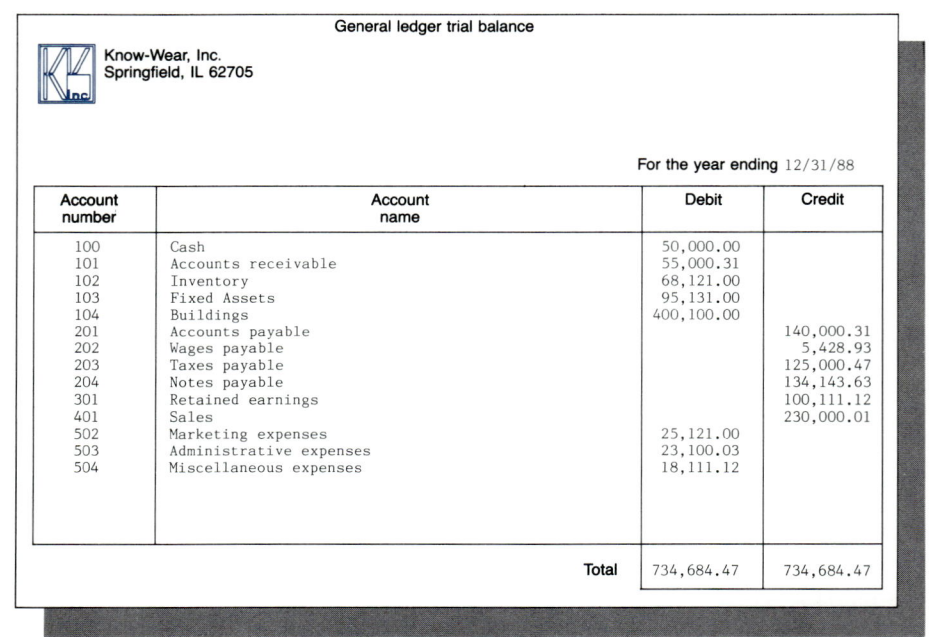

Figure 12-10 General ledger–oriented processing: trial balance. *Top:* All the OIS applications described so far (plus some manual entries not discussed) have been input to the general ledger. *Bottom:* When credits and debits are totaled separately for a trial balance, they should come out the same, as shown here for an end-of-year statement for Know-wear.

SUMMARY

- The purpose of an **operations information system (OIS),** the lowest level of computer-based information system, is to perform processing and transmit messages to help an organization keep track of its resources—its materials, money, employees, and facilities. The word "operations" refers to *clerical* operations such as accounts payable, accounts receivable, and payroll.
- An OIS fits the four functional departments of the business organization—

Marketing, Accounting and Finance, Production, and Research and Development. **Marketing,** the department responsible for sales of the product, is the customer's link to the organization. **Accounting and Finance** records the organization's monetary activities, providing financial statements and daily records of the organization's well-being. **Production** is the department that processes the resources input to the organization—materials, money, employees, and facilities—into finished goods or services. **Research and Development,** often abbreviated R & D, creates new products to meet future customer needs and improve the firm's market share.

- A **transaction** is any action or event dealing with the firm's clients, creditors, or its own resources, anything that needs to be recorded for later use—a sale, a purchase, a firing, a customer complaint. **Transaction processing** is done to generate outputs that assist the firm in its operations and to create data bases to support company-wide decision making and control. Transaction processing has four activities: (1) data entry, (2) data processing, (3) data storage, and (4) output generation.
- The purpose of **data entry** is to collect necessary data in a cost-effective, error-free, timely, and convenient way. Data entry can be either manual or automatic.
- Data entry and data processing may be coupled in three ways: (1) batch entry and batch processing, (2) direct entry and batch processing, and (3) direct entry and direct (immediate) processing.
- In the first way, *batch entry and batch processing,* individual transactions are stored on **source documents,** original documents (such as a daily time sheet) from data is copied. The source documents are collected and processed together at one time. The least expensive method, this is appropriate for payroll, accounts payable, and customer billing. However, it is the least accurate and up-to-the-minute method of processing.
- In *direct entry and batch processing,* transactions are stored immediately by direct (also known as on-line) data entry, often on magnetic tape or disk, but processed later. Typical applications include inventory control and retail sales, as grocery sales recorded on a POS terminal at the checkout counter and sent to the store's computer for storage on tape. At the end of the day, all sales are processed and inventory updated. This arrangement is more current than batch entry plus batch processing.
- In *direct entry and direct (immediate) processing,* a transaction is entered and processed immediately as it occurs. It is as accurate as the preceding method and even more current. However, the equipment is expensive, the computer must be immediately accessible, and if it fails, the entire data entry operation must be shut down. Typical applications are in quality and inventory control.
- The two systems for storing data are file management and data base management. In a file management system, independent files are created for

specific applications. In a data base management system, files are created for multiple applications. They can be organized in various ways and accessed by different users. Since business organizations now use their files for broader purposes, transaction processing must create data that can be stored so it is accessible to many users; in other words, businesses must build a data base management system.

- Transaction processing must create two types of data reports: (1) Computer-generated documents such as payroll checks or customer invoices, which are more economical and reliable than manual documents. (2) Reports of events, such as transactions listings of customers who have not paid their bills.
- An OIS consists of seven elements: (1) payroll, (2) order entry, (3) accounts receivable, (4) purchasing, (5) accounts payable, (6) fixed assets, and (7) general ledger. These elements are ways the OIS monitors the four types of resources within the organization: (1) *Materials:* This resource is monitored in the **purchasing** and **order entry** sections. Raw materials acquisition is tracked in the purchasing section, and the demand for finished products is recorded in the order entry section. (2) *Money:* This resource is recorded in the **accounts payable** and **accounts receivable** sections. Payments are recorded in the accounts payable, and income is recorded in accounts receivable. (3) *Employees:* The people resources are recorded in the **payroll** section, which calculates employee salaries and wages and issues paychecks. (4) **Facilities:** This resource is recorded in the **fixed assets** section. Transactions for all four resources are formally recorded in the **general ledger** section.
- The elements of an OIS can be combined into five forms of processing: (1) vendor-oriented processing, which includes purchasing and accounts payable; (2) customer-oriented processing, which includes order entry and accounts receivable; (3) personnel-oriented processing, which includes payroll; (4) facility-oriented processing, which includes fixed assets; and (5) general ledger–oriented processing.
- In **vendor-oriented processing,** the OIS has two applications, corresponding to the two transactions involved in getting something from a vendor: ordering it and paying for it. **Vendors** or suppliers are businesses that provide the firm with raw materials or services. When a department needs an item, the purchasing section creates a **purchase order (PO),** to send to the vendor who supplies it. Copies of the PO, called **receiving reports,** are distributed within the firm to confirm that the order has been placed and to document the expected delivery date. Upon delivery, the materials are checked against the original receiving report and the bill is sent along with a confirmation of the receipt of materials to the purchasing and accounting sections. Purchasing notifies the originator of the request that the materials have arrived. Accounting records both the receipt of the order and the bill in the general ledger.
- **Customer-oriented processing** concerns getting orders from customers for products or services and receiving payment for them. The two activities of customer-oriented processing are order entry and accounts receivable. The

source document that makes up the input for the order entry application is the customer order. It is used to create internal documents in the company that result in shipment of the products ordered. Accounts receivable monitors payments received from the customers. It updates the customer data base to reflect the change in status of the account, updates the general ledger data base to show the change in the accounts receivable balance, and produces a receipt or statement of account to send to the customer.

- **Personnel-oriented processing** concerns monitoring a company's employee resources. It makes sure employees are paid the right amount for their jobs and the hours they work and that the proper deductions are made. The OIS supports personnel-oriented processing through the payroll application. An employee's identification number is used to access the payroll data base and determine the employee's wage or salary, deductions, and other information necessary to calculate the paycheck. Both the payroll and the general ledger data bases are updated to reflect the latest payroll transactions.
- **Facility-oriented processing** concerns monitoring the acquisition of facilities or fixed assets used by a firm—office equipment, production equipment, buildings, whatever the U.S. Government allows to be depreciated or diminished in value for tax purposes. Acquisitions are recorded through a general ledger entry. The output is a **property inventory,** which describes the fixed assets and states who is responsible for them.
- The **general ledger** is a data base designed to record all of the financial transactions of the business. It is a series of entries that are balanced against one another. For example, when a company spends $100 for a fixed asset, the general ledger **debits**—adds—$100 to the financial account known as "fixed assets" and **credits**—subtracts—$100 from another account known as "cash." This is called a **double entry bookkeeping system,** because a single transaction creates a general ledger entry involving two or more financial accounts whose debit entries equal the credit entries. To check for errors in the general ledger, the Accounting and Finance department periodically runs **trial balances**—all the credits are totaled and all the debits are totaled, and if the two totals are not equal, then it means a mistake has been made.

KEY TERMS

REVIEW QUESTIONS

1. Describe the purpose of the OIS. What type of tasks does this system perform?
2. What are the four resources within an organization?
3. What are the four activities of transaction processing? Describe each.
4. Name the seven elements of an OIS.
5. Describe vendor-oriented processing.
6. Describe customer-oriented processing. How is a customer order filled and billed?
7. How are paychecks generated by the OIS?
8. What is the general ledger?

CASE PROBLEMS

Case 12-1: Treat the Customer Right

"You can't do enough for customers," writes New Hampshire consultant Jack Falvey in the *Wall Street Journal* (May 23, 1983). "The rule is that you get paid for everything you do for customers."[2] Technology, buildings, balance sheets, and the other elements that make up a business "must support the central theme of doing something for someone. When that someone no longer pays for what we do, we are out of business."

Falvey tells the story of a customer who, attracted by TV advertising, took some film to an air freight office to ship overnight to Chicago. It was important that the film arrive the next day, but "Absolutely, positively, in spite of many next-day phone calls," and so on, the film did not get there. It was found two days later and returned.

Then the company proceeded to turn the customer into a customer for the competition. When he received an invoice for the cost of shipment both ways, the customer wrote explaining the air freight shipper's failure to perform and the resultant cost to his business and asked that the invoice be canceled. But, Falvey writes, "the customer was no longer a customer but an accounts receivable credit number." The credit department began sending multiple dunning notices and eventually hired an outside collection agency to harass him further.

Your assignment: Clearly, the air freight company should have apologized to the customer and given him a free next shipment, thus, says Falvey, "retaining the person who provides the income from which we run our business." On the principle that every part of a company—delivery, service, credit people, and so on—are effectively sales representatives for that company, can you conceive of ways to design an order entry/accounts receivable system that will not have the unpleasant effects described here?

Case 12-2: Finding the Transactions for Trimming Travel Costs

Recently, many companies have been taking a hard look at how they can save travel dollars when they send their executives around the country. Airfares, for example, can range widely even on the same routes (the lowest one-way fare from San Francisco to Los Angeles is $30, the highest $198). Travel experts say that, with discount airfares, bulk hotel rates, and rental-car contracts, a company can lower its travel costs by 15% to 40% a year.[3] Before this can happen, however, a firm must have hard statistics to bargain with. Travel agents, hotels, and airlines will not negotiate unless they know what a company's usual travel patterns are.

Your assignment: Saving money starts with gathering data. Suppose you have been hired as a travel consultant to help trim travel costs for a company. You need to find out which cities the people in the company usually travel to and how many trips they make each year. Most of this information is on expense accounts, reports submitted by employees for their supervisors' approval and for reimbursement of expenses for travel, meals, and hotels. Some of the expenses are billed directly through the vendor-oriented processing part of the company's OIS. You want to put these travel transactions in a separate report. Can you determine how you might begin to do this, using the OIS?

CHAPTER 13

Management Information Systems

Useful Facts for Middle Managers

PREVIEW

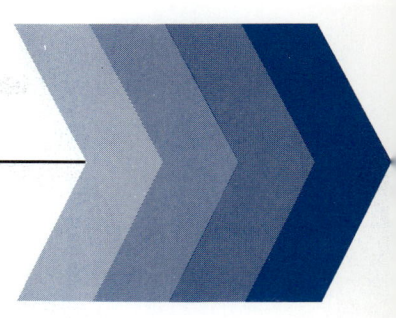

A business organization's appetite for information seems insatiable. In part, as we have been suggesting throughout this book, this appetite is stimulated by the increased complexity and rate of change in the business environment. In part, the complexity derives from the growth of business in the national and international marketplace, which has increased the need of many businesses for more information. How can a company and its all-too-human employees handle the rising tide of information?

One answer is to make better use of what is already pouring into it. The OIS is a first step. Nearly all large organizations have been operating with successful computerized operations information systems for the past several years to handle clerical tasks that previously were handled manually, such as payroll preparation, writing of purchase orders, and maintaining of inventory. The next step, as the case study shows, is to find a way to make this system useful for "the people in the middle."

The Basics of MIS

After an OIS is in place, the next step for the efficient handling of business information is to install a **management information system (MIS).** An OIS is certainly useful to handle standard clerical and accounting applications, but it can do very little to support management decision making. A management information system is designed to assist managers in the performance of their work; it is a network of computer-based processing procedures that are integrated with manual and other procedures to provide timely, effective information to support managerial planning and control.

CASE STUDY: MAKING DATA MEANINGFUL

Information for People in the Middle

In the best of all possible worlds, microcomputers would provide corporate users with autonomous processing power as well as a friendly link to the resources of larger computers. Users could download [unload] information from the mainframe to their machines, generate a report using VisiCalc or Lotus 1-2-3, upload the result to the mainframe, integrate it into a more complex financial model. . . .

But users are still out in the cold because products to open up mainframe resources to micros are not appearing fast enough. Andrew Langlois, director of management information services at Moore McCormack Resources Inc., having searched for and tested such products, summarizes: "There is a lot more hype than substance." . . .

Small businesses without in-house data processing departments must wait for the products they need. But Fortune 500 corporations such as Moore McCormack have the resources to fill in the gaps the vendors have left behind. Langlois' group was able to link up the company's microcomputers and mainframes by supplementing commercial products with in-house programming. The story of their efforts illustrates what such products can, and cannot, do.

Moore McCormack is made up of four subsidiaries. One subsidiary manufactures cement, ready-mix and concrete products. Ocean Bulk Transport carries oil and liquefied natural gas. M.M. Energy produces oil and gas and locates new sources. A fourth subsidiary mines and transports iron ore and coal.

Langlois' group spent more than a year choosing and implementing a standardized corporatewide system for collecting, consolidating and massaging [manipulating] data from the four subsidiaries into five-year profit plans. . . .

Langlois and his group set up help services for Moore McCormack employees who want to use microcomputers. Management information services tests various microcomputers and software packages and features the ones they like in a catalog.

Departments are urged to choose among such products, and, as an added incentive, Moore McCormack passes on quantity discounts to subsidiaries. For users who get into difficulties, each subsidiary has its own help desk and hot line offering advice and troubleshooting.

At Moore McCormack, the greatest need for microcomputers

occurred among the "people in the middle" who convert data provided them by subordinates into information which their superiors would use for financial planning, yearly forecasts and so on. Says Langlois: "One person's data is another person's information. Information is data organized, distilled and processed so additional meaning is available to the recipient."

At the bottom of the information hierarchy, clerks enter transactions such as "Customer *X* needs four widgets type 342" into the corporate data base. They only key data, so they do not need microcomputers. At the top of the hierarchy, presidents of subsidiaries and the president of the corporation use information in the form of hard-copy reports, graphs and charts presented to them by financial professionals and middle managers. . . .

Langlois wants to provide managers, executives, financial professionals and management information service people with software powerful enough for the work they are doing, yet not too complex for their level of technical expertise. He thinks he has a good mix. For instance, division managers can consolidate revenues, expenditures, debts, and other information about different product lines into a subsidiary report using a Lotus 1-2-3 spreadsheet. Financial managers at corporate headquarters can use Micro-FCS, mainframe FCS-EPS's "little brother," to consolidate division reports into a corporate model which a vice president might use to do forecasting.

—Elisabeth Horwitt,
Business Computer Systems,
February 1984

To fully understand MIS, let us describe three important concepts:

- The basic tasks of management.
- Management information needs.
- The desirable properties of an MIS.

What Managers Do: The Classic Tasks of Management

Management is the process of transforming resources—materials, money, employees, facilities—into products or services. As we mentioned back in Chapter 3, the primary activity of all managers is to make decisions in five areas: organizing, communicating, staffing, planning, and controlling. Let us describe these again.

- **Organizing:** Managers need to make decisions about organizing or coordinating people and resources, including what structures and

The tasks of management. Three of the most important activities of being a manager are communicating requirements to others (*top left*), planning short- and long-range goals (*right*), and controlling or monitoring performance (*bottom left*).

procedures should be set up, what authority delegated, what system of responsibility and accountability should be arranged.

- **Communicating:** Managers must be able to communicate their requests and requirements to subordinates and superiors. As we have seen, this management task is now receiving a good deal of computerized assistance, in the form of word processing, electronic mail, and telecommunications.
- **Staffing:** Decisions about staffing are decisions about hiring workers and managers and training them to achieve the organization's goals.

These three management tasks are important, but the most crucial are the two that follow, planning and controlling. Without these, there will probably be chaos in the organization. Planning and controlling are the two management tasks that an MIS is specially designed to support.

- **Planning:** In planning, managers formulate short-range and long-range goals for the organization, including policies, procedures, and standards necessary to achieve them. Planning also concerns identifying opportunities, problems, and alternative courses of action.
- **Controlling:** Managerial control concerns continually monitoring, with the help of performance measures, the organization's progress in reaching its goals. This means managers must keep track of employee performance as well as other resources and make any necessary adjustments.

What Managers Need: Not Data but Information

Managers need information not only about events in the outside business environment—about competitors, political events, economic trends, and technological advances—but also about internal events so that they can monitor the organization's resources and do efficient planning and controlling. A great amount of information is brought into the organization through the OIS and, in fact, has led to the problem of information overload. Because the data from transaction processing is so extensive and so quickly retrievable electronically, many managers are overwhelmed with quantities of data. Managers do not need just data; they need data that is analyzed and synthesized into useful form—in short, turned into information. An MIS should be able to offer this kind of help.

Better facts. An effective management information system should produce information that is accurate, timely, and complete yet concise. Spreadsheets and graphics can help summarize facts into more understandable form.

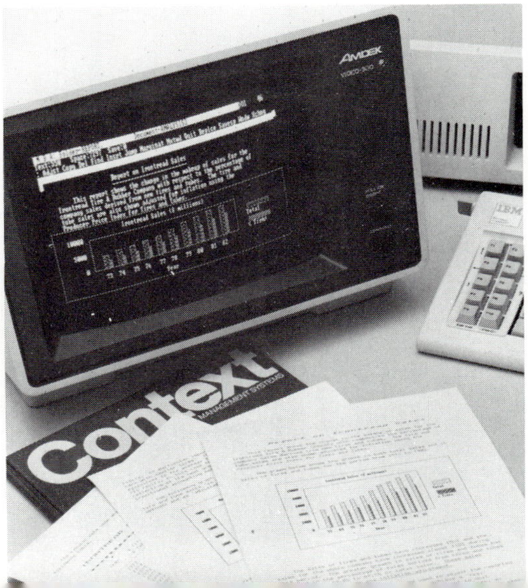
Context

An MIS: What Should It Do?

Not more facts but *better* facts are what a manager needs. What do we mean by "better"? An effective MIS should produce information that is *accurate, timely,* and *complete yet concise.* Let us describe what we mean:

- **Accuracy:** High accuracy—that is, completely error-free information—is usually expensive. For example, true accuracy might require that every time a clerk enters information into a data base the information must be verified by another clerk. Obviously, this would double the data entry costs. Sometimes high accuracy is cost-justifiable, but often it is not. Ninety percent accuracy might be fine for inventory of pencils in Know-wear's stockroom, but 90% accuracy is too low for the billing of accounts receivable.
- **Timeliness:** Given the rapid pace of business, what is considered information today may not be information tomorrow. Information, then, should be supplied quickly. A quality-control manager on a production line of men's shirts cannot wait three days to discover that a defect is producing shirts with 40-inch sleeves and size 13 collars, or Know-wear may well find itself with 96,000 oddball shirts to dispose of somehow.
- **Completeness with conciseness:** A report is not useful if it is accurate and timely but incomplete. A manager needs *all* the facts. However, the trick is not to overwhelm managers with unnecessary and unwanted facts. Some managers may require more details than others; thus, one of the more difficult responsibilities of a systems analyst is to determine what is essential and nonessential information for a particular manager. The accountant at Know-wear who monitors customers who are late paying their bills needs information about all overdue customers and their balances and due dates. The accountant does not need balances and due dates for all customers in accounts payable, however. These customers need to be given a civilized amount of time (such as 30 days) to remit payment.

The Parts of a Management Information System

Now that we have described the tasks of managers, their need for information, and the properties they need in an information system, let us see how a management information system works. As we stated at the outset, an MIS is a network of computer-based processing procedures integrated with manual and other procedures to provide timely, effective information to support managerial planning and control.

To more fully understand what an MIS is, let us examine its parts:

- Management
- Information
- Systems

The Management in an MIS

Recall from the last chapter that there are two ways to view a business. On the one hand, it can be viewed as a vertical organization of the four business functions of Marketing, Accounting and Finance, Production, and Research and Development. On the other hand, it can be viewed from a horizontal perspective of three levels of management: top, middle, and lower. Both these perspectives are presented in Figure 13-1.

The responsibilities of the three levels of management are as follows:

Top Management. Top management includes only a few of the most powerful managers in the organization, the typical title being vice president of one of the four business functions, such as shown in Figure 13-1. Their primary responsibility is *strategic planning*—establishing the overall direction of the company through long-range planning. They have the task of establishing firm performance goals and coordinating the activities of the entire organization to achieve these goals. Their problems are unstructured and their activities vary greatly—for example, establishing financial goals for the firm, determining new markets and products, and evaluating potential mergers and acquisitions.

Clearly, the decisions of top managers will have the greatest effect on the organization, although the effect may not be felt for several years. In order to make such decisions, top managers need both external and internal information.

Middle Managers. There are many more middle managers than there are top managers, and their responsibilities are to do *tactical planning and control*—to implement the plans of top management and to monitor the firm's current operations. Typical titles for managers at this level are regional sales manager, public relations manager, training and development coordinator, and director of employee relations.

In establishing the means for achieving the overall strategic plan, middle managers perform fairly structured activities—formulating budgets, doing production scheduling, making short-term forecasts, and monitoring sales, production, and personnel performances. They rely more on internal information than on external, and the effect of their decisions is felt much sooner than those of top management.

Lower or Supervisory Management. By far the largest group, supervisory managers are responsible for *operational control*—for implement-

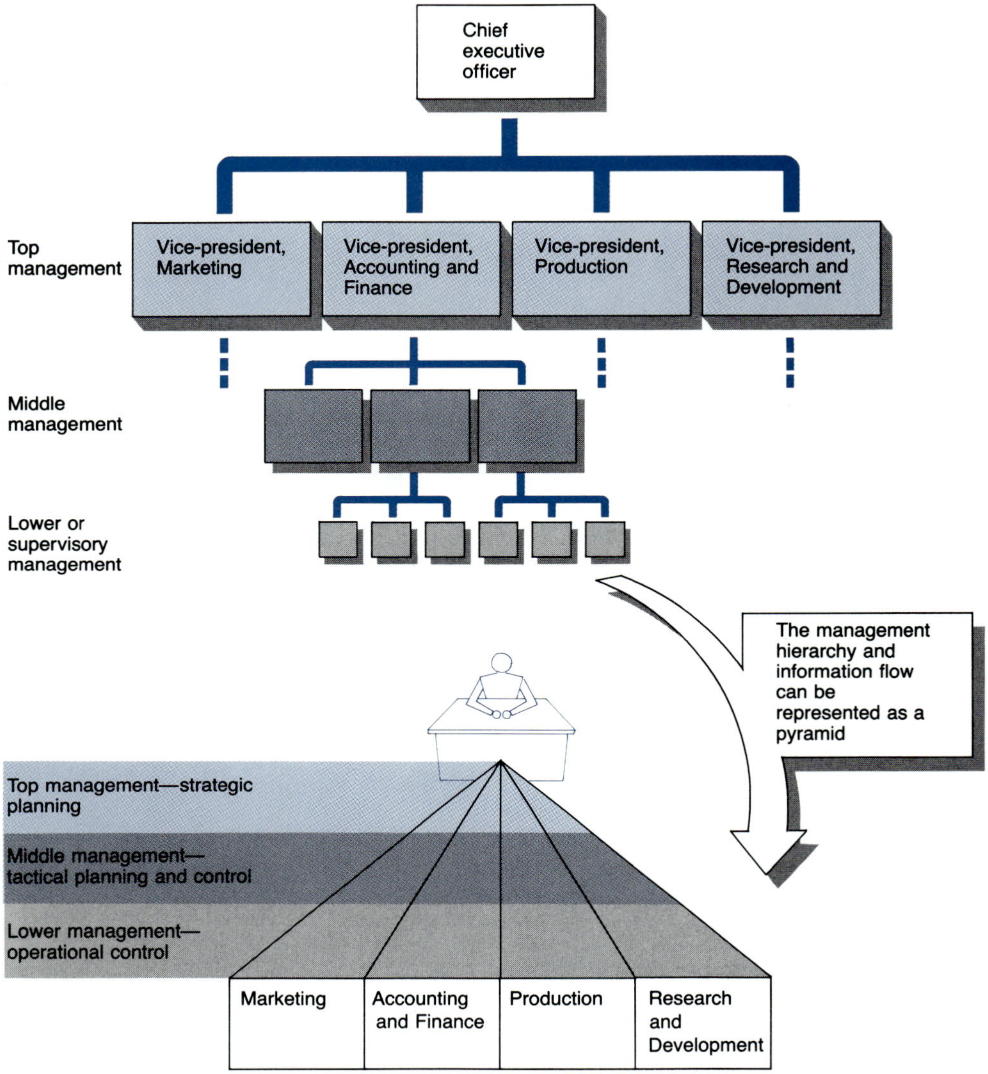
Chief executive officer
Top management
Vice-president, Marketing
Vice-president, Accounting and Finance
Vice-president, Production
Vice-president, Research and Development
Middle management
Lower or supervisory management
The management hierarchy and information flow can be represented as a pyramid
Top management—strategic planning
Middle management—tactical planning and control
Lower management—operational control
Marketing
Accounting and Finance
Production
Research and Development

Figure 13-1 Two perspectives of an organization. *Top:* An organization can be viewed as being made up of four business functional areas—Marketing, Accounting and Finance, Production, and Research and Development. (This is considered a vertical perspective.) *Bottom:* An organization may also be viewed as having three levels of management—top, middle, and lower. (This is considered a horizontal perspective.)

ing the plans of middle management and controlling day-to-day operations. The first-line supervisors who directly oversee the actual operations of a business, supervisory managers have titles such as local sales manager, accounts receivable manager, word processing supervisor, records supervisor, and group leader.

Middle managers. Such managers—regional sales managers, public relations managers, directors of employee relations, and the like—are concerned with tactical planning and control. This involves formulating budgets, doing production scheduling, monitoring sales performance, and other tasks that help implement the plans of top management.

The activities of lower-level managers are structured, routine, and oriented toward the present—for example, meeting production and marketing schedules, maintaining inventory records, determining raw material requirements, controlling quality, and otherwise seeing to the achievement of well-defined short-term objectives.

What Kind of Information for MIS?

Each management level requires a unique kind of information to support decision making:

- Top managers need information that is highly summarized, future oriented, and external as well as internal. This information is needed to support strategic planning.
- Middle managers need information that is summarized but contains enough detail to allow effective control. Such information has a past orientation to describe recent business activity.
- Supervisory managers need information that is very current. This information is needed to control day-to-day business operations.

These three management information needs are supported by separate, yet closely related, information systems:

- Top management has information needs that are supported primarily by decision support systems, which are described in Chapter 14.
- Middle managers need management information systems, which are described in this chapter.
- Supervisory managers need operations information systems, as described in Chapter 12.

The Data Base Management System as Part of MIS

Management information systems evolved out of operations information systems. The MISs were not intended to replace or to improve on the OISs but rather to satisfy another information need altogether—to serve middle management. However, for an MIS to exist, an OIS had to be in place in order to make computer-accessible data bases available.

Except by looking at what kind of managers the system serves, how can you tell the difference between an OIS and an MIS? One way is this: An OIS usually operates only within *one* functional area of the organization—Marketing, for instance, but not Production. The transaction processing that goes on in OIS produces data bases that are specialized for the functional areas. An MIS, by contrast, frequently requires access to data from *more* than one functional area—for example, from both Marketing *and* Production.

Getting data from more than one data base requires some sophisticated software known as data base management system software. Let us show how this works.

As we mentioned in Chapter 9, programs were originally written for applications within a particular department or functional area. This was called a *file management system*: Marketing people would write programs for their data files and Production people would write for theirs. Unfortunately, this led to more and more separate data files, with frequent duplication of data about customers, employees, and products. The file management system not only led to high storage and maintenance costs—one transaction might require updates of several different files—but also, of course, restricted people from having access to each other's files.

Data base management systems were developed to resolve these problems. A **data base management system (DBMS)** consists of programs that act as an interface between data bases and users and that allow users easy access to data. A DBMS is particularly valuable to an MIS because middle managers must be able to cross departments in an organization in order to get data—for Marketing people, for instance, to have access to data bases in Production or Research and Development. Figure 13-2 shows how the pyramidal arrangement of data bases that support transaction processing—each department with its own data base—may be rethought in a DBMS arrangement so that a user can view all four data bases as a single large integrated organizational data base.

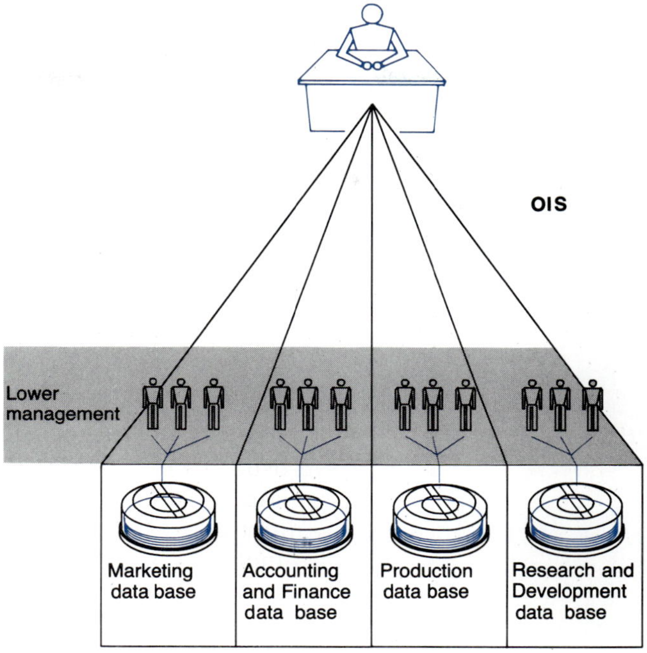
OIS
Lower management
Marketing data base
Accounting and Finance data base
Production data base
Research and Development data base

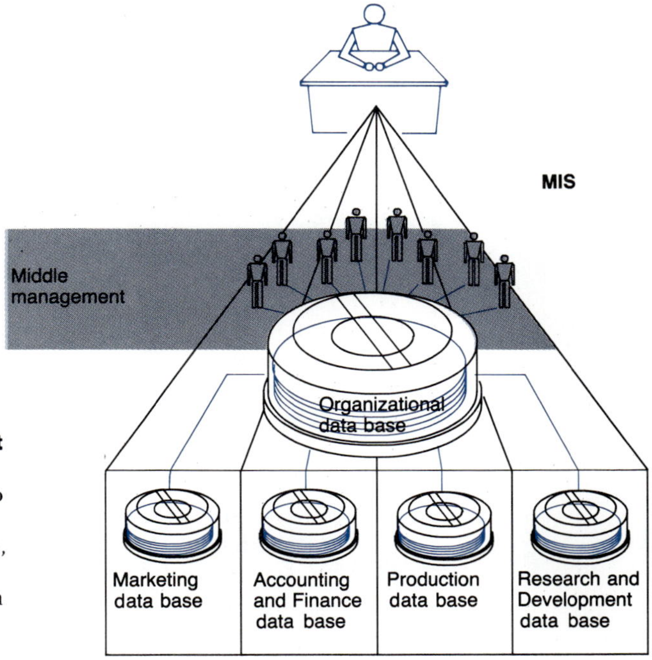
MIS
Middle management
Organizational data base
Marketing data base
Accounting and Finance data base
Production data base
Research and Development data base

Figure 13-2 The data base management system. *Top:* In an operations information system, four separate data bases correspond to the four separate business departments. *Bottom:* Under the data base management system, the four data bases may be thought of as integrated into an organizational data base, which gives middle managers more flexibility in a management information system.

Data Base Management Systems

There are three kinds of data base management systems that you probably will encounter routinely as a manager:

- Relational
- Hierarchical
- Network

A **relational** data base is made up of many tables, and data is stored on those tables according to relationships that the parts have to the whole. For example, when you were considering moving from Atlantic-Pacific Bank in Boston to Know-wear in Springfield, Illinois, you could have had a data base composed of a log of telephone calls that you made to Springfield inquiring about apartments. On that data base, you could have entered the address of the apartment, the phone number, the date you called, the apartment owner's name, the rent, the number of rooms, the distance in miles from work, and anything else of interest. As the illustration shows, these items are linked in relations or *pairs* in several tables—address/phone, address/date, distance/rent, and so on. You could then have retrieved data about any of those apartments simply by referring to the particular fields of data—rent, number of rooms, or whatever. Clearly, a relational data base management system can be useful because of its ability to cross reference data and retrieve data automatically.

A **hierarchical** data base management system is like the root system of a tree, with units of data structured in multiple levels. The units farther down the system are subordinate to the ones above, like the hierarchy of employees in a corporation or soldiers in the military. Finding a record usually requires you to start at the top of the hierarchy—you have to go through the generals, as it were, before you can get to the footsoldiers. One drawback is that deleting a root deletes all the subordinate units, and a subordinate unit cannot be added without a root. Thus, you might have had an apartment address as the root and the owner's name and phone number as subordinate units in the hierarchy. You might delete the apartment address (because it was too expensive, say), but that would delete all subordinate units—and suppose you wanted to stay in touch with the owner because he or she had other apartments? Or suppose you had the same owner listed under several different root-addresses, and his or her telephone number was changed? You would have to search the entire data base to change the telephone number in all places.

A **network** data base has records in hierarchi-

Relational data base. Tables of pairs.

Address/phone pairs	
Address	Phone
1269 4th Ave.	750-3606
19 Encline Ct.	282-3430
160 Manchester	326-1951

Address/distance pairs	
Address	Distance
1269 4th Ave.	3 miles
19 Encline Ct.	7 miles
160 Manchester	30 miles

Distance/rent pair	
Distance	Rent
3 miles	$650
7 miles	$350
30 miles	$400

etc.

cal arrangements, but the record can participate in several relationships. That is, there are additional links besides the root system of the hierarchy. Whereas in the hierarchical data base, each subordinate has only one superior, in the network data base each subordinate may have more than one superior. Thus, you can extract information by starting with any record.

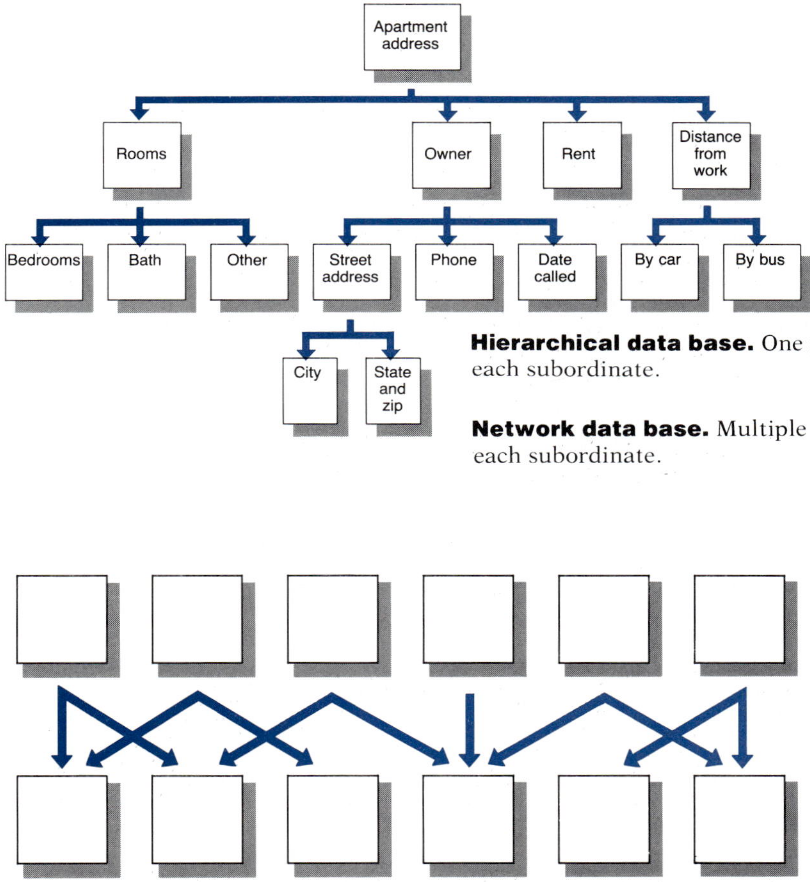
Apartment address
Rooms
Owner
Rent
Distance from work
Bedrooms
Bath
Other
Street address
Phone
Date called
By car
By bus
City
State and zip

Hierarchical data base. One superior for each subordinate.

Network data base. Multiple superiors for each subordinate.

A data base management system has several advantages:

- Data redundancy is reduced—that is, duplicate files of the same data are not necessary.
- The same data can be accessed by different application programs.
- Updating of data need only be done in one place instead of in numerous files.
- Application programs requiring data from more than one functional area can be developed more efficiently.
- Company-wide data is made more available to users.

Despite these marvelous benefits, there are a few disadvantages to a DBMS:

- One error in data entry causes problems not just in one file but throughout the entire organizational data base.
- To establish and maintain a DBMS requires highly skilled and well-trained people.
- Keeping data secure from unauthorized users becomes more of a problem, since corporate data is more accessible to more people.
- It can take longer to do traditional data processing jobs with a DBMS than with the old file management system.

Typical MIS Reports

A great deal of a manager's job involves making reports to his or her supervisor. Even at the top of the pyramid, the CEO must make reports—to the stockholders or the board of directors.

Sometimes reports are given orally; at other times they are given in writing. However, if you are one of those people for whom speaking or writing is not easy, you will be pleased to learn that a great deal of this activity has been computerized. The reports we are concerned with here are those produced by computer-based business information systems.

As we saw in the last chapter, an OIS produces reports of day-to-day operations—specific, detailed information that helps lower-level managers maintain close operation control. OIS reports are not very helpful to middle managers, however. Since middle managers are more concerned with planning and controlling, they need information that is more summarized and that has a wider perspective than that offered by an OIS. An MIS provides this. By giving managers access to all departmental data bases in the organization, an MIS can provide managers with reports summarizing the organization's performance, which can give them a basis for making organizational plans.

There are many kinds of MIS reports, some of which are specialized for certain industries. A pharmaceutical house, for instance, might have a report that carefully tracks the shelf life of certain types of drugs which deteriorate after a period of time. A shoe manufacturer, on the other hand, would have no need for such a program. However, both firms will most likely have MIS reports that summarize past due customer accounts.

The most significant attribute of MIS reports is that their format and their informational content is predetermined. There are three categories of MIS reports:

- Periodic
- Exception
- Demand

Every time one of these reports is to be generated, the MIS programs gain access to the organizational data base and calculate, summarize, and report the required information.

Let us see what these reports are and how they are used at Know-wear.

Periodic Reports

Periodic reports are reports generated at regular intervals—quarterly, monthly, or weekly. Examples of periodic reports include quarterly financial reports, monthly sales analyses, and weekly production reports. An example of a periodic report for Know-wear is a profitability report, as shown in Figure 13-3.

Two of the most common periodic reports are:

- The income statement.
- The balance sheet.

Both are used a great deal in business.

The Income Statement. An **income statement** is a statement of the organization's financial performance—income, expenses, and the difference between them—for a given period of time. A yearly income statement, for example, would report all income generated by the firm through sales and other sources for the preceding 12 months, all expenses for that period, and the net income—that is, the difference between income and expenses.

An example of an income statement for Know-wear is shown in the top part of Figure 13-4.

The Balance Sheet. The income statement is for a fixed period of time. The **balance sheet** reports the *overall* financial condition of the firm on a specific date, listing assets, liabilities, and the owner's share (proprietor's equity) in the firm. As the bottom half of Figure 13-4 shows, total

Know-Wear, Inc. — Customer profitability analysis — Page 1

Date: 12/31/88 Salesperson: John Foster

Customer number	Customer name	Current month: Net sales	Current month: Gross margin	Current month: Margin percent of sales	Year-to-date: Net sales	Year-to-date: Gross margin	Year-to-date: Margin percent of sales
0025	Thriller Threads	9,640	3,411	35.4	108,003	37,411	34.6
Last year		7,500	2,411	32.1	102,481	36,511	35.6
Percent change		28.5	41.5	10.3	5.4	2.5	-2.8
0314	Clothing World	10,789	4,691	43.5	121,613	45,631	37.5
Last year		11,411	5,032	44.1	124,713	51,711	41.5
Percent change		-5.5	-6.8	-1.4	-2.5	-11.8	-9.6
Salesperson total		20,429	8,102	39.7	229,616	83,042	36.2
Last year		18,911	7,443	39.4	227,194	88,222	38.8
Percent change		8.0	8.9	0.8	1.1	-5.9	-6.7

Figure 13-3 A periodic report: the customer profitability report. This report, which is issued on a regular basis, does two things: it analyzes the profitability of customers and it evaluates a salesperson's performance. Note that Know-wear's profitability for the second customer has decreased substantially compared to sales a year earlier, and that the salesperson, John Foster, may be well advised to keep closer track of sales there. Foster's sales efforts show some positive results for the current month, but he is behind for the year to date. ("Net sales" means Foster's total sales minus any allowances made to him and minus any items he sold that were returned by the customer. "Gross margin" means sales revenue minus the cost of goods sold. "Margin percent of sales" describes how much—what percentage—each customer is contributing to the profitability of the firm.)

Figure 13-4 (opposite page) Periodic reports: the income statement and balance sheet. *Top:* Income statement for Know-wear. The top line expresses all the income generated for the year, all of it through sales revenue. The cost of goods sold, operating expenses, and taxes are then subtracted from sales revenue in order to arrive at the net income after taxes—the profit for the firm. Note that these are abbreviated figures: the net income is not really $1,117 but is expressed in thousands of dollars—that is, $1,117,000. *Bottom:* Balance sheet for Know-wear. This shows the financial status of the firm as of the date indicated. Assets consist of cash on hand, cash owed by customers (accounts receivable), and value of inventory or products on hand, equipment, and buildings. Liabilities are money owed to vendors (accounts payable), employees, tax collectors, and holders of long-term loans (notes payable). The owner's equity consists of total assets minus total liabilities; since it is also expressed in thousands, this is $3,311,000.

Figure 13-4

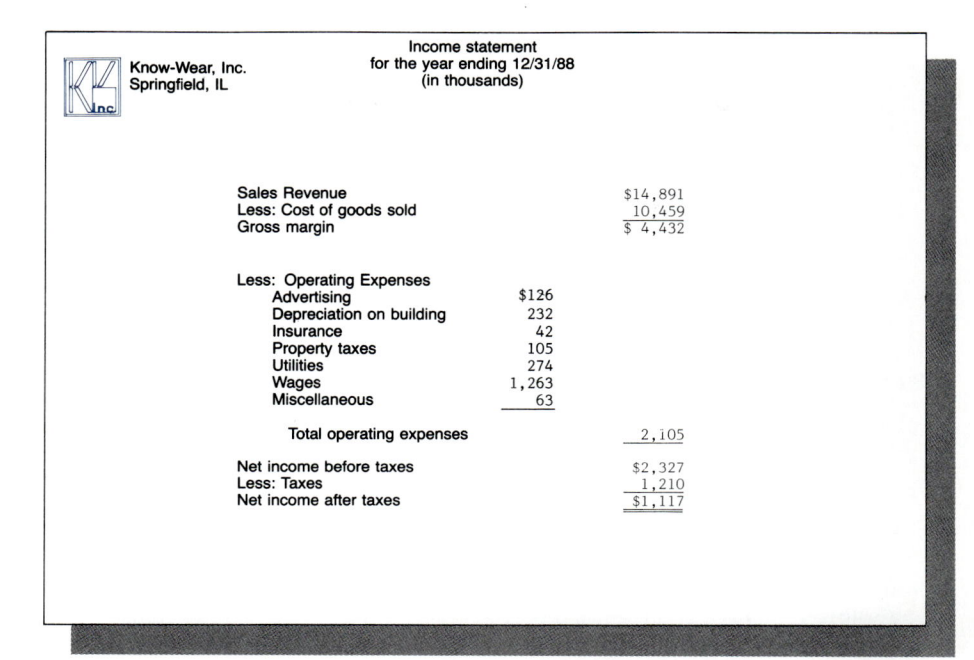

Know-Wear, Inc.
Springfield, IL

Income statement
for the year ending 12/31/88
(in thousands)

Sales Revenue		$14,891
Less: Cost of goods sold		10,459
Gross margin		$ 4,432
Less: Operating Expenses		
Advertising	$126	
Depreciation on building	232	
Insurance	42	
Property taxes	105	
Utilities	274	
Wages	1,263	
Miscellaneous	63	
Total operating expenses		2,105
Net income before taxes		$2,327
Less: Taxes		1,210
Net income after taxes		$1,117

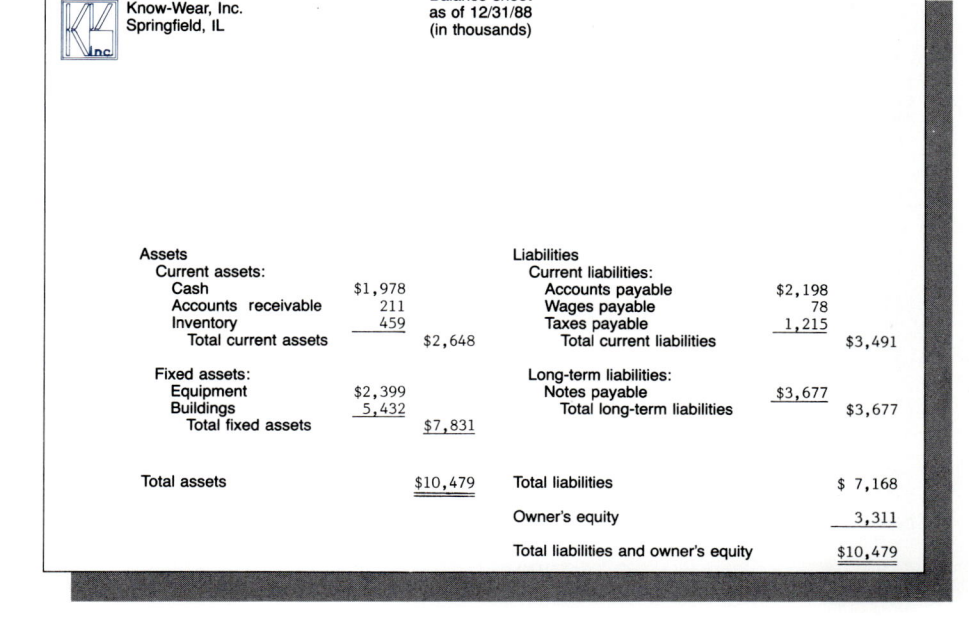

Know-Wear, Inc.
Springfield, IL

Balance sheet
as of 12/31/88
(in thousands)

Assets		
Current assets:		
Cash	$1,978	
Accounts receivable	211	
Inventory	459	
Total current assets		$2,648
Fixed assets:		
Equipment	$2,399	
Buildings	5,432	
Total fixed assets		$7,831
Total assets		$10,479

Liabilities		
Current liabilities:		
Accounts payable	$2,198	
Wages payable	78	
Taxes payable	1,215	
Total current liabilities		$3,491
Long-term liabilities:		
Notes payable	$3,677	
Total long-term liabilities		$3,677
Total liabilities		$ 7,168
Owner's equity		3,311
Total liabilities and owner's equity		$10,479

assets for Know-wear are equal to the sum of liabilities and proprietor's equity.

Exception Reports

Exception reports call attention to unusual situations. They are put out by the MIS when certain predefined conditions occur, such as when inventory levels drop dangerously low, production output is behind schedule, sales are low throughout an entire region, or the amount in accounts receivable is beyond an acceptable level.

An example of an exception report for Know-wear appears in Figure 13-5.

Demand Report

A **demand report** is the opposite of a periodic report; as its name implies, it is prepared on an as-needed, nonscheduled basis—that is, "on demand." Examples of demand reports are revised sales forecasts, employee salary reviews, and current production performance reports.

Figure 13-5 Exception report: aged receivables. An aged receivables report is produced by Know-wear's MIS whenever customers' accounts receivables have "aged" beyond a certain acceptable level—that is, customers are late in payment. By monitoring the payment history of a customer, Know-wear may increase or decrease that customer's credit limit, the maximum amount that customer will be sold on account. The aged receivables report may also be produced as a periodic report.

Know-Wear, Inc.

Aged accounts receivable

Page 1

Date: 10/31/88

Customer number	Customer name	Credit limit	Current balance	* —— Days past due —— * 1–30	31–60	61–90	Over 90	Total due
0025	Thriller Threads	18,000	6,431	5,569				12,000
0131	Fashion-Go-Round	7,500	2,111			1,123	2,121	5,355
0311	Miracle Mile Stores	12,000	4,000					4,000
0314	Clothing World	14,500	7,123	969	458			8,550
Company total			19,665	6,538	458	1,123	2,121	29,905
Percent of total due			65.8	21.9	1.5	3.8	7.1	100.0

Figure 13-6 shows two demand reports used at Know-wear. The national sales manager in the Marketing department, for example, may request a demand report called an "employee salary review" because competitiveness in recruiting sales people means that newly hired employees must be paid more than older employees—but older employees must also be paid enough to keep them from being lured away to other companies (assuming they have earned a pay hike).

Onward to DSS

Know-wear went from OIS to MIS because it was growing and its managers, including the CEO, Mr. Douglas, felt they were losing control of

Figure 13-6 Demand reports: employee salary review and insurance evaluation. Two instances of demand reports—reports produced on demand by the MIS at the request of managers—at Know-wear. *Below:* The employee salary review shows that three of the four sales people were doing acceptable or better jobs and so were given a raise in annual salary; Mike Davis was not performing well enough to deserve a raise. See insurance evaluation report on following page.

Employee salary review

Page 1

Know-Wear, Inc.

Department number: 120 Department name: Marketing

Date: 10/31/88

Employee number	Employee name	Hire date	Current annual salary	Rating	New annual salary	Percent change
6112	Adams, Ann	5/12/83	20,133	Good	21,663	7.6
1312	Davis, Mike	4/18/85	18,431	Unsatisfactory	18,431	0.0
9002	Foster, John	7/ 7/86	16,138	Satisfactory	16,961	5.1
4138	Scott, Ellen	2/ 1/86	23,311	Outstanding	26,038	11.7
Department summary						
Totals			78,013		83,093	
Averages			19,503	2.5	20,773	6.1
Number of employees: 4						

Key:

Rating	Points
Outstanding	4.0
Good	3.0
Satisfactory	2.0
Unsatisfactory	1.0

Department insurance evaluation

Page 1

Know-Wear, Inc.

Department name: Marketing

Date: 10/31/88

Property number	Description	Acquisition date	Original cost	Book value	Percent of accumulated depreciation	Replacement cost	Insurance value
01010	Typewriter	12/10/84	550.00	110.00	80.0	585.00	117.00
01077	Artificial Plants	12/11/86	600.00	315.00	47.5	615.00	322.88
01098	Calculator	4/12/87	750.00	487.00	35.1	775.00	502.98
01123	Desk	10/15/87	1,002.00	459.00	54.2	1,090.00	499.22
02246	Cabinet	9/10/88	410.00	376.00	8.3	460.00	421.82
03111	Automobile	7/21/88	6,432.00	5,832.00	9.3	7,141.00	6,476.89
Department totals			9,744.00	7,579.00		10,666.00	8,340.79

Figure 13-6 (continued) An insurance evaluation demand report, which describes the value and insurance coverage for equipment in the Marketing department.

the operation. They felt the need for more information and more reports. With an MIS installed, middle managers have computer-based assistance for tactical planning and control. Now it is time to move on to helping the top managers with strategic planning. It is time to consider DSS.

SUMMARY

- A **management information system (MIS),** which is designed to assist managers in the performance of their work, is a network of computer-based processing procedures that are integrated with manual and other procedures to provide timely, effective information to support managerial planning and control.
- **Management** is the process of transforming resources—materials, money, employees, facilities—into products or services. The primary task of managers is to make decisions in five areas: organizing, communicating, staffing,

planning, and controlling. Planning and controlling are the two management tasks that an MIS is specially designed to support.

- **Organizing** decisions include what structures and procedures should be set up, what authority delegated, what system of responsibility and accountability arranged.
- **Communicating** consists of transmitting requests and requirements to subordinates and superiors. Current computerized communicating assistance includes word processing, electronic mail, and telecommunications.
- **Staffing** consists of decisions about hiring and training employees to achieve the organization's goals.
- **Planning** is the formulation of short- and long-range goals for the organization—including policies, procedures, and standards necessary to achieve them. Planning is also concerned with identifying opportunities, problems, and alternative courses of action.
- **Controlling** is monitoring of the organization's progress toward its goals—keeping track of employee performance and other resources and making necessary adjustments.
- An effective MIS produces information that is accurate, timely, and complete yet concise. *Accuracy*—completely error-free information—is usually expensive, but sometimes the cost is justified. *Timeliness*—quickly supplied information—is necessary to keep up with the rapid pace of business. *Complete but concise* information includes all relevant facts, not unnecessary and unwanted facts.
- A management information system consists of three parts: management, information, and systems.

- *Management* in an organization has three levels: top, middle, and supervisory (lower).
- Top management, which includes a few of the most powerful managers, has the primary responsibility of strategic planning—establishing the overall direction of the company through long-range planning. The problems of these managers are unstructured and their activities are varied, such as establishing new markets and products and evaluating potential mergers and acquisitions. To make decisions, top managers need both external and internal information.
- Middle managers, who are more numerous than top managers, are responsible for tactical planning and control—implementing the plans of top management and monitoring the firm's operations. They perform fairly structured activities—formulating budgets, doing production scheduling, making short-term forecasts, and monitoring sales, production, and personnel performance. Middle managers rely more on internal information than on external, and their decisions take effect much sooner than those of top managers.

- Supervisory or lower management, by far the largest group, is responsible for operational control—implementing the plans of middle management and controlling day-to-day operations. Their activities are structured, routine, and oriented toward the present—such as meeting production and marketing schedules, maintaining inventory records, determining raw material requirements, controlling quality, and monitoring the achievement of well-defined short-term objectives.
- Each management level requires a unique kind of information to support decision making. Top managers need information that is highly summarized, future-oriented, and external as well as internal. Middle managers need information that is summarized but contains enough detail to allow effective control; such information has a past orientation to describe recent business activity. Supervisory managers need information that is not summarized but is very current to control day-to-day business operations.
- These three management information needs are supported by three separate, yet related, information systems: top management—by decision support systems (DSSs); middle management—by management information systems (MISs); supervisory management by operations information systems (OISs).
- A **data base management system (DBMS)** is a set of programs that act as interface between data bases and users and that allow users easy access to data. A DBMS is valuable to an MIS because middle managers must be able to cross departments in an organization in order to get data.
- A DBMS has five advantages: (1) Data redundancy is reduced. (2) The same data can be accessed by different application programs. (3) Updating of data needs to be done in only one place. (4) Application programs can be developed more efficiently. (5) Company-wide data is made more available to users.
- A DBMS has four disadvantages: (1) One error in data entry causes problems throughout the entire organizational data base. (2) To establish and maintain a DBMS requires highly skilled and well-trained people. (3) Keeping data secure from unauthorized users is more difficult because data is accessible to more people. (4) Traditional data processing jobs can take longer with a DBMS than with an old file management system.
- MIS reports have predetermined format and informational content. The three categories of MIS reports are periodic, exception, and demand. Every time a report is to be generated, the MIS programs access the organizational data base and calculate, summarize, and report the required information.
- **Periodic reports** are reports generated at regular intervals—quarterly, monthly, or weekly—such as quarterly financial reports, monthly sales analyses, and weekly production reports.
- Two of the most common periodic reports are the income statement and the balance sheet. An **income statement** is a statement of the organization's

financial performance—income, expenses, and the difference between them, or net income—for a given period of time. The **balance sheet** reports the *overall* financial condition of the firm, listing assets, liabilities, and the owner's share in the firm.

- **Exception reports** are put out by the MIS when certain predefined unusual conditions occur, such as when inventory levels drop dangerously low, production output is behind schedule, sales are low throughout an entire region, or the amount in accounts receivable is beyond an acceptable level.
- A **demand report** is the opposite of a periodic report; it is prepared on an as-needed, nonscheduled basis. Examples of demand reports are revised sales forecasts, employee salary reviews, and current production performance reports.

KEY TERMS

Balance sheet, p. 473
Communicating, p. 462
Controlling, p. 463
Data base management system (DBMS), p. 468
Demand report, p. 476
Exception report, p. 476
Income statement, p. 473
Management information system (MIS), p. 459
Organizing, p. 461
Periodic report, p. 473
Planning, p. 463
Staffing, p. 462

REVIEW QUESTIONS

1. What do managers do? Describe the classic tasks of management.
2. To aid managers in decision making, the MIS needs to produce information with what three attributes?
3. Describe the three levels of management. What type of information is needed at each level?
4. Compare the MIS to the OIS. How are they alike and how do they differ?
5. Describe the functions, advantages, and disadvantages of a data base management system.
6. Name and describe the three categories of MIS reports.
7. Describe the income statement and balance sheet.

CASE PROBLEMS

Case 13-1: JIT—The "Just-in-Time" Approach to Reducing Inventories

At the Harley-Davidson motorcycle-engine plant in Milwaukee, the system is called Material-as-Needed. At the T. D. Shea Manufacturing plant in Troy, Michigan, which makes plastic products, it is called Nick-of-Time. In most other places, according to *Inc.* magazine (March 1984), it is called Just-in-Time—JIT. Generally regarded as a development of the Japanese automobile manufacturers, JIT is a system used in repetitive manufacturing operations in which every station on the production line gets the parts or components it needs just when it needs them—"just in time," but not earlier. The idea is to avoid a build-up of piles of inventory waiting by the machines, which take up space, get in the way of workers, and cost extra to move about. JIT is the opposite of the point of view that a company must protect itself against human error, machine breakdown, and defective parts by always having huge inventories on hand.

JIT does not work for all manufacturing situations, but it seems to do well, according to *Inc.*, when the following exist: "There are significant levels of inventory to begin with; demand and production can be forecast accurately; suppliers are located nearby, manufacture quality parts, and are willing to cooperate."[1] The system means changes in ways of doing business: moving parts of the manufacturing process closer together, identifying the number of steps and bottlenecks in operations, sharing information with vendors—indeed, having exclusive relationships with suppliers, who will have to cover themselves with extra inventory and be willing to make more frequent deliveries to customers.

Your assignment: Top management may decide a JIT system should be installed in a plant, but it is middle management that will have to implement it—do the tactical planning and control. As a middle manager for a company that makes a product—sporting goods, drilling bits, wooden furniture, or whatever interests you—how would an MIS be helpful to you in implementing a JIT system?

Case 13-2: Using MIS for Marketing—Building a Mailing List

Mailing lists can be the sales and marketing lifeblood of a business, an effective way of targeting advertising that is less a "shotgun" approach, as ads in newspapers and on television often are. While one probably would not advertise hamburgers or breakfast cereals via direct mail, this channel can be successful for trying to reach customers for specialty or specialized products. *Inc.* magazine (September 1984) reports, for instance, on the efforts of the new owner of the London Wine Co. in Brookline, Massachusetts, when he took over the family business and decided he wanted to increase sales 50% to $1.5 million in only one year. Since the store had limited shelf and floor space and almost no parking, he realized that more business could not come from increasing foot traffic into the store. By obtaining a direct-mail management program designed to run on a personal computer, however, London Wine was able "to track each response and tailor its mailing to the tastes and needs of the individual recipients."[2]

Your assignment: One secret of a successful direct-mail computer program is its ability to compile very detailed records on customers, so that you can select customers with specific characteristics and then shape the advertising accordingly. Suppose you were instructed to develop a sophisticated mailing list for Know-wear, based on its present customer list of retail clothing stores and chains. What kind of information could be provided by the MIS that would be helpful for this purpose?

CHAPTER 14

Decision Support Systems

Helping Executive Managers Handle Uncertainty

"We are drowning in information but starved for knowledge." This, says J. Daniel Couger, a professor of computer and management science at the University of Colorado, Colorado Springs, is the corollary to the proposition stated by futurist John Naisbitt three chapters ago—that our industrial society is becoming an information society.

"This level of information is clearly impossible to handle by present means," says Couger. "Uncontrolled and unorganized information is no longer a resource in an information society. Instead, it becomes the enemy of the information worker. . . . Information technology brings order to the chaos of information pollution and, therefore, gives value to data that would otherwise be useless."[1]

The third stage of evolution in information technology—and the most valuable in coping with "information pollution"—is the decision support system (DSS). OIS and MIS are helpful in dealing with the structured and predictable, but 80% of all managerial decision making is in response to the unpredictable. As the case study on the next page indicates, most important decisions of the sort handled by a DSS are of the "What if...?" variety.

P R E V I E W

Decision Support: Why We Need It

"What if there is a strike?" a manager may want to know. "How would that affect inventory levels?" Or, "What if there is a downturn in the national economy? How would that affect sales?" The stuff of management is making decisions about unexpected problems, sudden opportunities, unique alternatives—situations that are unanticipated, rarely repeated, and need quick analysis and resolution.

CASE STUDY: THE DECISION AID

Decision Support Systems: Management Finally Gets Its Hand on the Data

The easiest way to provide an overview of decision support systems is to give some examples of what they can do.

- A U.S. mining company was faced with a major capital budgeting decision. Should it develop a new copper mine in Africa? Assessing the potential payback of such a 20-year project required hundreds of assumptions about cost, price, and demand variables. To handle this task, the company developed a decision support system that could handle all the variables and the "what-if" questions necessary to assess the project.
- With more than 100 operating units keeping separate financials [financial records] over different periods of time, a large multinational electronics company found it almost impossible to compile current financial data that reflected overall corporate performance. The company solved the problem with a decision support system that allowed it to produce a consolidated financial statement within hours of closing the books on worldwide operations.
- A large money-center bank wanted to develop its portfolio management business without significantly increasing its staff. The bank also wanted to assist its portfolio managers in evaluating a wide range of investment strategies for its clients, a very time-consuming task using traditional methods. The bank addressed both problems by implementing a decision support system that allowed bank personnel to evaluate the status of portfolios, investigate alternative investment strategies, and improve client presentations.

These examples illustrate the diverse applications of a decision support system, one of the most misunderstood terms of today's "information age."

Simply stated, a decision support system is a complex set of computer programs and equipment that allows end users—usually managers and professionals—to analyze, manipulate, format, and display data in different ways. The analysis and manipulation usually help in decision making, because the user can pull together data from different sources and view them in ways that may differ from the original formats. The system also makes it possible for the data to be printed out, or to be prepared in the form of charts or graphs.

—Carl Wolf and Jim Treleaven, *Management Technology*, November 1983

Moreover, because managers often feel they are drowning in a sea of data, what they need is not more data or more information, but tools that will help them analyze and make decisions about the information they have. The answer is not only OIS and MIS but DSS—a decision support system.

A **decision support system (DSS)** is a set of computer programs and hardware that helps managers arrange information from various sources in new and different ways. Middle-level managers can use a DSS for analysis and research, but the system is principally intended to help high-level managers in their decision making. Thus, the system must be *flexible* and *interactive*—that is, the user must be able to obtain immediate access to data through an interactive computer terminal.

Most DSSs are designed for large computer systems, which are able to process and store large amounts of data quickly and efficiently. However, one of the oldest DSSs is VisiCalc, which, as we saw back in Chapter 4, was designed to operate on microcomputers. More powerful DSSs are now available for microcomputers—for example, Interactive Financial Planning System (IFPS), marketed by Execucom Systems of Austin, Texas. IFPS has a version designed for mainframe use as well.

"The many potential benefits of DSS," says one commentary, "include examining many alternative business situations, gaining a better understanding of the business, and obtaining better control of information. But all this depends upon putting together a well-designed system that is easy to learn and use. Though the high cost of a DSS is sometimes difficult to justify, it is worthwhile where a broader spectrum of data would expand and improve decision making, or when timely access to information is critical."[2]

We will take a detailed look at what constitutes a DSS. First, however, let us quickly review the distinctions among the three kinds of management systems:

- **OIS**: Focusing on data generated by the firm's transactions and operations, OIS is exemplified by the payroll system that processes employee time cards, produces employee paychecks, and records the appropriate journal accounting entries.
- **MIS**: Designed to provide management with structured reports, MIS is illustrated by quarterly labor analysis reports that summarize labor costs.
- **DSS**: Intended to support management decision making in the analysis of semistructured and unstructured problems, DSS is exemplified by information that helps managers quickly evaluate trends in salaries of employees within a particular job classification over the last five years. DSS, then, is a natural evolution from OIS and MIS.

VIEWS ON OIS, MIS, AND DSS

Are There Really Differences Among Information Systems?

When we state in this book that OISs are for supervisory managers, MISs for middle managers, and DSSs for top managers, we have used this division as a way of presenting basic concepts. In point of fact, however, the three systems overlap, and there is some dispute as to whether, for example, there are truly differences between MIS and DSS. Here is how Ralph H. Sprague, Jr. and Eric D. Carlson describe the controversy. Note that they use EDP (electronic data processing) for what we have been calling OIS.

We seem to be on the verge of another "era" in the relentless advancement of computer-based information systems in organizations. Designated by the term decision support systems (DSS), these systems are receiving reactions ranging from "a major breakthrough" to "just another buzzword."

One view is that the natural evolutionary advancement of information technology and its use in the organizational context has led from electronic data processing (EDP) to management information systems (MIS) to the current DSS thrust. In this view, DSS pick up where MIS leave off. An alternative view portrays DSS as an important subset of what MIS have been and will continue to be. Still another view recognizes a type of system that has been developing for several years and "now we have a name for it." Meanwhile, the skeptics suspect that DSS is just another buzzword to justify the next round of visits from the vendors. . . .

A decision support system may be defined by its capabilities in several critical areas. . . .

- They tend to be aimed at the less well structured, underspecified problems that upper-level managers typically face.
- They attempt to combine the use of models or analytic techniques with traditional data access and retrieval functions.
- They specifically focus on features that make them easy to use by noncomputer people in an interactive mode.
- They emphasize flexibility and adaptability to accommodate changes in the environment and decision-making approach of the user. . . .

DSS represent not merely an evolutionary advancement of EDP and MIS, and certainly will not replace either. Nor are they merely a type of information system aimed exclusively at top management, where other information systems seem to have failed. Rather, DSS comprise a class of information system that draws on transaction processing [EDP] systems and interacts with the other parts of the overall information system to support the decision-making activities of managers and other knowledge workers in organizations. There are, however, some subtle but significant differences between DSS and traditional EDP or so-called MIS approaches. Moreover, these systems require a new combination of information systems technology to satisfy a set of heretofore unmet needs.

—Ralph H. Sprague, Jr. and Eric D. Carlson, *Building Effective Decision Support Systems*

The Three Parts of DSS: Decision, Support, System

It was not always possible to provide computerized support for decision making about unanticipated problems, but recent technological advances have changed all that. Microprocessors, telecommunications, large storage capacity, user-friendly software, and data base management systems have helped to extend the range of the ordinary manager's control over information.

To understand DSS and how it fits in with other information systems, let us examine each of its parts:

- Decision
- Support
- Systems

Decisions: Making Things Happen

service

Nearly everyone in business has to make decisions, but obviously the decisions are different the higher you go in the organization. As a Knowwear sales representative, for example, you will have to make different decisions than you will if you become the Vice President of Marketing—whose types of decisions will be different from those of the Vice President of Production.

Despite these differences, there are seven activities common to decision making. Whatever kind of manager you are or become, you will probably perform the following tasks:

- **Searching:** The decision process typically begins with a *search* for available data—facts, figures, and reports.
- **Specifying:** The data uncovered may allow you to *specify* the problem more precisely, eliminating some alternatives and revealing new ones.
- **Computing:** The data may have to be manipulated in some way; that is, you may have to do some mathematical and statistical *computing*.
- **Assimilating:** After the computations, you *assimilate* or pull together the accumulated facts, reports, and summaries.
- **Drawing inferences:** After assimilating the facts, you draw conclusions or *inferences* from the data.
- **Deciding:** The assimilating and inferring steps will allow you to *decide*—to formulate a decision.
- **Communicating:** Finally, you *communicate* the decision to the people who are to be affected by it in some way.

These seven activities constitute the brain work of a manager. They describe how a manager spends his or her day.

Support: Getting Help with the Information Glut

"We've got information coming out our ears!" is the cry of many managers. "What we need now is some way to make sense of it." What is needed, in other words, is some way to take hold of it so a manager can make decisions about it.

Because MIS reports tend to be passive and predetermined, they are not as helpful in supporting managerial planning and decision mak-

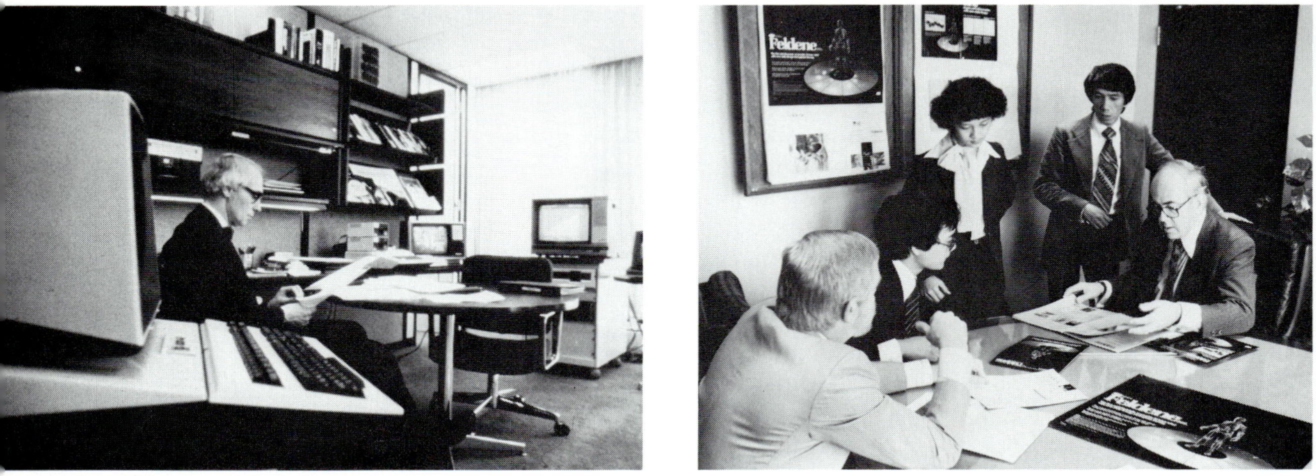
Feldene
Feldene

Decision making The task of decision making has seven activities: searching for data, specifying the problem, computing data, assimilating facts (*left*), drawing inferences, formulating a decision, and (*right*) communicating the decision to the people affected by it.

ing. Something more active and flexible is needed, something that will better support the seven decision-making tasks above.

A number of components of computer technology can assist in these tasks. For example:

- *Searching* for facts, figures, and reports can be enhanced by large data bases containing numeric and text data.
- *Specifying* and *computing* are helped by computational models, such as electronic spreadsheets or statistical packages.
- *Assimilating, drawing inferences,* and *deciding* are helped by computer graphics.
- *Communicating* is given a boost with word processing and with telecommunications, such as teleconferencing with other managers about a problem.

Perhaps the *need* for decision support is best demonstrated by the increasing use of microcomputers in business organizations. With their increasingly easy-to-use software and good graphics, microcomputers give managers immediate, convenient access to data and analytical tools that help them with their decision making. And, although microcomputers alone are limited in their ability to store, manipulate, and quickly process large amounts of data, when they are connected to mainframes these drawbacks disappear.

The manager can have the best of both worlds. He or she can access the mainframe and use its tremendous power and data storage capability. Selected data and programs can be retrieved and stored in the manager's microcomputer. With the mainframe freed for other tasks, the manager has the freedom and convenience of examining and analyzing the selected information on his or her personal microcomputer.

Systems: Elimination of the Limitations

Computers are limited in what they can do. So are people. When computers and people are put together in a system, however, their combined strengths are powerful. Computers offer speed, access, and computational power. People offer creativity, reasoning, and perspective. Paired in a DSS, they provide a system for increasing the effectiveness of management decisions.

A DSS, then, does not produce a product. Whereas an OIS may produce a list of transactions and an MIS a report, a DSS does neither. Rather it is designed to produce a *service* that will affect the quality of management decisions.

The Model Way of Doing Things

To OIS, MIS, and DSS let us add another set of initials—**MS**. It stands for **management science,** defined as the application of quantitative techniques or models to the analysis of management problems. Decision support systems are actually related to a combination of MIS and MS. MIS provides managers with structured reports; MS provides them with models. By models, we do not mean something you buy in a hobby store. **Models** are ideas, hypothetical notions that consist of technical recommendations and procedures for analyzing and solving complex management problems. Although management science by itself has had only limited effects on managerial decision making—the complexity of MS techniques has restricted their widespread use—it has shown the value of using models as a problem-solving tool.

There are three types of management science models:

- **Optimization**: **Optimization** models are used to identify the best—that is, optimal—solution in very specialized problems. The best known and widely used such model is *linear programming,* used in the oil industry for scheduling refinery operations, as well as in banking, transportation, and public utilities.
- **Heuristics**: A model that probably will be used more in the future, **heuristics** consist of a set of rules or guidelines that lead to a solution to a particular type of problem. For example, in the banking industry, guidelines are set up for loan officers to follow when authorizing

loan applications; the applicant must meet certain criteria for income level, credit rating, and so on.

- **Simulation:** The most used and most effective in business organizations, **simulation** models are used to represent complex problems by conceptualizing them and describing them mathematically. More flexible than other models and capable of analyzing a wider range of problems, simulation models can be used to determine allocations of a firm's resources. For example, a model may consider external factors such as current economic conditions and internal factors such as available investment capital in order to arrive at a projected solution. Simulation is one of the most widely used tools of middle- and top-level managers for planning and decision making.

Models like these are used frequently in business to formulate strategies for making decisions.

An Ideal DSS

What would an ideal DSS look like? Let us say that Know-wear has been on a surge of growth. New offices have been opened around the United States and Canada, and the CEO, Mr. Douglas, finds that he needs help in making strategic decisions. It is time, he begins to see, for him and his vice presidents to take advantage of a complete computer-based business information system—namely, to install a decision support system. Once again, Mr. Douglas taps you to help do the spadework of putting such a system in place.

In setting up a DSS, a company must consider three aspects:

- Which of two types of DSS to use—ad hoc or institutional.
- The performance objectives required of the DSS.
- The building blocks of the DSS—hardware, software, and decision makers.

The Two Types of DSS

Decision support systems are of two types:

- Ad hoc
- Institutional

The **ad hoc DSSs,** also known as general DSSs, are designed to handle a wide variety of management decision problems and are especially suited to unexpected, nonrecurring management problems. The Generalized Planning System (GPLAN) is one example of an ad hoc DSS. It is used by business people to support a wide variety of decisions ranging from inventory control to financial management.

Institutional DSSs are specialized and use terminology and analysis procedures established within certain areas, such as medicine or advertising. Because of their lack of flexibility, they are not able to support organization-wide decision making. Examples of institutional DSSs are MYCIN, which is used by physicians for assistance in diagnosing patient symptoms (see Figure 14-1); IRIS, used in personnel and labor relations; and IMS, used for evaluating advertising strategies.

Financial planning languages (FPLs) evolved from high-level languages into institutional decision support systems and from there into ad hoc DSSs. Although they have a definite financial orientation, they have attained a great deal of flexibility and now are used in a variety of decision support roles, including mathematical, statistical, and forecasting procedures; sensitivity and "what-if" analyses; goal seeking and optimization; report generation and graphic displays. Figure 14-2 lists some common applications of FPLs in the four business areas of Marketing, Accounting and Finance, Production, and Research and Development.

The questions that FPLs are able to address are those "what-if" types of questions that arise so frequently in business: "What if fuel prices increase 20% next year?" "What if interest rates increase 2% next month?" "How sensitive is net income to changes in sales price? labor costs? interest rates?"

For instance, at Know-wear, the CEO learns that certain garment workers are considering going on strike. Management forms a negotiation team in preparation for the strike, but prior to the negotiations, the team is asked to evaluate how long the company could survive profitably on its inventories before being affected by the strike. Armed with this information, the team has a better grasp of its strategy by knowing how hard to negotiate with the union.

The DSS is used in the following manner. The team uses historical data to predict sales for the next three months. A model is chosen, a data base is accessed, and a prediction equation formulated. Based on this equation, "what-if" questions are asked—"What if inventory decreases by 80 percent? What would be the effect on sales?" With the results of this projection, the negotiation team informs management to build up inventories by a certain amount before the strike. From answers to related questions, the team informs the CEO how badly the strike could affect the company, depending on its length.

service

At Know-wear, the Marketing vice president hears that the CEO is considering a DSS and suggests that the company acquire IMS—which, of course, would be useful for her in her advertising decisions but will not be useful to anyone else. The CEO refers the matter to a systems analyst and asks you to be the liaison in the matter.

The systems analyst disagrees with the Marketing vp's choice,

```
      NAME                                AGE          SEX          RACE
1) ** JOHN DOE                            34           MALE            CAUCASIAN


2)  ARE THERE ANY POSITIVE CULTURES OBTAINED FROM JOHN DOE?
**  NO

3)  ARE THERE ANY PENDING CULTURES OF JOHN DOE?
**  YES

        SITE           DATE               STAIN          :METHOD OF
                       COLLECTED          EXAMINED?      :COLLECTION
                                                         :URINE, SPUTUM ONLY]
  4)  **CSF            30 JAN 77          YES
              STAIN OF SMEAR  MORPH
              (TYPE NONE IF NO ORGANISM WAS SEEN ON THE SMEAR)
        5)  ** NONE
        [NO OTHER PENDING CULTURES.]

[CONSIDERING ORGANISMS (OTHER THAN THOSE ISOLATED FROM CULTURES) WHICH MIGHT BE
PRESENT...]

13) HAS JOHN DOE RECENTLY HAD SYMPTOMS OF PERSISTENT HEADACHE OR OTHER ABNORMAL
NEUROLOGIC SYMPTOMS (DIZZINESS, LETHARGY, ETC.)?
** YES

(14) HAS JOHN DOE RECENTLY HAD OBJECTIVE EVIDENCE OF ABNORMAL NEUROLOGIC SIGNS
    (NUCHAL RIGIDITY, COMA, SEIZURES, ETC.) DOCUMENTED BY PHYSICIAN
    OBSERVATION OR EXAMINATION?
** YES

THE CSF CULTURES WILL BE CONSIDERED TO BE ASSOCIATED WITH MENINGITIS
15) PLEASE GIVE THE DATE ON WHICH CLINICAL EVIDENCE (SYMPTOMS, SIGNS, OR
    LABORATORY TESTS) OF MENINGITIS FIRST APPEARED.

PLEASE ENTER CSF FINDINGS IN THE FOLLOWING TABLE

        CSF            PERCENT        PROTEIN        CSF            PERIPHERAL
        WBC            PMN                           GLUCOSE        GLUCOSE
23) **  100            99             280            5              UNKNOWN

34) IS MENINGITIS A HOSPITAL-ACQUIRED INFECTION?
** WHY?
```

Figure 14-1 An institutional DSS. MYCIN was developed to aid physicians during the crucial first 24 or 48 hours when much decision making about patients is imprecise because not all the relevant information is in hand. The program's record for correct diagnoses and treatments for meningitis and bacteremia has equaled the performance of human experts. The physician holds an interactive dialogue with MYCIN about a particular patient. Questions from MYCIN are preceded by 1), 2), and so on; the answers keyed in by the physician are preceded by **. If the user types WHY, a program is triggered which leads the physician through the line of reasoning that produced MYCIN's diagnosis.

```
[2.0] THIS WILL AID IN DETERMINING THE ORGANISMS (OTHER THAN THOSE SEEN ON CULTURES OR
      SMEARS) WHICH MIGHT BE CAUSING THE INFECTION.  IT HAS ALREADY BEEN ESTABLISHED THAT
        [2.1] THE INFECTION WHICH REQUIRES THERAPY IS MENINGITIS, AND
        [2.2] ORGANISMS WERE NOT SEEN ON THE STAIN OF THE PENDING CSF CULTURE, AND
        [2.3] THE TYPE OF THE INFECTION IS BACTERIAL, AND
        [2.4] NEUROSURGERY IS NOT ONE OF THE RELEVANT ITEMS FROM THE
              HISTORY OF JOHN DOE, AND
        [2.5] THE AGE OF JOHN DOE IS GREATER THAN 10 DAYS
      THEREFORE, IF
        [2.6] THE INFECTION WAS ACQUIRED WHILE THE PATIENT WAS HOSPITALIZED
              THEN THERE IS EVIDENCE THAT THE ORGANISMS (OTHER THAN THOSE
              SEEN ON CULTURES OR SMEARS) WHICH MIGHT BE CAUSING THE
              INFECTION ARE E. COLI ( 75) STAPHYLOCOCCUS-COAG-POS ( 3)
              PSEUDOMONAS-AERUGINOSA ( 3) KLEBSIELLA-PNEUMONIAE ( 5)

(BACK TO QUESTION 34...)
** YES

        MY THERAPY RECOMMENDATIONS WILL BE DESIGNED TO TREAT FOR ORGANISMS
THAT EITHER ARE VERY LIKELY OR, ALTHOUGH LESS LIKELY, WOULD HAVE A SIGNIFICANT
EFFECT ON THERAPY SELECTION IF THEY WERE PRESENT. IT IS IMPORTANT TO COVER
FOR THE FOLLOWING PROBABLE INFECTION(S) AND ASSOCIATED ORGANISM(S).

INFECTION-1 IS MENINGITIS

  + <ITEM-1>  E. COLI (FROM CLINICAL EVIDENCE ONLY)
  + <ITEM-2>  PSEUDOMONAS-AERUGINOSA [FROM CLINICAL EVIDENCE ONLY]
  + <ITEM-3>  KLEBSIELLA-PNEUMONIAE [FROM CLINICAL EVIDENCE ONLY]
  + <ITEM-4>  DIPLOCOCCUS-PNEUMONIAE [FROM CLINICAL EVIDENCE ONLY]

40) DOES JOHN DOE HAVE A CLINICALLY SIGNIFICANT ALLERGIC REACTION TO ANY ANTIMICROBIAL
AGENT?
** NO
[CONSIDERING AMPICILLIN-AND-GENTAMICIN FOR USE AGAINST INFECTION-1...]
41) DO YOU HAVE REASON TO SUSPECT THAT JOHN DOE MAY HAVE IMPAIRED RENAL FUNCTION?
** NO

42) JOHN DOE'S WEIGHT IN KILOGRAMS (OR <NUMBER> POUNDS)
** 70
[REC-1] MY PREFERRED THERAPY RECOMMENDATION IS AS FOLLOWS:
   IN ORDER TO COVER FOR ITEMS <1 2 3 4>
        GIVE THE FOLLOWING IN COMBINATION:
        (1) AMPICILLIN
        DOSE: 3.5 G (28.0 ML) Q4H IV [CALCULATED ON BASIS OF 50 MG/KG]

        (2) GENTAMICIN
        DOSE: 119 MG (3.0 ML, 80 MG/2 ML AMPULE) Q8H IV (CALCULATED ON
              BASIS OF 1.7 MG/KG) PLUS CONSIDER GIVING 5 MG Q24H
              INTRATHECAL
        COMMENTS: MONITOR SERUM CONCENTRATIONS

        SINCE HIGH CONCENTRATIONS OF PENICILLINS CAN INACTIVATE AMINOGLYCOSIDES,
        DO NOT MIX THESE TWO ANTIBIOTICS IN THE SAME IV BOTTLE.
```

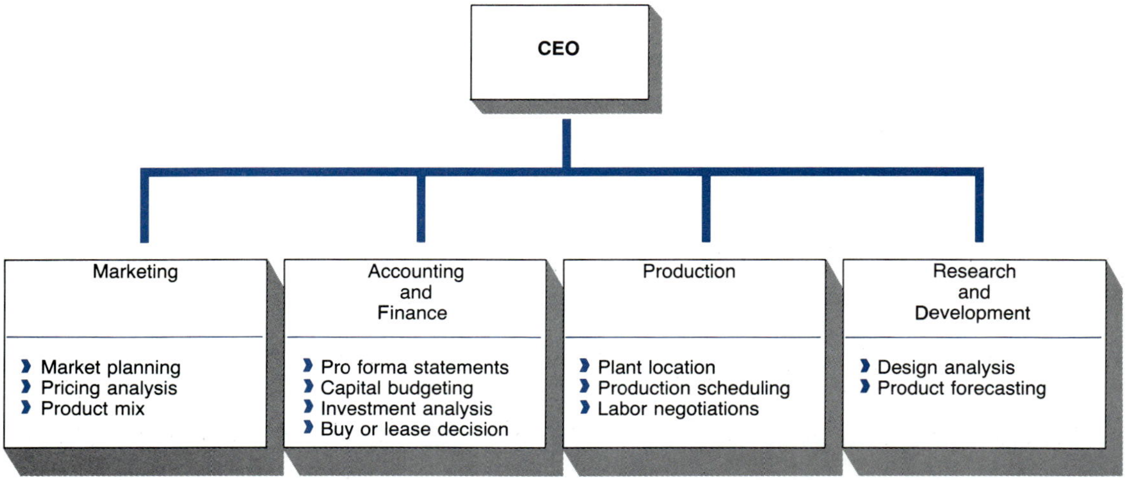
CEO
Marketing
Market planning
Pricing analysis
Product mix
Accounting and Finance
Pro forma statements
Capital budgeting
Investment analysis
Buy or lease decision
Production
Plant location
Production scheduling
Labor negotiations
Research and Development
Design analysis
Product forecasting

Figure 14-2 The uses of FPLs. Common applications of Financial Planning Languages are shown for the four principal business areas.

believing that a more general or ad hoc DSS would better serve the organization. He suggests the use of an ad hoc system called IFPS—Interactive Financial Planning System. After a thorough systems analysis and design, Know-wear adopts IFPS.

Performance Objectives for a DSS

In general, the objectives of a DSS are to provide a flexible, powerful tool to support management decision making. More precisely, the objectives are:

- To support all management levels—top, middle, and supervisory—in all phases of decision making.
- To analyze unexpected problems.
- To integrate information flow and decision-making activities.
- To be easy to use yet powerful and flexible.

Let us look at these more carefully.

Management Levels. DSSs are designed to support the *planning* activities of middle and upper level managers as well as the *decision-making* activities of all managers in all phases of decision making. Thus, DSSs are used not only for data collection and analysis but also to support decision-making tasks: searching, specifying, computing, assimilating, drawing inferences, forming decisions, and communicating.

Unexpected Problems. Perhaps only 20% of the problems that managers encounter are standard and routine, and these can be evaluated effectively using MIS reports. However, as we mentioned at the outset of this chapter, 80% of all managerial decision making is in response to problems that are unexpected. Moreover, these problems usually require action within a very short period of time.

Information Flow and Decision-making Activities. As we have mentioned, the flow of information within an organization is both vertically within a department (for example, between management levels in Marketing) and horizontally between departments (for example, between Marketing and Production vice presidents). A DSS should facilitate this flow, especially horizontally at the higher management levels. Generally, the information is in the form of reports that communicate decisions and coordinate problem-solving activities. This means that the information must flow easily in and out of the organization's data base and that the DSS must be able to quickly update and access the data base.

Ease of Use. Users of a DSS are managers, not computer programmers; thus, one of the most crucial performance objectives of a DSS is that it must be easy to use. If the DSS is not powerful, flexible, and easy to use, then it simply will not be used. Commands should be English-like—for example, "BROWSE" might allow a manager to examine the contents of a data base.

DSS Building Blocks: Hardware, Software, Decision Maker

Decision support systems have become effective because of technological advances in hardware and software and because managers have become more sophisticated about using management science techniques and computers for help in making decisions. Let us, therefore, examine the three building blocks of a DSS:

- Hardware
- Software
- Decision maker

Hardware. The DSS software is typically located in a mainframe computer to which are attached terminals used by the company's managers. Therefore, probably the two most crucial pieces of hardware in the system are interactive graphic terminals and telecommunications networks:

- **Interactive graphic terminals:** Graphics capabilities are essential because charts and graphs aid decision making ("a picture is worth a thousand words"). An interactive graphic display terminal allows

REGIONAL PRODUCTION

Decision support systems. Two crucial pieces of hardware in a DSS are interactive graphic terminals, which permit managers to display charts and graphs (*upper left*) and window or split screens (*right*), and telecommunications equipment, which lets managers share data and reports with other managers (*lower left*).

the decision maker to have a natural, responsive interaction with the DSS software.

- **Telecommunications networks:** Such networks, which allow sophisticated time-sharing computer systems to be developed, let managers share data and reports with other managers, quickly coordinate problem-solving activities, and have access to far-flung data bases within the organization and to data bases outside the organization.

Software. Four types of software are needed in a DSS:

- **Data base management system:** A DBMS extends the range of data that can be collected, retrieved, and analyzed. It allows a manager to interact with the firm's internal data bases as well as with external data bases. The internal data will have been recorded primarily through the activities of transaction processing. The external data will be obtainable from commercially available data bases.
- **Simulation and application languages:** These specialized languages allow decision makers to do model building—to develop their own management science models and to purchase custom-made models. The models are contained within the data base as preprogrammed structures. The most common models are for financial statement simulations, risk analysis, and forecasting.
- **A DSS query language:** A query language that is understandable to managers is necessary if decision makers are to communicate easily with the DSS. The query language should use such commands as—add, graph, chart, calculate, select, browse, get, and so on. Such commands perform basic arithmetic operations, create bar graphs and charts, calculate ratios, perform statistical operations, and numerous other activities.
- **DSS executive software:** This acts like an operating system in that it handles many of the operational duties for the DSS, sparing the user these chores. The executive software is essential to monitor and to coordinate DSS activities. One of the most important functions of the DSS executive software is the coordination and control of the other three types of software.

Decision Maker. A decision maker is the human element, of course—the manager at his or her desk, eyes on the terminal screen, fingers on the keyboard. There are three roles in interacting with the DSS, and they can be performed by the same person or by three different persons:

- **The model builder:** This is the person who conceptualizes and develops the model.
- **The model user:** This is the person who actually runs the model. He or she specifies the inputs and evaluates the alternatives.
- **The decision maker:** This is the person who analyzes the results of the model, makes any modifications, and comes to the final decision.

For the most effective interaction between human and machine, and thus the most effective support of human decision making, one person should perform all three roles.

Models and Micros for Managers

Although many decision support systems require the use of mainframe computers, microcomputers can also be used. Here Chase Manhattan Bank vice president Hannah Blank describes how managers can use microcomputers to construct financial models to aid in their decision making.

Without large capital outlays and without adding personnel, managers can improve their companies' revenues almost immediately with a microcomputer. . . .

The exercise of formulating a model itself can be useful: Focusing on the relationship between one factor and another can sharpen decisions, even if one later chooses not to use a computer. But if it is used, it can save days or weeks of labor. . . .

Many kinds of business decisions could be modeled—whether to lease or buy a facility; how many bolts of Irish tweed will be enough but not too much; whether to support a particular research and development project; whether or not to hire for a peak period. Because of deadline pressures, these decisions often are made by management judgment alone, without sufficient quantification. . . .

Clearly, the manager beginning to use a micro must invest some time up front. He has to learn how to handle the microcomputer hardware—half an hour. He has to read a manual so that he can find what he needs when he needs it—two hours. He has to learn how to use an electronic worksheet—one day for getting started, more for advanced uses. And he has to give some thought to the structure of his model. But once having done all that, he can reapply the model many times.

Micros can help a manager close a profitable transaction that otherwise would have been impossible to arrange. Example: A lending officer at a bank was working on a large and complex transaction involving numerous quantifiable variables and complex calculations. And it was a sensitive situation. Differing, somewhat conflicting interests had to be served:

- The client wanted the transaction only on terms more favorable than could be obtained elsewhere;
- The lending officer wanted the transaction because of the client's prestige and size, and because of the magnitude of the deal;
- The loan committee of the bank sternly insisted that any arrangement, no matter how attractive the potential profit, meet all of its risk and quality criteria without exception.

Furthermore, it was necessary that the bank present its proposal quickly, because of potential competition.

After review by the various players, the complex document required 11 changes. Making the changes with hand calculators would have required another two or three weeks. During that time the competition could have come in with a better proposal. But with the model and all the data already on the microcomputer, only the changes needed to be entered—a matter of minutes—and a new printed document, attractive and accurate, not requiring proofreading, was ready in a matter of minutes. The client was served, the loan committee was satisfied, the transaction was completed.

Financing is not the only area where complex calculations are needed quickly and accurately. Tax planning, mergers and acquisitions, and investment decisions are but a few other examples.

One bond trader earned the price of his micro in a single trade. Before he began using a micro, he would arrive at his bids on secondaries by gut-feel decisions: He would look at the issue's rating and its degree of acceptance, consider the state of the market, calculate yield on a hand-held calculator and then come up with a bid. In order to utilize his micro, he had to codify his intuition into a bidding model. And once he did so, he made a profit in an hour that exceeded by more than the cost of the micro what he would have gained with the gut-feeling approach.

—Hannah I. Blank, *Wall Street Journal*, February 13, 1984

DSS Output: Graphic Display and Reports

The output for a DSS is highly diverse and depends on what problem you are investigating. The output may be:

- In pictorial format, such as charts and graphs displayed on a graphic terminal.
- In a report format, such as the expected sales of a product or production output of a factory.

Two common forms of output of DSSs are **pro forma**—which means "projected"—balance sheets and pro forma income statements, both of which predict the future financial position of the firm.

At Know-wear, the CEO has used the new DSS to develop a projected income statement (Figure 14-3) and a projected balance sheet (Figure 14-4).

Two common decision-making activities using these projected statements are:

- Performing **"what-if" analysis**—changing assumptions to see what might result. (We examined "what-if" analysis with spreadsheets in Chapter 4.)
- Performing **goal-seeking analysis**—stating a goal and the variables influencing it to see what is required to achieve that goal.

service

The Know-wear CEO and the Vice President of Accounting and Finance had to make many forecasts and projections to develop the projected financial statements shown in Figures 14-2 and 14-3; however, these are simply projections and not definite. The CEO wants to do some "what-if" analysis—change a few of the assumptions and see what the results are. Mr. Douglas wonders, for example, what would be the effect on net income in the year 1993 if sales in that year increased by 10%; of course expenses are sure to increase with sales. Costs of goods sold, for example, increase as more of Know-wear products are sold. Mr. Douglas esti-

Know-Wear, Inc.

Five-year financial plan
(in thousands)

Page 1

Date: 12/31/89

Income statements for the year ending

	Actual 1989	Budget 1990	* Projections 1991	1992	1993	1994	1995 *
Sales	$17,600	$23,100	$28,600	$34,100	$39,000	$44,500	$50,000
Cost of goods sold	11,820	13,000	15,000	18,000	19,412	21,000	23,000
Gross margin	$ 5,780	$10,100	$13,600	$16,100	$19,588	$23,500	$27,000
Marketing expenses	$ 1,300	$ 1,900	$ 2,600	$ 3,800	$ 4,131	$ 4,900	$ 5,250
Administrative expenses	986	1,100	1,300	1,400	1,500	1,750	1,980
Miscellaneous expenses	371	480	560	640	700	790	810
Total expenses	$ 2,657	$ 3,480	$ 4,460	$ 5,840	$ 6,331	$ 7,440	$ 8,040
Net income before taxes	$ 3,123	$ 6,620	$ 9,140	$10,260	$13,257	$16,060	$18,960
Federal taxes	1,624	3,442	4,753	5,335	6,894	8,351	9,859
Net income after taxes	$ 1,499	$ 3,178	$ 4,387	$ 4,925	$ 6,363	$ 7,709	$ 9,101

Figure 14-3 Projected income statement. These are projected ("pro forma") financial statements of income for Know-wear for the years 1991–1995. The numbers were derived using a DSS.

mates these increased costs and the results are shown in Figure 14-5: projected sales increased from $39 million to $42.9 million while net income went from about $6.4 million to $6.8 million. (Note that to obtain higher sales, higher expenses must be projected, also.)

The CEO is also interested in goal seeking—setting net income at a certain value and determining what level of sales is needed to achieve that specific net income. This is shown in Figure 14-6: if the goal is a net income of $7 million in 1993 and a large increase in expenses is assumed in that year, the DSS shows that sales of over $74 million are needed. Note that if expenses continue to increase in the years 1994 and 1995, the company's net income will drop severely.

Know-Wear, Inc.	Five-year financial plan (in thousands)						Page 1
	Balance sheets as of year end						Date: 12/31/89
	Actual 1989	Budget 1990	Projections 1991	1992	1993	1994	1995
Current Assets:							
Cash	$ 2,100	$ 2,500	$ 2,600	$ 2,700	$ 2,900	$ 3,300	$ 3,700
Accounts receivable	2,800	3,000	3,200	3,600	4,200	4,700	4,900
Inventory	3,100	3,900	4,200	4,500	4,800	5,300	5,500
Total current assets	$ 8,000	$ 9,400	$10,000	$10,800	$11,900	$13,300	$14,100
Fixed assets:							
Equipment	$ 1,200	$ 2,000	$ 2,200	$ 2,300	$ 2,600	$ 2,700	$ 2,900
Buildings	1,200	1,600	1,900	1,998	2,103	2,211	2,314
Total fixed assets	$ 2,400	$ 3,600	$ 4,100	$ 4,298	$ 4,703	$ 4,911	$ 5,214
Total assets	$10,400	$13,000	$14,100	$15,098	$16,603	$18,211	$19,314
Current liabilities:							
Accounts payable	$ 2,400	$ 2,600	$ 2,900	$ 3,300	$ 3,700	$ 3,750	$ 3,950
Wages payable	84	96	102	108	141	148	156
Taxes payable	1,411	1,712	1,950	2,111	2,300	2,450	2,510
Total current liabilities	$ 3,895	$ 4,408	$ 4,952	$ 5,519	$ 6,141	$ 6,348	$ 6,616
Long-term liabilities:							
Notes payable	$ 3,400	$ 4,600	$ 4,511	$ 4,700	$ 5,000	$ 6,111	$ 6,211
Total long-term liabilities	$ 3,400	$ 4,600	$ 4,511	$ 4,700	$ 5,000	$ 6,111	$ 6,211
Total liabilities	$ 7,295	$ 9,008	$ 9,463	$10,219	$11,141	$12,459	$12,827
Owner's equity	3,105	3,992	4,637	4,879	5,462	5,752	6,487
Total liabilities and owner's equity	$10,400	$13,000	$14,100	$15,098	$16,603	$18,211	$19,314

Figure 14-4 Projected balance sheet. The projected balance sheet of Know-wear's assets and liabilities and owner's equity covers the years 1991–1995.

Beyond DSS

So far in this book, we have written about computer-based information systems that aid or support decision making. Is it possible systems could be devised to *replace* human decision making? The answer is: They already have been.

Programmed decision systems (PDSs), which use operational data to produce decisions, are effective in situations that are so structured that decisions can be clearly defined without intervening judgment. Unlike DSSs, which support decision making, typical programmed decision systems make decisions that once were handled by human decision mak-

Know-Wear, Inc.

Five-year financial plan
(in thousands)

Page 1

Income statements for the year ending

Date: 12/31/89

	Actual	Budget	*		Projections		*
	1989	1990	1991	1992	1993	1994	1995
Sales	$17,600	$23,100	$28,600	$34,100	$42,900	$44,500	$50,000
Cost of goods sold	11,820	13,000	15,000	18,000	21,000	21,000	23,000
Gross margin	$ 5,780	$10,100	$13,600	$16,100	$21,900	$23,500	$27,000
Marketing expenses	$ 1,300	$ 1,900	$ 2,600	$ 3,800	$ 4,524	$ 4,900	$ 5,250
Administrative expenses	986	1,100	1,300	1,400	2,000	1,750	1,980
Miscellaneous expenses	371	480	560	640	1,208	790	810
Total expenses	$ 2,657	$ 3,480	$ 4,460	$ 5,840	$ 7,732	$ 7,440	$ 8,040
Net income before taxes	$ 3,123	$ 6,620	$ 9,140	$10,260	$14,168	$16,060	$18,960
Federal taxes	1,624	3,442	4,753	5,335	7,367	8,351	9,859
Net income after taxes	$ 1,499	$ 3,178	$ 4,387	$ 4,925	$ 6,801	$ 7,709	$ 9,101

Figure 14-5 What-if analysis: revised income statement. Using the DSS, Know-wear top management has changed the figures in the column for the year 1993 to reflect a 10% sales increase.

ers. Common uses of PDSs include loan and credit approval, inventory reordering, and IRS audit decisions. Such decisions have become so routine and defined that they now can be programmed by precisely stating decision rules that will dictate the decision for every combination of circumstances. These decision rules are incorporated into software so that certain operational input data will cause the appropriate action to be taken.

To demonstrate the different uses of OIS, MIS, DSS, and now PDS, consider Know-wear's inventory of raw materials—in this case, bolts of Irish tweed. The receipt and use of raw materials is recorded in an OIS through transaction processing. A report summarizing the level of raw material inventory is produced by the MIS. An analysis of the length of time over a year that the Irish tweed is held in inventory is performed

Know-Wear, Inc.

Five-year financial plan
(in thousands)

Page 1

Income statements for the year ending

Date: 12/31/89

	Actual	Budget	*		Projections		*
	1989	1990	1991	1992	1993	1994	1995
Sales	$17,600	$23,100	$28,600	$34,100	$74,472	$76,000	$78,000
Cost of goods sold	11,820	13,000	15,000	18,000	35,851	36,011	37,499
Gross margin	$ 5,780	$10,100	$13,600	$16,100	$38,621	$39,989	$40,501
Marketing expenses	$ 1,300	$ 1,900	$ 2,600	$ 3,800	$10,252	$14,000	$14,100
Administrative expenses	986	1,100	1,300	1,400	7,611	9,700	9,700
Miscellaneous expenses	371	480	560	640	6,175	8,613	8,620
Total expenses	$ 2,657	$ 3,480	$ 4,460	$ 5,840	$24,083	$32,313	$32,420
Net income before taxes	$ 3,123	$ 6,620	$ 9,140	$10,260	$14,583	$ 7,676	$ 8,081
Federal taxes	1,624	3,442	4,753	5,335	7,583	3,992	4,202
Net income after taxes	$ 1,499	$ 3,178	$ 4,387	$ 4,925	$ 7,000	$ 3,684	$ 3,879

Figure 14-6 Goal-seeking analysis. Know-wear's CEO has set net income at $7 million in 1993 and assumed a large increase in expenses. The DSS shows that sales of over $74 million are needed to achieve that goal. (Numbers in Figures 14-3 through 14-6 are expressed in thousands of dollars: 74,472 means "$74,472,000.") Note that if expenses continue to increase in the years 1994 and 1995, net income will drop.

using a DSS. Finally, the automatic reordering of the cloth once its inventory has reached a certain specified level is accomplished by the PDS.

The Need for Strategic Vision

Where is a company going? This is the biggest "what-if" question of all. A company needs a strategic plan, and a decision support system is critical in helping explore the alternatives to achieving that plan, as we have suggested throughout this chapter.

But something more than a strategic plan is required. "We are restructuring from a society run by short-term considerations and rewards in favor of dealing with things in much longer time frames." This is another one of the so-called megatrends or "restructurings" identified by futurist John Naisbitt. This trend will also have an important effect on information systems, says the University of Colorado's Professor Couger:

> Short-term approaches are turning to long-term. We must reconceptualize what business we are in, or conceptualize what business it would be useful for us to think we are in. . . .
>
> Strategic planning is worthless unless there is first a strategic vision. A strategic vision is a clear image of what you want to achieve, which then organizes and instructs every step toward that goal. The extraordinarily successful strategic vision for the National Aeronautics and Space Administration was, "Put a man on the moon by the end of the decade." That vision gave magnetic direction to the entire organization. Nobody had to be told or reminded of where the organization was going. Contrast the organizing focus of putting a man on the moon by the end of the decade with, "We are going to be the world leader in space exploration."
>
> In a constantly changing world, strategic planning is not enough; it becomes planning for its own sake. Strategic planning must be geared to a strategic vision with a clarity that remains in spite of the confusion natural to the first stages of change.

This may mark the end of your apprenticeship at Know-wear. Whether you stay on and begin a climb through the management ranks or move on to another company or industry, at least you have some basic knowledge of the new tools available to a manager. Of course, there is always more to learn, and in Part 5 we will move on to information resource management, security and privacy, and exciting possibilities for the future.

SUMMARY

- A **decision support system (DSS)** is a set of computer programs and hardware intended primarily to help top managers arrange information from various sources in new and different ways. A DSS must be flexible and interactive— immediately accessible through an interactive terminal.
- The distinctions among the three kinds of management systems are: (1) OIS generates data from the firm's transactions and operations—such as a payroll system that processes employee time cards, produces employee paychecks, and records appropriate journal accounting entries. (2) MIS provides structured reports for management—for example, quarterly labor analysis reports that summarize labor costs. (3) DSS supports management decision

making with analysis of semistructured and unstructured problems—for example, trends in salaries within a particular job classification over the last five years.

- A DSS has three parts: decision, support, and system.
- The *decision* part includes seven activities: searching, specifying, computing, assimilating, drawing inferences, deciding, communicating. (1) Searching is for available facts, figures, and reports. (2) Specifying means defining the problem precisely, eliminating some alternatives and revealing new ones. (3) Computing is a mathematical and statistical manipulation of data. (4) Assimilating is pulling together of the accumulated facts, reports, and summaries. (5) Drawing inferences is arriving at conclusions from the data and computations. (6) Deciding is decision making based on the assimilated facts and inferences. (7) Communicating is conveying the decision to those people who are affected by it.
- The *support* aspect of the DSS helps managers make sense of the information glut by facilitating the seven decision tasks: (1) Searching is enhanced by large data bases containing numeric and text data. (2) Specifying and (3) computing are helped by computational models, such as electronic spreadsheets. (4) Assimilating, (5) drawing inferences, and (6) deciding are helped by computer graphics. (7) Communicating is assisted with word processing and telecommunications.
- The *system* part of a DSS combines the strengths of both people and computers: the speed, access, and computational power of computers and the creativity, reasoning, and perspective of people. Paired in a DSS, they increase the effectiveness of management decisions.
- **Management science (MS)** is the application of quantitative techniques or models to the analysis of management problems. **Models** are ideas, hypothetical notions that consist of technical recommendations and procedures for analyzing and solving complex management problems.
- The three types of MS models are: (1) **Optimization** models, used to identify the optimal (best) solution in very specialized problems. The best known such model is linear programming, used in the oil industry for scheduling refinery operations. (2) **Heuristics** is a set of rules for solving a particular type of problem—for example, authorizing loan applications. (3) **Simulation** models represent complex problems by conceptualizing them and describing them mathematically. Simulation models are used to determine allocations of a firm's resources, such as projecting a company's capital available for investment.
- In setting up a DSS, a company must consider three aspects: (1) which of two types of DSS, ad hoc or institutional; (2) the performance objectives; and (3) the building blocks of the DSS—hardware, software, and decision makers.

- The two *types of DSS* are: (1) **Ad hoc,** or general, DSSs, designed to handle a variety of management problems, especially those that are unexpected and nonrecurring. (2) **Institutional** DSSs, specialized systems using terminology and analysis procedures established within certain areas, such as medicine or advertising.
- The *performance objectives* of a DSS are: (1) To support all management levels—top, middle, supervisory—in all phases of decision making. DSSs support the planning activities of middle and upper management and the decision-making activities of all managers in all phases of decision making. (2) To analyze unexpected problems, which account for about 80% of all managerial decision making and which usually require action in a very short period of time. (3) To integrate information flow and decision-making activities, especially horizontally at the higher management levels; generally the information is in the form of reports communicating decisions and coordinating problem-solving activities and so must flow easily in and out of the organization's data base. (4) To be easy to use yet powerful and flexible—a crucial matter because DSS users are managers, not programmers.
- The three *building blocks* of a DSS are: (1) hardware, (2) software, and (3) the decision maker.
- The two most important pieces of *hardware* in a DSS are: (1) Interactive graphic terminals, since graphics capabilities are essential to produce charts and graphs and managers must have a natural, responsive interaction with the DSS software. (2) Telecommunications networks, which let managers share data and reports, quickly coordinate problem solving activities, and have access to data bases within and outside the organization.
- Four types of *software* are needed in a DSS: (1) A data base management system (DBMS), which extends the range of data that can be collected, retrieved, and analyzed and which allows managers to interact with the firm's transaction data bases as well as with external data bases. (2) **Simulation and application languages,** which allow decision makers to do model building—to develop their own models and to purchase custom-made models. (3) **DSS executive software,** which acts like an operating system in that it handles many of the operational duties for the DSS and monitors and coordinates DSS activities. (4) A DSS **query language,** an easily understood language that is necessary for managers to communicate with the DSS.
- The *decision maker* is the human element, playing one or more of the three roles for interacting with the DSS: (1) the model builder, who conceptualizes and develops the model; (2) the model user, who actually runs it; and (3) the decision maker, who analyzes the results of the model, makes any modifications, and comes to the final decision.
- The output for a DSS depends on the problem under investigation. It may be in (1) pictorial format, such as charts or graphs on a graphic terminal, or (2) report format, such as expected sales or output.

- Two common forms of DSS output are pro forma balance sheets and pro forma income statements. **Pro forma** means "projected." Pro forma statements are used for performing (1) **what-if analysis,** changing assumptions to see what might result, and (2) **goal-seeking analysis,** stating a goal and the variables influencing it to see what is required to achieve that goal.
- **Financial planning languages (FPLs)** evolved from high-level languages into institutional DSSs and from there into ad hoc DSSs. FPLs have a financial orientation but are flexible, and they now are used in a variety of decision support roles.
- **Programmed decision systems (PDSs)** use operational data to produce decisions in structured situations with clearly defined judgment criteria. Unlike DSSs, which support decision making, PDSs *replace* human decision making.

KEY TERMS

Ad hoc DSS, p. 492
Decision support system, p. 487
DSS executive software, p. 499
Financial planning language (FPL), p. 493
Goal-seeking analysis, p. 501
Heuristics, p. 491
Institutional DSS, p. 493
Management science (MS), p. 491
Model, p. 499
Optimization model, p. 491
Pro forma, p. 501
Programmed decision system (PDS), p. 503
Query language, p. 499
Simulation, p. 492
Simulation and application languages, p. 499
What-if analysis, p. 501

REVIEW QUESTIONS

1. What percentage of a manager's decision making is in response to unexpected problems?
2. Describe a DSS. What types of situations and decisions does it support that an MIS would not?
3. What are the distinctions among the three kinds of management systems: OIS, MIS, DSS?
4. What are the seven activities common to decision making? How are these activities supported by the DSS?
5. What is a model?

6. Name the three types of models. Which is most effective in business organizations?
7. Describe the two types of DSS.
8. Describe the four types of software needed in a DSS.

CASE PROBLEMS

Case 14-1: DSS for Sales and Merchandising

In Chicago, retail giant Sears, Roebuck "is constantly searching to learn who its customers are, what they like, what they are avoiding, how they are changing," reports *Time* magazine (August 20, 1984). "Through one of the largest systems of IBM computers outside the U.S. Government, the company keeps track of what is being bought and where."[3] The head of the Merchandising Group each morning calls up on his CRT terminal a display that can tell him the dollar volume of all Sears stores the previous day. "He can also look at sales figures by region, specific store or product line." In Rocky Mount, North Carolina, Boddie-Noell Enterprises, Inc., which operates 208 Hardee's fast-food restaurants, has an information system that is tied to each restaurant's own computer and each cash register. As an article in *Inc.* (September 1984) describes it, "Number of transactions, nonfood sales, net sales, paid insurance, total cash, promotion, eat in, eat out, drive through, cash short, tax—every action of the [restaurant] unit's life is chronicled in glowing green."[4] In Visalia, California, considered a microcosm of the West Coast's "Middle America," a supermarket checkout scanner "notes every brand, package size and price and logs the information in a computer file on [a customer's] family's buying habits."[5] Detailed information on the family's purchases is sent to Chicago, where, along with information on other families, it is studied by marketing experts. (All families have volunteered for the project.) The data is used by many consumer product companies, including General Foods, General Mills, and Procter & Gamble, to measure how new-product sales compare to that of competitors and to analyze consumer buying trends.

Your assignment: These examples show how some of the biggest names in American business use computer-based information systems to make major decisions about merchandising. Let us suppose you are the owner of a muffler shop or of a fabric and yardage store and are considering expanding into a chain of stores. You thus have some sales and merchandising experience to go by, but you clearly have a number of strategic what-if and goal-seeking questions to ask. What kinds of questions would they be and what kinds of information variables might you have to manipulate?

case problems continue on p. 511.

CORPORATE REPORT 5

Computers for Decision Making: The Tasks of Business

What is the task of a manager? Management is the process of transforming resources—materials, money, employees, and facilities—into products or services. This means that the primary activity of managers is to *make decisions*. The decisions are in five areas: organizing people and resources; communicating requirements to subordinates and superiors; staffing, including hiring and training; planning, including identifying opportunities and problems; and controlling, including monitoring performance.

To make these kinds of decisions, of course, managers need information. But the *kind* of information managers need depends on their level—supervisory, middle, or top. It also depends on the department they are in: Marketing, Accounting and Finance, Production, Research and Development—or a new one, Information Processing. The Information Revolution promises to change the character of these departments. This Corporate Report takes a look at the use of computers as a business tool for decision making.

The Business Pyramid and the Information Pyramid

A business may be viewed as a pyramid with three levels of management divided into four business departments. Information systems, consisting of data bases of relevant information, can be designed to resemble the pyramidal organization:

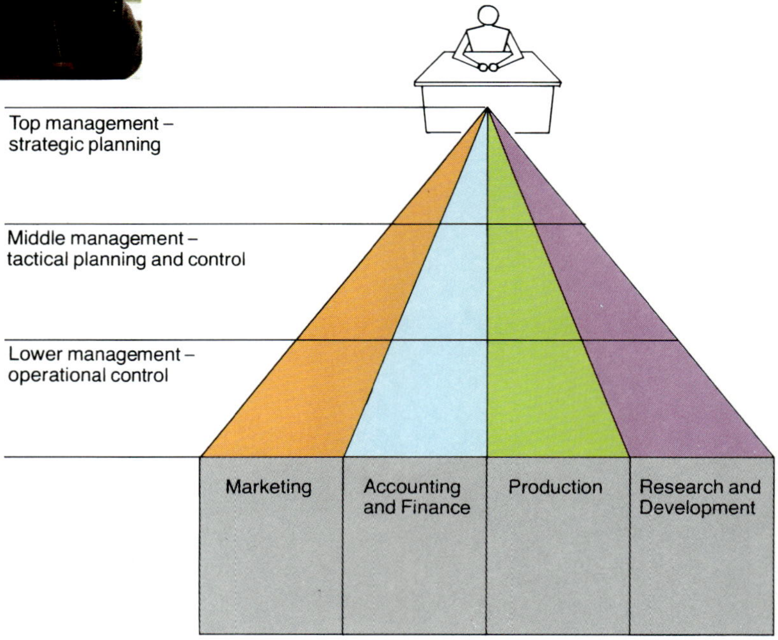
Top management – strategic planning
Middle management – tactical planning and control
Lower management – operational control
Marketing
Accounting and Finance
Production
Research and Development

- Operations information systems (OISs) are for supervisory managers, who need highly structured, routine, and present-oriented information, such as production schedules and inventory records. OISs provide detailed, specific information on day-to-day operations.
- Management information systems (MISs) are for middle managers, who need more internal than external information, such as budgets and sales forecasts. Because MISs have access to all departmental data bases, they provide reports that are more summarized to assist in tactical planning and control.
- Decision support systems (DSSs) are for top managers, who have the greatest uncertainty and so need both internal and external information. DSSs provide information for strategic planning—support for "what-if" questions and goal-seeking analysis that will help top managers make decisions about new markets and new products.

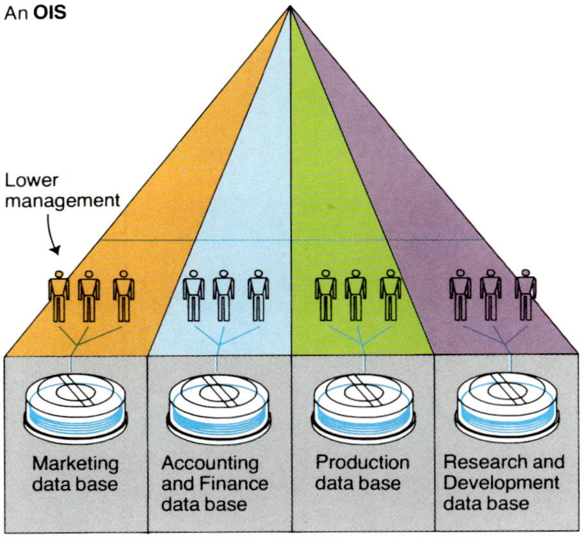
An OIS
Lower management
Marketing data base
Accounting and Finance data base
Production data base
Research and Development data base

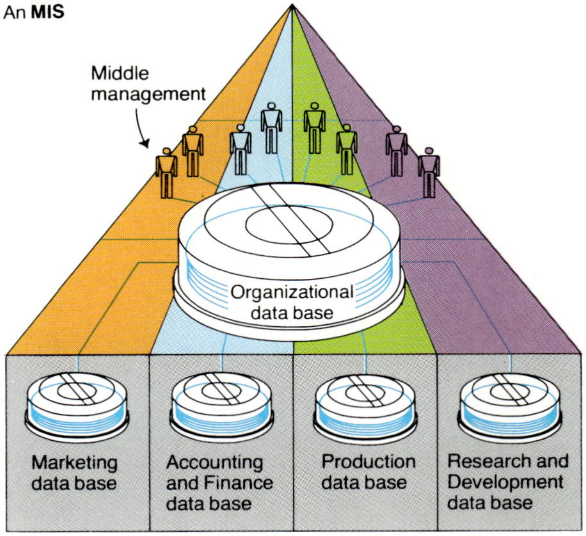
An MIS
Middle management
Organizational data base
Marketing data base
Accounting and Finance data base
Production data base
Research and Development data base

Marketing

Marketing is concerned with sales forecasting, advertising, pricing, selling, and the movement of goods to market. Top managers find that computers are limited for making marketing decisions—but then so are people. Combined in a DSS, however, they are powerful: people offer creativity, reasoning, and perspective, and computers offer speed, access, and computational power. Together they produce a service that affects the quality of management decisions.

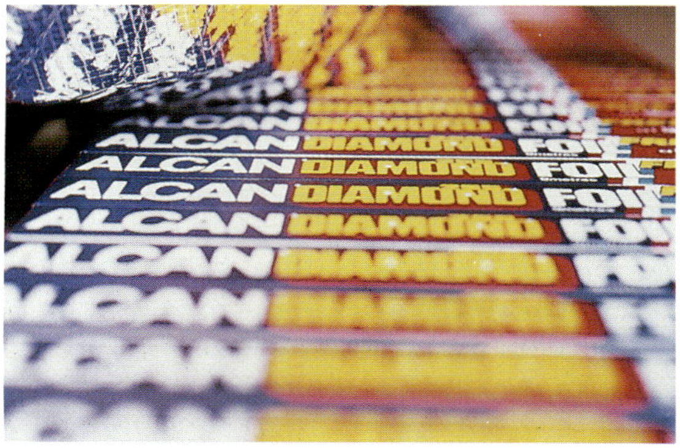
ALCAN
DIAMOND

Accounting and Finance

The Accounting and Finance department is concerned with generating and investing capital—that is, money—and with such tasks as payroll, accounts receivable, and accounts payable. Accounting and finance decision-makers, then, can make good use of electronic spreadsheets, statistical packages, and—as shown here—computer graphics.

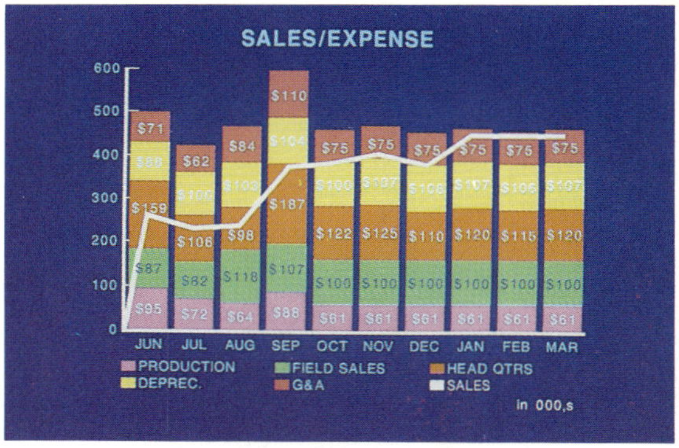
SALES/EXPENSE
600
500
400
300
200
100
0
$71 $159 $87 $95
$62 $106 $82 $72
$84 $98 $118 $64
$110 $104 $187 $107 $88
$75 $100 $122 $100 $61
$75 $107 $125 $100 $61
$75 $110 $100 $61
$75 $107 $120 $100 $61
$75 $115 $100 $61
$75 $107 $120 $100 $61
JUN JUL AUG SEP OCT NOV DEC JAN FEB MAR
PRODUCTION
FIELD SALES
HEAD QTRS
DEPREC.
G&A
SALES
in 000,s

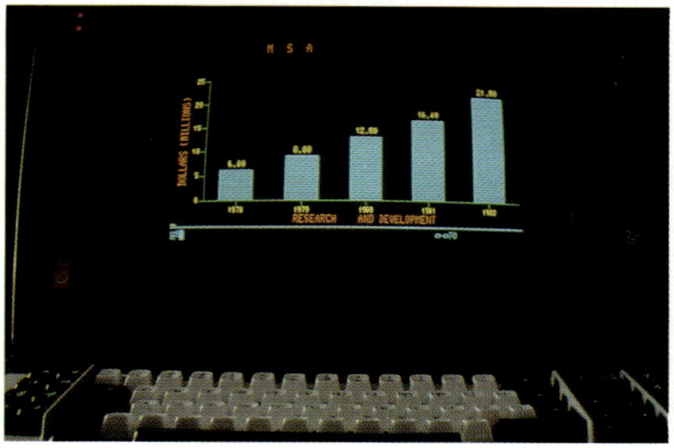

MANAGING THE MICRO MIX

One of the classic complaints against the data processing department has been that it is slow to get reports and information to other departments, such as Marketing or Accounting and Finance. The availability of microcomputers and business applications software has begun to alleviate this problem—but it has created others.

In many companies, individuals and departments have bought computers one by one, without any overall plan for their use. The result has been uncontrolled costs and computers that are unable to work together.

Recently, as companies have begun to realize the importance of information as a corporate resource—as evidenced by establishing the position of information resource manager *(see last page of this Corporate Report)*—top executives have taken the long-range view and encouraged policies that make microcomputers interact smoothly with other parts of the corporate information system.

Production

The Production Department of a company is concerned with purchasing raw materials, production scheduling, and inventory control (monitoring goods on hand). Whether the goods being produced are capsules, croissants, or Cummins engines, computer-based information systems help managers compare prices, determine the number of units in a warehouse, and anticipate bottlenecks on production lines. Of course computers—factory robots, for instance—are also widely used in the physical production of the goods themselves.

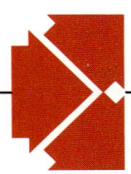

Research and Development

The lifeblood of a company, innovation—development of new products and improvement of existing ones—is the job of Research and Development. Here is where top managers may benefit by the "what-if" capability of a DSS. Although it can be quite difficult to estimate the cost of something that has not happened yet, a manager must try to gauge the gap between what may be too risky and what may be missed opportunity: What if there is no oil discovered within *x* months? What if it costs *y* dollars to develop this drug? Computers are also used in the actual research and development process: design of new drugs, geological explorations, development of new computer chips.

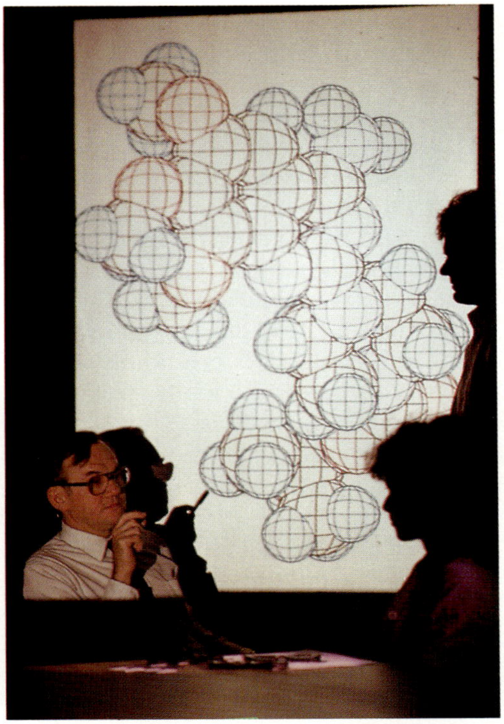

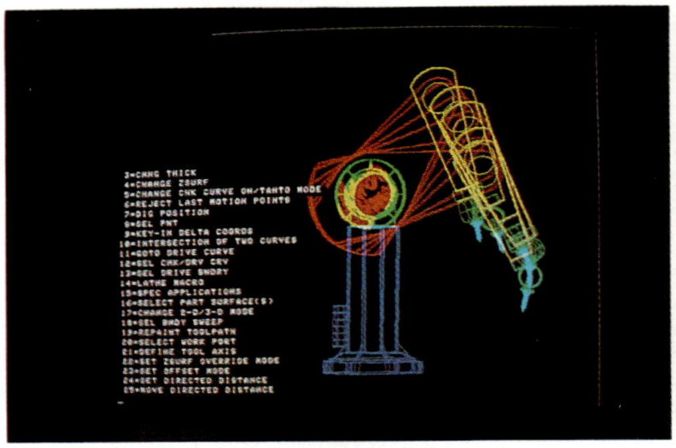

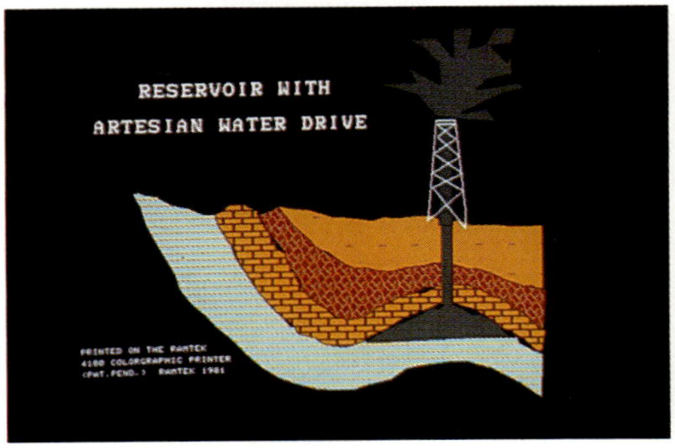
RESERVOIR WITH
ARTESIAN WATER DRIVE
PRINTED ON THE RAMTEK
4100 COLORGRAPHIC PRINTER
(PAT. PEND.) RAMTEK 1981

Information Resource Management

The decisions of the top executives of Marketing, Accounting and Finance, Production, and Research and Development can be no better than the business information on which they are based. Many companies have begun to realize, therefore, that information must be treated as a corporate asset—an asset as valuable as any other, if not more so. This means that someone in a position of authority must be in charge of corporate information.

Accordingly, forward-looking companies usually have a manager of information resources—someone who coordinates and directs managers of office systems, data base systems, and systems analysis and design activities; who makes sure the company's information remains secure and private; who keeps current with the technology; and who acts as a source of advice and training for others within the organization. Clearly, this is an important job, and many companies have recognized this fact by elevating the manager of information resources to the same level as the heads of the other principal departments—that is, to the vice-presidential level.

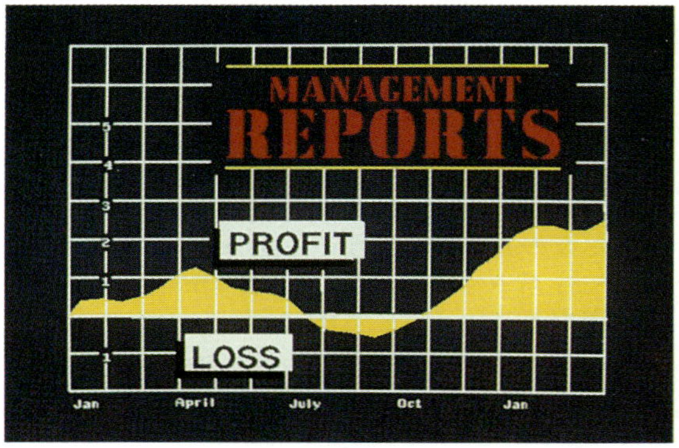
MANAGEMENT
REPORTS
PROFIT
LOSS
Jan
April
July
Oct
Jan

Case 14-2: Creating Your Own Models

In a September 1984 article in *Business Computing,* Professor David Ness, of the Wharton School at the University of Pennsylvania, states he believes that many people do not really want decision support software; rather, they want to enter data relating to their problem into their computer and have the computer make the decision for them. Ness argues that "the real value of any decision support activity is very often in the modeling stage rather than in the results stage. Because numbers are simply numbers. But by learning and talking about your business, you start to understand how to make decisions regardless of what the numbers say."[6] Creating your own models helps you become a better decision maker. Lotus 1-2-3, for example, though not promoted as a decision support tool, helps a manager get used to thinking about problem solving by thinking about each unique level of the management hierarchy—supervisory (operations decisions), middle management (tactical decisions), and top management (strategic decisions). This kind of decision support software is the reverse of the kind that step the user through a series of questions about his or her business.

Your assignment: Do you agree with Ness's reasoning? Why or why not?

Part 5

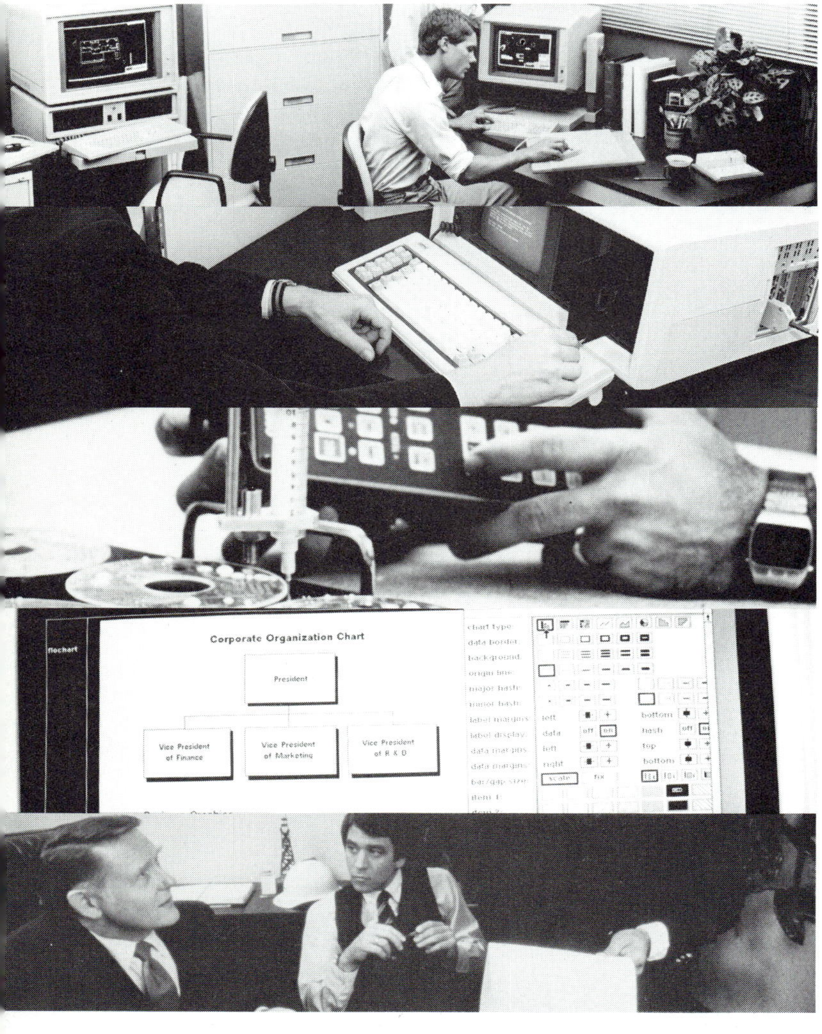
flochart
Corporate Organization Chart
President
Vice President of Finance
Vice President of Marketing
Vice President of R & D
chart type
data border
background
origin line
major hash
minor hash
label margins
label display
data margins
bar/gap size
item 1
left
data
right
scale
fix
bottom
hash
top
off
on

The Rewards and Risks of the Information Age

The value of information is, like beauty, in the eye of the beholder or user. Data that is meaningless to one person may be pure gold to another. Regardless, information *is* one of the most valuable assets today—both to you personally and to business organizations generally.

However, the problem with information is not the lack of it, as we have seen. The problem is to better understand the information that is usually already there. The need is for increased *productivity*—to make better use of people's time. Although it is difficult to measure productivity improvements of managers and other professionals, it is among this group that the greatest gains are possible.

Clearly, the computer offers one of the best opportunities here—for improving both personal productivity, as in the use of word processing and electronic spreadsheets, and corporate productivity, as in providing access to the data generated by an OIS, MIS, or DSS. It is important to recognize the computer for what it is. It is an exceptionally powerful tool for today and an indispensable tool for tomorrow. However, though it is an incredibly fast and accurate device, the computer has no intelligence. Humans are what give it intelligence.

In the next three chapters, we will describe both the rewards and the dangers of the information revolution. First we will describe the evolution in information systems. Then we will describe security of information. Finally, we will consider the future, including robotics, artificial intelligence, expert systems, query languages—and what these all mean for your future career.

CHAPTER 15

Managing Information Resources

More Integration, More Ease of Use, More Business Power

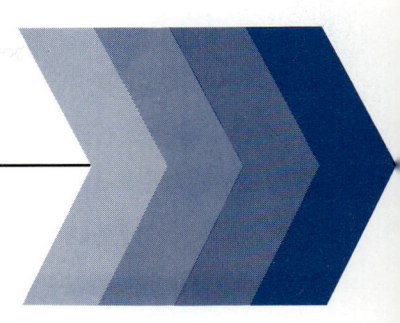

There are all kinds of myths and misconceptions about technology. Lowell Steele, a veteran of 29 years at General Electric, points out that many managers think the "best possible" technology should be obtained, expect most innovative efforts to be successful, put greater reliance on the development of new technology than on extensions of what is currently available, and trust that companies are indeed competent to make use of technical advances.[1] Such misconceptions can have long-term consequences.

Yet if new technology—in particular, information technology—offers the risk of vulnerability, it also offers the opportunity for a competitive edge, as the box on the next page shows.

PREVIEW

The Challenge of Using Information Technology

Should a company try to adopt information technology as a strategic resource? F. Warren McFarlan suggests only if it can answer "yes" to the following five questions:[2]

- **Can information technology keep your competitors away from your customers?** McFarlan points out that customers do not want devices from different vendors on their premises, nor do they want to go to the trouble of learning complex software all over again after they have already learned another package. Thus, if a financial services company installs or sells its customers an attractive financial product that depends on sophisticated software, competitors will find it difficult to catch up—particularly if the original company keeps on improving the product and software, making itself a moving target.

CASE STUDY: INFORMATION OF VALUE

Information Technology Changes the Way You Compete

- To solve customer service problems, a major distributor installs an on-line network to its key customers so they can directly enter orders into its computer. The computer's main purpose is to cut order-entry costs and to provide more flexibility to customers in the time and process of order submission. The system yields a larger competitive advantage, adding value for customers and a substantial rise in their sales. The resulting sharp increase in the company's market share forces a primary competitor into a corporate reorganization and a massive systems development effort to contain the damage, but these corrective actions have gained only partial success.
- A regional airline testifies before the U.S. Congress that it has been badly hurt by the reservation system of a national carrier. It claims that the larger airline, through access to the reservation levels on every one of the smaller line's flights, can pinpoint all mutually competitive routes where the regional is performing well and take competitive pricing and service action. Since the regional airline lacks access to the bigger carrier's data, it allegedly is at a decided competitive disadvantage.
- A large aerospace company has required major suppliers to acquire CAD (computer-aided design) equipment to link directly to its CAD installation. It claims this has dramatically reduced total cost and time of design changes, parts acquisition, and inventory, making it more competitive.

These examples are not unusual. With great speed, the sharp reduction in the cost of information systems (IS) technology (i.e., computers, remote devices, and telecommunications) has allowed computer systems to move from applications for back-office support to those offering significant competitive advantage. Particularly outstanding are systems that link customer and supplier. Though such links offer an opportunity for a competitive edge, they also bring a risk of strategic vulnerability. In the case of the aerospace manufacturer, operating procedures have shown much improvement, but this has been at the cost of vastly greater dependence, since it is now much harder for the manufacturer to change suppliers.

In many cases, the new technology has opened up a singular, one-time opportunity for a company to redeploy its assets and rethink its strategy. The technology has given the organization the potential for forging sharp new tools that can produce lasting gains in market share.

—F. Warren McFarlan, *Harvard Business Review,* May–June 1984

- **Will the information technology make it difficult for customers to switch to competitors?** "Are there ways to encourage customers to rely increasingly on the supplier's electronic support," asks McFarlan, "building it into their operations so that increased operational dependence and normal human inertia make switching to a competitor unattractive?" An example, he points out, is electronic home banking. When a customer has learned to use the system and coded all the creditors for that system, he or she will find it inconvenient to change banks.
- **Can the technology change the basis of competition?** Some competition is based on costs, and information technology may help to lower costs. Other competition is based on product differentiation, but "dramatic cost reduction can significantly alter the old ground rules of competition," McFarlan says. An example, he says, is the situation of airlines that are trying to get their on-line reservations systems into travel agencies; by positioning their flight recommendations on the CRT screen, the airlines can influence the travel agent's purchase recommendations.
- **Can information technology change the balance of power in supplier relationships?** Interorganizational systems can redistribute power between buyer and supplier. A furniture retailer was linked to order-entry systems of different sofa suppliers, and the one with the lowest rate got the order. The retailer also, said McFarlan, continually monitors the suppliers' finished-goods inventories, factory scheduling, and commitments against the schedule to make sure inventory will be available to meet his unexpected demand, giving him considerable control over the suppliers.
- **Can information technology generate new products?** Information systems technology, says McFarlan, "can lead to products that are

of higher quality, that can be delivered faster, or that are cheaper. Similarly, at little extra cost, existing products can be tailored to customers' needs."

These are the challenges that may well confront you as a future decision maker.

Past as Prologue: Where Are We Heading?

Sometimes it is difficult to see the forest for the trees. Let us, therefore, briefly review where we have been in order to have a clearer idea of where we are going.

Toward Integration and Ease of Use

In the last eleven chapters, we have examined software, hardware, and systems separately. Let us now reexamine them and see how they are evolving and how they fit together into an information processing system.

Software. All the advances in computers would be of limited value without software to instruct the computers to perform operations. Historically, businesses developed their own software, mainly to run large computers and operations information systems. Recently, the trend has been toward purchasing integrated packages, both for microcomputers and for mainframes. As we have seen, integrated software packages combine word processing, electronic spreadsheets, and file management as well as graphics capabilities. Such packages are capable of creating a data base of information, maintaining it, and retrieving information from it.

For both users and programmers, structured programming concepts have greatly improved the efficiency of the programming process. Applications languages also are being developed that are very high level and much more user friendly, which benefits nontechnical users. The evolution in software is toward integrated software packages and higher-level user-friendly languages. The key words are "integration" and "ease of use."

Hardware. Technology is the driving force of the information revolution, and this technology is centered on improvements in hardware. Here are some of the recent developments:

- **Input devices:** These are now designed to eliminate data entry steps by allowing direct data entry from source documents, thereby reducing human errors and removing the need for batch data entry.
- **Output devices:** These are becoming more varied, more reliable, and faster. High-quality output devices are readily affordable for low-

cost computer systems. Graphics terminals and printers have greatly extended the capability of presenting output.

- **CPUs:** Integrated circuits are less expensive, faster, and more reliable—microcomputers have CPUs that surpass the power of mainframe CPUs of only a few years ago. The processors of tomorrow promise to be even more powerful.
- **Secondary storage devices:** These allow more information to be stored and retrieved than would have been thought possible a few years ago; large data bases now can be created and maintained relatively easily.
- **Data communications:** The communication links that allow the integration and common sharing of various information resources are constantly improving.
- **Microcomputers:** One of the most dramatic hardware advances, the microcomputer, when combined with communication links, can give users a wide variety of powers, from solving individual problems locally to calling up information from large centralized data bases. The microcomputer is a tool that enhances personal productivity, whereas the mainframe or minicomputer is a corporate tool.

As with software, the evolution in hardware has been toward integration of equipment, using communication systems, and the development of ever more user-friendly capabilities. Especially important is the capability to integrate microcomputers into an organization's total computer information system through data communication links.

Systems. As we have seen, within large organizations, computer applications can be categorized into three areas—operations information systems (OISs), management information systems (MISs), and decision support systems (DSSs). OISs focus on record keeping and clerical operations. MISs focus on management reports. DSSs focus on supporting decision-making and planning activities. Although each system is separate and performs a distinct function within the organization, all require and use a common data base of corporate information. The revolution in information systems is in the development of DSSs and the use of common data bases inside and outside the organization. The result is, once again, making information more integrated and user friendly. The key to this integration has been the recent development of powerful yet easy to use data base management systems that allow OIS, MIS, and DSS systems to efficiently share common data.

The Tripod of Information Processing

Software, hardware, and systems describe the architecture or tools used in information processing, but they do not describe the *activity* of information processing. What is it, in fact, that users actually *do* when they process information?

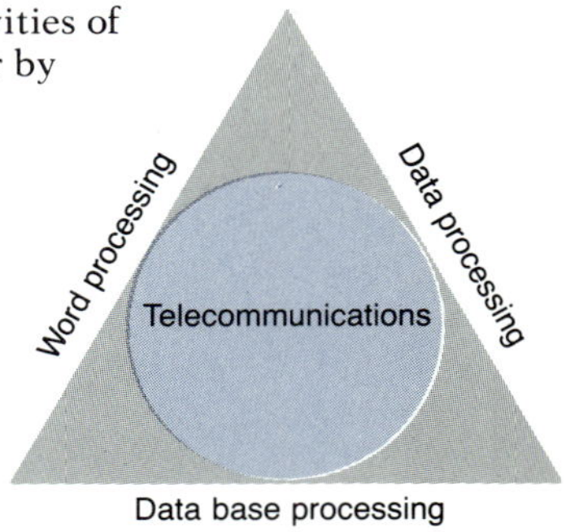
Word processing
Data processing
Telecommunications
Data base processing

Figure 15-1 Tripod. These three activities of information processing are tied together by telecommunications.

As Figure 15-1 shows, there are three activities of processing information:

- Word processing
- Data processing
- Data base processing

These three legs form a "tripod" of information processing that is connected by a common element: telecommunications. Let us review these activities.

Word Processing. Because one hears the phrase "data processing" so often, it is tempting to think that computers process numbers all the time. Actually, 90% of all symbols processed by a company are *words*. Ninety percent of all information is recorded by characters, not numbers. Thus, word processing—by which we mean any creation, storage, and retrieval of textual data or information—is truly a most significant use of computers.

Data Processing. There is a great deal of difference between word processing and data processing. Data processing operates on data according to a logical set of instructions (the program) and requires human interaction primarily for monitoring. Word processing, on the other hand, is concerned with words, sentences, and paragraphs and requires constant human interaction to interpret and manipulate the text; logical definitions and instructions will not suffice. When compared to word processing tasks, data processing tasks seem to have had more importance attached to them. The reasons may lie in the fact that "data processing" had its origins in government military and space projects, whereas "word processing" evolved out of clerical and secretarial work. But, as we have shown, word processing is no longer just for secretaries. Managers and professionals of all types use both data and word processing, but particularly the latter. They spend much more time creating and retrieving text—written reports, management directives, sales forecasts—than analyzing pure numeric data.

Data Base Processing. Data base systems capable of storing both numeric and text data are the foundation of any information processing system. Data processing and word processing provide the data that make up a data base. If you are a sales manager, for instance, you will want to be able to pull sales figures (numeric data) and long-range sales promotions (text data) from a data base. Originally, computer files were organized like the paper-records files that preceded them, but when it was discovered that this only led to increased volumes of files and inefficient computer use, data base management systems were developed to make optimal use of computers and their storage devices. Nearly all data base systems currently operate principally on numeric data. However, text management systems are being rapidly developed, and records in the form of data, text, image, and voice are a certainty in the future.

Telecommunications. The importance of telecommunications to information processing cannot be overstated. It is what integrates the three activities of information processing: word processing, data processing,

Telecommunications. Telephonic and data communications technology—represented by Chicago's Sears Tower antennas—provides the means for networks, which in turn lead to new business activities such as home banking.

and data base processing. As we have been demonstrating, it allows users at various locations to have access to common information as well as to each other.

In Search of Synergism

The significance of telecommunications can truly be expressed in the word **synergism:** the total effect of the activities of information processing is greater than the sum of the effects taken independently. In other words, one technology not only allows another technology to develop but also expands its capability and influence.

The synergistic effect is seen in networks, which allow users to gain access to data on computers, text on word processors, images on microfilm, and voice on the network itself. The telecommunications permitted by the network is the underlying technology of the automated office. It is what allows us to use electronic mail, voice messaging, teleconferencing, data base access, and so on.

All these marvels are possible today. The question is: just how advanced are most organizations in this scheme of things? We turn, therefore, from this review of past concepts to a consideration of the present.

Where Is Information Processing Today?

If you have any contact with present business organizations, it may seem to you we are describing some fairly idealized concepts. How many executives are in fact using teleconferencing, executive workstations, and the like?

An organization with a full-blown integrated, user-friendly information processing system does not develop overnight, of course. It is achieved in stages. This evolutionary process is shown in Table 15-1. In general, progressive computer-using organizations have followed four stages of evolution:

- Initiation
- Contagion
- Control
- Integration

As the table shows, these have roughly paralleled developments of the last four decades and have gone from little user involvement to more user involvement, from loose planning and control of information to tighter planning and control. However, some firms today, those that have just purchased their first computers, will be just beginning—in the

Table 15-1 **Stages in the Evolution of Information Processing Systems.** The four stages in the history of this evolution also correspond to the four stages a company goes through when implementing a computer-based information system.

Characteristic	I Initiation	II Contagion	III Control	IV Integration
Time	1950s	1960s	1970s	1980s
Applications	OIS	OIS	MIS	DSS
User involvement and awareness	None	Superficially enthusiastic	Accountable, with limited control	Accountable and controllable
Planning and control of information processing department (computer resources)	Loose budget, minimal controls	Internal planning and control	Formalized control and planning	Long-range planning and improved control

initiation stage. Most firms are in either the second or third stage. Only the most advanced are in the last.

Let us see what happens in these four stages.

Stage 1: Initiation

In the **initiation** stage, an organization has purchased its first computer, and there is a great deal of excitement. There are high expectations—usually too high—which must be brought into line.

Applications programs are purchased or developed which focus on elementary transaction processing for accounting and clerical operations. Because the company's interest is in replacing manual procedures, there is usually some employee concern and even unrest.

Access to the computer and involvement by users generally is carefully controlled and in fact typically discouraged. Computer technical support people are hired, which generally proves upsetting to the existing salary scale for noncomputer technical personnel, since computer support people command higher salaries. The computer department—which later will probably come to be known as the information processing department—has very free reign and loose managerial budget control.

Stage 2: Contagion

In this stage, computer applications become infectious. Although the focus is still on transaction processing, computer applications spread into areas other than accounting. The full range of operations information systems (OISs) technology is brought in to support accounting and other selected applications.

Computerization and displacement. In the contagion stage in the evolution of an information system, some employees—such as certain garment or automobile workers—may be displaced from their jobs by automation. Often they are transferred to other jobs or simply not replaced when they quit or retire.

Many manual operations are computerized, resulting in the loss of some jobs. Some employees are displaced from their jobs, usually by being transferred to other activities or by not being replaced when they leave. Although users' expectations are not as high as they were during the initiation stage, there is still a great deal of enthusiasm. Upper management is now better able to control operations in the computer department, and some formal internal planning and control begin to emerge.

Stage 3: Control

Once an OIS has been developed and is operating well, the next step in the evolution of information processing is the development of an MIS, a management information system to control operations. In this stage, management has a better tool to control corporate resources. User involvement also increases greatly; there is a high degree of interaction between the computer department and the various other functional business areas, at least at the managerial level. Information processing is freed from "the computer room," which is no longer considered a mysterious cave.

Users now are held more accountable for the computer resources that they request and require, and this requires more careful planning and control of the computer department. In fact, control of the department begins to increase significantly. Systems analysts begin to be quite active. Requests for services for systems analysis and design exceed capabilities, and backlogs result. This in turn forces more accountability from the computer department—which by now probably has been upgraded to the information processing department.

Stage 4: Integration

In the final stage, the organization builds on the previous OIS and MIS to develop more fully integrated information systems. This is the stage at which decision support systems (DSSs) emerge.

Networks that were introduced in the previous stage are now heavily used and effectively integrate hardware, software, and systems. Users have easy access to the information system and interact with it on a regular basis. Correspondingly, they are also held accountable for the system's use.

The information processing system becomes much more of a user-oriented system, with the computer department—now information systems department—allocating much of its resources toward maintaining existing programs and data bases. The management of the department becomes more actively involved with long-range planning and developing improved methods of controlling their operations.

Telecommunications systems allow convenient access to people and information located at various remote sites, with external as well as internal data bases. The computer is used much more effectively as a tool for decision making by managers.

Want Ad: The Need for Management

Very few companies are yet into the integration stage. Indeed, even for firms in this stage, the pace of evolution toward highly integrated systems is rather slow.

Why have so few companies achieved what is technologically feasible and so clearly beneficial to their operations? It is certainly not because of hardware limitations. Advances in hardware have outpaced applications. Software *could* be a reason for holding back, but, as we have seen, the activity and pace of software development has been accelerating. Systems could also be a limitation. However, OIS and MIS are well-developed concepts; only DSS still needs some refining, although the pace of development here is accelerating also.

The *real* reason for the slow progression toward integrated information processing systems can be expressed in one word: management. There is a lack of management support for and understanding of high technology and a lack of managers with capabilities in this area.

Although information is crucial to every manager's operations—indeed, crucial to everyone within the organization—no one is really

Wanted: forward-looking managers. The biggest reason for the slow progression toward integrated information processing systems is that there is a lack of management support for and understanding of high technology and a lack of managers with capabilities in this area.

managing information in most companies. Rather, everyone assumes that "information is everybody's business"—which means, paradoxically, it is really *nobody's* business. There is a strong need for managerial expertise to control and plan for information processing. The technology needs to be managed by people who will look at it not as an end but as a means—as a tool for improving the organization's performance and productivity.

What kind of people would make such managers? (Would *you* make such a manager?) Data processing people would seem to be the most natural source, since they know the technology and are usually good at applying it. However, their business knowledge is usually limited.

The problem stems from the fact that the philosophy of most organizations has been to isolate the technical people, taking them out of the mainstream of business operations so that they can concentrate on developing and implementing computer technology—which means, of course, that they become more involved with technology than with business.

The need, then, is for information managers who possess managerial and business skills as well as knowledge of technology. Actually, the problem is twofold:

- There is a need to establish managerial positions within the organization—managerial positions with real clout—with the responsibility for information processing.
- There is a need to find individuals with the correct combination of technical and managerial skills to fill these positions.

To address these needs, a new concept has recently emerged—that of information resource management.

Information Resource Management

Information resource management recognizes that information systems technology changes the way you do business and the way you compete. It realizes that computer resources have shifted from closed-shop DP departments to open, user-oriented organizations. It recognizes that there is a real need for business people to understand how to use information.

Information resource management (IRM) is the concept that information should be viewed as a corporate resource and managed accordingly. This means that computer hardware, software, systems, and personnel require careful management for the benefit of the entire organization. Fragmented and overlapping information functions should be combined and placed under the control of a senior information executive, a director of information management.

The Director of Information Management

What would be the job description of a director of information management? He or she would have at least four responsibilities:

- Coordinate and give direction to the managers of data base systems, systems analysis and design activities, management science applications, telecommunications, and office systems. The supervisors or middle managers in charge of these tasks are shown in Figure 15-2.
- Help other people in the company cope with change in technology, information needs, and health concerns. **Ergonomics,** the study of human factors related to computing, is discussed in the box on pp. 528–529.
- Keep up with changes in technology. However, the director of information management is a generalist—the details of new technology are left to the specialists.
- Keep information secure and private files private. This issue will be discussed further in Chapter 16.

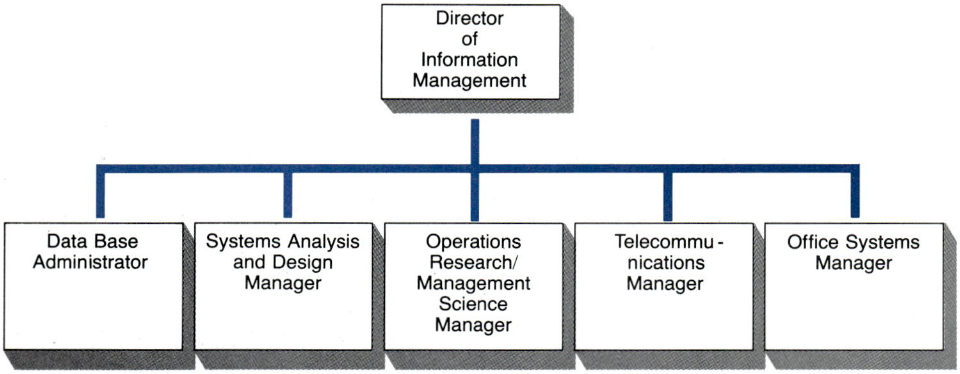
Director
of
Information
Management
Data Base Administrator
Systems Analysis and Design Manager
Operations Research/ Management Science Manager
Telecommu-nications Manager
Office Systems Manager

Figure 15-2 The tasks of the director of information management. The supervisors reporting to the director of information management are shown in this chart.

ERGONOMICS IN THE OFFICE

Workstations, Productivity, and Health

People such as clerical workers who work long hours at CRT screens—also called video display terminals (VDTs)—may complain of eye strain, headaches, back and neck problems, and feelings of irritability and stress. Some have even expressed concerns about the long-range effects of low-level radiation, and others have worried about the possibility of pregnant VDT operators having miscarriages or giving birth to babies with birth defects.

Such concerns have contributed to *ergonomics*, the study of human factors related to computing. "Ergonomics" has become a buzzword in the advertising of computer-related equipment, because business customers are vitally interested in purchasing equipment that will increase the productivity of the people using it. One recent ergonomic furniture design is the Jefferson lounge chair designed by industrial designer Niels Diffrient. This $3500 system pivots much as the body does at the waist and hips; the headrest supports the neck, and surfaces can be lifted or lowered, tilted or joined in various ways so that one is actually leaning back and stretched out while working—even for executive-style desk work. Diffrient's invention represents ergonomics in its more radical form; however, the National Institute for Occupational Safety and Health (NIOSH) has made some recommendations about such matters as heights of keyboards and positioning of CRT screens (see illustration).

Many postural and vision-related complaints are the result of improperly arranged workstations and faulty equipment. Chairs should provide back support and be easily adjustable; when seated, one's feet should be flat on the floor, legs clearing the underside of the worktable, and thighs parallel to the floor. Keyboards should be detachable. Workstations should be located so that there is no glare on the CRT screen from bright overhead lights or windows; an adjustable, shaded copy lamp should be provided for the operator. The screen should be adjustable for brightness, contrast, and flicker control. Green

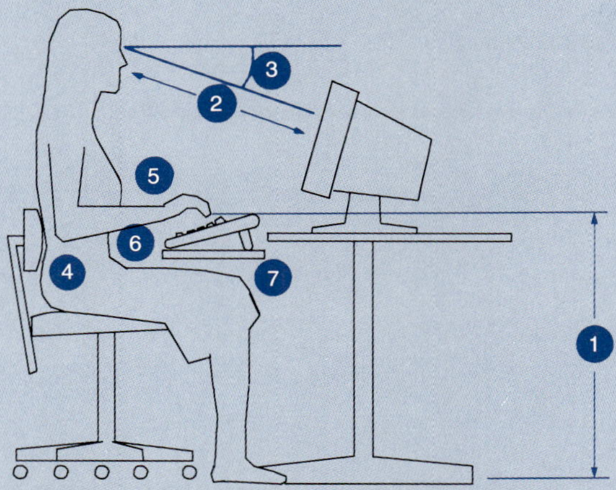
3
2
5
6
4
7
1

Workstation design. In its publication *Potential Health Hazards of Video Display Terminals*, the National Institute for Occupational Safety and Health makes the following recommendations: ❶ The European recommmendation for the height of the home row keys is $28\frac{1}{4}$ to $29\frac{1}{2}$ inches. The U.S. military standard is $29\frac{1}{4}$ to 31 inches. ❷ The viewing distance should be between $17\frac{1}{4}$ and $19\frac{3}{4}$ inches, with a maximum of $27\frac{1}{2}$ inches. ❸ Generally, the center of the screen should be at a position between 10 and 20 degrees below the horizontal plane at the operator's eye height. One researcher recommends that the top of the screen be below eye height, another that the top line of the display be 10 to 15 degrees below the horizontal, with no portion of the screen at an angle greater than 40 degrees below the horizontal. ❹ One researcher recommends that the angle between the upper and lower arms be between 80 and 120 degrees. ❺ The angle of the wrist should be no greater than 10 degrees. ❻ The keyboard should be at or below elbow height. ❼ Don't forget enough room for your legs—feet should be flat on the floor and thighs parallel to the floor.

on black or amber on black are the best CRT screen color combinations; white on black is legible, but may have more flicker than green displays.

NIOSH recommends eye-care exams before people start working on CRT screens. Operators should not wear sunglasses, tinted lenses, or phototropic lenses that adjust to brightness while working with CRTs.

Reasonably frequent movement or breaks are important. CRT operators do not move as much as previously because the machines eliminate much of the need to get up and down for files, paper, and so on. Sitting in one place for a long period of time can induce fatigue. Operators should not work for more than an hour and a half without a break, and some experts believe operators should not use computers for more than four or five hours a day.

Computer-related stress, it has been found, is not as apt to occur among managers, who generally find that computers enhance their jobs by reducing tedium and giving them more information. However, many clerical workers have found that CRTs can make their jobs more tedious and stressful. The stress often comes about because the computer can keep count of the operator's keystrokes and thus constantly evaluates the operator's productivity—even when he or she is having some off days. Some clerical operators feel over-monitored by their supervisors.

At one point there were some suggestions that low-level radiation emitted from CRTs might cause eye problems, in particular cataracts. However, the radiation is well below present government standards, and the issue remains unsettled. (Some newspapers have put radiation-reducing shields around the CRTs used by their reporters and editors.) There have also been concerns that CRTs may have been the cause of miscarriages and birth defects among newborns of pregnant women. Although female CRT operators are asking to change job assignments during pregnancy, there is no evidence yet that CRTs are injurious in this respect.[3]

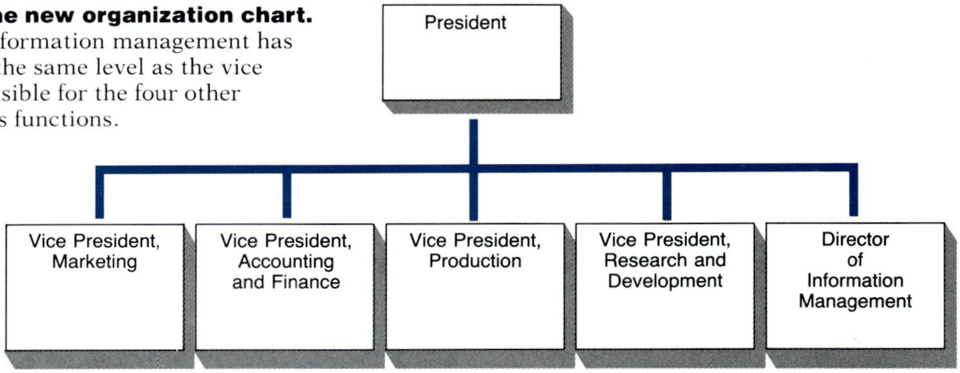
President
Vice President, Marketing
Vice President, Accounting and Finance
Vice President, Production
Vice President, Research and Development
Director of Information Management

Figure 15-3 The new organization chart. The director of information management has been elevated to the same level as the vice presidents responsible for the four other principal business functions.

Organization: The Need for Clout

It is not enough just to *have* a director of information management. That director must have clout within the organization.

Clout does not come from having brains or energy or strong personality; it comes from having power within the organization. Power stems from position. The lack of a high organizational position for a director of information management has been identified by many observers as one of the major obstacles to the rapid evolution of integrated information processing.

In many firms, the information processing department reports directly to the vice president of Accounting and Finance, a logical outgrowth of the time when information processing consisted mainly of OIS and clerical and accounting operations. However, this kind of reporting limits the perspective and capabilities of the information processing system.

In other firms, the information processing department reports to *all* the functional vice presidents—not just Accounting and Finance, but Marketing, Production, and Research and Development as well. This scheme, however, has the drawbacks of a servant trying to serve too many masters.

Companies that have adopted an IRM orientation as a philosophical position have elevated the director of information management to the vice presidential level, with the same access to the company president as that of other vice presidents (see Figure 15-3). From this position, the company's information processing system can evolve in an integrating fashion, under the direction of a manager with organizational clout and broad perspective.

Onward: Is IRM Big Brother?

If IRM is so good, why have more firms not adopted it? The signs are that the vast majority will in the near future. Those that do not are simply not ready to accept the intangible nature of information; they have difficulty acknowledging that it should be treated as a resource like any other corporate resource. However, one interesting reason there may be some reluctance is that to many people IRM sounds like a dictatorial Big Brother watching. In management, information means power: the more you know, the more secure your position. Other managers fear that a director of information management might have the potential to limit, control, and select the information available to others in the organization—and thereby limit their power.

Security and privacy are responsibilities of the director of information management but should be major concerns of everyone who deals with computers—including you. We turn to these issues in the next chapter.

SUMMARY

- A company should adopt information technology as a strategic resource if it can answer yes to the following five questions: (1) Can information technology keep your competitors away from your customers? (2) Will the information technology make it difficult for customers to switch to competitors? (3) Can the technology change the basis of competition? (4) Can the technology change the balance of power in supplier relationships? (5) Can information technology generate new products?
- Software is what makes the advances in computers valuable. Historically, businesses developed their own software, mainly to run large computers and operational information systems. Recently, businesses have been purchasing integrated packages, for both microcomputers and mainframes. The evolution in software is toward integrated packages and higher-level user-friendly languages. The key words are "integration" and "ease of use."
- Technological improvements in hardware are central to the information revolution: (1) Input devices now are designed to allow direct entry from source documents, thereby reducing human error and removing the need for batch data entry. (2) Output devices are becoming more varied, more reliable, and faster. High-quality output devices such as graphics terminals and printers are readily affordable for low-cost computer systems. (3) CPUs have integrated circuits that are less expensive, faster, and more reliable; today's microcomputers have CPUs that surpass those of mainframes only a few years ago. (4) Secondary storage devices allow storage and retrieval of more information than imaginable a few years ago; large data bases now can be created and maintained relatively easily. (5) Data communications, which allow the integration and common sharing of various information resources, are constantly improving. (6) Microcomputers, a dramatic advance,

can be combined with data communications to give users a wide variety of powers, from solving individual problems locally to calling up information from large centralized data bases.

- Computer applications systems can be categorized into three areas: (1) Operations information systems (OISs) focus on record keeping and clerical operations. (2) Management information systems (MISs) focus on management reports. (3) Decision support systems (DSSs) focus on supporting decision-making and planning activities. Each separate system performs a distinct function, but all use a common data base of corporate information. The revolution in information systems is in the development of DSSs and the use of common data bases inside and outside the organization.
- The three activities of processing information are: (1) word processing, (2) data processing, (3) data base processing. This "tripod" of information processing is connected by a common element: telecommunications.
- Word processing—the creation, storage, and retrieval of textual data or information—is by far the most significant use of computers, accounting for 90% of all symbols processed by a company.
- Data processing—work with numerical data—operates according to a logical set of instructions, or program, with little human interaction; it makes up the remaining 10% of a company's activity.
- Data base processing—the storing of both numeric and text data—is the foundation of any information processing system. Computer files organized like the paper files that preceded them led to increased file volume and inefficient computer use, so data base management systems were developed to make optimal use of computers and their storage devices. Nearly all data base systems currently operate on numeric data, but text management systems and records in the form of data, text, image, and voice are a certainty in the near future.
- Telecommunications is what integrates word processing, data processing, and data base processing. It allows users at various locations to have access to common information as well as to each other.
- **Synergism** expresses the significance of telecommunications: the total effect of information processing activities is greater than the sum of the effects taken independently. One technology not only allows another technology to develop but also expands its capability and influence.
- An organization with a full-blown integrated, user-friendly information processing system develops in stages, generally: (1) initiation, (2) contagion, (3) control, and (4) integration.
- In stage 1,**initiation,** an organization purchases its first computer and purchases or develops applications programs for elementary transaction processing of accounting and clerical operations. This stage is characterized by high expectations (usually too high), some employee concern or even

unrest, controlled access to the computer, hiring of computer technical support people, and loose managerial budget control of the computer department.

- In stage 2, **contagion,** computer applications spread into other areas besides accounting. The full range of OIS technology is brought in to support accounting and other applications. Many previously manual operations are replaced, some employees are displaced, and although expectations are more realistic, enthusiasm is still high. Upper management has better control of operations in the computer department, and some formal internal planning and control begin to emerge.
- Stage 3, **control,** occurs with the development of an MIS to control operations after the OISs have been developed. Management now has a better tool to control corporate resources. User involvement with the computer department increases, especially at the managerial level. Users are held more accountable for the computer resources they use, necessitating more planning and control of the computer department. Systems analysts become quite active, requests for services for systems analysis and design exceed capabilities, and backlogs result. This forces more accountability from the computer department—which now may be called the information processing department.
- In stage 4, **integration,** the organization builds on the OIS and MIS to develop more fully integrated information systems such as DSSs. Networks integrating hardware, software, and systems are heavily used; users have regular access to and interaction with the information system and are accountable for its use; and managers use the computer more effectively for decision-making support. The computer department allocates much of its resources toward maintaining existing programs and data bases, and department management is more actively involved in long-range planning and control of their operations. Through telecommunications, remote hardware is integrated with both internal and external data bases.
- **Information resource management (IRM)** is the concept that information should be viewed and managed as a corporate resource. Computer hardware, software, systems, and personnel require careful management to benefit the entire organization; information functions should be under the control of a senior information executive, a director of information management.
- The director of information management has four major responsibilities: (1) Coordinate and direct managers of data base systems, systems analysis and design activities, management science applications, telecommunications, and office systems. (2) Help other people in the company cope with change in technology, information needs, and health concerns, including **ergonomics**—the study of human factors related to computing. (3) Keep up with changes in technology. (4) Keep information secure and private.

KEY TERMS

Contagion, p. 523
Control, p. 524
Ergonomics, p. 527
Information resource management (IRM), p. 527
Initiation, p. 523
Integration, p. 525
Synergism, p. 522

REVIEW QUESTIONS

1. Describe some of the recent developments in software. In hardware. In systems.
2. What are the three activities that make up the tripod of information processing?
3. What is the synergistic effect of telecommunications on information processing?
4. Describe the developing information processing system in an organization as it passes through the four stages of evolution.
5. What is the real reason for the slow progression toward integrated information systems in most companies today?
6. Define information resource management.
7. What are the four basic duties of the director of information management?

CASE PROBLEMS

Case 15-1: The Interrupt-Driven Day

A phrase that describes the environment of many office workers is the "interrupt-driven day." One writer characterizes such people thus: "Teeming with ideas and eager to tackle them, these people are incessantly pestered by phone calls, meetings, conferences, loquacious co-workers, visitors and more phone calls."[4] The result, unfortunately, is that they have trouble getting work done because they cannot get time to think. Other observers just find this a characteristic of the way people do things: "There's a tremendous need to be able to work on an interrupt basis. . . .That's how humans work. They get started on one project, get interrupted and then have to spend five minutes on another project."[5]

However the "interrupt-driven day" is viewed, some enterprising spirits see some new technological ways of coping with it. One is the portable computer, which allows people to be productive whenever and wherever they can get time. The other is "windowing" or the "desktop environment," software that allows one to be involved with several applications programs—spreadsheets, word processing, data base, and so on—at once through overlapping windows on the CRT screen. Most windowing software allows the user to "zoom in" on one window and hide the others. Often a mouse is used to move the cursor, rather than a series of keystrokes. What is important here is the ease with which one may interchange programs—something that has not been possible with microcomputers in the past.

Your assignment: Manpower Inc., one of the world's largest providers of temporary typists and stenographers, has operated since 1948 by testing people looking for part-time work and then placing them in jobs. The *Wall Street Journal* (February 6, 1984) reported that recently Manpower started a program to train temporaries to use word processors in an effort to become the dominant supplier of operators for these machines.[6] Suppose you were an executive in a temporary-help firm like Manpower. You would probably have a high interrupt-driven day, as calls came in for temporary help (from different industries with different seasonal and personnel needs), as training programs were instituted, and as people called on you for new estimates, budgets, planning memos, and other demands. How would you use the tools described in this chapter to handle your work load and extend the services your firm has to offer?

Case 15-2: The Reading Computer

An interesting and relatively new form of data-entry technology is a device, marketed by Kurzweil Computer Products of Cambridge, Massachusetts, which has the ability to recognize letters and numbers in a great variety of typefaces, a task conventional computers cannot do. According to the *New York Times* (August 19, 1984), the computer "optically examines all sorts of letters for their pattern before recording them at a rate of up to 70 characters a second."[7] The machine is finding use among institutions that need large banks of computerized texts. A Boston publisher, for instance, uses the Kurzweil scanner to record the contents of books that it reprints in large-type editions for the visually impaired. The Nexus news information network uses it to scan newspapers and magazines. The Federal Government is using it to read documents printed in Russian and other languages.

Your assignment: In this chapter, we mentioned the concept of synergism—how one technology not only allows another to develop but also expands its capability and influence. Suppose you were able to acquire the Kurzweil scanner and link it with a large data base and telecommunications capability. How might these be used in some new form of enterprise? Think of the kinds of information that now exist in typewritten or printed form: patent records, legal cases, political speeches, training manuals, geological data, medical histories, recipes, and so on.

CHAPTER 16

Privacy, Security, and Ethics

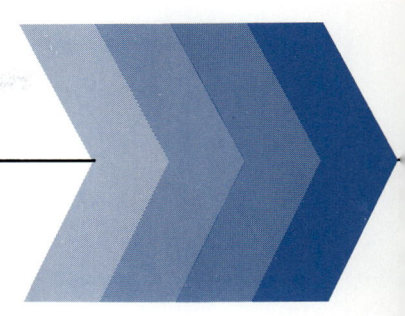

Keeping Information Safe

PREVIEW

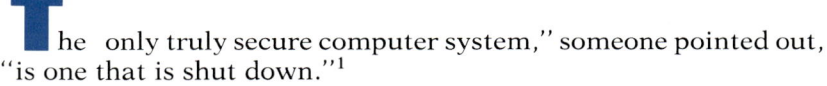

"The only truly secure computer system," someone pointed out, "is one that is shut down."[1]

The remark came in the wake of the discovery in mid-1984 that a subscriber's **password**—the secret words or numbers that must be keyed in before the system will operate—to a major credit bureau had been stolen, making it possible for unauthorized people to cash in on other people's good credit. The credit bureau was TRW Information Services, based in Anaheim, California, with information on the credit histories of over 90 million people—a computerized data base and communications service second in size only to that of the federal government.

What did the thief or thieves, whoever they were, do with the password? Interestingly, they did not keep it to themselves; they allegedly posted it on "electronic bulletin boards" available to microcomputer hobbyists with telephone connections. This meant that **hackers**—the term started out to mean "computer enthusiasts" but now seems to mean people with more malicious intent who invade other people's files and data bases—could have used someone else's credit history to apply for credit cards or charge up bills against that person's credit card account number. In other words, credit fraud would have been possible.

Although hackers would not have been able to enter information to change a file and although no fraud was actually uncovered, the story illustrates just how vulnerable the computer industry remains to breaches in security. It also shows why there is such business interest in security, including, as the box on the next page describes, the new field of **biometrics**—the measurement and use of individual characteristics such as fingerprints as unique identifiers.

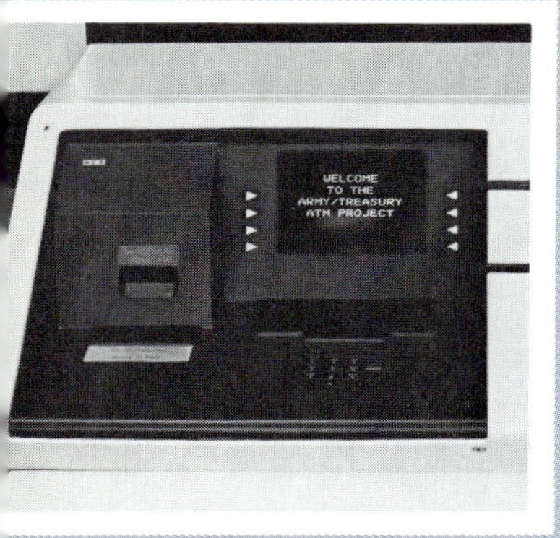
WELCOME
TO THE
ARMY/TREASURY
ATM PROJECT

CASE STUDY: WHAT PRICE SECURITY?

Planning to Outfox Office Security? This Handy Device May Finger You

Michael Schiller, the president of Fingermatrix Inc., is betting on the fingerprint. Other companies are marketing devices based on recognition of signatures, palm geometry, voice patterns, even retinas. All of them hope that the new high-tech biometric security field will burgeon.

One Fingermatrix scanner has been designed for building and room security. To get inside, a worker places two fingers in succession against an electro-optical plate. A laser scans the fingerprints and compares them with images already in its memory bank. When used with an identification number, the odds against an imposter fooling the machine are estimated at 10,000 to one (100,000 to one in the case of the computer device, which is more precise).

Winning the machine's approval isn't easy. People who are careless and don't line up their fingertips precisely may get turned away. At U.S. Navy facilities in Norfolk, Va., for example, Fingermatrix machines barred three out of 10 authorized workers, Mr. Schiller says. Some reacted with open hostility; one man threatened to punt the offending scanner into oblivion. Recently, however, the rate of misreadings has dropped to 5%.

Fingermatrix, based in North White Plains, N.Y., has been in the business since 1976. Barely out of its research and development phase, it has sales of less than $1 million so far, mostly to the government. According to Mr. Schiller, it will take a major breach of present security to rouse the commercial market. "When the first big hit clobbers one of them," says Mr. Schiller, "they're not going to be so particular."

Chase Manhattan Bank experimented with a Fingermatrix device for a year. "It works as well with the toes, by the way," says Richard Beck, a Chase vice president. At First National Bank of Chicago, which purchased four in 1980, executives are still casting about for the best way to use them, says Vice President Donald G. Miller.

First Chicago currently gets one incorrect rejection per 1,000 attempts. Mr. Miller thinks the odds would have to be trimmed to one in 10,000 or one in 100,000 before banks would be prepared to use the device in automatic teller machines.

> While employees can be required to learn to use the machine correctly, the public isn't so malleable, Mr. Miller says. "A customer would blow his stack," he adds, "if this thing came back and told him he isn't who he is."
>
> —Elaine Johnson, *Wall Street Journal*, July 1, 1984

Privacy and Security: Where Personal and Business Meet

Credit checking has become a big business. According to one writer, Robert Heuer, "someone peeks at someone's credit history about a million times a day."

Most such peeks are possible because of the some 2,000 credit bureaus around the country, which gather data on people's bill-paying practices from banks, merchants, and other creditors. Most of these credit bureaus are tied to massive data bases of five major firms (of which TRW is one of the largest). The importance of these big information services has been stated by Heuer as follows:

> Credit grantors rely on credit information services to help reduce bad debt losses, accelerate cash flow, and expand profitable sales. . . .
>
> Accounts receivables for nonfinancial corporations in the United States are becoming an increasingly important item on America's balance sheets, totaling about $500 billion a year, up from $464 billion in 1980. Business bankruptcy is also rising. During 1979, 7,564 failed businesses owed a total of $2.7 billion; a year earlier, 6,691 businesses owed $2.4 billion.
>
> In the last two decades, the average time it takes for a manufacturer to collect receivables has risen from 33 to 43 days. . . . As a result, credit managers are being pressed to speed up their methods for gaining information on a potential client, as well as increasing the number of credit decisions.[2]

Clearly, there is no going back on the trend toward large credit data bases. But the integrity of such data bases depends on two important issues: privacy and security. **Privacy** is primarily a personal concern; it is the assurance to individuals that personal information is accurate, is used properly, and is protected against improper access. Some credit reports include not only credit history, but personal history, including payment records, delinquencies, marital status, employment history, credit card numbers, and credit account limits.

Security is primarily a business concern; it is a system of safeguards designed to protect a computer system and data from deliberate or accidental damage and from access by unauthorized persons. Security is thus concerned with protection against fire, sabotage, and espionage, as well as various kinds of thefts—thefts of computer time, of programs, of data, and of passwords.

The reputed unauthorized use of a password from a TRW client (a Sears store in Sacramento, Calif.) is both a breach of privacy and a breach of security. According to one story, the credit information service itself printed computer access codes and passwords right on the printed reports sent to subscribers, apparently a holdover from a time when such practices presented no problem because home microcomputers were not widely used.[3] The company's computer security, then, appeared to be behind the times. While there were no reported instances of actual violations of privacy, the potential was there.

Let us explore the issues of privacy and security in more detail.

Privacy: How Much Do We Have Left?

Already a great deal of your life is no doubt in a number of computer files and data banks. And there is nothing wrong with that as long as it is kept in the limited form for which it was intended. Employers, physicians, and financial aid officers need to know different things about you; they do not need to know *everything*. Moreover, few of us get through life without having some embarrassments, relationships, financial indiscretions, medical matters, and so on, that we would just as soon not share with most others. We have the legal right to keep such matters to ourselves.

Data Banks: Reaching Beyond the Manila Folder

Keeping personal information private has always been a concern, of course. However, as Harvard Law School professor Arthur Miller has said, "The manila folder just doesn't travel as far as the computer entry."[4] Miller was referring to government surveillance by computers, in which information about citizens is now disseminated more widely than it was during times when information was kept mainly in filing cabinets. There are, for instance, *nine* federal intelligence-gathering agencies (CIA, FBI, National Security Agency, Army, Navy, Air Force, Defense Department, IRS, Secret Service). According to reports filed under the Privacy Act of 1974, there are 3.9 billion records on individuals stored in some 4575 data systems of 97 federal agencies. The smallest number of records is the 23 million in the Department of Labor; the largest is the 853 million

Government data banks. The U.S. Census is a necessary foundation of American democracy. However, a concern of democratic governments is that information be kept private and not be used for unauthorized surveillance of citizens.

in the Treasury Department, which includes the Internal Revenue Service. Of course, state and local governments also have their files, based on taxes, voter and car registration, and so on.

Miller's concern about the way information is treated may be extended to nongovernmental institutions as well. As a *New York Times* writer put it:

> Concern about possible misuse of computers has been growing in the last few years. The questions now being raised center on one aspect of these powerful machines: their use by political groups, private companies and law-enforcement agencies to compile dossiers on virtually anyone by taking bits of information from such sources as telephone directories, drivers' licenses, vehicle registrations, voter registration lists, land ownership records, and birth, marriage and death certificates.
>
> These dossiers are frequently used for purposes far different from those for which the information was originally volunteered.[5]

As an example, the *Times* reported that a major clothing company was able to obtain, for advertising purposes, a list of 63 million licensed drivers to find names and addresses of women under 5 feet 3 inches and less than 120 pounds who were between 21 and 40 years old. In a reverse development—a government agency using business sources—the Internal Revenue Service, in a move to locate tax cheaters, experimented with obtaining lists of high-income households from a commercial marketing company to see if names also appeared on official federal tax rolls.

All you have to do to see how data moves around is subscribe to a magazine or contribute to a worthwhile cause. Sure enough, your mailbox soon becomes stuffed with solicitations to subscribe to other magazines and to contribute to other charities. Indeed, it makes an interesting test to misspell your name slightly or use it in an unusual way (dropping the first name and using only the middle name, for instance), then watch how much unsolicited mail comes to you in that form. But this experiment also shows how *erroneous* information can be entered into computer files and widely circulated—a fact that should give one pause when considering how misinformation in government or credit files can go uncorrected for years.

It is quite likely that a lot of information about you will get into data bases because you volunteer it—for instance, by giving your job history to a computerized employment service. This will become particularly true as computers are used for more and more purposes. While this has some dangers, more worrisome is the kind of data that might be collected about you without your knowledge—from point-of-sale terminals, from teleshopping linked to a home computer, from electronic banking. Indeed, this is a downside risk of the automated office. A Yale University sociologist reports that some major American corporations "collect detailed and apparently trivial data to detect the flow of communication in their organizations," according to the *New York Times*. "Using computers, they gather data such as which executives receive copies of internal memorandums, eat lunch together or converse on the internal telephone system."[6]

Privacy and the Law

"The right to be let alone is the most comprehensive of rights and the right most valued by civilized men," wrote U.S. Supreme Court Justice Louis Brandeis in 1928. Can this right still be protected? Critics say that computer technology includes some methods of information use that currently outstrip the ethical and legal standards for their use. Even so, there are some privacy laws:

- **Fair Credit Reporting Act:** Passed into law in 1970, this law gives you the right to gain access to records kept about you by credit bureaus—and to challenge the records if you think they are inaccurate. This is important because some believe that the credit-reporting business has a poor reputation for maintaining accuracy in its information. TRW Inc., the firm referred to earlier, is said to estimate that a third of the one million people who each year demand to see their records challenge the information they see.[7]

- **Freedom of Information Act:** Also passed in 1970, this law gives ordinary people the right to have access to data gathered by federal agencies about them. Sometimes a lawsuit may be required, and it often takes a great deal of time to obtain the information. In addition, an individual may find that the photocopies of his or her file have been heavily censored—information blacked out—in the interests of national security or some other consideration.
- **Federal Privacy Act:** This act was passed in 1974 in the wake of the Watergate abuses, in which federal agencies were used to try to "get" the Nixon administration's political enemies. The act prohibits secret personal files, stipulates that individuals must be allowed to know what is stored in files about them and how it is used, and extends the restrictions not only to government agencies but also to private contractors dealing with the government. Organizations may not launch "fishing expeditions" for collecting data about individuals; they must justify the effort.

Keeping information private is of vital concern. Part of keeping it private is keeping it secure. Let us examine this aspect next.

Computer Crime, Piracy, and Industrial Espionage: End Runs on Ethics

As Figure 16-1 shows, there are a number of ways by which computer security may be compromised and a number of people in a position to do the compromising. For our purposes, security covers the following multitude of sins and possible problems:

- Computer crime—use of computers to steal money, goods, information, or computer time.
- Piracy—stealing or unauthorized copying of programs or software.
- Industrial espionage—stealing of computer industry trade secrets.

Let us examine each of these.

Computer Crime

Computer crime is big business and is becoming bigger. The American Bar Association (ABA) found in a 1984 survey of 283 business and governmental institutions that *half* were struck by incidents of computer crime in the preceding year. The crimes included unauthorized use of business computers for personal purposes, theft of tangible and intangible assets, and destruction of data. Although the institutions were not

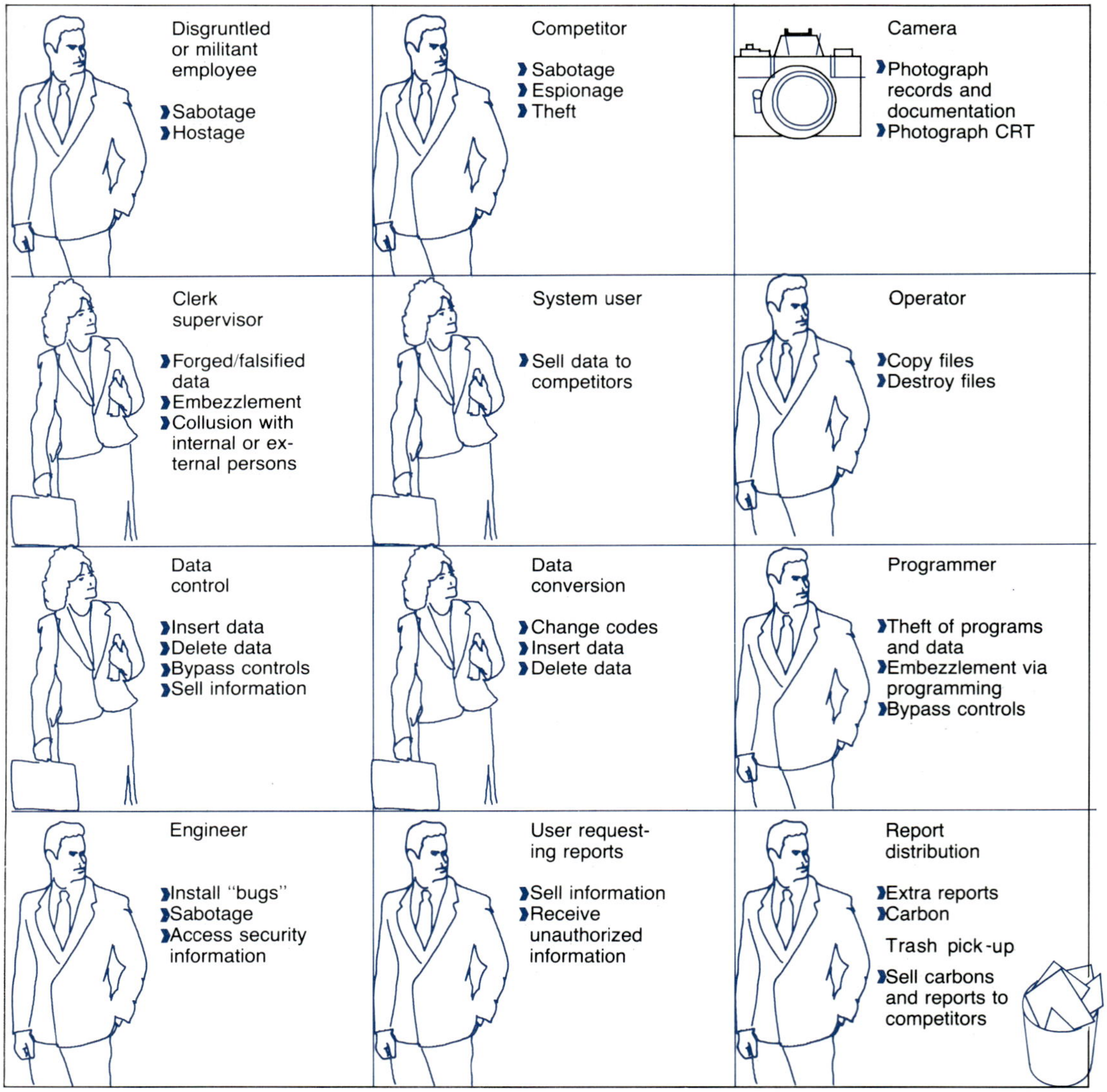
Disgruntled or militant employee
›Sabotage
›Hostage
Competitor
›Sabotage
›Espionage
›Theft
Camera
›Photograph records and documentation
›Photograph CRT
Clerk supervisor
›Forged/falsified data
›Embezzlement
›Collusion with internal or external persons
System user
›Sell data to competitors
Operator
›Copy files
›Destroy files
Data control
›Insert data
›Delete data
›Bypass controls
›Sell information
Data conversion
›Change codes
›Insert data
›Delete data
Programmer
›Theft of programs and data
›Embezzlement via programming
›Bypass controls
Engineer
›Install "bugs"
›Sabotage
›Access security information
User requesting reports
›Sell information
›Receive unauthorized information
Report distribution
›Extra reports
›Carbon
Trash pick-up
›Sell carbons and reports to competitors

Figure 16-1 Computer vulnerabilities. The number of people with access to corporate files and the number of ways at getting at sensitive data are extensive. A company's director of information security must take into account all these possibilities.

a representative sample of public and private institutions, so many of the organizations reported large losses that the ABA felt the problem to be enormous. Indeed, it cited estimates of nationwide losses caused by computer crime that ran as high as $45 billion a year.[8]

What are the various types of computer crime? Some of them are as follows:

- **Theft of computer time:** This happens frequently, and may range from the trivial—people using their employers' computers to type term papers or figure their bowling averages—to the serious, as in the case of two programmers convicted of stealing $244,000 worth of their employer's computer time to rescore music for a private business they were operating on the side.
- **Manipulation of computer programs or data:** This can range from changing one's grades in college computer files to, as happened with the Penn Central computer system, changing instructions so that box cars are sent to deserted tracks where they can be looted. Two tricks of data manipulation are **Trojan Horse,** in which a programmer adds instructions to someone else's program that allow it to work normally but also to do additional illegal things, and **data diddling,** in which data is modified before it goes into a computer file. In one instance, a 17-year-old hacker inserted dirty words into a company's computerized sales lists; the company went out of business until the system was (literally) cleaned up.
- **Theft of data:** This category includes the crimes of hackers who use microcomputers to break into large data banks and data bases, as in the TRW case mentioned earlier. It also includes embezzlements; in one famous case, a former computer consultant for Security Pacific Bank in Los Angeles obtained an electronic funds transfer code and arranged to divert $10 million to a Swiss bank account. One trick of embezzlers, called the **salami method,** is to take only a few cents ("slices") from many bank accounts, so that the small sums will not be missed but the aggregate will be quite large.

The list of crimes using computers is nearly endless. As an example, let us look at the potential security problems for an agency that sells tickets to various musical, theatrical, and sporting events through department stores and other outlets. What can prevent dishonest employees from reserving tickets in fraudulent names, then selling them or "scalping" them at reduced rates? What is to prevent disgruntled employees from sabotaging or erasing ticket reservations for events that are months away—and that will not show up until long after the employees have left? What is to prevent hackers who might work in the ticket outlets from breaking into the agency's system through their home computers? Such are the concerns with which a business now must deal.

ETHICS IN COMPUTING

Criminals and Copiers

What are computer criminals like? Interestingly, they are people you would probably find it easy to socialize with. They are often young, likely to be regarded as ideal employees, usually in positions of trust in their organizations, and usually without previous law-breaking experience. They do not see themselves as stealing but as simply "borrowing." They see the crimes not as crimes but as challenges, all the more so because they are clean and nonviolent acts and because quite often the crimes are reasonably easy to accomplish.

By "computer criminals," we are referring to the white-collar rogues mentioned previously. However, what if you are doing a friend a favor and making a copy on a blank diskette of a microcomputer game that he or she has admired? This may seem like a nice thing to do—except that you have broken the law. Although you are permitted to make a copy for your own backup purposes in case the original is damaged, making duplicate diskettes for other uses is a federal offense, a violation of the U.S. Copyright Code. Yet bootleg copying is so widespread that it is believed there may be as many as ten illegal copies for every legitimate program sold.

"Just one copy can't hurt," people argue, but the copies add up, and the effects are felt in the prices manufacturers must charge for their software. The effects may also be felt in the reluctance of such manufacturers to develop new software packages. Copiers may try to argue that "everyone does it" (so their individual illegal acts of copying will barely be felt or will only make them "even" with everyone else). They may also feel it unlikely that they will be prosecuted, and indeed most software manufacturers find that costly legal fees make court cases impractical.

The real point, however, is that copying software is simply unethical. A lot of effort by programmers and others went into developing the disk, and the developers deserve to be paid for their efforts. Not doing so puts them in the position of a student who spent weeks writing a term paper, only to have someone else photocopy it and turn it in for a grade.

Piracy

Piracy is illegal copying of software. At the level at which you probably will first encounter it, if you have not already, a floppy disk of a commercially developed program is bought at a microcomputer store; the diskette is then duplicated onto a blank diskette (using a microcomputer) for use by others—games for friends, word processing software for fellow students, electronic spreadsheet programs for business colleagues, or whatever. Duplicated disks may be given to friends or, worse yet, sold for a profit. Many software manufacturers try to build in software protection codes to prevent duplication, but there are many computer hobbyists around who enjoy cracking the codes and there is even software available that can break codes.

Piracy also describes the activity of programmers who steal programs from their employers. Although programmers might feel the programs "belong" to them because they developed them, the law states

Industrial espionage. Pharmaceutical companies are particularly vulnerable to industrial espionage—theft or misappropriation of trade secrets—because of the technical nature of their secrets.

that programs belong to the employer. The U.S. Supreme Court has also ruled that software can be patented. The **Copyright Act of 1976** states that flowcharts, source code, and assembly code are copyrightable.

Industrial Espionage

Industrial espionage—the misappropriation of company trade secrets, either by theft or by more subtle means—has always been a problem in the business world. Aerospace, electronics, pharmaceutical, and cosmetic companies are particularly vulnerable because of the technical nature of their secrets.

There are perfectly legitimate ways to gather business intelligence; IBM, for instance, has an elaborate system that relies on detailed reports from its sales force as well as published sources to scout the competition. However, it is quite a step from this to photographing a competitor's factory layout or breaking into another company's data bases. As a company becomes more vested in technology, it must become more watchful of industrial espionage.

In a famous case, IBM security people helped the FBI in 1982 arrest two employees of Japanese computer maker Hitachi, Ltd., who were trying to obtain IBM trade secrets. Hitachi and its employees later pleaded guilty in federal court to conspiring to transport stolen IBM property out of the United States and were given fines of several thousand dollars.

Security Controls

As we indicated earlier in the book, the trend is toward making computers easier to use and information easier to obtain. How, then, does a company keep unauthorized people from getting into its computer system?

There are a number of measures, whose descriptions follow:

Passes and Passwords

Authorized employees may need to have some sort of pass, such as a badge or a card, which they must show to company security guards. Or the card may be magnetized, like the ones used to gain access to an automatic teller machine. This will at least keep unauthorized people away from the computer room. As we mentioned at the beginning of this chapter, the field of biometrics is now being pursued as a way of creating unique identification systems.

In addition, every computer system should require special passwords for access. Passwords should not be obvious—a group of Los Angeles teenagers once penetrated part of a bank's computer system just by trying a few logical passwords. It is advisable to have passwords of at least six characters, which mathematically increases the odds against guessing. Moreover, passwords should be changed randomly and frequently, especially if a great deal of money is at stake.

Technical Controls

As Figure 16-2 shows, security **dial-back devices** can eliminate the problems of access by hackers and former employees. In one such system, when someone dials the computer by telephone and gives a password, the computer then disconnects the caller, checks its files, and dials back the authorized telephone number indicated by the password in the files. This may come to be a standard technical solution in future computer systems.

Encryption devices are another possibility. Data sent over telecommunications lines is encrypted or scrambled—put in code that can be decoded only by an authorized person. The American National Standards Institute has endorsed the **Data Encryption Standard (DES),** a stan-

COMMUNICATIONS CONTROL CENTER
Racal-Milgo
COMMUNICATIONS CONTROL CENTER

Data encryption. Protection of messages during transmission between locations may be accomplished by data encryption devices (such as those shown here with keys), which transform messages into unintelligible form at the point of transmission, then translate them into intelligible form again at their destination.

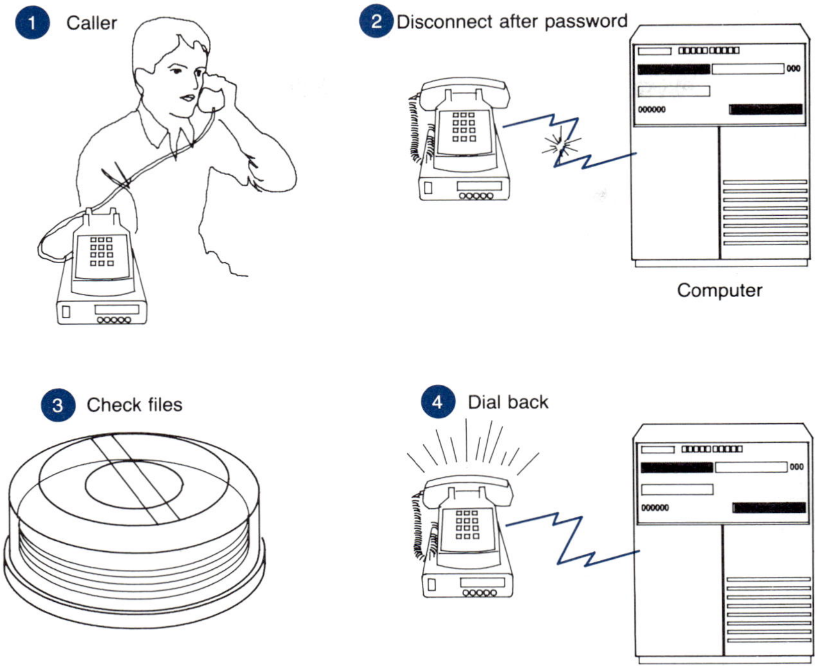
1 Caller
2 Disconnect after password
Computer
3 Check files
4 Dial back

Figure 16-2 Dial-back system. This system prevents unauthorized outsiders from breaking into a company's information system using microcomputers and phone lines. One such system works as follows: ❶ A person dials up the computer, using a touch-tone phone. ❷ The computer acknowledges the call, asks for a password, which the person gives. The computer then disconnects. ❸ The computer checks its files to see if the password matches an authorized phone number, then calls the number back. Only then is the person able to get on-line with the system. ❹ If the call came from an unauthorized number, the computer dials the authorized location and warns the user that there has been an attempt to use that password.

dardized code which, though it can be broken, is most widely used because the method of interception by outsiders is expensive. Few companies are using any encryption packages, however.

Some software has built-in access restrictions, so that users are limited only to certain parts of the program. Or the software may have a user profile—information about regular users, such as job, budget number, access privileges, supervisor, and even loss-causing potential—which can be checked if there is a problem. Such software may also provide an **audit trail**—a means by which auditors can see whether someone has had access to the data and, if so, to what parts.

Management Controls

There are a number of straightforward steps by which managers can try to ensure computer security:

- **Screen applicants:** Employers should verify resumes and check recommendations when hiring.
- **Separate employee functions:** A programmer should not also be allowed to be a computer operator, since this would put him or her in the position of running as well as writing unauthorized programs. Separating functions is not always possible in smaller companies, however.
- **Keep a log system:** A log should be kept of all transactions regarding access to data within the company.
- **Train employees:** Executives and other employees need to have a clear understanding of standards, and should be required to sign statements on proper computer use. Employees must be made to realize that information belongs to the company and otherwise educated about pitfalls and penalties.
- **Provide grievance channels:** The company's general counsel or an internal auditor or even a corporate ombudsman—a grievance counselor—is a good person to listen to employee complaints outside the normal supervisor-reporting channels. This can diminish employee resentments that can translate into computer crime or other security lapses.

Law Enforcement Controls

About one-third of the states have enacted their own computer crime laws, but for years there have been attempts to get legislation passed at the federal level. Law enforcement efforts have also dragged behind, handicapped by a lack of definition of "property" and "value" as they relate to computerized information. Oftentimes prosecutors have been reluctant to prosecute hackers or other computer thieves because company security has been slipshod or naive. To further law enforcement efforts, it has been suggested that information systems should be designed to collect evidence of unauthorized access and the systems should be made so secure that prosecutors will be willing to prosecute security violators.[9]

All of the above may reduce the possibility of unauthorized access to a company's important data and equipment. However, the worst *can* happen, of course—particularly that resulting from natural disasters. What if essential data is destroyed?

Computer Disasters

"Today, money is just a blip on a transistor," says one banker."Without power, we're paralyzed." Indeed, for some banks, even a brief loss of electrical power could mean the loss of hours of transactions. A severe dislocation such as an earthquake, flood, or concentrated act of terrorism or sabotage could shut down a bank for a few hours and have an

Disaster. The destruction of data processing programs and files can be even more harmful to a company than the destruction of physical goods. The tornado damage to this supermarket in Grand Island, Nebraska, is serious enough, but it has been calculated that an average size distributing company would go out of business in only 3.3 days if it lost all its data processing facilities. Companies thus must take steps to guard against destruction of their information processing by natural disasters, terrorism, and sabotage.

immediate impact on state and even national economies, since banks cannot survive more than a few days of confused accounting.[10]

Studies from the banking industry show that if a small bank is deprived of its data processing system for three days it will go bankrupt. A large bank such as Bank of America would be bankrupt by the eighth day. A study by the Graduate School of Business at the University of Minnesota determined it would take a distributing company of average size 3.3 days to go out of business if it lost all its data processing facilities; a manufacturing company, 4.8 days; and an insurance company, 5.6 days.[11]

Some companies, say security specialists, give more attention to the security of their parking garage than of their computer systems and files. But, as the above numbers show, it is crucial that companies take steps to make their information assets secure from fires, floods, earthquakes, and sabotage, as well as from hackers, dishonest insiders, and disgruntled former employees.

Disaster Recovery

Disaster recovery will not "just happen"; it has to be planned for. A **disaster recovery plan** is a plan for rapid resumption of essential data processing operations that have been interrupted by destruction or major damage. In anticipation of damage from natural disasters such as hurricanes, tornados, floods, fires, or earthquakes or damage from civil disorder, a disaster recovery plan specifies the following:

- **Who does what:** Employees are given specific assignments. Some are members of a disaster recovery team. A system of alerting employees during a disaster is set up.
- **What equipment is needed:** The plan specifies what hardware is needed and from where it can be borrowed or leased in event of emergency.
- **What programs have priority:** This is a critical decision. A bank might decide it has to put processing of customer checks before anything else.
- **What facilities and supplies are needed:** The plan must designate temporary buildings, air conditioning for large computers, and so on, that will be required in case of a disaster. The plan must also indicate what forms and paperwork will keep the work flow moving during the recovery period.

- **How input and output should be handled:** The disaster recovery plan must specify how input data should be gathered and how processed information should be distributed during the recovery time.

At first you might think that the biggest loss might be of an institution's expensive hardware—all that input and output equipment, computers, and telecommunications gear. Equipment is insurable, however, and can be replaced. What is more important is the loss of processing *time*; as mentioned, a bank could go out of business in three days if it lost its data processing capability. More significant than that is the loss of processing *data*. How would an institution the size of an insurance company reconstruct its files if they were destroyed?

The trick is to continue to do business while the telephone lines are still down and the broken glass is still being swept up. To this end, companies have devised two ways of continuing operations in the event their own offices are wrecked:

- Use of disaster recovery centers.
- Mutual aid pacts.

Disaster recovery centers consist of alternative computer setups that go unused except during emergencies. A typical arrangement would have computer, disk drives, communications network, and guaranteed power. A disaster recovery center may be either a **hot site,** which is a fully equipped center, with security, fire protection, telecommunications, and so on, or a **cold site,** which is simply an empty shell with power, water, and air conditioning in which a company may install its own equipment.

A disaster recovery center may be supported by a consortium of companies, since the centers go unused except during emergencies. However, companies may also join forces in mutual aid pacts. That is, they agree to lend each other computer time and facilities should one of their members be hit by disaster. For instance, in the Washington, D.C., area, a number of banks formed Bancon as a nonprofit organization to assist each other in processing checks—one bank alone processes half a million checks a day—in the event of emergency. Members have agreed to share check MICR (magnetic ink character-recognition) encoding equipment during certain hours if a member suffers a setback, and the processing would then be done by an outside service bureau.

Whatever disaster recovery plan is adopted, a company should have a storage area away from its main computer facility in which to house backup copies of hardware inventory, program listings, master and transaction files, and program and operating systems documentation, as well as the disaster plan manual.

The Birth of an Industry

In the 1950s and early sixties, when companies began to install mainframe computers, security of computerized information was not much of an issue. As one old DP hand from those days said, "There was only one group of people who knew how to diddle with a computer—our group. Now, with a number of micro and personal computers and large numbers of people becoming computer literate, there's a much broader understanding of use and how to get into corporate records."[12]

As we contemplate the problems of security, it is clear that we are witnessing the birth of a new industry. This is not just any industry, however, for there are many important legal and moral issues that must be resolved. How these are handled today will determine a great deal about how we live tomorrow.

Tomorrow—that is the subject of the next and final chapter.

SUMMARY

- **Privacy** is primarily a personal concern; it is the assurance to individuals that personal information is used properly and protected against improper access. **Security** is primarily a business concern; it is a system of safeguards designed to protect a computer system and data from deliberate or accidental damage or access by unauthorized persons.
- Concern has been growing about possible invasion of privacy by computer misuse. Computer technology may include methods of information use that outstrip the current ethical and legal standards for their use. Even so, there are some privacy laws: (1) The **Fair Credit Reporting Act,** passed in 1970, gives individuals the right to gain access to records kept about them by credit bureaus—and to challenge the records that may be inaccurate. (2) The **Freedom of Information Act,** also passed in 1970, gives ordinary people the right to have access to data about them gathered by federal agencies. This sometimes requires a lawsuit, may be time-consuming, and may result in heavily censored photocopies. (3) The **Federal Privacy Act,** passed in 1974, prohibits secret personal files, stipulates that individuals must be allowed to know the content and use of files about them, and extends the restrictions beyond government agencies to include private contractors dealing with the government. Government organizations may not launch "fishing expeditions" to collect data about individuals; they must justify the effort.
- Three problems that might compromise computer security are: (1) Computer crime—use of computers to steal money, goods, information, or computer time. (2) Piracy—stealing or unauthorized copying of programs or software. (3) Industrial espionage—stealing of computer industry trade secrets.

- *Computer crime* includes various activities, among them: (1) Theft of computer time ranges from the trivial—people using their employers' computers for games or personal use—to the serious, such as people using their employers' computers to operate their own businesses. (2) Manipulation of computer programs or data ranges from changing grades in college computer files to altering important instructions in a business system for personal gain. Two tricks of data manipulation are **Trojan Horse,** which is adding instructions to someone else's program so it works normally but also does additional illegal things, and **data diddling,** in which data is modified before it goes into a computer file. (3) Theft of data includes using microcomputers to break into large data banks and data bases. It also includes embezzlement; one trick, called the **salami method,** is to take from many accounts only a few cents ("slices") that will not be missed but that will add up to quite a large sum.
- **Piracy** is illegal copying of software, which is in violation of the **Copyright Act of 1976**. It includes the copying of commercially developed software by private individuals, who give or sell copies to their friends. Many manufacturers build in software protection codes to prevent duplication, but these codes can be cracked. Piracy also describes the activity of programmers who steal programs they write for their employers. Programs legally belong to the employers of the programmers who develop them.
- **Industrial espionage** is the misappropriation of company trade secrets, either by theft or by more subtle means. Legitimate ways for a business to gather intelligence include getting reports from its sales force as well as from published sources about the competition. However, photographing a competitor's factory layout or breaking into another company's data bases is espionage.
- Passes and passwords are two security measures to prevent unauthorized computer access. A pass, such as a badge or a card, perhaps with magnetized coding, may be required of authorized employers by computer room security guards. The new field of **biometrics**—the measurement and use of individual characteristics such as fingerprints as unique identifiers—may provide new forms of identification systems. Every computer system also should require special **passwords**—secret words or numbers that must be keyed into the system before it will operate. Passwords should not be obvious, should be at least six characters long, and should be changed randomly and frequently.
- Technical controls can improve security against unauthorized system entry: (1) Security **dial-back devices,** which call back the caller, assuming the correct password has been submitted, and connect him or her to the computer, may eliminate the problems of access by former employees and by hackers. **Hackers** used to mean "computer enthusiasts" but now seems to apply to people who invade other people's files and data bases. (2) Encryption devices scramble or encode data sent over telecommunications lines so it can be

decoded only by an authorized person. The **Data Encryption Standard (DES),** endorsed by the American National Standards Institute, is one such code. (3) Some software has built-in access restrictions to limit users to certain parts of a program. (4) Software may have a user profile—information about regular users, such as job, budget number and access privileges, which can be checked if there is a problem. (5) Such software can also provide an **audit trail**—a means by which auditors can see who has had access to what parts of the data.

- The following management controls can help to ensure computer security: (1) Screen applicants by verifying résumés and checking recommendations before hiring. (2) Separate employee functions so programmers are not also computer operators, able to run as well as write unauthorized programs. (3) Keep a log system of all transactions regarding access to data within the company. (4) Train employees so they have a clear understanding of standards; require them to sign statements on computer use, acknowledging that information belongs to the company. (5) Provide grievance channels, such as a grievance counselor or internal auditor, for employee complaints in order to diminish resentment that might translate into computer crime or other security lapses.
- Law enforcement controls of computer crime have lagged behind; about one-third of the states have enacted computer crime laws, but so far no legislation has been passed at the federal level. Law enforcement efforts are handicapped by lack of definition of "property" and "value" relating to computerized information, and prosecutors are reluctant to prosecute when company security has been slipshod or naive.
- Data processing facilities are not immune to being hit by disasters. Even a brief loss of electrical power to a bank, for example, could mean loss of hours of transactions; a severe dislocation such as an earthquake, flood, act of terrorism, or sabotage could shut down a bank for a few hours with immediate impact on state and even national economies.
- A **disaster recovery plan** is a plan for rapid resumption of essential data processing operations that have been interrupted by destruction or major damage. It specifies the following: (1) Who does what—employees are assigned specific activities and a system is set up to alert employees during a disaster. (2) What equipment is needed—what hardware and where it can be borrowed or leased in an emergency. (3) What programs have priority when disrupted processing operations are being resumed. (4) What facilities, such as temporary buildings, and what supplies, such as forms, will be needed during the recovery period. (5) How input and output should be handled—how data should be gathered and how output should be distributed during recovery.
- A **disaster recovery center** is an alternative computer setup that is used only during emergencies. Typically, it would have a computer, disk drives, com-

munications network, and guaranteed power. A **hot site** is a fully equipped center; a **cold site** is simply an empty shell with power, water, and air conditioning in which a company installs its own equipment. A disaster recovery center may be supported by a consortium of companies, or the companies may join in mutual aid pacts to lend each other computer time and facilities if one of their members is hit by disaster.

KEY TERMS

Audit trail, p. 550
Biometrics, p. 537
Cold site, p. 553
Copyright Act of 1976, p. 547
Data diddling, p. 545
Data Encryption Standard (DES), p. 549
Dial-back device, p. 548
Disaster recovery center, p. 553
Disaster recovery plan, p. 552
Fair Credit Reporting Act, p. 542
Federal Privacy Act, p. 543
Freedom of Information Act, p. 543
Hacker, p. 537
Hot site, p. 553
Industrial espionage, p. 547
Password, p. 537
Piracy, p. 539
Privacy, p. 546
Salami method, p. 545
Security p. 540
Trojan Horse, p. 545

REVIEW QUESTIONS

1. How does the theft of passwords from TRW involve the problems of privacy and security?
2. What are some of the concerns about the possible misuse of computers dealing with personal information?
3. Describe one of the recent privacy laws.
4. What are the three areas of concern for computer security?
5. What is a possible computer crime? What steps could be taken to prevent it?
6. What can be gained by the use of passes and passwords?
7. Describe the steps by which managers can ensure computer security.
8. What is a hot site? What is a cold site?

CASE PROBLEMS

Case 16-1: Can You Make Money from Murphy's Law?

One of the interesting things about the computer industry is the number of third-party companies that have sprung up to serve particular needs that did not exist before. For instance, in 1981 when Laurence Murphy was a vice president of Brinks, Inc., the armored-car company, he failed to convince the company that the time was right to enter the information security marketplace, so he and another man joined forces to establish the Vault Co. of Atlanta. What makes the Vault different from other data storage and disaster recovery facilities, according to Murphy, as quoted in an article in *Computerworld* (February 6, 1984), is that it is not just a warehouse but also provides total physical and environmental security. The data library, which can store up to 100,000 computer tapes at $1 a month each, is watched over by closed-circuit television monitors and bonded security guards behind bulletproof glass. States the article: "Only a trained data librarian utilizing a computerized tape retrieval system has access to the tapes stored in the library, which is both temperature and humidity controlled and equipped with a Halon fire-protection system. Clients must undergo a signature-matching process to verify their authority to take delivery of tapes."[13]

Your assignment: Long ago, another Murphy offered his famous Murphy's Law—"If anything can go wrong, it will." Look back over this chapter and, playing devil's advocate, think of things someone might do that are illegal but might beat the system—ways of stealing data, selling pirated software, and so on, or ways to compromise or destroy a data processing system—that is, Murphy's Law in operation. (If you can think of a "scam," probably others have, too.) Now think of some solutions to these security holes. You may have the basis for starting up a new enterprise.

Case 16-2: Hiring by Computer—and the Privacy Issue

Will "pounding the pavement" and classified advertising become obsolete employment techniques? Perhaps so, if the growth in computerized employer-employee matchmaking services continues. According to press reports, computerized employment agencies "have helped fill thousands of jobs for engineering, data processing, marketing, finance and other professionals."[14] Using telecommunications, employers connect with the employment service's data base and specify requirements such as skills, salary, and education. Within seconds, the computer provides them with people matching those characteristics.

Employers can conduct a search of several states or narrow it to a single zip code, if they do not want to pay employee relocation costs. Some services also do part of the job interviewing process, pre-screening job applicants by asking them 80 to 100 multiple-choice questions. The advantage of computerized recruitment services to job hunters is that they give them the opportunity to apply for thousands of jobs all over the country. The services believe this will be the primary method of recruitment in the coming years.

Your assignment: This whole topic is worth your serious concern if computerized recruitment services become as important in the employment process as some people think they will. Think about the issues: How do you feel about being interviewed by questionnaire instead of face to face? Résumés often are written to emphasize certain types of experience, depending on the job, but how would you deal with this aspect if you could put only one résumé in a data base? What privacy guarantees would you want?

CHAPTER 17

The Future

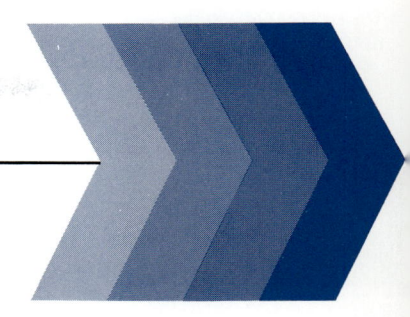

The Computer as an Expression of Enterprise

P R E V I E W

A new spirit of enterprise has begun to emerge. Entrepreneurship—the willingness to seek business opportunities despite the risks—seems to be on the rise. "Entrepreneurship will be the major impetus of the decade immediately ahead of us," says Donald C. Burr, the 42-year-old founder of People Express Airlines, "and what's ahead is terrifically exciting."[1]

Opinion analyst Daniel Yankelovich finds evidence for this forecast. The dominant value of Americans before the 1960s, he says, was concern with economic security; in the 1970s, this gave way to the value of enhancing one's material well-being. Now, however, there is a new group called the Expressives: "They are the trailblazers, I believe, who mark the way into our future." This group is interested in the values of personal development, of style and challenge, of life as adventure. Self-denial and self-satisfaction, then, are giving way to self-expression, and with it a drive toward creativity and enterprise in the workplace.[2]

Often this impulse takes shape as a desire to be one's own boss, but more and more businesses are also creating arrangements whereby entrepreneurship can be made to happen within their own companies. In 1980, for instance, IBM organized a number of quasi-autonomous independent business units; one of them created the IBM Personal Computer, one of today's greatest corporate success stories.

The Computer as Career Tool

The computer is part of this spirit of enterprise, as the case study on the next page makes clear. Whereas in the sixties the computer was a symbol of depersonalization ("Do not fold, spindle, or

CASE STUDY: ENTREPRENEURS MAKE COMPUTING MORE INTUITIVE

User Friendlier

With the advent of the desktop personal computer, ease-of-use has emerged as the critical element needed to open computing to the masses, and entrepreneurs are flooding the marketplace with all kinds of hardware gadgets and software tricks to make these machines, if not more human, then at least less intimidating.

Today, innovative companies are bringing out products to liberate the computer user from the tyranny of the keyboard. Hard-to-remember written codes are evolving into familiar graphic symbols. Computerese is becoming less arcane, and computing is becoming more *intuitive.*

At advanced research centers, computer scientists are testing the "user-interface" concepts of the future. Massachusetts Institute of Technology's architecture machine group developed a system that simulates visually on a wall-sized screen the act of walking down a hall, opening a file cabinet, and pulling out documents. Its computer is controlled with hand motions detected by wrist-mounted sensors. Much university research today explores artificial intelligence (AI) techniques that could let a computer interpret speech or body gestures. "The real problem of the future is to build a computer with common sense," observes MIT professor Marvin Minsky, a pioneering AI theorist. "You want a system to make a guess why you did something, and act accordingly."

Devices already on the market are making it easier to interact with personal computers:

- San Diego engineer Dennis Kuzara builds an inexpensive "light pen" that can locate or draw electronic images directly on a computer screen. He heads Design Technology, the manufacturing end of the business. His wife, Sherry, runs Inkwell Systems, the software and marketing arm.
- Pierlugi Zappacosta is president of two-year-old Logitech Inc., a Redwood City, Calif., maker of a mouse, the little rolling box championed by Apple Computer for control of its Lisa and Macintosh.
- In Woburn, Mass., Jim Logan runs Microtouch Systems Inc., a two-year-old manufacturer of a video monitor that lets a user

run a computer by just touching commands on the screen surface.

- In Fremont, Calif., Ron Stephens is president of Votan, a five-year-old firm whose product lets users control an IBM PC with voice commands.
- Founder Keith Plant's Speech Plus of Mountain View, Calif., is involved in speech synthesis. Computers that talk make it easier for production-line workers to understand data. . . .

New technologies let people do a lot more than merely point and talk to their video screens. The same devices making computers easier to use are simultaneously unleashing the power of computers for people who never had much use for them. From its conventional role as a calculation machine, the computer is evolving into a tool of creativity.

Some psychologists say the human brain parcels its thinking into two regions. The left hemisphere of the brain deals with logic, step-by-step analysis, and verbal thinking; the right side is the seat of intuition, metaphorical thinking, and visual comparison. The thought processes of chess masters and mathematicians are linked with the left side of the brain; those of artists and musicians with the right. By virtue of the electronic logic etched into their circuits, computers have been excellent tools for "left-brain thinkers." Most computing tasks such as word processing and financial modeling are typical left-brain functions. But the very qualities that make computers so good at logic make them intimidating to people who are not mathematically inclined. In their efforts to make computing easier—through the use of intuitive devices like touch screens, mice, and light pens—engineers have made the machines more responsive to the right side of the brain. Now, entrepreneurs are responding with products tailored to intuitive thinkers.

"We've talked about our product as a computer for the right side of the brain," acknowledges Chris Berg, marketing manager of Mindset Corp. of Sunnyvale, Calif., which has developed an IBM-compatible personal computer with the ability to process complex color graphic images at high speeds. It can be controlled with a mouse or touch tablet. "Intuition is not plodding. It's spontaneous, erratic. Speed is very important," Berg explains.

—Sabin Russell,
Venture, July 1984

mutilate"), in the 1980s, points out Yankelovich, "The microcomputer has become a tool of personal power."

The computer as tool—that is the idea we have stressed repeatedly throughout this book. Although we might like to think otherwise, human beings "are only occasionally productive, only occasionally goal-oriented. . . ," as humanist William Chace writes. "Much of the time humans daydream, waste time, spin their wheels and, in general, prove inefficient and prodigal of their abilities. . . .Not so with computers."[3] This does not mean computers are better than we are. Rather, they are the tools that make *us* better—more productive, more efficient, more quickly able to achieve our goals.

How will the computer figure in your career as we rapidly approach the end of the century? Let us consider this next.

The Outlook in High-Technology Jobs

Many students are considering a high-technology career—in electronics, computers, engineering, and the like—on the theory that these industries will be a major new source of jobs. Certainly there will continue to be great demands for people in these fields, as Figure 17-1 shows. The demand will be particularly strong for those in electrical engineering and computer science.

But there are some important things to note about high technology:

- Only 6% of new jobs—1.5 million—created from now until 1995, according to the Federal Bureau of Labor Statistics, will be for high-technology workers—engineers, life and physical scientists, mathematical specialists, engineering and science technicians, and computer specialists.[4]
- High-tech jobs tend to be polarized, with highly skilled, highly paid jobs at one end and low-skilled, low-paid jobs at the other end. Computer systems analysts—a well-paying occupation—will increase 85%, as Figure 17-1 shows. This occupation requires a college degree, but only about 200,000 new jobs are expected in this category. On the other hand, computer operators are expected to increase about 76%, but the jobs do not require more than a high school education.
- There is a great deal of flux and change in high-tech jobs. One three-year study of such jobs in California found that for every three high-tech jobs created each year in the state, one was lost, owing to intense competition that resulted in mergers, movement of assembly-line jobs overseas, and so on.[5]

High technology has been compared to potatoes: potato farming employs few people and is unlikely to employ a great many more in the next decade or so. Yet there are hundreds of thousands more people who earn a living by making and selling French-fried and baked potatoes.[6] Tech-

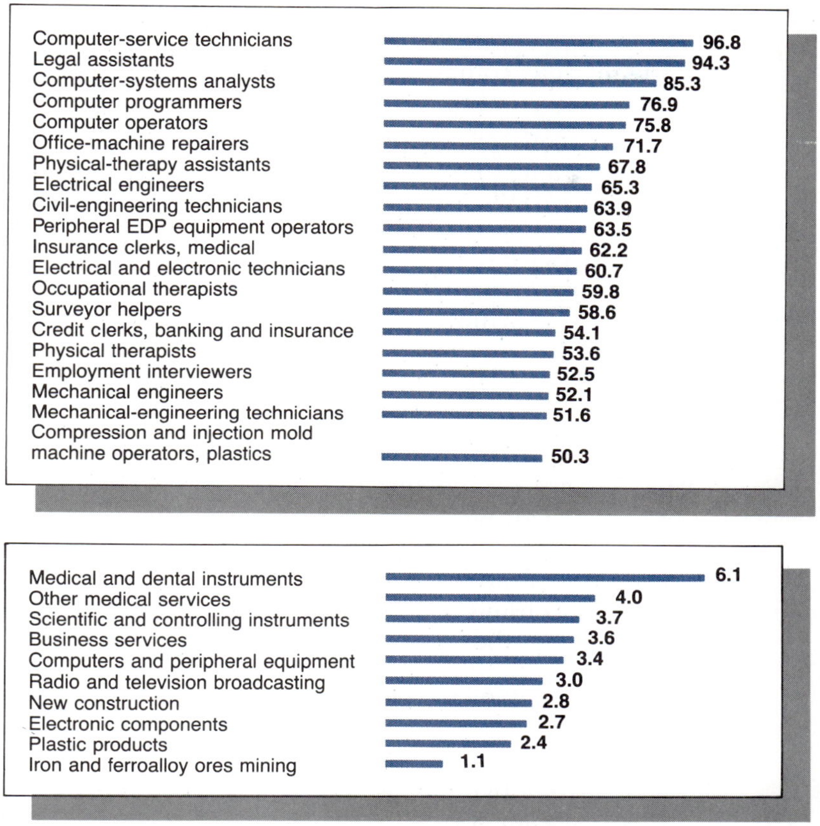
Computer-service technicians 96.8
Legal assistants 94.3
Computer-systems analysts 85.3
Computer programmers 76.9
Computer operators 75.8
Office-machine repairers 71.7
Physical-therapy assistants 67.8
Electrical engineers 65.3
Civil-engineering technicians 63.9
Peripheral EDP equipment operators 63.5
Insurance clerks, medical 62.2
Electrical and electronic technicians 60.7
Occupational therapists 59.8
Surveyor helpers 58.6
Credit clerks, banking and insurance 54.1
Physical therapists 53.6
Employment interviewers 52.5
Mechanical engineers 52.1
Mechanical-engineering technicians 51.6
Compression and injection mold machine operators, plastics 50.3
Medical and dental instruments 6.1
Other medical services 4.0
Scientific and controlling instruments 3.7
Business services 3.6
Computers and peripheral equipment 3.4
Radio and television broadcasting 3.0
New construction 2.8
Electronic components 2.7
Plastic products 2.4
Iron and ferroalloy ores mining 1.1

Figure 17-1 **Fast-growing jobs.** *Top*: The 20 fastest-growing occupations in the United States, 1982–1995. Chart shows the percentage growth in employment as projected by the Federal Bureau of Labor Statistics (includes only detailed occupations with 1982 employment of 25,000 or more people). *Bottom*: Projected employment changes for fastest-growing industries, 1990–1995. Chart shows average annual percentage rate of change as projected by the Bureau of Labor Statistics.

nology seems to operate the same way. "There are not going to be a lot of jobs in technology per se," states one economist, "but there will be a lot of high-technology jobs." In other words, the growth of jobs in the future will occur more in industries that arise to make use of the technology rather than to create it.

Jobs that Use Technology

It is the intelligent use of technology or innovation, concludes MIT researcher David Birch, that generates employment. Innovation is the use of technology to create new or replacement goods or processes.[7]

Where will the new jobs be? If trends continue, nearly 75% of all new jobs through 1995 will come from service-producing industries, according to the Bureau of Labor Statistics. Indeed, as Figure 17-2 shows, service jobs are already outpacing manufacturing or goods-producing industries. Service jobs, which are usually more interesting and rewarding than factory jobs, include working for retail shops, airlines, fast-food chains, public utilities, and a host of other occupations.

A quarter of the expected employment by 1995—31 million jobs—will be in an area the Bureau of Labor Statistics calls "miscellaneous services." This category is expected to provide one out of every three new jobs in the decade ahead. Miscellaneous services include business services, recreation, hotels, and medical care. Says the *New York Times*:

> Business services—which include consultants, personnel services, public relations, security systems, computer and data processing services—will be one of the hottest growth areas, with employment expected to double, to about 6.2 million by 1995. A related industry, "miscellaneous professional services," which includes lawyers, engineers, accountants and architects, will add about 850,000 jobs, to top 3 million by 1995. And medical care should employ some 3 million new people by 1995, or about 12 percent of all new jobs generated in the next decade.[8]

Figure 17-2 Where the workers are. Index of employment in the United States from 1978 to 1984, by major sector—service-producing industries versus goods-producing industries. (1978 = 100.) Note the steady rise in service-producing industries.

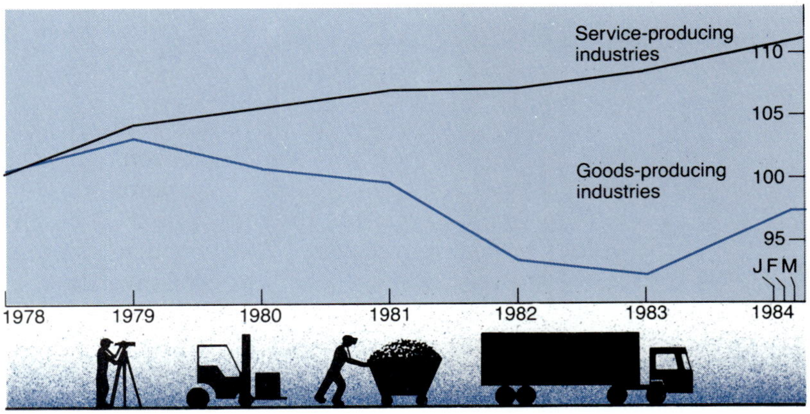
Service-producing industries
Goods-producing industries
110
105
100
95
J F M
1978
1979
1980
1981
1982
1983
1984

Career growth area. Law is an area that is expected to provide a great many jobs in the next decade—and law in turn will rely heavily on computer technology.

As we have been suggesting throughout this book, all these kinds of white-collar, managerial, or professional occupations will be making great use of computers in the future. The question is: How much computer training is necessary?

No High-Tech Skills Needed?

The computer is a high-tech tool, to be sure. But it does not necessarily require high-tech skills to use it. In this sense, it does not follow the experience of industrial workers earlier in this century, when industrial machinery made many unskilled jobs semiskilled. Although, as we have seen, computerization is being introduced into millions of office jobs with the help of packaged software—word processing, spreadsheets, data base, and so on—one can learn to use a microcomputer without having to learn programming, for instance. Perhaps, as we suggested earlier, computer skills will be needed in up to three-quarters of all jobs by the end of this decade, but it does not follow that high-tech skills will be required to use the computer as a tool. Indeed, some think that many service-sector jobs will call for a level of computer expertise that can be acquired in only a week or two of practical instruction.[9]

The Threat of Automation

Perhaps, you think, it all sounds too easy. After all, you *have* heard about the threat of automation.

Indeed, automation gives rise to some serious concerns. In France, for instance, medical students have been advised to consider going into specialties that depend heavily on manual dexterity, such as obstetrics and surgery; other medical specialties that depend more on intellectual judgment may be vulnerable to being displaced by computers. In Japan, where the robot revolution has rolled through industry, there has developed labor resistance to cooperation in further factory automation—this in a country where large firms have adopted a lifetime employment guarantee for workers. And in the United States, some middle managers find themselves in the difficult situation of implementing factory automation systems that will eliminate their present jobs.

There is no doubt that computer automation will change the workplace. The Congressional Budget Office estimates that by the end of the decade 15% of today's manufacturing jobs will have disappeared, owing to automation and robotization. The use of industrial robots is expected to grow at an annual rate of 33 to 44% through 1990. However, many argue that the automated machines will create more jobs than they eliminate; there will be a need for robot production technicians, for technicians to maintain and operate robots, for programmers, and for computer-assisted manufacturing specialists.

As for the effects of automation on managers, a survey of 608,000 high-technology jobs across the United States by the Computer and Business Equipment Manufacturers' Association found that automation did not cause middle management dropout. "Middle management jobs are highly necessary to coordinate projects and take in a lot of information to make decisions," said an association representative. "They [managers] work directly with people, and people respond better to a person than a machine."[10]

Training. Many companies are finding out that the way to handle a work force threatened by layoffs from automation is to retrain people in order to retain existing talent. The people here analyze advantages of computers for other departments of the company and train personnel in basic concepts.

Computers, robots, and other forms of high-tech automation will have complex effects. Some jobs, of course, *are* being eliminated. Others are being made more complicated and some are becoming more compartmentalized. But there are ways of dealing with the jobs issue. As a future manager, you need to realize that enhancements in productivity brought about by automation can be wiped out by a work force resisting machine encroachments or by back-stabbing competition for remaining jobs. A better idea is to retain the talent and expertise of the employees by retraining them for computer-related jobs and communicating to them the future job opportunities available to them once automation is in place.

Again, points out MIT's David Birch, innovation can drive the U.S. economy forward and keep it competitive in world markets. However:

> Most innovation does not create new products; rather, it involves finding a better and, often, more efficient way of doing something—making steel, for example. While innovation is absolutely essential to keep American steel companies in business, it is just as essential to find something else for laid-off steel workers to do. If we don't, organized steel workers facing unemployment won't allow innovation to go forward, and eventually the United States will be out of the steel business altogether.[11]

Automation, then, is a manageable social problem, if we want to take hold of it. But we must look to see if there are other problems that may not be solvable.

Should We Really Trust Computers?

Remember HAL, the computer in *2001, A Space Odyssey*, that ran amok and killed all but one man on its spaceship? HAL almost seemed to symbolize an earlier generation's worst fears as to what computers could become—independent thinking, apparently friendly, but also insane and homicidal. Today, however, about six out of ten Americans say they "trust" computers, when dealing with them in a business relationship. Indeed, nearly three-quarters of adult Americans under the age of 35 say they have some trust when dealing with computers, as opposed to only 45% of those over age 50.[12]

Are we wise to have such trust in computers? There are at least three areas over which we should cast a cautious eye:

- Health and stress
- "Computer error"
- Changes in quality of life

EVIL COMPUTERS?

Do You Fear Computers?

Heading into the Orwellian "Big Brother" year of 1984, a Louis Harris public opinion poll found a great deal of fear on the part of Americans about computers. Answer the following questions and see how your responses compare with those of most Americans. (The poll responses are given upside down at the bottom of the box.)

1. Do computers threaten your privacy?
2. Do you believe personal information about you is being kept in files for purposes unknown to you?
3. Do you believe it is possible that computerized information will be taken over by the federal government and combined with electronic surveillance of individuals to control the population under a totalitarian state?
4. If you are a factory worker, do you believe robots will hurt your livelihood?
5. Are you worried that in offices "people will end up working for machines instead of using their brains and creativeness to do an effective job"?

—Louis Harris opinion poll on impact of technology, reported in "Statistics Accentuate the Positive and Negative of High Tech," *Computerworld,* December 12, 1983

Clearly, there are grave concerns about "evil" computer systems. Morally reprehensible uses of computer systems may not be the result of greed or malice so much as ignorance and negligence. Nevertheless, computers may serve many masters and every use suggests a misuse.

Poll responses: The proportion of Americans surveyed who answered "yes" was as follows: 1. 51%; 2. 67%; 3. 63%; 4. 60%; 5. 67%.

Health and Stress

Could computers be hazardous to your health? Take, for a moment, the locations where computers are made, such as California's "Silicon Valley," Santa Clara County, about 30 miles south of San Francisco. There are no smokestacks in Silicon Valley, and the plants that produce computers look like college campuses. Indeed, computer makers have enjoyed the reputation of being a "clean" industry. Yet 20 years after the first computer firms started up, there are lawsuits by manufacturing workers who say their health has been damaged by toxic chemicals used in making microprocessors, air quality officials have discovered that semiconductor firms release several tons of smog-producing gases into the atmosphere every day, and local cities have found that their underground water supplies have been tainted by toxic chemicals from chip-producing firms. Computer makers, however, argue that their industry is still one of the cleanest around, and this may well be true compared to traditional heavy industries such as steel and automaking.

As we saw in the box on page 528 in Chapter 15, some people have raised concerns that computers—particularly CRT terminals—may be hazardous to users. Although there is no evidence of any risk to pregnant women or that low-level radiation levels are hazardous, there are legitimate concerns that operators may suffer from eye and back strain and stress. As we mentioned in Chapter 15, however, these have little to do with computer technology and much to do with improper adjustment and location of equipment and, most especially, unrealistic productivity demands made of clerical workers. Health and stress have become labor issues among office workers, only 10% of whom are unionized. These concerns may well increase when the estimated 7 million workers using CRT terminals rises to 40 million by 1990.[13]

"Computer Error"

The expression "computer error" is often used to blame on a machine what are really human errors. However, computer-related failures can have a number of causes, as follows:

- **Faulty equipment:** This is what people often want us to believe is the cause when they say there is a computer error or the computer is "down." Usually, semiconductor manufacturers put chips through extremely rigorous tests so that failure is rare, although there was

Silicon Valley. Cradle of the Computer Revolution, this area of hills and red rooftops in which so many computers are made lies in Santa Clara County, 30 miles south of San Francisco.

a good deal of furor a few years ago when it was discovered that National Semiconductor had supplied the military with chips that were not satisfactorily tested. But even if chips are relatively reliable, other computer-related equipment can sometimes go awry: air-conditioning systems break down, printers quit, antiquated switching plants in the public telephone system fail, and so on. Sometimes such faulty equipment produces spectacular results: in June 1980, a faulty integrated circuit in a communications multiplexor wrongly signaled the North American Air Defense Command that a wave of Russian missiles was headed toward the North American continent. The mistake was detected, but not before Strategic Air Command bomber crews had been sent aloft.

- **Interrupted power supply and electronic "hash":** Power fluctuations and "noise"—static or electromagnetic pollution—are serious enemies of computers. A 25% voltage drop for even a tenth of a second can shut down many computers. Indeed, a great deal of time is spent trying to recover data lost from an electrical problem. Obviously, in the computerized future we will be highly dependent on electric power; however, some people worry that, with demand for electricity growing at 4% to 5% a year, we will start to exhaust available supplies between 1988 and 1990.[14] In addition, a rise in electronic "hash" or "noise" is producing an epidemic of static that disrupts communications equipment and destroys data. Many firms have been forced to install expensive screens to shield computer hardware.
- **Equipment design flaws:** Often hardware and software manufacturers simply do not allow for the mistakes users might make on their equipment. If one is using an IBM Personal Computer XT with a hard disk drive, for instance, and does not indicate which drive to format (prepare to receive information), the machine could format the hard disk and wipe all data off it. Also, microcomputer software is usually made without so-called audit trail reports, which indicate who was the last person to use the software and what changes he or she made—features that are usually included with mainframe software. Experts say that today's microcomputer hardware and software offer inadequate backup facilities, so that it is easier to lose data.
- **Programmer errors:** Here is where the time-honored DP phrase "garbage in, garbage out" applies. Programmers have several opportunities to discover and fix program errors, but some may go undetected—particularly if the programmers are working under pressure to meet deadlines.
- **Data-entry errors:** This is not a "computer error" but human error, and it is the most common source of mistakes. If you have ever been victimized by a computer billing foul-up, this is probably the cause

of it—as it was for the Salt Lake City woman who was mistakenly credited with $161 billion to her Sears, Roebuck charge account.

While a great deal of activity can still be done manually in the event of computer failure, albeit with difficulty, there are some situations in which activity ceases until the power comes back on. In some telephone areas, for instance, directory-assistance operators cannot give customers information because their directories exist only in computer form. Banks, airlines, and retail stores usually have various backup systems in case a mainframe computer should fail. If there is a power outage, there are emergency generators and batteries. If a mainframe computer goes down, there is often an alternative computer. In New York, Citibank has two main computers, each serving different regions but each capable of handling the entire system in an emergency. In Phoenix, when the reservations computer for Best Western's 2800 hotels goes out, the system can be switched onto a computer used for back-office business. In Los Angeles, each store in the Ralph's supermarket chain is paired with another store, so that if the controller for the checkout scanning system goes out at one store, the sister store can take over.[15]

Ralphs
24 HOUR superstore

Backup. Stores like those in the Ralph's supermarket chain are paired with sister stores, so that if the controller for the checkout system fails in one store, the controller in the other store can take over.

Changes in Quality of Life

Computers will change the quality of life. During the 1950s when television was a novelty in American living rooms, critics speculated that television would produce a nation of unimaginative zombies. Likewise with computers—some scholars speculate that computers can reduce curiosity and imagination because computers formalize the way we think. For the society as a whole, computers may widen the gap between first-class and second-class citizens: the former may be those with inside knowledge, access to data banks, credit cards, and so on; the latter will be the poor and unemployed and those living in the illegal "underground" cash-and-barter economy that the computer cannot penetrate.

These are some of the downside issues of the automated future facing us. However, there is a plethora of new, exciting challenges ahead. Let us turn to them.

Artificial Intelligence and Other High-Tech Aids for Future Enterprise

"If you really want your people to innovate, buy a science fiction book, take the cover off and tell them it's history." The advice came from Atari, Inc. founder Nolan Bushnell to a conference of information industry representatives. "The future is not totally dependent on innovation. Most of the ideas are out there. Just read science fiction; most of the things they write about are going to come true."[16]

Bushnell was talking partly tongue in cheek, but certainly a lot of the hardware and software around today *do* seem like science fiction come true. What are some of the innovations of the future that will affect how we live and work? Let us look at some possibilities.

Primary Storage

In a 1945 *Atlantic Monthly* article, Vannevar Bush, inventor of analog computers at MIT, took a look at things he thought would happen in the next 20 years. One of them was a gadget called a "Memex," which was a desk-size information machine that would have the capacity of about 10,000 books—the size of a small-town library—which people would be able to have in their homes. By the end of the present decade, it is speculated, a processor with a cubic meter of space would be able to contain all the information in the Library of Congress. Whereas today a single 3- or 6-inch silicon wafer is used to make hundreds of small chips, in the future such a wafer may be used to make *one* large chip—and such large chips may be joined to others as building blocks to make "chip machines." From these could be produced "component institutions"—component schools, component libraries, even "offices on a wafer."

In addition, as we mentioned in Chapter 8, researchers are proposing biochips, which, using recombinant-DNA genetic engineering tech-

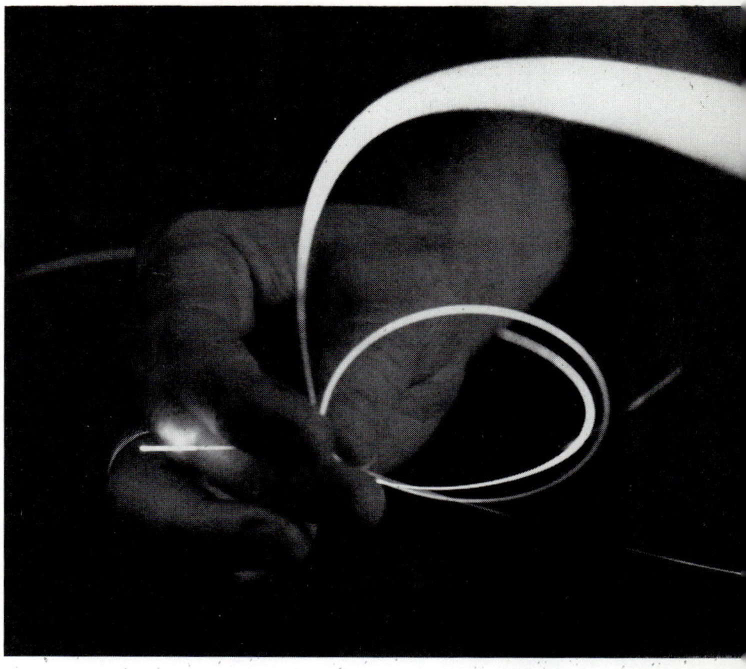

Fiber optics. Loops of a hair-thin glass fiber, illuminated by laser light, represent the transmission medium of fiber optics, which will probably greatly increase the flexibility of telecommunications. A cable with such fibers can carry more than 40,000 voice channels.

niques, would permit computers to be grown as biological molecules. Perhaps in the future computers will be based on carbon rather than silicon.

Storage Technology

The floppy disk may well become the punched card of the 1980s, some experts think, as more and more microcomputers begin using hard disk as secondary storage devices. Microcomputer storage devices will also continue to shrink in size, with more microfloppy disks and micro-Winchester hard disks that will hold millions of bytes of information.

As we mentioned in Chapter 9, we also probably will see a trend toward optical storage devices.

Printers

Future generations of copiers may be so good at duplication that the U.S. Treasury Department is already looking into what will have to be done to make paper money less vulnerable to easy counterfeiting on a photocopying machine. Printers also will doubtless have better quality. Low-cost ink jet printers and laser printers with outstanding graphics capabilities will soon be readily available.

Graphics Capabilities

About 30% of all software packages now sold are for graphics applications, and sales are expected to continue to grow perhaps 40 to 50% a year for the next five years, as managers become their own graphic artists.[17] More microcomputer manufacturers are also building graphics capabilities into their products.

8786
8786
8786
SANTA
CATS-1

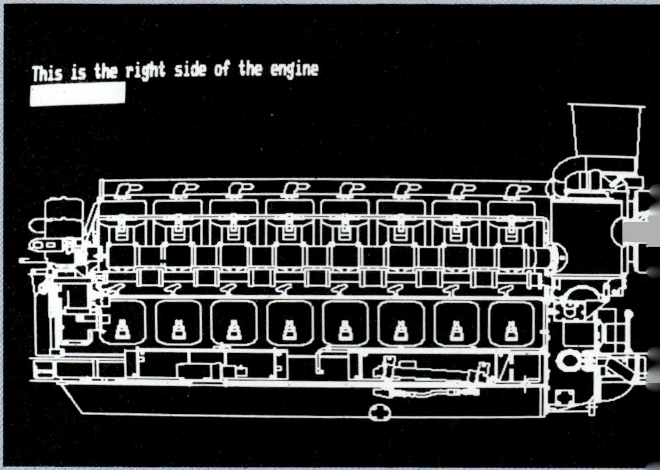
This is the right side of the engine

In addition, new high-resolution video screens are being developed, which will show finely developed detail. Although high-resolution color screens are available now, so far they have been too expensive for the general market.

Networking Networking and data communications may well turn out to be more important than any of the above technologies. As one writer points out, "data communications enables a global exchange of information. There are no bounds to it, and its functions are worldwide, driven by reasons of profit and even national security."[18]

Fiber optics, cheaper modems, and more frequencies providing more communication channels will probably greatly increase the extent and flexibility of telecommunications. In addition, we may expect cellular telephone services using networks of radio towers interspersed in "cells" throughout a city to expand the use of portable and mobile phones.

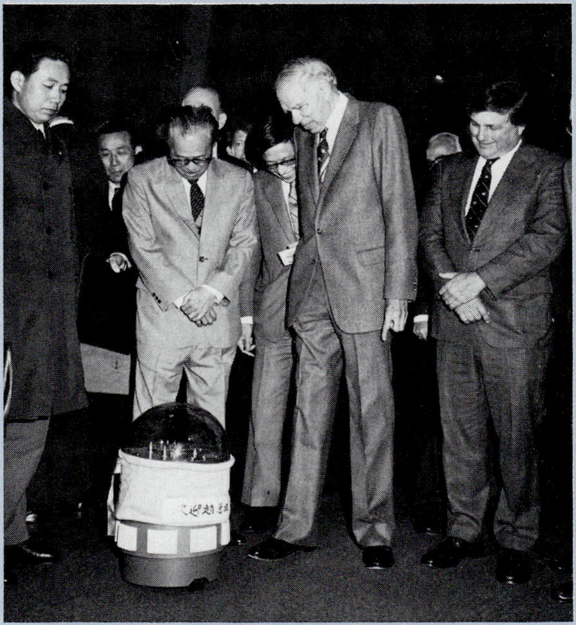

New intelligence. General Electric's expert system *(opposite page, left and right)* used the results of several months of interviews with GE's top locomotive field service engineer (David Smith, at right) to devise a software program that would put Smith's accumulated diagnostic expertise into a computer. Now inexperienced locomotive mechanics can type in responses to questions concerning a malfunction, and the system will even demonstrate repair procedures on the CRT screen. Thus, the system troubleshoots by reasoning, much the way a human expert would. Another form of computer intelligence, robots, may simply be of the cute R2D2 variety *(above left)*, but they also have practical uses. The picture here *(above right)* shows the view through a robot camera; the boxes outline the points the robot is tracking. If it can follow the points from one step to the next, the apparent motion of the points can be used to give the actual motion of the robot.

Artificial Intelligence, Expert Systems, and Knowledge-Based Systems

If the developments above are revolutionary, artificial intelligence (AI) promises to be superrevolutionary. "AI will change civilization in a profound way," states Nils J. Nilsson, director of the AI center at SRI International in Menlo Park, California. "It will change the way we work, the way we learn, and even the way we think about ourselves."

Artificial intelligence—the field of study that explores how computers can be used for tasks requiring the human characteristics of intelligence, imagination, and intuition in order to perform specific tasks—is already here, and it has three subspecialties: robotics, natural language inquiry, and knowledge engineering. Knowledge engineering in turn has yielded two applied fruits:

- **Expert systems:** These begin with a specialist in knowledge engineering who "debriefs" or extensively interviews a recognized authority in a particular field such as geology. That expert's knowledge is then codified into rules, which are represented symbolically, then transferred to a computer program which mimics the expert's problem-solving strategies.
- **Knowledge-based systems:** These systems draw not only on experts but also on books, computer manuals, or other subject matter that requires no special aptitude or education to master.

Both expert and knowledge-based systems draw on pools of collected information and use inferences to reach informed conclusions, and these systematic simulations of human thinking have now begun to find their way into business. Diesel locomotives built by General Electric are tested for malfunctions with an automated diagnostic aid. Faulty AT&T phone lines in Texas are fixed with the help of an Automated Cable Expertise system. A molybdenum ore field in eastern Washington was located with the help of an "electronic geologist" hundreds of miles away in Menlo Park, California. As expert and knowledge-based systems emerge from the laboratory, it is estimated that the market for them will explode from $20 million in 1984 to $2.5 *billion* by 1993.

Hello to the Information Age

Computers give us many choices. Still, the choices are those that only human beings can put there. When computers sometimes seem awesome to contemplate, we would do well to consider humanist William Chace's observation:

> The computer is, when all is said and done, a tool, no more than a tool, and it is *our* tool. We will use it after craftsmen have made it available to us. So it was once with the hammer, cannon and the knife; so once it was with the automobile, the radio and the airplane. Originally objects of awe, curiosity, and even terror—we have exerted our full authority over them all.
>
> So now it is with the digital computer. We will, certainly in the 21st century, claim it as one more man-made instrument that we have controlled and demystified.[19]

SUMMARY

- In the 1980s, the computer as a tool has become an integral part of an emerging spirit of entrepreneurship—the willingness to seek business opportunities despite the risks.
- The future job market in the high-tech field seems less secure than commonly thought: only 6% of new jobs created between now and 1995 will be for high-technology workers. High-tech jobs tend to be polarized, with highly skilled, highly paid jobs at one end and low-skilled, low-paid jobs at the other. The high-tech job market also fluctuates widely, with mergers, relocations, and so on, eliminating some jobs as others are created.
- Employment opportunities for the future will be in the service-producing fields such as retail, airlines, and public utilities. One in three jobs created in the next decade will be in "miscellaneous services," including business services, recreation, hotels, and medical care.
- Computer skills may be required in up to three-quarters of all jobs by the end of the decade, but these skills need not be high-tech. The computer expertise required for many service-sector jobs probably can be learned in a week or two of practical instruction.
- There is no doubt that computer automation will change the workplace. By the end of the decade, 15% of today's manufacturing jobs will have disappeared, owing to automation and robotization. Many argue, however, that the automated machines will create more jobs than they eliminate.
- To deal with the jobs issues, managers must realize that enhancements in productivity can be wiped out by a work force resisting machine encroachments or by back-stabbing competition for remaining jobs. It is better to retain the talent and expertise of employees by retraining them for computer-related jobs and the future job opportunities available after automation.
- Today most Americans trust computers, but three areas should be examined: (1) health and stress, (2) "computer error," and (3) changes in the quality of life.
- *Health and stress* have not been thought a problem in the computer industry. Yet 20 years after the first computer firms started up, there are lawsuits by manufacturing workers charging that toxic chemicals used in making microprocessors have damaged their health; air quality officials have discovered that semiconductor firms release smog-producing gases; and cities have discovered water supplies tainted by toxic chemicals from nearby chip-producing firms.

- Questions of health and stress have also been raised by computer users. Some have worried about the effect of radiation on pregnant women from CRT terminals, but the level of radiation is deemed not harmful according to present government standards. Visual and postural problems usually have to do with the positioning of CRTs and users. Stress has less to do with computer technology than with working conditions involving computers and unrealistic expectations by management for productivity by clerical workers.
- *"Computer error"* is often used to blame on a machine what are really human errors. However, computer-related failures can have a number of causes: (1) Faulty equipment. (2) Interrupted power supply, power fluctuations, and "noise"—static or electromagnetic pollution. A 25% voltage drop for even a tenth of a second can shut down many computers. A rise in electronic "hash" or "noise" is producing an epidemic of static that disrupts communications equipment and destroys data. (3) Equipment design flaws. (4) Programmer errors. (5) Data-entry errors.
- *Changes in quality of life* may be a downside risk of an automated future. Some scholars speculate computers may reduce curiosity and imagination because they formalize the way we think. For the society as a whole, computers may widen the gap between first- and second-class citizens: the former may have access to data banks, credit cards, and so on; the latter may be the poor and unemployed.
- Some of the technological innovations we may expect in the future include improvements in primary storage, storage technology, printers, graphics capabilities, and networking: (1) Primary storage capacity may be increased dramatically by chips that fill entire wafers and that can be joined together as "chip machines" that could be used to produce "component institutions" such as an office on a wafer. Biochips, using recombinant-DNA genetic engineering, may permit computers to be grown as molecules. (2) Hard disk may replace floppy disks as the most popular storage device for microcomputers; floppy disks themselves will continue to shrink in size. There will probably be a trend toward optical storage. (3) Future printers will have outstanding graphics capabilities. (4) Microcomputer manufacturers are building graphics capabilities into their products, and graphics software will continue to gain in popularity. Affordable high-resolution video screens are being developed. (5) Networking and data communications will be enhanced by fiber optics, cheaper modems, more frequencies to provide more communication channels, and cellular telephone systems to expand use of portable and mobile phones.
- **Artificial intelligence (AI)**—the field of study that explores how computers can be used to perform specific tasks that require the human characteristics of intelligence, imagination, and intuition—has three subspecialties: robotics, natural language inquiry, and knowledge engineering. Knowledge engi-

neering has yielded two applications: (1) **Expert systems** are based on the knowledge of a recognized authority in a particular field such as geology. That expert's knowledge is codified into rules, which are represented symbolically, then transferred to a computer program that mimics the expert's problem-solving strategies. (2) **Knowledge-based systems** draw not only on experts but also on books, computer manuals, or other subject matter that requires no special aptitude or education to master.

KEY TERMS

Artificial intelligence, p. 577
Expert systems, p. 578
Knowledge-based systems, p. 578

REVIEW QUESTIONS

1. How much training will be required to fill the majority of computer-related jobs in the near future?
2. What field is going to offer the greatest number of new jobs in the near future?
3. What are the three areas of computer technology over which we should cast a critical eye?
4. Take one of these areas and describe the dangers therein.
5. What is a possible solution to the question of job loss due to automation?
6. Describe one of the positive future possibilities of computer technology.
7. What is AI?
8. What is the difference between expert systems and knowledge-based systems?

CASE PROBLEMS

Case 17-1: New Management Ideas

A great deal is going on that will affect the way managers will have to manage in the future. Consider the following reports:

- A three-year study of the American workplace finds that American workers want to do high-quality work, but this desire is seriously undermined by management practices. The Public Agenda Foundation of New York found that many workers report that lack of stress, convenient location, and good fringe benefits make their jobs more satisfying, but what makes them work harder are potential for advancement, a chance to develop abilities, and a challenging job.[20]
- The coauthor of the best-selling book *In Search of Excellence* told a conference that managers are out of touch with their employees and customers because they are not paying attention to quality needs, to the people on the production line. Thomas Peters said it is essential to instill a sense of trust within a company. "If you insist on treating the people in your organization like children, do not be surprised when they respond that way."[21]
- Futurist Alvin Toffler (author of *The Third Wave*) says that people of the industrial society which is now beginning to fade were comfortable with uniformity, wanted to be like their next-door neighbors, accepted permanence, and were guided by their employers. People in the new society protest routine, want to feel they are doing something valuable, are diverse, improvise, mistrust experts and authority, have multiple bosses, and set themselves in motion.[22]
- Yale economics professor Jennifer Roback says that a number of fast-track professional women in their 30s who have become new mothers find they want more time off to spend with their children and more flexible working hours than their employers are accustomed to offering. Since many companies have difficulties accommodating these desires, Roback says the answer lies in self-employment, that such women should start their own firms and become entrepreneurs.[23]

Your assignment: As a manager during the next several years, you may be dealing with a different kind of employee than in the past, including many who will not want to work under normal hours or office conditions. How can you use the new technology discussed in this book to give such employees the kind of independence they may want yet still be able to ensure productivity?

Case 17-2: How Computers Can Shape Government History

A fascinating look at how technology changes our perceptions and ways of doing business was reported in an August 26, 1984 *New York Times* story.[24] Government administrators are worried that several computer technologies will have an adverse effect on the collection and storage of government documents, such as drafts of speeches and preliminary memorandums outlining policy options. These early drafts are of value not only to historians but also to new government agency heads who want to know the reasoning behind a predecessor's decision and to Federal judges trying to weigh the issues in lawsuits over government files.

Here are some of the ways information technology can hamper systematic collection of such records:

- Paper, once used, cannot be reused, so it almost automatically gets stored. However, floppy disks used in microcomputers are expensive, and so there is pressure to erase old data and reuse the disks.
- The information stored on disks frequently is not labeled properly.
- Information stored on computer tapes cannot be guaranteed for more than 20 years, because the electronic signal deteriorates.
- Information is recorded in a form that becomes obsolete (such as a kind of microfilm) and the machines used to make the information available are dropped from the government inventory.

Your assignment: Clearly, some new policies for handling such information must be established. (The government is in the process of establishing them.) Suppose you were an information consultant to the Government Services Administration, the government's warehouse and supply agency (or to the National Bureau of Standards or to the U.S. Congress). What kinds of procedures would you suggest for preserving documents? Suppose you were making recommendations to a large insurance company, whose interest in preserving records is no less critical. Would your recommendations be any different?

APPENDIX
Structured Programming in BASIC

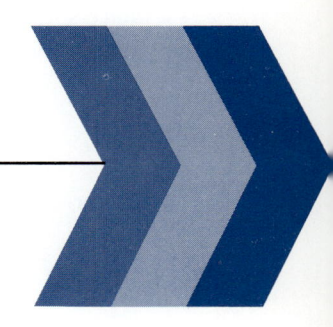

An Introduction

The Preliminaries

What Is a Program?

Consider the many ways people communicate ideas. We speak to one another to voice our thoughts. We write to make thoughts last and we read to learn something new. We use symbols to represent ideas and make them real. A piece of paper with green print represents far greater wealth than the paper's actual value, but its meaning is clearly understood. These symbols are abstractions of what is real; they are all tools that give substance to ideas.

A computer program is just another of these tools. By arranging a series of instructions in a carefully planned manner, you can direct a computer to a specific action. Instructions are just text formulated by the programmer and input to a computer. When the text, converted to machine-readable form, is run, the program allows the computer to accept information, process it, and produce results as instructed.

Programming in BASIC is one way you can formulate computer instructions. The BASIC language includes a set of specific statements that you use with proper syntax and ordering to produce a program. A typical BASIC program (shown in Figure A-1) instructs the computer to accept a temperature in degrees Fahrenheit. It then converts the number to Celsius and prints it.

Communicating with the Computer

A BASIC program is a block of text, and it can be read as such. However, you must take some steps before the computer can use the program. First you type the program into the computer, and then you review what you have typed, save the program, change it, or run it. Several commands, called system commands, make all of these things possible. System commands are typically one-word commands that you key in, then press the ENTER or RETURN key.

```
100 REM FAHRENHEIT TO CELSIUS -- T. COURY
110 REM
120 REM THIS PROGRAM WILL ACCEPT A NUMBER THAT IS THE TEMPERATURE
130 REM IN DEGREES FAHRENHEIT AND WILL CONVERT AND PRINT
140 REM IT IN CELSIUS.
150 REM
160 REM OUTPUT: C = DEGREES CONVERTED TO CELSIUS
170 REM INPUT:  F = DEGREES INPUT IN FAHRENHEIT
180 REM PROCESS: THE CONVERSION FORMULA IS
190 REM          C = (5 / 9) x (F - 32)
200 REM
210 REM
220 PRINT "ENTER TEMPERATURE IN DEGREES FAHRENHEIT."
230 INPUT F
240 LET C = (5 / 9) * (F - 32)
250 PRINT F; "DEGREES FAHRENHEIT IS"; C; "DEGREES CELSIUS"
9999 END

RUN

ENTER TEMPERATURE IN DEGREES FAHRENHEIT.
? 32
32 DEGREES FAHRENHEIT IS 0 DEGREES CELSIUS.

RUN

ENTER TEMPERATURE IN DEGREES FAHRENHEIT.
? 98.6
98.6 DEGREES FAHRENHEIT IS 37 DEGREES CELSIUS.
```

Figure A-1 A program in BASIC.

Program Entry Mode. System commands are often different on different computers, but they accomplish the same functions. To start, the computer must be in some form of program entry mode. This establishes a user work area that will accept a program that is typed into the computer. Some editing may also be available and minimally consists of deleting the last character typed and replacing an entire line. Check the documentation for your system, or ask an instructor for more details on how to do this.

Let's enter a simple BASIC program. You do not have to understand how the program works to do this. When past the program entry mode, type in the following program just as presented; end each line by pressing the RETURN or ENTER key:

```
100 REM A SAMPLE PROGRAM TO TYPE IN
110 REM
120 PRINT "WHAT IS YOUR NAME"
130 INPUT N$
140 PRINT "HELLO "; N$
9999 END
```

The program is now stored in the user work area, which is a part of the computer's memory. If one of the lines you entered is not identical to the corresponding line above, retype the line. The computer matches the lines you type by the numbers that start them; in the case of duplicate numbers, it saves the latest version you typed in.

LIST. The computer can print the program you entered as it currently exists in the work area using the system command LIST. Simply enter:

```
LIST
```

and you will see the program that you typed in.

RUN. Simply entering a program does not make it perform. The RUN command tells the computer to execute the statements of the program contained in the work area. Enter:

```
RUN
```

The computer should print:

```
RUN

WHAT IS YOUR NAME
?
```

The question mark indicates that the computer needs an entry from you. Answer the question "WHAT IS YOUR NAME" by typing in your name followed by the RETURN or ENTER key. The program will finish running and the system will wait for your next command as shown below:

```
WHAT IS YOUR NAME
? TOM
HELLO TOM
```

SAVE. At a later date you may want to have the computer say "HELLO" again, but you will probably not want to retype the program, so you will need to store it on a secondary storage medium—usually a disk. Since the user work area is only temporary storage, what you entered will disappear when you end your current session.

The SAVE command will transfer the program from the user work area to secondary storage where you can recall it sometime in the future. The SAVE command varies considerably from system to system but usually has a form similar to the following:

```
SAVE "filename"
```

where "filename" is the name of the file under which you want to store the program. Consult your system's reference manual for the specifics and then try saving your program.

Other System Commands. Many other system commands help programmers develop a good working program. Look for them in the reference manual for your particular computer installation. They are often very system-dependent, for example:

- Preparing the user work area for new program entry.

```
NEW
CLEAR
```

- Recalling a file from secondary storage and placing it in the user work area.

```
LOAD "filename"
OLD filename
```

- Listing the files currently stored on the secondary storage device.

```
FILES
DIR
```

- Removing from secondary storage files that are no longer needed.

```
KILL "filename"
DELETE filename
```

- Renaming a file currently on secondary storage.

```
NAME "old filename" AS "new filename"
RENAME old filename new filename
```

- Editing a file using a system editor.

```
EDIT filename
```

ASIDE: How to Read a Syntax Description

Throughout this appendix when you see a BASIC statement presented, a syntax description will generally follow. Its purpose is to help explain the statement and to present a framework for using it. Just glance at the definitions now and refer to them when needed.

Syntax Description Elements and Definitions

[ ]	The brackets indicate that whatever is contained within them is optional.
. . .	Three periods indicate that whatever immediately precedes them may be repeated a number of times.
CAPITALIZED	Words that are completely capitalized are BASIC statements, i.e., GOTO, INPUT, LET, PRINT
condition	This is replaced by a valid condition as described under the IF statement, i.e., A < B
constant	This is replaced by a valid constant, i.e., 1, 34, "JOE"
expression *expn1* *expn2* etc.	These are replaced by a numeric or string expression, variable, or constant, depending on the context, i.e., A / 2, C, B * (4 * A), A$, LEN(A$)
line number	This is replaced by a valid number that introduces a BASIC statement.
line number *line number1* *line number2*	Each is replaced by the line number for a BASIC statement that is to be branched to.
variable	This is replaced by a valid variable name, i.e., A, C, A$, B$

The Basics

You have seen a few BASIC programs and know how to enter and run them on a computer, so what's next? It is time to write them! BASIC programs include several elements whose arrangement must follow specific rules. Knowing where to place the numbers, spaces, commas, statements, and other components of a program is the science of BASIC programming, and this science is our focus. But programming is also an art, and this art involves combining the components in an effective and logical fashion. You will learn the art as well as the science of programming in the pages that follow.

Some BASIC Programming Considerations

Line Numbers. A BASIC program generally executes sequentially, each statement in line number order. These line numbers start each statement; they act as a label for the entire line.

Legal line numbers are usually numbers between 1 and 99999, but the maximum number differs from system to system. Commonly, BASIC programmers number programs in increments of 10 starting at 100. This allows a neat and easily readable program. It's also easy to maintain because you can insert a new statement between existing statements by starting it with a line number that fits numerically between the two existing line numbers. For example, we could add to our "HELLO" program by typing the following line:

```
145 PRINT "HOW ARE YOU TODAY?"
```

After executing a LIST command the modified program would appear as:

```
100 REM A SAMPLE PROGRAM TO TYPE IN
110 REM
120 PRINT "WHAT IS YOUR NAME?"
130 INPUT N$
140 PRINT "HELLO ", N$
145 PRINT "HOW ARE YOU TODAY?"
9999 END
```

If you type a new line with the same line number as one that exists, the new line will replace the old line.

Spacing. Spacing, while unimportant to many computers, matters to programmers. Only spaces that will appear in the output are critical since the computer will not insert spaces; it interprets all print commands literally. Use spaces as much as possible to improve readability since any statement line that does not contain spaces is difficulttoread!

DO

Show spaces that are part of a literal string.

```
200 PRINT "HELLO JOE"
                  ^
```

Space between the line number and the rest of the statement

```
130 INPUT N$
   ^
```

Space between components of the statement line.

```
140 PRINT "HELLO";  N$
   ^     ^        ^
```

Space between values and operators of an expression (more on this later).

```
500 LET Y = (3 * X) / (X - 5)
         ^ ^  ^ ^  ^ ^  ^ ^
```

DO NOT

Insert spaces between the digits of a line number.

```
1 00 REM A SAMPLE PROGRAM TO TYPE IN
 ^
```

Insert spaces between statement words.

```
130 IN PUT N$
      ^
```

Insert spaces between the digits of a number in an expression. (Do not insert commas either.)

```
500 LET X = Y + 1 000
                 ^
```

The End of the Program. You tell the computer that it's reached the end of a program with the—you guessed it—END statement. It is the last statement in any program and occurs only once. END does not necessarily show where program execution ends; it shows where the computer stops interpreting the program. Always use the highest possible line number for the END statement to ensure that it will be the last line of the program. The number 9999 represents the highest line number in our examples so this line will contain each program's END statement.

Stopping Execution. Very often, execution shouldn't stop at the last line of a program. If a program contains data, or a subroutine or function, execution should stop before the END statement. Put a STOP at the proper place in a program to terminate execution at the appropriate time; you can use STOP as often as needed. This statement's value will become clearer to you later.

Program Remarks. Documenting a program will help you with not only its development but also its maintenance. The REM statement lets you put remarks within a program. REM tells the computer to ignore the line when it executes the program. The examples presented here make generous use of remarks as program documentation. REM documentation also makes it easier for others to read and understand your program, but too many remarks can become annoying and obscure the actual statements, of course.

Variables

BASIC programming involves storing, generating, and manipulating information, and variables help make all this work possible. Variables

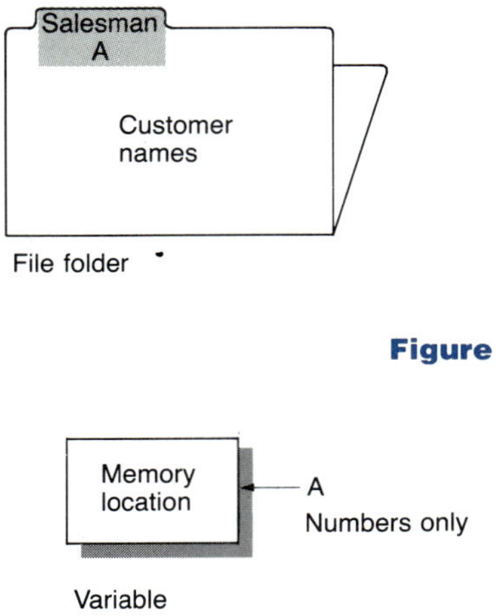
Salesman
A
Customer
names
File folder
Memory
location
A
Numbers only
Variable

Figure A-2 A file folder and a variable.

allow data to be stored and retrieved from a computer's memory; the variable acts as a label for the data and both points to where it is stored and describes the type of information it contains. One way to visualize this is shown in Figure A-2. The file folder represents a part of the computer's memory, and the label represents the variable. The label can identify the correct folder for storing or retrieving files, and it can also indicate the type of file to be stored. Similarly, a variable identifies the correct memory location for storing or retrieving data, and it too identifies the type of data stored in the memory location.

Variable Types. The two most common variable types are numeric and alphanumeric variables. We subdivide the numeric type into integer or real variables, and the two types may be subdivided further still. For our purposes we will define both integers and real numbers as numeric, and any variable that will be used to store a number for computations belongs to the numeric type. The alphanumeric variable, also called a string or character variable, can store any sequence of characters but cannot be used for computations.

When programming, there is a big difference between numbers and characters. If you want to store a person's name in a character variable, you would represent the name as "JOE." The letters *J* - *O* - *E* are stored without the quotation marks (or the dashes and spaces) since the quotes only tell the computer that the characters contained within them are to be interpreted literally. These three letters, called a literal string, would be stored in an alphanumeric variable.

You could also use an alphanumeric variable to store Joe's street address. If his address is 16050 you could store the string "16050" in an alphanumeric variable. The number 16050, shown without the quotes, can only be stored in a numeric variable. You can add 1 to 16050 but you cannot do arithmetic operations with the string "16050". In other words, 16050 represents the number sixteen thousand and fifty, while "16050" represents five characters which just happen to be numbers.

Naming Variables. To create a variable name you choose some combination of characters that the program will use to represent the memory location where the variable's information is to be stored. In previous examples, we used F, C, and N$ as variable names. F in line 230 of Figure A-1 stores the number representing the temperature in degrees Fahrenheit. This numeric variable is used in line 240's computation. N$ in line 130 of the "HELLO" program, an alphanumeric variable, will store the user-entered name; the print instructions follow in line 140. You cannot use an alphanumeric variable for computations even if you enter numbers.

The rules for naming variables vary from system to system, but most systems allow numeric names to have one letter (optionally followed by one digit), and alphanumeric names have one letter and an optional digit. You must end an alphanumeric variable's name with a dollar sign ($). For example, A, B, Z, A1, and B9 are legal numeric variables and A$, B$, Z$, A1$, and B9$ are legal alphanumeric variables.

Many versions of BASIC allow longer variable names (six, eight, 30, or more characters) and some allow special characters (such as the period or underline). If this is the case, use names that describe the data the variable will contain: e.g., CUSTOMER.NAME$, CUSTOMER.ADDRESS$, and ITEM$ for alphanumeric variable names, and PRICE, TOTAL, and GRAND.TOTAL for numeric variable names. If you can use only one or two characters, it is still good practice to think carefully when you select a name. Can you imagine the confusion if the program in Example A-1 used C for degrees Fahrenheit and F for degrees Celsius?

Assigning Values to Variables

There are various ways to assign values to variables. A numeric variable can receive a constant value directly, or it can receive the result of a computation. The program can also use a variable as a counter, either within a loop or as a part of the program control. You can assign a literal string to alphanumeric variables. Though they cannot be used for arithmetic computations, these alphanumeric strings have string manipulation statements and functions.

Assignment Using the LET Statement. The LET statement assigns values to all types of variables. Look at Figure A-3 briefly and then continue reading. Each type of assignment will be discussed in greater detail as we continue.

```
100 LET A = 5
200 LET B = A
300 LET C = (5 / 9) * (F - 32)
400 LET K = K + 1
500 LET A$ = "LITERAL STRING"
600 LET N$ = "JOE"
700 LET B$ = A$
```

The LET is optional on many systems, so:

```
400 K = K + 1
```

is equivalent to line 400 above.

Figure A-3 Some typical LET statements.

The LET statement has the following general syntax:

line number [LET] *variable* = *expression*

This shows that *variable* will be assigned the value of *expression*, and *expression* must be either numeric or alphanumeric depending on the type of *variable*. In most versions of BASIC, the word LET is optional as indicated, but it may be required in yours, so check to be sure.

When reading the LET statement in a program, think of the equal sign as "become" rather than "equal," to avoid confusion with an algebraic equal sign. Line 400 above would then be read "Let K become K plus one" rather than "Let K equal K plus one." This makes sense since the statement uses the previous value of K, adds one to it, and replaces it in K—that is, the new value of K becomes the old value of K plus one. Algebraically, "K equals K plus one" is impossible, so think of equal in association with conditional statements only (more on conditional statements later).

Line 400 of Figure A-3 shows a common use of the LET statement, and in this statement the variable K is being used as a counter. Each time the statement executes, the value of K increases by one. This use is usually found within some sort of looping structure in a program, where the variable indicates the number of times the loop has been executed.

Figure A-3 shows direct assignment of a constant (line 100), assignment of one numeric variable's value to another variable (line 200), and assignment of a computation result to a variable (line 300). Other lines illustrate literal string assignments (lines 500 and 600) and alphanumeric variable value assignment (line 700). You can assign a new value to a variable simply by executing another LET statement with the same variable. When this occurs, the previous value of the variable on the left of the equal sign is lost.

Constants. Constants, like variables, fit into one of two types—numeric or alphanumeric; we have already seen both in use. Numeric constants are simply numbers that you can use as part of an assignment, computation, condition, or other BASIC statement. Valid constants may start with a minus sign (−), must contain digits, and may include one decimal point. They may not have commas or dollar signs. Valid numeric constants include: 1, 2, 10, 10000, 1.78, −34.765, and 4.00.

An alphanumeric constant or literal string is a group of characters within quotes. You can assign, compare, and even manipulate these strings. Examples of alphanumeric constants are: "JOE", "Deanna", "16050", and "". The last example, the "", is a special alphanumeric constant called the null string; it contains nothing. It differs from the string " ", which is a literal string containing one space. Both of these strings have frequent applications in BASIC programming.

Arithmetic Computations. Computers in general—and BASIC in particular—can perform rapid and accurate computations. Though not identical to algebraic equations, arithmetic computations may be constructed to represent most any relation needed. The equations use the LET statement to assign the value of the equation to the right of the equal sign to the variable on the left of the equal sign. You can use numbers, numeric variables, and operators to construct the equations, which must fit on one line. Other components of an equation—such as BASIC or user-defined functions—will not be covered at this time.

BASIC symbols represent each of the major arithmetic operations, and the hierarchy for each is similar to algebraic hierarchy. Equations are evaluated first on this hierarchy and then in left-to-right order. Unary operators such as negative and positive signs (−1, +2) come first, followed by exponentiation, which is expressed as two asterisks (**), an upward arrow (↑), or a caret (^), depending on your system. Next comes multiplication (*) and division (/), which are of equal level. Addition (+) and subtraction (−) are the last to be evaluated and are also of equal level. Parentheses will override the standard hierarchy and may also be inserted for clarity. Figure A-4 summarizes the operations.

Input and Output

For our purposes input and output describe the process of making user-entered information available to a program while it is running, and allowing the program to convey information back to the user. In BASIC, the INPUT and PRINT statements allow user input and computer output.

The INPUT Statement. When BASIC sees an INPUT statement while a program is running, the program temporarily stops and waits for you

Level	Operation	Symbol	Comment
1	Unary	+, -	When used to show a number's sign.
2	Exponentiation	↑, ^, or **	In algebra: X^y
3	Multiplication	*	{Same level
3	Division	/	
4	Addition	+	{Same level
4	Subtraction	-	

Parentheses may be used to override the level of hierarchy shown.

Examples

Algebra	BASIC
$C = \frac{5}{9}(F - 32)$	`LET C = (5 / 9) * (F - 32)`
$Y = MX + B$	`LET Y = M * X + B`
$X = \frac{-B + \sqrt{B^2 - 4AC}}{2A}$	`LET X = (-B + (B ** 2 - 4 * A * C) ** .5) / (2 * A)`

Figure A-4 Summary of arithmetic operations in BASIC.

to enter something from the keyboard. The computer prints some type of prompt character (usually a question mark) and execution continues after you enter a response. This response is assigned to the variable associated with the INPUT statement.

The general syntax for the INPUT statement is:

line number INPUT *variable* [, *variable*] . . .

As shown, the statement may be used to accept values for more than one variable, and execution will not continue until a value has been entered for each. *Variable* may be either numeric or alphanumeric; you can have more than one *variable* for each INPUT statement. Enter a number when the prompt is for a numeric variable, a string when BASIC expects an alphanumeric variable, and remember that alphanumeric variables cannot be used in calculations. The following program fragment illustrates several uses of the INPUT statement:

```
230 INPUT F
130 INPUT N$
300 INPUT X, Y, Z
400 INPUT C$, P
500 INPUT A$, B$, C$
```

As you have seen in previous examples, a message informed the user of a needed entry. This communication forms a necessary link between the program and the person, and the PRINT statement creates the link. Many versions of BASIC also allow a prompt to be included within the INPUT statement itself. This method is not as flexible as using a PRINT statement, but it merits further study because of its convenience.

The PRINT Statement. The PRINT statement sends output to the user's terminal. This statement can print many types of expressions, in several different ways. It can print the value of all types of variables, literal strings, or even the result of an arithmetic expression contained within the PRINT statement itself. The format for the PRINT statement is:

line number PRINT [*expression*] [; or , *expression*] . . . [;]

The PRINT statement uses two special characters to separate expressions, and each character has a different effect on the appearance of the output. The semicolon (;) causes each item to be printed directly next to the previous item without skipping any spaces. The comma (,) acts like the tab key on a typewriter, forcing the next item into a new "zone." The actual size of the zone varies from computer to computer, but most use zones of 15 characters. This is illustrated in Figure A-5.

Figure A-5 Uses of the PRINT statement.

Assume the following have been executed:

```
100 LET A = 287
110 LET B = 5
120 LET C = 1000
130 LET N$ = "JOE"
140 LET H$ = "HELLO"
```

PRINT Statement	How It Will Appear	
`200 PRINT A, B`	`287`	`5`
`210 PRINT A; B, C`	`287 5`	`1000`
`220 PRINT "A = "; A, "B = "; B`	`A = 287`	`B = 5`
`230 PRINT H$; N$`	`HELLOJOE`	
`240 PRINT H$; " "; N$`	`HELLO JOE`	
`250 PRINT H$, N$`	`HELLO`	`JOE`
`260 PRINT H$; A`	`HELLO 287`	

Note: Notice the space that precedes numbers. This is the place for a sign if one were to be printed. For example:

150 LET D = −55

`270 PRINT A; D`	`287-55`	
`280 PRINT A; ","; D`	`287,-55`	

Assume the variables have the same values as in Figure A-3.

Program statements	Program output
200 PRINT A; 210 PRINT B	287 5
220 PRINT "ENTER YOUR NAME "; 230 INPUT N$	ENTER YOUR NAME ? JOE (JOE entered by user.)
240 PRINT "HELLO "; 250 PRINT N$	HELLO JOE

Figure A-6 Examples of line feed suppression.

As indicated in the syntax description just given, the PRINT statement may end with a semicolon (;), which causes line feed suppression. When an INPUT or PRINT statement follows a PRINT statement that ends with a semicolon, any output or prompt associated with the second statement will be printed on the same line as the first. Examples of this are illustrated in Figure A-6. Line feed suppression is frequently used when issuing prompts before an INPUT statement. This allows user entry on the same line as the prompt.

Two Programming Tasks

Up to this point we have covered enough topics to allow us to write some simple BASIC programs. You will be presented with two programming problems, and you will solve them step by step, using the three BASIC statements presented so far.

The EBIT Problem. You are the financial wizard at your favorite multimillion dollar company, and you want to program a recently purchased personal computer to calculate earnings before interest and taxes. How do you begin?

The best way to start is to outline the problem and identify what is required. Always start with the output. What information will the computer give to the user? In this case, the program must output a value for EBIT. Next, identify the input. What information does the computer need to calculate the output, and what is available? Taking a look at the financial information available (Figure A-7), we notice values for fixed cost, a variable cost fraction of sales, the number of units sold, and the price received for each unit. Finally, we must identify the process needed to change the inputs to the desired output. A summary of the output, input, and process is illustrated in Figure A-8.

Fixed cost:	$50,000.00
Variable cost:	60% of Total Sales
Quantity sold:	10,436 units
Price per unit:	$20

EBIT = Total Sales − Fixed Cost − Variable Cost

Figure A-7 Information for earnings before interest and taxes.

Output:	The value calculated for EBIT
Input:	Fixed cost (in dollars) Variable cost fraction (as a percent of sales) Quantity sold Unit price
Process:	Sales = Quantity sold × Unit price Variable Cost = Sales × Variable cost fraction EBIT = Sales − Fixed cost − Variable cost

Figure A-8 Output, input, and process summary for the EBIT problem.

Now that the components have been identified, let's rearrange them to act as guide in writing the program. The output, input, process order—appropriate for program planning—should be changed to input, process, output. This is the order of program execution, and will allow more rapid program development.

To fulfill the input requirements, the program will use the PRINT statement to issue a prompt and the INPUT statement to receive the user entry. The LET statement will perform calculations, and the PRINT statement, once again, will create output. That's it! Remember to add remarks for clarity and have an END as the last statement, and your program should be ready to run.

A flowchart is a useful means of communicating the execution of a program. Programs often are written from flowcharts that are created by a systems analyst; sometimes they are just used to help document the program for future maintenance. In any case, it is good to become familiar with flowcharts for even small programs. This will help you when you have to confront the larger tasks. Figure A-9 shows the flowchart for the EBIT problem.

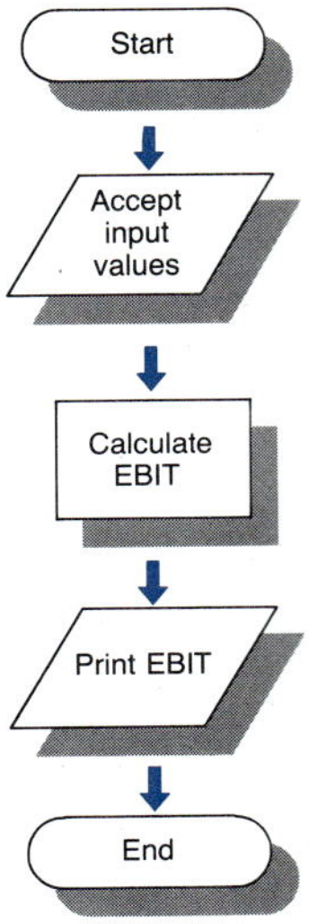
Start
Accept input values
Calculate EBIT
Print EBIT
End

Figure A-9 Flowchart for the EBIT program.

Now let's review the program. Look at Figure A-10, a listing and sample run for the EBIT problem. The program starts with a series of remarks to explain what is to be done. These may be more extensive than this small program required, but they provide a good example. Lines 290 to 390 issue prompts and accept input from the user. Lines 300 and 390 (PRINT statements) are used only to skip a line in the output. Since the statement includes no expressions, nothing but a blank line will print. The other PRINT statements in this range—used with INPUT statements—issue prompts so the user knows what number is needed. The semicolon that ends each PRINT statement causes the user entry to appear on the same line as the prompt. Once all the data has been entered, the values are calculated in lines 400 to 420, and the answer is finally output in line 430.

Figure A-10 The EBIT program and execution.

```
100 REM EBIT CALCULATION -- T. COURY
110 REM
120 REM THIS PROGRAM WILL CALCULATE EARNINGS BEFORE
130 REM INTEREST AND TAXES BASED ON FIXED COST,
140 REM VARIABLE COST, AND SALES.
150 REM
160 REM OUTPUT: E = EBIT CALCULATED
```

continued

```
170 REM INPUT:  F = FIXED COST IN DOLLARS
180 REM         V = VARIABLE COST AS A FRACTION OF TOTAL SALES
190 REM         Q = NUMBER OF UNITS SOLD
200 REM         P = UNIT PRICE
210 REM PROCESS:  EBIT IS CALCULATED BY THE FOLLOWING FORMULA,
220 REM         EBIT = TOTAL SALES - VARIABLE COSTS - FIXED COSTS
230 REM
240 REM OTHER VARIABLES:
250 REM         S = TOTAL SALES
260 REM         V2 = VARIABLE COST IN DOLLARS
270 REM
280 REM
290 PRINT "CALCULATION OF EBIT"
300 PRINT
310 PRINT "ENTER FIXED COST IN DOLLARS ";
320 INPUT F
330 PRINT "ENTER VARIABLE COST AS A FRACTION OF SALES (IE. .7) ";
340 INPUT V
350 PRINT "ENTER QUANTITY SOLD ";
360 INPUT Q
370 PRINT "ENTER UNIT PRICE ";
380 INPUT P
390 PRINT
400 LET S = Q * P
410 LET V2 = S * V
420 LET E = S - V2 - F
430 PRINT "EARNINGS BEFORE INTEREST AND TAXES >> $"; E
9999 END

RUN

CALCULATION OF EBIT

ENTER FIXED COST IN DOLLARS ? 50000
ENTER VARIABLE COST AS A FRACTION OF SALES (IE. .7) ? .6
ENTER QUANTITY SOLD ? 10436
ENTER UNIT PRICE ? 20

EARNINGS BEFORE INTEREST AND TAXES >> $ 33487.99
```

Now that your program is complete, you can calculate EBIT whenever you need to. Another useful calculation would be the break-even sales amount. Let's now write a program to perform this calculation.

Break-even Analysis. The break-even sales level occurs when EBIT equals zero. The equation may be algebraically simplified to:

$$\text{Break-even sales} = \text{Fixed cost} / (1 - \text{Variable cost fraction})$$

The sales level is the output, fixed cost and variable cost fraction are the inputs, and the processing is described by the above equation. The program is actually simpler than the previous one, and its flowchart is almost identical. Figure A-11 shows a listing and sample run.

Figure A-11 The break-even program.

```
100 REM BREAK-EVEN ANALYSIS -- T. COURY
110 REM
120 REM THIS PROGRAM WILL FIND THE BREAK-EVEN
130 REM SALES LEVEL BASED ON FIXED COST AND
140 REM VARIABLE COST.
150 REM
160 REM OUTPUT: S = BREAK-EVEN SALES
170 REM INPUT:  F = FIXED COST IN DOLLARS
180 REM         V = VARIABLE COST AS A FRACTION OF SALES
190 REM PROCESS:  THE BREAK-EVEN EQUATION IS FOUND BY ALGEBRAICALLY
200 REM         SOLVING THE EBIT EQUATION FOR SALES AT EBIT = 0.
210 REM         THE EQUATION IS:
220 REM         BREAK-EVEN SALES = FIXED COST / 1 - VARIABLE
                FRACTION
230 REM
240 REM
250 PRINT "BREAK-EVEN ANALYSIS"
260 PRINT
270 PRINT "ENTER FIXED COST IN DOLLARS ";
280 INPUT F
290 PRINT "ENTER VARIABLE COST AS A FRACTION OF SALES (IE. .7) ";
300 INPUT V
310 PRINT
320 LET S = F / (1 - V)
330 PRINT "BREAK-EVEN SALES LEVEL >> $"; S
9999 END
```

continued

```
RUN

BREAK-EVEN ANALYSIS

ENTER FIXED COST IN DOLLARS ? 50000
ENTER VARIABLE COST AS A FRACTION OF SALES (IE. .7) ? .6

BREAK-EVEN SALES LEVEL >> $ 125000
```

Branching—Moving from Place to Place

The EBIT problem was solved easily with only a few INPUT statements, some calculations, and the output statement, but as problems become more complex, so do the solutions. Branching within a program can perform these difficult tasks, and can make some seemingly impossible programs simple. In BASIC, a program normally executes sequentially from line to line, but branching allows a variation to the sequential execution.

Branching can occur in one of several ways. A program may execute a few lines, then skip to another line and continue there. It may execute only certain lines depending on a condition, or it may repeatedly execute lines a specific number of times. Each common type of branching has an application that suits it best.

The GOTO Statement. The GOTO statement creates an unconditional branch. The format for this statement is:

line number GOTO *line number*

When a GOTO occurs in a program, execution continues at the *line number* specified in the statement. Any lines between the GOTO statement and the *line number* are skipped and are not executed. As a caution, be sure that the *line number* you meant to branch to exists! Figure A-12 shows the GOTO statement.

The GOTO statement usually works in tandem with some other type of branching statement, and we will be covering these shortly. GOTO is the easiest to use, and its applications will be presented with the statements usually associated with it.

The IF Statement. The IF statement allows conditional branching based on the comparison of two expressions. The format for this statement is:

line number IF *condition* THEN *line number*

When an IF statement occurs, the condition is evaluated and, if true,

```
100 REM START OF A PROGRAM
110 REM
120
130    part of a
140         program
150
160 GOTO 200
170 these
180      lines are
190             skipped
200 execution continues here
```

Figure A-12 The GOTO statement.

execution will continue at *line number*. The *condition* is the comparison of the two expressions, and it has the following format:

expression1 conditional operator *expression2*

where the conditional operator is one of the following symbols:

Symbol	Meaning	Symbol	Meaning
=	equal to	<>	not equal to
>	greater than	>=	greater than or equal to
<	less than	<=	less than or equal to

Also, *expression1* and *expression2* must both be of the same type, either both numeric or both alphanumeric. The expressions may be constants, variables, or equations, and they are evaluated before their values are compared. This may seem somewhat complicated at first, but don't give up. Figure A-13 illustrates several examples of the IF statement.

Lines 200 to 220 of Figure A-13 illustrate the comparison of a numeric variable with a constant. These types of statements typically control execution based on a value that has been calculated or entered for N. Lines 230 to 240 are similar, but these compare the results of two calculations. Line 250 illustrates the comparison of an equation and a constant. This might be found in a program used for calculating grades. If M and N were test scores, then line 250 would cause a branch to line 500 if the average of the scores were less than or equal to 50.

Figure A-13 also shows the comparison of alphanumeric expressions. As a programmer you have to remember how a computer evaluates these comparisons to avoid errors in programming. Line 260 compares the value of A$ with the string "END", and branching occurs if

Comparing a numeric variable and a constant:

```
200 IF N = 1 THEN 500
210 IF N > 1 THEN 500
220 IF N <> 1 THEN 500
```

Comparing two numeric variables:

```
230 IF N = M THEN 500
240 IF N < M THEN 500
```

Comparing an equation and a constant:

```
250 IF (N + M) / 2 <= 50 THEN 500
```

Comparing an alphanumeric variable and a constant:

```
260 IF A$ = "END" THEN 500
270 IF N$ < "L" THEN 500
```

Comparing two alphanumeric variables:

```
280 IF A$ = N$ THEN 500
290 IF A$ < N$ THEN 500
```

Figure A-13 IF statement examples.

they are equal. This will be true only if "END" is contained in A$, and false if not. Computers are very particular about equality, of course; "END" is not equal to " END" or "E N D", which contain spaces.

For comparisons other than equality, the alphanumeric expressions are ordered alphabetically. For example, "AAA" is less than "BBB," and "JOE" is less than "JOHN." The only time this rule cannot be used is when a nonalphabetic character is a part of the comparison. In this case you must understand how the computer represents all characters in order to know what sequence will be used for evaluation. For now, we will use only alphabetic characters in any alphanumeric expression.

Line 270 compares the variable N$ with the constant "L". If N$ contains "A", "DEANNA", or "KZZZZ" then the condition is true and execution transfers to line 500. If it contains "L", "MOTHER", or "THERESA", it is false and execution does not transfer.

The final two lines of the example compare the contents of two variables, not a variable and a constant. Transfer will occur in line 280 only if the content of A$ is identical to the content of N$, and in line 290 if the content of A$ is less than the content of N$.

Additional IF Statement Forms. A few additional forms of the IF statement are available with many of the more recent versions of BASIC. An ELSE option may be available, allowing the following additional format:

line number IF *condition* THEN *line number1* ELSE *line number2*

This option allows branching to *line number1* if the *condition* is true, and to *line number2* if the *condition* is false. For example, in the following statement:

```
100 IF N = 1 THEN 500 ELSE 600
```

if N = 1 is true then the program will branch to line 500 and execution will continue there. If it is false, execution will continue at line 600. Also note that any lines between 100 and 500 would not be executed unless branched to by a different statement.

If the ELSE option is not available in a particular version of BASIC, you can still use a GOTO statement in the line following the IF/THEN statement to create the same type of control. For example, the following two statements:

```
100 IF N = 1 THEN 500
110 GOTO 600
```

will function just as the IF-THEN-ELSE statement in line 100 of the previous example. To ensure compatibility with most versions of BASIC, we will use the latter method in the examples presented.

Another option often available with the IF statement is direct statement execution rather than transfer to a line number. The new forms for both the IF-THEN and the IF-THEN-ELSE are:

line number IF *condition* THEN statement
line number IF *condition* THEN *statement* ELSE *statement*

and examples of these are:

```
100 IF A = B THEN PRINT "A EQUALS B"
100 IF A = B THEN PRINT "A EQUALS B" ELSE PRINT "A DOES NOT EQUAL B"
```

This IF statement is convenient if only one statement is to be executed contingent upon the evaluation of the condition. Sometimes multiple statements or segments of a program that are functionally related must be controlled by a condition, and one of the structured branching techniques fits this niche.

Structured Branching. In structured programming, it is common to use the IF statement to form one of the four logical patterns that are illustrated in Figure A-14. The patterns are not a required part of the BASIC language, but they help you to produce a structure for accurate and consistent program development. The GOTO statement with the IF helps

Pattern 1: The IF-THEN Structure

```
100 REM
110 REM
120
130     part of a
140             program
150
160 IF A < B THEN 180
170 GOTO 220
180 REM IF A < B THEN BEGIN
190             statement
200             statement
210             statement
220 REM END IF A < B
230 program continues here
```

Pattern 2: The IF-THEN-ELSE Structure

```
240 REM
250 REM
260
270     part of a
280             program
290
300 IF A < B THEN 320
310 GOTO 370
320 REM IF A < B THEN BEGIN
330             statement
340             statement
350             statement
360      GOTO 410
370 REM ELSE
380             statement
390             statement
400             statement
410 REM END IF A < B
420 program continues here
```

Pattern 3: The WHILE Structure

```
430 REM
440 REM
450
460     part of a
470             program
480
490 IF A < B THEN 510
500 GOTO 560

510 REM WHILE A < B THEN BEGIN
520             statement
530             statement
540             statement
550      GOTO 490
560 REM END WHILE A < B
570 program continues here
```

Pattern 4: The UNTIL Structure

```
580 REM
590 REM
600
610     part of a
620             program
630
640 REM REPEAT
650             statement
660             statement
670             statement
680 REM UNTIL A < B
690 IF A < B THEN 710
700 GOTO 640
710 program continues here
```

Note: The condition A < B is an example. Any condition may be used.

Figure A-14 IF statement structures.

to produce the patterns, and the combination of the two will add structure to an otherwise unstructured language.

The techniques presented and the examples in which they are used are by no means the only way to write programs, and they are often not the shortest and most efficient method of programming. These patterns will help you to maintain a modular and structured program for logical and accurate development, which saves you a great deal of time and effort in the long term.

The first pattern is the IF-THEN structure. If the condition is true, then execute one or more statements; otherwise continue normal execution. In other words, a series of statements is associated with the condition. These statements will be executed only if the condition is true; if it is not true, they will be ignored.

In Figure A-14 the condition of Pattern 1 is actually tested in line 160. If the condition (A less than B) is true, then the statements of lines 190 to 210 will be executed, and the program will continue at line 230. If false, they will be ignored, and execution will then immediately continue at line 230. The GOTO statement at line 170, used with the IF statement, allows this transfer of control. When the condition is false, the GOTO forces a branch around the statements of lines 190 to 210, and execution continues at line 230. The GOTO won't execute if the condition is true.

The remarks shown in the structure are not a required part of the BASIC language, but you should always include them because they add clarity. Remarks associate the proper statements with the conditions and make the programmer's intent more obvious to anyone else who reads the program. The statements within the structure itself, such as those in lines 190 to 210, are indented to further clarify the associations. Following these guidelines will make you a structured programmer and save you time and effort by helping you avoid errors.

The second pattern has two parts and is called an IF-THEN-ELSE structure. If the condition is true, then one or more statements execute. This is similar to the previous pattern, but if the condition is false, then another set of statements is performed. The branch will return to the main program stream only after one set of statements or the other executes. In this case, picture two sets of instructions associated with the condition. One set executes if the condition is true and the other if it is false. Unlike the first pattern, part of the structure will always execute; then the branch returns.

In Pattern 2 of Figure A-14, lines 330 to 350 are the statements that execute when the condition is true, and lines 380 to 400 execute when the condition is false. When true, the IF will force transfer to line 320 as the statement of line 300 indicates. After lines 330 to 350 execute, the GOTO of line 360 branches to continue program execution at line 420. You must do this to bypass the statements associated with the ELSE portion of this structure. When the condition of the IF statement in line 300 is false, the GOTO of line 310 will force transfer to line 370. The statements associated with the ELSE will then execute and the program will continue.

The third pattern is the WHILE structure; WHILE will execute a block of statements as long as (while) a condition is true. This is illustrated in lines 430 to 570 of Figure A-14. The statements of lines 520 to 550 execute as long as A is less than B. The condition is tested in line 490 and if it's true the statements that follow it will execute. Line 550 then transfers control back to line 490 where the condition is checked once again. This will continue until A is no longer less than B, and the GOTO of line 500 will then force transfer to line 570, where the program continues. It should be noted that one of the statements within the structure must change the value of either A or B to allow the condition to become false. If not, the condition of A less than B will never change, and you will have created an infinite loop, a troublesome and embarrassing programming error.

The final pattern is the UNTIL structure, which you can consider as the opposite of the WHILE structure. UNTIL allows execution of a block of statements until a condition is met. UNTIL also differs from the WHILE structure in that it does not check the condition until after the statements have been executed, whereas the WHILE checks it before execution. This means that in an UNTIL structure, the associated statements will always be executed at least once; they may not be executed at all in the WHILE structure if the condition is false at the initial trial. These structures are called pretest (WHILE) or posttest (UNTIL) conditional looping structures. The differences account for many subtle programming errors.

Lines 650 to 670 of Figure A-14 contain the statements of the UNTIL structure, and as you can see, they execute before line 690 checks the condition. If A is less than B, then the program continues at line 710. If A is not less than B, then the GOTO of line 700 forces transfer back to line 640, and the statements of the UNTIL execute again. The caution regarding an infinite loop applies here. Somewhere within the body of the structure the condition must change to allow transfer to line 710 and program continuation.

As a final note concerning all four patterns, each of the statements within the structures may actually represent another structure. An IF structure may be contained within another IF, a WHILE within a WHILE, an IF within a WHILE, or any other combination that you may require. Nesting of structures occurs frequently in well-designed programs, and if the patterns established are followed, the programs will remain clear and accurate.

Financial Analysis Revisited. We have already written two simple financial analysis programs, EBIT Calculation and Break-Even Analysis. With the new programming techniques just presented, a more useful single program could combine the calculations of the previous two. The

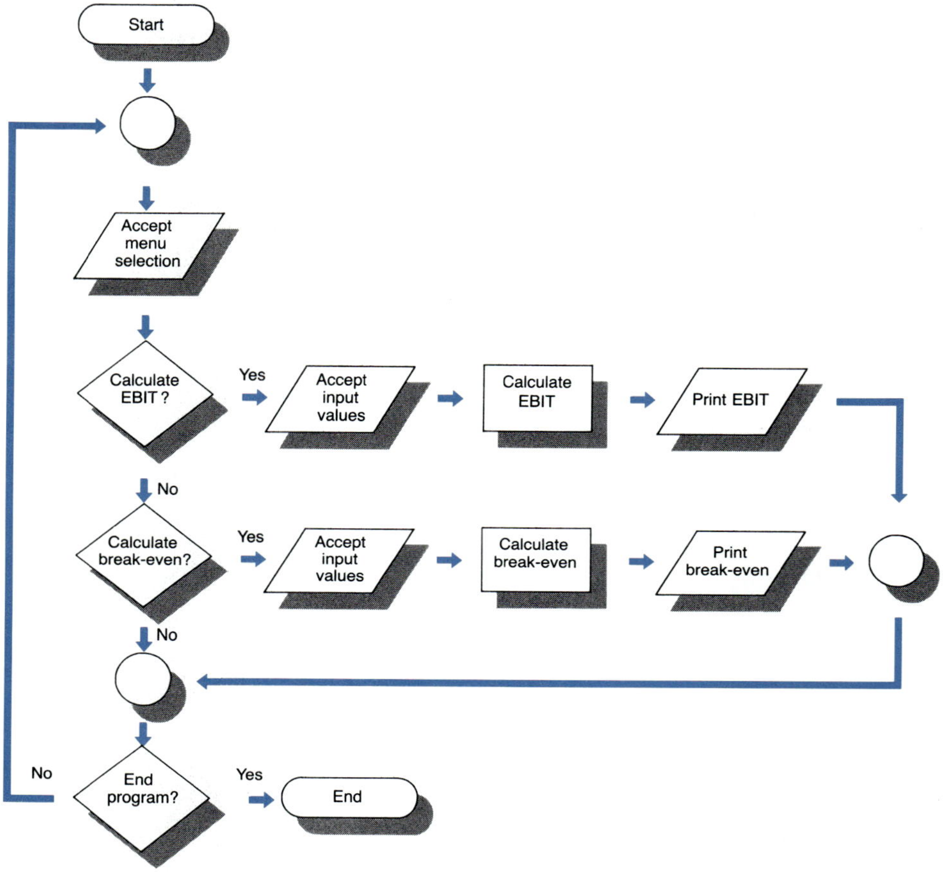
Start
Accept menu selection
Calculate EBIT?
Yes
Accept input values
Calculate EBIT
Print EBIT
No
Calculate break-even?
Yes
Accept input values
Calculate break-even
Print break-even
No
No
End program?
Yes
End

Figure A-15 Flowchart for the financial analysis program.

new program will present a menu with three possible selections, one for each of the two previous analyses and one to end the program. Based on the user's choice, the program will request proper inputs and it will then calculate and display the results.

The flowchart of Figure A-15 illustrates the logic needed for this program. The first process will print the menu and accept the selection. Selections 1, 2, and 3 correspond to calculate EBIT, calculate break-even sales, and end program, respectively. Once the selection has been entered, the program must evaluate it and perform the necessary functions. This process repeats until the user chooses a 3, which signals the end of the program.

```
100 REM FINANCIAL ANALYSIS 1 -- T. COURY
110 REM
120 REM THIS PROGRAM WILL FIND EITHER EBIT OR BREAK-EVEN
130 REM SALES LEVEL DEPENDING ON A MENU SELECTION.
140 REM
150 REM OUTPUT: E = EBIT CALCULATED
160 REM      OR  S = BREAK-EVEN SALES
170 REM INPUT:  F = FIXED COST IN DOLLARS
180 REM         V = VARIABLE COST AS A FRACTION OF TOTAL SALES
190 REM         Q = QUANTITY OF UNITS SOLD
200 REM         P = UNIT PRICE
210 REM PROCESS:  EBIT IS CALCULATED BY:
220 REM         EBIT = TOTAL SALES - VARIABLE COSTS - FIXED COSTS
230 REM           BREAK-EVEN SALES IS CALCULATED BY:
240 REM         BREAK-EVEN SALES = FIXED COST / (1 - VARIABLE FRACTION)
250 REM
260 REM OTHER VARIABLES:
270 REM         S = TOTAL SALES IN EBIT ONLY
280 REM         V2 = VARIABLE COST IN DOLLARS IN EBIT ONLY
290 REM         C = MENU CHOICE
300 REM
310 REM
320 REM ***************      PROGRAM BEGINS     ***************
330 REM REPEAT
340     PRINT
350     PRINT "1. CALCULATE EBIT"
360     PRINT "2. CALCULATE BREAK-EVEN SALES"
370     PRINT "3. END PROGRAM"
380     PRINT
390     PRINT "ENTER THE NUMBER OF YOUR CHOICE ==> ";
400     INPUT C
410     PRINT
420     IF C = 1 THEN 440
430     GOTO 620
440     REM IF C = 1 THEN BEGIN
450         REM **********     CALCULATE EBIT     **********
460         PRINT "CALCULATION OF EBIT"
470         PRINT
480         PRINT "ENTER FIXED COST IN DOLLARS ";
490         INPUT F
500         PRINT "ENTER VARIABLE COST AS A FRACTION OF SALES (IE. .7) ";
510         INPUT V
520         PRINT "ENTER QUANTITY SOLD ";
530         INPUT Q
```

continued

Figure A-16 The financial analysis program.

```
540         PRINT "ENTER UNIT PRICE ";
550         INPUT P
560         PRINT
570         LET S = Q * P
580         LET V2 = S * V
590         LET E = S - V2 - F
600         PRINT "EARNINGS BEFORE INTEREST AND TAXES >> $"; E
610         GOTO 770
620     REM ELSE
630         IF C = 2 THEN 650
640         GOTO 760
650         REM IF C = 2 THEN BEGIN
660             REM *****     CALCULATE BREAK-EVEN     *****
670             PRINT "BREAK-EVEN ANALYSIS"
680             PRINT
690             PRINT "ENTER FIXED COST IN DOLLARS ";
700             INPUT F
710             PRINT "ENTER VARIABLE COST AS A FRACTION OF SALES (IE. .7) ";
720             INPUT V
730             PRINT
740             LET S = F / (1 - V)
750             PRINT "BREAK-EVEN SALES LEVEL >> $"; S
760         REM END IF C = 2
770     REM END IF C = 1
780 REM UNTIL C = 3
790 IF C = 3 THEN 810
800 GOTO 330
810 PRINT
820 PRINT "PROGRAM COMPLETE..."
9999 END

RUN

1. CALCULATE EBIT
2. CALCULATE BREAK-EVEN SALES
3. END PROGRAM

ENTER THE NUMBER OF YOUR CHOICE ==> ? 1

CALCULATION OF EBIT

ENTER FIXED COST IN DOLLARS ? 50000
ENTER VARIABLE COST AS A FRACTION OF SALES (IE. .7) ? .6
ENTER QUANTITY SOLD ? 10436
ENTER UNIT PRICE ? 20

EARNINGS BEFORE INTEREST AND TAXES >> $ 33487.99
```

```
1. CALCULATE EBIT
2. CALCULATE BREAK-EVEN SALES
3. END PROGRAM

ENTER THE NUMBER OF YOUR CHOICE ==> ? 2

BREAK-EVEN ANALYSIS

ENTER FIXED COST IN DOLLARS ? 50000
ENTER VARIABLE COST AS A FRACTION OF SALES (IE. .7) ? .6

BREAK-EVEN SALES LEVEL >> $ 125000

1. CALCULATE EBIT
2. CALCULATE BREAK-EVEN SALES
3. END PROGRAM

ENTER THE NUMBER OF YOUR CHOICE ==> ? 4

1. CALCULATE EBIT
2. CALCULATE BREAK-EVEN SALES
3. END PROGRAM

ENTER THE NUMBER OF YOUR CHOICE ==> ? 3

PROGRAM COMPLETE...
```

The program listed in Figure A-16 uses three of the structures described in the previous section. Almost the entire program is contained within the UNTIL structure starting in line 330 with the REPEAT comment. The menu prints and the choice is accepted in lines 340 to 410. An IF-THEN-ELSE structure occurs next, with the condition C = 1. If true, the program accepts data for the EBIT calculation and calculates the output (lines 450 to 600). If false, the ELSE portion of the statement will execute, and it contains an IF-THEN structure with the condition C = 2. If this condition is true, then break-even sales will be calculated in lines 660 to 750, and if false, both IF structures end. At this point, the UNTIL condition is checked (C = 3); the program will end if the condition proves true and it will repeat otherwise. If the user enters a number other than 1, 2, or 3, the UNTIL will ignore the entry and repeat to allow a new prompt. Your programs should always include techniques to ensure that the program will process only valid entries and ignore those that are invalid. Verify all data entry to prevent unexpected results!

This program demonstrates the use of nested structures and the advantage of the UNTIL structure's posttest in some situations. The UNTIL contains an IF-THEN-ELSE, which contains an IF-THEN. One condition is checked in the first IF, and the second is checked only if the first is false. The UNTIL will then repeat the checking as long as its condition is not met. The posttest allows you to enter the choice before any checking is done. If a WHILE structure were used in its place, the user's choice of an entry would have to occur both before the structure is entered and within the structure itself, since the condition cannot be checked until a choice is entered. To avoid this "priming" problem, use the UNTIL structure. With a WHILE, the condition would change from UNTIL C = 3 to WHILE C <> 3.

The FOR/NEXT Looping Structure. Another popular structure is the FOR-NEXT loop, used when a series of statements is to be executed a specific number of times. Unlike the WHILE or UNTIL structures, the FOR-NEXT loop does not have a condition, and it does have a specific syntax that is part of the BASIC language. The first part of the syntax initiates the loop and is:

line number FOR *variable* = *expn1* TO *expn2* [STEP *expn3*]

The second part of the syntax designates the end of the loop, and the statements between the two parts are those that are executed repeatedly. The syntax description for this part is:

line number NEXT *variable*

The *variable* and all expressions (*expn1, expn2, expn3*) are numeric, and *variable* is the same in both the FOR and the NEXT statements of the structure.

When the computer encounters the FOR statement during program execution, *variable* is assigned the value of *expn1*. Execution then continues with the statements following the FOR. When the computer reaches the NEXT statement, the program branches back to the FOR statement of the loop. The value of *expn3* is added to *variable* and the execution once again proceeds with the statements in the body of the loop. This looping continues until *expn3* is added to *variable* and *variable* becomes greater than *expn2* if *expn3* is positive, or less than *expn2* if *expn3* is negative. At this point execution continues with the statement directly following the NEXT with the associated *variable*. As indicated in the syntax structure, STEP *expn3* is optional. If it is omitted, *expn3* is assumed to be a +1, and this is added to *variable* during each iteration of the loop.

There are a few more facts that you need to know about the FOR-NEXT structure, but since quite a bit has been presented already, let us discuss a few examples to help clarify its use. Study Figure A-17 briefly and continue reading. Each of the examples will be discussed as we proceed.

The first example of Figure A-17 illustrates a simple loop that will print the numbers from 1 to 10 with each on a separate line. The structure starts with the FOR of line 100. When this executes, the variable K

Figure A-17 The FOR-NEXT loop.

A simple loop to count from 1 to 10:

```
100 FOR K = 1 TO 10
110 PRINT K
120 NEXT K
```

This is the same as:

```
130 FOR K = 1 TO 10 STEP 1
140 PRINT K
150 NEXT K
```

A loop containing a variable as the initial value:

```
160 FOR I = J TO 100
170 PRINT I
180 NEXT I
```

A loop containing a variable as the initial and terminal value:

```
190 FOR I = J TO K
200 PRINT I
210 NEXT I
```

A loop that will count by fives:

```
220 FOR K = 1 TO 20 STEP 5
230 PRINT K
240 NEXT K
```

A loop that will count backward:

```
250 FOR K = 10 TO 1 STEP -1
260 PRINT K
270 NEXT K
```

A loop that contains an equation:

```
280 FOR J = 1 TO 100 - K
290 PRINT J
300 NEXT J
```

will be assigned the value of 1, and execution will then continue with the PRINT of line 110. A 1 is printed and the NEXT forces transfer back to line 100. Since STEP has been omitted, it has an assumed value of +1, and this is now added to K giving it a value of 2. The cycle continues with the PRINT, the NEXT and the transfer back to the FOR with 1 being added to K each time. Now assume we are at line 120 and K has the value of 10. Transfer occurs to the FOR in line 100, but since K already has the value of 10, the loop does not execute again; execution now transfers to the line directly following the NEXT of line 120 since the NEXT indicates the end of the looping structure. The last value for K printed within the loop was a 10.

The value of K after the FOR-NEXT structure has completed differs from system to system. In some computers the value will be 10 and in some 11. You can test this by running the short program of Figure A-18. (Some versions of BASIC do not actually add the value of the STEP expression to the variable unless the loop is to be executed again. Instead, the sum of the STEP expression and the variable is compared with the terminal value, and stored in the variable only if the condition requires another iteration of the loop.)

Look once again at the examples of Figure A-17. The loop illustrated in lines 130 to 150 is identical to the one preceding it. As previously mentioned, if STEP is omitted it is assumed to be STEP 1. The third example (lines 160 to 180) uses a variable as the initial value assigned to I. By changing its assignment before the loop is executed, you can use the value of J to determine the initial value of the counting. If J is 50, then the loop will count from 50 to 100. If J is greater than or equal to 100, then the loop will not execute at all. Lines 190 to 210 present a similar example, but both the initial value and terminal value are variables and determined by a previous assignment.

Write a short program that will accept J and K as input and then execute the loop of lines 190 to 210. This will allow you to try different values and observe the results. The best way to learn BASIC is to experiment with it!

The example of lines 220 to 240 in Figure A-17 illustrates the use of

Figure A-18 Is it 10 or 11?

```
100 FOR K = 1 TO 10
110 PRINT K
120 NEXT K
130 PRINT "THE LOOP HAS ENDED. THE VALUE OF K IS "; K
```

the STEP option to allow increments other than 1. In this example, the variable K will begin with 1 and be raised by increments of 5 with each iteration. The next value for K will be 6 (1 + 5), followed by 11, and ending with 16. Did you notice that 20 is never actually reached? This happens because the STEP value is added to the variable, and the loop terminates when the sum is greater than the terminal value. In this case, 16 + 5 is greater than 20, so the loop ends.

If the STEP is negative, the objective of the loop is to count backward, as illustrated in lines 250 to 270. K is initialized (begins) with 10 and will count down to 1, where the loop ends.

The final example illustrates the use of a short equation as one of the expressions. An equation may replace any of the expressions, and this use is common in applications such as sorting, which we will discuss later.

An Application of the FOR-NEXT. We have already discussed a program to solve EBIT. Let's add another dimension to the program to make it even more useful. When trying to predict EBIT for sales that have not occurred, you don't know the actual quantity sold. You can usually determine a range of possible quantities, but this range will also have a range of EBIT values associated with it. We should modify the original EBIT program to allow it to print a table that represents an entire range of values for quantity sold. Total sales and total cost also change with quantity and these too may be added to the table. Figure A-19 illustrates this program and a sample run.

Figure A-19 EBIT with variable quantity.

```
100 REM EBIT CALCULATION WITH A VARIABLE QUANTITY -- T. COURY
110 REM
120 REM THIS PROGRAM WILL CALCULATE AN EBIT TABLE
130 REM BASED ON FIXED COST, VARIABLE COST, AND
140 REM A SALES LEVEL WITH A VARIABLE QUANTITY.
150 REM
160 REM OUTPUT: Q = QUANTITY INDEX
170 REM         S = TOTAL SALES
180 REM         F + V2 = TOTAL COST
190 REM         E = EBIT
200 REM INPUT:  F = FIXED COST IN DOLLARS
```

continued

```
210 REM          V = VARIABLE COST AS A FRACTION OF TOTAL SALES
220 REM          Q1 = MINIMUM QUANTITY TO BE SOLD
230 REM          Q2 = MAXIMUM QUANTITY TO BE SOLD
240 REM          I = QUANTITY INCREMENT
250 REM          P = UNIT PRICE
260 REM PROCESS:  EBIT IS CALCULATED BY THE FOLLOWING FORMULA,
270 REM          EBIT = TOTAL SALES - VARIABLE COSTS - FIXED COSTS
280 REM
290 REM OTHER VARIABLES:
300 REM          V2 = VARIABLE COST IN DOLLARS
310 REM
320 REM
330 PRINT "CALCULATION OF EBIT TABLE BASED ON VARIABLE QUANTITY"
340 PRINT
350 PRINT "ENTER FIXED COST IN DOLLARS ";
360 INPUT F
370 PRINT "ENTER VARIABLE COST AS A FRACTION OF SALES (IE. .7) ";
380 INPUT V
390 PRINT "ENTER MINIMUM QUANTITY TO BE SOLD ";
400 INPUT Q1
410 PRINT "ENTER MAXIMUM QUANTITY TO BE SOLD ";
420 INPUT Q2
430 PRINT "ENTER QUANTITY INCREMENT ";
440 INPUT I
450 PRINT "ENTER UNIT PRICE ";
460 INPUT P
470 PRINT
480 PRINT " POSSIBLE", "   TOTAL", "   TOTAL"
490 PRINT " QUANTITY", "   SALES", "   COST", "   EBIT"
500 PRINT "----------", "----------", "----------", "----------"
510 FOR Q = Q1 TO Q2 STEP I
520     LET S = Q * P
530     LET V2 = S * V
540     LET E = S - V2 - F
550     PRINT Q, S, F + V2, E
560 NEXT Q
9999 END
```

RUN

```
CALCULATION OF EBIT TABLE BASED ON VARIABLE QUANTITY
```

continued

```
ENTER FIXED COST IN DOLLARS ? 50000
ENTER VARIABLE COST AS A FRACTION OF SALES (IE. .7) ? .6
ENTER MINIMUM QUANTITY TO BE SOLD ? 5000
ENTER MAXIMUM QUANTITY TO BE SOLD ? 15000
ENTER QUANTITY INCREMENT ? 500
ENTER UNIT PRICE ? 20

 POSSIBLE        TOTAL           TOTAL
 QUANTITY        SALES           COST            EBIT
----------     ----------     ----------     ----------
 5000           100000         110000         -10000
 5500           110000         116000         -6000
 6000           120000         122000         -2000
 6500           130000         128000          2000
 7000           140000         134000          6000
 7500           150000         140000          10000
 8000           160000         146000          14000
                         *
                         *
                         *
 14000          280000         218000          62000
 14500          290000         224000          66000
 15000          300000         230000          70000
```

This program works like the original EBIT program. Instead of a specific quantity, a minimum, maximum, and incremental quantity are entered. This allows the FOR-NEXT structure of lines 510 to 560 to generate a table. Go over the function of all of the statements in the program until you understand them all, including the quantities in the FOR statement and in the calculation of line 520. Did you observe the print formatting using the comma? More elegant methods of formatting are available, but this method works easily and simply.

This program could be added as choice 3 to the financial analysis program of Figure A-16, with the end as program choice 4. As new types of calculations are developed and choices added, the financial analysis program could develop into a very useful tool.

Branching and Nesting with the FOR-NEXT. Any type of branching structure including another FOR-NEXT can fit within the body of a FOR-NEXT structure, but you have to observe certain rules. First, an IF statement cannot branch into the structure between the FOR and the NEXT. For example, the following is not legal:

Illegal

```
100 IF A < B THEN 120
110 FOR K = 1 TO 10
120 PRINT K
130 NEXT K
```

A FOR-NEXT structure may only be entered by first executing the FOR statement. It is, however, permissible to exit a structure using an IF statement. An example of this is:

Legal

```
100 FOR K = 1 TO 10
110 IF K = 5 THEN 130
120 NEXT K
130 PRINT K
```

Though the example is legal, it makes no sense, but there are applications which require this kind of branch; one such application is presented in Figure A-20.

Figure A-20 The square root program.

```
100 REM CALCULATE SQUARE ROOT -- T. COURY
110 REM
120 REM THIS PROGRAM WILL CALCULATE THE SQUARE ROOT
130 REM OF A POSITIVE REAL NUMBER USING NEWTON'S METHOD.
140 REM
150 REM OUTPUT: S = SQUARE ROOT OF NUMBER ENTERED
160 REM INPUT:  N = REAL NUMBER ENTERED
170 REM PROCESS: THE SQUARE ROOT IS CALCULATED USING ONLY THE
180 REM          FOUR BASIC ARITHMETIC FUNCTIONS AND NEWTON'S
190 REM          FORMULA, WHICH IS:
200 REM          NEW X = OLD X - (OLD X * OLD X - I) / (2 * OLD X)
210 REM          A MAXIMUM OF 100 ITERATIONS WILL BE ALLOWED.
220 REM          K IS USED AS A LOOP COUNTER VARIABLE.
230 REM          X IS USED AS A TEMPORARY VARIABLE.
240 REM          THE FIRST GUESS WILL BE N / 2.
250 REM
260 REM NOTE: THIS IS A NUMERIC METHOD AND IS SIMILAR TO MANY
270 REM       COMPUTATION METHODS USED IN CALCULATORS AND COMPUTERS.
280 REM
290 REM
```

continued

```
300 PRINT "THIS WILL FIND THE SQUARE ROOT OF"
310 PRINT "A REAL NUMBER GREATER THAN ZERO."
320 PRINT
330 PRINT "ENTER THE NUMBER ";
340 INPUT N
350 IF N <= 0 THEN 300
360 LET X = N / 2
370 FOR K = 1 TO 100
380 LET S = X - (X * X - N) / (2 * X)
390 IF S = X THEN 420
400 LET X = S
410 NEXT K
420 PRINT "THE SQUARE ROOT OF"; N; "IS"; S
9999 END

RUN

THIS WILL FIND THE SQUARE ROOT OF
A REAL NUMBER GREATER THAN ZERO.

ENTER THE NUMBER ? 144
THE SQUARE ROOT OF 144 IS 12

RUN

THIS WILL FIND THE SQUARE ROOT OF
A REAL NUMBER GREATER THAN ZERO.

ENTER THE NUMBER ? 2
THE SQUARE ROOT OF 2 IS 1.414214
```

It is also possible to branch within the FOR-NEXT structure, or even to the NEXT statement itself, as long as the FOR has already been executed. When an IF statement forces branching from within a loop to the FOR statement, the FOR will initiate the loop once again. Consider the following example:

An infinite loop

```
100 FOR K = 1 TO 10
110 IF K = 5 THEN 100
120 NEXT K
```

Look at the example above. When K is assigned the value of 5, the IF in line 110 will force a transfer back to line 100 and the loop will start from 1 again—another example of the infamous infinite loop! An example that may be of use is:

Skip the 5

```
100 FOR K = 1 TO 10
110 IF K = 5 THEN 130
120 PRINT K
130 NEXT K
```

In this example the loop will print the numbers from 1 to 4 and 6 to 10. The IF in line 110 will prevent a 5 from being printed. Branching to the NEXT simply causes another iteration of the loop if its condition permits.

As mentioned previously, FOR-NEXT structures may be nested. The number of nested structures is limited by various systems, but most support the nesting of at least a few FOR-NEXT structures. When these are nested, be sure not to cross the loops. In other words a FOR-NEXT structure must be completely contained within the loop of another FOR-NEXT structure, for example:

A legal nested FOR-NEXT structure

```
100 FOR I = 1 TO 10
110     FOR J = 1 TO 10
120         FOR K = 1 TO 10
130             PRINT I, J, K
140         NEXT K
150     NEXT J
160 NEXT I
```

This, however, is an illegal nested FOR-NEXT structure:

An illegal nested FOR-NEXT structure

```
100 FOR I = 1 TO 10
110     FOR J = 1 TO 10
120         FOR K = 1 TO 10
130             PRINT I, J, K
140         NEXT I
150     NEXT J
160 NEXT K
```

Now you know all there is to know about the FOR-NEXT loop!

The Final Revision to the EBIT Program. Yes, it's the same program again, but wait until you see what we do with it this time! Let's add another variation to the execution. In addition to a variable quantity, a variable price would increase the program's usefulness in certain situations. The program should now include a range of quantities for each value in a range of prices. This new program could evaluate a pricing policy in relation to an uncertain sales quantity. A table would be printed and could be used for the evaluation.

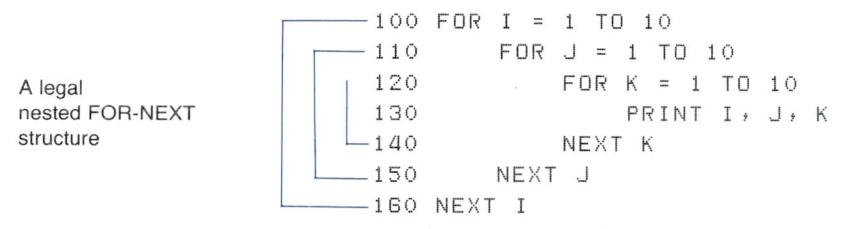

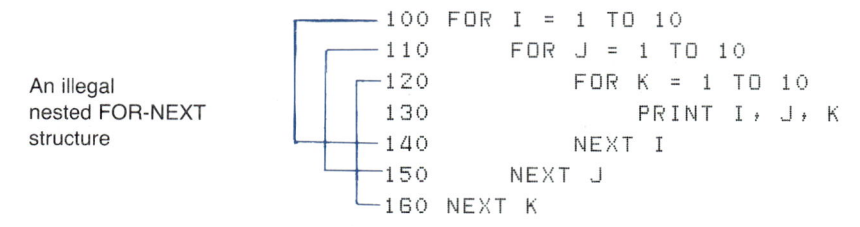

Since the table is likely to be large, and a display terminal may be used for output, it would be desirable to pause when printing output if the display is full. Otherwise the values would keep printing and could not be evaluated properly. This situation is easily resolved using the structure programming techniques previously presented.

Figure A-21 shows the logic for the program. The program uses two nested FOR-NEXT structures and an IF-THEN-ELSE structure to control the output. The calculations for EBIT remain the same but occur more frequently.

Figure A-22 shows the listing and demonstrates several interesting features. The constant L2, initialized in line 400, represents the number of lines that are contained on a display page. The program uses number of lines as a constant rather than just a value so that it may be changed easily to be used with various display sizes. By simply changing this assignment, the program will alter the number of lines displayed before a pause occurs. This type of tool will allow easy maintenance of your programs.

Minimum, maximum, and increment values are entered for both quantity and price, and these values then appear as the expressions in two FOR-NEXT loops. The quantity loop is contained within the price loop to allow the entire range of quantities to be printed for each price. We made this choice because it has the most likely applications.

After all the required input has been accepted and the initial heading printed, the price loop begins (line 630). A new price prints each time it changes (line 640). Note the semicolon ending the line to suppress line feed. The quantity loop starts in line 650, followed by the EBIT calculations. Before the results print, the program determines if it needs a pause. This is tested in line 690, and it pauses if the number of lines that have been printed equals the number of lines on the display. If this is true, then the statements in lines 720 to 810 execute, and if false, lines 830 to 840 execute. After one of the two blocks of statements completes execution, the program continues with another iteration of the quantity loop. It ends when Q1 is equal to Q2. You then encounter the NEXT P of line 870, and the price loop executes once again. This assigns a new price, and the quantity loop starts again from its initial value. The entire process continues until the price loop is complete, and the program finally ends.

Adding special features between pages of information is called a page break—a common programming feature. This occurs with displays and when it is desirable to print headings on separate pages of a printout. Notice the assignment in lines 390 and 800. This initializes the line counter for the page break. It is assigned a 6 since that number of lines is accounted for by the three lines of the heading, the two lines of the pause prompt, and the one line of the values (called a detail line) to be printed.

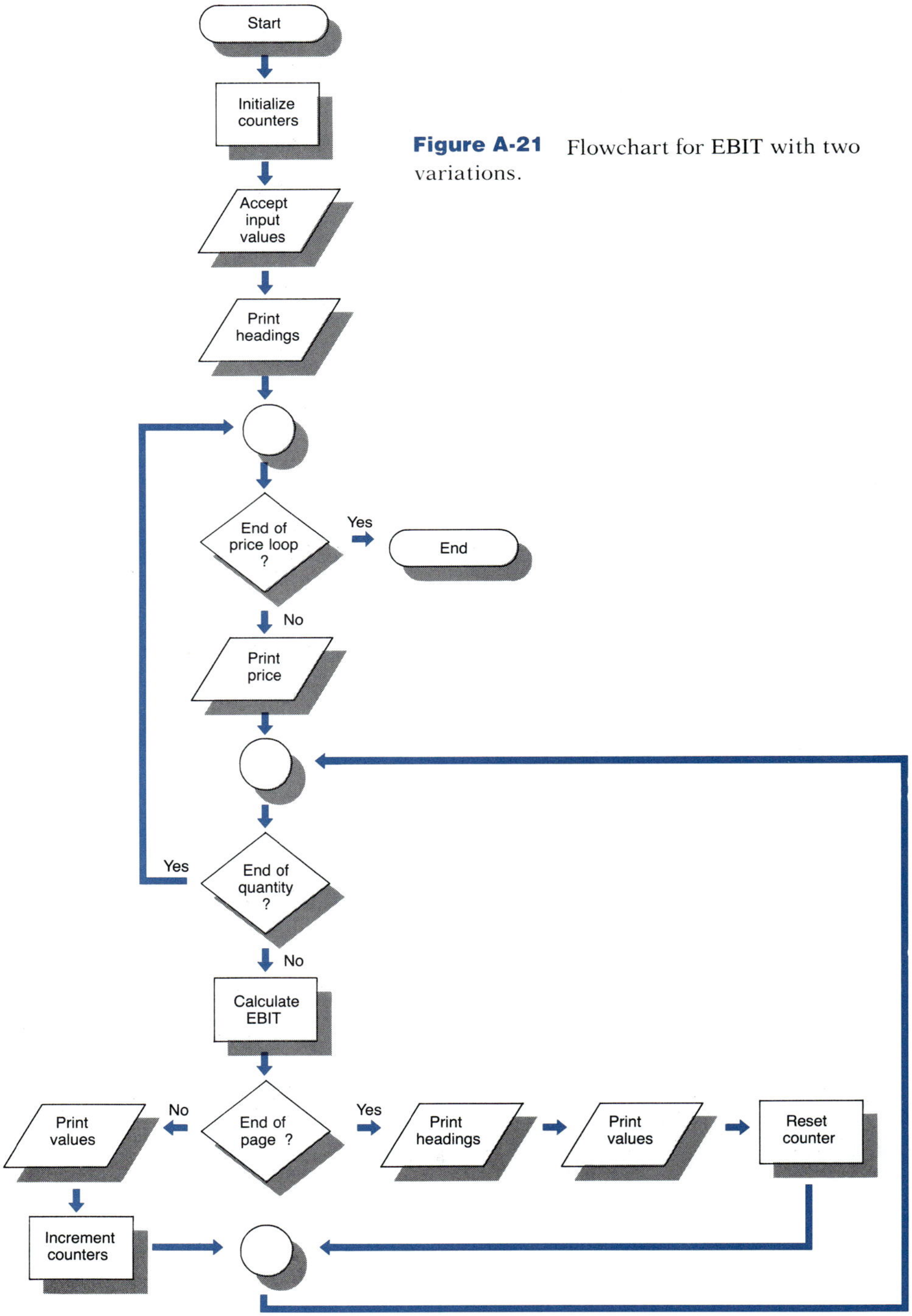
Start
Initialize counters
Accept input values
Print headings
End of price loop ?
Yes
End
No
Print price
Yes
End of quantity ?
No
Calculate EBIT
No
End of page ?
Yes
Print values
Increment counters
Print headings
Print values
Reset counter

Figure A-21 Flowchart for EBIT with two variations.

```
100 REM EBIT CALCULATION WITH A VARIABLE PRICE & QUANTITY -- T. COURY
110 REM
120 REM THIS PROGRAM WILL CALCULATE AN EBIT TABLE
130 REM BASED ON FIXED COST, VARIABLE COST, AND A SALES
140 REM LEVEL WITH A VARIABLE PRICE & QUANTITY.
150 REM
160 REM OUTPUT: P = CURRENT PRICE
170 REM         Q = QUANTITY INDEX
180 REM         S = TOTAL SALES
190 REM         F + V2 = TOTAL COST
200 REM         E = EBIT
210 REM INPUT:  F = FIXED COST IN DOLLARS
220 REM         V = VARIABLE COST AS A FRACTION OF TOTAL SALES
230 REM         Q1 = MINIMUM QUANTITY TO BE SOLD
240 REM         Q2 = MAXIMUM QUANTITY TO BE SOLD
250 REM         I1 = QUANTITY INCREMENT
260 REM         P1 = MINIMUM PRICE SET
270 REM         P2 = MAXIMUM PRICE SET
280 REM         I2 = PRICE INCREMENT
290 REM PROCESS:  EBIT IS CALCULATED BY THE FOLLOWING FORMULA,
300 REM         EBIT = TOTAL SALES - VARIABLE COSTS - FIXED COSTS
310 REM
320 REM OTHER VARIABLES:
330 REM         V2 = VARIABLE COST IN DOLLARS
340 REM         L1 = CURRENT LINE COUNTER
350 REM         L2 = NUMBER OF LINES PER PAGE
360 REM
370 REM
380 REM INITIALIZE COUNTERS AND CONSTANTS
390 LET L1 = 6
400 LET L2 = 24
410 PRINT "CALCULATION OF EBIT TABLE BASED ON VARIABLE PRICE & QUANTITY"
420 PRINT
430 PRINT "ENTER FIXED COST IN DOLLARS ";
440 INPUT F
450 PRINT "ENTER VARIABLE COST AS A FRACTION OF SALES (IE. .7) ";
460 INPUT V
470 PRINT "ENTER MINIMUM QUANTITY TO BE SOLD ";
480 INPUT Q1
490 PRINT "ENTER MAXIMUM QUANTITY TO BE SOLD ";
500 INPUT Q2
510 PRINT "ENTER QUANTITY INCREMENT ";
520 INPUT I1
530 PRINT "ENTER MINIMUM UNIT PRICE ";
540 INPUT P1
550 PRINT "ENTER MAXIMUM UNIT PRICE ";
560 INPUT P2
570 PRINT "ENTER PRICE INCREMENT ";
580 INPUT I2
590 PRINT
600 PRINT "   UNIT", " POSSIBLE", "   TOTAL", "   TOTAL",
610 PRINT "   PRICE", " QUANTITY", " SALES", "   COST", "     EBIT"
620 PRINT "----------", "----------", "----------", "----------", "----------"
630 FOR P = P1 TO P2 STEP I2
640     PRINT P;
```

continued

Figure A-22 EBIT with two variations.

```
650      FOR Q = Q1 TO Q2 STEP I1
660          LET S = Q * P
670          LET V2 = S * V
680          LET E = S - V2 - F
690          IF L1 = L2 THEN 710
700          GOTO 820
710          REM IF L1 = L2 THEN BEGIN
720              PRINT
730              PRINT "HIT ENTER TO CONTINUE ";
740              INPUT Z$
750              PRINT "   UNIT", " POSSIBLE", "   TOTAL", "   TOTAL"
760              PRINT "   PRICE", " QUANTITY", "   SALES", "   COST", "   EBIT"
770              PRINT "----------", "----------", "----------", "----------", "----------"
780              PRINT P;
790              PRINT , Q, S, F + V2, E
800              LET L1 = 6
810              GOTO 850
820          REM ELSE
830              PRINT , Q, S, F + V2, E
840              LET L1 = L1 + 1
850          REM END IF L1 = L2
860      NEXT Q
870 NEXT P
9999 END

RUN

CALCULATION OF EBIT TABLE BASED ON VARIABLE PRICE & QUANTITY

ENTER FIXED COST IN DOLLARS ? 50000
ENTER VARIABLE COST AS A FRACTION OF SALES (IE. .7) ? .6
ENTER MINIMUM QUANTITY TO BE SOLD ? 5000
ENTER MAXIMUM QUANTITY TO BE SOLD ? 15000
ENTER QUANTITY INCREMENT ? 1000
ENTER MINIMUM UNIT PRICE ? 15
ENTER MAXIMUM UNIT PRICE ? 25
ENTER PRICE INCREMENT ? 5

   UNIT       POSSIBLE       TOTAL        TOTAL
   PRICE      QUANTITY       SALES        COST          EBIT
----------   ----------   ----------   ----------   ----------
 15             5000        75000        95000        -20000
                6000        90000        104000       -14000
                7000        105000       113000       -8000.004
                              *
                              *
                              *
                15000       225000       185000        40000
 20             5000        100000       110000       -10000
                              *
                              *
                              *
                11000       220000       182000        38000

HIT ENTER TO CONTINUE ?
```

continued

```
UNIT        POSSIBLE      TOTAL        TOTAL
PRICE       QUANTITY      SALES        COST         EBIT
----------  ----------  ----------  ----------  ----------
20           12000       240000       194000       46000
             13000       260000       206000       54000
             14000       280000       218000       62000
             15000       300000       230000       70000
25           5000        125000       125000       0
                           *
                           *
                           *
             15000       375000       275000       100000
```

Now that this program is complete, why not add this to the financial analysis package we have been building? You would then have a program with five selections and much variety. At this point, the EBIT problem has probably been solved in more ways than one would care to think about.

SUGGESTED PROGRAMMING CHALLENGES

1. You have some friends who love junk food but are concerned about gaining weight. They want you to help prevent them from consuming more Calories than they use—an easy task since the only foods they consume are Big Whop McBurgers at 500 Calories each, slices of pizza at 200 Calories, and milkshakes at 300 Calories. Also, each of your friends will jog as long as needed to burn any Calories in excess of their normal daily allowance. Assume that this allowance is 2000 Calories for women and 3000 Calories for men, and that a person burns six Calories for every minute of jogging time.

   Write a program to accept the sex of your friend and the quantity of each of the above foods he or she consumed. Calculate the total Calorie intake and the appropriate allowance. The program should then determine whether the intake is greater or less than the allowance and display the number of minutes the person should jog to keep from gaining weight, or it should display the message, "YOU MAY KEEP ON EATING!"

2. A program is needed to help assess common stock transactions. Write a program to accept the price per share for which some stock was purchased, the number of shares purchased, the selling price per share, the time in months that the stock was owned, and the commission rate the broker charged as a percent of the transaction amount.

   The program should then calculate and display the total commission paid. Assume that total commission is the commission rate times the sum of the total purchase amount and the total selling amount. It should also display the amount of profit or loss and the percentage rate of the profit or loss on an annualized basis.

3. Assume you are an agent who helps organize giant oil shipments. Typically you try to find buyers for contracts that call for delivery of between 100,000 and 500,000 barrels of oil per day, and you generally receive a commission of between $0.0025 and $0.05 per barrel. A contract is usually labeled by terms such as $6 \times 3 \times 1$, which means that the selling price per barrel may be adjusted every six months, that the contract is subject to renewal every three months, and that the maximum length is one year. You receive your commission at a prenegotiated amount per barrel for the number of barrels actually delivered.

   Write a program to accept the commission rate per barrel, the number of barrels per day that is expressed in the contract, the renewal period, and the maximum length of the contract. Then calculate and display the amount of the commission and the cumulative amount for each period until the end of the contract.

4. Write a program to determine what equal payment is needed, compounded at some interest rate, to provide a required future sum (this is commonly referred to as the sinking fund problem). For example, assume you have a $10,000 loan that is due in five years. What equal, annual amount should be deposited in a savings account that pays 8% interest in order to pay the loan when it becomes due? The formula for solving this problem is:

   Payment per period = Amount needed / Annuity compound factor
   where annuity compound factor (ACF) for period, n, at a k percent interest rate (ACF k,n) is

   $$\text{ACF } k,n = (1 + k)^{n-1} + (1 + k)^{n-2} + \ldots + (1 + k)^1 + 1$$

   For example, the ACF for the above problem would be

   $$\text{ACF } .08,5 = 1.08^4 + 1.08^3 + 1.08^2 + 1.08 + 1 = 5.867$$

   and the annual deposit for each of five years should then be

   Payment per period = $10,000 / 5.867 = $1704.45

   Your program should accept the amount needed, the number of periods, and the interest rate received per period. It should then calculate the annuity compound factor and the payment required per period with the latter being displayed.

5. The factorial function has many applications in mathematics and statistics. If n is some positive integer, then *n factorial* (commonly seen as $n!$) is defined as the product of all integers between 1 and n. For example, 4! would be computed as

   $$1 \times 2 \times 3 \times 4 = 24$$

Also, by definition, 0! is equal to 1.

Write a program to accept a positive integer and display its factorial.

6. There is a unique sequence of integers known as the Fibonacci sequence, which is

0, 1, 1, 2, 3, 5, 8, 13, 21, . . .

Each integer of the sequence is the sum of the previous two integers, and the first two elements are 0 and 1.

Write a program to accept an element position and give the corresponding Fibonacci number. For example, if a 7 were accepted, the number 8 would be displayed since it is the seventh Fibonacci number.

The Next Step

Now that we've reviewed the basics of BASIC programming, it's time for the next step. There are several more features of the language that will boost your power in developing better and more useful programs. These include methods for using tables, for storing data within the program itself, for using subroutines, and for processing a case structure. We'll cover each of these tools.

Arrays

Table Storage with Arrays. We have seen how BASIC uses variables to store and access information, but in order to take full advantage of a computer's processing power, you need to store related information in an array. If a variable is analogous to a file folder, then an array is analogous to an accordion file. As illustrated in Figure A-23, the array name is the label on the file, and—like the file—the array has a different slot for each of several elements. Actually, an array is a subscripted variable, with each subscript representing another storage position.

Single-dimension array variables appear as:

```
A$(5), B$(2), T(10), P3(5)
```

These are simply variables that have been defined as arrays; they are variable names followed by a number in parentheses. Each position within the array has a number (called its index), and the numbers start at one and end with the maximum number of storage positions (the array's dimension). An array is often called a table since the number that serves as an index can be used to find the element to which it refers.

The DIM statement sets the dimensions of an array. Rather than using a syntax description, we'll use the following example to describe the DIM statement:

```
100 DIM A$(10), T2(20)
```

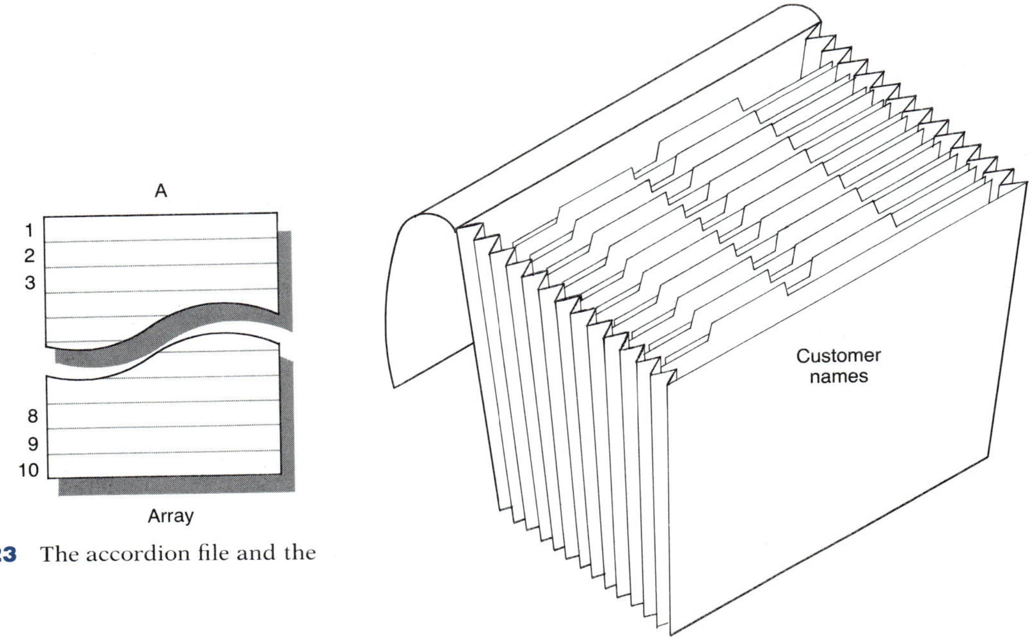
A
1
2
3
8
9
10
Array
Customer
names

Figure A-23 The accordion file and the array.

Used to define the size of an array, the DIM line belongs near the beginning of a BASIC program. This is necessary because an array must be defined in most versions of BASIC before you can use it. In other words, an element of any array may not be assigned a value before the DIM statement has defined the array. In addition to declaring that an array exists, the DIM statement also indicates the total number of elements that you can put in the array. In the example, A$(10) defines the A$ array with enough storage for ten elements; you address each element by using the variables A$(1) to A$(10).

Once the array has been defined, you treat each array variable just as any other variable. A$(1) or A$(5) may be used just as B$ or C$ would be. An array can, however, be much more desirable in some applications. The numbers that act as an index to the variable can be replaced by an expression—that is, another variable or even an equation. Consider the following example:

```
100 DIM A$(10)
110 PRINT "ENTER 10 NAMES."
120 FOR K = 1 TO 10
130 INPUT A$(K)
140 NEXT K
```

```
150 PRINT "THE NAMES YOU ENTERED WERE:"
160 FOR K = 1 TO 10
170 PRINT A$(K)
180 NEXT K
9999 END
```

The example simply accepts ten names from a user, places them into the A$ array, and prints them back. Imagine trying to write this short program without using an array! It would require ten separate variables, ten INPUT statements, and ten PRINT statements, just to accept and print the names, and the FOR-NEXT loops could not be used.

Using FOR-NEXT loops is common with array processing because the variable of the loop acts as an index for the array elements. Let us now consider a variation of the previous program that demonstrates the use of an array and FOR-NEXT loops. In addition to accepting and printing ten names as demonstrated, we will now write a program that will accept them, sort them alphabetically, and then print them.

Figure A-24 includes the program and a sample run. The array sort in lines 340 to 450 uses a bubble sort, so-called because as the loops are executed, the names that should alphabetically appear first in the array "bubble" to the top. The two loops needed for this sort are nested one within the other. The outer loop—the K loop—starts at 1 and ends at 9,

Figure A-24 The sort program.

```
100 REM NAME SORT -- T. COURY
110 REM
120 REM THIS PROGRAM WILL ACCEPT 10 NAMES, SORT THEM
130 REM AND PRINT THEM IN ALPHABETICAL ORDER.
140 REM
150 REM OUTPUT: N$() = THE ARRAY CONTAINING THE SORTED NAMES
160 REM INPUT:  N$() = THE ARRAY THAT WILL CONTAIN THE NAMES
170 REM PROCESS:  A BUBBLE SORT WILL BE USED TO ALPHABETIZE
180 REM           THE NAMES.
190 REM
200 REM OTHER VARIABLES:
210 REM         I = A LOOP COUNTER
220 REM         J = A LOOP COUNTER
230 REM         T$ = TEMPORARY NAME STORAGE
240 REM
250 REM
260 REM DIMENSION ARRAY
```

continued

```
270 DIM N$(10)
280 REM ACCEPT INPUT
290 PRINT "ENTER 10 NAMES:"
300 FOR K = 1 TO 10
310     PRINT "ENTER NAME NUMBER "; K; " ";
320     INPUT N$(K)
330 NEXT K
340 REM SORT NAMES
350 FOR K = 1 TO 9
360     FOR J = 1 TO 10 - K
370         IF N$(J) > N$(J + 1) THEN 390
380         GOTO 430
390         REM IF N$(J) > N$(J + 1) THEN BEGIN
400             LET T$ = N$(J)
410             LET N$(J) = N$(J + 1)
420             LET N$(J + 1) = T$
430         REM END IF N$(J) > N$(J + 1)
440     NEXT J
450 NEXT K
460 REM PRINT NAMES
470 PRINT
480 PRINT "THE SORTED NAMES ARE:"
490 FOR K = 1 TO 10
500 PRINT , N$(K)
510 NEXT K
9999 END

RUN

ENTER 10 NAMES:
ENTER NAME NUMBER  1  ? ZACHARY
ENTER NAME NUMBER  2  ? ANTHONY
ENTER NAME NUMBER  3  ? DEANNA
ENTER NAME NUMBER  4  ? ROBERT
ENTER NAME NUMBER  5  ? TERI
ENTER NAME NUMBER  6  ? JOHN
ENTER NAME NUMBER  7  ? BETH
ENTER NAME NUMBER  8  ? TRACI
ENTER NAME NUMBER  9  ? FRANCES
ENTER NAME NUMBER  10  ? MARY
```

continued

```
THE SORTED NAMES ARE:
              ANTHONY
              BETH
              DEANNA
              FRANCES
              JOHN
              MARY
              ROBERT
              TERI
              TRACI
              ZACHARY
```

which is one less than the number of elements in the array. As each iteration of the K loop completes, one more element has been sorted. The J loop indexes the comparisons, allowing two successive elements to be compared during each of its iterations. Did you notice that each time the K loop executes, the J loop's terminal value decreases by one? This is because each time the J loop completes, the last element it indexes ends up in its proper place.

The actual sorting occurs in lines 370 to 430. The IF statement compares the two successive elements currently being indexed by the J loop. If the predecessor is greater than the successor, then the items are switched; otherwise they are not. This repeats until all the needed elements have been compared.

Let's examine the bubble sort in Figure A-25. When the loops start with K and J equal to 1, the first comparison is made between items 1 and 2, which contain the names Zachary and Anthony. Since Zachary is "greater" than Anthony (alphabetically speaking), their positions are exchanged. The J loop moves to the next item, and the process continues until Zachary is in the tenth position. At this point the J loop ends, and the K loop continues with its next iteration. The J loop starts again from 1, but since its terminal value is dependent upon the current value of K, it will execute one less time than it did previously. This makes sense since Zachary is correctly in the last position, and we don't need a comparison for this position.

Two-Dimensional Arrays. Up to this point we have been working with single-dimension arrays, but BASIC also uses two-dimensional arrays. These are often called matrices (singular: matrix). Using the DIM statement to define a matrix:

```
100 DIM A$(10,10), B$(4,10), S(3,6)
```

Unsorted names

1	ZACHARY
2	ANTHONY
3	DEANNA
4	ROBERT
5	TERI
6	JOHN
7	BETH
8	TRACI
9	FRANCES
10	MARY

After first iteration
K=1, J=1

1	ANTHONY
2	ZACHARY
3	DEANNA
4	ROBERT
5	TERI
6	JOHN
7	BETH
8	TRACI
9	FRANCES
10	MARY

After second iteration
K=1, J=2

1	ANTHONY
2	DEANNA
3	ZACHARY
4	ROBERT
5	TERI
6	JOHN
7	BETH
8	TRACI
9	FRANCES
10	MARY

After last iteration
K=1, J=9

1	ANTHONY
2	DEANNA
3	ROBERT
4	TERI
5	JOHN
6	BETH
7	TRACI
8	FRANCES
9	MARY
10	ZACHARY

After fourth iteration
K=2, J=4

1	ANTHONY
2	DEANNA
3	ROBERT
4	JOHN
5	TERI
6	BETH
7	TRACI
8	FRANCES
9	MARY
10	ZACHARY

After fifth iteration
K=2, J=5

1	ANTHONY
2	DEANNA
3	ROBERT
4	JOHN
5	BETH
6	TERI
7	TRACI
8	FRANCES
9	MARY
10	ZACHARY

Note: Positions are switched for all values of J when K is 1, but when K becomes 2, switching occurs only for J values of 4, 5, 7, and 8, and TRACI ends up in the ninth position. Try it by hand and it will become clear.

Figure A-25 What is a bubble sort?

The matrix has a row and a column, with the first number in the parentheses representing the maximum number of rows and the second the maximum number of columns. If C$ is defined as C$(5,5), then this matrix may contain a total of 25 items, and each could be referenced by indexing the two numbers of the array variable.

Figure A-26 shows a matrix. To access the first row and first column of the C$ array, use the variable C$(1,1). Each pair of numbers shown in the matrix refers to that position in the two-dimensional array variable C$.

Just as in the single-dimension array, the index number can be a

Row \ Column	1	2	3	4	5
1	1,1	1,2	1,3	1,4	1,5
2	2,1	2,2	2,3	2,4	2,5
3	3,1	3,2	3,3	3,4	3,5
4	4,1	4,2	4,3	4,4	4,5
5	5,1	5,2	5,3	5,4	5,5

Figure A-26 The matrix.

numeric expression. The following example demonstrates how 25 numbers would be entered into a matrix:

```
100 DIM C(5,5)
110 FOR I = 1 TO 5
120 FOR J = 1 TO 5
130 PRINT "ENTER NUMBER "; I; ","; J; " ";
140 INPUT C(I,J)
150 NEXT J
160 NEXT I
```

An example of this type may be used if a program is to perform matrix arithmetic. Matrices are not as useful as single-dimension arrays for business processing.

As a final note concerning one- and two-dimensional arrays: the variable name that you use in a DIM statement is not the same as the name of the nonarray variable. Even though C(5,5) was defined in line 100 above, your program could also include a numeric variable named C. Since the C *array* always appears as C(num,num), the computer can't confuse it with the C *variable,* so you can use both in the same program.

Storing Data Within a Program

The READ and DATA Statements. In business programming, you generally use the READ and DATA statements to store information that you will use within a table. For example, if you write a program to calculate the depreciation of a fixed asset, you could store the standard depreciation values in the program and read them into a table for reference when needed. These statements often appear in place of file processing. Using READ-DATA to simulate reading from a file works well enough when you are new to BASIC, but it is not realistic for genuine applications.

Using the READ-DATA statements to access information is easy. The READ statement works as the INPUT statement does, but instead of accepting a user entry, the system retrieves information from the DATA statement. The syntax of the READ statement is:

line number READ *variable* [*,variable*] . . .

The syntax of the DATA statement is:

line number DATA *constant* [*,constant*] . . .

These would commonly appear in a program as:

```
100 READ N1$, N2$, A
110 PRINT N1$, N2$, A
         .
         .
         .
600 DATA "BRIAN", "JEWELL", 24
610 END
```

When the program is run, the READ statement will assign "BRIAN" to N1$, "JEWELL" to N2$, and the number 24 to A. These would then be printed in line 110.

Notice that the DATA statement is near the end of the program. Actually, you can place this statement anywhere since it does not affect program execution, but placing all the DATA statements at the end keeps the executable portion of the program readable. Make sure that you have enough data within the DATA statement for all the variables.

The READ statement may appear more than once—and usually does. When another READ executes, it takes the next item of data from the DATA statement. Picture a pointer that indicates the last data item that was retrieved by a READ statement. This pointer does not reset with a new READ; instead, it continues retrieving data where it left off. You're always allowed to have more than enough data but you can't have too little. Consider the following example:

```
100 READ  N1$, N2$, A
110 PRINT N1$, N2$, A
120 READ  N1$, N2$, A
130 PRINT N1$, N2$, A
          .
          .
          .
600 DATA "BRIAN", "JEWELL", 24, "JOHN", "STANOVICH", 31
610 DATA "JOHN", "SROKA", 30, "JOE", "BLOW", 31
9999 END
```

As before, the first READ will retrieve BRIAN, JEWELL, and 24, and these will be printed by line 110. The second READ will then retrieve JOHN, STANOVICH, and 31, and these will be printed by line 130. If another READ existed, it would continue with the next DATA statement and so on.

We haven't mentioned it until now, but the data types within the READ and DATA statements must match. An error will occur if an alphanumeric constant is read into a numeric variable or, in some cases, if a number that is not within quotes is read into a string variable. Remember to maintain proper ordering in both the variables of the READ and the constants of the DATA to ensure matched assignments.

Observing these BASIC program examples will help you to develop a clear understanding of the applications. Figure A-27 presents a program that uses table processing with arrays and READ-DATA state-

Figure A-27 A program to calculate depreciation.

```
100 REM ACCELERATED DEPRECIATION CALCULATOR -- T. COURY
110 REM
120 REM THIS PROGRAM WILL CALCULATE AN ACCELERATED
130 REM DEPRECIATION TABLE BASE ON THE ACRS RECOVERY
140 REM TABLE FOR AN ASSET OF 1985.
150 REM
160 REM OUTPUT: D = DEPRECIATION AMOUNT FOR THE YEAR
170 REM INPUT:  O = ORIGINAL BASIS
180 REM         C = CLASS LIFE IN YEARS
190 REM PROCESS:  THE DEPRECIATION FOR EACH YEAR IS CALCULATED BY:
200 REM        DEPRECIATION = ACRS VALUE X BASIS
210 REM
220 REM OTHER VARIABLES:
230 REM          T1(3) = THREE-YEAR TABLE
240 REM          T2(5) = FIVE-YEAR TABLE
250 REM          T3(10) = TEN-YEAR TABLE
260 REM          I = INDEX
270 REM          Q$ = RECEIVE ANSWER TO REDO QUESTION
280 REM
290 REM
300 REM DIMENSION ARRAYS
310 DIM T1(3), T2(5), T3(10)
320 REM INITIALIZE THREE-YEAR TABLE
330 FOR I = 1 TO 3
340     READ T1(I)
350 NEXT I
360 REM INITIALIZE FIVE-YEAR TABLE
370 FOR I = 1 TO 5
380     READ T2(I)
```

continued

```
390 NEXT I
400 REM INITIALIZE TEN-YEAR TABLE
410 FOR I = 1 TO 10
420     READ T3(I)
430 NEXT I
440 REM ACCEPT INPUT
450 PRINT "ENTER ORIGINAL BASIS ";
460 INPUT O
470 PRINT "ENTER CLASS LIFE IN YEARS (3, 5, OR, 10) ";
480 INPUT C
490 PRINT
500 PRINT "    YEAR", "DEPRECIATION"
510 PRINT "------------", "------------"
520 REM CALCULATE DEPRECIATION
530 IF C = 3 THEN 550
540 GOTO 610
550 REM IF C = 3 THEN BEGIN
560     FOR I = 1 TO 3
570         D = T1(I) * O
580         PRINT I, D
590     NEXT I
600     GOTO 830
610 REM ELSE
620     IF C = 5 THEN 640
630     GOTO 700
640     REM IF C = 5 THEN BEGIN
650         FOR I = 1 TO 5
660             D = T2(I) * O
670             PRINT I, D
680         NEXT I
690         GOTO 820
700     REM ELSE
710         IF C = 10 THEN 730
720         GOTO 790
730         REM IF C = 10 THEN BEGIN
740             FOR I = 1 TO 10
750                 D = T3(I) * O
760                 PRINT I, D
770             NEXT I
780             GOTO 810
790         REM ELSE
800             GOTO 470
```

continued

```
810         REM END IF C = 10
820     REM END IF C = 5
830 REM END IF C = 3
840 PRINT
850 PRINT "DO YOU WANT ANOTHER CALCULATION (Y OR N) ";
860 INPUT Q$
870 IF Q$ = "Y" THEN 440
880 PRINT
890 PRINT "PROGRAM COMPLETE..."
900 DATA .29, .47, .24
910 DATA .18, .33, .25, .16, .08
920 DATA .09, .19, .16, .14, .12
930 DATA .10, .08, .06, .04, .02
9999 END

RUN

ENTER ORIGINAL BASIS ? 20000
ENTER CLASS LIFE IN YEARS (3, 5, OR, 10) ? 3

    YEAR      DEPRECIATION
------------ ------------
 1             5800
 2             9400
 3             4800

DO YOU WANT ANOTHER CALCULATION (Y OR N) ? Y
ENTER ORIGINAL BASIS ? 20000
ENTER CLASS LIFE IN YEARS (3, 5, OR, 10) ? 5

    YEAR      DEPRECIATION
------------ ------------
 1             3600
 2             6600
 3             5000
 4             3200
 5             1600

DO YOU WANT ANOTHER CALCULATION (Y OR N) ? Y
ENTER ORIGINAL BASIS ? 20000
ENTER CLASS LIFE IN YEARS (3, 5, OR, 10) ? 10
```

continued

```
     YEAR      DEPRECIATION
------------ ------------
 1              1800
 2              3800
 3              3200
 4              2800
 5              2400
 6              2000
 7              1600
 8              1200
 9              800
 10             400

DO YOU WANT ANOTHER CALCULATION (Y OR N) ? N

PROGRAM COMPLETE...
```

ments. The data contained within the program are the recovery percentages used for calculating accelerated depreciation using the *Accelerated Cost Recovery System* standard. The program will accept the original basis for an investment along with its class life, and it will calculate and display each year's depreciation allowance.

The program initializes three tables in lines 320 to 430 by reading the data from the DATA statements of lines 900 to 930. The index to each of the tables represents the corresponding year of the depreciation percentage contained within the table. That's why the three-year table contains three elements, the five-year contains five elements, and so on. Once you've determined the proper class with the nested IF's of lines 530 to 820, each year's depreciation is calculated with the corresponding FOR-NEXT loop performing the table indexing. Finally, you see the value printed.

Using RESTORE with READ-DATA. Remember the data pointer mentioned earlier? The RESTORE statement resets that pointer. This statement has the following very short syntax:

line number RESTORE

When a RESTORE executes, the READ statement that follows it will start reading from the first constant of the first DATA statement just as it would on an initial READ. Consider a slight modification to an example used above:

```
100 READ  N1$, N2$, A
110 PRINT N1$, N2$, A
120 READ  N1$, N2$, A
130 PRINT N1$, N2$, A
140 RESTORE
150 READ  N1$, N2$, A
160 PRINT N1$, N2$, A
          .
          .
          .
600 DATA "BRIAN", "JEWELL", 24, "JOHN", "STANOVICH", 31
610 DATA "JOHN", "SROKA", 30, "JOE", "BLOW", 31
9999 END
```

After execution of the RESTORE of line 140, the data pointer resets to "BRIAN", and the READ of line 150 will retrieve this name along with "JEWELL" and 24. With no RESTORE at 140, the READ of 150 would assign "JOHN", "SROKA", and 30 to its variables.

The RESTORE is most commonly used in an application that requires multiple use of the same constants in a DATA statement, for example, a process that uses the READ-DATA combination to do a table search rather than reading the data into an array.

Subroutines in BASIC

GOSUB and RETURN. A subroutine in BASIC gives you another way of branching, with the added advantage of an unconditional return. The GOSUB and RETURN statements create this type of subroutine branching. The syntax for the GOSUB is:

line number GOSUB *line number*

and the RETURN:

line number RETURN

The GOSUB works much like the GOTO, but isn't used in the same situations. The *line number* referenced by GOSUB is actually the start of a group of statements that end with a RETURN. When BASIC sees a GOSUB, execution transfers to *line number* and the program proceeds from that point until it encounters a RETURN. The RETURN then forces transfer back to the line immediately following the GOSUB statement that initiated the branch.

Consider the following example:

```
100 REM A PROGRAM TO SQUARE A NUMBER
110 INPUT N
```

```
120 GOSUB 150
130 PRINT S
140 STOP
150 REM START OF THE SUBROUTINE
160 LET S = N * N
170 RETURN
9999 END
```

This shows the use of both a subroutine and the STOP statement introduced earlier. The GOSUB of line 120 forces transfer to the subroutine of line 150. The value of S is calculated and the RETURN statement branches back to the PRINT of line 130.

Be careful when you use subroutines. An error will occur if a RETURN executes without a GOSUB. This would happen without the STOP in the example. Recall that the STOP terminates the program at that point. Also, if a GOTO is used to branch to the subroutine, an error would occur since the RETURN is not matched by a calling GOSUB. A subroutine may be called within another subroutine, but various systems limit the level of nesting. A few levels are generally safe as is a well-structured program.

A Case Structure

The ON . . . GOTO Statement. A case structure selects an alternative based on some determination value. In BASIC, the ON . . . GOTO statement does the work and the determination value is contained within a numeric expression. The syntax for this statement is:

line number ON *expression* GOTO *line number* [,*line number*] . . .

The statement will force branching to one of the *line numbers* within it, and *expression* determines to which *line number* control branches. For example, if the value of *expression* were 3, then the GOTO would transfer to the third *line number* in the list. Make sure that you account for all possible values of *expression* in the ON . . . GOTO statement. That is, there should be enough *line numbers* to match the maximum value for *expression*, and *expression* should never be less than one or have a non-integer value. Also—as you may have guessed—*expression* is always numeric.

One of the most common uses for the ON . . . GOTO statement is in processing a menu selection (this may be used in place of the nested IF's in the financial analysis program). The following example illustrates this concept:

```
100 REM MENU PROCESSING USING A CASE STRUCTURE
110 PRINT "ENTER YOUR CHOICE (1, 2, OR 3) ";
120 INPUT C
```

```
130 IF C < 1 THEN 110
140 IF C > 3 THEN 110
150 ON C GOTO 160, 200, 300
160 REM PROCESS C = 1
                    .
                    .
                    .
200 REM PROCESS C = 2
                    .
                    .
                    .
300 REM PROCESS C = 3
                    .
                    .
                    .
9999 END
```

As the example illustrates, you will branch to line 160, 200, or 300 based on the value input for C—a 1, 2, or 3, respectively. Also, the IF statements ensure that a valid entry was accepted. And finally, ON . . . GOTO statements need comments for each section that will be branched to. This enhances a program's clarity and helps to keep it structured.

A Little Bit of Everything in a Payroll Program

Now that you have the bulk of what you need to produce useful BASIC programs, it is time to put what you've learned to use once again. A payroll program is a good application for this purpose, and it also introduces some concepts that will be beneficial in your future software development.

The next program contains many familiar components, as well as some that may not be so familiar. File processing is simulated using the READ-DATA statements. The program starts by reading a line of data that could represent what is known as a record in a sequential file. The record contains the employee's name, department, hourly wage, and the number of hours worked in the week. Each simulated record is processed to calculate the wages earned, and certain data are then stored in arrays for later use. This procedure continues until all of the employees' records have been processed, and the entire payroll is stored.

You want to display the results of the payroll calculations as they are produced, but you also want to present sorted payroll listings. Based on a menu selection, you choose to list the payroll either in alphabetical order by name, or in order by department. (You need array storage to give you this output option.) The program will end when the final menu item is selected.

Figure A-28 presents a summary of what you need to produce the payroll program. As a programming challenge, use this summary to write the program.

You will need some creative thinking to write the payroll program, based on the topics we have covered. Most of what is shown in Figure A-29 is familiar, but there are a few things that need to be discussed.

Figure A-28 The payroll program challenge.

Required outputs:

Name, department, overtime pay per employee, total hours per employee, total pay per employee, total company regular pay, total company overtime pay

Data inputs:

Name, department, pay rate, hours worked

User inputs:

Menu selection

Process:

1. Print headings.
2. While not end of data:
   Calculate overtime and regular pay for each employee.
   (Overtime pays time and one-half.)
   Print the output.
   Store the items in arrays.
   Read the next data line.
3. Print the "Total" line.
4. Print the menu and accept choice:
   If the choice is "Print Payroll Sorted by Name" then:
      Sort arrays by name.
      Print the output.
   If the choice is "Print Payroll Sorted by Department" then:
      Sort arrays by department.
      Print the output with department first.
   If the choice is "End Program" then:
      Print message.
      End program.

continued

Hints:

- Place an "END" mark in the data and read until it is found.
- Count the number of items that were read.
- Use a separate array for each item to be stored.
- Dimension the arrays to a number larger than the anticipated number of employee data records.
- Perform a sort only if the array is not in the required order.
- Remember to exchange the items of all arrays when required during the sort.

Good luck!

Figure A-29 The payroll program.

```
100 REM PAYROLL WITH SORTED OUTPUT -- T. COURY
110 REM
120 REM THIS PROGRAM USES THE READ-DATA STATEMENT TO SIMULATE
130 REM READING PAYROLL RECORDS.  IT THEN CALCULATES THE PAYROLL
140 REM AND ALLOWS SORTED OUTPUT BASED ON A MENU SELECTION.
150 REM
160 REM  OUTPUT: N$ = EMPLOYEE NAME
170 REM          D$ = DEPARTMENT
180 REM          H  = NUMBER OF HOURS WORKED
190 REM          O  = AMOUNT OF OVERTIME PAY
200 REM          P  = AMOUNT OF TOTAL PAY
210 REM          T1 = OVERTIME PAY FOR ALL EMPLOYEES
220 REM          T2 = TOTAL PAY FOR ALL EMPLOYEES
230 REM INPUT FROM DATA:
240 REM          N$ = EMPLOYEE NAME
250 REM          D$ = DEPARTMENT
260 REM          R  = PAY RATE
270 REM          H  = NUMBER OF HOURS WORKED
280 REM INPUT FROM USER:
290 REM          C  = MENU CHOICE
```

continued

```
300 REM PROCESS:  OVERTIME IS CALCULATED BY: 1.5 x (H - 40) x R
310 REM           REGULAR PAY IS: HOURS (<= 40) x R
320 REM           TOTAL PAY IS: REGULAR PAY + OVERTIME (IF ANY)
330 REM           ITEMS ARE SORTED USING A BUBBLE SORT.
340 REM
350 REM OTHER VARIABLES:
360 REM         N   = EMPLOYEE COUNTER
370 REM         S$  = SORT ORDER FLAG
380 REM         I   = LOOP COUNTER
390 REM         J   = LOOP COUNTER
400 REM         T3  = TEMPORARY STORAGE
410 REM         T$  = TEMPORARY STORAGE
420 REM         N$() = ARRAY OF NAMES
430 REM         D$() = ARRAY OF DEPARTMENTS
440 REM         H()  = ARRAY OF HOURS
450 REM         O()  = ARRAY OF OVERTIME
460 REM         P()  = ARRAY OF PAY
470 REM
480 REM
490 REM DIMENSION ARRAYS
500 DIM N$(20), D$(20), H(20), O(20), P(20)
510 REM INITIALIZE ACCUMULATORS AND FLAG
520 LET N = 0
530 LET T1 = 0
540 LET T2 = 0
550 LET S$ = "NOT SORTED"
560 REM ***************     START OF MAIN ROUTINE     ***************
570 REM
580 PRINT "                          PAYROLL REPORT"
590 PRINT
600 PRINT , ,"   TOTAL", " OVERTIME", "   TOTAL"
610 PRINT "   NAME", "DEPARTMENT", "   HOURS", "    PAY", "    PAY"
620 PRINT "----------", "----------", "----------", "----------", "----------"
630 READ N$, D$, R, H
640 IF N$ <> "END" THEN 660
650 GOTO 880
660 REM WHILE N$ <> "END" BEGIN
670     LET N = N + 1
680     IF H > 40 THEN 700
690     GOTO 750
700     REM IF H > 40 THEN BEGIN
710         LET O = 1.5 * (H - 40) * R
720         LET T1 = T1 + O
730         LET P = 40 * R + O
740         GOTO 780
750     REM ELSE
760         LET O = 0
770         LET P = H * R
```

continued

```
780      REM END IF H > 40
790      LET T2 = T2 + P
800      PRINT N$, D$, H, O, P
810      LET N$(N) = N$
820      LET D$(N) = D$
830      LET H(N) = H
840      LET O(N) = O
850      LET P(N) = P
860      READ N$, D$, R, H
870   GOTO 640
880 REM END WHILE N$ <> "END"
890 PRINT
900 PRINT "TOTAL OVERTIME PAID FOR ENTIRE PAYROLL = "; T1
910 PRINT
920 PRINT "                TOTAL PAYROLL AMOUNT = "; T2
930 REM PROCESS THE MENU ITEMS
940 PRINT
950 PRINT "1.  PRINT PAYROLL SORTED BY NAME."
960 PRINT "2.  PRINT PAYROLL SORTED BY DEPARTMENT."
970 PRINT "3.  END PROGRAM"
980 PRINT
990 PRINT "ENTER NUMBER OF YOUR CHOICE (1, 2, OR 3) ";
1000 INPUT C
1010 IF C < 1 THEN 990
1020 IF C > 3 THEN 990
1030 ON C GOTO 1040, 1070, 1100
1040 REM CASE: C = 1 BEGIN
1050     GOSUB 1160
1060     GOTO 930
1070 REM CASE: C = 2 BEGIN
1080     GOSUB 1660
1090     GOTO 930
1100 REM CASE: C = 3 BEGIN
1110     PRINT
1120     PRINT "PROGRAM COMPLETE..."
1130     STOP
1140 REM****************     END OF MAIN ROUTINE     ***************
1150 REM
1160 REM SUBROUTINE TO PRINT PAYROLL SORTED BY NAME
1170 PRINT
1180 PRINT "PAYROLL SORTED BY NAME:"
1190 PRINT
1200 IF S$ <> "NAME" THEN 1220
1210 GOTO 1520
1220 REM IF S$ <> "NAME" THEN BEGIN
1230    FOR I = 1 TO N - 1
1240        FOR J = 1 TO N - I
1250            IF N$(J) > N$(J + 1) THEN 1270
1260            GOTO 1480
```

continued

```
1270             REM IF N$(J) > N$(J + 1) THEN BEGIN
1280                     REM EXCHANGE NAMES
1290                 LET T$ = N$(J)
1300                 LET N$(J) = N$(J + 1)
1310                 LET N$(J + 1) = T$
1320                     REM EXCHANGE DEPARTMENTS
1330                 LET T$ = D$(J)
1340                 LET D$(J) = D$(J + 1)
1350                 LET D$(J + 1) = T$
1360                     REM EXCHANGE HOURS WORKED
1370                 LET T3 = H(J)
1380                 LET H(J) = H(J + 1)
1390                 LET H(J + 1) = T3
1400                     REM EXCHANGE OVERTIME PAY
1410                 LET T3 = O(J)
1420                 LET O(J) = O(J + 1)
1430                 LET O(J + 1) = T3
1440                     REM EXCHANGE TOTAL PAY
1450                 LET T3 = P(J)
1460                 LET P(J) = P(J + 1)
1470                 LET P(J + 1) = T3
1480             REM END IF N$(J) > N$(J + 1)
1490         NEXT J
1500     NEXT I
1510     LET S$ = "NAME"
1520 REM END IF S$ <> "NAME"
1530 PRINT , ,"   TOTAL", " OVERTIME", "   TOTAL"
1540 PRINT "   NAME", "DEPARTMENT", "   HOURS", "     PAY", "     PAY"
1550 PRINT "----------", "----------", "----------", "----------", "----------"
1560 FOR I = 1 TO N
1570     PRINT N$(I), D$(I), H(I), O(I), P(I)
1580 NEXT I
1590 PRINT
1600 PRINT "TOTAL OVERTIME PAID FOR ENTIRE PAYROLL = "; T1
1610 PRINT
1620 PRINT "                    TOTAL PAYROLL AMOUNT = "; T2
1630 RETURN
1640 REM ***************     END OF SORT BY NAME     ***************
1650 REM
1660 REM SUBROUTINE TO PRINT PAYROLL SORTED BY DEPARTMENT
1670 PRINT
1680 PRINT "PAYROLL SORTED BY DEPARTMENT:"
1690 PRINT
1700 IF S$ <> "DEPT" THEN 1720
1710 GOTO 2020
1720 REM IF S$ <> "DEPT" THEN BEGIN
1730     FOR I = 1 TO N - 1
1740         FOR J = 1 TO N - I
```

continued

```
1750              IF D$(J) > D$(J + 1) THEN 1770
1760              GOTO 1980
1770              REM IF D$(J) > D$(J + 1) THEN BEGIN
1780                      REM EXCHANGE DEPARTMENTS
1790                  LET T$ = D$(J)
1800                  LET D$(J) = D$(J + 1)
1810                  LET D$(J + 1) = T$
1820                      REM EXCHANGE NAMES
1830                  LET T$ = N$(J)
1840                  LET N$(J) = N$(J + 1)
1850                  LET N$(J + 1) = T$
1860                      REM EXCHANGE HOURS WORKED
1870                  LET T3 = H(J)
1880                  LET H(J) = H(J + 1)
1890                  LET H(J + 1) = T3
1900                      REM EXCHANGE OVERTIME PAY
1910                  LET T3 = O(J)
1920                  LET O(J) = O(J + 1)
1930                  LET O(J + 1) = T3
1940                      REM EXCHANGE TOTAL PAY
1950                  LET T3 = P(J)
1960                  LET P(J) = P(J + 1)
1970                  LET P(J + 1) = T3
1980              REM END IF D$(J) > D$(J + 1)
1990          NEXT J
2000      NEXT I
2010      LET S$ = "DEPT"
2020 REM END IF S$ <> "DEPT"
2030 PRINT , ,"   TOTAL", " OVERTIME", "   TOTAL"
2040 PRINT "DEPARTMENT", "   NAME", "   HOURS", "     PAY", "     PAY"
2050 PRINT "----------", "----------", "----------", "----------", "----------"
2060 FOR I = 1 TO N
2070    PRINT D$(I), N$(I), H(I), O(I), P(I)
2080 NEXT I
2090 PRINT
2100 PRINT "TOTAL OVERTIME PAID FOR ENTIRE PAYROLL = "; T1
2110 PRINT
2120 PRINT "                  TOTAL PAYROLL AMOUNT = "; T2
2130 RETURN
2140 REM ***************     END OF SORT BY DEPARTMENT     ***************
2150 REM
2160 REM PAYROLL DATA
2170 REM
2180 DATA "ZACHARY", "MARKETNG", 7.25, 44
2190 DATA "ANTHONY", "FINANCE", 10.50, 40
2200 DATA "DEANNA", "MARKETING", 9.25, 35
2210 DATA "ROBERT", "MARKETING", 8.75, 40
2220 DATA "TERI", "FINANCE", 10.50, 50
2230 DATA "JOHN", "FINANCE", 10.00, 40
```

continued

```
2240 DATA "BETH", "PRODUCTION", 7.75, 30
2250 DATA "TRACI", "PRODUCTION", 7.00, 45
2260 DATA "FRANCES", "MARKETING", 7.50, 48
2270 DATA "MARY", "PRODUCTION", 7.25, 40
2280 DATA "END", "ZZZZZ", 0, 0
9999 END

RUN

                              PAYROLL REPORT

                                     TOTAL        OVERTIME        TOTAL
   NAME         DEPARTMENT           HOURS          PAY            PAY
----------    ----------     ----------     ----------     ----------
ZACHARY       MARKETING        44             43.5           333.5
ANTHONY       FINANCE          40             0              420
DEANNA        MARKETING        35             0              323.75
ROBERT        MARKETING        40             0              350
TERI          FINANCE          50             157.5          577.5
JOHN          FINANCE          40             0              400
BETH          PRODUCTION       30             0              232.5
TRACI         PRODUCTION       45             52.5           332.5
FRANCES       MARKETING        48             90             390
MARY          PRODUCTION       40             0              290

TOTAL OVERTIME PAID FOR ENTIRE PAYROLL =  343.5
                  TOTAL PAYROLL AMOUNT =  3649.75

1.  PRINT PAYROLL SORTED BY NAME.
2.  PRINT PAYROLL SORTED BY DEPARTMENT.
3.  END PROGRAM

ENTER NUMBER OF YOUR CHOICE (1, 2, OR 3) ? 1

PAYROLL SORTED BY NAME:

                                     TOTAL        OVERTIME        TOTAL
   NAME         DEPARTMENT           HOURS          PAY            PAY
----------    ----------     ----------     ----------     ----------
ANTHONY       FINANCE          40             0              420
BETH          PRODUCTION       30             0              232.5
DEANNA        MARKETING        35             0              323.75
FRANCES       MARKETING        48             90             390
JOHN          FINANCE          40             0              400
MARY          PRODUCTION       40             0              290
ROBERT        MARKETING        40             0              350
TERI          FINANCE          50             157.5          577.5
TRACI         PRODUCTION       45             52.5           332.5
ZACHARY       MARKETING        44             43.5           333.5
```

continued

```
TOTAL OVERTIME PAID FOR ENTIRE PAYROLL =  343.5
                  TOTAL PAYROLL AMOUNT =  3649.75

1.  PRINT PAYROLL SORTED BY NAME.
2.  PRINT PAYROLL SORTED BY DEPARTMENT.
3.  END PROGRAM

ENTER NUMBER OF YOUR CHOICE (1, 2, OR 3) ? 2

PAYROLL SORTED BY DEPARTMENT:

                                  TOTAL        OVERTIME       TOTAL
DEPARTMENT       NAME             HOURS          PAY           PAY
----------    ----------       ----------    ----------    ----------
FINANCE       ANTHONY          40            0             420
FINANCE       JOHN             40            0             400
FINANCE       TERI             50            157.5         577.5
MARKETING     DEANNA           35            0             323.75
MARKETING     FRANCES          48            90            390
MARKETING     ROBERT           40            0             350
MARKETING     ZACHARY          44            43.5          333.5
PRODUCTION    BETH             30            0             232.5
PRODUCTION    MARY             40            0             290
PRODUCTION    TRACI            45            52.5          332.5

TOTAL OVERTIME PAID FOR ENTIRE PAYROLL =  343.5

                  TOTAL PAYROLL AMOUNT =  3649.75

1.  PRINT PAYROLL SORTED BY NAME.
2.  PRINT PAYROLL SORTED BY DEPARTMENT.
3.  END PROGRAM

ENTER NUMBER OF YOUR CHOICE (1, 2, OR 3) ? 3

PROGRAM COMPLETE...
```

When dealing with a record-processing situation, you need some method to detect the end of the records. In the payroll program the literal string "END" was placed as the last data name in line 2280, and records are read using a WHILE loop until the computer reaches this item. You check for "END" in line 640. A counter—the variable N—keeps track of the number of names being read from the DATA statements. You need a WHILE loop, rather than an UNTIL loop, to prevent an error from occurring if no records existed, because encountering a file without records is a possibility in genuine record processing. A "priming" READ for the WHILE condition exists in line 630.

The calculations and IF-THEN-ELSE structure of lines 680 to 780 promote the program's clarity, as do the calculations and assignments of lines 790 to 850. The WHILE loop ends with another READ and the process continues until the "END" string occurs.

The menu items are processed using the ON . . . GOTO statement and the case structure it produces. Two GOSUB's do the requested sorting and printing, and the program ends directly.

In the subroutines, a flag is checked (lines 1220 and 1700) before the array sorts. If the flag indicates that the last sort to occur is the current one, the array is printed just as it is. If another sort is needed, then the sort criteria are used for the comparison (lines 1250 and 1750). When an exchange is needed, an item in one of the arrays exchanges with one in the second array, and they maintain their association (lines 1280 to 1470, and 1780 to 1970). Finally, you print the array.

If you're not sure about how something works or why it is needed, go ahead and play with it! Add, change, or eliminate statements; the results will be very educational.

SUGGESTED PROGRAMMING CHALLENGES

1. Write a program to read and sort the following unordered numbers into an array of 20 elements. Your program should then ask the user to enter a number from 1 to 50, and it should search the array and display the position where the number was found. It should also indicate if the number is not in the list.

```
DATA 4, 2, 19, 5, 20, 1, 35, 42, 46, 29
DATA 34, 23, 50, 21, 11, 44, 47, 32, 39, 26
```

2. Write a program to help your friend, Kay the DJ, keep track of playing times for her albums. The data below contains names of albums and the playing times for each. Your program should read this data into two arrays and produce output that contains two lists. One list shows the albums in alphabetical order with the corresponding times, and the other list shows the albums in order from shortest to longest time. It should also display—separately—the shortest album, the longest album, and the average time for all the albums.

```
DATA "TRESPASS – GENESIS", 43
DATA "BORN IN THE U.S.A. – BRUCE SPRINGSTEEN", 46
DATA "WINELIGHT – GROVER WASHINGTON JR.", 39
DATA "ARC OF A DIVER – STEVE WINWOOD", 40
```

```
DATA "THE BEST OF GILBERT & SULLIVAN", 54
DATA "SHANGO – SANTANA", 46
DATA "WHAT'S NEW – LINDA RONSTADT", 37
DATA "FAMILY – HUBERT LAWS", 41
```

3. A program is needed to maintain the inventory for a restaurant's fine wine cellar. The data below contains the names of a few of the wines with the corresponding bin numbers, quantity on hand, and cost per bottle. Develop a program that reads this data into several arrays, displays the information for the wines, and processes each of the following menu selections

1. REMOVE WINE FROM THE CELLAR
2. ADD WINE TO THE CELLAR
3. INDICATE NEEDED ORDERS
4. END THE PROGRAM

Menu items 1 and 2 should allow selection and adjustment of the appropriate array elements. For item 3, an order is needed if the quantity on hand for one of the items is less than or equal to 3. All wine is ordered by the case (12 bottles). When item 3 is selected, the information for each of the wines that needs to be ordered should be displayed along with the cost for each order, and the total cost for all cases ordered. The program should end only after item 4 has been selected.

```
DATA "CHATEAU LAFITE-ROTHSCHILD", 1, 3, 99
DATA "CHATEAU MARGAUX", 2, 5, 95
DATA "CHATEAU HAUT-BRION", 3, 7, 90
DATA "CHATEAU LATOUR", 4, 2, 93
DATA "CHATEAU MOUTON ROTHSCHILD", 5, 1, 91
DATA "CHATEAU TALBOT", 6, 9, 60
```

4. Four of your close friends—Chris, Jimmy, John, and Martina—are avid tennis players whom you have been observing for some time. You have noticed definite trends in their games and have devised a rating system that will help determine who will win various matches in different situations. The system assigns points to the type of court surface, the outcome of an immediately previous match, and the opponent. Add the points associated with each of the criteria, and the player with the greatest number of points will be the predicted winner. The data is as follows:

	Surface		Last Match		This Opponent			
Player	Clay	Grass	Won	Lost	Chris	Jimmy	John	Martina
Chris	6	5	7	3	—	5	3	7
Jimmy	9	7	8	5	9	—	5	8
John	9	8	9	6	9	6	—	9
Martina	6	6	7	6	8	6	3	—

For example, if Jimmy and John are going to have a match on grass and both won their last matches, Jimmy would be given a rating of 7 + 8 + 5 = 20, and John would be given a rating of 8 + 9 + 6 = 23. John would then be predicted as the winner.

Write a program to accept the players of a match, the court type, and the outcome of the last match for each of the players. The program should then predict a winner. There are situations where a tie may occur and no winner can be predicted.

The Final Step

The final step to becoming a proficient BASIC programmer is learning the many additional language statements and functions that are both a standard part of BASIC and unique to the system that you will use. The final step also involves the more difficult task of refining the art of programming itself. Learning the additional language techniques requires little more than some added study, but refining the art is probably best accomplished by practice and experience.

The remaining sections of this appendix present some typical features that you will find in one form or another in most versions of BASIC. These statements tend to be less standard than those we have presented, but this section will act as an overview to what is available.

Formatted Printing

The PRINT USING Statement. The PRINT USING statement will format the output of variables, allowing a programmer to define such things as the number of decimal places and insertion of commas in numeric variables, and the positioning of characters in alphanumeric variables. Two of the more common formats for the PRINT USING statement are:

> line number PRINT USING *string expn*; *expression*
> [; *expression*] . . .

and:

> line number PRINT USING *line number*, *expression*
> [, *expression*] . . .

In the first form of the statement the *string expn* is an alphanumeric variable or literal string containing a group of characters that will allow the formatting. Those characters are contained in the line numbered *line number* in the second form. The characters differ from system to system, but the pound sign (#) is generally used for number formatting. Some simple examples are:

> Form One: PRINT USING "###.##"; 498.45690
>
> Will Print: 498.46

Form Two: 100 PRINT USING 110, 498.45690
110:###.##
(The colon is required in this format.)

Will Print: 498.46

This statement has many additional features, and with a bit of practice you'll be using it to enhance the appearance of your program output.

The TAB Function. Another enhancement to print formatting is the TAB function, used with the normal PRINT statement. Like the comma, it acts as a tab key, with the advantage of variable tabbing. For example:

```
100 PRINT TAB(10); "THIS STARTS IN COLUMN 10"
```

The "T" of "THIS" will print in column 10 as indicated by the TAB function. The function may be used more than once in a PRINT statement, with different values for the column position.

Functions in BASIC

Arithmetic Functions. BASIC includes several arithmetic functions that you can incorporate into a program. These functions work like one of the function keys on a pocket calculator. Based on the value you enter into a function, you get different results. A function typically appears as:

```
100 LET S = SQR(X)
```

The SQR function will return the square root of the value contained in X. Figure A-30 summarizes several of the more common arithmetic functions.

Figure A-30 BASIC arithmetic functions.

Function	Returns
ABS(X)	The absolute value of X
ATN(X)	The arctangent (in radians) of
COS(X)	The cosine of X where X is in radians
EXP(X)	The value of e raised to the X power
FIX(X)	The value of X with any fractional portion truncated
INT(X)	The greatest integer in X
LOG(X)	The base e log of X
RND(X)	A random number between 0 and 1
SIN(X)	The sine of X where X is in radians
SQR(X)	The square root of X
TAN(X)	The tangent of X where X is in radians

String Functions. String functions selectively retrieve the characters contained in an alphanumeric variable, or they generate character strings based on values that direct the function. These functions tend to differ from system to system, so any that are presented here may not have the same form or function in a particular version of BASIC. Figure A-31 summarizes some of the string functions that may be available on your system.

User-Defined Functions. If one of the available standard BASIC functions fails to supply what you need for an application, then you may define your own, using the DEF FN statement. The syntax for defining functions is:

line number DEF FN*variable*(*arg* [,*arg*] . . .) = *expression*

Figure A-31 BASIC string functions.

Function	Returns
ASC(A$), ASCII(A$)	The ASCII value of the first character in A$
CHR$(N)	The character with the ASCII code N
INSTR(N,A$,B$)	The position of the first occurrence of B$ in A$ starting with the Nth character of A$
LEN(A$)	The length of A$
LEFT$(A$,N), LEFT(A$,N)	The leftmost N characters of A$
MID$(A$,N,M), MID(A$,N,M)	The M characters of A$ starting with the Nth character
RIGHT$(A$,N), RIGHT(A$,N)	The rightmost N characters of A$, or the rightmost characters of A$ starting from the Nth position
SPACE$(N)	A string of N spaces
STRING$(N,M) STRING$(N,A$)	A string of N characters with the ASCII value of M or the first character in A$
VAL(A$)	The numeric value of A$ when A$ contains all numeric characters

Note: Functions defined twice indicate two commonly implemented versions that are system dependent.

Variable is the name of the function and may be numeric or alphanumeric. The *expression* returns a result based on the *arg* values assigned, and the *expression type must match that of the variable.*

The following example illustrates the use of the DEF FN statement to find a quadratic root (although this will not find complex roots):

```
100 DEF FNQ(A, B, C) = (-B + SQR(B^2 - 4 * A * C)) / (2 * A)
110 PRINT "ENTER COEFFICIENTS A, B, C ";
120 INPUT A, B, C
130 PRINT "THE ROOT = "; FNQ(A, B, C)
9999 END
```

The DEF FN statement is also useful for many types of string manipulations. You can define functions to justify numbers that are stored as strings, or words that need to be of a uniform size. When you're using a video display for output, you can control the print position (cursor position) with certain sequences of characters. This is also easily handled in a user-defined function.

Functions, like so many of the topics we've discussed, differ from system to system. Some versions of BASIC support multiple line functions which allow the development of program modules that may be executed with a function call. You can also vary the location of a function in a program. Some versions require you to define a function before you use it, and some do not. The specific type of user-defined function that your system supports would be documented in a user's manual.

Using functions can save you time and increase the modularity and clarity of your BASIC programs.

File Processing

Any programming language would be of limited use if it did not include some method for storing data external to a program. File processing describes a method for reading, processing, and writing data that is stored on some secondary storage medium. If we had used a file in the previous payroll program instead of the READ-DATA combination, the information could be added to or changed as well as read. This isn't possible when the data is stored within the program. If another program could use the same data for a different process, this would create a link between the two. In the payroll example, one program could store the employee information on a file, and the second program could then create the payroll information. Commonly called batch processing, this uses a sequential file structure. That is, the records of the file are read one after another in the order they occur.

BASIC provides a modified INPUT and PRINT statement to allow sequential file processing; they need some means of identifying the associated file and other related information. Additional statements allow what is referred to as Random I/O, Record I/O, or Direct I/O processing.

This is a method of reading the records of a file in a selective or random order, and not necessarily in the order they were stored.

Many other statements and techniques associated with file processing will help you as you develop applications for business. Once you're proficient in their use, you will have all the tools you need to be a master BASIC programmer.

SUGGESTED PROGRAMMING CHALLENGES

1. The executive decision maker—Create this simple program by loading an alphanumeric array with a group of phrases and randomly displaying one of those phrases when a user presses the RETURN key. The idea is that a question would be considered and the random phrase would answer the question. If you use an array with ten elements, the following statement would create a random index for one of those phrases on most systems.

```
LET I = INT(RND(X) * 10) + 1
```

2. Write a program to accept a letter and a phrase and display the number of occurrences of the letter in the phrase. For example

```
ENTER A LETTER > ? E
ENTER A PHRASE > ? COMPUTERS ARE FUN

THERE ARE 2 E'S IN THE PHRASE.
```

3. Write a program to accept two dates (month, day, year), and display the number of days between those dates. Remember to account for leap years.
4. Write a program to accept a date in numeric form (08/12/86), convert the month to a word, and display it formally (September 12, 1986).
5. This is a challenge—Create a Vegas-style Blackjack program. The program could keep a deck of cards in DATA statements and shuffle by randomly filling an array. You deal the cards by reading the array. The program should also maintain a bank to allow for betting. The program becomes more exciting if you allow the computer to play the game.
6. This is very challenging—the eight queens problem. This problem is frequently encountered in the study of data structures. The challenge is to write a program that will indicate how to place eight queens on a chess board with none of them in check against another. Good Luck!

Notes

Prologue

[1]Data taken from Theodore Anton Sande, *Industrial Archeology: A New Look at the American Heritage* (New York: Penguin Books, 1978), p. 48.

Chapter 1

[1]Peter Dworkin, "Hard Times for a Law Firm that Went Big on Advertising," *San Francisco Chronicle,* August 6, 1982, pp. 6–7.

[2]"Business Week/Harris Poll: Middle Managers Still Think Positively," *Business Week,* April 25, 1983, p. 64.

[3]Mary Bralove, "Computer Anxiety Hits Middle Management," *Wall Street Journal,* March 7, 1983, p. 16.

[4]Evan Peelle, "The Well Tempered Risk," *Personal Computing,* July 1982, p. 28.

[5]Kent A. MacDougall, "The Complete Paper Clip and Other Fables," *Los Angeles Times,* reprinted in the *San Francisco Chronicle,* January 16, 1984, pp. 53–54.

[6]William J. Broad, "The Digital Revolution: Smart New Appliances," *New York Times,* March 8, 1984, pp. 17–18.

Chapter 2

[1]Richard N. Foster, "To Exploit New Technology, Know When to Junk the Old," *Wall Street Journal,* May 2, 1983, p. 26.

[2]William Serrin, "Electronic Office Conjuring Wonders, Loneliness and Tedium," *New York Times,* March 28, 1984, p. 10.

[3]Novelist Ernest Hebert, quoted in G. Berton Latamore, "A Fluid Well for Your Words," *Personal Computing,* January 1983, p. 106.

[4]"Typewriters Said No Match for WP," *Computerworld,* June 28, 1982, p. 13.

[5]Louis T. Hagopian, "Does Accounting Pry When You Fly?", *Wall Street Journal,* January 5, 1984, p. 16.

[6]Thomas Jenkins, "Teleconferencing: How to Make It Work," *Infosystems,* 1982, vol. 9, pp. 14–17.

[7]Same as above.

[8]Further information about Dvorak is available from ANSI, 1430 Broadway, New York, New York 10018, and from Dvorak International Federation, 11 Pearl Street, Brandon, Vermont 03733.

[9]Reprinted by Serrin, New York Times.

Chapter 3

[1]Conclusions reported by Stanford University psychologist Amos Tversky at symposium of National Academy of Sciences, in article by Philip M. Boffey, *New York Times,* reprinted in *San Francisco Chronicle,* December 14, 1983, p. 43.

[2]Robert N. Veres, "Flying Low," *Inc.,* November 1983, p. 25.

[3]S. Norman Feingold, "Emerging Careers: Occupations for Post-Industrial Society," *The Futurist,* February 1984, pp. 9–10.

Chapter 4

[1]Abby Solomon, "Climbing to the Top of the Charts," *Inc.,* September 1983, p. 141.

[2]Robert A. Mamis, "Unlocking Management Creativity," *Inc.,* June 1983, p. 103.

[3]David Tarrant, vice president of Graphic Communications, quoted in Paul Bonner, "Communicating with Presentation Graphics," *Personal Computing,* July 1983, p. 174.

[4]Reported in Paul Bonner, "When You'd Rather Switch Than Swap . . . ," *Personal Computing,* August 1983, p. 73.

[5]An excellent article on how farmers and other small business people can manage cash flow using spreadsheets has been written by Craig Zarley, "Managing Cash Flow for the Profit of It," *Personal Computing,* November 1983, pp. 127–135, 235.

[6]John Bussey, "Training Firms for Computers Are Growing," *Wall Street Journal,* May 4, 1984, p. 23.

Chapter 5

[1]Edsger Dijkstra, quoted in Steve Olson, "Sage of Software," *Science 84,* January/February 1984, p. 75.

[2]We are indebted to Carole Colaneri of Mid-Florida Technical College for her analogy here for pseudocode.

[3]Elli Holman, "When Your Time Is the Bottom Line," *Personal Computing,* September 1983, pp. 95, 96.

[4]Source of information: *San Francisco Chronicle, This World* magazine, March 18, 1984, p. 3.

Chapter 6

[1]Bohdan O. Szuprowicz, "DOD Push of Ada Spawns Business Bonanza," *Computerworld,* February 6, 1984, p. 94.

[2]Material reported in John Gallant, "University Launches 'Turing,' " *Computerworld,* February 20, 1984, pp. 43, 49.

Part 3

[1]Susan Fraker, "High-Speed Management for the High-Tech Age," *Fortune,* March 5, 1984, p. 62.

Chapter 7

[1]Tom Henkel, "Oldies Still Goodies, but Change to Come," *Computerworld,* January 23, 1984, pp. 73–74.

[2]Ted Nelson, *The Home Computer Revolution,* 1977. Published by the author and available from The Distributors, 702 South Michigan, South Bend, Ind. 46618.

[3]Andrew Pollack, "Computers Learn to Listen," *New York Times,* reprinted in *This World* (supplement to *San Francisco Chronicle*), February 5, 1984, p. 13.

[4]National Research Council, quoted in *U.S. News & World Report,* December 5, 1983, p. 59.

[5]Eleanor Johnson Tracy, "How to Sell Robots in Robotland," *Fortune,* August 6, 1984, p. 60.

[6]John Eckhouse, "A Useful Robot Is Intelligent—and Ethical," *San Francisco Chronicle,* June 30, 1964, p. 51.

[7]H. J. Maidenberg, "Pinning Down the Job Trend," *New York Times,* March 25, 1984, sec. 3, p. 1.

[8]Paul Hawken, "Surviving in Small Business," *Co-Evolution Quarterly,* Spring 1984, p. 15.

[9]Leslie Wayne, "A Pioneer Spirit Sweeps Business," *New York Times,* March 25, 1984, sec. 3, p. 12.

Chapter 8

[1]Peter Laurie, *The Joy of Computers* (Boston: Little, Brown, 1983), p. 16.

[2]The same.

[3]Jonathan B. Tucker, "Biochips: Can Molecules Compute?" *High Technology,* February 1984, p. 36.

[4]Patricia Keefe, "Leading Micro Operating Systems Threatened," *Computerworld,* February 6, 1984, p. 15.

[5]William M. Bulkeley, "Multiuser Computer Systems Seen Emerging as a Big Force in Market," *Wall Street Journal,* August 6, 1984, p. 19.

[6]Paul Truax, "Generic Operating Systems: Bringing the Pieces Together in Office Systems," *Computerworld,* November 29, 1982, In Depth/9.

[7]Rick Cook, "Unix: Emerging Business Tool," *CAP,* September 1984, pp. 75–77.

[8]Jean L. Yates, president of Yates Ventures, quoted in "Major Leaguers Join the Fray Over Operating Systems," *Business Week,* April 16, 1984, p. 122.

Chapter 9

[1]"Microcomputers Impacting Storage, Report Says," *Computerworld,* January 24, 1983, p. 62.

[2]Milton Moskowitz, "Feeding People Is Big Business," *San Francisco Chronicle,* July 28, 1984, p. 52.

[3]"Football Star Tracks Fans, Manages Restaurant with Computer," *Computerworld,* August 6, 1984, p. 19.

[4]David Gabel, "Creating a Fail-Safe Hard Disk System," *Personal Computing,* August 1984, pp. 137–44.

Chapter 10

[1]Richard A. Shaffer, "A Global Data System Is Seen as Telephones Use More Digital Gear," *Wall Street Journal,* December 23, 1983, p. 1.

[2]John Markoff, "Coping with the Data Dilemma," *San Francisco Examiner,* May 18, 1984, p. D1.

[3]Arthur M. Louis, "The Great Electronic Mail Shootout," *Fortune,* August 20, 1984, pp. 167–72.

[4]Charles H. Nobs of Bankers Trust Co., New York, quoted in "Linking Office Computers: The Market Comes of Age," *Businessweek,* May 14, 1984, p. 140.

[5]John M. Allswang, "Local Area Networks: Making the Right Connections Depends on Asking the Right Questions," *CAP,* April 1984, pp. 39–44.

Part 4

[1]John Naisbitt, *Megatrends: Ten New Directions Transforming Our Lives* (New York: Warner Books, 1982), p. 1.

[2]Estimated by J. Daniel Couger, "DP Megatrends," *Computerworld,* February 6, 1984, p. 34.

[3]James J. Renier, quoted in "Academia, Business Called Upon to Combat 'Cyberphobia,' " *Computerworld,* May 7, 1984, p. 26.

Chapter 11

[1]David Margolick, "Store's Demise Marks End of an Era," *New York Times,* April 24, 1984, p. 11.

[2]Donald K. White, "Metric System's Slow Pace in U.S.," *San Francisco Chronicle,* April 24, 1984, p. 47.

[3]Jerry FitzGerald, Ardra F. FitzGerald, and Warren D. Stallings, Jr., *Fundamentals of Systems Analysis,* 2d ed. (New York: John Wiley & Sons, 1981), p. 57.

[4]Charles J. McDonough, "Meanwhile, Back at the Paper Work Ghetto . . . ," *Wall Street Journal,* May 21, 1984, p. 28.

[5]Michael J. Powers, David R. Adams, and Marlan D. Millers, *Computer Information Systems and Development* (Cincinatti: South-Western, 1984) p. 118.

Chapter 12

[1]Theodore Levitt, *The Marketing Imagination;* quoted by Bill Abrams, "Putting the Customer Ahead of Profit," *Wall Street Journal,* December 2, 1983.

[2]Jack Falvey, "So Wrapped Up in Business, We Forget the Customer," *Wall Street Journal,* May 23, 1983, p. 26.

[3]Gail E. Schares, "Tricks of the Travel Trade," *San Francisco Chronicle,* August 27, 1984, pp. 55, 57.

Chapter 13

[1]Craig R. Waters, "Why Everybody's Talking About 'Just-in-Time,' " *Inc.,* March 1984, p. 80.
[2]Jeffrey L. Seglin, "The Direct Approach," *Inc.,* September 1984, pp. 149–54.

Chapter 14

[1]J. Daniel Couger, "DP Megatrends," *Computerworld,* February 6, 1984, p. 38.
[2]Summary preceding article by Carl Wolf and Jim Treleaven, "Decision Support Systems: Management Finally Gets Its Hand on the Data," *Management Technology,* November 1983, p. 44.
[3]"Sears' Sizzling New Vitality," *Time,* August 20, 1984, p. 90.
[4]Craig R. Waters, "Franchise Capital of America," *Inc.,* September 1984, p. 108.
[5]Laurie Itow, "What U.S. Gets May Depend on Whether Visalia Likes It," *San Francisco Examiner,* September 2, 1984, pp. A1, A20.
[6]David Collopy, "Can Decision Support Systems Solve Your Problems?" *Business Computing,* September 1984, p. 27.

Chapter 15

[1]Lowell Steele, "Managers' Misconceptions About Technology," *Harvard Business Review,* November-December 1983, pp. 133–40.
[2]F. Warren McFarlan, "Information Technology Changes the Way You Compete," *Harvard Business Review,* May-June 1984, pp. 99–101.
[3]Data taken from "VDTs—A New Social Disease?", *Harvard Medical School Newsletter,* April 1983, p. 3; "Clearing Up Those VDT Complaints," *Graphics Journal,* May 1984, p. 13; Jonathan King, "VDT: How to Prevent 'Terminal Illness,' " *Medical Self Care,* Spring 1984, pp. 27–32, 48; *Potential Health Hazards of Video Display Terminals* (Cincinnati, Ohio: National Institute for Occupational Safety and Health, 1981), p. 23.
[4]C. W. Miranker, "Top Targets for Computers," *San Francisco Examiner,* June 24, 1984, p. D1.
[5]Jeff Elpren, in Paul Bonner, "The Desktop Environment," *Personal Computing,* August 1984, p. 64.
[6]Frank E. James, "Manpower Inc. Seeks a Niche in High Tech," *Wall Street Journal,* February 6, 1984, p. 23.
[7]Colin Campbell, "Reading Computer Finding Many Uses," *New York Times,* August 19, 1984, p. 15.

Chapter 16

[1]Delia Fernandez, TRW, Inc.'s, Information Services Division's public affairs director, quoted in Jeffry Beeler, "TRW Password Theft Refocuses

Attention on Security," *Computerworld,* July 2, 1984, p. 2.

[2]Robert Heuer, "A Million Peeks a Day," *Link-Up,* June 1984, p. 46.

[3]Reported in *Newsday;* reprinted in *San Francisco Chronicle,* July 5, 1984, pp. 59, 64.

[4]Quoted in *Computerworld,* March 7, 1983, p. 17.

[5]David Burnham, "Computer Dossiers Prompt Concern," *New York Times,* June 10, 1984, p. 20.

[6]Scott A. Boorman, reported in Burnham, p. 20.

[7]Reported by Robert Ellis Smith, publisher of *The Privacy Times,* in testimony before House Judiciary Subcommittee on Civil Liberties, in *New York Times;* reprinted in *San Francisco Chronicle,* "Credit Records Open to U.S. Scrutiny Soon," April 11, 1984, p. 17.

[8]David Burnham, "Survey of Businesses and Agencies Says Computer Crime Struck Half," *New York Times,* June 11, 1984, pp. 1, 14.

[9]Banker Dale C. Hatfield, quoted in Gale E. Schares, "Quake a Big Peril to Computers," *San Francisco Chronicle,* April 17, 1984, p. 46.

[10]Statistics from Jane Ferrell, *San Francisco Examiner,* December 18, 1983, p. D2.

[11]Bettie Steiger, vice-president of information resources for Reference Technology, Inc., in Jake Kirchner, "Naivete Seen as Hurdle to On-line Security," *Computerworld,* March 12, 1984, p. 17.

[12]Bob Leach of Management Information Consulting Division of Arthur Andersen & Co., quoted in United Press story, "Expert Says 'Hackers' Threatening Computer Industry," *San Francisco Chronicle,* February 21, 1984, p. 57.

[13]John Gallant, "Vault Takes Page from Brinks," *Computerworld,* February 6, 1984, p. 8.

[14]John Eckhouse, "Employment Goes Electronic," *San Francisco Chronicle,* July 9, 1984, p. 54.

Chapter 17

[1]Quoted in Leslie Wayne, "A Pioneer Spirit Sweeps Business," *New York Times,* March 25, 1984, sec. 3, p. 1.

[2]Quoted in T George Harris, "From Hedonism to Health," *American Health,* March/April 1984, p. 56.

[3]Prof. William Chace, associate dean of humanities and sciences, Stanford University, "Intelligence, Artificial, and Otherwise," speech reprinted in *The Stanford Observer,* May 1984, p. 4.

[4]Andrew Pollack, "Job Outlook for the 80s Is Generally Optimistic," *New York Times,* March 25, 1984, Sec. 12, "Employment Outlook in High Technology," pp. 12, 14.

[5]Data from Plant Closures Research Group, University of California, Berkeley, reported in Allyn Stone, "High-Tech Jobs Called a Gamble," *San Francisco Chronicle,* February 17, 1984, p. 6.

[6]Tom Richman, "Does Technology Really Create Jobs?" *Inc.,* August 1984, p. 26.

[7]David Birch, quoted in Richman, p. 26.

[8]Leslie Wayne, "America's Astounding Job Machine," *New York Times,* June 17, 1984, sec. 3, p. 25.

[9]Douglas Noble, "The Underside of Computer Literacy," *Raritan* (Rutgers University quarterly), Spring 1984; reprinted as "The Myth of Computer Literacy," *Harper's,* August 1984, pp. 23–24.

[10]Charlotte LeGates, Computer and Business Equipment Manufacturers' Association director of communications, quoted in "Comments from the Sidelines," *InfoWorld,* May 28, 1984, p. 25.

[11]David Birch, paraphrased by Richman, p. 26.

[12]Survey by Audits and Surveys, Inc., reported by Alijandra Mogilner, "Americans Under 35 Trust Computers," *Infoworld,* December 6, 1982.

[13]Data from William Serrin, "Computers in the Office Change Labor Relations," *New York Times,* May 22, 1984, p. 11.

[14]John Siegel and John Silin, "Dimming Our Electric Future," *Wall Street Journal,* May 4, 1984, p. 20.

[15]Data from S. J. Diamon, "How People Cope When the Computer Can't," *Los Angeles Times;* reprinted in *San Francisco Chronicle Sunday Punch,* March 20, 1983, p. 7.

[16]Quoted in Peter Bartollk, "Atari Founder Heralds the Unorthodox for Innovation," *Computerworld,* January 16, 1984, p. 12.

[17]"The Growing Power of Computer Graphics," *San Francisco Chronicle,* July 24, 1984, p. 59.

[18]Ronald M. Groenke, "Network Evolution: Putting It in Perspective," *Computerworld,* February 27, 1984, p. SR/3.

[19]Chace, p. 4

[20]"Report Faults Managers on Work Quality," *New York Times,* reported in *San Francisco Chronicle,* September 5, 1983, p. 2.

[21]Robert Blatt, "Attention to Quality Stressed for High-Tech Executives," *Computerworld,* March 26, 1984, p. 102.

[22]Alvin Toffler in speech to American Medical Association's National leadership Conference, reported in United Press story, "Author Toffler Talks of New Individualism," *San Francisco Chronicle,* February 25, 1984, p. 5.

[23]Jennifer Roback,"Torn Between Family and Career? Give Birth to a Business," *Wall Street Journal,* November 14, 1983, p. 26.

[24]David Burnham, "Experts Fear Computers' Use Imperils Government History," *New York Times,* August 26, 1984, pp. 1, 17.

Credits and Acknowledgments

P. 8, excerpt from David E. Sanger, "S.E.C.'s Computer Revolution," *New York Times*, April 4, 1984, pp. 25–26. Copyright © 1984 by The New York Times Company. Reprinted by permission.

P. 9, excerpt from Peter Dworkin, "Hard Times for a Law Firm that Went Big on Advertising," *San Francisco Chronicle*, August 6, 1982, pp. 6–7. © San Francisco Chronicle, 1982. Reprinted by permission.

P. 18, excerpt from Mary Bralove, "Computer Anxiety Hits Middle Management," *Wall Street Journal*, March 7, 1983, p. 16. Reprinted by permission of the *Wall Street Journal*. © Dow Jones & Company, Inc., 1983. All rights reserved.

Pp. 25, 27–28, paraphrase and direct quote from Richard N. Foster, "To Exploit New Technology, Know When to Junk the Old," *Wall Street Journal*, May 2, 1983, p. 26. Reprinted by permission of the *Wall Street Journal*. © Dow Jones & Company, Inc., 1983. All rights reserved.

Pp. 26–27, 46, excerpts from Harvey L. Poppel, "Who Needs the Office of the Future?" *Harvard Business Review*, November-December 1982, pp. 146, 150. Copyright © 1982 by the President and Fellows of Harvard College; all rights reserved. Reprinted by permission of the Harvard Business Review.

P. 40, excerpt from Louis T. Hagopian, "Does Accounting Pry When You Fly?", *Wall Street Journal*, January 5, 1984, p. 16. Reprinted by permission of the *Wall Street Journal*. © Dow Jones & Company, Inc., 1984. All rights reserved.

P. 56, excerpt from Paul Korzenlowski, "Videotex Eyed as Traffic Stopper," *Computerworld*, January 23, 1984, p. 7. Copyright 1984 by CW Communications/Inc., Framingham, MA 01701. Reprinted from *Computerworld*.

Pp. 83–84, excerpt from Robert N. Veres, "Flying Low," *Inc.*, November 1983, p. 25. Reprinted with permission, *Inc.* magazine, November 1983. Copyright © 1983 by Inc. Publishing Corporation, 38 Commercial Wharf, Boston, MA 02110.

Pp. 84–85, excerpt from S. Norman Feingold, "Emerging Careers: Occupations for Post-Industrial Society," *The Futurist*, February 1984, pp. 9–10. By permission of *The Futurist* and Dr. S. Norman Feingold. Dr. Feingold is co-author with Norma R. Miller of *Emerging Careers: New Occupations for the Year 2000*, published in 1983 by Garrett Park Press, Garrett Park, MD 20896.

Pp. 90–91, excerpt from "Making the Most of the Money You Raise," *Personal Computing*, November 1983, p. 22. Reprinted with permission from *Personal Computing*. Copyright 1983, Hayden Publishing Company.

P. 94, excerpt from Daniel Farber, "A Mouse in the Hand," *Macworld*, March/April 1984, p. 28. Reprinted by permission of *Macworld* from Premier (March/April) issue, 1984, published at 555 De Haro Street, San Francisco, California 94107.

P. 101, excerpt from Robert A. Mamis, "Unlocking Management Creativity," *Inc.*, June 1983, p. 103. Reprinted with permission of *Inc.* magazine, June 1983. Copyright © 1983 by Inc. Publishing Corporation, 38 Commercial Wharf, Boston, MA 02110.

P. 121, excerpt from *LIST*, Spring 1983, p. 130. Reprinted by permission from *LIST*, the business software magazine, Vero Beach, Florida 32963.

P. 122, excerpt from Paul Bonner, "When You'd Rather Switch Than Swap . . . ," *Personal Computing*, August 1983, p. 73. Reprinted with permission from Personal Computing. Copyright 1983, Hayden Publishing Company.

P. 129, excerpt from John Bussey, "Training Firms for Computers Are Growing," *Wall Street Journal*, May 4, 1984, p. 23. Reprinted by permission of the *Wall Street Journal*. © Dow Jones & Company, Inc., 1984. All rights reserved.

P. 132–33, excerpt from Steve Olson, "The Sage of Software," *Science 84*, January/February 1984, pp. 75–76. Reprinted by permission of *Science 84* magazine, © the American Association for the Advancement of Science.

P. 142, excerpt from Paul Bonner, "Computer Programming: What's in It for You?", *Personal Computing*, August 1983, p. 128. Reprinted by permission from *Personal Computing*. Copyright 1983, Hayden Publishing Company.

P. 162, table 5–1, "Saving for College," from *This World, San Francisco Chronicle*, March 18, 1984, p. 3. © San Francisco Chronicle, 1982. Reprinted by permission.

Pp. 166–67, excerpt from Bart Eisenberg, "Who Grows the Software?", *LIST*, Spring 1983, pp. 82–84. Reprinted by permission from *LIST*, the business software magazine, Vero Beach, Florida 32963.

Pp. 177–78, excerpts from William H. Bulkeley, "Originators of Basic Computer Language Seek to Profit from Success of Their Work," *Wall Street Journal*, December 16, 1983, p. 29. Reprinted by permission of the *Wall Street Journal*. © Dow Jones & Company, Inc. 1983.

P. 198, excerpt from Bohdan O. Szuprowicz, "DOD Push of Ada Spawns Business Bonanza," *Computerworld*, February 6, 1984, p. 94. Copyright 1984 by CW Communications/Inc., Framingham, MA 01701. Reprinted from *Computerworld*.

P. 198, material from John Gallant, "University Launches 'Turning' ", *Computerworld*, February 20, 1984, pp. 43, 49. Copyright 1984 by CW Communications/Inc., Framingham, MA 01701. Reprinted from *Computerworld*.

P. 204, excerpt from Susan Fraker, "High-Tech Management for the High-Tech Age," *Fortune*, March 5, 1984, pp. 63–64. © 1984 Time Inc. All rights reserved.

Pp. 231–32, excerpt from Christopher Lofting, *Journal of Commerce*, reprinted in *San Francisco Sunday Examiner and Chronicle*, February 26, 1984, travel section, p. 4. Excerpted from "Executive Travel" column, *The Journal of Commerce*.

P. 232, excerpt from Susan Blakeney, "French Town to Try Out Medical Smart Card," *Computerworld*, February 27, 1984, p. 24. Copyright 1984 by CW Communications/Inc., Framingham, MA 01701. Reprinted from *Computerworld*.

P. 233, excerpt from Ronald J. Ostrow, "Automated Banking Called Ripe for Abuse," *Los Angeles Times*, February 20, 1984; reprinted in *San Francisco Chronicle*, February 20, 1984, p. 3. Copyright 1984, Los Angeles Times. Reprinted by permission.

Pp. 266–67, excerpt from David Myers, "Banks and the Holiday Rush," *Computerworld*, December 19, 1983, p. 10. Copyright 1983 by CW Communications/Inc., Framingham, MA 01701. Reprinted from *Computerworld*.

Pp. 288–89, excerpt from Tom Alexander, "Reinventing the Computer," *Fortune*, March 5, 1984, pp. 86, 88. © 1984 Time Inc. All rights reserved.

P. 310, excerpt from Jane Wollman, "Videodisc Applications," appearing in the April 1983 issue of *Popular Computing* magazine, pp. 81–82. Copyright © 1983 Byte Publications, Inc. Used with permission of Byte Publications Inc.

P. 344, excerpt from Manuel Schiffres, "The Big Rush to Videotex—and Its Big Risks," *U.S. News & World Report*, February 13, 1984, p. BC–3. Copyright, 1984, U.S. News & World Report, Inc.

Pp. 369, 370, excerpts from Richard A. Shaffer, "A Global Data System Is Seen as Telephones Use More Digital Gear," *Wall Street Journal*, December 23, 1983, p. 1. Reprinted by permission of the *Wall Street Journal*, © Dow Jones & Company, Inc. 1983. All rights reserved.

P. 382, excerpt from "Closing the Valve on Inventory Mistakes," *Computerworld*, January 30, 1984, p. SR/10. Copyright 1984 by CW Communications/Inc., Framingham, MA 01701. Reprinted from *Computerworld*.

P. 428, excerpt from Jerry FitzGerald, Ardra F. FitzGerald, and Warren D. Stallings, Jr., *Fundamentals of Systems Analysis*. 2d ed. (New York: John Wiley & Sons, 1981), p. 57. Copyright © 1973, 1981 by John Wiley & Sons, Inc. Reprinted by permission of John Wiley & Sons, Inc.

P. 428, excerpt and paraphrase from Charles J. McDonough, "Meanwhile, Back at the Paper Work Ghetto . . . , *Wall Street Journal*, May 21, 1984, p. 28. Reprinted by permission of the *Wall Street Journal*, © Dow Jones & Company, Inc. 1983. All rights reserved.

P. 429, excerpt from Figure 4–12, p. 118, from *Computer Information Systems Development: Analysis and Design* by Michael J. Powers, David R. Adams, and Harlan D. Millers. Copyright 1984, published by South-Western Publishing Co., Cincinnati, OH 45227.

P. 432, excerpt from "Telephone Company Automates Its Billing Process," *Computerworld*, May 14, 1984, p. 57. Copyright 1984 by CW Communications/Inc., Framingham, MA 01701. Reprinted from *Computerworld*.

P. 457, paraphrase and quotations from Jack Falvey, "So Wrapped Up in Business, We Forget the Customer," *Wall Street Journal*, May 23, 1983, p. 26. Reprinted by permission of the *Wall Street Journal*, © Dow Jones & Company, Inc. 1983. All rights reserved.

Pp. 460–461, excerpt from Elisabeth Horwitt, "Making Connections," Business Computer Systems, February 1984, pp. 48, 50–51. Copyright 1984 by Cahners Publishing Company, Division of Reed Holdings Inc. Reprinted with permission from *Business Computer Systems*, February 1984.

P. 482, paraphrase of ideas in Craig R. Waters, "Why Everybody's Talking about 'Just-in-Time,'" *Inc.*, March 1984, pp. 77-90. Reprinted with permission, *Inc.* magazine, March 1984. Copyright © 1984 by Inc. Publishing Corporation, 38 Commercial Wharf, Boston, MA 02110.

P. 482, paraphrase of ideas in Jeffrey L. Seglin, "The Direct Approach," *Inc.*, September 1984, pp. 149-54. Reprinted with permission, *Inc.* magazine, September 1984. Copyright © 1984 by Inc. Publishing Corporation, 38 Commercial Wharf, Boston, MA 02110.

P. 486, excerpt from Carl Wolf and Jim Treleaven, "Decision Support Systems: Management Finally Gets Its Hand on the Data," *Management Technology*, November 1983, pp. 44, 46. Reprinted by permission of the publisher and authors from *Management Technology Magazine*, 135 W. 50th Street, 12th floor, New York, N.Y. 10020.

P. 490, excerpt from Ralph H. Sprague, Jr. and Eric D. Carlson, *Building Effective Decision Support Systems* (Englewood Cliffs, N.J.: Prentice-Hall, 1982), pp. 4, 6, 9–10. © 1982. Reprinted by permission of Prentice-Hall, Inc., Englewood Cliffs, N.J.

Pp. 500–01, excerpt from Hannah I. Blank, "Throw Out Your Pencils and Plug in Your Micro," *Wall Street Journal*, February 13, 1984, p. 22. Reprinted by permission of the *Wall Street Journal*, © Dow Jones & Company, Inc. 1984. All rights reserved.

Pp. 515–517, excerpt and paraphrase from F. Warren McFarlan, "Information Technology Changes the Way You Compete," *Harvard Business Review*, May-June 1984, pp. 98–99. Copyright © 1984 by the President and Fellows of Harvard College; all rights reserved. Reprinted by permission of the Harvard Business Review.

P. 539, excerpt from Robert Heuer, "A Million Peeks a Day," *Link-Up*, June 1984, p. 46. Reprinted by permission of *Link-up*, the magazine for small computer communications.

Pp. 538–39, article from Elaine Johnson, "Planning to Outfox Office Security? This Handy Device May Finger You," *Wall Street Journal*, July 2, 1984, p. 17. Reprinted by permission of the *Wall Street Journal*, © Dow Jones & Company, Inc. 1984. All rights reserved.

P. 541, excerpt from David Burnham, "Computer Dossiers Prompt Concern," *New York Times*, June 20, 1984, p. 20. Copyright © 1984 by The New York Times Company. Reprinted by permission.

Pp. 562–63, excerpt from Sabin Russell, "User Friendlier," *Venture*, July 1984, pp. 48, 52. Reprinted from the July 1984 issue of *Venture*, The Magazine for Entrepreneurs, by special permission. © 1984 Venture Magazine, Inc., 521 Fifth Avenue, New York, NY 10175.

P. 566, excerpt from Leslie Wayne, "America's Astounding Job Machine," *New York Times*, June 17, 1954, sec. 3, p. 25. Copyright © 1984 by The New York Times Company. Reprinted by permission.

Photo and Illustration Credits

We are indebted to the many people and organizations who contributed photographs and illustrations to this book. The page numbers and contributors are listed below.

PART AND CHAPTER OPENING PHOTOGRAPHS

6 Eagle Computer.

24 Bunker Ramo Information Systems.

54 Satellite Business Systems.

88 Texas Instruments Incorporated.

130 Tektronix, Inc.

164 Management Science America, Inc.

202 Courtesy of Motorola, Inc.

264 Courtesy Racal-Vadic.

308 Courtesy of IBM Corporation.

342 TRW, Inc.

380 Consolidated Foods Corporation, Photographer Bob Day.

430 Courtesy of IBM Corporation.

458 TRW, Inc.

484 From Honeywell, Inc.

514 Photo Courtesy Anacomp, Inc.

536 Chevron U.S.A. Inc.

560 Sperry Corporation.

4, 86, 200, 378, 512 Part openings were constructed (from top to bottom) of photographs from the following sources: Tektronix, Inc.; Computerland; Courtesy of Motorola Inc.; Photograph Courtesy of Interleaf, Inc.; Boeing Computer Services Company.

TEXT PHOTOGRAPHS AND LINE ART

2 Library of Congress.

8 ITT Corporation.

11 Unimation Inc.

13 Courtesy of Hayes Microcomputer Products, Inc.

15 *Clockwise from top left,* Smithsonian Institution Photo No. 61758E; Courtesy of AT&T Bell Laboratories; Courtesy Intel Corporation.

17 F1-1 adapted from table by Gallup Organization, *New York Times,* May 11, 1983, p. 25. Copyright © by The New York Times Company. Reprinted by permission.

26 © 1984 Nita Winter.

35 F2-2 Codex Corporation.

37 F2-3 *Counterclockwise from top right,* Bell & Howell Business Equipment Group; 3M; 3M.

41 F2-4 *Left,* National Semiconductor Corporation; *right,* Codex Corporation.

43 F2-5 *Left,* Courtesy of AT&T Information Systems; *right,* Courtesy of AT&T Information Systems.

44 Courtesy of Burroughs Corporation.

46 © 1984 Nita Winter.

56 Hawaii Visitor's Bureau.

67 *Top,* Courtesy of International Business Machines Corporation; *bottom,* The Bettman Archive.

68 *Top,* Historical Pictures Service, Chicago; *bottom,* British Crown Copyright–reproduced with permission of the Controller of Her Britannic Majesty's Stationery Office.

70–71 F3-6, illustration of supercomputer and microcomputer from Edward Lipinski, *New York Times,* February 1, 1983, p. 19. Copyright © 1983 by The New York Times Company. Reprinted by permission.

70 *Top,* Cray Research, Inc.; *bottom,* Courtesy of International Business Machines Corporation.

71 *Top,* Courtesy Wang Laboratories, Inc.; *bottom,* Harris Corporation.

90 Christian Child Help Foundation Photo by J. Stephen Sandifer.

92 F4-1 Redrawn from illustration by Dan Collins, "Top 10 in Business Software," in article by Abby Solomon, "Climbing to the Top of the

Charts," *Inc.*, September 1983, p. 141. Reprinted with permission, *Inc.* magazine, September 1983. Copyright © 1983 by Inc. Publishing Corporation, 38 Commercial Wharf, Boston, MA 02110.

94 Mouse Systems Corporation.

95 *Top,* Public Domain; F4-2 Courtesy of Apple Computer, Inc.

102 *Top,* Courtesy of VISICORP; *bottom,* Software Arts Inc.

103 Public Domain.

113 F4-12 Context Management Systems.

115 Public Domain.

118 F4-15 *Top,* Courtesy of Hewlett-Packard Company; *bottom,* Matrox Electronic Systems Ltd.

119 F4-15 *Both,* ISSCO.

130 Old Tucson.

132 NASA.

139 Old Tucson.

144 F5-5 Redrawn from H. L. Capron and Brian K. Williams, *Computers and Data Processing,* 2d ed. (Menlo Park, Calif.: Benjamin/Cummings Publishing Co., 1984). p. 218.

152 Old Tucson.

153 © Ian Yeomans/Susan Griggs Agency Ltd.

156 Mohawk Data Systems.

166 John Foraste, Brown University.

169 Hollywood Movie Posters.

178 Hollywood Movie Posters.

185 F6-6 Courtesy of International Business Machines Corporation.

186 Hollywood Movie Posters.

204 Courtesy of Hewlett-Packard Company.

205 © Van Bucher/Photo Researchers, Inc.

206 © Van Bucher/Photo Researchers, Inc.

208 *Top,* The Bettman Archive; *bottom,* Courtesy of International Business Machines Corporation.

211 F7-1 Reprinted from H. L. Capron and Brian K. Williams, *Computers and Data Processing,* 2d ed. (Menlo Park, Calif.: Benjamin/Cummings Publishing Co., 1984), p. 86.

212 *Top left,* Courtesy Judi Lee.

213 F7-2 *Top,* Wells Fargo Bank; *bottom,* Sperry Corporation.

215 *Top,* New Century Bank Corporation; *bottom,* Texas Instruments Incorporated.

218 © Van Bucher/Photo Researchers, Inc.

219 F7-4 *Bottom left and right,* NCR Corporation.

221 F7-5 Recognition Equipment Incorporated, Dallas.

222 F7-6 Courtesy of AT&T Bell Laboratories.

224 F7-7 *Photograph,* Courtesy of IBM Corporation.

226 F7-8 GTE; 7-9 Courtesy of IBM Corporation.

227 F7-10 *Bottom,* Courtesy Stacey C. Sawyer.

228 F7-11 Interstate Voice Products.

230 F7-12 *Top,* Exchange Bank.

231 Wells Fargo Bank.

235 F7-13 Qume Corporation, A Subsidiary of ITT Corporation.

237 F7-14 Courtesy of IBM Corporation.

243 F 7-17 *Top left and right,* Qume Corporation, A Subsidiary of ITT Corporation.

244 F7-18 *Top,* Anderson Jacobson, Inc.; *Bottom,* Sperry Corporation.

246 F7-19 *Left,* Sanders Associates, Inc.; *right,* Courtesy of Nicolet Instrument Corporation.

247 F7-19 Courtesy of Hewlett-Packard Company.

250 F7-21 Courtesy Chrysler Corporation.

251 F7-21 *Top,* General Motors Corporation; *bottom,* Bell & Howell Business Equipment Group.

266 New York Convention & Visitors Bureau.

269 Courtesy of Reuben H. Donnelley.

277 Compliments of the Crocker Bank.

280 *ALL,* Harvard University, Cruft Photo Lab.

281 *Left to right,* Wide World Photos, Inc.; Iowa State University.

282 *Left to right,* Institute for Advanced Study, Princeton, N.J.; The Bettman Archive.

284 F8.4 *Left,* Courtesy of International Business Machines Corporation.

285 F8-5 © Dan McCoy/Rainbow.

288 F8.6 Courtesy of AT&T Bell Laboratories.

289 Illustration redrawn from artwork by Daniel Pelavin, in *Fortune* Magazine, March 5, 1984, p. 89; by permission of Daniel Pelavin.

291 F8-7 *Photograph,* Oakland Symphony Orchestra/Ron Scherl Photographer.

293 F8.8 *Photograph,* Oakland Symphony Orchestra/Ron Scherl Photographer.

294 F8.9 *Photograph,* Oakland Symphony Orchestra/Ron Scherl Photographer.

296 Compliments of the Crocker Bank.

297 F8-10 Adapted from chart by Strategic, Inc., from article by Patricia Keefe, "Leading Micro Operating Systems Threatened," *Computerworld,* February 6, 1984, p. 15. By permission of Strategic, Inc., San Jose, CA.

310 N.A.P. Consumer Electronics Corp., A North American Phillips Company.

314 F9.2 *Top left,* Courtesy of International Business Machines Corporation.

315 Compliments of the Crocker Bank.

318 F9-6 *Left,* 3M; *right,* Sun Company.

319 F9-7 *Top right,* 3M; *lower left,* reprinted from H. L. Capron and Brian K. Williams, *Computers and Data Processing,* 2d ed. (Menlo Park, Calif.: Benjamin/Cummings Publishing Co., 1984), p. 159; *lower right,* 3M.

320 Illustration of floppy disk handling and storage tips courtesy of Maxell Corporation of America.

321 F9-8 *Clockwise from top left,* Seagate; Courtesy of IBM Corporation; Courtesy of International Business Machines Corporation.

323 F9-9 *Top left,* from p. 146 and *bottom left* from 148, H. L. Capron and Brian K. Williams, *Computers and Data Processing,* 2d ed. (Menlo Park, Calif.: Benjamin/Cummings Publishing Co., 1984); *right,* Memorex Corporation.

325 F9-10 *Top,* adapted from p. 151, H. L. Capron and Brian K. Williams, *Computers and Data Processing,* 2d ed. (Menlo Park, Calif.: Benjamin/Cummings Publishing Co., 1984).

327 F9-11 *Top,* Courtesy of IBM Corporation; *bottom,* Courtesy of IBM Corporation.

328 F9-12 *Top,* Xerox Corporation/ComputerWorld.

329 Exchange Bank.

330 Compliments of the Crocker Bank.

334 F9-14 Adapted from p. 157, H. L. Capron and Brian K. Williams, *Computers and Data Processing,* 2d ed. (Menlo Park, Calif.: Benjamin/Cummings Publishing Co., 1984).

344 *Both,* Copyright Viewdata Corporation of America, Inc. 1984.

345 Courtesy of IBM Corporation.

346–47 F10-1 Redrawn from John McHale, *The Changing Information Environment.* Reprinted by permission of Westview Press. Copyright © 1976 by Elek Books, Ltd., London, England.

348 *Bottom left,* Courtesy Racal-Vadic; *bottom right,* Computone Systems.

351 Courtesy of IBM Corporation.

352 F10-4 *Bottom left,* Courtesy of COMSAT; *bottom right,* HughesAircraft Company.

353 F10-4 *Top left and right,* Courtesy of AT&T Bell Laboratories; *bottom,* New York Port Authority.

355 *Top,* Sperry-Univac, a Division of Sperry Corporation; *bottom,* Courtesy of IBM Corporation.

356 *Top,* Courtesy of IBM Corporation; *bottom,* Courtesy AT&T Information Systems.

367 *Top,* Courtesy of AT&T Information Systems; *bottom,* Western Union Telegraph Corporation.

369 Exxon Office Systems Company.

382 Crane USA.

384 Bill Blass, Ltd.

385 *Clockwise from top left,* Waldenbooks, Walden Book Co., Inc.; Pfizer, Inc.; Ramtek Corporation; American Trucking Associations, Inc.

393 Bill Blass, Ltd.

400 Bill Blass, Ltd.

416 *Top left,* System Industries; *top right,* Courtesy of Hewlett-Packard Company; *middle left,* Courtesy of Hewlett-Packard Company; *middle right,* System Industries; *bottom right,* Exxon Office Systems Company.

418 Bill Blass, Ltd.

432 Satellite Business Systems.

437 *Clockwise from top right,* Photo Courtesy Mervyn's; Photo Courtesy Mervyn's; Ralphs Grocery Company; Consolidated Foods Corporation, Photographer Bob Day; Courtesy of IBM Corporation.

439 ILGWU.

442 *Top,* Courtesy of Hewlett-Packard Company; *bottom,* ILGWU.

444 ILGWU.

448 ILGWU.

460 Moore McCormack Resources, Inc.

462 *Counterclockwise from bottom left,* NASA; Photo Courtesy of Wetterau Incorporated; Carter Hawley Hale.

463 *Left,* Kaypro Corporation; *right,* Context Management Systems.

464 ILGWU.

467 Courtesy of Apple Computer, Inc.

473 ILGWU.

486 Exxon Office Systems Company.

489 Photo Courtesy Mervyn's.

490 *Left,* Westinghouse Electric Corporation; *right,* Pfizer, Inc.

493 Photo Courtesy Mervyn's.

494–95 F14-1 Illustration on MYCIN reprinted with permission of the Heuristic Programming Project, Stanford University. MYCIN was developed under grant support from the National Institutes of Health.

498 *Counterclockwise from bottom left,* Anderson Jacobson, Inc.; Courtesy of Hewlett-Packard Company; Courtesy of Hewlett-Packard Company.

516 PSA, Inc.

521 *Left,* Sears, Roebuck and Co.; *right,* Bank of America.

524 *Left,* ILGWU; *right,* American Motors.

526 First Interstate Services Company.

538 Stellar Systems.

541 U.S. Dept. of Commerce.

544 F16-1 Redrawn from illustration "Data Security," *Infosystems,* June 1982, p. 54; Infosystems, copyright Hitchcock Publishing Co., 1983. Adapted from schematic,

"Computer System—Threats and Vulnerabilities"; reprinted with permission of Assets Protection Publishing, Madison, WI.

547 Pfizer, Inc.

548 Courtesy Racal-Milgo.

551 U.S. Dept. of Interior/Bureau of Reclamation.

562 Photo Courtesy of Zilog, Inc. ©1983.

565 F17-1 Both redrawn from illustrations in *New York Times,* March 25, 1984, sec. 12, p. 12 and 14. Copyright © 1984 by The New York Times Company. Reprinted by permission.

566 F17-2 Redrawn from illustration in *New York Times,* June 17, 1984, sec. 3, p. 1. Copyright © 1984 by The New York Times Company. Reprinted by permission.

567 Exxon Office Systems Company.

568 Warner-Lambert Company.

571 LIGHTHOUSE MEDIA, INC.

573 Ralphs Grocery Company.

575 Courtesy of AT&T Bell Laboratories.

576 *Left,* Courtesy of General Electric Research & Development Center; *right,* Courtesy of General Electric.

577 *Left,* Robotics Institute of Carnegie-Mellon University; *right,* Lawrence Hall of Science.

CORPORATE REPORT CREDITS

Corporate Report 1—by photo number

1. Courtesy of IBM Corporation.
2. Grid Systems Corporation.
3. Courtesy of IBM Corporation.
4. Advanced Micro Systems, Inc.
5. Sperry Corporation.
6. Courtesy of Hewlett-Packard Company.
7. Corvus Systems, Inc.
8. Courtesy of IBM Corporation.
9. Sperry Corporation.
10. Sperry Corporation.
11. Exxon Office Systems Company.
12. Photo Compliments of the Crocker Bank.
13. Bunker Ramo Information Systems.
14. Photo Compliments of the Crocker Bank.
15. New Century Bank Corporation.
16. Datapoint Corporation.
17. MAGI.
18. MAGI.
19. Westinghouse Electric Corporation.
20. Evans & Sutherland and Boeing Aerospace Center.
21. Colorgraphics Systems, Inc.
22. Satellite Business Systems.
23. Westinghouse Electric Corporation.
24. Southern California Edison Company.
25. Southern California Edison Company.
26. Southern California Edison Company.
27. Southern California Edison Company.
28. The Foxboro Company.
29. Chevron U.S.A. Inc.
30. Reprinted with permission of Computervision, Bedford, MA.
31. Courtesy of Motorola Inc.
32. © Charles Harbutt, Archive Pictures, Inc.
33. Courtesy of Hewlett-Packard Company.
34. Ramtek Corporation.
35. Hughes Aircraft Co.
36. Courtesy Chrysler Corporation.
37. Photo Courtesy of Megotek Corporation, San Diego, California.
38. Credit information unavailable.
39. Sperry Corporation.
40. Courtesy of General Electric.
41. Courtesy of General Electric.
42. Courtesy of General Electric.
43. Courtesy of General Electric.
44. Reprinted with permission of Computervision, Bedford, MA.
45. Credit information unavailable.
46. McDonnel Douglas Automation Company.
47. International Space Hall of Fame.
48. International Space hall of Fame.

PL1-1 and 1-2 Artwork redrawn from figures prepared as part of paid advertisements by International Data Corporation entitled "Underlying Circuit Technology Drives the Market," from *Fortune,* May 16, 1983, p. 32; "The Meteoric Rise of the Personal Computer," from *Fortune,* January 23, 1984, p. 98. By permission of International Data Corporation and *Fortune.*

PL1-3 Artwork adapted from drawing, "An Avalanche of Devices," prepared by International Data Corporation as part of paid advertisement in *Fortune,* October 15, 1984, p. 100. By permission of International Data Corporation and *Fortune.*

PL1-4 Artwork redrawn from figure prepared by Gartner Group entitled "Office Systems Evolution," on p. 36 of "Office Today," supplement to *The New York Times,* September 1984. Reprinted by permission of Gartner Group, Inc. Copyright © 1984 by The New York Times Company. Reprinted by permission.

Corporate Report 2

All photographs © Peeter Vilms 1984. ASK photos and line art reproduced with kind permission of Allison Hartman and ASK Computer Systems, Inc., 730 Distel Drive, Los Altos, CA 94022.

ART: 2-7 *top,* Sippican Ocean Systems; *middle,* Hewitt Soap Company; *bottom,* NMB HI-TEK Corporation, Garden Grove, California: Low profile and standard profile computer keyboards.

Corporate Report 3—by page number

All photographs except those listed below © Peter Menzel 1984. El Camino Hospital photos reproduced by kind permission of Karen Fischer and Andrew Letterer and El Camino Hospital, 2500 Grant Road, Mountain View, CA 94039.
3-4 *Top,* From Honeywell, Inc.; *bottom,* MSI Data Corporation.
3-5 *Lower right,* Hospital Corporation of America.
3-6 *Top left and right,* Pfizer, Inc.; *bottom left,* Pfizer, Inc.; *bottom right,* Monmouth Medical Center.
3-7 *Top left,* © Dan McCoy/ Rainbow; *top right,* Courtesy Digital Effects, Inc.; *middle left,* American Heart Association; *lower right,* American Heart Association; *lower left,* Intergraph Corporation.

Corporate Report 4—by page number

All photographs © Peeter Vilms 1984. PC World and Macworld photos reproduced by kind permission of David Bunnell, Janet McCandless, and PC World, 555 De Haro Street, San Francisco, CA 94107. Covers and illustrations from Macworld by permission.
4-3 Artwork redrawn from figure "Monthly Computer Magazine Circulation" based on data from *Communications Trends,* Larchmont, New York, copyright 1984, Communications Trends, Inc. Figure prepared by International Data Corporation as part of paid advertisement in *Fortune,* January 23, 1984, p. 136. By permission of *Communications Trends,* International Data Corporation, and *Fortune.*

Corporate Report 5—by page number

5-1 Courtesy of IBM Corporation.
5-2 Consolidated Foods Corporation, Photographer Bob Day.
5-4 *Top,* Photo Courtesy of Alcan Aluminum Limited; *middle,* MAGI; *bottom,* Courtesy of Management Science America, Inc.
5-5 Cray Research, Inc.
5-6 *Top,* Warner-Lambert Company; *middle right,* Consolidated Foods Corporation, Photographer Bob Day; *bottom left,* Cummins Engine Company, Inc.; *bottom right,* ITT. 5-7 *Top right,* Pfizer, Inc.; *bottom right and top left,* Reprinted with permission of Computervision, Bedford, MA; *bottom left,* Ramtek Corporation.
5-8 *Top,* Ramtek Corporation; *bottom,* Courtesy of Hewlett-Packard Company.

Glossary/Index

A small "f" following a page number refers to a figure; the abbreviation "CR" refers to "Corporate Reports" (color sections).

Access arm: Device in a disk drive unit that moves a read/write head over a particular track. 322–24, 323f, 337

Access time: Time between when the computer requests data from a secondary storage device and when the data transfer is complete. 324, 337

Accounting and Finance: Department in an organization that maintains a financial record of all activities. 58, 78, 453, CR5:1, CR5:5, CR5:8
  operations information systems and 433, 440f

Accounts payable: Money owed, spent, or paid out by an organization. 439, 440, 454
  vendor-oriented processing and 444, 445f

Accounts receivable: Income or money received by or owed to an organization. 439, 440, 454
  customer-oriented processing and 447–48, 447f

Accumulator: Register in the ALU that holds accumulated data. 286, 302

Acoustic coupler: Cradle that allows a modem to accept a standard telephone handset. 41f, 349, 371

Ada: Programming language developed under the sponsorship of the Department of Defense and named for Lady Ada Augusta Byron. 168, 189–92, 195–98

Address 299–300

Address register: Register located in the controller that holds the address of a location containing data called for by an instruction. 286, 302

Ad hoc DSS: Decision support system designed to handle management decision problems that are unexpected or nonrecurring. 492, 508

Aegis Systems Corporation 56

Aetna Life and Casualty Insurance Company 354

Aged receivables 476f

AI; see Artificial intelligence

Aiken, Howard H. 279, 280

Alexander, Tom 289

ALGOL: Algorithmic programming language designed for mathematical and scientific applications. 187, 196

ALGOrithmic Language; see ALGOL

Allnet Communications 356

Allswang, John M. 377

Alphanumeric terminals: Terminals that display alphanumeric output. 234, 256

ALU; see Arithmetic/logic unit

Amdahl, Gene 355

Amdahl 470V/6 355

American National Standards Institute (ANSI) 52, 181, 194, 548

American Robot Corporation 261

American Satellite Company 354

American Standard Code for Information Exchange (ASCII): Eight-bit code used in data communications, most microcomputers, and some large computers. 276f, 277, 300

American Telephone & Telegraph; see AT&T

Americom 354

Analog signal: Electronic signal that will represent a range of frequencies. 348, 371

Analytical engine 68

Analytical graphics: Graphics that help the user analyze compiled data. 120, 127, CR1:7

Annotation flag 147f

ANSI; see American National Standards Institute

ANSI-COBOL: Version of COBOL standardized by the American National Standards Institute. 181, 194

APL: Programming language introduced by IBM that is useful for processing tables and arrays. 187, 196

Apple Computer 11, 16–17, 47, 187, 196, 298, 355, CR2:1

Apple II 13, 90, 103, 126, 267

Apple IIc 217

Apple IIe, word processing with 95, 95f

Apple Lisa 122, 127, 187, 196, 562

Apple Macintosh 94, 122, 127, 187, 196, 562, CR4:1–5

Apple Writer II 94

Applications languages, developments in 518

Applications programs: Programs designed to perform specific data processing and computational tasks. 133, 157

A Programming Language; see APL

Arcs: Lines joining points in a network. 362

Arithmetic computations, BASIC 595

Arithmetic functions, BASIC 655, 655f

Arithmetic/logic unit (ALU): Electronic circuitry that controls all

Chase Manhattan Bank 267, 500, 538
Check bit: An additional bit attached to a byte that allows the computer to tell if a bit in the byte has been lost. 277–78, 278f, 300
Checklist: List of questions used to ensure that the user and systems analyst address key issues when they are evaluating the present system. 405, 405f, 425
Chemical Bank 266
C-I-L 19
Citibank 573
CLEAR command 588
Coaxial cable: Improved transmission line in which multiple wires are replaced by a single solid core. 351, 352f, 371
COBOL: Most frequently used high-level business programming language. 148, 155, 165, 168, 172–73, 176–83, 179f, 192–94, 197–98, 295, 343
  sample output of 180f
COBOL-8X 181
Coding: Writing of statements in programming language. 133, 157, 159
  structured 150–52
Cold site: Disaster recovery center that is simply an empty shell with power, water, and air conditioning in which a company may install its own equipment. 553, 557
COM; see Computer output microfilm
Commodore 16–17, 355
Common Business-Oriented Language; see COBOL
Common carrier: An organization such as AT&T or Western Union that has been approved by the Federal Communications Commission and state regulatory agencies to offer communications services to the public. 367–68, 374
Communicating: Sharing information between people. 61, 79, CR5:1
  management and 462, 479
Communication, microcomputers and 19
Communications interface: Sending and receiving instrument that converts ideas into electronic signals to be transmitted, such as a telephone handset or telegraph key. 345–49, 370–71
Communications processor: Processor similar to a CPU that serves solely to enhance data communications between two points. 359–61, 372–73
Communications satellite: Satellite used as a microwave relay station in space. 351–54, 352f, 371–72, CR1:8-9
Compiler: High-level programming language translator that translates programs into machine language code. 295, 304
Compiler language: Language such as COBOL or FORTRAN in which a translation program converts each high-level language program statement into machine language code. 172, 193
Compiling run: Process of translating high-level language programs into machine language code. 172, 193
CompuServe 17
Computer-aided design (CAD): System used by engineers, architects, and others to design products, buildings, and manufacturing processes. 236, 256, CR1:13
Computer-aided engineering (CAE): Variant on CAD/CAM in which graphics are used to assist in developing complicated products, such as airplanes. 236, 256, CR1:13
Computer-aided manufacturing (CAM): System used to physically manufacture products. 236, 256, CR1:13
Computer-assisted instruction (CAI): System whereby the computer is used to present instructional materials to students. 236, 256
Computer-based information systems 73–77
Computer conferencing: Conferencing in which participants have access to the same computer file and can communicate—without all being present at the same time—by typing on their keyboards. The conference is stored in a computer file. 40–42, 50
Computer crime 543–46, 555
Computer disaster 551–52
Computer disaster recovery 552–53
Computer disaster recovery center: An alternative computer setup that is used only during emergencies. 553, 556–57
Computer disaster recovery plan: A plan for rapid resumption of essential data processing operations that have been interrupted by destruction or major damage. 552, 556
Computer error 571–73, 580
Computer graphics 115–20, 118f, 127
Computerization, job displacement and 524f
Computerized axial tomography (CAT) CR3:6
Computer message switching: Form of electronic mail in which messages are sent to be displayed on or stored in a computer. 39, 49
Computer output microfilm (COM): Computer-generated documents photographically reduced in size for later use. 36, 49, 245–47, 248f, 259
  systems 37f
Computers
  career planning and 561–69
  decision making and CR5:1-5
  health and stress and 570–71
  quality of life and 574
  telecommunications and 345
Computer systems 61–73, 62f
  hardware components of 311f
Computer time, theft of 545
Computer training firms 129
Computerworld CR4:6
COMSAT: United States representative to INTELSAT (International Telecommunications Satellite Consortium). 354, 372
Concentrator: Multiplexer that can be programmed and that has increased processing capability and greater flexibility. 359, 373
Connector symbol 147f
Constants, BASIC 595
Contagion: Stage in the development of an integrated, user-friendly information processing system in which computer applications spread into areas other than accounting. 523–24, 533
Context MBA 113
Continental Telephone Company 354
Control: Stage in the development of an information processing system in which the development of an MIS to control operations occurs. 524–25, 533
Control Data Corporation 354

dures along with a list of test data and solutions. 155, 157, 160
PROM; see Programmable read-only memory
Property inventory: The output of facility-oriented processing, which describes the fixed assets and states who is responsible for them. 450, 455
Protocols: In data transmission, a set of rules for the exchange of information between sender and receiver. 357–58
Pseudocode: A narrative form of describing structure program logic. It focuses on the logic of the program rather than on the details of programming and flowcharting. 147–48, 149f, 159, 174f
Punched cards: Stiff paper cards punched with holes that represent data. 209–11, 210f, 253
Purchase order (PO): An order issued by the purchasing department and sent to a vendor for an item requested by a department in the organization. 441–42, 454
Purchasing: Element in an operations information system concerned with raw materials acquisition. 454
  vendor-oriented processing and 442, 442f

Query languages: In decision support systems, a language that is easily understood by managers so that they can communicate with the system. 499, 508
Questionnaires: Used frequently by systems analysts to obtain more responses in shorter time concerning the information system presently in use. 403

RAM; see Random-access memory
Random-access memory (RAM): Storage in which data and programs not only can be obtained from primary storage but also can be put into it. 285, 302
Rate of return: Ratio between the estimated benefits and estimated costs of something. 394, 424
RCA Corporation 310, 354, 355, 366, CR1:8
Read: Retrieve data from. 313, 335
Read-only memory (ROM): Firmware in which programs are built into the primary storage and cannot be changed by the user. 285, 302
READ statement 635–40
Read/write head: An electromagnet that reads magnetized areas on magnetic tape or disks, converts them into electrical signals, and sends them to the CPU. It also can write data from the CPU onto the magnetic tape or disks. 313, 335
Real-time processing: Transaction processing. 206, 252
Receiving report: Copy of a purchase order distributed within an organization to confirm that the order has been placed and to document the expected delivery date. 441, 454
Record: In referring to data, a collection of related fields. 315, 336
Registers: Temporary, special-purpose holding locations in the CPU for instructions and data. 286, 302
Relational data base 470
Remington, Philo 5
Remington Rand 354
REM statement 591
RENAME command 588
Report Program Generator; see RPG
Reports, management information system 472–77, 474f, 476f
Research and development: Department concerned with improving products and developing new ones. 59, 78, 453, CR5:1, CR5:7, CR5:8
  operations information systems and 433
Reserved words: In COBOL, words with exact meanings that cannot be used for variable names. 183, 194
RESTORE statement 640–41
RETURN statement 585, 641–42
Reverse video 216
Richie, Dennis 297
Ring network: A distributed data processing system in which connected computers do their own processing in various locations, usually via telephone lines. 363f, 364–65, 373
Roback, Jennifer 582
Robotics: The study of the design, construction, and use of robots. 248–50, 251f, 259
Robots CR1:1
  personal CR1:16
ROM; see Read-only memory
Rotational delay 337
Rotational delay time: The time for a particular record to be positioned under the read/write head. 324
RPG: A problem-oriented language designed to generate business reports. 168, 173, 184–86, 185f, 192, 195
RPG II: An updated version of RPG introduced in 1970 that extends the language's capabilities. 186
RPG III: A modern interactive language that presents the programmer with menus allowing choices of various types of programming specifications. 186
RUN command 587

Salami method: Form of embezzlement in which a few cents are taken from many accounts, so that the small sums will not be missed but the aggregate will be quite large. 545, 555
Sales and merchandising, decision support systems for 510
Sanger, David E. 8
Satellite Business Systems 354, CR1:9
Satellite communications CR1:8-9
SAVE command 587–88
Schulhof, Nathan M. 166–67
ScreenWriter II 94
Scripsit 94
Scrolling 216
Seaborg, Glenn 261
Sealed data modules: A hard disk drive, which has disks, access arms, and read/write heads sealed inside it. The read/write heads float on a cushion of air over the disk surfaces. 322, 336–37
Search and replace: In word processing, a function that instructs the computer to automatically search for and replace, in the entire document, any words the user wants to change. 97, 125
Sears, Roebuck & Co., 343, 510, 573
SEC; see Securities and Exchange Commission
Secondary storage: Storage located physically outside the processor. The most common types of secondary storage are magnetic tape, hard disks, and flexible disks. 62, 66, 79– 80, 309–13, 335